Texts in Computer Science

Series Editors

David Gries, Department of Computer Science, Cornell University, Ithaca, NY, USA

Orit Hazzan⬤, Faculty of Education in Technology and Science, Technion—Israel Institute of Technology, Haifa, Israel

Titles in this series now included in the Thomson Reuters Book Citation Index!

'Texts in Computer Science' (TCS) delivers high-quality instructional content for undergraduates and graduates in all areas of computing and information science, with a strong emphasis on core foundational and theoretical material but inclusive of some prominent applications-related content. TCS books should be reasonably self-contained and aim to provide students with modern and clear accounts of topics ranging across the computing curriculum. As a result, the books are ideal for semester courses or for individual self-study in cases where people need to expand their knowledge. All texts are authored by established experts in their fields, reviewed internally and by the series editors, and provide numerous examples, problems, and other pedagogical tools; many contain fully worked solutions.

The TCS series is comprised of high-quality, self-contained books that have broad and comprehensive coverage and are generally in hardback format and sometimes contain color. For undergraduate textbooks that are likely to be more brief and modular in their approach, require only black and white, and are under 275 pages, Springer offers the flexibly designed Undergraduate Topics in Computer Science series, to which we refer potential authors.

Quentin Charatan • Aaron Kans

Programming in Two Semesters

Using Python and Java

 Springer

Quentin Charatan
School of Architecture, Computing
and Engineering
University of East London
London, UK

Aaron Kans
School of Architecture, Computing
and Engineering
University of East London
London, UK

ISSN 1868-0941   ISSN 1868-095X (electronic)
Texts in Computer Science
ISBN 978-3-031-01328-7   ISBN 978-3-031-01326-3   (eBook)
https://doi.org/10.1007/978-3-031-01326-3

This Springer imprint is published by the registered company Springer Nature Switzerland AG
The registered company address is: Gewerbestrasse 11, 6330 Cham, Switzerland

In loving memory of Jimmy Glass (1951–2021) and Nigel Maudsley (1953–2021)

—Quentin Charatan

In loving memory of our beloved Brigadier Yashpal Mohan (1953–2021)

—Aaron Kans

Preface

Accompanying website: *Go to the publisher's website,* https://link.springer.com, *and search for this textbook. From that page you will be directed to a link that allows you to download the resources you need for this book.*

This book is designed for university students taking a first module in software development or programming, followed by a second, more advanced module. This book takes a unique approach of covering these topics using *two* popular programming languages—Python *and* Java. Python is the vehicle for the teaching of fundamental programming concepts that would align with the first introductory programming module and Java as the vehicle for teaching more advanced programming concepts that would align with the second more advanced module. Design concepts are explained throughout using the UML notation. The topics are taught from first principles and assume no prior knowledge of the subject.

The book is organized so as to support two twelve-week, one-semester modules, which might typically comprise a two-hour lecture, a one-hour seminar and a one or two-hour laboratory session. The outcomes at the start of each chapter highlights its key learning objectives, the self-test questions at the end of each chapter (which would be ideal as the basis for seminar sessions) ensure that the learning objectives for that chapter have been met, while the programming exercises that follow (which would be ideal for laboratory sessions) allow these learning objectives to be applied to complete different programs. In addition to these exercises and questions, a case study is developed in each semester to illustrate the use of the techniques covered in the text to develop a non-trivial application. Lecturers who teach on modules that run for fewer than twelve weeks in a semester could treat these case studies as a self-directed student learning experience, rather than as taught topics.

The approach taken in this book is ideal for all students, including those entering university with little or no background in the subject matter, perhaps coming from pre-degree courses in other disciplines, or perhaps returning to study after long periods away from formal education. It is the authors' experience that such students have enormous difficulties in grasping the fundamental programming concepts the first-time round and therefore require a simpler and gentler introduction to the subject than is presented in most standard texts.

The book takes an integrated approach to software development by covering such topics as basic design principles and standards, testing methodologies and the user interface, as well as looking at detailed implementation topics.

In the first semester, considerable time is spent concentrating on the fundamental programming concepts such as declarations of variables and basic control structures, functions and collections, prior to introducing students to classes and objects, inheritance, file handling, graphics and event-driven programming. Python is chosen as the vehicle to teach these first semester topics as it is a programming language very well suited to students who have had no prior programming experience. Instructions are also provided on how to download and use the Python interpreter for writing and running Python programs.

Since Java is often found to be challenging programming language for students completely new to programming Java is chosen instead as the vehicle to cover more advanced *second semester* topics (such as, arrays, interfaces and lambda expressions, exceptions, collection classes, advanced graphics using JavaFX and packages). A smooth transition is provided from Python to Java by revisiting some fundamental concepts such as variables, control structures, file handling and classes and objects in Java and highlighting differences and similarities between the two languages.

The accompanying website contains all the code from the text book and instructions for using some common development tools, while the book itself includes an appendix that contains a guide to the various ways of writing and running Java programs.

We would like to thank our publisher, Springer, for the encouragement and guidance that we have received throughout the production of this book. Additionally, we would especially like to thank the Computing students of the University of East London for their thoughtful comments and feedback. For support and inspiration, special thanks are due once again to our families and friends.

London, UK   Quentin Charatan
                                                                                                       Aaron Kans

Contents

Part I
Semester One: Python

Python: The First Step

1

Outcomes

By the end of this chapter you should be able to:

- *explain the meaning of the terms **software**, **program**, **source code**, **program code**;*
- *distinguish between **application software** and **system software**;*
- *describe the different ways in which source code can be converted to machine code;*
- *explain how Python programs are compiled, interpreted and run;*
- *write Python programs that display text on the screen;*
- *add comments to your programs.*

1.1 Introduction

Like any student starting out on a first programming module, you will be itching to do just one thing—get started on your first program. We can well understand that, and you won't be disappointed, because you will be writing programs in this very first chapter. Designing and writing computer programs—or **coding**, as its often referred to nowadays—can be one of the most enjoyable and satisfying things you can do, although it can seem a little daunting at first because it is like nothing else you have ever done. But, with a bit of perseverance, you will not only start to get a real taste for it, but you may well find yourself sitting up till two o'clock in the

---

Supplementary Information The online version contains supplementary material available at https://doi.org/10.1007/978-3-031-01326-3_1.

Table 1.1 PYPL popularity of programming language[1]

Worldwide, October 2021, compared to a year ago			
Rank	Language	Share (%)	Trend (%)
1	Python	29.66	−2.1
2	Java	17.18	+0.8
3	JavaScript	8.81	+0.4
4	C#	7.3	+1.1
5	C/C++	6.48	+0.7
6	PHP	5.92	+0.1
7	R	4.09	+0.2
8	Objective-C	2.24	−1.2
9	TypeScript	1.91	+0.1
10	Kotlin	1.9	+0.3

morning trying to solve a problem. And just when you have given up and you are dropping off to sleep, the answer pops into your head and you are at the computer again until you notice it is getting light outside! So, if this is happening to you, then don't worry—it's normal!

In this book we are going to cover two of the most popular programming languages in current use—Python in this semester and Java in the second semester. Both Python and Java are extremely popular programming languages, by whatever metric you use. At the time of writing, they came first and second, respectively, in the language tutorials most searched in Google (see Table 1.1). They both score at or near the top of tables that record the skills needed for jobs in the industry, and they are both used extensively for teaching programming skills at schools, colleges and universities around the world.

This semester we will be using Python. The development of Python began in the 1980s. The first release—Python 1.0—was in 1994. Version 2.0 was released in 2000, and 2008 saw the release of version 3.0. Python has since then become an extremely popular and widely used language. It is becoming more and more popular in schools, colleges and universities as a first programming language, mostly because of its simplicity and easy-to-read code. However, it is also very widely used in industry, particularly in the fields of web development, artificial intelligence and data science.

As we have said, it will not be long before you write your first program. However, before you start writing programs we need to make sure that you understand what we mean by important terms such as *program, software, code* and *programming languages*.

---

[1] https://pypl.github.io/PYPL.html.

1.2 Software

A computer is not very useful unless we give it some instructions that tell it what to do. This set of instructions is called a **program**. Programs that the computer can use can be stored on electronic chips that form part of the computer, can be stored on devices like magnetic or solid-state disk drives, or on optical media such as CDs or DVDs—and nowadays we often talk about "cloud" storage, which really just means remote storage devices whose type and location are hidden from us.

The word **software** is the name given to a single program or a set of programs. There are two main kinds of software:

- **Application software**. This is the name given to useful programs that a user might need; for example, word processors, spreadsheets, accounts programs, games and so on. Such programs are often referred to simply as **applications** or **apps**.
- **System software**. This is the name given to special programs that help the computer to do its job; for example, operating systems (such as UNIX™ or Windows™, which help us to use the computer) and network software (which helps computers to communicate with each other).

Of course, software is not restricted simply to computers themselves. Many of today's devices—from mobile phones to microwave ovens to games consoles—rely on computer programs that are built into the device. Such software is referred to as **embedded software**.

1.3 Programming

Both application software and system software are built by writing a set of instructions for the computer to obey. **Programming,** or **coding**, is the task of writing these instructions. These instructions have to be written in a language specially designed for this purpose. These **programming languages** include C++, Visual Basic, Python, Java and many more. In the first half of this book—the first semester—we will be using Python. In the second semester we will be moving on to Java.

Like most modern programming languages, both the Python language and the Java language consist of instructions that look a bit like English. For example, words such as **`while`** and **`if`** are part of both languages. Words that form part of the language are referred to as **keywords**, and in this text we are going to write keywords in bold fixed-width font so you can easily recognize them. The set of instructions written in a programming language is called the **program code** or **source code**.

---

[1] https://pypl.github.io/PYPL.html.

Ultimately these instructions have to be translated into a language that can be understood by the computer. The computer understands only **binary** instructions—that means instructions written as a series of 0s and 1s. So, for example, the machine might understand 01100111 to mean add. The language of the computer is often referred to as **machine code**.

There are different ways in which program code can be converted into machine code. In the case of languages such as C and C++, the whole thing is converted by using a piece of software called a **compiler**; once the program has been successfully compiled we end up with something we call an **executable** file, which can be run on a computer. This is illustrated in Fig. 1.1.

It should be noted that because binary instructions are different for particular computer operating systems (Windows™, macOS™, Unix™, etc.) an executable file has to be compiled for a specific operating system. Because of this, languages like Python and Java have been developed so that the compilation process is slightly different to the above.

In this chapter we will talk about the programming process for Python—but as you will see in Chap. 13, in Java the process is very similar, with only some slight differences.

When we code in Python we use a special program called an **interpreter**. You will see how to download and install that in the next section. When we run a Python program, we normally do so in what is known as **script mode**. In this mode the interpreter (which includes a compiler) translates our source code into special instructions called **byte code.** Byte code, which, like machine code, consists of 0s

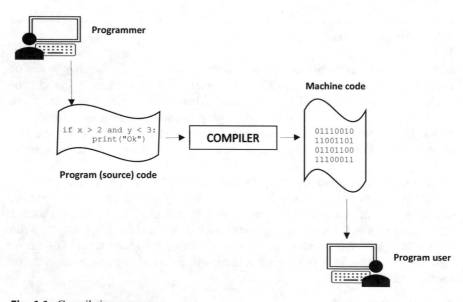

Fig. 1.1 Compilation process

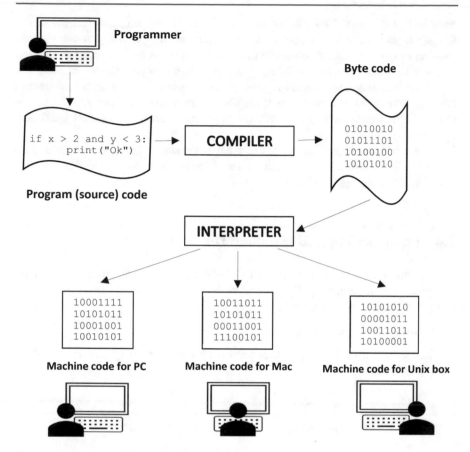

Fig. 1.2 Compiling and interpreting Python programs

and 1s, contains instructions that are exactly the same irrespective of the type of computer—it is *universal*, whereas machine code is specific to a particular type of computer.

Along with the interpreter comes a special program called a **virtual machine**. The job of the virtual machine is to translate each byte code instruction for the computer it is running on, before the instruction is performed. This process is known as **interpretation**. This is illustrated in Fig. 1.2.

As you will see later, in Python the source code is always saved in a file with a.py extension. The whole process of compiling and running the program is completely seamless—the byte code is in fact automatically saved into a file (with a.pyc extension), but this takes place in the background.

Programming languages have a very strict set of rules that you must follow. Just as with natural languages, this set of rules is called the **syntax** of the language. Before a program can be compiled, or can be run with an interpreter, the program must be free of errors. You will see when you start writing programs that the sort of things that can cause such errors are the incorrect use of special Python keywords, missing brackets and many others. When you try to run a Python program that has syntax errors, the interpreter will help you correct them, as you will see in Sect. 1.5.

If, at a later stage, we wanted to deploy our programs to computers that weren't running the Python interpreter, there are some easy-to-use third-party tools such as Pyinstaller™ that allow us to convert our programs to executable code for different operating systems.

Python programs can also be run in what is known as **interactive mode**. This mode provides a quick way of running lines of Python code without saving the code first. You will see this in action in Sect. 1.5.

1.4   Downloading and Installing the Interpreter

So, the first thing we need to do is to download and install the correct Python interpreter for our computer. Updated versions of Python appear regularly, and you can get the latest version from here:

https://www.python.org/downloads

Follow the instructions given there for downloading the interpreter and installing it on your machine.

1.5   Your First Program

As we have said, the normal way to write a program in Python is to create a file containing the program code. However, as we told you above, Python can also be run in interactive mode. The Python interpreter comes with a program called IDLE, and it is possible simply to type instructions at the prompt without saving them. You will probably realize immediately that this isn't a sensible way to run a whole program, as the instructions would have to be typed in each time. However, it is a very useful way to test a few quick lines of code, and it is something you can try out in future. And to demonstrate how this works, we will start off by running our first program—which contains only one line of code—in this way.

Now, anyone who knows anything about programming will tell you that the first program that you write in a new language has always got to be a program that displays the words 'Hello world' on the screen; so we will stick with tradition, and your first program will do exactly that!

Open your Python interpreter—you will see that the IDLE program appears (Fig. 1.3).

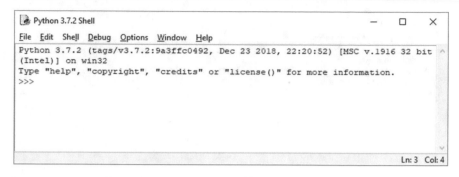

Fig. 1.3 IDLE program

The code for our first program is written out for you below—as you can see it consists of just one line:

```
print('Hello world')
```

The `print` command is always the way we get text printed on the screen—we will tell you a lot more about this in the next chapter. For now, just notice that whatever we want to be printed is enclosed in single quotes.

Type the above code at the prompt, exactly as you see it, press *Enter*, and you will see the words 'Hello world' displayed, as shown in Fig. 1.4.

As we have said, if we type commands like this at the prompt they can be run straight away, but if we want to run them again we would have to retype them each time. So, the normal way of doing things is to save the commands in a file once and then run this file as many times as we like. To do that, choose **File|New File** from the top menu bar of the IDLE program. You will be presented with a text editor into which you can type your program. So, type the above single line of code, and save your file, naming it `helloworld.py` (all Python scripts have the extension `.py`). See Fig. 1.5.

Run the program by choosing **Run|Run Module**, or simply by pressing F5 in a Windows™ environment, or (usually) Fn + F5 on a Mac™. The words 'Hello world' will appear on the IDLE screen as before.[2]

In Sect. 1.3 we told you that the interpreter will help you to correct any syntax errors that you make when you run the program. Try this out by leaving out the final bracket after 'Hello world' and then running the program again. The position of the error is highlighted, and a pop-up window appears telling you the nature of your error (Fig. 1.6).

---

[2] If you try to run the program without first saving it, you will be prompted to save it.

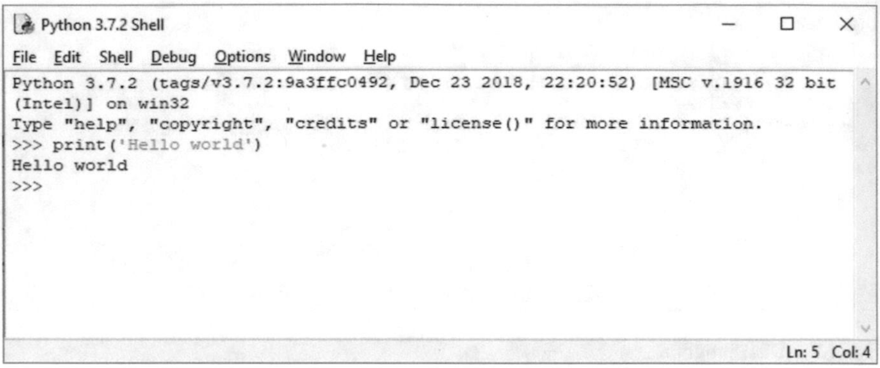

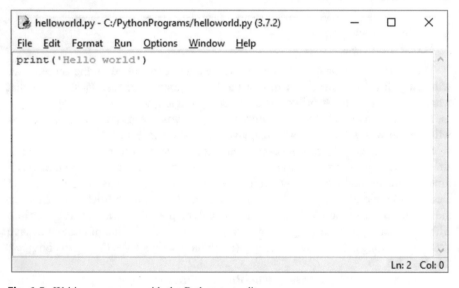

Fig. 1.4 Your first program

Fig. 1.5 Writing a program with the Python text editor

Now, it is true that the message in the window isn't all that helpful at the moment, but you will get used to working out what is wrong, particularly as the position of the error is indicated. Also, if we tell you that EOF stands for "End of file", you could probably work out that the compiler is saying that it has suddenly reached the end of the file before the brackets were closed. By the way, "parsing" simply means checking the grammar, as it does with natural languages. Try making another error such as leaving out the end quote, and see what the message says.

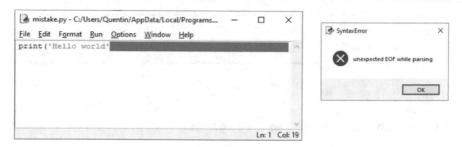

Fig. 1.6 Trying to run a program that contains a syntax error

Certain errors—**run-time errors**—will not be picked up by the compiler, but will only become apparent when the program is running. An example might be trying to perform a numerical calculation on something that isn't a number but is perhaps a piece of text like "banana".

It is also possible to make errors in your program that will never be picked up. These errors—known as **logical errors**—are the ones that involve writing code that has valid syntax, but does not do what you intended it to do. A simple example might be adding two numbers together when what was called for was to subtract one number from the other one. When you get to our case study in Chap. 12, you will see how we can develop testing strategies that pick up these sorts of logical errors.

The simple program above consisted of just one line. Normally, of course, programs will consist of many lines of code—so let's add in one more line as shown below and run the program again:

```
print('Hello world')
print('Hello world again')
```

As you have probably guessed—and as you will see for yourself when you run the program—this code results in the following output:

```
Hello world
Hello world again
```

As we said, you are going to find out a lot more about this in the next chapter. But we will tell you one more thing here—if you want a blank line in your program, you just need to leave the brackets empty. Try changing your program to this, and see what happens:

```
print('Hello world')
print()
print('Hello world again')
```

1.6 Adding Comments to a Program

When we write program code, we will often want to include some comments to help remind us what we were doing when we look at our code a few weeks later, or to help other people to understand what we have done.

Of course, we want the interpreter to ignore these comments when the code is being run. There are two different ways of doing this. For short comments we use a hashtag (#) to start the comment—everything after this hashtag, up to the end of the line, is then ignored by the interpreter.

For longer comments (i.e. ones that run over more than a single line) we usually use another approach. The comment is enclosed between two special symbols, which consist of three single quotes ('''). Everything between these two symbols is ignored when the program is run. The program below shows examples of both types of comment; when you run this program, you will see that the comments have no effect on the code, and the output is exactly the same as that of the original program.

```
# this is a short comment, so we use the first method

print('Hello world')  # we can also place a comment here

'''
this is the second method of including comments - it is more convenient to use this method here,
because the comment is longer and goes over more than one line
'''
```

Now that you have taken your first steps and have written your first program, you are ready to move on to the next chapter. There you will learn to write programs that not only output messages on the screen, but are also capable of processing information that is input by the user of your program, thereby making your programs truly interactive.

1.7   Self-test Questions

1. Explain the meaning of the following terms:
   - program;
   - software;
   - application software;
   - system software;
   - machine code;
   - source code;
   - embedded software.

2. Explain how Python programs are compiled, interpreted and run.
3. Describe two different ways of adding comments to a Python program.
4. Consider the program below, which will not run because it has syntax errors:

```
# this program has errors
print(Hi)                    .
print('Hope you are well)
print 'I am fine')
print 'Hope you are fine too'
```

Correct it so that it will output the following:

```
Hi
Hope you are well
I am fine
Hope you are fine too
```

1.8   Programming Exercises

1. Test out the program you adapted in question 4 above.
2. Write a program that displays your name, address and telephone number, each on separate lines.
3. Adapt the above program so that there is a blank line between your name and address.

4. Write a program that displays your initials in big letters made of asterisks. For example:

Do this by using a series of `print` commands, each printing one row of asterisks with spaces in the correct positions.

Python: Building Blocks

2

Outcomes

By the end of this chapter you should be able to:

- *write Python programs that display text on the screen;*
- *join messages in output commands by using the **concatenation** (+) operator;*
- *write programs that allow a user to input data into a program;*
- ***create** and **assign** values to **variables** and explain the concept of a **data type**;*
- *utilize the basic arithmetic operators available in Python;*
- *explain how to **type cast** from one data type to another;*
- *format strings in order to display information in different ways.*

2.1 Introduction

Now it is time to start writing your own programs. In this chapter, you will learn fundamental concepts that underpin the art of programming. You will learn how to display information on the screen, you will find out about the types of data that you can use in your programs, how to manipulate that data and how to make your programs interactive. It is vitally important that you study this chapter very carefully, because, although it is specific to Python, it nonetheless provides the fundamental building blocks that you need when coding in any language.

Supplementary Information The online version contains supplementary material available at https://doi.org/10.1007/978-3-031-01326-3_2.

© Springer Nature Switzerland AG 2022
Q. Charatan and A. Kans, *Programming in Two Semesters*,
Texts in Computer Science, https://doi.org/10.1007/978-3-031-01326-3_2

2.2 Output in Python

As you have seen from the *Hello world* program in Chap. 1, to output a message onto the screen in Python we use the following command:

print(*message to be printed on screen*)

For example, we have already seen:

```
print('Hello world')
```

Messages such as 'Hello world' are in fact what we call **strings**. A string is a sequence of characters. It can contain letters, numbers or characters such as question mark (?), exclamation mark (!) or currency symbols such as £ or €.

In Python, literal strings like this are always enclosed in quotes—they can be double quotes or single quotes.

So in fact we could have written the above command like this:

```
print("Hello world")
```

You can choose whichever one you like, but it's best to be consistent. In this text, we will use single quotes.

In Python, two strings can be joined together with the plus symbol (+). When using this symbol for this purpose, it is known as the **concatenation operator**. For example, instead of printing the single string 'Hello world', we could have joined two strings, 'Hello' and 'world', for output using the following command:

```
print('Hello ' + 'world')
```

Note that spaces are printed by including them within the single quotes ('Hello '), not by adding spaces around the concatenation operator (which has no effect at all).

By default, the print command ends with an instruction to start a new line. Consider, for example, the following two instructions:

```
print('Hello world')
print('Hello world again')
```

This would give is the following output:

```
Hello world
Hello world again
```

If we don't want to end with a new line, we can specify how we want the output to terminate by using a special end instruction as follows:

```
print('Hello world', end = '')
print('Hello world again')
```

Here, the end = ' ' after the string says that we do not want any character or instruction added to the string (the single quotes are empty). We would get:

Hello worldHello world again

If, instead, we wanted it to end with a few spaces we would write:

```
print('Hello world', end= '    ')
print('Hello world again')
```

which would result in:

Hello world   Hello world again

If we wanted the string to end with a symbol such as a dash, we would write:

```
print('Hello world', end= '-')
print('Hello world again')
```

This would give us:

Hello world-Hello world again

Remember, if we want a blank line then we simply use print with empty brackets:

```
print()
```

2.3 An Interactive Program

So now we have seen how to display something on the screen. But of course, we want our programs to do much more than just that. In particular, we will want our programs to be able to get data from the user and process it. So let's look at the very simple program below, which is stored in a file called inputdemo1.py. From now on we will present our programs as we have done below—with the file name at the top and the code below it. You can download this program from our website (see preface) or simply type it in. Run the program a couple of times, then we will discuss it.

---

inputdemo1.py

```
myName = input('What is your name? ')
print('Hello ' + myName)
```

As you will have seen, running this program would result in a dialogue like this:

```
What is your name? Ahmed
Hello Ahmed
```

The program asks the user to enter a name, and then responds to that with a message, using the name that was entered. Now, although this is very simple, there are loads important concepts and techniques to learn about just in those two lines. The first line, for example, displays a prompt on the screen and waits for the user to enter his or her name. And, as we shall see in a moment, it also stores that name in the computer's memory. The second line uses the data that has been stored to display a personal greeting. In the sections that follow, we are going to explore a lot of very important programming principles, and from time to time we will refer to this short program to illustrate them.

2.4 Variables and Types

Imagine a computer game that requires a piece of data to record the player's score as secret keys are found in a haunted house. The value of this item of data will vary as more keys are found. This piece of data would be referred to as a **variable**, because its value can vary.

Can you spot a variable in the inputdemo1.py program from the last section? The answer is that myName is a variable. Every time the program runs, it can hold a different value, depending on what the user enters.

In Python, when we create a variable such as myName, it is stored in the computer's memory and is "tagged" with a name in order that we can refer to it in our program. If the value of the variable is changed, that value is stored in a different memory location and the tag is directed at the new location.[1]

To create a variable in your program you must:

- give the variable a name (of your choice);
- give it an initial value.

---

[1] We should point out here that this is rather different from the way that variables are stored in most other computer languages such as C++ or Java. In the second semester you will be able to explore this in more detail.

There are some rules that we must observe when naming a variable in Python:

- a variable name must start with a letter or the underscore character;
- a variable name cannot be a Python keyword. Python keywords are special words that form part of the language itself (such as **if, for, while** that you will come across later). As we mentioned in the last chapter, in this text we will always use a bold fixed-width font for keywords.
- a variable name may contain only alpha-numeric characters and underscores (that is A–Z, 0–9 and _).

It is very important to remember that variable names are **case-sensitive**—so for example month, Month and MONTH are all different variables.

In this text we are going to stick with the convention of using lower case for variable names—but when the variable consists of two words joined together we will capitalize the first letter of the second word: For example, employeeName or studentNumber.

So what would be a suitable name for the variable in our haunted house game? We could simply call it score.

In Python, we have to give a variable an initial value. Since the score will be a whole number a suitable initial value might be zero.[2] We assign this value with the equality symbol (=). With our score variable we would do this as follows:

```
score = 0
```

So now score will have been given a value of zero. If we wanted it to start off with a value of 10, for example, we would do this:

```
score = 10
```

Giving a variable a value is known as **assignment**. As we stated above, assignments are written in Python with the use of the equality symbol (=). This symbol is known as the **assignment operator**. In general, simple assignments take the following form:

```
variableName = value
```

The above assignment should be read as '*set* the value of score *to* 10' or alternatively as 'score *becomes equal to* 10'.

We often talk about the **type** of a variable, which refers to the type of data that a variable holds. Having assigned a value of 10 to score, it currently holds an integer value. In Python, a variable that holds an integer is said to be of type int.

---

[2] Many languages such as C++ and Java require us to state explicitly state the type of value that a variable will hold. This is called **declaring** a variable. But in Python the all we have to do is give it an initial value.

Now, imagine we initialize a variable called `price` as follows:

```
price = 10.54
```

In this case, `price` will hold a floating point number (a decimal number). In Python, a variable that holds a floating point number is of type `float`.

What if we wanted a variable to hold a string? We would have to place the value in quotes—for example, using the `myName` variable from our example program we could write:

```
myName = 'Linda'
```

Although we are using single quotes in this text, double quotes could also be used, as we mentioned earlier:

```
myName = "Adewale"
```

Here, `myName` is of type `str`.

It is very helpful if we understand what is going on in the computer's memory when we create and assign values to variables. The way that this works in Python is actually quite different to the way it works in most common languages such as C++ and Java. Take a look at Fig. 2.1.

As you can see, when we create a variable such as `score` and give it a value, then a small part of the computer's memory is set aside to hold that value (0 in this case), and this location is "tagged" with our chosen name. When we assign a new

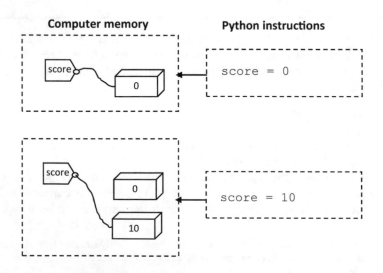

Fig. 2.1 Effect of creating and assigning variable in Java

value, a new location is created in memory to hold the new value (10 in this case) and the tag is now changed to that location. The old location is no longer available to us, and it becomes available for the system to use again.

The data types that we have come across so far (int, float and str) are all said to be **immutable**. This means that the value held in the particular memory location that is tagged with that variable's name cannot be changed. So, unlike the process in a language such as Java, in Python, when the variable is assigned a new value, that value is put into a new location and the tag is moved. So now, effectively, the variable holds a new value.

This might also mean that the *type* of the variable has changed.

As an example, consider a variable x. Let's assign this an initial value of 100:

```
x = 100
```

After this assignment, x is of type int and it holds a value of 100.

Now we make the following assignment:

```
x = 3.4
```

Now, x is of type float and it holds a value of 3.5.

2.5 Arithmetic Operators

Rather than just assign simple values (such as 24 and 2.5) to variables, it is often useful to carry out some kind of arithmetic in assignment statements. Python has the four familiar arithmetic operators, plus three others, for this purpose. These operators are listed in Table 2.1.

You can use these operators in assignment statements, much like you might use a calculator. For example, consider the following instructions:

```
x = 10 + 25
```

After these instructions, the variable x would contain the value 35: the result of adding 10–25. Terms on the right-hand side of assignment operators (like 10 + 25) that have to be *worked out* before they are assigned are referred to as **expressions**. These expressions can involve more than one operator.

Let's consider a line of code that works out the perimeter of a rectangle with a length of 4.5 and a height of 7.5. The perimeter is found by adding the length to the height and multiplying by 2, so the following line of code would do the job:

```
perimeter = 2 * (4.5 + 7.5)
```

Table 2.1 Arithmetic operators of Python

Operation	Python operator	Notes
Addition	+	The result is an int if all operands are ints, but a float if any of them are floats
Subtraction	–	
Multiplication	*	
Division	/	The result is always a float
Modulo	%	This gives us the remainder (an int) when one integer is divided by another For example: 8%3 = 2
Floor division	//	This rounds the answer to a division *down* to the nearest whole number (an int) for example 14//5 = 2
Exponent	**	This will calculate the value of a number raised to a power. The result is an int or float depending the type of the operands For example: 5**2 = 25

In case you are wondering, the order in which expressions such as these are evaluated is the same as in arithmetic: terms in brackets are calculated first, followed by division and multiplication, then addition and subtraction. So, in fact, we could have written our line of code like this:

```
perimeter = 2 * 4.5 + 2 * 7.5
```

In both cases the expression evaluates to 24.0.

Let's take a further look at a couple of the operators in Table 2.1. First is the **modulo** operator (%). This operator calculates the *remainder* after *integer division* (often referred to as the **modulus**). Table 2.2 illustrates some examples of the use of this operator together with the values returned.

Next let's look at **floor division** (//). This rounds the answer to a division *down* to the nearest whole number. Some examples are shown in Table 2.3.

As an illustration of the use of both the floor division operator and the modulo operator, consider the following example:

A large party of 30 people is going to attend a school reunion. The function room will be furnished with a number of tables, each of which seats four people.

To calculate how many tables of four are required, and how many people will be left over, the floor division and modulo operators could be used as follows:

```
tablesOfFour = 30//4 # number of tables
peopleLeftOver = 30%4 # number of people left over
```

Table 2.2 Examples of using the modulo operator in Python

Expression	Value
29% 9	2
6% 8	6
40% 40	0
10% 2	0

Table 2.3 Examples of using the floor division operator in Python

Expression	Value
7 // 2	3
50.3//3	16.0
41 // 2.0	20.0
56.7 // 21.1	2.0

After these instructions the value of `tablesOfFour` will be 7 (the result of dividing 30 by 4, rounded down) and the value of `peopleLeftOver` will be 2 (the remainder after dividing 30 by 4).

2.6   Expressions in Python

So far, variable names have appeared only on the left-hand side of assignment statements. However, the expression on the right-hand side of an assignment statement can itself contain variable names. If this is the case then the name does not refer to *the location*, but to *the contents of the location*. For example, the assignment to calculate the perimeter of the rectangle could have been rewritten as follows:

```
length = 4.5 # set length
height = 7.5 # set height
perimeter = 2 * (length + height) # calculate perimeter
```

Here, the variables `length` and `height` that appear in the expression

```
perimeter = 2 * (length + height)
```

are taken to mean *the values contained in* `length` and `height` respectively. This expression evaluates to 24.0 as before.

The first time we are using the variable name `perimeter` is in the third line above. So how do we know what type it is? The answer is that because the variables used in the expression are both decimal numbers then `perimeter` will be a float.

It is very common to find the name of the variable to which you are assigning an expression in the expression itself. This would just mean that the old value of the variable is being used to calculate its new value. Think again about the previous example in which a computer game keeps track of a player's score, which increases as secret keys are located. Imagine that finding a particular key adds 5 to a player's score.

Having created a variable called `score`, there is no need to create a new variable to store the value when the key has been located—instead, the calculation can update the *original* score as follows:

```
score = score + 5
```

Let's look at this assignment a bit more closely.

When reading this instruction, the score in the right-hand expression is to be read as the *old value* of `score`, whereas the score on the left-hand side is to be read as *the new value* of `score`.

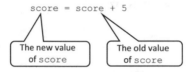

If `score` had initially been given a value of 0, then after executing this instruction it would have a value of 5. If we executed the same instruction again, its value would be 10.

You might be wondering what would happen if we used a variable in the right-hand side of an expression before it had been given a value. In this case you would get a run-time error caused by the fact that you are trying to use a variable before it has been created and initialized.

Before we move on, we will mention that there are a couple of short cuts that you might come across in other texts (we be won't be using them here, because they can be confusing to new programers):

The following expression:

```
y += x
```

is shorthand for:

```
y = y + x
```

Similarly

```
y -= x
```

is shorthand for:

```
y = y - x
```

2.7   More About Output

We have already seen how the `print` command allows us to display a message on
the screen. But as well as displaying messages, Python also allows any numerical
values or expressions to be used with the `print` command.

For example, the square of 10 can be displayed on the screen as follows:

```
print(10*10)
```

This instruction prints the number 100 on the screen.

However, if we want to concatenate (join) a numerical value to a string we need to
explicitly convert it to a string. We do this by placing `str` in front of the variable,
which is placed in brackets. You will see an example of this in a moment—it is called
type casting, and you will understand it more fully when you get to Sect. 2.10.

So as an example, let's return to the party of 30 people attending their school
reunion that we discussed in Sect. 2.5. If each person is charged a fee of 7.50 for the
evening, the total cost to the whole party could be displayed as follows:

```
print('cost = ' + str(30*7.5))
```

Here the concatenation operator (+), is being used to join the string, 'cost = ',
onto the value of the expression, the string equivalent of (30*7.5).

This would result in the following output:

```
cost = 225.0
```

Bear these ideas in mind and look at this little program which calculates the
amount of sales tax payable on a particular item:

```
findtax.py

# a program to calculate and display the sales tax on a product

print('*** Product Tax Check ***')
price = 500.0
taxRate = 17.5
tax = price * taxRate/100
print ('The amount of tax = ' + str(tax))
```

This program produces the following output:

```
*** Product Tax Check ***
The amount of tax = 87.5
```

Of course, in reality, the above program wouldn't actually be of much use to us: the problem is that it can only calculate the cost of products when the sales tax rate is 17.5% and the initial price is 500!

What is required is not to fix the rate of sales tax or the price of the product but, instead, to get the *user of your program* to *input* these values as the program runs.

2.8 Input in Python

As you saw in our first interactive program in Sect. 2.3, Python allows a user to input information at the keyboard by making use of the `input` command. For example, if the following line is executed in a program, the program will pause to allow the user to enter some information, and whatever is entered will be assigned to the variable `myName` *in the form of a string*.

```
myName = input()
```

However, it is almost always the case that when we want the user to enter something, we should prompt them to do so, rather than just leave them with a flashing cursor! So, one way of achieving this could be:

```
print('What is your name? ')
myName = input()
```

However, as we saw in Sect. 2.3, Python provides a very neat way of doing this, by simply allowing the text of the prompt to be placed in the brackets. For example:

```
myName = input('What is your name? ')
```

Let's remind ourselves of the program in which this line appeared:

inputdemo1.py
```
myName = input('What is your name? ')
print('Hello ' + myName)
```

We saw that a possible run of this program could look like this

```
What is your name? Ahmed
Hello Ahmed
```

Let's look at this a bit more carefully now. Firstly, notice that, in the print instruction, we have left spaces in the text so that it reads nicely. And notice, in particular, how we have concatenated the variable myName onto the string 'Hello'. We do not need to convert myName, because, as we have said, the return value of an input statement is always a string.

Let's extend this program so that now we ask the user for their age as well as their name:

---

inputdemo2.py

```
myName = input('What is your name? ')
print('Hello ' + myName)
print()
age = input('How are old are you? ')
print('When I was ' + age + ' I was older than you!')
```

Here is a possible run of this program:

```
What is your name? Mary
Hello Mary

How are old are you? 12
When I was 12 I was older than you!
```

Since the result of an input operation is a string, when the following line of code is executed the variable age will be of type str. Its value, in the above example, will be '12'.

```
age = input('How are old are you? ')
```

In the next line we concatenate it to two other strings:

```
print('When I was ' + age + ' I was older than you!')
```

Since all we are doing with this variable is to join it to other strings and display the result, this is fine. But what if we wanted to perform a calculation on this variable? Then it would have to be of type int or float.

As an example, consider the program below. Take a look at it, then we will go through it with you:

inputdemo3.py

```
myName = input('What is your name? ')
print('Hello ' + myName)
print()
age = int(input('How are old are you? ')) # convert input to integer
age = age + 1 # increase age by 1
print('When I was your age I was ' + str(age)) # convert age to string for printing
```

Although this is a rather short program there are some important learning points here.

As you can see in the last but one line, we are going to add 1 to the age that the user inputs. In order to do this, we need age to be an integer rather than a string. So when we obtain the input, we do so like this:

```
age = int(input('How are old are you? '))
```

We have placed the entire input instruction in brackets, and preceded it with the word int. The input string that is entered will be converted to an int and assigned to the variable age. Once again, this will be explained more fully in Sect. 2.10.

You might be asking yourself what would happen if the user entered something that didn't look like an integer (such as 'Hello' or '4.56'). The answer is that you would get an error at run time. In Chap. 4 we will show you how to make sure that the user enters information in the correct form.

Now look at the final line:

```
print('When I was your age I was ' + str(age))
```

As we mentioned before, the concatenation operator (+) can only be used with strings, so we have converted age to string so that it can be concatenated onto the first string. You should notice, however, that age remains an integer after this line is executed: we have not *assigned* anything to the variable itself. If we wanted to convert age to a string we would write:

```
age = str(age)
```

Below is a sample program run:

```
What is your name? Leroy
Hello Leroy

How are old are you? 9
When I was your age I was 10
```

As another example, let us rewrite our previous program—findtax.py—that calculated the amount of sales tax payable on an item; this time the price of the product and the rate of sales tax are not fixed in the program, but are input from the keyboard.

```
findtax2.py

'''
a program to input the initial price of a product and the rate of tax, and then calculate and display
the amount of tax to be paid
'''

print('*** Product Tax Check ***')
price = float(input('Enter initial price: ')) # get user to input price
taxRate = float(input('Enter tax rate: ')) # get user to input tax rate
tax = price * taxRate/100 # perform the calculation
print('The amount of tax = ' + str(tax))
```

Note that, by looking at this program code alone, there is no way to determine what the final price of the product will be, as the initial price and the tax rate will be determined *only when the program is run*.

Here is a possible run from this program:

```
*** Product Tax Check ***
Enter initial price: 1200
Enter tax rate: 12.5
The amount of tax = 150.0
```

2.9 Formatting Strings

Let's run our previous program again, but with some different inputs from the user:

```
*** Product Tax Check ***
Enter initial price: 130.99
Enter tax rate: 17.5
The amount of tax = 22.923250000000003
```

This time, the figures entered by the user resulted in a number that wasn't a nice round value. Since we are dealing with currency here, we would want our final figure to be shown to two decimal places only.

In order to achieve this we need to look at an alternative way to format our strings. We have rewritten our findtax.py program below. You can see that the last line has been changed. Take a look at it, then we will explain it to you.

---

findtax3.py

```
'''
a program to input the initial price of a product and the rate of tax, and then calculate and display
the amount of tax to be paid. This time the output will always be formatted neatly

'''

print('*** Product Tax Check ***')
price = float(input('Enter initial price: ')) # get user to input price
taxRate = float(input('Enter tax rate: ')) # get user to input tax rate
tax = price * taxRate/100 # perform the calculation
print('The amount of tax = %0.2f' %(tax))
```

With the same inputs as before, we now get

```
*** Product Tax Check ***
Enter initial price: 130.99
Enter tax rate: 17.5
The amount of tax = 22.92
```

As you can see, our new output has been achieved with this line of code:

```
print('Cost after tax = %0.2f' %(price))
```

The string that we are printing contains this rather strange-looking %0.2f. What is this all about? The answer is that a group of characters starting with the percentage sign (%) represents a *place holder*. Something will be inserted here. The information following the percentage sign tells the interpreter what type of quantity is to be expected and how it should be formatted. The f at the end indicates that we are expecting a float. The 0.2 stipulates how it should be formatted. The number after the decimal point—in this case 2—says that there must be two figures after the decimal point. The number before the decimal point specifies the minimum length of the outputted value (including the decimal point). This is useful if we want to line up a few outputs, because it will pad out the number with spaces at the beginning, if the length is less than that specified. In the above case we have a zero before the decimal point, so it will simply print the number with no leading spaces.

The value, or values, that replace the place holders are listed after the string, in brackets that follow another percentage sign. These can be actual values, or can be names of variables.

If the value is going to be a string or an integer we use s and d respectively instead of f. Again, numbers can indicate the minimum length.

Now this all sounds a bit complicated, but really it isn't. A few examples should make it all clear:

This line of code

```
print('My name is %s and I am %d years old' %('Olu', 7))
```

will result in the following output:

```
My name is Olu and I am 7 years old
```

Here we could have used variables instead of actual values:

```
myName = 'Olu'
age = 7
print('My name is %s and I am %d years old' %(myName, age))
```

Notice the difference if we specify minimum lengths for the string and integers:

```
print('My name is %6s and I am %10d years old' %('Olu', 7))
```

This causes the values in the string to be padded with leading spaces:

```
My name is    Olu and I am          7 years old
```

Finally, let's look at another float example:

```
num = 6.9865
print('The number to three decimal places is: %6.3f' %(num))
```

This gives us:

```
The number to three decimal places is:  6.987
```

Another way we could do this is, of course, to create our string and assign it to a variable, and then print the string. For example:

```
x = 4.5
y = 2.0
message = 'If we multiply %0.2f by %0.2f, we get %0.2f' %(x, y, x*y)
print (message)
```

The output is:

```
If we multiply 4.50 by 2.00, we get 9.00
```

One other thing to point out here. If we had initialized x and y as integers, this would still work. Python would do some implicit type casting and convert them to floating point numbers.

So now we have seen two ways of creating longer strings from variables—concatenation, and using a place holder that contains formatting instructions.

There is also another way, using the format function, which we will show you in Chap. 5.

2.10 Type Casting

You have seen in previous sections that it is often necessary to change the type of a variable. This is usually referred to as **type casting**.

In Python this is normally achieved by the use of one of three built-in *functions*. Now, we won't actually study functions until Chap. 5, but for now all you need to know is that a function is a routine for doing a particular job—and that when we execute a function it often calculates a result that it returns to us so that we can then assign it to a variable, or use it in other expressions.

You have already seen some of these functions in action. They are called int, float and str; you see that they have exactly the same name as the types themselves. They will, respectively, convert a variable to an integer, a decimal number or a string.

Here, we will also make use of another function, which is called type, that will report the type of a particular variable.

This is best understood by looking at some examples. Take a look at this little program:

```
typedemo.py

x = 5.7 # initialize x - it will start off as a float
y = int(x)  # type cast x to an int, and assign that value to y
z = str(x)  # type cast x to a str, and assign that value to z
print(type(x))# display the type of the variable x
print(type(y))  # display the type of the variable y
print(type(z))  # display the type of the variable z
```

We start off by initializing x with the value of 5.7. So x is initialized as a float.

Next we use the int function to return an integer version of x, and we assign this to y.

We then use the str function to return the string equivalent of x, and assign it to z.

Finally we use the type function to display the type of each of the variables in turn.

The output of the program is as follows:

```
<class 'float'>
<class 'int'>
<class 'str'>
```

You will see that the word *class* is used here instead of *type*. Don't worry about this right now—we will deal with classes when we get to Chap. 8.

There are occasions when Python does some type casting in the background, without us being aware of it. One example is in the print statement. This statement, as we have seen, expects to receive a string. But it is perfectly ok for us to write a statement like this, where x is an integer or a decimal number for example:

```
print(x)
```

The reason this works is that Python converts x to a string before displaying it. In this way, Python allows numbers, the value of variables, or the value of expressions to be displayed with the print command. This is often referred to as *implicit* type casting. Other examples of implicit type casting can be seen in Table 2.1, where, for example, a division operation will always result in a float, even if the two operands are integers—similarly if an int is added, subtracted or multiplied by a float the result is a float.

Let's use this fact to adapt our typedemo program so that instead of printing the *type* of each variable on the screen, we print its value:

typedemo2.py

```
x = 5.7 # initialize x as a float
y = int(x) # type cast x to an int, and assign that value to y
z = str(x) # type cast x to a str, and assign that value to z
print(x) # display the value x
print(y) # display the value y
print(z) # display the value z
```

Running this program will result in the following output:

```
5.7
5
5.7
```

Notice that when the float to int conversion is done, 5.7 becomes 5: the decimal part is simply chopped off.

As we mentioned above, by using the int and float functions we can type cast a string to a floating point number or an integer. However, in this case the string has to be in the correct form—in other words, something that looks like a decimal number or an integer.

So this would be fine:

```
s = '78.98'
x = float(s)
```

And so would this:

```
s = '78'
x = int(s)
```

But if we placed these lines in a program, we would get an error message:

```
s = 'Hello'
x = float(s)
```

There is also another very important point to notice. Using a function such as int, float or str *does not change the value of the variable itself*. The function simply returns a value which we can then use by, for example, assigning it to another variable.

Now, in fact, Python allows us to do something that many other programming languages do not—and this is because of its unusual method of assigning values to variables by "tagging", as we explained in Sect. 2.4. It allows us to effectively re-initialize the variable so that it becomes a different type. So we are able to do this sort of thing without getting an error:

```
x = 'Hello'
x = 5
x = 7.98
```

When it was first created, x held string. Then it held an integer, then finally a decimal number.

Because we are allowed to do this, we can effectively use our functions to change the type of a variable. For example we could write:

```
x = '37.5' # x is of type str
x = float(x) # x is now of type float
x = int(x) # x is now of type int
```

2.11 Escape Sequences

Imagine that we needed to include a single or double quote in a string—for example if we wanted the following output:

```
She typed 'Hello world'
```

We would have a problem, because as soon as the interpreter encountered the quote, it would think that the quote was meant to begin or end the string. To get round this, we use a special character, the backslash (\). This is known as the **escape character**. Any sequence of characters immediately following the backslash is called an **escape sequence**.

The escape character is also used if we want to include a tab or a newline in our string: '\t' inserts a tab, while '\n' inserts a new line.

Table 2.4 shows the escape sequences we can use to insert the characters we need.

Table 2.5 shows examples of how these are used, with the corresponding output.

Table 2.4 Escape characters

Escape character	Meaning
\n	Inserts a new line
\t	Inserts a tab
\'	Inserts a single quote
\"	Inserts a double quote
\\	Inserts a backslash

Table 2.5 Using the escape characters

Code	Output
`print('Hello\tWorld')`	`Hello    World`
`print('Hello\t\tWorld')`	`Hello        World`
`print('Hello\nWorld')`	`Hello` `World`
`print('Hello\n\tWorld')`	`Hello` `  World`
`print('\'Hello World\'')`	`'Hello World'`
`print('\"Hello World\"')`	`"Hello World"`
`print('C:\\python\\projects')`	`C:\python\projects`
`print('%s\t\t%s' %('Hello', 'World'))`	`Hello        World`

2.12 Self-test Questions

1. Which of the following would be valid names for a variable in Python?
   - `ticket`
   - `cinema ticket`
   - `cinemaTicket`
   - `cinema_ticket`
   - `if`
   - `Ticket`

2. What is the final value of z in the following program?

```
z = 20
x = 5
y = x + 2
x = 10
z = y * x
```

3. Take a look at each of the following short programs. What would be displayed on the screen in each case?

(a)

```
print('Hello %s. The car you want will cost £%0.2f' %('Ms Smith', 5000))
```

(b)

```
message = 'Hello %s. The car you want will cost £%0.2f' %('Ms Smith', 5000)
print (message)
```

(c)

```
x = 4
message = '%d squared = %d' %(x, x**2)
print (message)
```

4. What would be the final output from the program below if the user entered the number 10 when prompted.

```
num2 = 6
num1 = int(input('Enter value '))
num1 = num1 + 2
num2 = num1 / num2
print('result = %0.2f' %(num2))
```

5. The program below was written in an attempt to swap the value of two variables. However it does not give the desired result:

```
'''
This program attempts to swap the value of two variables
It doesn't give the desired result however!
'''

# enter values
x = int(input('Enter value for x '))
y = int(input('Enter value for y '))

# code attempting to swap two variables
x = y
y = x

#display results
print('x = %d' %(x))
print('y = %d' %(y))
```

(a) Can you see why the program doesn't do what we hoped?
(b) What would be the actual output of the program?

6. How could you modify the program in question 5 so that the values of the two variables are swapped successfully?
7. Create a program that asks the user to enter values for the length and height of a rectangle and then displays the area and perimeter of that rectangle.

2.13   Programming Exercises

1. Implement the programs from self-test questions 2 to 5 above in order to verify your answers to those questions. Then implement your corrected version of the program in question 6.
2. Implement the rectangle program that you designed in self-test question 7.
3. Create a program that allows the user to enter an amount in pounds, and then converts the amount to kilos (1 kilo = 2.2 pounds).
4. An individual's Body Mass Index (BMI) is a measure of a person's weight in relation to their height. It is calculated as follows:
   • divide a person's weight (in kg) by the square of their height (in metres).
   Design and implement a program to allow the user to enter their weight and height and then display their BMI.
5. A group of students has been told to get into teams of a specific size for their coursework. Design and implement a program that prompts for the number of students in the group and the size of the teams to be formed and displays how many teams can be formed and how many students are left without a team.
6. Design and implement a program that asks the user to enter a value for the radius of a circle, then displays the area and circumference of the circle.
   Note that the area is calculated by evaluating πr^2 and the circumference by evaluating $2\pi r$. You can take the value of π to be 3.1416—and ideally you should assign this to a variable at the start of the program.[3]

---

[3] Of course you will not be able to use the Greek letter π as a name for a variable. You will need to give it a name like PI.

Python Control Structures: Selection

3

Outcomes

By the end of this chapter you should be able to:

- *explain the difference between **sequence** and **selection**;*
- *use an **if** statement to make a single choice in a program;*
- *use an **if…else** statement to make a choice between two options in a program;*
- *use **elif** statements to make multiple choices in a program.*

3.1 Introduction

One of the most rewarding aspects of writing and running a program is knowing that *you* are the one who has control over the computer. But looking back at the programs you have already written, just how much control do you actually have? Certainly, it was you who decided upon which instructions to include in your programs but *the order in which these instructions were executed* was *not* under your control. These instructions were always executed in **sequence**, that is one after the other, from the beginning to the end of the program. You will soon find that there are numerous instances when this order of execution is too restrictive and you will want to have much more control over the order in which instructions are executed.

3.2 Making Choices

Very often you will want your programs to make *choices* among different courses of action. For example, a program processing requests for airline tickets could have the following choices to make:

Supplementary Information The online version contains supplementary material available at https://doi.org/10.1007/978-3-031-01326-3_3.

Q. Charatan and A. Kans, *Programming in Two Semesters*,
Texts in Computer Science, https://doi.org/10.1007/978-3-031-01326-3_3

- display the price of the seats requested;
- display a list of alternative flights;
- display a message saying that no flights are available to that destination.

A program that can make choices can behave *differently* each time it is run, whereas programs in which instructions are just executed in sequence behave the *same way* each time they are run.

As we have already mentioned, unless you indicate otherwise, program instructions are always executed in sequence. **Selection**, however, is a method of program control in which a choice can be made about which instructions to execute.

For example, consider the following program, which welcomes customers queuing up for a roller-coaster ride:

---
rollercoaster.py

```
age = input('How old are you? ')
print('Hello Junior!')
print('Enjoy your ride')
```

As you can see, there are three instructions in this program. Remember that at the moment these instructions will be executed in sequence, from top to bottom. Consider the following interaction with this program:

```
How old are you? 10
Hello Junior!
Enjoy your ride
```

This looks fine but the message 'Hello Junior!' is only meant for children. Now let's assume that someone older comes along and interacts with this program as follows:

```
How old are you? 45
Hello Junior!
Enjoy your ride
```

The message 'Hello Junior!', while flattering, might not be appropriate in this case! In other words, it is not always appropriate to execute the following instruction:

```
print('Hello Junior!')
```

What is required is a way of deciding (while the program is running) whether or not to execute this instruction. In effect, this instruction needs to be *guarded* so that it is only executed *when appropriate*. In other words (assuming that a child is defined to be a person who is 12 or under) we are saying that the print statement above is executed only *if* the user is under 13.

This is something we can do quite easily in Python, and indeed in any programming language. It is an example of the form of control known as **selection**. Let's now look at how to code this selection in Python.

3.3 The 'if' Statement

The particular form of selection discussed above is implemented by making use of Python's **if** statement.

A generalized version of an **if** statement would look like this:

```
if '''test goes here ''':
    # instruction(s) to be guarded go here
```

To understand what this means, let's adapt our roller-coaster program.

rollercoaster2.py

```
age = int(input('How old are you? '))
if age < 13: # the test controls if the next instruction is executed
    print('Hello Junior!')
print('Enjoy your ride')
```

What we are doing here is performing a *test* to see if we should execute the guarded instructions.

In this case the test is to see whether or not the user is under 13 years of age. But in general, a test is any expression that is going to be either *true* or *false*. In our example age < 13 is indeed a test as it is an expression that is will be either true or false, depending upon the value of age. In mathematics, we call an expression that evaluates to true or false a **boolean** expression.

In Python, **True** and **False** are keywords (note the upper-case initial letter), and a variable that holds one of these values is of type **bool**. We will see more of this later.

Examples of tests in everyday language are:

- this password is valid;
- there is an empty seat on the plane;
- the temperature in the laboratory is too high.

The test must follow the **if** keyword, and end with a colon (:). When the test gives a result of **True**, the instructions that are *indented* after the **if** statement are executed (in our case there is only one instruction—but there can be more, as we shall see later). The program then continues by executing the instructions after the indentation as normal. If, however, the **if** test gives a result of **False** the indented instructions are *skipped* and not executed.

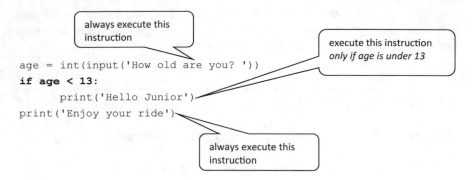

Fig. 3.1 The *if* statement allows a choice to be made in programs

Indentation is a very important part of the Python language, and we will see many more examples as we move forward.

So now, when we run our roller-coaster program, the message 'Hello Junior!' will be executed only if the test (`age<13`) is true; otherwise, it will be skipped (see Fig. 3.1).

Let's assume we run the above program with the same values that were entered when running the previous version. First, the child approaches the ride:

```
How old are you? 10
Hello Junior!
Enjoy your ride
```

In this case, the **if** statement has allowed the 'Hello Junior!' message to be displayed as the age entered is less than 13. Now the adult approaches the ride:

```
How old are you? 45
Enjoy your ride
```

In this case the **if** statement has not allowed the given instruction to be executed as the associated test was not true. The message is skipped, and the program continues with the following instruction to display 'Enjoy your ride'.

3.3.1 Comparison Operators

In the example above, the 'less than' operator (<) was used to check the value of the `age` variable. This operator is often referred to as a **comparison operator** as it is used to compare two values. Table 3.1 shows all the Python comparison operator symbols.

Since comparison operators give a result of **True** or **False** they are often used in tests such as those we have been discussing. For example, consider a temperature variable being used to record the temperature for a particular day of the week.

Table 3.1 Comparison operators of Python

Operator	Meaning
= =	Equal to
! =	Not equal to
<	Less than
>	Greater than
> =	Greater than or equal to
< =	Less than or equal to

Assume that a temperature of 18° or above is considered to be a hot day. We could use the 'greater than or equal to' operator (>=) to check for this as follows:

```
if temperature >= 18: # test to check for hot temperature
    # this line executed only when the test is true
    print('Today is a hot day!')
```

You can see from Table 3.1 that a double equals (= =) is used to check for equality in Python and not the single equals (=), which, as you know, is used for assignment. *To use the single equals is a very common error!* For example, to check whether an angle is a right angle the following test should be used:

```
if angle == 90: # note the use of the double equals
    print('This IS a right angle')
```

To check if something is *not equal* to a particular value we use the exclamation mark followed by an equals sign (! =). So to test if an angle is *not* a right angle we can have the following:

```
if angle != 90:
    print('This is NOT a right angle')
```

3.3.2 Multiple Instructions Within an 'if' Statement

So far we have only seen one instruction being guarded by an **if** statement. But that doesn't have to be the case.

Do you remember the example from the previous chapter that calculated the amount of tax on a product of a product? Here it is again:

---

findtax2.py

```
'''
a program to input the initial price of a product and the rate of tax, and then calculate and
display the amount of tax to be paid
'''
print('*** Product Tax Check ***')
price = float(input('Enter initial price: ')) # get user to input price
taxRate = float(input('Enter tax rate: ')) # get user to input tax rate
tax = price * taxRate/100 # perform the calculation
print('The amount of tax = ' + str(tax))
```

Now assume that a special promotion is in place for those products with an initial price over 100. For such products the company pays half the tax. The program below makes use of an **if** statement to apply this promotion, as well as informing the user that a tax discount has been applied. Take a look at it, and then we will discuss it.

findtaxwithdiscount.py

```
print('*** Product Tax Check ***')

price = float(input('Enter initial price: '))
taxRate = float(input('Enter tax rate: '))

# the following 'if' statement allows a selection to take place
if price > 100:   # test the price to see if a discount applies
                # these two instructions executed only when the test is true
                print('Special Promotion: We pay half your tax!')
                taxRate = taxRate * 0.5

# the remaining instructions are always executed
tax = price * taxRate/100
print('The amount of tax = %0.2f' %(tax))
```

Now, the user is still always prompted to enter the initial price and tax as before:

```
price = float(input('Enter initial price: '))
taxRate = float(input('Enter tax rate: '))
```

The next two instructions are then indented following an **if** statement. This means they might not always be executed:

```
if price > 100:
                print('Special Promotion: We pay half your tax!')
                taxRate = taxRate * 0.5
```

Since both these instructions are indented, they will be executed only when the test (price > 100) returns a result of **True**. So, for example, if the user had entered a price of 150 the discount would be applied; but if the user entered a price of 50 these instructions would not be executed and a discount would not be applied.

Regardless of whether or not the test was **True** and the instructions in the **if** statement were executed, the program always continues with the remaining instructions:

```
tax = price * taxRate/100
print('The amount of tax = %0.2f' %(tax))
```

Here is a sample program run when the test returns a result of **False** and the discount is not applied:

```
*** Product Tax Check ***
Enter initial price: 100
Enter tax rate: 10
The amount of tax = 10.00
```

In this case the program appears to behave in exactly the same way as the original program. Here, however, is a program run when the test returns a result of **True** and a discount does apply:

```
*** Product Tax Check ***
Enter initial price: 1000
Enter tax rate: 10
Special Promotion: We pay half your tax!
The amount of tax = 50.00
```

3.4 The 'if...else' Statement

Using the **if** statement in the way that we have done so far has allowed us to build the idea of a choice into our programs. In fact, the **if** statement made one of two choices before continuing with the remaining instructions in the program:

- execute the conditional instructions, or
- do not execute the conditional instructions.

The second option amounts to 'do nothing'. Rather than do nothing if the test returns **False**, an extended version of an **if** statement exists in Python to state an *alternative* course of action. This extended form of selection is the **if...else** statement. As the name implies, the instructions to be executed if the test evaluates to **False** are preceded by the Python keyword **else**. To illustrate how this works, take a look at the program below:

displayresult.py

```
print ('***Check your result ***')
print ()
mark = int(input('What exam mark did you get? '))

if mark >=40:
    # executed when test is true
    print('Congratulations, you passed')
else:
    # executed when test is false
    print('I'm sorry, but you failed')

print('Good luck with your other exams')
```

The syntax should be clear from the program. The statements following the **else** are indented as with the **if**. Notice also the colon after the **else**.

This program checks a student's exam mark and tells the student whether or not he or she has passed (gained a mark greater than or equal to 40), before displaying a good luck message on the screen. Let's examine this program a bit more closely.

Prior to the **if…else** statement the following lines are executed in sequence:

```
print ('***Check your result ***')
print ()
mark = int(input('What exam mark did you get? '))
```

Then the following condition is tested as part of the **if…else** statement:

```
mark >= 40
```

When this test returns **True** the following line is executed:

```
print('Congratulations, you passed')
```

When the test evaluates to **False**, however, the following line is executed *instead*:

```
print('I'm sorry, but you failed')
```

Finally, whichever path was chosen the program continues by executing the last line:

```
print('Good luck with your other exams')
```

The **if...else** form of control has allowed us to choose from *two* alternative courses of action. Here is a sample program run:

```
What exam mark did you get? 52
Congratulations, you passed
Good luck with your other exams
```

Here is another sample run where a different course of action is chosen.

```
What exam mark did you get? 35
I'm sorry, but you failed
Good luck with your other exams
```

3.5 Logical Operators

As we've already pointed out, the test in an **if** statement is an expression that produces a result of **True** or **False**. Often it is necessary to join two or more tests together to create a single more complicated test.

As an example, consider a program that checks the temperature in a laboratory. Assume that, for the experiments in the laboratory to be successful, the temperature must remain between 5 and 12 °C. The **if** statement will be required to combine the following two tests in order to ensure that the temperature is safe:

1. check that the temperature is greater than or equal to 5 (temperature >= 5);
2. check that the temperature is less than or equal to 12 (temperature <= 12).

Both of these tests need to evaluate to **True** in order for the temperature to be safe. When we require two tests to be **True** we use the following keyword to join the two tests:

and

Those of you who are familiar with mathematical logic will see that this corresponds to the logical AND operator ($\land$).

So the correct test is:

```
if temperature >= 5 and temperature <= 12:
```

Let's incorporate this into a little program:

---
laboratory.py

```
temperature = float(input('Enter tempertature: '))
if temperature >= 5 and temperature <= 12:
    print('TEMPERATURE IS SAFE!')
else:
    print('UNSAFE: RAISE ALARM!!')
```

Now, if the temperature were below 5, the first test (temperature >= 5) would evaluate to **False** giving a final result of **False**; the **if** statement would be skipped and the **else** statement would be executed:

UNSAFE: RAISE ALARM!!

If the temperature were greater than 12 the second part of the test (temperature <= 12) would evaluate to **False** also giving an overall result of **False**—and again the **if** statement would be skipped and the **else** statement would be executed.

However, when the temperature is between 5 and 12 *both* tests would evaluate to **True** and the final result would be **True** as required; the **if** statement would then be executed instead:

TEMPERATURE IS SAFE!

Notice that the two tests must be *completely* specified as each needs to return a boolean value of **True** or **False**. It would be wrong to try something like the following:

```
# wrong! second test does not mention 'temperature'!
if temperature >= 5 and <= 12
```

This is wrong as the second test (<= 12) is not a legal expression.

Symbols that join tests together to form longer tests are known as **logical operators**. There are three logical operators available in Python: **and**, **or** and **not**. Table 3.2 shows how they work:

Table 3.2 Logical operators of Python

Logical operator	Explanation
x **and** y	This will evaluate to **True** only if x and y are both **True**. Otherwise it evaluates to **False**
x **or** y	This will evaluate to **True** if either x or y (or both) are **True**. Otherwise it evaluates to **False**
not x	This will evaluate to **True** if x is **False**, and **False** if x is **True**

Table 3.3 Logical operators: some examples

Expression	Result	Explanation
10>5 and 10>7	**True**	Both tests are true
10>5 and 10>20	**False**	The second test is false
10>15 and 10>20	**False**	Both tests are false
10>5 or 10>7	**True**	At least one test is true (in this case both tests are true)
10>5 or 10>20	**True**	At least one test is true (in this case just one test is true)
10>15 or 10>20	**False**	Both tests are false
not 10>5	**False**	Original test is true
not 10>15	**True**	Original test is false

While both the **and** operator and the **or** operator join two tests together to give a final result, the **not** operator flips a value of **True** to **False** and a value of **False** to **True**. Table 3.3 gives some examples of the use of these logical operators:

To illustrate the use of the **not** operator, first take a look at this piece of code:

```
ok = True
if ok:
    print('ok is True')
```

Because the variable ok is a **bool**, with a value of **True**, the test of the **if** statement is **True** and we will get an output of:

ok is True

Now we will negate ok in the test with the **not** operator:

```
ok = True
if not ok: # ok is negated
    print('ok is False')
```

Now our output is:

ok is False

In other words:
'**if** ok' is the same as: '**if** ok == True'
'**if not** ok' is the same as: '**if** ok == **False**'
For another example of the use of the **not** operator, let us return to the temperature example of Sect. 3.3.1. We said that we were going to assume that a temperature of greater than 18° was going to be considered a hot day. To check that the day is not a hot day we could use the **not** operator as follows:

```
if not temperature > 18: # test to check if temperature is not hot
    print('Today is not a hot day!')
```

Of course, if a temperature is not greater than 18° then it must be less than or equal to 18°. So, another way to check the test above would be as follows:

```
if temperature <= 18: # test to check if temperature is not hot
    print('Today is not a hot day!')
```

3.6 Nested 'if...else' Statements

Instructions within **if** and **if...else** statements can themselves be *any* legal Python commands. In particular they could contain other **if** or **if...else** statements. This form of control is referred to as **nesting**. Nesting allows multiple choices to be processed.

As an example, consider the following program, which asks a student to enter his or her tutorial group (A, B or C) and then displays on the screen the time of the software lab.

Timetable.py

```
print('***Lab Times***') # display header

group = input('Enter your group (A,B,C): ')

# check tutorial group and display appropriate time
if group == 'A':
    print('10.00 a.m') # lab time for group A
else:
    if group == 'B':
        print('1.00 p.m') # lab time for group B
    else:
        if group == 'C':
            print('11.00 a.m') # lab time for group C
        else:
            print('No such group') # invalid group
```

As you can see, nesting can result in code with many indents and could soon become difficult to read. Such code can be made easier to read by using the Python keyword **elif**, which joins the **else if** together. We do this in the second version of the timetable program shown below:

timetableversion2.py

```
print('***Lab Times***') # display header

group = input('Enter your group (A,B,C): ')

# check tutorial group and display appropriate time
if group == 'A':
    print('10.00 a.m') # lab time for group A
elif group == 'B':
    print('1.00 p.m') # lab time for group B
elif group == 'C':
    print('11.00 a.m') # lab time for group C
else:
    print('No such group') # invalid group
```

You'll agree that this version looks a lot neater!

You might have noticed that in this program we have included some basic **error checking**. That is, the program does not *assume* that the user of this program will always type the *expected* values. If the wrong group (not A, B or C) is entered, an error message is displayed saying '*No such group*'.

```
# valid groups checked above
else:
    print('No such group') # error message
```

Error checking like this is a very good habit to get into.

There is one other point to notice here. The program is set up so that only the upper-case letters, 'A', 'B' and 'C' are accepted as valid. If the user were to enter 'a' for example, then 'No such group' would be displayed. Can you think how to fix this? You will have the opportunity to do that in the exercises at the end of the chapter.

3.7   Self-test Questions

1. Explain the difference between *sequence* and *selection*.
2. When would it be appropriate to use
   - an **if** statement?
   - an **if…else** statement?
   - an **elif** statement?
3. Consider the following Python program, which is intended to display the cost of a cinema ticket. Part of the code has been replaced by a comment:

```
price = 10.00
age = input('Enter your age: ')

# code to reduce ticket price for children goes here

print('Ticket price = %5.2f' %(price))
```

Replace the comment so that children under the age of 14 get half price tickets.

4. Consider the following program:

```
x = int(input('Enter a number: '))
if x > 10:
    print('Green')
    print('Blue')
print('Red')
```

What would be the output from this program if
(a) the user entered 10 when prompted?
(b) the user entered 20 when prompted?

5. Consider the following program:

```
x = int(input('Enter a number: '))
if x > 10:
    print('Green')
else:
    print('Blue')
print('Red')
```

What would be the output from this program if
(a) the user entered 10 when prompted?
(b) the user entered 20 when prompted?

6. Consider the following program:

```
x = int(input('Enter a number: '))
if x == 1 or x == 2:
    print('Green')
elif x == 3 or x == 4 or x == 5:
    print('Blue')
else:
    print('numbers 1-5 only')
print('Red')
```

What would be the output from this program if
(a) the user entered 1 when prompted?
(b) the user entered 2 when prompted?
(c) the user entered 3 when prompted?
(d) the user entered 10 when prompted?
(e) the first line of the program was replaced by the following and the user entered 1?

```
x = input('Enter a number: ')
```

3.8 Programming Exercises

1. Implement and run the programs from self-test questions 3—6 above to test your answers.
2. Design and implement a program that asks the user to enter two numbers and then displays the message 'NUMBERS ARE EQUAL', if the two numbers are equal and 'NUMBERS ARE NOT EQUAL', if they are not equal.

   Hint : Don't forget to use the double equals (==) to test for equality.
3. Adapt the program developed in the question above so that as well as checking if the two numbers are equal, the program will also display 'FIRST NUMBER BIGGER' if the first number is bigger than the second number and display 'SECOND NUMBER BIGGER' if the second number is bigger than the first.
4. Design and implement a program that asks the user to enter two numbers and then guess at the sum of those two numbers. If the user guesses correctly a congratulatory message is displayed; otherwise, a commiseration message is displayed along with the correct answer.
5. Implement the `displayresult.py` program from Sect. 3.4 which processed an exam mark, and then adapt the program so that marks of 70 or above are awarded a distinction rather than a pass.
6. In programming exercise 5 of the previous chapter you were asked to calculate the BMI of an individual. Adapt this program so that it also reports on whether the BMI is in a healthy range, or if it indicates the person is underweight or overweight, using the following table:

BMI	Classification
<18.5	Underweight
18.5–24.9	Healthy
>24.9	Overweight

7. Write a program to take an order for a new computer. The basic system costs 375.99. The user then has to choose from a 38 cm screen (costing 75.99) or a 43 cm screen (costing 99.99). The following extras are optional.

Item	Price
Antivirus software	65.99
Printer	125.00

   The program should allow the user to select from these extras and then display the final cost of the order.
8. Implement the `timetableversion2.py` program (Sect. 3.6) so that it accepts both upper-case and lower-case letters for the group

9. Consider a bank that offers four different types of account ('A', 'B', 'C' and 'X'). The following table illustrates the annual rate of interest offered for each type of account.

Account	Annual rate of interest (%)
A	1.5
B	2
C	1.5
X	5

Design and implement a program that allows the user to enter an amount of money and a type of bank account, before displaying the amount of money that can be earned in one year as interest on that money for the given type of bank account.

Hint: be careful to consider the case of the letters representing the bank accounts. You might want to restrict this to, say, just upper case. Or you could enhance your program by allowing the user to enter either lower-case or upper-case letters.

10. Consider the bank accounts discussed in exercise 9 again. Now assume that each type of bank account is associated with a minimum balance as given in the table below:

Account	Minimum balance
A	250
B	1000
C	250
X	5000

Adapt the program in exercise 9 above so that the interest is applied only if the amount of money entered satisfies the minimum balance requirement for the given account. If the amount of money is below the minimum balance for the given account an error message should be displayed.

Python Control Structures: Iteration

4

Outcomes

By the end of this chapter you should be able to:

- *explain the term* **iteration**;
- *repeat a section of code with a* **for** *loop;*
- *repeat a section of code with a* **while** *loop;*
- *select the most appropriate loop for a particular task;*
- *use a* **break** *statement to terminate a loop;*
- *use a* **continue** *statement to skip an iteration of a loop;*
- *explain the term* **input validation** *and write simple validation routines;*
- *use a* **try** ... **except** *statement to catch run-time exceptions.*

4.1 Introduction

One of the advantages of using computers rather than humans to carry out tasks is that they can repeat those tasks over and over again without ever getting tired. With a computer we do not have to worry about mistakes creeping in because of fatigue, whereas humans would need a break to stop them becoming sloppy or careless when carrying out repetitive tasks over a long period of time. Neither sequence nor selection allows us to carry out this kind of control in our programs. As an example,

Supplementary Information The online version contains supplementary material available at https://doi.org/10.1007/978-3-031-01326-3_4.

Q. Charatan and A. Kans, *Programming in Two Semesters*,
Texts in Computer Science, https://doi.org/10.1007/978-3-031-01326-3_4

consider a program that needs to display a square of stars (five by five) on the
screen as follows:

```
* * * * *
* * * * *
* * * * *
* * * * *
* * * * *
```

This could be achieved with five output statements executed in sequence, as
shown in below in a program which we have called `drawpattern.py`:

drawpattern.py

```
print('*****') # instruction to display one row
print('*****') # instruction to display one row
print('*****') # instruction to display one row
print('*****') # instruction to display one row
print('*****') # instruction to display one row
```

While this produces the desired result, the program actually consists just of the
following instruction to print out one row, but repeated five times:

```
print('*****') # this instruction is written five times
```

Writing out the same line many times is somewhat wasteful of our precious time
as programmers. Imagine what would happen if we wanted a square 40 by 40!

Rather than write out this instruction five times, it would be preferable if *the
program* were to execute the line five times.

Iteration is the form of program control that allows us to instruct the computer
to carry out a task several times by repeating a section of code. For this reason, this
form of control is often also referred to as **repetition**. The programming structure
that is used to control this repetition is often called a **loop**; we say that the loop
iterates a certain number of times. There are two types of loop in Python:

- **for** loop;
- **while** loop.

We will consider each of these in turn.

4.2 The 'for' Loop

If we wish to repeat a section of code a *fixed* number of times (five in the example
above), we would use Python's **for** loop. For example, the program below rewrites
`drawpattern.py` by making use of a **for** loop. Take a look at it and then we
will discuss it:

drawpattern2.py

```
for i in range(0, 5, 1): #  loop to repeat 5 times
    print('*****') # instruction to display one row
```

The **for** loop tells the program to repeat some instructions a specific number of times. The instructions to be repeated (only one in the above program) are indented after the **for** statement.

The first line, which in this case instructs the program to repeat an action five times, looks rather unfamiliar—so let's take a closer look.

The i that you see is an integer variable which acts as a **counter** that counts the number of times we go round the loop. It is called i here, but we could have given it any name we chose.

If we were to write out a generalized version of the **for** loop, it would look like this:

```
for i in range(start, end , step): # start, end and step are integer variables
    # instruction(s) to be repeated go here
```

As you can see there are three integers in the brackets following the word range; each is separated by a comma.

The first of these determines the initial value of the counter, **i**. In the draw-pattern2.py program we have initialized it to 0.

Each time we go round the loop, i is increased by the amount specified by the third integer value, step. This has been specified as 1 in our drawpattern2.py program. Before the loop is repeated the value of i is tested—if it has reached the value specified by the second integer, end, then the repetition stops and the program moves on to carry out the instructions in the rest of the program.

In the drawpattern2.py program end has been specified as 5. So on the first iteration of the loop i starts at 0—this is less than 5, so the instruction to print the row of stars is executed. The counter is then increased to 1, and the value is tested. As it has not reached the end value, 5 the instruction inside the loop is carried out again. This continues while i is increased to 2, then 3, then 4. But after five iterations (0, 1, 2, 3, 4), when i is tested it will be equal to 5 so the loop stops and the program moves on past the loop.

To illustrate what we have just told you, we have changed our drawpattern. py program so that instead of printing out a row of stars, each time we go round the loop, we print the value of i:

counterdemo.py

```
for i in range(0, 5, 1):
    print(i)
```

The output from this program is:

```
0
1
2
3
4
```

In our programs so far, only one statement is required to be repeated. In the next version of drawpattern.py, *two* lines are executed every time we go round the loop. As you can see, we have also changed the number of iterations to three instead of five.

---

drawpattern3.py

```
for i in range(0, 3, 1): # loop to repeat 3 times
    print("++++++")
    print("xxxxxx")
```

The output from this program is:

```
++++++
xxxxxx
++++++
xxxxxx
++++++
xxxxxx
```

It is very useful to know that it is possible to specify the range function within the **for** loop with fewer items in the brackets. For example:

```
for i in range(5):
```

When there is only one item specified it refers to the end value. In such a case the start value is set at 0 and the step at 1. In other words, it can be used when all we wish to do is repeat a set of instructions a certain number of times, which is often the case. We will be using this version of the range function in later examples; in effect, it simply says repeat a given number of times (5 in the above example).

So rewriting our original drawpattern.py program in this way, we would have:

---

drawpattern4.py

```
for i in range(5): #  loop to repeat 5 times
    print('*****') # instruction to display one row
```

There is also a version with two items, for example:

```
for i in range(2, 10):
```

These values specify the start and end values of the counter; the step will again be set at 1.

4.2.1 Varying the Loop Counter

The drawpattern programs illustrated a common way of using a **for** loop; start the counter at 0 and add 1 to the counter each time the loop repeats. However, you may start your counter at *any* value and change the counter in any way you choose when constructing your **for** loops.

For example, we could have rewritten the **for** loop of the above program so that the counter starts at 1 instead of 0. In that case, if we wish the **for** loop to still execute the instructions 5 times, the loop must finish when the counter reaches 6 and not 5:

```
# this counter starts at 1 and goes up to 6 so the loop still executes 5 times
for i in range(1, 6, 1): #  loop to repeat 5 times
    print('*****') # instruction to display one row
```

We can also change the way we modify the counter after each iteration. Returning to the original **for** loop, we could increment the counter by 2 each time instead of 1. If we still wish the loop to repeat 5 times, we could start at 2 and get the counter to go up to 11—in other words, the loop should repeat as long as the counter does not reach 11:

```
# this loop still executes 5 times
for i in range(2, 11, 2): # the counter moves up in steps of 2
    print('*****')
```

Finally, counters can move down as well as up. As an example, look at the following program that prints out a countdown of the numbers from 10 down to 1.

countdown.py
```
print('*** Numbers from 10 to 1 ***')
for i in range(10, 0, -1): # counter moving down from 10 to 1
    print(i)
```

Here the counter starts at 10 and is reduced by 1 each time. The loop stops when the counter falls to 0.

```
*** Numbers from 10 to 1 ***

10
9
8
7
6
5
4
3
2
1
```

4.2.2   The Body of the Loop

The body of the loop can contain any number and type of instructions, including assignments, **if** statements, or even another loop! For example, the dis-playeven.py program below modifies our countdown.py by including an **if** statement inside the **for** loop so that only the *even* numbers from 10 to 1 are displayed:

---

displayeven.py

```
print('*** Even numbers from 10 to 2 ***')
for i in range(10, 0, -1): # counter moving down from 10 to 1
    if i%2 == 0:
        print(i)
```

You can see that the body of the **for** loop contains within it an **if** statement. The test of the **if** statement checks the current value of the loop counter i to see if it is an even number:

```
if i%2 == 0:
    printi(i)
```

An even number is a number that leaves no remainder when divided by 2, so we use the modulo operator (%) to check this. Now the loop counter is displayed only if it is an even number. Running the program gives us the obvious results:

```
*** Even numbers from 10 to 1 ***

10
8
6
4
2
```

In this example we included an **if** statement inside the **for** loop. It is also possible to have one **for** loop inside another. When we have one loop inside another we refer to these loops as **nested** loops. As an example of this consider the program drawpattern5.py below, which displays a square of stars as before, but this time uses a pair of nested loops to achieve this:

---

drawpattern5.py

```
for i in range(5): # outer loop controlling the number of rows
    for j in range(5): # inner loop controlling the number of stars in one row
        print('*', end = '')
    print()
```

You can see that the outer **for** loop is the same as the one used previously in drawpattern2.py, although this time we have used the shorter version that only requires the end value of the counter (remember this means the counter starts at 0, with a step of 1, so that the loop will execute 5 times). Whereas in the original program we had a single instruction to display a single row of stars inside our loop:

```
print('*****') # original instruction inside the 'for' loop
```

---

in drawpattern5.py we have replaced this instruction with *another* **for** loop, followed by a blank print instruction:

```
# new instructions inside the original 'for' loop to print a single row of stars
for j in range(5):
    print('*', end = '')
print()
```

Notice first of all that when we place one loop inside another, we need a fresh name for the loop counter in the nested loop. In this case we have called the counter j.

Notice also the form of the print statement which has the expression end = '' after the string to be printed, which in this case is a single star. As we saw in Chap. 2, this has the effect of causing the cursor to remain on the same line after printing, rather than starting a new line. The **for** loop now needs to be followed by an instruction to start a new line, print().

These instructions together allow us to display a single row of 5 stars and move to a new line, ready to print the next row.

Let's look at how the control in this program flows. First the outer loop counter is set to 0, so the instructions within the **for** loop are executed. The first instruction is another loop which displays five stars in a row:

```
* * * * *
```

The second instruction moves the cursor to a new line.

Now the outer loop counter, i, is increased to 1, and the outer loop is again executed so that a second row of stars is displayed. This continues until i becomes equal to 5, and the loop finishes.

drawpattern5.py displayed a five by five square of stars. Now take a look at the next program and see if you can work out what it does. Look particularly at the header of the inner loop:

---

drawpattern6.py

```
for i in range(5): # outer loop controlling the number of rows
    for j in range(i+1): # inner loop controlling the number of stars in one row
        print('*', end = '')
    print()
```

You can see this is very similar to the previous program, except that in that program the inner loop displayed 5 stars each time. In this case the number of stars is not fixed to a particular number, but instead to the value of the outer loop counter i, plus 1.

So let's work out what this will do. The first time around the counter of the outer loop, i, is 0. The counter of the inner loop, j, starts at 0 and ends at 1 (the value of i + 1). So it will display one star, but then stop because next time round j is equal to 1.

The second time round the loop, i is equal to 1, so the inner loop again starts at 0, but this time the end value is 2; so two stars will be displayed. The third time 3 stars will be displayed, and so on until 5 stars are displayed. At this point i will be equal to 6 and the process will stop. Effectively this means the program will display a *triangle* of stars as follows:

```
*
*  *
*  *  *
*  *  *  *
*  *  *  *  *
```

4.2.3 Revisiting the Loop Counter

Before we move on to look at other kinds of loops in Python it is important to understand that, although a **for** loop is used to repeat something a fixed number of times, you don't necessarily need to know this fixed number when you are writing the program. This fixed number could be a value given to you by the user of your program, for example. This number could then be used to test against your loop counter. The program below modifies drawpattern5.py by asking the user to determine the size of the square of stars. Notice in this case we have chosen to use the form of the range function that takes just one parameter.

---

drawpattern7.py

```
# prompt and get user reply
num = input('Size of square? ')
num = int(num)
for i in range(num):  # loop to repeat num times
    for j in range(num):
        print('*', end = '')  # instruction to display one row
    print()
```

In this program you cannot tell from the code exactly how many times the loops will iterate, but you can say that they will iterate num number of times—whatever the user may have entered for num. So in this sense the loop is still fixed. Here is a sample run of drawpattern7.py:

```
Size of square? 7
* * * * * * *
* * * * * * *
* * * * * * *
* * * * * * *
* * * * * * *
* * * * * * *
* * * * * * *
```

Here is another sample run:

```
Size of square? 3
* * *
* * *
* * *
```

4.3 The 'while' Loop

Much of the power of computers comes from the ability to ask them to carry out repetitive tasks, so iteration is a very important form of program control. The **for** loop is an often-used construct to implement fixed repetitions.

Sometimes, however, a repetition is required that is *not fixed* and a **for** loop is not the best one to use in such a case. Consider the following scenarios, for example:

- a racing game that repeatedly moves a car around a track until the car crashes;
- a ticket issuing program that repeatedly offers tickets for sale until the user chooses to quit the program;
- a password checking program that does not let a user into an application until he or she enters the right password.

Each of the above cases involves repetition; however, the number of repetitions is not fixed but depends upon some condition. The **while** loop provides the means of implementing non-fixed iteration. The syntax for constructing this loop in Python is as follows:

```
while ''' test goes here ''' :
    # instruction(s) to be repeated go here
```

As you can see, this loop is much simpler to construct than a **for** loop; as this loop is not repeating a fixed number of times, there is no need to create a counter to keep track of the number of repetitions. The loop will repeat so long as the test (which is a **bool** expression) evaluates to **True**.

When might this kind of loop be useful? The first example we will explore is the use of the **while** loop to check data that is input by the user. Checking input data for errors is referred to as **input validation**.

For example, look back at a fragment of the program `displayresult.py` in the last chapter, which asked the user to enter an exam mark:

```
mark = int(input('What exam mark did you get? '))
if mark >=40:
    # rest of code goes here
```

The mark that is entered should never be greater than 100 or less than 0. At the time we assumed that the user would enter the mark correctly. However, good programmers never make this assumption!

Before accepting the mark that is entered and moving on to the next stage of the program, it is good practice to check that the mark entered is indeed a valid one. If it is not, then the user will be allowed to enter the mark again. This will go on until the user enters a valid mark.

An error message should be displayed every time the user enters an invalid mark. The user may enter an invalid mark many times, so an iteration is required here.

However, the number of iterations is not fixed as it is impossible to say how many, if any, mistakes the user will make.

This sounds like a job for the **while** loop:

```
mark = int(input('What exam mark did you get? '))

while mark < 0 or mark > 100: # check if mark is invalid
    mark = int(input('Invalid mark: please re-enter: '))
# rest of code goes here
```

The program below shows the whole of the displayresult.py rewritten to include the input validation. Notice how this works—we ask the user for the mark; if it is within the acceptable range, the **while** loop is not entered and we move past it to the other instructions. But if the mark entered is less than zero or greater than 100 we enter the loop, display an error message and ask the user to input the mark again. This continues until the mark is within the required range.

displayresult2.py

```
print('***Check your result ***')
print()
mark = int(input('What exam mark did you get? '))

while mark < 0 or mark > 100: # check if mark is invalid
    mark = int(input('Invalid mark: please re-enter: '))

# by this point the loop is finished and mark will be valid
if mark >= 40:
    print('Congratulations, you passed')
else:
    print('I'm sorry, but you failed')
print('Good luck with your other exams')
```

Here is a sample program run:

```
What exam mark did you get? 101

Invalid mark: please re-enter: -10

Invalid mark: please re-enter: 10

I'm sorry, but you failed

Good luck with your other exams
```

Let's look at another example. Think about all the programs you have written so far. In each case, once the program has done its job it terminates—if you want it to perform the same task again, you have to go through the whole procedure of running the program again.

In many cases a better solution would be to put your whole program in a loop that keeps repeating until the user chooses to quit the program. This would involve asking the user each time if he or she would like to continue repeating the program, or to stop.

A **for** loop would not be the best loop to choose here as this is more useful when the number of repetitions can be predicted; a **while** loop is a better choice:

```
response ='y'
while response == 'y' or response == 'Y':
    # program instructions go here
```

There is something important to notice here. The user's reply will be assigned to the variable response—however, before we enter the **while** loop we need to initialize this to a value that will make the test evaluate to **True** and hence allow the loop to be entered. So, in this case we have given it an initial value of 'y'.

As an example of this, the program below amends the findtax2.py program of Chap. 2, which calculated the cost of a product, by allowing the user to repeat the program as often as he or she chooses.

findtax3.py
```
print('*** Product Tax Check ***')
response ='y'
while response == 'y' or response == 'Y':

    price = float(input('Enter initial price: '))
    taxRate = float(input('Enter tax rate: '))

    tax = price * taxRate/100;
    print('The amount of tax = %0.2f'  %(tax))

    # now see if user wants another go
    print()
    response = input('Would you like to enter another product(y/n)? ')
```

Here is sample program run:

```
*** Product Tax Check ***
Enter initial price: 50
Enter tax rate: 10
The amount of tax = 5.00

Would you like to enter another product(y/n)? y
Enter initial price: 70
Enter tax rate: 5
The amount of tax = 3.50

Would you like to enter another product(y/n)? y
Enter initial price: 200
Enter tax rate: 15
The amount of tax = 30.00

Would you like to enter another product(y/n)? n
```

Another way to allow a program to be run repeatedly using a **while** loop is to include a *menu* of options within the loop (this was very common in the days before windows and mice.). The options themselves are processed by a series conditional statements. One of the options in the menu list would be the option to quit, and this option is checked in the **while** condition of the loop. The program below is a reworking of the timetable program of the previous chapter using this technique.

---

timetablewithloop.py

```
response = '1' # initialize to a value that allows the loop to be entered

print('***Lab Times***')

while response != '4':  # put code in loop
    # offer menu of options
    print()
    print('[1] TIME FOR GROUP A')
    print('[2] TIME FOR GROUP B')
    print('[3] TIME FOR GROUP C')
    print('[4] QUIT PROGRAM')
    print('enter choice [1,2,3,4]: ')

    print()

    response = input()

    if response == '1':
        print('10:00am')
    elif response == '2':
        print('1:00pm')
    elif response == '3':
        print('11:00am')
    elif response == '4':
        print('Goodbye')
    else:
        print('Options 1-4 only')
```

Notice that the menu option is treated as a string here, rather than an integer. So, option 1 would be interpreted as the string '1' rather than the number 1, for example. The advantage of treating the menu option as a string rather than a number is that an incorrect menu entry would not result in a program crash if the value entered was non-numeric. Here is a sample run of this program:

```
***Lab Times***

[1] TIME FOR GROUP A
[2] TIME FOR GROUP B
[3] TIME FOR GROUP C
[4] QUIT PROGRAM
enter choice [1,2,3,4]: 2

1.00pm

[1] TIME FOR GROUP A
[2] TIME FOR GROUP B
[3] TIME FOR GROUP C
[4] QUIT PROGRAM
enter choice [1,2,3,4]: 5

Options 1-4 only

[1] TIME FOR GROUP A
[2] TIME FOR GROUP B
[3] TIME FOR GROUP C
[4] QUIT PROGRAM
enter choice [1,2,3,4]: 1
10.00am

[1] TIME FOR GROUP A
[2] TIME FOR GROUP B
[3] TIME FOR GROUP C
[4] QUIT PROGRAM
enter choice [1,2,3,4]: 3

11.00am

[1] TIME FOR GROUP A
[2] TIME FOR GROUP B
[3] TIME FOR GROUP C
[4] QUIT PROGRAM enter choice [1,2,3,4]: 4

Goodbye
```

4.4 The 'break' Statement

The **break** statement is used to terminate a loop before it reaches its natural end. For example, consider a program that allows the user a maximum of three attempts to guess a secret number. This is an example of a non-fixed iteration—but the iteration does have a fixed upper limit of three.

We could use either of the loop types to implement this. If we wished to use a **for** loop, however, we would need to make use of the **break** statement. Take a look at the following program that does this for a secret number of 27:

---

secretnumber.py

```
# This program demonstrates the use of the 'break' statement inside a 'for' loop

SECRET = 27 # secret number - we often use upper case for variable name that will remain constant
guessed = False # so far number not guessed

print('You have 3 goes to guess the secret number')
print('HINT: It is a number less than 50!')
print() # blank line

# look carefully at this loop
for i in range(3): #  loop to repeat 3 times
        num = int(input('Enter guess: '))
        # check guess
        if num == SECRET: # check if number guessed correctly
                guessed = True # record number has been guessed correctly
                break    # exit loop

# now check to see if the number was guessed correctly or not
if guessed:
    print('Number guessed correctly')
else:
    print('Number NOT guessed')
```

The important part of this program is the **for** loop. You can see that it has been written to repeat three times. Each time around the loop the user gets to have a guess at the secret number. We need to do two things if we determine that the guess is correct. Firstly, set a **bool** variable to **True** to indicate a correct guess. Then, secondly, we need to terminate the loop, even if this is before we reach the third iteration. We do so by using a **break** statement if the guess is correct:

```
for i in range(3): #  loop to repeat 3 times
        num = int(input('Enter guess: '))
        # check guess
        if num == SECRET: # check if number guessed correctly
                guessed = True # record number has been guessed correctly
                break    # exit loop
```

Here is a sample program run:

```
You have 3 goes to guess the secret number
HINT: It is a number less than 50!

Enter guess: 49
Enter guess: 27
Number guessed correctly
```

Here the user guessed the number after two attempts and the loop terminated early due to the **break** statement. Here is another program run where the user fails to guess the secret number:

```
You have 3 goes to guess the secret number
HINT: It is a number less than 50!

Enter guess: 33
Enter guess: 22
Enter guess: 11
Number NOT guessed
```

Here the **break** statement is never reached so the loop iterates three times without terminating early.

4.5 The 'continue' Statement

Whereas the **break** statement forces a loop to terminate, a **continue** statement forces a loop to skip the remaining instructions in the body of the loop and to *continue* to the next iteration. As an example of this, here is a reminder of the earlier program that displayed the even numbers from 10 down to 1:

---

displayeven.py – a reminder

```
print('*** Even numbers from 10 to 2 ***')
for i in range(10, 0, -1): # counter moving down from 10 to 1
    if i%2 == 0:
        print(i)
```

Here the body of the loop displayed the loop counter if it was an even number. An alternative approach would have been to skip a number if it was odd and move on to the next iteration of the loop. If the number is not skipped, then it must be even, so can be displayed. This is what we have done in the following program:

---

displayeven2.py

```
print('*** Even numbers from 10 to 1 ***')
print()
for i in range(10, 0, -1):
    if i%2 != 0: # check if number is NOT even
        continue # skips the rest of this iteration and moves to the next iteration
    print(i) # even number displayed only if we have not skipped this iteration
```

The **if** statement checks to see if the number is odd (not even). If this is the case the rest of the instructions in the loop can be skipped with a **continue** statement, so the loop moves to the next iteration:

```
if i%2 != 0: # check if number is NOT even
    continue # skips the rest of this iteration and moves to the next iteration
print(i) # even number displayed only if we have not skipped this iteration
```

The last `print` instruction is only executed if the number is even and the iteration has not been skipped. Of course, the result of running this program will be the same as the result of running the original program.

4.6 A Couple of Pitfalls

You have seen that with both **for** loops and **while** loops it is very important to make sure that your start conditions and end conditions are correct. As an example, look at this **for** loop:

```
for i in range(4, 3, 1):
    print('i')
```

Can you see the problem here? The counter starts off with a value of 4, which is already greater than the end value, so the instruction in the loop will never be executed.

And what about this?

```
i = 5
while i != 4:
    i = i + 1
    print(i)
```

Here the loop is designed to stop when i is not equal to 4. But it starts at 5, and increases by 1 each time round the loop—so the end condition is never met and the loop just goes on repeating. This is known as an **infinite loop**, and needless to say should be avoided.

4.7 The 'try ... except' Statement

When a program is running there are times when something goes wrong and the program crashes, or at least doesn't behave as we would expect. In Chap. 10, when we cover file handling, you will see that one of these things that could go wrong is that we are trying to open a file that doesn't exist, or to save a file when there is no space on the disk. Sometimes a printer could go wrong, or a keyboard could get stuck. Sometimes the program instructs the computer to perform an operation that causes an error—like division by zero for example. And as we mentioned in Chap. 2, sometimes a user can input information which causes a problem.

The **try ...except** construct allows the program to anticipate these problems and organize things so that the error is dealt with smoothly and the program continues to run.

Look at the following lines of code that ask the user to enter a number, then a calculation is performed in which 5 is divided by that number, and the result is displayed:

```
x = float(input('Enter a number: '))
result = 5/x
print(result)
```

There are two potential problems here. Firstly, the user could enter something like 'xyz' that doesn't look like a float, causing the program to terminate because the conversion from float to str cannot take place. You would see this message:

ValueError: could not convert string to float: 'xyz'

Secondly the user could enter zero, causing the program to crash because division by zero is not a legal operation. This time you would get the following:

ZeroDivisionError: float division by zero

Errors during run-time are usually referred to as **exceptions**. The following short program makes use of the **try** ... **except** statement to handle these exceptions neatly:

```
tryexceptdemo.py
try:
    x = float(input('Enter a number: '))
    result = 5/x
    print(result)
except:
    print('Oops ... something went wrong!')
```

This time, if the user enters a non-zero number, the program will print the result and the **except** clause will never be entered. But if he or she enters something that is not a number, or is zero, then control will move to the **except** clause and the message will be printed. Here are three possible runs from this program:

Here the user enters something that is not a number:

Enter a number: 4myef
Oops ... something went wrong!

This time the user enters zero:

Enter a number: 0
Oops ... something went wrong!

But now the user enters a number:

```
Enter a number: 10
0.5
```

A very common way to incorporate this construct into an input validation routine is to use it in conjunction with a **while** loop, as the following program demonstrates:

tryexceptdemo2.py

```
ok = False
while not ok:
    try:
        x = float(input('Enter a number: '))
        result = 5/x
        ok = True
    except:
        print('Something went wrong - make sure you enter a non-zero number in the correct form')
print(result)
```

We have declared a **bool** variable, ok, and initialized it to **False**. The **while** statement is defined so that the loop will continue as long as ok is **False**. The two potentially problematic statements are placed in the **try** block—if these execute successfully, then ok is set to **True**, and the loop terminates. If, however, there is a problem, then the program enters the **except** clause. The message is printed, and ok remains **False**, so that the loop continues until such time that the user enters an acceptable value.

Here is a sample run:

```
Enter a number: 1..2
Something went wrong - make sure you enter a non-zero number in the
correct form
Enter a number: 0
Something went wrong - make sure you enter a non-zero number in the
correct form
Enter a number: 1
5.0
```

In one of the programming exercises that follow you can have a go at using a **try... except** construct to validate input for one of our previous programs.

4.8   Self-test Questions

1. Consider the following program:

```
for i in range(1, 4, 1):
    print('YES')
print('OK')
```

(a) How many times does this **for** loop execute?

(b) What would be the output of this program?

2. Consider the following program:

```
for i in range(1, 3, 1):
    print('YES')
    print('NO')
print('OK')
```

(a) How many times does this **for** loop execute?

(b) What would be the output of this program?

3. Consider the following program:

```
num = int(input('Enter a number: '))
for i in range(1, num, 1):
    print('YES')
    print('NO')
print('OK')
```

(a) What would be the output of this program if the user entered 5 when prompted?

(b) What would be the output of this program if the user entered 1 when prompted?

4. Consider the following program

```
for i in range(1, 16, 2):
    print(i)
```

(a) How many times does this **for** loop execute?

(b) What would be the output of this program?

(c) What would be the consequence of changing the end value of the loop to 15?

5. Consider the following program:

```
for i in range(5, 1, -1):
    if i == 1 or i == 3:
        print('YES')
    elif i == 2 or i == 4 or i == 5:
        print('NO')
print('OK')
```

(a) How many times does this **for** loop execute?

(b) What would be the output of this program?

(c) What would be the consequence of changing the loop counter to 1 instead of −1?

6. What would be the output from the following program?

```
for i in range(1, 3, 1):
    for j in range(1, 8, 1):
        print('*', end = '')
    print()
```

7. Examine the program below that aims to allow a user to guess the square of a number that is entered. Part of the code has been replaced by a comment:

```
num = int(input('Enter a whole number '))
square = int(input('Enter the square of this number '))
# loop to check answer
while ''' test to be completed''':
    print('Wrong answer, try again');
    square = int(input('Enter the square of this number '))
print('Well done, right answer')
```

(a) Why is a **while** loop preferable to a **for** loop here?

(b) Replace the comment with an appropriate test for this loop.

8. What would be the output of the following program?

```
for i in range(1, 11, 1):
    if i > 5:
        break
    print(i)
```

9. What would be the output of the following program?

```
for i in range(1, 11, 1):
    if i <= 5:
        continue
    print(i)
```

4.9 Programming Exercises

1. Implement a few of the programs from this chapter and then implement the programs from the self-test questions above in order to verify your answers to those questions.

2. (a) Modify the `displayeven.py` program from Sect. 4.2.2 so that the program displays the even numbers from 1 to 20 instead of from 10 down to 1.
   (b) Modify the program further so that the user enters a number and the program displays all the even numbers from 1 up to the number entered by the user.
   (c) Modify the program again so that it identifies which of these numbers are odd and which are even. For example, if the user entered 5 the program should display something like the following:

   1 is odd
   2 is even
   3 is odd
   4 is even
   5 is odd

3. Write a program that makes use of nested **for** loops to display the following shapes:

   (a) * * * * * *
        * * * * * *
        * * * * * *

   (b) * **
        * **
        * * * * * * * **
        * * * * * * * **
        * **
        * **

   *Hint: make use of an **if...else** statement inside your **for** loops.*

   (c) *   *   *   *
        *   *   *
        *   *
        *

4. (a) Using a **for** loop, write a program that displays a '6 times' multiplication table; the output should look like this:

```
1 × 6 = 6
2 × 6 = 12
3 × 6 = 18
4 × 6 = 24
5 × 6 = 30
6 × 6 = 36
7 × 6 = 42
8 × 6 = 48
9 × 6 = 54
10 × 6 = 60
11 × 6 = 66
12 × 6 = 72
```

   (b) Adapt the program so that instead of a '6 times' table, the user chooses which table is displayed

   (c) Modify the program further by making use of a **while** loop to carry out some *input validation* that ensures that the user enters a number that is never less than 2. If a number less than 2 is entered, an error message should be displayed and the user is asked to enter another number.

   (d) Finally, make use of a **while** loop so that the user is asked to enter 'y' or 'n' to indicate if they wish to run the program again. Ideally the program should run again if the user enters 'y' or 'Y'.

5. Implement the program `drawpattern7.py` from Sect. 4.2.3 (which allows the user to determine the size of a square of stars) and then
   (a) adapt it so that the user is allowed to enter a size only between 2 and 20;
   (b) adapt the program further so that the user can choose whether or not to have another go.

6. Modify programming exercise 6, from Sect. 2.12, that carries out some calculations related to a circle as follows:
   (a) Add input validation to ensure that the radius entered is always non-negative
   (b) Provide a menu interface for this program. For example:

```
[1] Set radius
[2] Display radius
[3] Display area
[4] Display perimeter
[5] Quit
```

7. Consider a vending machine that offers the following options:

```
[1] Get gum
[2] Get chocolate
[3] Get popcorn
[4] Get juice
[5] Display total sold so far
[6] Quit
```

Design and implement a program that continuously allows users to select from these options. When options 1–4 are selected an appropriate message is to be displayed acknowledging their choice. For example, when option 3 is selected the following message could be displayed:

Here is your popcorn
When option 5 is selected, the number of each type of item sold is displayed. For example:

```
3 items of gum sold
2 items of chocolate sold
6 items of popcorn sold
9 items of juice sold
```

When option 6 is chosen the program terminates. If an option other than 1–6 is entered, an appropriate error message should be displayed, such as:

```
Error, options 1-6 only!
```

8. By making use of the **try** … **except** construct, amend the findtax3.py program from Sect. 4.3 so that the user is not allowed to enter non-numerical values for the price and tax.

Python: Functions and Modules

5

Outcomes

By the end of this chapter you should be able to:

- *explain the meaning of the term **function**;*
- *declare and define functions;*
- ***call** a function;*
- *explain the meaning of the terms **arguments** and **parameters**;*
- *distinguish between **local** and **global** variables, and identify the **scope** of a particular variable;*
- *use Python's built-in functions and modules and create your own modules;*
- *make use of a variety of string functions.*

5.1 Introduction

In Chap. 2 you were introduced to the term **function**. A function is a set of instructions that together perform a single well-defined task. Examples of the many sorts of task that a function could perform are calculating the area of a circle, displaying a particular message on the screen, converting a temperature from Fahrenheit to Celsius and many more. Python provides a number of built-in functions, a few of which you have already come across—input, print, float, int, str for example.

But we can also write our own functions, and in this chapter you will see how we can collect the instructions for performing these sorts of tasks together to form a single function.

Supplementary Information The online version contains supplementary material available at https://doi.org/10.1007/978-3-031-01326-3_5.

You will also see how, once we have written a function, we can get it to perform its task within a program. When we do this, we say that we are **calling** the function. When we call a function, what we are actually doing is telling the program to jump to a new place (where the function instructions are stored), carry out the set of instructions that it finds there, and, when it has finished (i.e. when the function has terminated), return and carry on where it left off.

So, in this chapter you will learn how to write a function within a program, how to call a function from another part of the program and how to send information into a function and get information back.

5.2 Declaring and Defining Functions

Let's illustrate the idea of a function by thinking about a simple little program. The program prompts the user to enter his or her year of birth, month of birth and day of birth; each time the prompt is displayed, it is followed by a message, consisting of a couple of lines, explaining that the information entered is confidential. This is shown in the program below. The program would obviously then go on to do other things with the information that has been entered, but we are not interested in that, so we have just replaced all the rest of the program with a comment.

```
dataentry.py

year = input('Please enter the year of your birth: ')

# display confidentiality message
print('Please note that all information supplied is confidential')
print('No personal details will be shared with any third party')

month = input('Please enter the month of your birth: ')

# display confidentiality message
print('Please note that all information supplied is confidential')
print('No personal details will be shared with any third party')

day = input('Please enter the day of your birth: ')

# display confidentiality message
print('Please note that all information supplied is confidential')
print('No personal details will be shared with any third party')

# more code goes here
```

You can see from the above program that we have had to type out the two lines that display the confidentiality message three times. It would be far less time consuming if we could do this just once, then send the program off to wherever these instructions are stored and then come back and carry on with what it was doing. You will probably have realized by now that we can indeed do this—by writing a *function*. The job of this particular function will be simply to display the confidentiality message on the screen. We need to give our function a name so that we can refer to it when required, so let's call it `displayMessage`. Here is how it is going to look:

```
def displayMessage():
    print('Please note that all information supplied is confidential')
    print('No personal details will be shared with any third party')
    print()
    return
```

The function is introduced by the keyword **def**. We give the function any name we choose, but must follow the same rules as those for naming variables, which we saw in Chap. 2. In this case we are calling it `displayMessage`. The function name is followed by a pair of brackets and finally a colon. Very soon you will learn that it is possible to send some information *into* a function—for example, some values that the function needs in order to perform a calculation. When we need to do that we list, in the brackets, data that we are going to send in; here, however, as the function is doing nothing more than displaying a message on the screen, we do not have to send in any data and the brackets are left empty.

The body of this function, which is indented, contains the instructions that we want the function to perform, namely to display two lines of text on the screen followed by a blank line.

Finally, we see the keyword **return**. When a function encounters a **return** instruction, it immediately ends, skipping any remaining instructions, and control reverts to the point in the program after the function was called.

In fact, in this particular example, we could have omitted the **return** statement because there is no information to send back, and, since there are no further instructions, the function would finish anyway. However, you will come across many examples where the **return** statement does not come at the end of the function: for example, it could come in one branch of an **if** statement, or within a loop, and the function ends only if this particular part of the function is reached. We have included it here for completeness even though it is not strictly required.

In Sect. 5.4 you will see that the **return** statement is also used to send back information from the function.

5.3   Calling a Function

Now that we have declared and defined our function, we can make use of it. The idea is that we get the function to perform its instructions as and when we need it to do so—you have seen that this process is referred to as *calling* the function. To call a function in Python, we simply use its name, along with the following brackets, which in this case are empty. So in this case our function call, which will be placed at the point in the program where we need it, looks like this:

```
displayMessage()
```

Now we can rewrite our `dataentry.py` program, replacing the appropriate lines of code with the simple function call. The whole program is shown below:

---
dataentry2.py

```python
def displayMessage():
    print('Please note that all information supplied is confidential')
    print('No personal details will be shared with any third party')
    print()
    return

year = input('Please enter the year of your birth: ')
displayMessage()

month = input('Please enter the month of your birth: ')
displayMessage()

day = input('Please enter the day of your birth: ')
displayMessage()
```

The function itself must be defined before it is used, and we normally declare all our functions before the body of the program.

We should emphasize again here that when a function is called, program control moves to the start of the function, then carries out the instructions in the called function. When it has finished doing this, it returns to the original point in the program, which then resumes. By the way, it is perfectly possible for any function to call another function—indeed, the called function could in turn call yet another function. This would result in a number of functions being 'chained'. When each function terminates, the control of the program would return to the function that called it. This is illustrated in the following program.

---
chain.py

```python
def function1():
    print('Welcome to function1')
    function2()

def function2():
    print('Welcome to function2')
    function3()

def function3():
    print('Welcome to function3')

# main body
function1()
print('Goodbye')
```

As you can see, `function1` is called in the main body of the program. This function displays a message, then calls `function2`, which again displays a message and then calls `function3`. This function simply displays a message and control returns to the main body at the point after `function1` was called. A final message is then displayed, and the program terminates.

The output is therefore:

```
Welcome to function1
Welcome to function2
Welcome to function3
Goodbye
```

5.4   Function Input and Output

We have already told you that it is possible to send some data into a function, and that a function can send data back when it terminates. Now we will look into this in more detail.

In order to do this we will use as an example a program that we wrote in Chap. 2. Here is a reminder of that program:

---

findtax3.py - a reminder

```
print('*** Product Tax Check ***')
price = float(input('Enter initial price: ')) # get user to input price
taxRate = float(input('Enter tax rate: ')) # get user to input tax rate
tax = price * taxRate/100 # perform the calculation
print('The amount of tax = %0.2f' %(tax))
```

The line that calculates the tax is this one:

```
tax = price * taxRate/100
```

Let's create a function that performs this calculation—in a real application this would be very useful, because we might need to call this function at various points within the program, and, as you will see, each time we do so we could get it to carry out the calculation for different values of the price and the tax. We will need a way to send in these values to the function. But on top of that, we need to arrange for the function to tell us the result of adding the new tax—if it didn't do that, it wouldn't be much use!

The function is going to look like this:

```
def calcTax(priceIn, taxRateIn):
    return priceIn * taxRateIn/100
```

The first thing to notice is that this time the brackets following the function name aren't empty. You can see that within these brackets we are naming two variables. The variables named in this way are known as the **parameters** of the function. Parameters are variables that are created exclusively to hold values sent into the function. They are going to hold, respectively, the values of the price and the tax that are going to be sent in (you will see how this is done in a moment). Of course, these variables could be given any name we choose, but we have called them priceIn and taxIn, respectively. We will use this convention of adding the suffix In to variable names in the parameter list throughout this book.

Now we can turn our attention to the body of the function, which as you can see, in this case, consists of a single line:

```
return priceIn * taxRateIn/100
```

As we have already seen, the word **return** in a function plays two very important roles. First it ends the function—as soon as the program encounters this keyword, the function terminates, and control of the program jumps back to the point at which it was called. The second role is to send back a value. In this case it sends back the result of the following calculation:

```
priceIn * taxRateIn/100
```

Now we can discuss how we actually call this function and use its return value. The whole program appears below:

findtax4.py
```
def calcTax(priceIn, taxRateIn):
    return priceIn * taxRateIn/100

price = float(input('Enter initial price: '))
taxRate = float(input('Enter tax rate: '))
tax = calcTax(price, taxRate)
print('The amount of tax = %0.2f' %(tax))
```

The line that calls the function is this one:

```
tax = calcTax(price, taxRate)
```

Look at the items in brackets after the function name. As you might have expected, there are two items in the brackets—these are the *actual* values that we are sending into our function. They are referred to as the **arguments** of the function.

In Python, the way this works is that the name tags of the parameters in the called function are set to point to the same location as that of the arguments and therefore contain the same values. This process, which is referred to as **passing** parameters, is illustrated in Fig. 5.1, which shows you the situation immediately after the function is called.

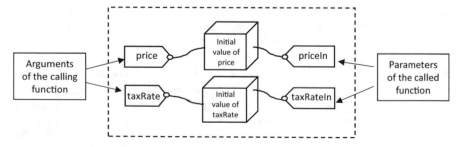

Fig. 5.1 What happens when we call a function in Python?

Fig. 5.2 Passing arguments into a function

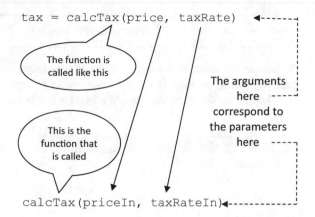

Of course, if, within the function, new values were assigned to `taxRateIn` or `priceIn`, then each tag would point to a new location in memory.

You might be wondering how the program knows which arguments correspond to which parameters. The answer is that it is the order that is the important. Although the variable names have been conveniently chosen, the names themselves have nothing to do with which argument corresponds to which parameter. This is illustrated in Fig. 5.2.

You might also be wondering what would happen if you tried to call the function with the wrong number of arguments. For example:

```
tax = calcTax(price)
```

The answer is that you would get a run-time error, because there is no function called `calcTax` that requires just one single variable to be passed into it.

We can now move on to looking at how we make use of the return value of a function.

The `calcTax` function returns the result that we are interested in, namely the tax to be paid. What we need to do is to assign this value to the variable `tax`. As you have already seen we have done this in the same line in which we called the function:

```
tax = calcTax(price, taxRate)
```

A function that returns a value can in fact be used just as if it were a variable! Here we have used it in an assignment statement—but in fact we could have simply dropped it into the `print` statement, just as we would have done with a simple `float` variable:

```
print('Cost after tax = %0.2f' %(calcTax(price, taxRate)))
```

Before we leave this section, there is one thing we should emphasize—when passing a variable of an immutable type as an argument, a function cannot change the *original* value of the variable. We will illustrate this with a very simple program indeed:

parameterdemo.py

```
def demoFunction(xIn):
        xIn = 25
        print(xIn)

x = 10;
demoFunction(x)
print(x)
```

You can see that in the main body of the program we declare an integer, x, which is initialized to 10. We then call a function called demoFunction, with x as a parameter. The parameter of this function—xIn—will now of course have the value 10. But the function then assigns the value of 25 to the parameter, so the output of the program is:

```
25
10
```

As expected, the original value of x is unchanged—integers are immutable.

5.5   More Examples of Functions

Just to make sure you have got the idea, let's define a few more functions. To start with, we will create a very simple function, one that calculates the square of a number. When we are going to write a function, there are four things to consider:

- the name that we will give to the function;
- the inputs to the function (the parameters);
- the output of the function (the value being returned, if any);
- the body of the function (the instructions that do the job required).

In the case of the function in question, the name square would seem like a sensible choice. We will define the function so that it will calculate the square of any number, so it should accept a single numerical value. Similarly, it will return a numerical value.

The instructions will be very simple—just return the square of the number.

```
def square(numberIn):
    return numberIn ** 2
```

Remember that we can choose any names we want for the input parameters; here we have stuck with our convention of using the suffix In for parameters.

To use this function in another part of the program is now very easy. Say, for example, we had declared and initialized two variables as follows:

```
a = 2.5
b = 9.0
```

Let's say we wanted to assign the square of a to a variable x and the square of b to a variable y. We could do this as follows:

```
x = square(a)
y = square(b)
```

After these instructions, x would hold the value 6.25 and y would hold the value 81.0.

For our next illustration we will choose a slightly more complicated example. We will define a function that we will call max; it will accept two values and will return the bigger value of the two (of course, if they are equal, it can return the value of either one). It should be clear that an **if...else** statement should do the job— if the first number is greater than the second, return the first number, if not return the second. Here is our function:

```
def max(firstIn, secondIn):
    if firstIn > secondIn:
        return firstIn
    else:
        return secondIn
```

You should note that in this example we have two **return** statements, each potentially returning a different value—the value that is actually returned is decided at run-time by the values of the variables firstIn and secondIn. Remember, as soon as a **return** statement is reached the function terminates.

Let's develop one more function. There are many instances in our programming lives where we might need to test whether a number is even or odd. Let's provide a function that does this job for us. We will call our function isEven, and it will report on whether or not a particular number is an even number. The function will accept a single parameter. The type of the item that is returned is interesting—the function will tell us whether or not a number is even, so it will need to return a value of type **bool**. It will return **True** if the number is even or **False** if it is not.

The instructions are quite simple to devise—again, an **if...else** statement should certainly do the job.

An even number will give a remainder of zero when divided by 2. An odd number will not. So we use the modulo operator here. Here is our function:

```
def isEven(numberIn):
    if numberIn % 2 == 0:
        return True
    else:
        return False
```

Actually there is a slightly neater way we could have written this function. The expression:

numberIn % 2 == 0

will evaluate to either **True** or **False**—and we could therefore simply have returned the value of this expression and written our function like this:

```
def isEven(numberIn):
    return numberIn % 2 == 0
```

A function that returns a value of type **bool** can be referred to as a **boolean function**. In Chap. 3 you came across boolean *expressions* (expressions that evaluate to **True** or **False**) such as:

temperature > 10

or

y == 180

Because boolean functions also evaluate to **True** or **False** (i.e. they return a value of **True** or **False**) they can—as with boolean expressions—be used as the test in a selection or loop.

For example, assuming that a variable called number had been initialized as an integer, we could write something like:

```
if isEven(number):
    # code here
```

or

```
while isEven(number):
    # code here
```

To test for a **False** value, we simply negate the expression with the **not** operator:

```
if not isEven(number):
    # code here
```

5.6 Variable Scope

When we write functions it is perfectly possible, and often necessary, to declare variables within that function. However there is a very important point here: variables declared within a function are *local to that function and cannot be accessed elsewhere in the program*. They are referred to as **local variables**. In contrast, variables declared within the main body of the program are accessible throughout the program and are therefore referred to as **global variables**. Because variables are not always accessible throughout an entire program, we say that variables have a **scope**.

The very simple program below illustrates this.

```
scopetest.py

def myFunction():
    x = 'Local variable' # x is accessible only within myFunction
    print(x)
    print(y)

y = 'Global variable' # y is accessible throughout the program
myFunction()
```

The output from this program, as you would expect, is:

```
Local variable
Global variable
```

However, if we were to try to access x in the main body of the program, this would cause an error at run-time. Try this out with the program below in which we have added an instruction at the end of the main body:

```
scopetest2.py

# This program will give rise to an error at runtime

def myFunction():
    x = 'Local variable' # x is accessible only within myFunction
    print(x)
    print(y)

y = 'Global variable' # y is accessible throughout the program
myFunction()
print(x) # this will cause an error because x is accessible only within myFunction
```

It is interesting to note that, since a function is completely unaware of what has been declared inside any other function, you could declare variables with the same name inside different functions. And, in addition, a local variable could have the same name as a global variable—but what would happen in this case? Well, take a look at the next program in which the local variable and the global variable have now both been called x. We have displayed the value x in the function and then in the main program.

---

scopetest3.py

```
def myFunction():
    x = 'Local variable'
    print(x)

x = 'Global variable'
myFunction()
print(x)
```

What we get when we run the program is this:

```
Local variable
Global variable
```

As you can see, the function thinks that we are referring to the local variable x rather than the global variable with the same name.

To understand why this is so, it helps to know a little about what goes on when the program is running. A part of the computer's memory called the **stack** is reserved for use by running programs. When a function is called, some space on the stack is used to store the values for that function's parameters and its local variables. That is why, whatever names we give them, they are local to their particular function. Once the function terminates, this part of the stack is no longer accessible, and the variables effectively no longer exist. And this might help you to understand even more clearly why the value of a variable passed as a parameter to a function cannot be changed by that function.

5.7 Global Variables: The Pitfalls

Having just told you about global variables, we are now going to tell you that it is never a good idea to make use of global variables within a function!

There are two very important reasons for this. The first reason is that allowing a function to access a global variable can easily lead to programming errors, because the function can inadvertently be made to change the value of that variable, thus affecting the entire program.

The second reason is that functions are designed to be used over and over again, often with different values being passed in as arguments. Not only can functions be called many times within one program, but they can also be stored as part of a *module* (as explained later in this chapter) for use in other programs. If a function makes use of a global variable it would be impossible to use that function in any other program.

You can see in the `circlecalculation.py` program in the next section how we carefully pass values into a function, which then returns a result to us.

5.8 Using Functions in Menu-Driven Programs

In Chap. 4 we developed a program that presented the user with a menu of choices; we pointed out that this was a very common interface for programs before the days of graphics.

Here is a reminder of that program:

---
timetablewithloop.py - a reminder

```
response = '1' # initialize to a value that allows the loop to be entered

print('***Lab Times***')

while response != '4':  # put code in loop
    # offer menu of options
    print()
    print('[1] TIME FOR GROUP A')
    print('[2] TIME FOR GROUP B')
    print('[3] TIME FOR GROUP C')
    print('[4] QUIT PROGRAM')
    print('enter choice [1,2,3,4]: ')

    print()

    response = input()

    if response == '1':
        print('10:00am')
    elif response == '2':
        print('1:00pm')
    elif response == '3':
        print('11:00am')
    elif response == '4':
        print('Goodbye')
    else:
        print('Options 1-4 only')
```

In this program, each conditional statement consisted of a single instruction, which simply displayed one line of text. Imagine, though, that we were to develop a more complex program in which each menu choice involved a lot of processing. The conditional statements would start to get very messy, and the program could easily become very unwieldy. In this situation, confining each menu option to a particular function will make our program far more manageable.

The next program, `circlecalulation`, is an example of such a program. The program allows a user to enter the radius of a circle and then enables the area and circumference of the circle to be calculated and displayed. Four menu options are offered. The first allows the user to enter the radius. The second displays the area of the circle and the third the circumference. The final option allows the user to quit the program.

Study it carefully, and then we will point out some of the interesting features.

---

circlecalculation.py

```python
# option1 gets the user to enter the radius of the circle
def option1():
    myRadius = float(input('Enter the radius of the circle: '))
    return myRadius

# option2 calculates and displays the area of the circle
def option2(radiusIn):
    if radiusIn == -999:
        print('Radius has not been entered')
    else:
        area = 3.1416 * radiusIn * radiusIn # calculate the area
        print('The area of the circle is: %0.2f' %(area))

# option3 calculates and displays the circumference of the circle
def option3(radiusIn):
    if radiusIn == -999:
        print('Radius has not been entered')
    else:
        circumference = 2 * 3.1416 * radiusIn # calculate the circumference
        print('The circumference of the circle is: %0.2f ' %(circumference))

''' The variable below is local to the main function; if the value is needed by another function,
    it must be passed in as a parameter '''

radius = -999 # initialize with a dummy value to show that nothing has been entered
choice = 0
while choice != '4':
    print()
    print('*** CIRCLE CALCULATIONS ***')
    print()
    print('1. Enter the radius of the circle')
    print('2. Display the area of the circle')
    print('3. Display the circumference of the circle')
    print('4. Quit')
    print()

    choice = input('Enter a number from 1 - 4: ')
    print()

    if choice == '1':
        radius = option1() # call function option1
    elif choice == '2':
        option2(radius); # call function option2
    elif choice == '3':
        option3(radius); # call function option3
    elif choice == '4':
        pass
    else:
        print('Enter only numbers from 1 - 4')
```

There is only one new programming technique in this program, which is the use of the **pass** command in option 4. This, as its name suggests, simply means "do nothing". The comments are self-explanatory; so we draw your attention only to a few important points:

- as we explained in the last section, we have avoided the use of global variables. The radius is passed as an argument to the functions which perform the calculations, and the result is returned. This is good programming practice;
- the radius is initialized with a 'dummy' value of -999. This allows us to check if the radius has been entered before attempting to perform a calculation;
- choosing menu option 1 causes the function `option1` to be called—the value of the radius entered by the user is returned;
- choosing menu option 2 causes the function `option2` to be called. The radius of the circle is sent in as an argument. After using the dummy value to check that a value for the radius has been entered, the area is then calculated and displayed;
- choosing menu option 3 causes the function `option3` to be called. This is similar to `option2`, but for the circumference instead of the area;

- choosing option 4 causes the program to terminate—this happens because the body of the **while** loop executes only while choice is not equal to 4. If it is equal to 4, the loop is not executed and the program ends.

Here is a sample run from this program:

```
*** CIRCLE CALCULATIONS ***

1. Enter the radius of the circle
2. Display the area of the circle
3. Display the circumference of the circle
4. Quit

Enter a number from 1 - 4: 1

Enter the radius of the circle: 10

*** CIRCLE CALCULATIONS ***

1. Enter the radius of the circle
2. Display the area of the circle
3. Display the circumference of the circle
4. Quit

Enter a number from 1 - 4: 2

The area of the circle is: 314.16

*** CIRCLE CALCULATIONS ***

1. Enter the radius of the circle
2. Display the area of the circle
3. Display the circumference of the circle
4. Quit

Enter a number from 1 - 4: 3

The circumference of the circle is: 62.83

*** CIRCLE CALCULATIONS ***

1. Enter the radius of the circle
2. Display the area of the circle
3. Display the circumference of the circle
4. Quit

Enter a number from 1 - 4: 4
```

5.9   Built-In Functions

As mentioned in the introduction, Python comes with a number of "built-in" functions that are always available. You have come across many of these already: `input`, `print`, `float`, `int`, `str` for example. They are able to act on many different types of data. The `str` function for example will accept both floats and integers as arguments and will convert them to strings.

There are also a great many functions that are associated with a particular object. We are using the word "object" here quite loosely to mean an item of a particular type such as a string. In the next chapters you will see how different functions are associated with the types that you will be introduced to there—lists, tuples and dictionaries. In actual fact, the word "object" has a more precise meaning than this, as you will discover in Chap. 8—but for now our loose description is good enough.

When using functions that are associated with a specific object, we use a full stop (known as the **dot operator**) along with the variable name. To help you understand this, we are going to look at the most common of the functions associated with the string type (those not included here can be found in the Python documentation). Example programs will demonstrate how you use them. Notice that we have included one built-in function here—`len`, which is extremely useful and can be used with other data types as you will see in the next chapter.

5.10   String Functions

In the examples below, we will refer to the position of a character in a string as the **index**. But you must make a note of the fact that the indexing starts at zero. So the first character in a string has an index of 0, the second an index of 1 and so on.

You should also note that when we talk of a start position and end position, counting begins at the start index, but the end index is not counted. So if we said we were going to count from index 3 to 6, we would count the characters at index 3, index 4 and index 5. The examples below will make this clear.

count

Returns the number of times a substring occurs in a string. This function is case-sensitive.

---
countexample.py
```
myString = 'Mary, Mary, quite contrary'
result = myString.count('ary')  # counts the number of times 'ary' appears in the string
print(result)
```

Notice the use of the dot operator here:

```
result = myString.count('ary')
```

Output

```
3
```

Optionally, we can specify a start position, or both a start and an end position. The table below shows the index of each character in the string and should help you understand the program that follows.

0	1	2	3	4	5	6	7	8	9	10	11	12	13	14	15	16	17	18	19	20	21	22	23	24	25
M	a	r	y	,		M	a	r	y	,		q	u	i	t	e		c	o	n	t	r	a	r	y

---

countexample1.py

```
myString = 'Mary, Mary, quite contrary'

''' counts the number of times 'ary' appears in the string, starting at
index 7 up to the end. '''
result = myString.count('ary', 7)
print(result)

''' counts the number of times 'a' appears in the string, starting at index 1,
up to, but not including index 7. '''
result = myString.count('a', 1, 7)
print(result)
```

Output

```
2
1
```

endswith and startswith

endswith returns **True** if the string ends with a specified suffix. Otherwise returns **False**. Once again, this function is case-sensitive.

---

endswithexample.py

```
myString = 'European Union'
print(myString.endswith('ion'))  # check if the string endswith 'ion'
print(myString.endswith('ION'))  # check if the string endswith 'ION'
print(myString.endswith('n'))    # check if the string endswith 'n'
```

Output

```
True
False
True
```

There is also a version that allows you to specify a start and end position for the part of the string you wish to search—this operates in a similar way to that shown in the count example above.

The startswith function behaves in exactly the same way, but checks whether the string starts with a particular prefix.

find and **index**

Both of these functions return the index in a string of the first occurrence of a specified substring. Find returns −1 if the substring is not present, whereas index raises a run-time error—which is why, in the program below, we have used a **try ... except** block to catch this error.

---
findexample.py

```
myString = 'Humpty Dumpty sat on a wall'
num = myString.find('ty') # return the index of first occurrence of 'ty' (using find)
print(num)
num = myString.find('xx') # return the index of first occurrence of 'xx' (using find)
print(num)

try:
    num = myString.index('xx') # return the index of first occurrence of 'xx' (using index)
    print(num)
except:
    print('Substring not found')
```

Output

```
4
-1
Substring not found
```

As usual, both these functions are case-sensitive.

format

The format method provides an additional way of formatting strings. It is best explained by example:

---
formatexample.py

```
myString = '{0:d} kilos of {1:s} will cost £{2:1.2f}'.format(3, 'apples', 5.5)
print(myString)
```

The parameters of the format method are the items we wish to be inserted; they will replace the braces that you see in the string. They are referred to by their positions, starting at zero; so in this example, 0 refers to 3, 1 refers to 'apples' and 2 refers to 5.5. Within the string itself, the braces contain two items, separated by a colon. The item before the colon refers to the particular parameter of the format method, while the second determines how it is formatted.

Output

```
3 kilos of apples will cost £5.50
```

isalnum, **isalpha** and **isdigit**

The isalnum function returns **True** if all the characters in a string are alphanumeric and **False** otherwise. It does not require any arguments.

---

isalnumexample.py

```
myString1 = 'xyz123'
myString2 = 'xyz123$%^'
print(myString1.isalnum()) # check if all the characters in myString1 are alphanumeric
print(myString2.isalnum()) # check if all the characters in myString2 are alphanumeric
```

Output

```
True
False
```

Similarly, the `isalpha` function returns **True** if all the characters in a string are alphabetic, and `isdigit` returns **True** if all the characters in a string are digits.

islower and isupper

The `islower` function returns **True** if all the alphabetic characters in a string are lower case, otherwise returns **False**. The `isupper` function does the same thing, but for upper case letters.

---

islowerisupperexample.py

```
myString = 'hello world'
print(myString.islower()) # check if all alphabetic characters are lower case
print(myString.isupper()) # check if all alphabetic characters are upper case

print()

myString = 'HELLO WORLD 1234'
print(myString.islower()) # check if all alphabetic characters are lower case
print(myString.isupper()) # check if all alphabetic characters are upper case
```

Output

```
True
False

False
True
```

There is also an `isspace` function that checks whether all the characters in a string are spaces, and an `istitle` function that checks whether each word in a string (separated by a space) consists of an initial upper case letter followed by all lower case letters (such as 'Hello World Again').

len

This is a built-in function, so does not use the dot operator, but takes the string as an argument. It returns the length of the string.

---

stringlengthexample.py

```
myString = 'hello world'
print(len(myString)) # prints the length of the string (including spaces)
```

Output

```
11
```

lower and upper

The lower function returns a copy of the string converted to lower case—the original string is unchanged. The upper function converts it to upper case.

---
lowerandupperexample.py

```
oldString = 'I have visited Brazil, but not Argentina.'

lowerString = oldString.lower() #return a string converted to lower case
upperString = oldString.upper() #return a string converted to upper case

print(oldString)
print(lowerString)
print(upperString)
```

Output

```
I have visited Brazil, but not Argentina.
i have visited brazil, but not argentina.
I HAVE VISITED BRAZIL, BUT NOT ARGENTINA.
```

replace

This function returns a copy of the original string with all the occurrences of a specified substring replaced with a new substring. The original string is unchanged. As with other string functions, replace is case-sensitive. An optional third argument, n, can be included to specify that only the first n substrings should be replaced.

---
replaceexample.py

```
oldString = 'That is his book, his desk, his chair, and his computer.'

#return a string with all occurrences of 'his' replaced with 'her'
newString1 = oldString.replace('his', 'her')

#return a string with the first 2 occurrences of 'his' replaced with 'her'
newString2 = oldString.replace('his', 'her', 2)

print(oldString)
print(newString1)
print(newString2)
```

Output

```
That is his book, his desk, his chair, and his computer.
That is her book, her desk, her chair, and her computer.
That is her book, her desk, his chair, and his computer.
```

strip

This function returns a copy of the string after removing specified characters from the beginning and end of the string. If no characters are specified, then any whitespace is removed. Whitespace refers to characters that you cannot see—for example spaces, newline characters and tabs.

---

stripexamples.py

```
testString = 'hello there'
print(testString.strip('hel')) # strip removes 'h' 'e' and 'l' from start and end
testString = '   hello   '
print(testString.strip() + testString.strip()) # strip removes spaces from start and end
testString = 'goodbye\n'
print(testString + testString.strip() + testString) # strip removes newline from end
```

Output

```
o ther
hellohello
goodbye
goodbyegoodbye
```

5.11   Modules

As we have seen, one of the advantages of functions is that we can call a function many times within a program, often with different arguments. But why stop there? Many of the functions we write are likely to be useful in other programs too. As just one example, imagine a function that calculates the area of a rectangle—and another that calculates its perimeter. Or we could have a function that calculates the volume of a cube and another to calculate its surface area. A very useful thing would be to write functions for these processes and keep them together in a file for future use. This is something that we can easily do in Python—such a file is called a module. We just write all the functions we need and save it with a .py extension.

The module shown below which we have called geometry.py keeps the four functions we have mentioned together in one place:

Module: geometry.py

```
# function to calculate the perimeter of a rectangle
def rectanglePerimeter(lengthIn, heightIn):
    return (lengthIn + heightIn) * 2

# function to calculate the area of a rectangle
def rectangleArea(lengthIn, heightIn):
    return lengthIn * heightIn

# function to calculate the surface area of a cube
def cubeArea(sideIn):
    return 6 * sideIn**2

# function to calculate the surface area of a cube
def cubeVolume(sideIn):
    return sideIn**3
```

Now, in order to use these functions in a program, we need to import the module (which should be in the same directory as the program); we do this with the following statement.

```
import geometry
```

The program below uses our geometry module.

calculations.py

```
import geometry

rLength = 3 # length of rectangle
rHeight = 4 # height of rectangle

cLength = 5 # length of the cube edges

rectA = geometry.rectangleArea(rLength, rHeight)
rectP = geometry.rectanglePerimeter(rLength, rHeight)
cubeA = geometry.cubeArea(cLength)
cubeV = geometry.cubeVolume(cLength)

print('The area of the rectangle is %d' %(rectA))
print('The perimeter of the rectangle is %d' %(rectP))
print('The surface area of the cube is %d' %(cubeA))
print('The volume of the cube is %d' %(cubeV))
```

The most important thing to notice here is that, when using the functions, we do so by using the module name and the function name joined with the dot operator:

```
rectArea = geometry.rectangleArea(rLength, rHeight)
rectPerimeter = geometry.rectanglePerimeter(rLength, rHeight)
cubeArea = geometry.cubeArea(cLength)
cubeVolume = geometry.cubeVolume(cLength)
```

As you would expect, the output from this program is as follows:

```
The area of the rectangle is 12
The perimeter of the rectangle is 14
The surface area of the cube is 150
The volume of the cube is 125
```

If you prefer not to have to write the whole module name each time, you can use an import statement such as:

```
import geometry as geo
```

Now, instead of writing the full function name you can simply write geo. For example:

```
rectArea = geo.rectangleArea(rLength, rHeight)
```

Another alternative is to import only the functions that you need, using a **from... import** statement. For example:

```
from geometry import rectangleArea, rectanglePerimeter
```

In this case the functions can be called using just the function name, without the module name. For example:

```
rectArea = rectangleArea(rLength, rHeight)
```

There is yet another alternative here—rather than naming the individual functions that we wish to import, we can import all of them by using what is known as a **wildcard**, represented by an asterisk (*):

```
from geometry import *
```

In our case this would be exactly the same as the statement below (so we could call the functions without preceding them with the module name).

```
from geometry import rectangleArea, rectanglePerimeter, cubeArea, cubeVolume
```

In this text we will avoid using the wildcard and instead use explicit imports for the items we require. One reason for this is that if we are importing from a number of different modules, it is not then clear in our code which function comes from which module.

Python is packaged with a number of built-in modules, also known as **libraries**. One of the most commonly used is the math module, which contains functions such as cos, sin, tan, radians (to covert from degrees to radians), degrees (radians to degrees) and many others. To use these, you would need to include the following **import** statement:

```
import math
```

You could then go on to write statements such as:

```
angle = math.radians(60)
print(math.cos(angle))
```

The math module also contains constants such as pi (the value of π, 3.141592 ...) and e (Euler's number, 2.718281...). An example of how you might use such a constant could be:

```
radius = 5
circumferenceOfCircle = 2 * math.pi * radius
```

You will have a chance to do this in the exercises that follow.

5.12   Self-test Questions

1. Explain the meaning of the term *function*.

2. What would be the output of the following program?

```
def function1():
    print('Wales')

def function2():
    print('Scotland')
    function1()

function1()
print('England')
function2()
print('Ireland')
```

3. Consider the following program:

```
def myFunction1(firstIn, secondIn, thirdIn):
    return firstIn + secondIn + thirdIn

def myFunction2(firstIn, secondIn):
    return firstIn - secondIn

print(myFunction2(3, 5))
print(myFunction1(3, 5, 10))
```

  (a) By referring to this program, distinguish between the terms *arguments* and *parameters*.

  (b) What would be displayed on the screen when this program was run?

  (c) Explain, giving reasons, the effect of adding the following line to the main body of the program:

```
print(myFunction1(3))
```

4. What would be displayed on the screen as a result of running the following program?

```
def myFunction(firstIn, secondIn):
    x = 10
    y = x + firstIn + secondIn
    return y

x = 3
y = 4
z = (myFunction(x, y))
print(z)
print(y)
```

5. What would be displayed on the screen as a result of running the following program?

```
def myFunction(a, x):
    y = 20
    return y - a - x

x = 2
y = 7
print(myFunction(x, y))
print(y)
```

5.13 Programming Exercises

1. Implement the programs from the self-test questions in order to verify your answers.
2. For one of the programming exercises in Chap. 2, you wrote a program that converted pounds to kilograms. Rewrite this program, so that the conversion takes place in a separate function which is called in the main body of the program.
3. In the exercises at the end of Chap. 2 you were asked to write a program that calculated the area and perimeter of a rectangle. Rewrite this program so that now the instructions for calculating the area and perimeter of the rectangle are contained in two separate functions.
4. (a) Design and implement a program that converts a sum of money to a different currency. The amount of money to be converted and the exchange rate are entered by the user. The program should have separate functions for:

   - obtaining the sum of money from the user;
   - obtaining the exchange rate from the user;
   - making the conversion;
   - displaying the result.

(b) Adapt the above program so that after the result is displayed the user is asked if he or she wishes to convert another sum of money. The program continues in this way until the user chooses to quit.

5. (a) Write a menu-driven program that provides three options:

- the first option allows the user to enter a temperature in Celsius and displays the corresponding Fahrenheit temperature;

- the second option allows the user to enter a temperature in Fahrenheit and displays the corresponding Celsius temperature;

- the third option allows the user to quit.

The formulae that you need are as follows, where C represents a Celsius temperature and F a Fahrenheit temperature:

$$F = \frac{9C}{5} + 32$$

$$C = \frac{5(F - 32)}{9}$$

(b) Adapt the above program so that the user is not allowed to enter a temperature below absolute zero; this is −273.15 C, or −459.67 F.

6. (a) Adapt the geometry module from section 5.11 by adding a function that calculates the circumference of a circle and another that calculates the area. You can use math.pi from the math module if you wish, but remember to import this module into the geometry module.

(b) Add some lines to the Calculations module to test out your new functions.

Python Collections: Lists and Tuples

6

Outcomes

By the end of this chapter you should be able to:

- *create a **list** and use various functions to modify the list;*
- *explain how lists are accessed using an index;*
- *use both iterable and non-iterable **for** loops to process a list;*
- *use lists as function inputs and outputs;*
- *distinguish between a stack and a queue implement both using a list.*

6.1 Introduction

In previous chapters we have shown you how to create variables and store data in them. In each case the variables you created could be used to hold only a *single* item of data. So how would you deal with a situation in which you had to create and handle a very large number of data items?

An obvious approach would be just to declare as many variables as you need. Declaring a large number of variables is a nuisance but simple enough. For example, let's consider a very simple application that records seven temperature readings (one for each day of the week). You could make use of seven variables, such as `temperature1`, `temperature2`, etc., right up to `temperature7`. But if you wanted to get the user to enter values for each of these temperatures, you would have to do so as follows:

Supplementary Information The online version contains supplementary material available at https://doi.org/10.1007/978-3-031-01326-3_6.

```
temperature1 = float(input('Max temperature for day 1? '))
temperature2 = float(input('Max temperature for day 2? '))
temperature3 = float(input('Max temperature for day 3? '))
temperature4 = float(input('Max temperature for day 4? '))
temperature5 = float(input('Max temperature for day 5? '))
temperature6 = float(input('Max temperature for day 6? '))
temperature7 = float(input('Max temperature for day 7? '))
```

Surely you've got better things to do with your time! And just imagine if we had 100 temperatures! Essentially, you want to repeat the same line seven times, but each time for a different variable—`temperature1`, `temperature2` and so on. And while at first glance you might think that a **for** loop is the answer, the problem we would then have is that each time round the loop, because of the change of variable name, the statement is slightly different.

What we need here is a data type that holds a *collection* of items. Python provides just such data types, the most common of which is a **list**. That is the one we will study first.

6.2 Creating Lists

A list is a special data type in Python that can be thought of as a *container* to store a *collection of items*. Its data type is **list**. These items are sometimes referred to as the **elements** of the list. A list keeps the values in order, so it is often referred to as a sequence.

To declare a list we use square brackets which contain the initial values of the elements. So in the temperature example we would have something like this:

```
temperature = [15.5, 16.0, 14.7, 13.0, 18.5, 17.8, 15.0]
```

This declares a list of seven temperatures. If we wanted our list to start off empty, we would simply use empty brackets:

```
temperature = []
```

A particular feature of Python lists (and other collection types that you will study in the next chapter) is that the elements of the list can all be of different types—something that may come as a surprise to those familiar with other languages such as Java or C++. So we could have, for example:

```
myList = [3.781, 'Hello', 5]
```

If you think about the temperature example, you will probably realize that initializing the values of each temperature when the list is created is actually quite unrealistic. It is much more likely that temperatures would be entered into the program as it runs, and each temperature is added to the list. Adding new items to the end of the list is easy: we simply use the append function. For example, if we wanted to add a new item to myList we would do so like this:

```
myList.append(987)
```

After this operation, mylist would have the value [3.781, 'Hello', 5, 987]

Lists can be used in conjunction with the print statement to display the whole list on the screen. So, using the temperature example:

```
print(temperature)
```

would result in the following output:

[15.5, 16.0, 14.7, 13.0, 18.5, 17.8, 15.0]

6.3   Accessing List Elements

Having learnt how to create a list, we now need to access the individual items in the list. This is done by an indexing system. Each element in a list shares the same name as the list, so in the case of our temperature list, each element is called temperature, but the individual elements are then *uniquely identified* by an additional **index value**. An index value acts rather like a street number to identify houses on the same street (see Fig. 6.1). In much the same way as a house on a street is identified by the street name and a house number, a list element is identified by the list name and the index value.

Fig. 6.1 Elements in a list are identified in much the same way as houses on a street

Like a street number, these index values are always contiguous integers. Note carefully that, in Python, *list indices start from 0 and not from 1*. This index value is always enclosed in square brackets, so the first temperature in the list is identified as `temperature[0]`, the second temperature as `temperature[1]` and so on.

This means that the size of the list and the last index value are *not* the same value. In this case the size is 7 and the last index is 6. There is no such value as `temperature[7]`, for example. Remember this, as it is a common cause of errors in programs. If you try to access an invalid element such as `temperature [7]`, the following program error will be generated at run-time:

```
IndexError: list index out of range
```

Once a list has been created, its elements can be used like any other variable of the given type in Python.

As with any variable, the assignment operator can be used to enter a value, but with a list you have to specify *which* element to place the value in. So once the list is created, we can use the assignment operator to change the value of a particular element.

For example, to allow the user of the program to enter a new value for the first temperature, the following assignment could be used:

```
temperature[0] = float(input('Enter value for first temperature: '))
```

Note again that, since list indices begin at 0, the first temperature is not at index 1 but index 0.

List elements could also be printed on the screen. For example, the following command prints out the value of the *sixth* list element:

```
print(temperature[5]) # index 5 is the sixth element!
```

Once again, note that a list index (such as 5) is just used to *locate* a position in the list; it is *not* the item at that position.

For example, assume that the value of the first temperature in the list is of 25.5. The following statement:

```
print('temperature for day 1 is %2.1f' % (temperature[0]))
```

would then print out the message:

```
temperature for day 1 is 25.5
```

Statements like the `print` command above might seem a bit confusing at first. The message refers to 'temperature for day **1**' but the temperature that is displayed is `temperature[0]`. Remember though that the temperature at index position 0 *is* the first temperature! After a while you will get used to this indexing system.

As you can see from the examples above, you can use list elements in exactly the same way you can use any other kind of variable of the given type. Here are a few more examples:

```
temperature[4] = temperature[4] * 2
```

This assignment doubles the value of the *fifth* temperature. The following **if** statement checks if the temperature for the *third* day was a hot temperature:

```
if temperatureList[2] >= 18:
        print('it was hot today')
```

Python also provides another, very useful way of accessing the variables in a list, which allows us to access the list from the end rather than the beginning. The last item in the list is given the index of −1. The last but one item is given the index −2 and so on.

Let's illustrate this with a new example—a list that contains a number of strings:

```
colours = ['Red', 'Blue', 'Yellow', 'Green', 'Pink', 'Purple', 'Orange']
```

The following statement:

```
print(colours[-1])
print(colours[-3])
```

would give us the following output:

```
Orange
Pink
```

Lists can be assigned to variables in the same way as any other variable. For example:

```
colours2 = colours
```

But we can also assign a part of the list only—this is known as a slice. The slice notation is as follows:

```
colours3 = colours[2:5]
```

Here the two numbers in the square brackets refer to the start and end index—but note that the item at the beginning is included, but the item at the end is excluded. But remember also that we are talking about the index here, rather than the position. In this case the item with the index 2 is 'yellow' and the one with index 4 (because 5 is excluded) is 'pink'.

So this statement:

```
print(colours3)
```

would give the following output:

```
['Yellow', 'Green', 'Pink']
```

So far, all we have done is to access particular elements of a list. However, one of the most common things we want to do is to **iterate** (loop) through a list from beginning to end in order perhaps to display all items or to select particular items that match some criterion.

A version of the **for** loop exists to make life very simple. It is known as an **iterable for** loop. It can be used with any object, such as a list, which is *iterable*— meaning it is possible to loop through from beginning to end. The little program below, which uses our `colours` list, illustrates how it works.

```
colours.py

# create list
colours = ['Red', 'Blue', 'Yellow', 'Green', 'Pink', 'Purple', 'Orange']
# display colours
print() # blank line
print('***Colours in list***');
print() # blank line
for x in colours:
    print(x)
```

As you can see, the header of the **for** loop takes the following form:

```
for x in colours:
```

The program loops through the `colours` list from beginning to end, and as it does so the variable x (which we could have been given any name of our choice) is assigned the value of each item in turn. So in our example, the first time round the loop, x is given the value 'red', then 'blue' and so on. This value is displayed on each iteration, so the output will be:

```
Red
Blue
Yellow
Green
Pink
Purple
Orange
```

In some cases, however, we cannot use this version of the **for** loop.

One case is when we need to *change* the value of an item. The reason for this should be clear—with this version of the **for** loop we only have access to the loop variable (x in our case), not to the item itself.

Another time when we can't use this **for** loop is when we want to use the index itself in the body of the loop. To illustrate this, we will return to out temperature example. Look at this program.

---

temperatures.py

```
temperature = [15.5, 16.0, 14.7, 13.0, 18.5, 17.8, 15.0]
# display temperatures
print() # blank line
print('***TEMPERATURES IN LIST***')
print() # blank line
for i in range(7):
    print('Day %d: %s' % (i + 1, temperature[i]))
```

The output from this program is as follows:

```
***TEMPERATURES IN LIST***

Day 1: 15.5
Day 2: 16.0
Day 3: 14.7
Day 4: 13.0
Day 5: 18.5
Day 6: 17.8
Day 7: 15.0
```

In this case, each time round the loop, we have used the index to display the particular day number (notice that this is $i + 1$ rather than i, because indexing starts at 0). This is why we have used the "in range" version of the **for** loop rather than the "for x in" version.

One more thing to note: in the range function of the **for** loop we have specified 7 as the end point, as we already knew the number of items in the list. It is often the case, however, that we do not know in advance how many items will be in the list, because a user of the program could be dynamically adding and removing items. In this case, we can make use of the very useful built-in len function, which returns the number of items in the list. If we had used this in the above program, the **for** loop would have looked like this:

```
for i in range(len(temperatureList)):
    print('Day %d: %s' %(i + 1, temperatureList[i]))
```

len is not the only function we can use in conjunction with lists. We have already seen how to use the append function in Sect. 6.2, and in Sect. 6.6 we will show you a number of other very useful functions. We will, however, introduce you to one more function here, namely the remove function. As its name suggests, it will remove a particular item from a list. So, for example, if a particular list, myList, was to be declared and initialized as follows:

myList = ['London', 'Edinburgh', Liverpool', Newcastle']

then after the following instruction:

myList.remove('Liverpool')

myList would look like this:

['London', 'Edinburgh', Newcastle']

If there were multiple occurrences of an item, then only the first one would be removed. If myList had been initialized as follows:

myList = [1]

Then the instruction

myList.remove[1]

would result in an empty list.

If the item was not in the list, then this would result in a run-time error. It, therefore, gives us a good opportunity to make use of the **try ... except** construct that we learnt about in Chap. 4.

You can see the remove function in action in the next section.

6.4 Passing Lists as Parameters

In Chap. 5 we looked at how functions can be used to break up a programming task into manageable chunks. Functions can receive data in the form of parameters and can send back data in the form of a return value. Lists can be used both as parameters to functions and as return values. In the next section we will see an example of a list as a return value from a function. In this section we will look at passing lists as parameters to a function. The following menu-driven program allows a user to add names to a waiting list, to remove names and to display the list. Notice that an empty list is declared, which the user can then fill.

waitinglist.py

```python
# function to enter names
def addName(waitingListIn):
        name = input('Enter named to add: ')
        waitingListIn.append(name)

# function to remove a name
def removeName(waitingListIn):
        name = input('Enter name to remove: ')
        try:
                waitingListIn.remove(name)
        except:
                print()
                print('That name is not in the list')

# function to display waitingList
def displayList(waitingListIn):
        print() # blank line
        print('***Waiting List***')
        print() # blank line
        for i in range(len(waitingListIn)):
                print('%d: %s' %(i + 1, waitingListIn[i]))
        print()

# create empty list
waitingList = []

response = '1' # initialize to a value that allows the loop to be entered


print()

while response != '4': # put code in loop
        # offer menu of options
        print()

        print(' [1] Add a name to the waiting list')
        print(' [2] Remove a name from the waiting list')
        print(' [3] Display the waiting list')
        print(' [4] Quit')
        print('enter choice [1,2,3,4]: ')
        print()

        response = input()

        if response == '1':
                addName(waitingList)
        elif response == '2':
                removeName(waitingList)
        elif response == '3':
                displayList(waitingList)

        elif response == '4':
                print('Goodbye')
        else:
                print('Options 1-4 only')
```

Let's look at each of our functions in turn.

Firstly the function that allows us to add names to the list:

```python
# function to enter names
def addName(waitingListIn):
        name = input('Enter named to add: ')
        waitingListIn.append(name)
```

Up until now, all the types we have dealt with are immutable, so the original value in the location of the variable cannot be changed. However, this is not true in the case of a list, which is said to be **mutable**. This means we can use a list function such as append to change the original value of the variable. So, the addName function above actually fills the *original* list. Remember that even though the receiving parameter (waitingListIn) has a different name to the original variable in the body of the program (waitingList), they are both pointing to the same place in memory so both are modifying the same list.

Now let's look at the function for removing a name from the list:

```
# function to remove a name
def removeName(waitingListIn):
        name = input('Enter name to remove: ')
        try:
                waitingListIn.remove(name)
        except:
                print()
                print('That name is not in the list')
```

Here we have made use of the remove function we talked about earlier. Notice, however, that the instruction to remove the name has been placed inside a **try** block in case the name is not in the list—in which case the **except** block is reached and the program continues without terminating, and a message is displayed on the screen telling the user that the name is not in the list.

The function that displays the list is as follows:

```
# function to display waitingList
def displayList(waitingListIn):
        print()  # blank line
        print('***Waiting List***')
        print()  # blank line
        for i in range(len(waitingListIn)):
                print('%d: %s' %(i + 1, waitingListIn[i]))
        print()
```

Two things to note here. Firstly, the form of the **for** loop has had to include the index, i, because we have used this in the print statement—we cannot use an iterable **for** loop here. Secondly, the parameter to the range function has to be the length of the list—found by using the len function—because the size of the list varies.

Below is a sample run from this program.

```
[1] Add a name to the waiting list
[2] Remove a name from the waiting list
[3] Display the waiting list
[4] Quit
enter choice [1,2,3,4]:

1
Enter named to add: Patel

[1] Add a name to the waiting list
[2] Remove a name from the waiting list
[3] Display the waiting list
[4] Quit
enter choice [1,2,3,4]:

1
Enter named to add: Smith

[1] Add a name to the waiting list
[2] Remove a name from the waiting list
[3] Display the waiting list
[4] Quit
enter choice [1,2,3,4]:

1
Enter named to add: Adebayo

[1] Add a name to the waiting list
[2] Remove a name from the waiting list
[3] Display the waiting list
[4] Quit
enter choice [1,2,3,4]:

3

***Waiting List***

1: Patel
2: Smith
3: Adebayo


[1] Add a name to the waiting list
[2] Remove a name from the waiting list
[3] Display the waiting list
[4] Quit
enter choice [1,2,3,4]:
```

```
2
Enter name to remove: Jones

That name is not in the list

[1] Add a name to the waiting list
[2] Remove a name from the waiting list
[3] Display the waiting list
[4] Quit
enter choice [1,2,3,4]:

2
Enter name to remove: Smith

[1] Add a name to the waiting list
[2] Remove a name from the waiting list
[3] Display the waiting list
[4] Quit
enter choice [1,2,3,4]:

3

***Waiting List***

1: Patel
2: Adebayo


[1] Add a name to the waiting list
[2] Remove a name from the waiting list
[3] Display the waiting list
[4] Quit
enter choice [1,2,3,4]:

4
Goodbye
```

6.5 Returning a List from a Function

A function can return a list as well as receive a list as a parameter.

To illustrate this, we have written a shorter version of the waiting list program, which simply allows the user to add three names to a list (by calling a function called addNames) and then displays the list. The point about this version, though, is that it does this by a different mechanism to the previous one.

---

waitinglist2.py

```
# function to enter names
def addNames():
        theList =[]
        for i in range(3):
                name = input('Enter name number %d: ' %(i + 1))
                theList.append(name)
        return theList


waitingList = addNames()
print() # blank line
print('***Waiting List***');
print() # blank line
for a in waitingList:
        print(a)
```

As you can see, we have an `addNames` function, the purpose of which is to create a list (which we have called `myList`), allow the user to add three names to the list and then *return* this list to the main body of the program.

```
def addNames():
        myList =[]
        for i in range(3):
                name = input('Enter name number %d: ' %(i + 1))
                myList.append(name)
        return myList
```

The return value is assigned to a variable called `waitingList`.

```
waitingList = addNames()
```

The program then proceeds to display the names in the list:

```
print() # blank line
print('***Waiting List***');
print() # blank line
for a in waitingList:
        print(a)
```

Below is a sample run from this program:

```
Enter  name  number  1:  Patel
Enter  name  number  2:  Swift
Enter  name  number  3:  Umunna

***Waiting List***

Patel
Swift
Umunna
```

6.6   More *List* Functions

We have already seen how to use the "built-in" len function with lists, and we have also seen how to use the specific list functions append and remove. We will also see that some functions are Python keywords. Here we present these again together with some other useful list functions, together with a short program in each case to illustrate their use. Notice that in some cases we use the function on its own (e.g. len and del, which are built-in functions), and with others we use the dot operator that we discussed in Chap. 5 when we studied strings.

So here are the functions that we can use with lists:

append

We have already seen this in action. It adds an item to the end of a list.

---

appendexample.py

```
myList = ['zero', 'one', 'two', 'three', 'four', 'five', 'six', 'seven']
myList.append('eight') # appends 'eight' to the list
print(myList)
```

Output

```
['zero', 'one', 'two', 'three', 'four', 'five', 'six', 'seven', 'eight']
```

del

This function removes an item or items from the list, based upon the index. Note that **del** is a Python keyword. The syntax, as you can see, is rather different from that which we have seen before.

DelExample.py

```
myList = ['zero', 'one', 'two', 'three', 'four', 'five', 'six', 'seven']
del myList[3] # deletes the fourth item (at index 3)
print(myList)


myList = ['zero', 'one', 'two', 'three', 'four', 'five', 'six', 'seven']
del myList[2:4]
print(myList) # deletes the items starting at index 2 up to, but not including, index 4


myList = ['zero', 'one', 'two', 'three', 'four', 'five', 'six', 'seven']
del myList[:5]
print(myList) # deletes the items starting at index 0, up to but not including index 5

myList = ['zero', 'one', 'two', 'three', 'four', 'five', 'six', 'seven']
del myList[3:]
print(myList) # deletes the items starting at index 3 up to the end
```

Output

```
['zero', 'one', 'two', 'four', 'five', 'six', 'seven']
['zero', 'one', 'four', 'five', 'six', 'seven']
['five', 'six', 'seven']
['zero', 'one', 'two']
```

extend

Joins two lists together.

extendexample.py

```
myList1 = ['zero', 'one', 'two', 'three']
myList2 = ['four', 'five', 'six', 'seven']
myList1.extend(myList2) #joins myList2 onto the end of myList1
print(myList1)
```

Output

```
['zero', 'one', 'two', 'three', 'four', 'five', 'six', 'seven']
```

in

Checks if the list contains a particular item. It will return **True** if it does, **False** if
it does not. Note the particular format of the expression in the program below:

InExample.py

```
myList = ['zero', 'one', 'two', 'three', 'four', 'five', 'six', 'seven']
result1 = 'two' in myList # check if 'two' is in the list
result2 = 'nine' in myList # check if 'nine' is in the list

print(result1)
print(result2)
```

Output

```
True
False
```

Like **del**, **in** is also a Python keyword.

Insert

This function adds an item to a list at a particular index.

insertexample.py

```
myList = ['zero', 'one', 'two', 'three', 'four', 'five', 'six', 'seven']
myList.insert(1, 'half') # adds 'half' at index 1
print(myList)
```

Output

```
['zero', 'half', 'one', 'two', 'three', 'four', 'five', 'six', 'seven']
```

len

We have already seen this in action—it returns the length of the list.

lenexample.py

```
myList = ['zero', 'one', 'two', 'three', 'four', 'five', 'six', 'seven']
print(len(myList))
```

Output

```
8
```

pop

Removes an item from the list, specified by the index, and returns the item removed. If no index is specified (the brackets are empty) it removes the last item. It will give rise to a run-time error if the index is out of range.

---

popexample.py

```
myList = ['zero', 'one', 'two', 'three', 'four', 'five', 'six', 'seven']

member = myList.pop(3) # removes the item at index 3
print(member)
print(myList)

member = myList.pop() # removes the last item
print(member)
print(myList)
```

Output

```
three
['zero', 'one', 'two', 'four', 'five', 'six', 'seven']
seven
['zero', 'one', 'two', 'four', 'five', 'six']
```

remove

We have already seen how this works—it removes a specified item from a list and causes a run-time error if the item is not in the list.

removeexample.py

```
myList = ['zero', 'one', 'two', 'three', 'four', 'five', 'six', 'seven']

myList.remove('four') # removes 'four' from the list
print(myList)
```

Output

```
['zero', 'one', 'two', 'three', 'five', 'six', 'seven']
```

reverse

Reverses the items in a list.

reverseexample.py

```
myList = ['zero', 'one', 'two', 'three', 'four', 'five', 'six', 'seven']

myList.reverse() # reverses the list
print(myList)
```

Output

```
['seven', 'six', 'five', 'four', 'three', 'two', 'one', 'zero']
```

sort

Will sort a list alphabetically or numerically.

sortexample.py

```
myList = ['zero', 'one', 'two', 'three', 'four', 'five', 'six', 'seven']
myList.sort() # will sort the list alphabetically
print(myList)

myList = [3, -1, 2, 10, 0, 5, 6, -7]
myList.sort() # will sort the list numerically
print(myList)
```

Output

```
['five', 'four', 'one', 'seven', 'six', 'three', 'two', 'zero']
[-7, -1, 0, 2, 3, 5, 6, 10]
```

sorted

This function is a built-in function, so does not use the dot operator, but takes the list as a parameter. It does not sort the original list, but returns a new sorted list.

sortedexample.py

```
myList = [3, -1, 2, 10, 0, 5, 6, -7]

myListSorted = sorted(myList) # returns a sorted list

print(myList)
print(myListSorted)
```

Output

```
[-7, -1, 0, 2, 3, 5, 6, 10]
```

The concatenation operator and the multiplication operator

The concatenator operator (+) will join two lists together.

concatenationexample.py

```
myList1 = [ 1, 2, 3]
myList2 = [4, 5]
myList = myList1 + myList2 # joins the two lists
print(myList)
```

Output

```
[1, 2, 3, 4, 5]
```

The multiplication operator (*) duplicates the list the specified number of times, and each time concatenates it to the end of the list.

multiplicationexample.py

```
myList = [ 1, 2, 3]
myList1 = myList * 4 # duplicates the list and concatenates it to the end each time
print(myList1)
```

Output

```
[1, 2, 3, 1, 2, 3, 1, 2, 3, 1, 2, 3]
```

6.7   Queues and Stacks

Those of you who have studied computer science will be familiar with two very important data structures, stacks and queues, both of which comprise a sequence of items, and which can, therefore, be implemented as a list. The difference between a stack and a queue lies not in the structure itself, but in the way the items are removed.

In a queue the items are removed in the same order in which they were added. The first item added is the first to be removed—rather like a queue of people at a bus stop. This is referred to as a first in first out or FIFO protocol.

In a stack it is the last item that was added that is the first to be removed. Imagine a stack of plates that is added to each time a plate is removed from the dishwasher. Each plate will be added to the top of the stack. When it comes to using the plates, the first one to be used will be the one on the top—in other words, the last one added. This is referred to as a last in first out or LIFO protocol. We usually use the words *push* and *pop,* respectively, to refer to the actions of adding and removing items to and from a stack.

The program below implements a stack.

stack.py

```
# function to push item onto the stack
def pushItem(stackIn):
        item = input('Enter item to push: ')
        stackIn.append(item)

# function to pop item from the stack
def popItem(stackIn):
        if len(stackIn) != 0:
                item = stackIn.pop()
                print("Item removed was: " + item)
        else:
                print("The stack is empty")

# function to display waitingList
def displayStack(stackIn):
        print()# blank line
        print('***Stack***');
        print()# blank line
        for a in stackIn:
                print(a)

# create an empty stack
stack = []

response = '1' # initialize to a value that allows the loop to be entered


print()

while response != '4': # put code in loop
        # offer menu of options
        print()

        print('[1] Push an item onto the stack')
        print('[2] Pop an item from the stack')
        print('[3] Display stack')
        print('[4] Quit')
        print('enter choice [1,2,3,4]: ')
        print()

        response = input()

        if response == '1':
                pushItem(stack)
        elif response == '2':
                popItem(stack)
        elif response == '3':
                displayStack(stack)
        elif response == '4':
                print('Goodbye')
        else:
                print('Options 1-4 only')
```

There is nothing very new here, but we should draw your attention to the function that pops the item from the stack:

```
# function to pop item from the stack
def popItem(stackIn):
        if len(stackIn) != 0:
                item = stackIn.pop()
                print("Item removed was: " + item)
        else:
                print("The stack is empty")
```

We are using the pop function of list without parameters—as we saw this simply removes an item from the end of the list—in other words from the top of the stack.

Converting the stack to a queue is simply a matter of changing this function (apart from the wording of the menu). This has been left as a programming exercise at the end of the chapter.

6.8 Creating a List Using Comprehension

List comprehension is a unique way of creating a list using a **for** statement. It provides a way of defining each item according to a formula.

As an example, consider the following statement, which creates a list containing the cubes of the numbers from 0 to 5:

```
cubes = [x ** 3 for x in range(6)]
```

The **for** loop iterates 6 times; as it iterates, the value of x is assigned 0, then 1, then 2, up to 5. The corresponding item in the list is calculated according to the instruction, in this case x ** 3. Thus the list looks like this:
[0, 1, 8, 27, 64, 125]

When using comprehension to create a list, it is also possible to place a condition on how the items are chosen. For example, if we wanted to adapt the list above so that only the even numbers were included, we would do so as follows:

```
cubes = [x ** 3 for x in range(6) if x%2 == 0]
```

This would result in the following list:
[0, 8, 64]

6.9 Tuples

Tuples are very similar to lists, but with one important difference. It is not possible to change a tuple once it has been created. It is useful to use a tuple instead of a list in circumstances where you would never wish the data to be altered. An example might be a tuple that holds the days of the week or the months of the year.

To declare a tuple you use round brackets instead of square brackets. For example:

```
days = ('Monday', 'Tuesday', 'Wednesday', 'Thursday', 'Friday', 'Saturday', 'Sunday')
```

Elements of the tuple are accessed in the same way as lists, using their indices, in square brackets, and starting at zero. So, in the above example, `days[0]` would be 'Monday', `days[1]` would be 'Tuesday' and so on.

There are no functions for modifying a tuple, but the functions **in** and **len** can be used in the same way as they can with lists. You can also use the addition and multiplication operators with tuples. Additionally, **del** can be used to delete the entire tuple.

It is also possible to convert a tuple to a list by using the `list` function, which returns the tuple as a list. For example:

```
myTuple = (1000, 'xyz', 5.7, 'abc')
myList = list(myTuple)
```

6.10   Variable Length Parameter Lists

Now that we know what a tuple is, and we can explore an additional aspect of functions that we didn't cover in the previous chapter. It is possible in Python to allow the number of arguments passed into a function to vary, so that each time the function is called, a different number of arguments can be sent in.

The following short program shows how this works.

```
variablelengthparameterlist.py

# a function with a variable number of parameters
def demoFunction(*args):
    for a in args:
        print(a)

# main body
demoFunction('Hello', 'World', 1, 3.7)
print()
demoFunction('Goodbye')
```

The asterisk before the parameter name, `args`, indicates that this will be a variable length parameter list. In fact, `args` will be a tuple, and as you can see in the definition of `demoFunction`, we can, therefore, iterate through this tuple as we have done in `demoFunction`.

In the main body we have called `demoFunction` twice—firstly with four arguments and then with just one.

The output is:
```
Hello
World
1
3.7

Goodbye
```

Incidentally, although it is common practice to name the function parameter `args`, any name could in fact be used.

In the next chapter, we are going to expand on this topic and explore a construct known as *keyworded* variable length parameter lists.

6.11   Self-test Questions

1   Give some examples of when you might use a list in a program.
2   Consider the following explicit creation of a list:

```
someList = [2,5,1,9,11]
```

(a) What would be the value of `len(someList)`?
(b) What is the value of `someList[2]`?
(c) What would happen if you tried to access `someList[6]`?
(d) Create the equivalent list by declaring an empty list and then assigning the value of each element individually.
(e) Write a **for** loop that will double the value of every item in `someList`.
(f) Explain why, in the above example, it would not be appropriate to use an iterable **for** loop.
(g) Use an iterable **for** loop to display the values inside the list.
(h) Modify the iterable **for** loop above so that only numbers greater than 2 are displayed.

3   Look back at the waiting list program from Sect. 6.4, which read in and displayed a series of names. Design and write the code for an additional function, `initialLetter`, which displays all the names beginning with a particular letter (sent in as a parameter). Write a new menu option to include this option that will allow the user to choose the letter.

4   Assume that a list has been declared in the main body of a program as follows:

```
studentMarks = []
```

This list is to be used to store a list of student exam marks. Now, for each of the following functions, write the code for the given function and the instruction to call this function:

(a) A function, enterExamMarks, that prompts the user to enter some exam marks (as integers) stores the marks in a list and then returns this list.

(b) A function, increaseMarks, that accepts a list of exam marks and increases each mark by 5.

(c) A function, allHavePassed, that accepts a list of exam marks and returns **True** if all marks are greater than or equal to 40, and **False** otherwise.

6.12 Programming Exercises

1 Write a program to test your answers to question 2 above.

2 Make the changes to the waiting list program that you designed in question 3 above.

3 Implement a program for entering and displaying student scores that tests your answers to self-test question 4 above.

4 Design and implement a program that allows the user to enter into a list the price of 5 products in pounds sterling. The program should then copy this list into another list but convert the price of each product from pounds sterling to euro. The program should allow the user to enter the exchange rate of pounds to euro and should, when it terminates, display the contents of both lists. Once again, make use of functions in your program to carry out these tasks.

5 Modify the stack program from Sect. 6.7 so that it implements a queue instead of a stack.

Python Collections: Dictionaries and Sets

7

Outcomes

By the end of this chapter you should be able to:

- *create a **dictionary** and use various functions to modify the dictionary;*
- *explain how dictionary **values** are accessed using **keys**;*
- *use a **for** loop to process a dictionary;*
- *use a variety of dictionary functions;*
- *create a dictionary using **comprehension**;*
- *create a **set** and use a variety of set functions;*
- *use a **for** loop to process a set.*

7.1 Introduction

In the last chapter you were introduced to the concept of a *list*. As you saw, a Python list contains an ordered collection of items. In this chapter we will introduce two new data types, which also hold collections of items. The first is called a **dictionary**, and the second a **set**.

7.2 Dictionaries

A Python dictionary is rather different to the collection types we have come across so far, namely lists and tuples; a dictionary contains *pairs* of items. Its data type is `dict`.

Supplementary Information The online version contains supplementary material available at https://doi.org/10.1007/978-3-031-01326-3_7.

Table 7.1 Network users

User name	Password
Ahmed	Apple123
Miguel	Jan23uarY
Sonia	pa55word
Jonny	paradox1950
Robinder	Heisenberg

The best way to understand this is by means of an example.

Imagine a system—a computer network, for example—that requires users to log on with a unique user name and a password. Table 7.1 shows an example set of six users and their corresponding passwords.

This is an ideal situation in which we can use a dictionary. As we have said, a dictionary is a collection of pairs—in this case it would be user names and their corresponding passwords. The first item in the pair is referred to as the **key**, and the second item as the **value**. The keys must all be unique—but the values can have repetitions. The mathematicians among you will recognize that a Python dictionary implements a mathematical *function*; it is a set of connections.

You should be able to see that our table of user names and passwords naturally obeys the rules of dictionaries. User names must be unique, but it might be possible for more than one user to have the same password.

7.3   Creating Dictionaries

A dictionary is created by using curly brackets—the key and value of each pair is separated by a colon. So, for example, to create a dictionary called `users` containing the first three entries in Table 7.1 we would write the following statement:

```
users = {'Ahmed' : 'Apple123', 'Miguel' : 'Jan23uarY', 'Sonia': 'pa55word'}
```

To print the entire dictionary, we would use:

```
print(users)
```

This would result in the following output:

```
{'Ahmed': 'Apple123', 'Miguel': 'Jan23uarY', 'Sonia': 'pa55word'}
```

If the brackets are left empty, then an empty dictionary is created.

The program below will help us to further understand dictionaries and also to become acquainted with the various functions that a dictionary can perform. It allows the user to add a user name and password pair to a system (such as a local network), to remove names, change a user's password, find a particular password and display all the users and their passwords. Take a look at it and then we will go through it in detail.

```
networkusers.py

# function to enter users
def addUser(usersIn):
        userName = input('Enter name of user: ')
        if userName in usersIn:
                print('User name already exists')
        else:
                password = input('Enter password: ')
                usersIn[userName] = password

# function to remove a user
def removeUser(usersIn):
        userName = input('Enter name to remove: ')
        if userName in usersIn:
                del usersIn[userName]
                print(userName + ' has been removed')
        else:
                print()
                print('That name is not in the list')

# function to retrieve a password
def findPassword(usersIn):
        userName = input('Enter name of user: ')
        password = usersIn.get(userName)
        if password == None:
                print('No such user')
        else:
                print('Password is: ' + password)

# function to change a password
def changePassword(usersIn):
        userName = input('Enter name of user: ')
        if userName not in usersIn:
                print('No such user')
        else:
                password = input('Enter new password: ')
                usersIn[userName] = password
                print('Password changed')


# function to display users
def displayAll(usersIn):
        usernames = usersIn.keys()
        print()# blank line
        print('***Network Users***');
        print()# blank line
        for name in usernames:
                print('Name: %s \t Password: %s' %(name, usersIn.get(name)))
        print()


# create empty dictionary
users = {}

response = '1' # initialize to a value that allows the loop to be entered


print()

while response != '6':  # put code in loop
        # offer menu of options
        print()

        print('[1] Add a user to the list')
        print('[2] Remove a user from the waiting list')
        print('[3] Find password')
        print('[4] Change password')
        print('[5] Display all users')
        print('[6] Quit')
        print('Enter choice [1,2,3,4,5,6]: ')
        print()

        response = input()

        if response == '1':
                addUser(users)
        elif response == '2':
                removeUser(users)
        elif response == '3':
                findPassword(users)
        elif response == '4':
                changePassword(users)
        elif response == '5':
                displayAll(users)
        elif response == '6':
                print('Goodbye')
        else:
                print('Options 1-6 only')
```

This is a menu-driven program—each option on the menu is served by a separate function. An initially empty dictionary is created in the main body of the program with the following line of code.

```
users = {}
```

This dictionary is sent to each function as an argument. So now let's look at each of these functions in turn.

Firstly the function that adds a user name and password to the dictionary—it receives the dictionary as a parameter, `usersIn`:

```
# function to enter users
def addUser(usersIn):
        userName = input('Enter name of user: ')
        if userName in usersIn:
                print('User name already exists')
        else:
                password = input('Enter password: ')
                usersIn[userName] = password
```

We prompt for the user name and then check whether or not this name already exists. We do this with the `in` function, which operates in a similar way to the way it works with lists, but this time checks the keys.

As long as the name does not already exist, we prompt for the password, then add this pair to the dictionary:

```
usersIn[userName] = password
```

As you can see, the name of the dictionary—`usersIn` in this case—is followed by the name of the key in square brackets; the corresponding value is then assigned.

You might be wondering what would happen if the user name already existed. The answer is that the corresponding value would then be changed to the new value —we have used this in option 4 below to change a user's password.

Now the function that removes a user and password pair from the dictionary.

```
# function to remove a user
def removeUser(usersIn):
        userName = input('Enter name to remove: ')
        if userName in usersIn:
                del usersIn[userName]
                print(userName + ' has been removed')
        else:
                print()
                print('That name is not in the list')
```

Having obtained the name of the user, we check that he or she exists, and if so delete that pair with the following statement:

```
del usersIn[userName]
```

We are using the built-in function **del**, which we already saw in relation to lists. In the case of dictionaries we send in the key, and the pair is deleted. If the user does not exist an appropriate message is displayed. Had we not prepared for this possibility and tried to use **del** to delete a non-existing key, we would have got a run-time error.

Now the function that finds a user's password:

```
# function to retrieve a password
def findPassword(usersIn):
        userName = input('Enter name of user: ')
        password = usersIn.get(userName)
        if password == None:
                print('No such user')
        else:
                print('Password is: ' + password)
```

Here we are using the get function of dict, which accepts a key and returns the corresponding value. If there is no such key, it returns the keyword **None**, which indicates a null (missing) value. As will be explained in the Sect. 7.4, you can change this return value if you wish.

The next function we will discuss is the one that changes a user's password:

```
# function to change a password
def changePassword(usersIn):
        userName = input('Enter name of user: ')
        if userName not in usersIn:
                print('No such user')
        else:
                password = input('Enter new password: ')
                usersIn[userName] = password
                print('Password changed')
```

As mentioned, we use the same construct as we did when we added a user—but in this case, because the user already exists, nothing is added, but the password is changed:

```
usersIn[userName] = password
```

Finally we come to the function that displays the user names and passwords:

```
# function to display users
def displayAll(usersIn):
        usernames = usersIn.keys()
        print() # blank line
        print('***Network Users***');
        print() # blank line
        for name in usernames:
                print('Name: %s \t Password: %s' %(name, usersIn.get(name)))
        print()
```

We need to iterate through the names (the keys) and each time display the user name and corresponding password.

To do this, we use the keys function of dict, which returns a list.

```
usernames = usersIn.keys()
```

It's now an easy matter to iterate through this list, displaying, nicely formatted, each name and the corresponding password, which we retrieve with the get function.

```
for name in usernames:
        print('Name: %s \t Password: %s' %(name, usersIn.get(name)))
```

Below is a sample run from the program:

```
[1] Add a user to the list
[2] Remove a user from the waiting list
[3] Find password
[4] Change password
[5] Display all users
[6] Quit
Enter choice [1,2,3,4,5,6]:

1
Enter name of user: Ahmed
Enter password: Apple123

[1] Add a user to the list
[2] Remove a user from the waiting list
[3] Find password
[4] Change password
[5] Display all users
[6] Quit
Enter choice [1,2,3,4,5,6]:

1
```

```
Enter name of user: Sonia
Enter password: pa55word

[1] Add a user to the list
[2] Remove a user from the waiting list
[3] Find password
[4] Change password
[5] Display all users
[6] Quit
Enter choice [1,2,3,4,5,6]:

1
Enter name of user: Robinder
Enter password: Heisenberg

[1] Add a user to the list
[2] Remove a user from the waiting list
[3] Find password
[4] Change password
[5] Display all users
[6] Quit
Enter choice [1,2,3,4,5,6]:

1
Enter name of user: Ahmed
User name already exists

[1] Add a user to the list
[2] Remove a user from the waiting list
[3] Find password
[4] Change password
[5] Display all users
[6] Quit
Enter choice [1,2,3,4,5,6]:

1
Enter name of user: Jonny
Enter password: paradox1950

[1] Add a user to the list
[2] Remove a user from the waiting list
[3] Find password
[4] Change password
[5] Display all users
[6] Quit
Enter choice [1,2,3,4,5,6]:

2
Enter name to remove: Sonia
Sonia has been removed

[1] Add a user to the list
[2] Remove a user from the waiting list
[3] Find password
```

```
[4] Change password
[5] Display all users
[6] Quit
Enter choice [1,2,3,4,5,6]:

3
Enter name of user: Jonny
Password is: paradox1950

[1] Add a user to the list
[2] Remove a user from the waiting list
[3] Find password
[4] Change password
[5] Display all users
[6] Quit
Enter choice [1,2,3,4,5,6]:

4
Enter name of user: Ahmed
Enter new password: orange456
Password changed

[1] Add a user to the list
[2] Remove a user from the waiting list
[3] Find password
[4] Change password
[5] Display all users
[6] Quit
Enter choice [1,2,3,4,5,6]:

5

***Network Users***

Name: Ahmed        Password: orange456
Name: Robinder     Password: Heisenberg
Name: Jonny        Password: paradox1950


[1] Add a user to the list
[2] Remove a user from the waiting list
[3] Find password
[4] Change password
[5] Display all users
[6] Quit
Enter choice [1,2,3,4,5,6]:

6
Goodbye
>>>
```

7.4   More Dictionary Functions

We now present some of the most common dictionary functions (some of which you have already seen). A short program is provided in each case to illustrate their use. Notice once again that in some cases we use the function on its own (e.g. `len` and **`del`**, which are built-in functions), while with others we use the dot operator.

clear

This function removes all items from the dictionary, leaving it empty.

```
clearexample.py

myDictionary = {'January' : 1, 'February' : 2, 'March' : 3}
myDictionary.clear() # clear the contents
print(myDictionary)
```

Output

```
{}
```

del

We have already come across this function in connection with lists, and we saw it working with a dictionary in the previous section. It removes an item with a specified key from the dictionary. If no key is specified it removes the entire dictionary.

```
dictionarydelexample.py

myDictionary = {'January' : 1, 'February' : 2, 'March' : 3}
del myDictionary['February'] # deletes the pair 'February' : 2
print(myDictionary)
print()

del myDictionary # deletes the entire dictionary
try:
    print(myDictionary)
except:
    print('myDictionary does not exist')
```

Output

```
{'January': 1, 'March': 3}

myDictionary does not exist
```

get

We have seen this function in action in Sect. 7.3. It returns the value associated with a particular key. If the key does not exist, it returns **None**. However, it is also possible to specify a different return value, by including a second argument. This is illustrated in the example below.

---

getexample.py

```
myDictionary = {'January' : 1, 'February' : 2, 'March' : 3}
value = myDictionary.get('March') # get value associated with 'March'
print(value)

value = myDictionary.get('April') # get value associated with 'April'
print(value)

# get value associated with 'April' and return 'No such key' if not found
value = myDictionary.get('April', 'No such key')
print(value)
```

Output

```
3
None
No such key
```

in

The keyword **in** is used with dictionaries as well as with lists (which we saw in the last chapter). In the case of dictionaries, however, it applies to the set of keys.

---

dictionaryinexample.py

```
myDictionary = {5 : 'five', 6 : 'six', 7: 'seven'}
result1 = 6 in myDictionary # check if 6 is one of the keys
result2 = 9 in myDictionary # check if 9 is one of the keys

print(result1)
print(result2)
```

Output

```
True
False
```

items

This function returns a list of the pairs in the dictionary, each pair being a tuple.

---

itemsexample.py

```
myDictionary = {'UK' : 'Europe', 'Ghana' : 'Africa', 'China' : 'Asia'}
contents = myDictionary.items()
for a in contents:
    print(a)
```

Output

```
('UK', 'Europe')
('Ghana', 'Africa')
('China', 'Asia')
```

When we have a list of ordered pairs, we can also use a **for** loop to select both items from the pair as follows:

itemsexample1.py

```
myDictionary = {'UK' : 'Europe', 'Ghana' : 'Africa', 'China' : 'Asia'}
contents = myDictionary.items()
for a,  b in contents:
    print('%s is in %s' %(a, b))
```

This gives us:

```
UK is in Europe
Ghana is in Africa
China is in Asia
```

keys

Returns the dictionary's keys as a list.

keysexample.py

```
myDictionary = {'UK' : 'Europe', 'Ghana' : 'Africa', 'China' : 'Asia'}
countries = myDictionary.keys() # returns a list of keys
for a in countries:
    print(a)
```

Output

```
UK
Ghana
China
```

values

Returns the dictionary's values as a list.

valuesexample.py

```
myDictionary = {'UK' : 'Europe', 'Ghana' : 'Africa', 'China' : 'Asia', 'India' : 'Asia'}
continents = myDictionary.values() # returns a list of the dictionary's values
for a in continents:
        print(a)
```

Output

```
Europe
Africa
Asia
Asia
```

len

As with lists, the built-in function `len` returns the number of items (pairs) in the dictionary.

dictionarylenexample.py

```
myDictionary = {'UK' : 'Europe', 'Ghana' : 'Africa', 'China' : 'Asia'}
print(len(myDictionary))
```

Output

3

update

This function adds the pairs contained on one dictionary to another dictionary. If there are any duplicate keys, the corresponding value is overridden (or effectively remains unchanged if the values are also the same).

---
updateexample.py
```
myDictionary1 = {5 : 'five', 6 : 'six', 7 : 'seven'}
myDictionary2 = {5 : 'cinco', 6 : 'six', 8 : 'eight'}

myDictionary1.update(myDictionary2) # adds the contents of myDictionary2 to myDictionary1

print(myDictionary1)
```

Output

```
{5: 'cinco', 6: 'six', 7: 'seven', 8: 'eight'}
```

7.5 Creating a Dictionary Using Comprehension

Dictionary comprehension, is similar to list comprehension and enables us to create a dictionary using a **for** statement. It provides a way of defining each value from its key, according to a formula.

As an example, consider the following statement, which creates a dictionary containing 10 pairs consisting of the numbers from 1 to 10 and the corresponding square.

```
squares = {x : x * x for x in range(1,11)}
```

The **for** loop iterates 10 times; the value of x—the key for each pair—is assigned the values 1, 2, and so on, up to 10. The corresponding value is calculated according to the instructions after the colon. Thus the dictionary looks like this:

$\{1: 1, 2: 4, 3: 9, 4: 16, 5: 25, 6: 36, 7: 49, 8: 64, 9: 81, 10: 100\}$

As a further illustration, consider the program below, which creates a multiplication table:

---
dictionarycomprehension.py
```
number = int(input('Enter multiplier: ')) # get multiplier from user
table = {x : x * number for x in range(1, 13)} # create the multipliction table
counter = 1 # start a counter at 1
#use a 'for' loop to print out a neatly formatted table
for n in table:
    print('%2i x %2i = %2i' %(n, number, table.get(n)))
    counter = counter + 1 # increment counter
```

A sample run from this program is:

```
Enter multiplier: 12
 1 x 12 = 12
 2 x 12 = 24
 3 x 12 = 36
 4 x 12 = 48
 5 x 12 = 60
 6 x 12 = 72
 7 x 12 = 84
 8 x 12 = 96
 9 x 12 = 108
10 x 12 = 120
11 x 12 = 132
12 x 12 = 144
```

When using comprehension to create a dictionary, it is also possible to place a condition on how the keys are chosen. For example, if we wanted to adapt the *squares* dictionary above so that only the even numbers were included, we would do so as follows:

```
evenSquares = {x : x * x for x in range(1,11) if x%2 ==0}
```

This would result in the following dictionary:

```
{2: 4, 4: 16, 6: 36, 8: 64, 10: 100}
```

7.6 Keyworded Variable Length Parameter Lists

Variable length parameter lists such as the one described in the previous chapter, in Sect. 6.10, which begin with a single asterisk, are known as **non-keyworded** lists lists. In contrast, a parameter list that starts with two asterisks is called a **keyworded** parameter list. This list is essentially a dictionary.

The program below demonstrates how we use such a list.

```
keywordedparameterlist.py

# a function with a keyworded parameter list
def demoFunction(**kwargs):
    for a, b in kwargs.items():
        print('Name: %s, Age: %s' %(a, b))

# main body
demoFunction(Kwame = 20, Dorothy = 25, Ahmed = 30)
```

In the main body of the program we send in three pairs, the first item in the pair being a variable and the second the value that is assigned to it. This is received by kwargs in the demoFunction. We saw in Sect. 7.4 how a **for** loop can be used in conjunction with a dictionary's `items` function, so you should be able to see that the output from this program will be as follows:

```
Name: Kwame, Age: 20
Name: Dorothy, Age: 25
Name: Ahmed, Age: 30
```

We have in fact seen this in action before, when we have used the following version of the `print` function:

```
print('Hello world', end ='')
```

We will see more examples in Chap. 11.

If we wish to set up a function to receive a normal argument, a non-keyworded variable length argument and a keyworded variable length argument, we should observe the following order.

```
def myFunction(arg, *args, **kwargs):
```

7.7   Sets

In mathematics, a set is an unordered collection of items in which duplicates are not recorded—so effectively all the items are unique. A Python set is an implementation of this concept.[1]

While it is true that there are some real-world situations that reflect this model—for example the registration numbers of cars registered to use a particular car park—you will find in practice that using a list or a dictionary is rather more practical and versatile than using a set. However, where the set type really comes into its own is when you want to perform mathematical operations on sets.

The most common operations that are performed on sets are *union*, *intersection* and *difference*. The union of a set *A* and a set *B* is a set containing the elements of both sets (duplicates, of course, will not be recorded). The intersection of set *A* and set *B* is a set containing the elements that are *common* to both sets. The difference of set *A* and set *B* is a set containing only those elements of set *A* that are not present in set *B*.

The program below demonstrates how to create a set and use these operations.[2]

---

[1] In mathematics, all elements of a set should be of the same, clearly defined, type. Python sets do, however, allow you to mix types - for example integers and strings.

[2] In this program we have followed the mathematical convention of naming sets with an upper case letter.

---

setexample.py

```
A = {'red', 'yellow', 'blue', 'green', 'pink'} # create a set
B = {'white', 'yellow', 'blue', 'orange'} # create a set

aUnionB = A.union(B); # A union B
aInteresctionB = A.intersection(B); # A intersection B
aDifferenceB = A.difference(B); # A difference B

print('Set A is:')
print(A)
print()
print('Set B is:')
print(B)
print()
print('A union B is:')
print(aUnionB)
print()
print('A intersction B is:')
print(aInteresctionB)
print()
print('A difference B is:')
print(aDifferenceB)
```

Notice that a set is created by enclosing the membership in curly brackets—which is exactly the same as the way in which a set is represented in mathematics.

The output from the above program is as follows:

```
Set A is:
{'pink', 'blue', 'yellow', 'red', 'green'}

Set B is:
{'orange', 'blue', 'white', 'yellow'}

A union B is:
{'pink', 'orange', 'blue', 'yellow', 'white', 'red', 'green'}

A intersection B is:
{'blue', 'yellow'}

A difference B is:
{'red', 'pink', 'green'}
```

Elements can be added to and removed from the set using the add function and remove function, respectively. In addition, the in function can be used to test whether the set contains a particular item (as we saw with lists). Also, **del** can be used to delete the entire set, and clear will remove all items, leaving an empty set. Other functions—such as symmetric_difference—that reflect set operations are also available.

A **for** loop can be used to iterate through the set—but remember that the order will be unpredictable.

Notice that the print function prints the set with curly brackets, each item separated by a comma. And finally, notice how the order of the items when printed is unpredictable and does not reflect the way in which the sets were created.

7.8   Creating a Set Using Comprehension

Set comprehension is very similar to list comprehension. The difference is only that we create the set with curly brackets instead of square brackets:

As an example, consider the following statement, which creates a set containing the cubes of the numbers from 0 to 5, as we did when we created a list:

```
cubes = {x ** 3 for x in range(6)}
```

This would create the following set:

```
{0, 1, 8, 27, 64, 125}
```

Bear in mind that, since this is a set and not a list, if you were to use a `print` statement to display each item in the set, the order in which they were displayed would be unpredictable.

As with lists and dictionaries, we can place a condition on which items are included by using an **if** statement. For example:

```
cubes = {x ** 3 for x in range(6) if x%2 != 0}
```

This would result in the folowing set:

```
{1, 27, 125}
```

7.9   Self-test Questions

1. In this and the previous chapter you learnt about the following collection types that are available in Python:

   - List;
   - Tuple;
   - Dictionary;
   - Set.

   Distinguish between these types of collections.

2. Identify, with reasons, the Python collection type (from those you encountered in both this and the previous chapter) that most closely resembles each of the following real-world collections:

(a)   An ordered collection of patient names waiting for a doctor;

(b)   An unordered collection of patient names registered to a doctor;

(c)   A collection of words and their corresponding definitions;

(d)   A collection of the months of the year.

3. Consider the following line of code that creates a set, `fruits`:

```
fruits = {'apple', 'banana', 'orange', 'plum', 'pineapple'}
```

Write a fragment of code that uses a **for** loop to display each of these fruits on a separate line.

4. What would be the output from the following programs? (Bear in mind that the order in which items appear is not predictable)

(a)

ages1.py
```
ages = {'Katherine' :21, 'Abdul' : 20, 'Maria' : 20}
sum = 0;
for a in ages:
    sum = sum + ages.get(a)
print(sum)
```

(b)

ages2.py
```
ages = {'Katherine' :21, 'Abdul' : 20, 'Maria' : 20}
ages['Abdul'] = 40
ages['Leroy'] = 25
del ages['Maria']
print(ages)
```

(c)

fruits.py
```
fruits = {'Apple', 'Orange', 'Lemon', 'Plum'}
for i in range(5):
    fruits.add('Banana')
print(fruits)
```

5. (a) Using set comprehension, write a line of code that would produce a set of the squares of the numbers from 1 to 10.

(b) Modify the above so that the set contains only numbers greater than 30.

7.10   Programming Exercises

1. Write a short program to check your answer to self-test question 3.
2. Implement the programs in self-test question 4 to test your answers.
3. Write a program that implements an English dictionary, with each pair being a word and its corresponding definition. When you have studied file handling in Chap. 10 you will be able to keep your definitions so that you don't lose them at the end of the program.

   The program could be menu driven, with the menu looking something like the following:

   ```
   Dictionary application
   [1] Add a definition to the dictionary
   [2] Remove a word from the dictionary
   [3] Look up a word
   [4] Change a definition
   [5] Quit
   Enter choice [1,2,3,4,5]:
   ```
4. Write a short program to check your answer to self-test question 5.

Object-Oriented Python: Part 1

8

Outcomes:

By the end of this chapter you should be able to:

- *explain the meaning of the term **object-oriented***;
- *explain and distinguish between the terms **class** and **object***;
- *use Python objects as data types;*
- *create and process collections of objects;*
- *call the methods of an object;*
- *use **UML** notation to make a preliminary design for a class;*
- *write the Python code for a particular class;*
- *distinguish between **instance variables** and **class variables***;
- *explain the purpose of **special methods** (**magic methods**) in Python.*

8.1 Introduction

In the 1990s it became the norm for programming languages to use special constructs called **classes** and **objects**. Such languages are referred to as **object-oriented programming languages**. In this chapter and the next one we will explain what is meant by these terms.

As you will find out, languages such as Java (as well as C++ and others) are often thought of as "pure" object-oriented languages—but in fact Python is itself based entirely on **classes** and **objects**. The reason that Python is not always mentioned in the context of such languages is that it is easy to hide the object-oriented nature from the user. In the previous chapters for example you have been pro-

Supplementary Information The online version contains supplementary material available at https://doi.org/10.1007/978-3-031-01326-3_8.

© Springer Nature Switzerland AG 2022
Q. Charatan and A. Kans, *Programming in Two Semesters*,
Texts in Computer Science, https://doi.org/10.1007/978-3-031-01326-3_8

gramming in a more traditional "procedural" fashion—however, Python fully supports the notion of **classes** and **objects** as we shall see in this chapter.

8.2   Classes and Objects

When we think of data types such as ints and floats, we tend to think about them as holding a *single* piece of information—and this was the case in the earliest programming languages—in fact, even in an object-oriented language such as Java, such data types do indeed hold only one single piece of information—they are often referred to as *primitive* types.

However, as programming became more complex it became apparent that we needed data types that held more than one piece of information. Think for example of a book—a book might have a title, an author, an ISBN number and a price—or a student might have a name, an enrolment number and marks for various subjects. Earlier languages such as C and Pascal got around this problem by allowing us to create a type that allowed more than one piece of information to be held—such types were known by various names in different languages, the most common being *structure* and *record*.

Object-oriented languages such as Java and C++ went one stage further, however. They enabled us not only to create types that stored many pieces of data, but also to define within these types the functions by which we could process that data. For example a book 'type' might have a function that adds tax to the sale price; a student 'type' might have a function to calculate an average mark. As we shall see later, we usually refer to functions as **methods** when they are part of a class.

In order to demonstrate how useful the object-oriented approach is, consider the little program below, which allows a user to enter the length and height of a rectangle, and then calculates the area and perimeter of the rectangle:

---

rectanglecalculations.py

```
# function to calculate area
def calculateArea(lengthIn, heightIn):
    return lengthIn * heightIn

# function to calculate perimeter
def calculatePerimeter(lengthIn, heightIn):
    return 2 * (lengthIn + heightIn)

# main body
length = float(input("What is the length of the rectangle? ")) # prompt for length
height = float(input("What is the height of the rectangle? ")) # prompt for height
area = calculateArea(length, height) # call calculateArea function
perimeter = calculatePerimeter(length, height) # call calculatePerimeter function
print("The area of the rectangle is " + str(area)) # display area
print("The perimeter of the rectangle is " + str(perimeter)) # display perimeter
```

Can you see how useful it might be if, each time we wrote a program dealing with rectangles, instead of having to declare several variables and write methods to calculate the area and perimeter of a rectangle, we could just use a rectangle 'type' to create a single variable, and then use its prewritten methods? In fact you wouldn't even have to know how these calculations were performed.

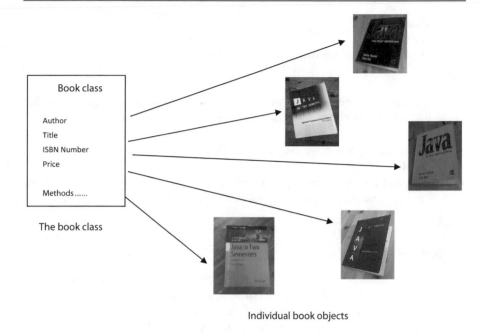

Individual book objects

Fig. 8.1 Many objects can be generated from a single class template

This is exactly what an object-oriented language allows us to do. You have probably guessed by now that this special construct that holds both data and methods is called a **class**. One of the biggest advantages of the object-oriented approach is that once we have written a class, such as a rectangle class, we can use the code as many times we want, in as many programs as we want.

In order to use the methods of a class you need to create an **object** of that class. To understand the difference between **classes** and **objects**, you can think of a class as a blueprint, or template, from which objects are generated, whereas an object refers to an individual *instance* of that class. For example, imagine a system that is used by a bookshop. The shop will contain many hundreds of books—but we do not need to define a book hundreds of times. We would define a book once (in a class) and then generate as many objects as we want from this blueprint, each one representing an individual book.

This is illustrated in Fig. 8.1.

In one program we may have many classes, as we would probably wish to generate many kinds of objects. A bookshop system might have books, customers, suppliers and so on. A university administration system might have students, courses, lecturers, etc.

Object-oriented programming, therefore, consists of defining one or more classes that may interact with each other.

8.3   Properties

You can see that there are two aspects to a class:

Attributes

These are the items of data that it holds—the *variables*. As we will discuss in more detail later, there are two types of attributes that a class can have:

- **Instance variables**—these are attributes that take on different values for each object of the class;
- **Class variables**—these belong to a class, rather than an object. A class variable will be the same for every object of the class, and if it changes for one object it changes for all objects.

Methods

These are the tasks it can perform—in other words the *functions*. In both Python and Java we usually call the functions of a class its **methods**.

Together the attributes and methods of the class are called the **properties** of the class; we access the properties by using the name of the object with the dot operator.

In Python, *everything* is a class, even simple data types such as **int** and **float**. You may remember that in Chap. 2 we used the type function to report on the type of a particular variable. We got outputs like this:

```
<class 'int'>
<class 'float'>
<class 'str'>
```

Now, while it might not be obvious that floats and integers are classes, in the case of a string it is easier to see. In Chap. 5 we showed you many of the functions associated with strings. These are the *methods* of the class. As you saw in that chapter, we invoke these methods with the dot operator. In Chaps. 6 and 7 you studied collections such as lists and dictionaries—these are also classes, and again you invoked their methods with the dot operator.

We will now illustrate all of this by creating and using our own objects. We are going to start by considering the example we discussed in Sect. 8.2, where we proposed a single "type" that dealt with calculating the area and perimeter of a rectangle.

8.4   The Rectangle Class

We have written a Rectangle class for you—classes in Python are by convention written with an initial uppercase letter, so we will follow this convention. The class we have created is saved in a module file called rectangle.py—you will need

Table 8.1 Attributes and methods of the *Rectangle* class

Instance variables	Description
Length	Holds the length of the rectangle. Could be an int or a float
Height	Holds the height of the rectangle. Could be an int or a float
Method	**Description**
calculateArea()	Calculates and returns the area of the rectangle (int or float)
calculatePerimeter()	Calculates and returns the perimeter of the rectangle (int or float)
The initializer	
This is a special method that is called when we create a Rectangle object In this case, it receives two parameters representing the length and height of the rectangle, and these are assigned to the length and height variables, respectively	

to download it from the website (see preface) and make sure that it is in the same folder as the program that is going to use it.

The great thing about object-oriented programming is that you can at this stage completely ignore the program code, because you can use a class without knowing anything about the details. Later in the chapter we will take a look inside the class and see how it is written—but for now we can just use it as we would any other 'type'.

What we do need to know, however, is some information about the data that a Rectangle object will hold and the methods available to process that information. This is given in Table 8.1.

Armed with this information we can proceed to write programs that use our Rectangle class.

8.5 Testing the *Rectangle* Class

The following program shows how we can create a Rectangle object and use its methods.

```
rectangletester.py

from rectangle import Rectangle

# get the values from the user
rectangleLength = float(input("Please enter the length of your rectangle: "))
rectangleHeight = float(input("Please enter the height of your rectangle: "))

# create a new rectangle object
myRectangle = Rectangle(rectangleLength, rectangleHeight)

'''
use the various methods of the rectangle class to display the length, height, area and perimeter of
the rectangle
'''

print("Rectangle length is " + str(myRectangle.length))
print("Rectangle height is " + str(myRectangle.height))
print("Rectangle area is " + str(myRectangle.calculateArea()))
print("Rectangle perimeter is " + str(myRectangle.calculatePerimeter()))
```

Let's take a closer look at this. First of all we import the `Rectangle` class from the module:

```
from rectangle import Rectangle
```

Remember that specifically importing the class (`Rectangle`) means that we can refer to its methods without having to use the name of the module (`rectangle`).

The first thing we do, once the class has been imported, is to get the user to specify the length and height of the rectangle; using those values we then create a `Rectangle` *object*, which we have called `myRectangle`:

```
myRectangle = Rectangle(rectangleLength, rectangleHeight)
```

This line causes our special initializer method to be called: the length and height as specified by the user are sent in as arguments, and these are assigned to the instance variables `length` and `height`, respectively. You will see later how we have coded the initializer to do this.

In the next two lines, we display the length and height of the rectangle:

```
print("Rectangle length is " + str(myRectangle.length))
print("Rectangle height is " + str(myRectangle.height))
```

As you can see, we access the instance variables with the dot operator, in the same way as we do with methods. Now, there may be some of you who are already familiar with object-oriented programming in other languages such as Java, and you might be surprised that we are directly accessing the instance variables in this way. This is discussed in more detail in Sect. 8.13.

Finally, we want to display the area and perimeter of the rectangle, which we do as follows:

```
print("Rectangle area is " + str(myRectangle.calculateArea()))
print("Rectangle perimeter is " + str(myRectangle.calculatePerimeter()))
```

We are calling the `calculateArea` and `calculatePerimeter` methods of `Rectangle` with the dot operator, as you have already seen us do with the methods (functions) of a list or a string.

Here is an example program run:

```
Please enter the length of your rectangle: 4
Please enter the height of your rectangle: 6
Rectangle length is 4.0
Rectangle height is 6.0
Rectangle area is 24.0
Rectangle perimeter is 20.0
```

8.6 The BankAccount Class

We have created a class called BankAccount, which you can download—it is saved in a file called bankaccount.py. This could be a very useful class in a real-world application—for example as part of a financial control system. Once again you do not need to look at the details of how this class is coded in order to use it. You do need to know, however, that the class holds three pieces of information —the account number, the account name and the account balance.

The properties are listed in Table 8.2.

The methods are straightforward, although you should pay particular attention to the withdraw method. Our simple BankAccount class does not allow for an overdraft facility, so unlike the deposit method, which simply adds the specified amount to the balance, the withdraw method needs to check that the amount to be withdrawn is not greater than the balance of the account; if this were to be the case then the balance would be left unchanged. The method returns a **bool** to indicate if the withdrawal was successful or not. A value of **True** would indicate success, and a value of **False** would indicate failure. This enables a program that uses the BankAccount class to check whether the withdrawal has been made successfully. You can see how this is done in the program that follows, which makes use of the BankAccount class.

---

bankaccounttester.py

```
from bankaccount import BankAccount

account1 = BankAccount ("99786754","Susan Richards") # create a new bank account
amount = float(input("Enter amount to deposit: ")) # get amount to deposit from user
account1.deposit(amount) # make deposit
print("Deposit was made")
print("Balance  = " + str(account1.balance)) # display new balance
print()
amount = float(input("Enter amount to withdraw: ")) # get amount to withdraw from user
ok = account1.withdraw(amount) # attempt withdrawal
if(ok):
    print("Withdrawal made") # success
else:
    print("Insufficient funds") # failure
print("Balance  = " + str(account1.balance)) # display new balance
```

The program creates a BankAccount object and then asks the user to enter an amount to deposit. It then confirms that the deposit was made and shows the new balance.

Table 8.2 Attributes and methods of the *BankAccount* class

Instance variables	Description
accountNumber	Holds the account number (a string)
accountName	Holds the name of the account holder (a string)
balance	Holds the current balance for this account (a float)
Method	**Description**
deposit(amountIn)	Adds amountIn to the balance
withdraw(amountIn)	If there are sufficient funds, subtracts amountIn from the balance and returns **True**. If there are insufficient funds, returns **False** and leaves the balance unchanged

The initializer
Receives two parameters representing the account number and account name. These are assigned to the accountNumber and accountName, respectively
Also, at the time the BankAccount object is created, balance is set to zero

It then does the same thing for a withdrawal. The withdraw method returns a **bool** indicating if the withdrawal has been successful or not, so we have assigned this return value to a **bool**, ok:

```
ok = account1.withdraw(amount);
```

Depending on the value of this variable, the appropriate message is then displayed:

```
if(ok):
    print("Withdrawal made") # success
else:
    print("Insufficient funds") # failure
print("Balance  = " + str(account1.balance)) # display new balance
```

Two sample runs from this program are shown below. In the first, the withdrawal was successful:

```
Enter amount to deposit: 1000
Deposit was made
Balance  = 1000.0

Enter amount to withdraw: 400
Withdrawal made
Balance  = 600.0
```

In the second, there were not sufficient funds to make the withdrawal:

```
Enter amount to deposit: 1000
Deposit was made
Balance = 1000.0

Enter amount to withdraw: 1500
Insufficient funds
Balance = 1000.0
```

8.7   Collections of Objects

It is very common occurrence that we want to create a collection—very often a `list`—of objects such as `BankAccount` objects. As you have seen, Python lists (and other collections) allow us to add items of any type to the list—including, of course, objects of our own classes.

This is what we do in the program below:

---

bankaccounttester2.py

```python
from bankaccount import BankAccount

# create an empty list
accountList = []

# add three new accounts to the list
accountList.append(BankAccount("99786754","Susan Richards"))
accountList.append(BankAccount("44567109","Delroy Jacobs"))
accountList.append(BankAccount("46376205","Sumana Khan"))

# make various deposits and withdrawals

accountList[0].deposit(1000);
accountList[2].deposit(150);
accountList[0].withdraw(500);

# print details of all three accounts

for account in accountList:
    print("Account number: " + account.accountNumber)
    print("Account name: " + account.accountName)
    print("Current balance: " + str(account.balance))
```

Let's take a look at this. First of all we create an empty list, to which we add three bank accounts.

```python
# create an empty list
accountList = []

# add three new accounts to the list
accountList.append(BankAccount("99786754","Susan Richards"))
accountList.append(BankAccount("44567109","Delroy Jacobs"))
accountList.append(BankAccount("46376205","Sumana Khan"))
```

We then deposit 100 and 150, respectively, into the first and last accounts in the list (index 0 and index 2) and withdraw 500 from the first.

```
accountList[0].deposit(1000);
accountList[2].deposit(150);
accountList[0].withdraw(500);
```

Finally, we use a **for** loop to display the details of each account.

```
for account in accountList:
    print("Account number: " + account.accountNumber)
    print("Account name: " + account.accountName)
    print("Current balance: " + str(account.balance))
```

As you might expect, the output from this program is as follows:

```
Account number: 99786754
Account name: Susan Richards
Current balance: 500.0

Account number: 44567109
Account name: Delroy Jacobs
Current balance: 0.0

Account number: 46376205
Account name: Sumana Khan
Current balance: 150.0
```

8.8   Designing and Implementing Classes in Python

Having used the Rectangle class and the BankAccount class as data types in our programs, we can now go on to show you how we implemented them. It is worth noting that, although we could have included the code in the same file as the programs that use these classes, we have—as you saw—saved the code for each class in a separate file. This is very good practice, because one of the main advantages of object-oriented programming is that we can use our classes over and over in our applications.

When we design classes, it is very useful to start off by using a diagrammatic notation. The usual way this is done is by making use of the notation of the **Unified Modeling Language (UML)**.[1] In this notation, a class is represented by a box divided into three sections. The first section provides the name of the class, the

---

[1] Martina Seidl et al., *UML @Classroom, An Introduction to Object Oriented Modeling*, Springer 2015.

Fig. 8.2 Design of the
Rectangle class

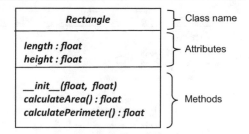

second section lists the attributes, and the third section lists the methods. The UML class diagram for the Rectangle class is shown in Fig. 8.2.

You can see that the UML notation requires us to indicate the names of the attributes along with their types, separated by a colon. When we move onto Java in the next semester, you will see that the types are fixed at the time the variables (or attributes) are declared. In Python, as you know, there is much more flexibility (it is *loosely typed*, whereas Java is *strongly typed*)—so here we have indicated the most appropriate type that we would use—in this case float for both length and height.

Now let's consider the notation for the methods, which are specified in the third box.

The first method specified is the initializer—it looks very strange, doesn't it? That is because it is what we call a **special method** or **magic method** in Python. Special methods always have two underscores at the beginning and end. They also have special names like init. Special methods are not called directly but are invoked when certain syntax is used. In the case of init it is called when we create a new object.

After the name you will see there are two items in brackets—these are the expected types of the arguments that will be sent into the method—in this case both floats.

Next comes the method for calculating the area of the rectangle. The brackets are empty because there are no inputs. But the expected output—in this case float—is specified after a colon. The method for calculating the perimeter is similar.

Now that we have designed our Rectangle class, the code is presented below. You will see from this that there are quite a few new concepts here, so we will go through it carefully once you have had a look at it.

Rectangle

```
class Rectangle:

    # the initializer
    def __init__(self, lengthIn, heightIn):
        self.length = lengthIn
        self.height = heightIn

    # method for calculating the area
    def calculateArea(self):
        return self.length * self.height

    # method for calculating the area
    def calculatePerimeter(self):
        return 2 * (self.length + self.height)
```

Let's start with the initializer. Its header, as we explained above, has rather a strange appearance—it also has an unexpected item—self—in the parameter list, which we will explain in a moment:

```
def __init__(self, lengthIn, heightIn):
```

This is the method that is called when we create a Rectangle object with a command such as this:

```
myRectangle = Rectangle(rectangleLength, rectangleHeight)
```

When this method is called it creates space in memory to hold a Rectangle object: as you will discover, it is equivalent to a **constructor** in Java. But it also carries out any instructions that we tell it to.

What you might find strange is that the method has three parameters, but we send in only two. The second and third parameters receive the arguments we send in —but the first is a special one called self.

So what is the purpose of self? As you have seen, when we refer to an instance variable or a method of a class we use the name of the object together with the dot operator. But if we are doing this while we are in the process of defining our class, what name should we give the object? That is where self comes in to play. The first parameter of the method declares the name we are going to use to refer to the object, which doesn't have to be self, but it is common to use this name. Now we can initialize the variables of the class by using this name:

```
self.length = lengthIn
self.height = heightIn
```

We are declaring the instance variables of the class and are initializing them by giving them the values of the arguments that were sent in. And as you see, we refer to the variables by joining them to the name self with the dot operator.

As we have said, the first variable doesn't actually have to be called self. We could give it any name, as long as we use that name in the method.

So now we can move on to the other methods. Firstly the method that calculates and returns the area of the rectangle:

```
def calculateArea(self):
    return self.length * self.height
```

The method doesn't expect to be sent any arguments—however, it still has one parameter, self, which we again use to refer to the variables of the class. The body of the method simply returns the area, calculated by multiplying the length by the height.

The method to calculate the perimeter is the same except for the calculation:

```
def calculatePerimeter(self):
    return 2 * (self.length + self.height)
```

8.9 Implementing the BankAccount Class

Having seen one class implemented, the next one—the BankAccount class—should not be too big a surprise.

Its UML diagram is shown in Fig. 8.3

Now for the code:

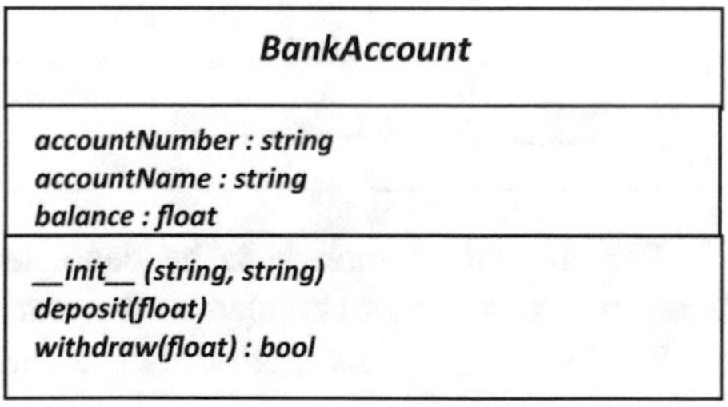

Fig. 8.3 Design of *BankAccount* class

BankAccount
accountNumber : string accountName : string balance : float
__init__ (string, string) deposit(float) withdraw(float) : bool

BankAccount

```
class BankAccount:
    # the initialzer
    def __init__(self, numberIn, nameIn):
        self.accountNumber = numberIn
        self.accountName = nameIn
        self.balance = 0.0

    # method to deposit money
    def deposit(self, amountIn):
        self.balance = self.balance + amountIn

    # method to withdraw money
    def withdraw(self, amountIn):
        if amountIn > self.balance:
            return False # no withdrawal was made
        else:
            self.balance = self.balance - amountIn
            return True # withdrawal successfully made
```

Let's take a look at this in a bit more detail. First the initializer:

```
def __init__(self, numberIn, nameIn):
    self.accountNumber = numberIn
    self.accountName = nameIn
    self.balance = 0.0
```

Once again we see three parameters. The first two instructions create and initialize the instance variables `accountNumber` and `accountName` using the values of the last two of the three parameters. The final instruction creates the `balance` variable and initializes it to zero. As before, the first parameter, `self`, enables us to refer to an instance of the class.

Next we have the method that allows us to deposit an amount of money into the account:

```
def deposit(self, amountIn):
    self.balance = self.balance + amountIn
```

The amount of money to be deposited is received as the second parameter, `amountIn`, and this is added to the current balance.

Finally we have the method that withdraws money from the account; this is a little more complicated:

```
def withdraw(self, amountIn):
    if amountIn > self.balance:
        return False # no withdrawal was made
    else:
        self.balance = self.balance - amountIn
        return True # withdrawal successfully made
```

Assuming there is no overdraft facility, the total we are allowed to withdraw must be no greater than the current balance. If it is greater, then a value of **False** is returned, indicating that the transaction was unsuccessful. If it is not greater than the current balance, then the amount is subtracted from the balance and a value of

True is returned. When the function is called, this return value can be used to test whether the transaction was successful or not, as we saw in Sect. 8.6.

8.10   A Bank Application

Let's write an application that allows a user to process a collection of bank accounts.

Before showing you the code for this application, we want to tell you something about the way we have chosen to implement it. We will need to create a variable that will hold a collection of accounts—you are probably guessing that this will be implemented as a list. This of course is perfectly possible, and you have already seen an example of how we created a method to deposit money in one of these accounts. However, in our application we have chosen to use not a list but a dictionary. You will recall that in a dictionary, the first item of a pair is a unique key. And in our BankAccount class, each account is identified by a unique account number. So in our dictionary, for each item, the key will be the account number and this will be associated with an account. As you will see this makes it possible to write very neat simple routines for processing our collection of accounts.

Here is our bank application—take a look at it, and then we will go over the important points.

bankapplication.py

```python
from bankaccount import BankAccount

#add account
def option1(accountsIn):
    # get details from user
    number = input('Enter account number: ')
    name = input('Enter account name: ')
    if number not in accountsIn: # check that account does not already exist
        # add new account
        acc = BankAccount(number, name)
        accountsIn[number] = acc
        print('Account created')
    else:
        print('Account number already exists')

# remove account
def option2(accountsIn):
    # get account number of account to remove
    number = input('Enter account number: ')
    if number in accountsIn: # if account exists
        del accountsIn[number]
        print('Account removed')
    else:
        print('No such account number')

# deposit money in an account
def option3(accountsIn):
    # get details from user
    number = input('Enter account number: ')
    amount = float(input('Enter amount to deposit: '))
    acc = accounts.get(number) # fetch account
    if acc == None: # if account does not exist
        print('No such account')
    else:
        acc.deposit(amount)
        print('Money deposited')

# withdraw money from an account
def option4(accountsIn):
    # get details from user
    number = input('Enter account number: ')
    amount = float(input('Enter amount to withdraw: '))
    acc = accountsIn.get(number) # fetch account
    if acc == None: # if account does not exist
        print('No such account')
    else:
        result = acc.withdraw(amount)
        if result:
            print('Withdrawal made')
        else:
            print('Insufficient funds')

# check account details
def option5(accountsIn):
    # get details from user
    number = input('Enter account number: ')
    acc = accountsIn.get(number)
    if acc == None: # if account does not exist
        print('No such account')
    else:
        print('Account number: ' + acc.accountNumber)
        print('Account name: ' + acc.accountName)
        print('Balance: ' + str(acc.balance))
        print()

# main body

accounts = {} # create an empty dictionary
```

```
choice = '1'
# offer menu
while choice != '6':
    print()
    print('Bank Application')
    print('1. Create new account')
    print('2. Remove an account')
    print('3. Deposit money')
    print('4. Withdraw money')
    print('5. Check account details')
    print('6. Quit')
    print()
    print('Enter choice [1-6]: ')

    # get choice
    choice = input()
    print()

    # process menu options
    if choice == '1':
        option1(accounts)
    elif choice == '2':
        option2(accounts)
    elif choice == '3':
        option3(accounts)
    elif choice == '4':
        option4(accounts);
    elif choice == '5':
        option5(accounts);
    elif choice == '6':
        print('Goodbye')
    else:
        print('Options 1-6 only')
```

We have seen this sort of menu-driven program before, where each choice calls a particular function. The main body of the program begins by creating an empty dictionary.

```
accounts = {} # create an empty dictionary
```

It then goes on to present and process the menu. We won't go into detail about this, because we are used to seeing this kind of approach.

Each menu choice calls the relevant function, sending in the `accounts` dictionary as an argument. Let us look, as an example of these functions, at choice 1, which adds a new account:

```
#add account
def option1(accountsIn):
    # get details from user
    number = input('Enter account number: ')
    name = input('Enter account name: ')
    if number not in accountsIn: # check that account does not already exist
        # add new account
        acc = BankAccount(number, name)
        accountsIn[number] = acc
        print('Account created')
    else:
        print('Account number already exists')
```

Notice how we have used the `in` function to check whether the account number already exists in the set of keys—this is an example of how using a dictionary is so useful here. Another example is `option3`, which makes a deposit:

```
# deposit money in an account
def option3(accountsIn):
    # get details from user
    number = input('Enter account number: ')
    amount = float(input('Enter amount to deposit: '))
    acc = accounts.get(number) # fetch account
    if acc == None: # if account does not exist
        print('No such account')
    else:
        acc.deposit(amount)
        print('Money deposited')
```

Here the `get` method of dictionary makes it a very easy matter to retrieve a particular account based on the account number. It also makes it easy to check if the account exists, by using the fact that it returns **None** if there is no such key.

Other functions are similar—look particularly at `option4` which makes a withdrawal:

```
# withdraw money from an account
def option4(accountsIn):
    # get details from user
    number = input('Enter account number: ')
    amount = float(input('Enter amount to withdraw: '))
    acc = accountsIn.get(number) # fetch account
    if acc == None: # if account does not exist
        print('No such account')
    else:
        result = acc.withdraw(amount)
        if result:
            print('Withdrawal made')
        else:
            print('Insufficient funds')
```

Notice how we make use of the return value of the `withdraw` method of `BankAccount` to check whether the withdrawal was made or not.

8.11   Class Variables

In Sect. 8.3 we introduced the idea of a class variable, which is an attribute that applies to the class rather than to an individual object, and which is, therefore, the same for every object of the class. As an example, think of our `BankAccount` class. Imagine that account holders earned interest on their accounts at a particular rate. This rate would be the same for all account holders—so we would want this attribute to be a class variable, rather than an instance variable.

Let's implement this example. A class variable is declared and initialized outside of any method. So, if we were to declare a class variable `interestRate` with an initial value of 2.5 (representing a percentage rate) we would do so as follows:

BankAccount

```
class BankAccount:
    # class variable
    interestRate = 2.5

    ...
    other definitions follow

        ............

    ...
```

When we want to access a class variable, we normally use the class name rather than the name of a particular object.

The following program demonstrates how to do this with our new bank account:

bankaccounttester3.py

```
from bankaccount import BankAccount

# create two bank accounts

account1 = BankAccount("99786754","Susan Richards")
account2 = BankAccount("44567109","Delroy Jacobs")

print('Before changing the interest rate')
print('Interest rate for account1 = %1.1f per cent' %account1.interestRate)
print('Interest rate for account2 = %1.1f per cent' %account2.interestRate)
print()

# set interest new interest rate (using the class name)
BankAccount.interestRate = 3.0

print('After changing the interest rate')
print('Interest rate for account1 = %1.1f per cent' %account1.interestRate)
print('Interest rate for account2 = %1.1f per cent' %account2.interestRate)
```

As hoped, the output from this program is:

```
Before changing the interest rate
Interest rate for account1 = 2.5 per cent
Interest rate for account2 = 2.5 per cent

After changing the interest rate
Interest rate for account1 = 3.0 per cent
Interest rate for account2 = 3.0 per cent
```

The interest rate has changed for both accounts.

To make use of the class variable we would probably wish to add a method to our bank account to apply the interest rate, which, at its most simple, would look like this:

```
# method to add interest
def addInterest(self):
    self.balance = self.balance + self.balance * BankAccount.interestRate/100
```

You should note that in UML notation class variables are indicated by underlining them.

8.12   The __str__ Method

In Sect. 8.8, we saw that the __init__ method is a special method (or magic method), and that such methods are prefixed and suffixed with two underscores. Here we will look at another special method, namely the _str__ method.

The __str__ method is a very useful method to include in a class for the purposes of testing. Rather than have to print each attribute of the class when testing it, it would save a lot of time if you could simply use the print command with the object name and see all the information you want. This is what the `__str__` method allows you to do. It will return a string of your choice, and this string will be displayed when the object name is used as an argument to the `print` function.

We will illustrate this with our `BankAccount` class. Let's add the following method to the class:

```
def __str__(self):
    return('Account number: %s, Name: %s, Balance: %0.2f' %(self.accountNumber, self.accountName, self.balance))
```

Now we can test it out:

strtester.py

```
from bankaccount import BankAccount

myAccount = BankAccount('98765432', 'Patel')
myAccount.deposit(100.0)
print(myAccount)
```

You can see that in the last line, we have simply used the name of the account object—`myAccount`—as the input to the `print` statement. We get the following result, as specified in the definition of `__str__`:

```
Account number: 98765432, Name: Patel, Balance: 100.00
```

8.13 Encapsulation

People who are already familiar with an object-oriented programming language will be asking whether Python supports the concept of **encapsulation** or information hiding. This is the technique of making attributes accessible only to the methods of the same class. As you will see when you study Java in the next semester, this is normally achieved by making the attributes of a class *private*. This means they cannot be directly accessed by the methods of another class, but only via carefully designed methods of their own class which are made public. By restricting access in this way, programmers can keep the data in their classes "sealed off" from other classes, because they are the ones in control of how it is actually accessed.

However, such a mechanism is not really available in Python, which is why you have seen us directly accessing the attributes by using the dot operator. Python does provide a way of indicating to a programmer that these attributes should not be accessed directly: this involves naming the attribute so that it is prefixed with a single underscore—for example `_balance`.

It is also possible to place a double underscore in front of the name, which would cause Python to rename the variable—this is known as **name-mangling**. For example, again referring to the `BankAccount` class, if we named an attribute `__balance`, the compiler would transform the name to `_BankAccount__balance`.

Imagine the initializer of our `BankAccount` class had been defined as follows:

```
def __init__(self, numberIn, nameIn):
    # notice double underscores
    self.__accountNumber = numberIn
    self.__accountName = nameIn
    self.__balance = 0.0
```

A program that used `BankAccount` would now need to do this sort of thing:

```
myAccount = BankAccount(10, 10)
print(myAccount._BankAccount__balance)
```

However, because the way it is renamed follows the same pattern in all cases, it does not really stop anyone from accessing the variable. It just sends a strong signal not to do so.

8.14 Self-test Questions

1. Examine the program below and then answer the questions that follow:

```
from rectangle import Rectangle

rectangle1 = Rectangle(3.34, 4.7)
rectangle2 =  Rectangle(5.123, 6.1)
print('The area of rectangle1 is %2.1f ' %(rectangle1.calculateArea()))
print('The area of rectangle21 is %2.1f ' %(rectangle2.calculateArea()))
```

   (a) By referring to the program above distinguish between a *class* and an *object*.
   (b) By referring to the program above explain the purpose of the initializer.
   (c) By referring to the program above explain how you call the method of a class.
   (d) What output would you expect to see from the program above?
2. Explain the difference between an *instance variable* and *class variable*.
3. (a) Declare a list called `rooms`. The list will hold `Rectangle` objects that represent the dimensions of rooms in an apartment.
   (b) There are three rooms in the apartment with the following dimensions:

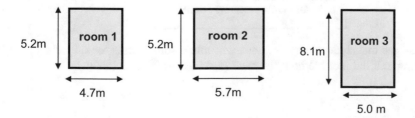

Add three appropriate `Rectangle` objects to the `rooms` list to represent these 3 rooms.

(c) Write the line of code that would make use of the `rooms` list to display the area of room 3 to the screen.

4. Consider a class that we could develop for calculating the area and circumference of a circle. The UML diagram for such a class, which we have called `CircularShape`, is shown below:

CircularShape
radius : float
__init__(float) *calculateArea() : float* *calculateCircumference() : float*

(a) Distinguish between *attributes* and *methods* in this class.

(b) For each method in the `CircularShape` class, determine.
   - the number of parameters;
   - the return type;
   - the equivalent method header in Python.

(c) Add an additional method into this UML diagram, `calculateDiameter`, which calculates and returns the diameter of the circle.

(d) Write the Python code for the `calculateDiameter` method.

5. The UML diagram below represents the design for a `Student` class.

Student
studentNumber : string *studentName : string* *markForMaths : int* *markForEnglish : int* *markForScience : int* *fee: float*
_init__(string, string) *enterMarks(int, int, int)* *calculateAverageMark() : float*

You can see that students have a name, a number, some marks for subjects they are studying and the fee. Methods are then provided to process this data.

(a) What is indicated by the fact that one of the attributes, `fee`, has been underlined?

(b) Write the Python code for the methods.

8.15 Programming Exercises

In order to tackle these exercises, make sure that the classes `Rectangle` and `BankAccount` have been downloaded from the website (see preface).

1. Implement the program given in self-test question 1 and run it to confirm your answer to part (d) of that question.

2. Design and implement a program that performs in the following way:
   - when the program starts, two bank accounts are created, using names and numbers which are written into the code;
   - the user is then asked to enter an account number, followed by an amount to deposit in that account;
   - the balance of the appropriate account is then updated accordingly—or if an incorrect account number was entered a message to this effect is displayed;
   - the user is then asked if he or she wishes to make more deposits;
   - if the user answers does wish to make more deposits, the process continues;
   - if the user does not wish to make more deposits, then details of both accounts (account number, account name and balance) are displayed.

3 (a) Implement the `CircularShape` class that was discussed in self-test question 4 above.

   (b) Add the `calculateDiameter` method into this class as discussed in parts 4c and 4d.

   (c) Write a program to test out your class. This program should allow the user to enter a value for the radius of the circle and then display the area, circumference and diameter of this circle on the screen by calling the appropriate methods of the `CircularShape` class.

   (d) Modify the tester program above so that once the information has been displayed the user is able to reset the radius of the circle. The area, circumference and diameter of the circle should then be displayed again.

4. (a) Write the code for the `Student` class discussed in self-test question 5 above.

   One thing to think about is what you choose for the initial values of the marks. If you chose to give each mark an initial value of zero, this could be ambiguous; a mark of zero could mean that the mark simply has not been entered—or it could mean the student actually scored zero in the subject! Can you think of a better initial value?

You can assume that the fees for the student are set initially to 3000.

(b) Write a tester class to test out your Student class; it should create two or three students (or even better a list of students), and use the methods of the Student class to test whether they work according to the specification.

5. A system is being developed for use in a store that sells electrical appliances. A class called StockItem is required for this system. An object of the StockItem class will require the following attributes:

- a stock number;
- a name;
- the price of the item
- the total number of these items currently in stock.

The first three of the above attributes will need to be set at the time a StockItem object is created—the total number of items in stock will be set to zero at this time.

The following methods are also required:

- a method that receives an integer and adds this to the total number of items of this type in stock;
- a method that returns the total value of items of this type in stock; this is calculated by multiplying the price of the item by the number of items in stock.

The design of the StockItem class is shown in the following UML diagram:

StockItem
stockNumber : string name : string price : float totalStock : int
__init__(string, string, float) increaseTotalStock(int) calculateTotalValue() : float

(a) Write the code for the StockItem class.
(b) Consider the following program, which uses the StockItem class, and in which most of the code has been replaced by comments:

```
from stockitem import StockItem

price = float(input('Enter the price of the item: '))

# Create a new item of stock using the values that were entered by the user

# Increase the total number of items in stock by 5

# Display the numer of items in stock, and the total value of the stock
```

Replace the comments with appropriate code.

(c) (i) A further attribute, salesTax, is required. The value of this attribute should always be the same for each object of the class. Write the declaration for this attribute.

(ii) Write a line of code that sets the sales tax for all objects of the class to 10 without referring to any particular object.

6. Consider a class that keeps track of the temperature within an incubator. The UML diagram is shown below:

Incubator
temperature : int
__init__ () *increaseTemperature(): bool* *decreaseTemperature(): bool*

When an Incubator object is created, the temperature is initially set to five degrees.

The increaseTemp method increases the temperature by 1, and the decreaseTemp method decreases the temperature by 1. However, the temperature must never be allowed to rise above a maximum value of 20 nor fall below a minimum value of -10. If an attempt is made to increase or decrease the temperature so it falls outside this range, then an alarm must be raised; the methods in this case should not increase or decrease the temperature but should return a value of **False**, indicating that the alarm should be raised. If the temperature is changed successfully, however, a value of **True** is returned.

(a) Write the code for the Incubatotor class.

(b) Develop an IncubatorTester program to test the Incubator class.

7. Write a program that creates a list of Rectangle objects to represent the dimensions of rooms in an apartment as described in self-test question 3. The program should allow the user to:

- determine the number of rooms;
- enter the dimensions of the rooms;
- retrieve the area and dimensions of any of the rooms.

8. In the previous question you were asked to develop a program to process a collection of rooms in an apartment. Now consider a separate class, Apartment, for this purpose. The Apartment class would hold a collection of Rectangle objects, where each Rectangle object represents a particular room in the apartment. The UML diagrams are are shown below: as you will discover in Chap. 12, the diamond and asterisk notation indicates that one class consists of objects of another class.

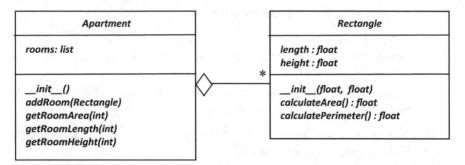

The single attribute of the Apartment class consists of a list of Rectangle objects representing rooms.

The methods of the Apartment class are described below:

__init__()

Creates an empty list as an attribute (instance variable).

addRoom(Rectangle)

Adds the given room to the list.

getRoomArea(int): float

Returns the area of the given room number sent in as a parameter. If an invalid room number is sent in as a parameter this method should send back some dummy value (e.g. −999).

getRoomLength(int): float

Returns the length of the given room number sent in as a parameter. If an invalid room number is sent in as a parameter this method should send back some dummy value (e.g. −999).

getRoomHeight(int): float

Returns the height of the given room number sent in as a parameter. If an invalid room number is sent in as a parameter this method should send back some dummy value (e.g. −999).

(a) Implement the Apartment class.

(b) Develop an ApartmentTester program that creates an object of the Apartment class, and tests its methods.

Object-Oriented Python: Part 2

9

Outcomes

By the end of this chapter you should be able to:

- *explain the term **inheritance***;
- *design inheritance structures using UML notation*;
- *implement inheritance relationships in Python*;
- *explain the term **method overriding***;
- *make use of built-in object functions.*

9.1 Introduction

One of the greatest benefits of the object-oriented approach to software development is that it offers the opportunity for us to *re-use* classes that have already been written—either by ourselves or by someone else. Let's look at a possible scenario. Say you wanted to develop a software system and you have, during your analysis, identified the need for a class called `Employee`. You might be aware that a colleague in your organization has already written an `Employee` class; rather than having to write your own class, it would be easier to approach your colleague and ask her to let you use her `Employee` class.

So far so good, but what if the `Employee` class that you are given doesn't quite do everything that you had hoped? Let's imagine for example (and we are keeping things *very* simple here) that the class has three attributes: an employee number (`number`), a first name (`givenName`) and a family name (`familyName`). In

Supplementary Information The online version contains supplementary material available at https://doi.org/10.1007/978-3-031-01326-3_9.

addition to an initializer that allows you to set these three values at the time an employee is created, it has a method called `createShortName`, which returns a short version of the name consisting of an initial and family name.

Now, assuming your employees are full-time employees, it would be most likely that you would want to record the employee's annual salary as part of the class and perhaps provide a method for calculating the monthly pay. This isn't currently available with the class as it stands.

You may think it would be necessary to go into the old class and start messing about with the code. But there is no need, because object-oriented programming languages provide the ability to extend existing classes by adding attributes and methods to them. This is called **inheritance**.

9.2   Defining Inheritance

Inheritance is the sharing of attributes and methods among classes. We take a class and then define other classes based on the first one. The new classes *inherit* all the attributes and methods of the first one, but also have attributes and methods of their own. Let's try to understand this by thinking about the `Employee` class.

As we have said, our `Employee` class has three attributes—an account number, a given name and a family name—together with an initializer and a method that returns a short version of the name. What we want to do is to provide a class—we will call it `FullTimeEmployee`—that contains one additional attribute (`annualSalary`) and one additional method (`calculateMonthlyPay`).

This is illustrated in Fig. 9.1 which uses the UML notation for inheritance, namely a triangle.

Fig. 9.1   Inheritance relationship

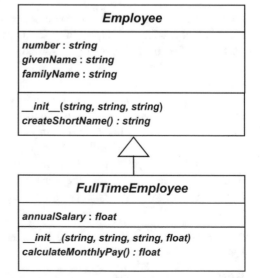

You can see from this diagram that an inheritance relationship is a *hierarchical* relationship. The class at the top of the hierarchy—in this case the Employee class —is referred to as the **superclass** (or **base class**) and the FullTimeEmployee as the **subclass** (or **derived class**).

The inheritance relationship is also often referred to as an *is-a-kind-of* relationship; in this case a FullTimeEmployee *is a kind of* Employee.

Before we go on, notice one thing: __init__ appears both in the superclass and in the subclass. This is because we will need each of these implementations to be slightly different. In the superclass, Employee, we will want to initialize three variables— number, givenName and familyName. However, in the subclass—FullTimeEmployee—we will also want to initialize annualSalary. Redefining a method in the subclass is known as **method overriding**—and as we shall see later, it isn't used just with special methods like the initializer, but with any method we want.

9.3 Implementing Inheritance in Python

So let's see how all this is achieved in Python. The code for the Employee class is shown below:

```
employee.py

class Employee:

    # the initializer
    def __init__(self, numberIn, givenNameIn, familyNameIn):
        self.number = numberIn
        self.givenName = givenNameIn
        self.familyName = familyNameIn

    # method to create short name formed of initial, plus full stop, plus famly name
    def createShortName(self):
        return self.givenName[0:1] + '.' + self.familyName
```

There is nothing new here, so let's get on with our FullTimeEmployee class. We will present the code first and analyse it afterwards.

```
fulltimeemployee.py

from employee import Employee

class FullTimeEmployee(Employee):

    # override the initializer
    def __init__(self, numberIn, givenNameIn, familyNameIn, annualSalaryIn):
        super().__init__(numberIn, givenNameIn, familyNameIn) # call the initializer of the superclass
        self.annualSalary = annualSalaryIn

    # method to calculate the monthly pay (one-twelfth annual salary)
    def calculateMonthlyPay(self):
        return self.annualSalary/12
```

The first line of interest—after importing the Employee class—is the class header itself:

```
class FullTimeEmployee(Employee):
```

Here you can see that the way we indicate that a class should be a subclass of some other class is by including the name of the superclass in brackets after the class name. In this case `FullTimeEmployee` is a subclass of `Employee`.

Now for the new version of the initializer:

```
def __init__(self, numberIn, givenNameIn, familyNameIn, annualSalaryIn):
    super().__init__(numberIn, givenNameIn, familyNameIn) # call the initializer of the superclass
    self.annualSalary = annualSalaryIn
```

As we should expect, the method has four parameters (apart from `self`) because we now need to declare and initialize an additional attribute, `annualSalary`.

In the first line we see the use of a very convenient built-in function called `super`. This function allows us to call a method of the superclass (in this case `__init__`). We do this when we have overridden a method in the subclass but we want to use the version that exists in the superclass. So, here the attributes `number`, `givenName` and `familyName` are all initialized. Then in the next line we initialize the `annualSalary` attribute, which is specific to the subclass.

Now we can define a method to calculate the monthly pay, which is specific to the `FullTimeEmployee` class. We have once again kept things very simple here and simply divided the annual salary by 12.

```
def calculateMonthlyPay(self):
    return self.annualSalary/12
```

Here is a little program that tests out our `FullTimeEmployee` class. It shows how we can access the properties of both the superclass, `Employee`, and the subclass, `FullTimeEmployee`.

fulltimeemployeetester.py

```
from fulltimeemployee import FullTimeEmployee

# get the details from the user
number = input("Employee Number? ")
givenName = input("Given name? ")
familyName = input("Family name? ")
salary = float(input("Annual Salary? "))

# create a new full-time employee
emp = FullTimeEmployee(number, givenName, familyName, salary)

# display full-time employee's details, including the monthly pay
print()

# the following three attributes have been inherited from the Employee class
print('Employee number : ' + emp.number)
print('Given name: ' + emp.givenName)
print('Family name: ' + emp.familyName)

# the following method has been inherited from the Employee class
print('Short name: ' + emp.createShortName())

# the following method is specific to the the FullTimeEmployee class
print('Monthly pay: ' + str(emp.calculateMonthlyPay()))
```

Here is a sample test run:

```
Employee Number? A123456
Given name? Walter
Family name? Wallcarpeting
Annual Salary? 24000.0

Employee number : A123456
Given name: Walter
Family name: Wallcarpeting
Short name: W.Wallcarpeting
Monthly pay: 2000.0
```

Thinking back to our example, many businesses would be likely to have some employees who were full-time and some who were part-time—and the part-time employees would not have an annual salary but an hourly rate, and their pay for a particular period would be calculated by multiplying this rate by the number of hours worked in that period. No problem—we can just define a `PartTimeEmployee` class, making our new inheritance hierarchy like that shown in Fig. 9.2.

Notice that the `calculatePay` method of `PartTimeEmployee` requires an integer argument, representing the number of hours worked in the particular period.

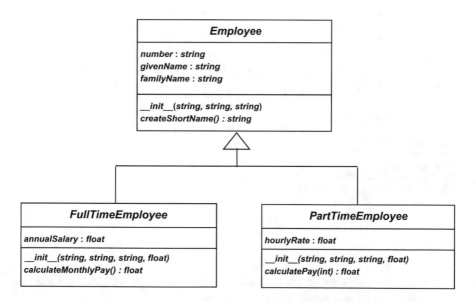

Fig. 9.2 Inheritance relationship showing the superclass *Employee* and the subclasses *FullTimeEmployee* and *PartTimeEmployee*

Here is the code for the `PartTimeEmployee` class:

parttimeemployee.py

```python
from employee import Employee

class PartTimeEmployee(Employee):

    def __init__(self, numberIn, givenNameIn, familyNameIn, hourlyRateIn):
        super().__init__(numberIn, givenNameIn, familyNameIn) # call the initialser of the superclass
        self.hourlyRate = hourlyRateIn

    def calculatePay(self, hoursWorkedIn):
        return hoursWorkedIn * self.hourlyRate
```

The following program uses the `PartTimeEmployee` class:

parttimeemployeetester.py

```python
from parttimeemployee import PartTimeEmployee

# get the details from the user
number = input("Employee Number? ")
givenName = input("Given name? ")
familyName = input("Family name? ")
rate = float(input("Hourly rate? "))
hours = int(input("Hours worked this week? "))

# create a new part-time employee
emp = PartTimeEmployee(number, givenName, familyName, rate)

# display part-time employee's details, including the weekly pay
print()

# the following three attributes have been inhereted from the Employee class
print(emp.number)
print(emp.givenName)
print(emp.familyName)

# the following method has been inhereted from the Employee class
print(emp.createShortName())

# the following method is specific to the the partTimeEmployee class
print(emp.calculatePay(hours))
```

Here is a sample run:

```
Employee Number? A123456
Given name? Sandy
Family name? Shaw
Hourly rate? 12.00
Hours worked this week? 40

A123456
Sandy
Shaw
S.Shaw
480.0
```

We can now move on to look at another inheritance example; let's choose the `Rectangle` class that we developed in the last chapter.

9.4 Extending the Rectangle Class

We are going to define a new class called `ExtendedRectangle`, which is a subclass of `Rectangle`. First, let's remind ourselves of the `Rectangle` class itself.

---

rectangle.py

```
class Rectangle:

    # the initializer
    def __init__(self, lengthIn, heightIn):
        self.length = lengthIn
        self.height = heightIn

    # method for calculating the area
    def calculateArea(self):
        return self.length * self.height

    # method for calculating the area
    def calculatePerimeter(self):
        return 2 * (self.length + self.height)
```

The original `Rectangle` class had the capability of reporting on the perimeter and area of the rectangle. Our extended class will have, in addition, the capability of sending back a string representation of itself composed of a number of symbols such as asterisks—for example:

```
*****
*****
*****
```

Now at first glance you might think that this isn't a string at all, because it consists of several lines. But if we think of the instruction to start a new line as just another character—which for convenience we could call < NEWLINE > then our string could be written like this.

```
*****<NEWLINE>*****<NEWLINE>*****
```

As we saw in Chap. 2, in Python we are able to represent this <NEWLINE> character with a special character that looks like this:

```
'\n'
```

The design of the `ExtendedRectangle` class is shown in Fig. 9.3.

Fig. 9.3 *Rectangle*
hierarchy

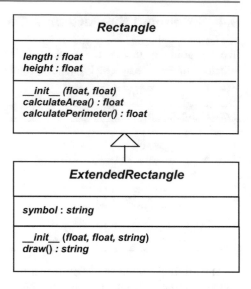

Now for the implementation:

```
extendedrectangle.py

from rectangle import Rectangle

class ExtendedRectangle(Rectangle):

    def __init__(self, lengthIn, heightIn, symbolIn):
        super().__init__(lengthIn, heightIn)
        self.symbol = symbolIn

    def draw(self):
        s = ''
        for i in range(int(self.height)): # outer loop - note the type cast to int
            for j in range(int(self.length)): # inner loop - note the type cast to int
                s = s + self.symbol; # add the symbol to the string
            s = s + '\n'; # add the <NEWLINE> character
        return s; # return the string representation
```

So let's take a closer look at all this. After the class header—which declares the class as a subclass of `Rectangle`—we have our initializer:

```
    def __init__(self, lengthIn, heightIn, symbolIn):
        super().__init__(lengthIn, heightIn)
        self.symbol = symbolIn
```

Once again we call the initializer of the superclass with the `super` function. We then create a new attribute, symbol, which will be set at the time that an object is created.

Next we have the `draw` method:

```
def draw(self):
    s = ''
    for i in range(int(self.height)): # outer loop - note the type cast to int
        for j in range(int(self.length)): # inner loop - note the type cast to int
            s = s + self.symbol; # add the symbol to the string
        s = s + '\n'; # add the <NEWLINE> character
    return s; # return the string representation
```

After creating an empty string, we use nested loops to build up the string which will, with the addition of newlines at the end of each row contain a rectangle made up of the specified symbol. You saw this technique used in Chap. 4. Notice that we have typecasted the height and length to integers, because we need whole numbers of rows and columns. Once the string is complete it is returned, and the function terminates.

The following program uses the `ExtendedRectangle` class. It creates a rectangle of length 10.6 and height 5.7, with an asterisk as the symbol; because of the typecast it then draws a rectangle of stars consisting of 10 columns and 5 rows. It then changes the symbol to a cross and draws the rectangle again.

---

extendedrectangletester

```
from extendedrectangle import ExtendedRectangle

er = ExtendedRectangle(10.6, 5.7, '*')
print(er.draw())
er.symbol = '+'
print(er.draw())
```

The output from this program is shown below:

```
**********
**********
**********
**********
**********

++++++++++
++++++++++
++++++++++
++++++++++
++++++++++
```

9.5 Method Overriding

In Sect. 9.2 you were briefly introduced to the idea of **method overriding**, which refers to the redefining of a method of the superclass in the subclass so that it behaves differently. There it referred to the initializer, but as we shall see here, any method of a superclass can be redefined—that is, overridden—in the subclass.

Method overriding is one way of achieving something that is a common feature of object-oriented languages, namely **polymorphism**. This refers to the ability to have methods (or operators) with the same name, but whose behaviour is different.

In order to explore this further, we are going to extend the BankAccount class that we developed in the previous chapter. You will recall that the class we developed there did not provide any overdraft facility—the withdraw method was designed so that the withdrawal would take place only if the amount to be withdrawn did not exceed the balance.

Now let's consider a special account which is the same as the original account, but allows holders of the account to be given an overdraft limit and to withdraw funds up to this limit. We will call this account GoldAccount. Since a Gold-Account *is a kind of* BankAccount, we can use inheritance here to design the GoldAccount class. In addition to the attributes of a BankAccount, a GoldAccount will need to have an attribute to represent the overdraft limit—and we need to reconsider the withdraw method. This will differ from the original method, because, instead of checking that the amount to be withdrawn does not exceed the balance, it will now check that the amount does not exceed the total of the balance plus the overdraft limit. So what we are going to do is to rewrite—or *override*—the withdraw method in the subclass.

The UML diagram for the BankAccount class and the GoldAccount class appears below in Fig. 9.4. You will notice that the withdraw method appears in both classes—this, of course, is because we are going to override it in the subclass.

Fig. 9.4 UML diagram for the *BankAccount* hierarchy

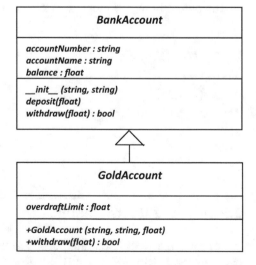

Here is the code for the `GoldAccount` class:

goldaccount.py

```
from bankaccount import BankAccount

class GoldAccount(BankAccount):
    def __init__(self, numberIn, nameIn, limitIn):
        super().__init__(numberIn, nameIn)
        self.overdraftLimit = limitIn
```

```
    # override the withdraw method
    def withdraw(self, amountIn):
        if amountIn > self.balance + self.overdraftLimit:  # can withdraw up to the overdraft limit
            return False;  # no withdrawal was made
        else:
            self.balance = self.balance - amountIn
            return True  # money was withdrawn successfully
```

Looking at the `withdraw` the method, the test in the **if** statement differs from the original method in the `BankAccount` class (as shown below), in order to take account of the fact that customers with a gold account are allowed an overdraft:

`withdraw` **method in** BankAccount **class**	`withdraw` **method in** GoldAccount **class**

`def withdraw(self, amountIn):`
　　`if amountIn > self.balance:`
　　　`return False`
　　`else:`
　　　`self.balance = self.balance - amountIn`
　　　`return True`
	`def withdraw(self, amountIn):`
	　　`if amountIn > self.balance + self.overdraftLimit:`
	　　　`return False;`
	　　`else:`
	　　　`self.balance = self.balance - amountIn`
	　　　`return True`

The methods have the same name and the same parameter list but belong to different classes—the superclass and the subclass—and their behaviour is different. They are distinguished by the *object with which they are associated*. We illustrate this in the program below.

OverridingDemo

```
from bankaccount import BankAccount
from goldaccount import GoldAccount

#declare a BankAccount object
bankAcc = BankAccount('123', 'Ordinary Account Holder')
#declare a GoldAccount object
goldAcc = GoldAccount('124', 'Gold Account Holder', 500)

bankAcc.deposit(1000)
goldAcc.deposit(1000)

ok = bankAcc.withdraw(1250)  # the withdraw method of BankAccount is called
if(ok):
    print('Money withdrawn. ')
else:
    print('Insufficient funds. ')

print('Balance of ' + bankAcc.accountName + ' is ' + str(bankAcc.balance))
print()

ok = goldAcc.withdraw(1250)  # the withdraw method of GoldAccount is called
if(ok):
    print('Money withdrawn. ')
else:
    print('Insufficient funds. ')

print('Balance of ' + goldAcc.accountName + ' is ' + str(goldAcc.balance))
```

In this program we create an object of the `BankAccount` class and an object of the `GoldAccount` class (with an overdraft limit of 500) and deposit an amount of 1000 in each:

```
#declare a BankAccount object
bankAcc = BankAccount('123', 'Ordinary Account Holder')
#declare a GoldAccount object
goldAcc = GoldAccount('124', 'Gold Account Holder', 500)

bankAcc.deposit(1000)
goldAcc.deposit(1000)
```

Next we attempt to withdraw the sum of 1250 from the `BankAccount` object and assign the return value to a variable, `ok`:

```
ok = bankAcc.withdraw(1250)  # the withdraw method of BankAccount is called
```

The `withdraw` method that is called here will be that of `BankAccount`, because it is called via the `BankAccount` object, `bankAcc`.

Once this is done we display a message showing whether or not the withdrawal was successful, followed by the balance of that account:

```
if(ok):
    print('Money withdrawn. ')
else:
    print('Insufficient funds. ')

print('Balance of ' + bankAcc.accountName + ' is ' + str(bankAcc.balance))
print()
```

Now the `withdraw` method is called again, but in this case via the `Gold-Account` object, `goldAcc`:

```
ok = goldAcc.withdraw(1250)  # the withdraw method of GoldAccount is called
```

This time it is the `withdraw` method of `GoldAccount` that will be called, because `goldAcc` is an object of this class. The appropriate message and the balance are again displayed.

The output from this program is shown below:

```
Insufficient funds.
Balance of Ordinary Account Holder is 1000.0

Money withdrawn.
Balance of Gold Account Holder is -250.0
```

As we would expect, the withdrawal from `BankAccount` does not take place —the balance is 1000, and since there is no overdraft facility a request to withdraw 1250 is denied.

In the case of the `GoldAccount`, however, a withdrawal of 1250 would result in a negative balance of 250, which is allowed, because it is within the overdraft limit of 500.

9.6   Built-in Object Functions

In previous chapters we have come across built-in functions such as `del` and `len`. There are some built-in functions that are specifically designed for objects, which we will now explore. In so doing, we will use the examples of `Employee` (superclass) and `FullTimeEmployee` (subclass) from Sect. 9.3.

isinstance

This functions takes two arguments, an object and a class, and checks whether or not the first is an instance of the second.

---

isinstanceexample.py

```
from employee import Employee
from fulltimeemployee import FullTimeEmployee

emp = Employee('123', 'Barbara', 'Jones') # create an Employee object
ftemp = FullTimeEmployee('456', 'Adenike',  'Oluran', 10000.0) # create a FullTimeEmployee object

print(isinstance(emp, FullTimeEmployee))
print(isinstance(emp, Employee))
print(isinstance(ftemp, FullTimeEmployee))
print(isinstance(ftemp, Employee))
```

Output

```
False
True
True
True
```

Look carefully at the final output here—it tells us that the `FullTimeEmployee` object, `ftemp`, is not only an instance of the `FullTimeEmployee` class, but is also an instance of the superclass `Employee`. This is because a full-time employee *is* a *kind of* employee.

issubclass

This function takes two classes as arguments and checks whether or not the first is a subclass of the second.

---

issubclassexample.py

```
from employee import Employee
from fulltimeemployee import FullTimeEmployee

print(issubclass(Employee, FullTimeEmployee))
print(issubclass(FullTimeEmployee, Employee))
print(issubclass(FullTimeEmployee, list))
```

Output

```
False
True
False
```

In the first case, `Employee` is not a subclass of `FullTimeEmployee`. In the second case, `FullTimeEmployee` is a subclass of `Employee`. In the final case, `FullTimeEmployee` is not a subclass of `list`.

hasattr

Takes two arguments—the first is the name of an object, and the second is the name of a property (attribute or method). It checks whether or not the instance has that particular property. You can see that the function is rather poorly named—a name like `hasproperty`—would be rather more accurate.

hasattrexample.py

```python
from employee import Employee
from fulltimeemployee import FullTimeEmployee

emp = Employee('123', 'Barbara', 'Jones') # create an Employee object
ftemp = FullTimeEmployee('456', 'Adenike',  'Oluran', 10000.0) # create a FullTimeEmployee object

print(hasattr(emp, 'familyName'))
print(hasattr(emp, 'annualSalary'))
print(hasattr(ftemp, 'annualSalary'))
print(hasattr(ftemp, 'calculateMonthlyPay'))
print(hasattr(ftemp, 'familyName'))
```

Output

```
True
False
True
True
True
```

Once again, it is worth taking note of the final output, which shows that `familyName` is indeed an attribute of a `FullTimeEmployee` object, despite the fact that it is not declared in that class; it is, of course, inherited from the superclass, `Employee`.

9.7   Some Benefits of Object-Oriented Programming

Below we have summarized some of the benefits that object-oriented programming has brought us.

- the object-oriented approach matches our natural view of the world;
- the object-oriented approach makes it far easier for us to *re-use* classes again and again. Having defined a `BankAccount` class or a `Student` class, for example, we can use them in many different programs without having to write a new class

each time. If systems can be assembled from re-usable objects, this leads to far higher productivity;

- with the object-oriented approach it is possible to define and use classes which are not yet complete. They can then be extended without upsetting the operation of other classes. This greatly improves the testing process. We can easily build prototypes without having to build a whole system before testing it and letting the user of the system see it;
- the object-oriented approach makes it far easier to make changes to systems once they have been completed. Whole classes can be replaced, or new classes can easily be added.

9.8   Self-test Questions

1. Below is a UML diagram for an inheritance relationship between two classes— Vehicle and UsedVehicle.

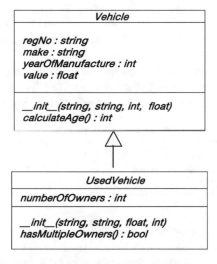

(a) By referring to the diagram, explain the meaning of the term *inheritance*.
(b) Write the header for the UsedVehicle class.
(c) Write the code for the initializer of the UsedVehicle class.

2. (a) Consider the following classes and arrange them into an inheritance hierarchy using UML notation:

(b) Write the top line of the class declaration for each of these classes when implementing them in Python.

9.9   Programming Exercises

1. (a) Download the `ExtendedRectangle` class from the website (see preface), then implement the `ExtendedRectangleTester` from Sect. 9.4.
   (b) Modify the `ExtendedRectangleTester` program so that the user is able to choose the symbol used to display the rectangle.
2. (a) Implement the `Vehicle` and the `UsedVehicle` classes of self-test question 1.
   You should note that:

   - the `calculateAge` method of `Vehicle` accepts an integer representing the current year and returns the age of the vehicle as calculated by subtracting the year of manufacture from the current year;
   - the `hasMultipleOwners` method of `UsedVehicle` should return **True** if the `numberOfOwners` attribute has a value greater than 1, or **False** otherwise.

   (b) Write a tester class that tests all the methods of the `UsedVehicle` class.
3. Write a menu-driven program that uses a mixed list to hold `Vehicles` and `UsedVehicles`, as defined in self-test question 1. The menu should offer the following options:

   ```
   1. Add a vehicle
   2. Display vehicles
   3. Quit
   ```

Notes

The `hasMultipleOwners` method should return **True** if there is more than one owner, **False** otherwise.

When adding vehicles, the user should be asked the number of previous owners, and this will determine whether to create a `Vehicle` (zero previous owners) or a `UsedVehicle`.

A possible output for option 2 could look something like this:

```
Registration number: AB14 C45
Make: Ford
Total price: 16800.00
Used vehicle with only one owner

Registration number: EN20 6TY
Make: Renault
Total price: 19200.00

Registration number: CN15 7UB
Make: Hyundai
Total price: 6000.00
Used vehicle with more than one owner
```

When iterating through the list, the isinstance method will be very useful in determining whether the vehicle is new or used.

Python: Working with Files

10

Outcomes

By the end of this chapter you should be able to:

- *explain the principles of **input** and **output** and identify a number of different input and output devices;*
- *explain the concept of an **I/O stream**;*
- *describe the basic file-handling techniques used in the Python language;*
- *distinguish between **text** and **binary** encoding of data;*
- *distinguish between **serial** access files and **random** access files;*
- *create and access both text and binary files in Python.*

10.1 Introduction

Do you remember the bank application that we developed in Chap. 8? Although it was very simple indeed, it should have given you an insight into the sort of thing that could be developed as part of a real-world application. There was one thing that was missing however. Once you close the program, all your information is lost—which of course, in a real-world setting, would render the whole thing useless. What we need is a means of storing the information once the application is closed and retrieving it when we open it again. We need to learn how to create a permanent record on some sort of storage device.

As you are probably already aware, a named block of externally stored data is called a **file**.

Supplementary Information The online version contains supplementary material available at https://doi.org/10.1007/978-3-031-01326-3_10.

© Springer Nature Switzerland AG 2022
Q. Charatan and A. Kans, *Programming in Two Semesters*,
Texts in Computer Science, https://doi.org/10.1007/978-3-031-01326-3_10

When we take an object-oriented approach, as we did in the two previous chapters, we don't separate the data from the behavior—we create a *class* that holds both; however, when it comes to storing information in files, then of course it is only the data that we are interested in storing. When referring to data alone, it is customary to use the terms **record** and **field**. A record refers to a single data instance—for example a person, a stock item, a student and so on; a **field** refers to what in the object-oriented world we would normally call an attribute—a name, a stock number, an exam mark, etc.

In this chapter we will learn how to create files, and write information to them, and to read the information back when we need it. We start by looking at this process in the overall context of input and output, or I/O as it is often called; you will then go on to learn a number of different techniques for keeping permanent copies of your data.

10.2   Input and Output

Any computer system must provide a means of allowing information to come in from the outside world (**input**) and, once it has been processed, to be sent out again (**output**). The whole question of input and output, particularly where files are concerned, can sometimes seem rather complex, especially from the point of view of the programmer.

As with all aspects of a computer system, the processes of input and output are handled by the computer hardware working in conjunction with the system software —that is, the operating system (Windows™, macOS™ or Linux™ for example). The particular application program that is running at the time normally deals with input and output by communicating with the operating system and getting it to perform these tasks in conjunction with the hardware.

All this involves some very real complexity and involves a lot of low-level details that a programmer is not usually concerned with; for example, the way in which the system writes to external media such as discs, or the way it reconciles the differences between the speed of the processor with the speed of the disk drive. Fortunately, Python hides all this complexity from us and makes file handling seem very easy. You will find out next semester that Java also provides the means to hide the programmer from the low-level detail—but it is not quite as neat as the Python solution.

10.3   Input and Output Devices

The most common way of getting data input from the outside world is via the keyboard; and the most common way of displaying output data is on the screen. Therefore, most systems are normally set up so that the *standard* input and output devices are the keyboard and the screen, respectively. However, there are many other devices that are concerned with input and output: magnetic, solid state and optical discs for permanent storage of data (both local and remote); flash drives; network interface cards and modems for communicating with other computers; and printers for producing hard copies. Today, of course, a lot of storage is "cloud based", which means that the storage devices are remote, and their precise nature is hidden from the user.

We should bear in mind that the process, in one sense, is always the same, no matter what the input or output device. All the data that is processed by the computer's central processing unit in response to program instructions is stored in the computer's main memory or Random Access Memory (RAM). Input is the transfer of data from some external device to main memory, whereas output is the transfer of data from main memory to an external device. In order for input or output to take place, it is necessary for a channel of communication to be established between the device and the computer's memory. Such a channel is referred to as a **stream**. The operating system will have established a **standard input stream** and a **standard output stream**, which will normally be the keyboard and screen, respectively. In addition to this, there is usually a **standard error stream** where error messages can be displayed; this is normally also set to the screen. All of these default settings for the standard streams can be changed via the operating system.

In this chapter, instead of dealing with input and output to the standard streams, we are going to be dealing with the input and output of data to external devices in the form of files—but, as you will see, the two processes are very similar.

10.4 File Handling

The output process, which consists of transferring data from memory to a file, is usually referred to as **writing**; the input process, which consists of transferring data from a file to memory, is referred to as **reading**. Both of these involve some low-level detail to do with the way in which data is stored physically on a disk or other device. As programmers, we do not want to have to worry more than is necessary about this process—which, of course, will differ from one machine to the next and from one operating system to the next. As we have said, fortunately Python makes it very easy for us to deal with these processes.

10.4.1 Encoding

Python supports two different ways of **encoding** data—that is, representing data on a disk or other storage device. These are **text** and **binary**.

In any computer system, each character is represented by an integer as defined by a particular encoding standard. In the early days of computing, this was the **ASCII**[1] system. ASCII defined 128 7-bit integers (0–127) each representing a particular character. For example, in ASCII, 65 represents 'A', and 97 represents 'a'.

As the need for more than 128 characters grew, it was necessary to develop other systems. **Unicode** is a superset of ASCII. There are different versions: UTF-8 (also known as extended ASCII) uses 8-bit storage (so 256 characters), whereas UTF-32 uses 32-bit storage. Python normally uses UTF-8 (UTF stands for Unicode Transformation Format).

Text encoding means that the data on the disk is stored as characters in the form used by the external system (usually ASCII). As an example, consider saving the number 107 to a text file—it will be saved as the character '1' in ASCII code (or whatever is used by the system) followed by the character '0', followed by the character '7'. A text file is therefore readable by a text editor (such as Windows™ Notepad).

Binary encoding, on the other hand, means that the data is stored in the same format as the internal representation of the data used by the program to store data in memory. So the number 107 would be saved as the binary number 1101011. A binary file could not be read properly by a text editor.

Normally we would use text encoding to store data that was purely text, and binary encoding for such things as images, videos and audio.

10.4.2   Access

In general, there are two ways in which files can be accessed—**serial** access and **random** access. In the first (and more common) method, each item of data is read (or written) in turn. The operating system provides what is known as a **file pointer**, which is really just a location in memory that keeps track of where we have got to in the process of reading or writing to a file.

Another way to access data in a file is to go directly to the record you want—this is known as random access and is a bit like going straight to the clip you want on a DVD; whereas serial access is like using an old-fashioned video tape, where you have to work your way through the entire tape to get to the bit you want. Random access requires that each item in the file is of equal length, so is not always suitable without some effort going into the structure of the data we are saving. When we study file handling in Java next semester, we will explore random access, but in this chapter we will deal only with serial access.

---

[1] *American Standard Code for Information Interchange.*

10.5 Reading and Writing to Text Files

Figure 10.1 shows a text file, verse.txt, which has been read by Windows™ Notepad.

Python makes it very easy for us to handle files by allowing us to create a file object that has a number of useful methods for reading and writing data. So, let's start off by writing a program that reads this file line by line and displays each line on the screen as it does so.

Take a look at the program, and then we'll explain what is going on.

---

readverse1.py

```
f = open('verse.txt', 'r') # open a text file for reading

# read each line of the file and print it on the screen
for i in range(4):
    item = f.readline()
    print(item, end = '')

f.close() # remember to close the file
```

Have a look at the first line.

```
f = open('verse.txt', 'r') # open a text file for reading
```

This line uses Python's built-in open function to open the file specified as the first argument in the brackets. Opening a file means that we establish a stream, as explained in Sect. 10.3. In this case it is an input stream, because the second parameter 'r' specifies that the file is opened in read mode. Using 'r' on its own means that the file will be opened as a text file (we could also have used 'rt' for this purpose as we shall see later).

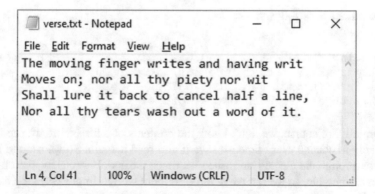

Fig. 10.1 Text file showing in a text editor

The Open command returns a file object, which we have assigned to a variable, f.

In this case, unusually, we know the contents of the file already—it consists of four lines of text. So in order to demonstrate how this works, we have simply used a **for** loop that iterates four times, each time reading a line of code and printing it on the screen:

```
for i in range(4):
    item = f.readline()
    print(item, end = '')
```

As you can see we are using the file's readline method. This method reads a line of text (that is to say, a portion of text terminated by a newline character) and returns this as a string. We have assigned this return value to the variable item. In order to keep track of where we are when moving through a file, the system maintains what is known as a file pointer, which, as explained above, is simply a location in memory that keeps track of where we have got to in the file. Each time readline is executed, the pointer is automatically moved to the beginning of the next line.

Each line that is read is subsequently displayed on the screen—you will notice that the print command also makes use of a second parameter, end = ' '. This, you will remember from Chap. 2, tells the print command not to add a new line after the string is printed. The reason for doing this is that readline actually picks up the newline character when it reads the string—so we don't want an additional newline character each time the line is printed.

Finally we need to remember to close the file—leaving it open could lead to the data being corrupted:

```
f.close()
```

The output is as follows:

```
The moving finger writes and having writ
Moves on; nor all thy piety nor wit
Shall lure it back to cancel half a line,
Nor all thy tears wash out a word of it.
```

Normally, of course, we don't know the contents of a file before we see it—and it is likely to change every time we save it and read it again. So we need to be able to move through the file and stop when we reach the end. Fortunately, file objects in Python are iterable, so we can move through them with a simple **for** loop as we do in the next program.

---

readverse2.py

```
f = open('verse.txt', 'r') # open a text file for reading

for item in f: # iterate through the file
    print(item, end = '')

f.close()
```

As you can see, this is a very elegant way of moving through the file. As with other iterable objects such as `lists`, the variable (in this case `item`) is assigned the value of each item in turn. Here, on each iteration the item is printed as before.

So what about writing a file? We do this in the next program:

---

writepoem.py

```
f = open('poem.txt', 'w') # open a text file for writing

f.write('Yesterday, upon on the stair,\n')
f.write('I met a man who wasn\'t there.\n')
f.write('He wasn\'t there again today.\n')
f.write('Oh, how I wish he\'d go away!\n')

f.close()
```

This time, when we use the `open` command, we have `'w'` as the second parameter. This means that we open the file in write mode. If a file of that name does not exist, then it will be created. Opening in write mode means that any data already in the file is deleted. If we want to keep the data and write our new data after the existing records, we should open the file in append mode, using `'a'` instead of `'w'`. As with write mode, append mode creates the file if it does not already exist.

As you can see, we write to the file using the file object's write method. We have written four lines separately and have terminated each with the newline character, `'\n'`.

You should also notice that some of our lines contain an apostrophe. We have had to precede this with a backslash—otherwise the apostrophe will be interpreted as the single quote which opens or closes a string.

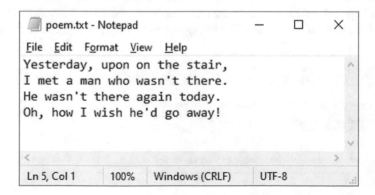

Fig. 10.2 `poem.txt` showing in a text editor

Figure 10.2 shows the result of running this program and viewing the file poem.txt in Windows™ Notepad.

10.6   Exceptions Associated with File Handling

In Chap. 4 you were introduced to the idea of an exception—an error that occurs when running a program. Handling exceptions is actually quite a complicated business, and we won't go into very much detail until we reach the second semester. But we do need to have some rudimentary skills in this area when it comes to file handling, because potentially there are a number of common errors, and we want our programs to handle these as smoothly as possible.

When it comes to reading and writing files, the two most common errors that occur are attempting to write a file to a disk (or other storage area) that does not have enough available space, and trying to open a file that does not exist.

There are other possible errors such as a file being corrupted, or a disk drive breaking down, but because of the complexity of distinguishing between different sorts of exceptions, in this chapter we will simply flag up the error and stop the program from crashing, without reporting on exactly what caused the problem. In reality it is very likely that any problem encountered is going to be caused by one of the two issues we just highlighted.

In the program below we have adapted our previous application and used the **try... except** construct that you learnt about in Chap. 4. All the instructions that could cause exceptions have been placed within the **try** block. The most likely one to cause an exception is the open instruction, because it could easily be the case that the file we were trying to open wasn't accessible. If this or any other exception occurs, then the **except** block is entered and a message is displayed on the screen. The program can then continue—although in this simple example there are no further instructions and the program would terminate smoothly. We should also point out here that there may be times in an application—as you will see in the next section—when it would be normal for the file not to exist because it is the first time the application runs, and no data has yet been created and saved. In this case, the technique used below would be very helpful—the message could be adapted accordingly.

---

readverse3.py

```
try:
    f = open('verse.txt', 'r') # open a text file for reading

    for item in f: # iterate through the file
        print(item, end = '')

    f.close()
except:
    print('An error occured while tryng to read the file')
```

Adapting the write application is similar:

```
writepoem2.py

try:
    f = open('poem.txt', 'w') # open a text file for writing

    f.write('Yesterday, upon on the stair,\n')
    f.write('I met a man who wasn\'t there.\n')
    f.write('He wasn\'t there again today.\n')
    f.write('Oh, how I wish he\'d go away!\n')

    f.close()
except:
        print('It was not possible to write the file')
```

10.7 Practical Examples

In this section we are going to revisit a couple of applications that we created in previous chapters and enable them to keep permanent records of the data that is created.

10.7.1 Adding File Handling to the Waiting List Application

Do you remember that in Chap. 6 we wrote a program that stored the names of people on a waiting list and allowed the user to add and remove names from the list as well as displaying a complete list on the screen? Wouldn't it be a nice idea if we could save this list so that each time we ran the program we could retrieve our data without having to start all over again?

In the program that follows we have done just that. We have added two new methods: one to write the list and one to read it. The former is called when the program terminates, and the latter when the program first starts up. We have emboldened the code that we have added.

waitinglistwithfiles.py

```python
# function to enter names
def addName(waitingListIn):
        name = input('Enter named to add: ')
        waitingListIn.append(name)

# function to remove a name
def removeName(waitingListIn):
        name = input('Enter name to remove: ')
        try:
                waitingListIn.remove(name)
        except:
                print()
                print('That name is not in the list')

# function to display waitingList
def displayList(waitingListIn):
        print() # blank line
        print('***Waiting List***');
        print() # blank line
        for i in range(len(waitingListIn)):
                print('%d: %s' %(i + 1, waitingListIn[i]))
        print()

# function to write the data to file (new)
def writeList(waitingListIn):
        try:
                f = open('waitinglist.txt', 'w') # open a text file for writing
                for item in waitingListIn:
                        f.write(item + '\n')
                f.close()
                return True
        except:
                return False

# function to read the data from the file (new)
def readList(waitingListIn):
        try:
                f = open('waitinglist.txt', 'r') # open a text file for reading
                for item in f:
                        waitingListIn.append(item.strip())
                f.close()
                return True
        except:
                return False

# main body

waitingList = [] # create empty list

# read the records from the file
readOk = readList(waitingList)
if not readOk:
        print('No records were read')

response = '1' # initialize to a value that allows the loop to be entered


print()

while response != '4':  # put code in loop
        # offer menu of options
        print()

        print('[1] Add a name to the waiting list')
        print('[2] Remove a name from the waiting list')
        print('[3] Display the waiting list')
        print('[4] Quit')
        print('enter choice [1,2,3,4]: ')
        print()
```

```
response = input()

if response == '1':
        addName(waitingList)
elif response == '2':
        removeName(waitingList)
elif response == '3':
        displayList(waitingList)
elif response == '4':

        # save the list to file (new)
        writtenOk = writeList(waitingList)
        if not writtenOk:
                print('There was a problem writing the file')

        print('Goodbye')
else:
        print('Options 1-4 only')
```

Let's look first of all at the method for writing the data to the file:

```
def writeList(waitingListIn):
        try:
                f = open('waitinglist.txt', 'w') # open a text file for writing
                for item in waitingListIn:
                        f.write(item + '\n')
                f.close()
                return True
        except:
                return False
```

As you can see we are using a **try... except** construct to deal smoothly with any problems that might arise when writing the file.

In the **try** block, we open the file in write mode and then use a **for** loop to iterate through the list, each time writing the entry to the file. As before we have added a newline character each time. When that is done, we return **True** to indicate success.

Should any problem arise during the process, the **except** block is entered, and **False** is returned, indicating failure.

Now the method for reading the file:

```
def readList(waitingListIn):
        try:
                f = open('waitinglist.txt', 'r') # open a text file for reading
                for item in f:
                        waitingListIn.append(item.strip())
                f.close()
                return True
        except:
                return False
```

This method is similar, except here the **for** loop iterates through the file and each time adds the name to the list. Here we have used the strip function of string to remove the newline character.

In the main body of the function, immediately after creating the empty list, we have added the following lines:

```
readOk = readList(waitingList)
if not readOk:
        print('No records were read')
```

We call the readList method and send it the empty list, so that when the program starts, the previous records are read from the file and the list is populated with the names that were saved. We have made use of the fact that readList returns **True** or **False** to indicate success or failure. In the latter case a message is displayed. We have chosen the wording of this message carefully because on the first run of the program it will be normal for there to be no file, so in this case failure to read the file is not actually an error.

Finally, the following lines have been added to the action that should take place if the user presses '4' to quit the application:

```
writtenOk = writeList(waitingList)
if not writtenOk:
        print('There was a problem writing the file')
```

The writeList method is called and the records are written to file before the program finally terminates. Again we have tested whether the method returned a value of **False** which would indicate that some sort of error occurred when trying to write the file.

An alternative strategy could be to write a new record to the file (using append mode) every time an item is added. In this case we would need to replace the writeList function with a function such as this:

```
# function to append the data to file
def appendName(nameIn):
        try:
                f = open('waitinglist1.txt', 'a') # open a text file in append mode
                f.write(nameIn + '\n') # append the new item
                f.close()
                return True
        except:
                return False
```

In the main body, the instruction to write the file when the program terminates should be removed; the addName function should now be adapted as follows:

```
# function to enter names
def addName(waitingListIn):
        name = input('Enter named to add: ')
        waitingListIn.append(name)

        # append the new entry to the file
        writtenOk = appendName(name)
        if not writtenOk:
                print('There was a problem saving the record')
```

10.7.2 Adding File Handling to the Bank Application

Do you remember the `bankapplication.py` program that we developed in Chap. 8? If you remember, we implemented the collection as a dictionary, which we named `accounts`. Each pair of the dictionary consisted of an account number mapping on to a `BankAccount` object. What we are going to do now is to add functions for saving and retrieving accounts in a similar way to the waiting list program above. It is going to be a little more complex this time because our records are now objects of a class rather than simple strings. It is also a little more complex because we are using a dictionary rather than a list. In the end of chapter exercises you will have the chance to do this using a simple list instead of a dictionary.

As far as the file is concerned, we will simply store each field of each record as a single text entry, so that each set of three entries in the file represents one bank account. The file will look similar to that showing below in Fig. 10.3.

So, when we write this file, we need to go through the accounts and save the account number, name and balance to the file. We need to bear in mind that the records were saved as a dictionary rather than a list—the second part of the pair (the value) was the whole account. We therefore need to retrieve the list of values. As you saw in Chap. 7, this is done with the `values` method of `dict`. Once we have this list, we can iterate through it.

This is the method that we will add to our `bankapplication.py` program:

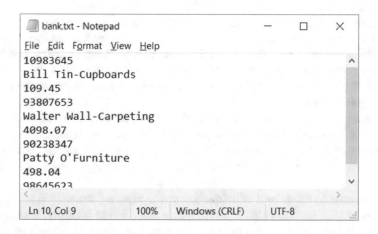

Fig. 10.3 File holding bank accounts, each field of each record stored as one entry in the file

```
def writeList(accountsIn):
    try:
        f = open('bank.txt', 'w')
        allAccounts = accountsIn.values() # returns a list containing all accounts
        for item in allAccounts:
            f.write(item.accountNumber + '\n')
            f.write(item.accountName + '\n')
            f.write(str(item.balance) + '\n') # convert balance to string
        f.close()
        return True
    except:
        return False
```

As before we are using a **try... except** construct to catch any input/output
errors. After opening the file in write mode, we use the `values` method of dictionary to retrieve the accounts as a list and assign this to a variable which we have
called `allAccounts`. We then iterate through this list and write each field in turn
to the file:

```
allAccounts = accountsIn.values() # returns a list containing all accounts
for item in allAccounts:
    f.write(item.accountNumber + '\n')
    f.write(item.accountName + '\n')
    f.write(str(item.balance) + '\n') # convert balance to string
```

Notice that we have, as before, added a newline character to the end of each
entry, and also that—because this is a text file—we have converted the balance
(which is a `float`) to a `string` before writing it to the file. As you will see in a
moment we must reverse this process when we read the file.

So now we come to the `readList` method. What we need to do here is to
create a loop that continuously retrieves three items from the file and then creates an
entry which we add to the dictionary. The question we have to ask is how do we
know when we have reached the end of the file. For a text file this is easy—we just
need to test if the item retrieved was blank. If this is the case, we terminate the loop
without going any further.

There are a couple of things to think about here. Firstly, if the file contains no
records, we want to stop as soon as we have read the first record, without even
entering the loop. Secondly, when we get to the end of the file and the field we have
read is empty, we want to stop straight away, without creating a new account for the
dictionary.

The way we do this is by a technique known as **reading ahead**. We read the first
item (the account number) before entering any loop. If that is empty, we stop right
there. If it is not, we enter the loop, read the next two entries and create an account
to add to the collection. We then read the next account number, and as long as that
is not empty, the loop starts its next iteration. This carries on until an empty item is
read.

Here is the method:

```
def readList(accountsIn):
    try:
        f = open('bank.txt', 'r')
        number = f.readline() # read ahead
        while number != '':
            name = f.readline()
            bal = f.readline()

            acc = BankAccount(number.strip(), name.strip()) # create new account
            acc.deposit(float(bal)) # add balance read to the account
            accountsIn[number.strip()] = acc # add account
            number = f.readline()
        f.close()
        return True
    except:
        return False
```

You can see how this method does exactly what we have described above. We test the **while** loop by checking that the item just read, which we assigned to the variable number, is not empty. Once we have read the account number, name and balance we create the new account which we add to the dictionary:

```
acc = BankAccount(number.strip(), name.strip()) # create new account
acc.deposit(float(bal)) # add balance read to the account
accountsIn[number.strip()] = acc # add account
```

First we create a new account with the account number and name we have just read. Notice that we use the strip method of string to remove the newline character. Remember that the account balance will be initialized to zero, so we must use the deposit method to add the balance that we read from the file. This has to be converted using the float function. We don't have to strip off the newline character, because the float function will take care of this.

Some of you might have been wondering if we could have used a **for** loop to iterate through the entire file instead of a **while** loop. This would certainly be possible, but we would need to count as went through; each time we read three items, we would add a new account as above. This has been left for you to do as an end of chapter exercise, where we give you some hints on how to go about it.

10.8 Reading into a Buffer

The two applications that we developed in the last section both read files that had been created by the application itself. Therefore we were aware of the structure of the files and knew that they consisted of single items, each starting on a new line. We were therefore able to use the readline function to retrieve these records.

However, it is sometimes the case that we are going to read a file the contents of which are completely unknown to us. We can't simply use `readline` in this case, because we don't know where the lines begin and end, and—very importantly—we don't know the size of the file. It could cause memory problems if we tried to read a massive file into memory all in one go.

In this case it is better to use what we call a **buffer**—a temporary storage space for chunks of the file to be read before they are processed. To do this, we can use the `read` method, which allows us to specify how many bytes to read. In the program that follows, we read the file in chunks of 20 bytes, printing each chunk as we go.

---

bufferexample.py

```
try:
    f = open('somefile.txt', 'r') # open a text file for reading

    buffer = f.read(20) # read ahead
    while len(buffer) != 0:
        print(buffer, end= '')
        buffer = f.read(20) # read the next 20 bytes
    f.close()

except:
    print('An error occurred')
```

It shouldn't be too hard to see what's going on here. We are using the 'read ahead' technique again; we read the first 20 bytes, which we assign to a variable called `buffer`. Then, as long as `buffer` is not of zero length, we enter the loop. We print the contents of `buffer` (without adding a newline character), then read the next 20 bytes. This continues until an empty string is read. The `read` method is quite helpful here—if there are fewer than 20 bytes remaining, it simply reads however much is left. On the next iteration, the string will be empty.

You can try this with a text file of your own.

10.9   Reading and Writing to Binary Files

When we refer to binary files, we are usually referring to non-text files such as video, audio or image files (although of course all files, including text files, are stored in binary format, so the process below could be used for any file). To open a file in binary mode, we use `'rb'` or `'wb'` (for reading and writing, respectively) as the second parameter. As we saw previously, without adding the `'b'` the mode defaults to text. Table 10.1 below shows all the possible ways we can open a file.

To demonstrate how to work with binary files, we have written a short program that copies an image file named `sunset.jpg` to another file called `copyof-sunset.jpg`. Take a look at it, then we will go through it with you:

Table 10.1 Python file modes

Mode	Meaning
r (or rt)	Opens a text file in read-only mode
w (or wt)	Opens a text file in write-only mode. Erases all existing data. Creates a new file if one with the same name doesn't exist
rb	Opens a binary file in read-only mode
wb	Opens a binary file in write-only mode. Erases all existing data. Creates a new file if one with the same name doesn't exist
a	Opens a text file for appending new data to it. Does not erase existing data. Creates a new file if one with the same name doesn't exist
ab	Opens a binary file for appending new data to it. Does not erase existing data. Creates a new file if one with the same name doesn't exist
r+	Opens a text file for reading and writing
w+	Opens a text file for writing and reading. Creates a new file if one with the same name doesn't exist
rb+	Opens a binary file for reading and writing
wb+	Opens a binary file for writing and reading. Creates a new file if one with the same name doesn't exist
a+	Opens a text file for both appending and reading. Creates a new file if one with the same name doesn't exist
ab+	Opens a binary file for both appending and reading. Creates a new file if one with the same name doesn't exist

copyfile.py

```
try:
    inputFile = open('sunset.jpg', 'rb') # open original file for reading
    outputFile = open('copyofsunset.jpg', 'wb') # open new file for writing

    buffer = inputFile.read(10) # read the first 10 bytes
    while len(buffer) != 0: # continue to read and write 10 bytes at a time
        outputFile.write(buffer)
        buffer = inputFile.read(10)
    inputFile.close()
    outputFile.close()
    print('File copied successfully')

except:
    print('An error occured')
```

We open an existing file for reading, then open a file with a different name for writing. Notice that we are using 'rb' and 'wb' this time as we are dealing with binary files.

Using the 'read ahead' method once again, we continuously read 10 bytes of the file and then write these bytes to our output file.

If you try this with a file of your own, you should see a copy of the file appear in your directory.

10.10   Deleting and Renaming Files

Two built-in functions exist for deleting and renaming files.
   To delete a file named myfile.txt, we would write:

```
remove('myfile.txt')
```

   To rename a file called oldfile.txt to newfile.txt, we would write:

```
rename('olfile.txt', 'newfile.txt')
```

10.11   Self-test Questions

1. Explain the principles of *input* and *output* and identify different input and output devices.
2. What is meant by the term *input/output stream?*
3. Distinguish between *text* and *binary encoding* of data.
4. What is the difference between *serial access* files and *random access* files?
5. Describe the technique of *reading ahead*, and say why it is necessary to use this method in certain situations.
6. Explain the difference between opening a file in wb mode and ab mode.
7. Write a line of code that would rename a file from thisFile.txt to thatFile.txt.

10.12   Programming Exercises

1. Implement the programs in Sects. 10.5 and 10.6 to see how file handling works in practice.
2. A class called Car is defined as follows:

```
class Car:

    def __init__(self, registrationIn, makeIn, priceIn):
        self.registration = registrationIn
        self.make = makeIn
        self.price = priceIn
```

Write a program that maintains a `list` of cars, and saves these records to a file, ready to be retrieved when the program starts again.

The program should allow the user to add and remove cars, and to display a list of all cars.

3. (a) Implement the changes to the waiting list program from Sect. 10.7.1 that are described at the end of that section so that the new item is added to the file each time a new entry is created.

   (b) Make similar changes to the `bankapplication.py` program as described in Sect. 10.7.2.

4. In Sect. 10.7.2 it was suggested that the `readList` method could have utilized a **for** loop to iterate through the entire file instead of a **while** loop. In order to do this we would need to do the following after opening the file for reading.

   - We would set a counter to zero before entering the **for** loop.
   - Once inside the **for** loop we would increment the counter by 1, and then, as the loop iterates, we would have three alternative actions:

   - If the counter was equal to 1, the item read would be assigned to a variable with a name such as `number`.
   - If the counter was equal to 2, the item read would be assigned to a variable with a name such as `name`.
   - If the counter was equal to 3, the item read would be assigned to a variable with a name such as `balance`. We would then add the account (using the number and name just read), deposit the `currentBalance` that was read (converting it to a float, as with the old version of the method). Finally we would reset the counter to zero.

   We would still need to close the file and return the appropriate values from the **try** and **except** blocks.

   See if you can write this alternative implementation.

5. Try copying a binary file such as an image or audio file, as explained in Sect. 10.9.

Python Graphics with Tkinter

11

Outcomes

By the end of this chapter you should be able to:

- *explain the relationship between **Tkinter** and **Tk**;*
- *describe the structure of a **Tkinter/Tk** application;*
- *identify, use and configure a number of common **Tk** widgets such as labels and buttons;*
- *explain the term event-handler (callback);*
- *bind a widget to a particular event and event-handler;*
- *build interactive graphics applications in Python using **Tkinter/Tk**;*
- *describe and utilize the **pack**, **grid** and **place** geometry managers;*
- *produce 2D graphical shapes using the **Canvas** widget;*
- *use the themed widgets provided in the **ttk** package.*

11.1 Introduction

Python comes with a package called **Tkinter** (pronounced "tee-kay-inter", and short for "Tk interface"), which provides access to a very rich graphics toolkit called **Tk**. Tk is a cross-platform toolkit and is the standard GUI (graphical user interface) for a number of programming languages including Python, Tcl and Perl. It provides us with all the common components (usually called **widgets**) that we are used to seeing—buttons, entry fields, check boxes and so on.

As we shall see, using Tkinter enables Python programmers to produce very attractive and modern looking graphical applications. In one chapter we can't possibly tell you everything there is to know about Tkinter/Tk—but we will cover

---

Supplementary Information The online version contains supplementary material available at https://doi.org/10.1007/978-3-031-01326-3_11.

Q. Charatan and A. Kans, *Programming in Two Semesters*,
Texts in Computer Science, https://doi.org/10.1007/978-3-031-01326-3_11

the basics, and hopefully that will whet your appetite and encourage you to explore other possibilities.

We should point out that in 2009, support was added to Tkinter for the newer "ttk" themed widgets, which are designed to give applications an even slicker look. For most of this chapter, however, we will deal only with the original Tk widgets, as they are very easy to configure. At the end of the chapter we will introduce the ttk widgets and show you how to use them if you wish to explore them further.

11.2   Tkinter: An Overview

You will already be very familiar with seeing components such as buttons and entry boxes in graphical applications—items like this which appear on your screen are collectively known as **widgets**. Figure 11.1 shows five commonly used widgets.

When we create a Tkinter program, we create a top level container (a window) in which all our widgets are arranged. It is also possible to create a container widget (a frame) that is usually invisible, but in which we can arrange other widgets that are then added to the main window as a group. In Fig. 11.1, for example, the label and the button are arranged horizontally in a frame, as are the check button and radio button.

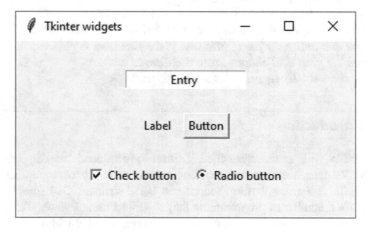

Fig. 11.1 Some common widgets

11.3 Your First Graphics Program

So let's get on with our first graphics program—and yes, you've guessed it, it's going to be a 'Hello world' program. Figure 11.2 shows how it will look.

Of course, this program isn't especially useful, and at this stage isn't particularly impressive—all it does is display a message in a window. But, as you will see, even this very simple application will help us begin to understand just how much we can achieve with Tk and Tkinter.

The code is shown below—we will take you through it once you have had a chance to look at it. But one thing you might notice straight away—just a few simple lines of code enable us to produce a graphical application such as this. This is one of the nice things about Tkinter and Python; we can do an enormous amount with a minimum amount of code.

---

helloworld1.py

```
from tkinter import Tk, Label

root = Tk() # create a window
label = Label(root, text = 'Hello world') # create a label
label.pack() # add the label to the window

root.mainloop() # create an event loop
```

So let's go through this. First the **import** statement:

```
from tkinter import Tk, Label
```

We are importing the two items that we need from the `tkinter` module. In many texts you will see that they choose to import the entire contents of the module using wildcards:

```
from tkinter import *
```

As we said in Chap. 5, we prefer to import only those items that we are going to use, so that it is clear which package they come from.

In some texts you will also see the following form of the **import** statement:

```
import tkinter
```

Fig. 11.2 Your first graphics program

In this case, as you already know, we would have to preface each item with the module name and the dot operator, so this is another reason for choosing to import only those items that we are going to use.

Now the next line:

```
root = Tk()
```

This line creates the window in which our graphic will appear. This window will be an object of the Tk class (note the capital letter in Tk). A reference to this window is assigned to a variable that we have called root. It is common (although clearly not mandatory) to use root to refer to our topmost window. The basic window that is created with this statement will contain icons for maximizing, minimizing and closing the window, as you can see from Fig. 11.2.

Next we create a Label, which is a widget that can hold either some text or an image.

```
label = Label(root, text = 'Hello world')
```

Tk widgets have initializers and methods which are set up to receive keyworded variable length parameter lists, which we explained in Chap. 7.

The first argument sent in is the name of the window (root) to which the label will be attached. After this, we can send in the variables and corresponding values which will define how the item will be configured when it is first created. In this case, we are specifying the text that appears on the label, 'Hello world'.

At this stage, the label will not actually appear. Before widgets can appear on the screen we have to instruct the window as to how the items should be arranged. This is done by calling what is known as a **layout manager**, or **geometry manager**. As you will see shortly there are three possible layout managers we can use (**pack**, **grid** and **place**), each of which arrange the widgets in a different way. Here we are using the pack layout manager.

```
label.pack()
```

The default position of the pack layout manager is to arrange the widgets vertically—here there is just one item, but shortly you will see how it works with multiple items.

The final statement looks like this:

```
root.mainloop()
```

The `mainloop` function should always be called once everything is set up. Its purpose is to create an **event loop** for the window—this is a loop that continually checks for **events**. As we shall see later, an event is some external action, like a mouse being clicked or moved, or a key being pressed on a keyboard. It is necessary to create an event loop because if it did not exist the program would not be able to respond immediately to events—it would have to wait for one event to be processed before responding to the next one. In our case the only relevant events that could take place would involve clicking on one of the three window icons. Later, however, we will create interactive programs that rely on many other sorts of events taking place.

11.4 Configuring Components

Our first program demonstrated a few basic principles very nicely, but what we ended up with didn't look all that special. So now we are going to make a couple of simple adjustments to our code and produce a graphic like the one shown in Fig. 11.3.

As you can see, our window now has a title. The label has a yellow background and red text, and there is some space around it so we can see exactly how it is placed in the window.

The code for the new program is shown below—we have emboldened the lines that have changed:

```
helloworld2.py

from tkinter import Tk, Label

root = Tk() # create a window
root.title('A simple program') # add a title to the window
label = Label(root, text = 'Hello world') # create a label
label.configure(bg = 'yellow', fg = 'red') # yellow background, red foreground
label.pack(padx = 100, pady = 100) # add the label to the window with some padding

root.mainloop() # create an event loop
```

The first change we made was to add a title to the window, using its `title` method:

```
root.title('A simple program')
```

Next we used the `configure` method of `Label`:

```
label.configure(bg = 'yellow', fg = 'red')
```

Fig. 11.3 Some simple
tweaks to the *Hello world*
program

As we explained above, methods such as this are set up to receive keyworded variable length argument lists, allowing us to set values for the attributes of the component. In this case, bg determines the background colour and fg the foreground colour (i.e. the colour of the text).

Tkinter allows us to use the names of the wide range of colours provided by both the Windows and Mac operating systems, and these should be fine for most of your needs. However, it is possible, if you wished, to create your own colours. Colours on screen are created by mixing red, green and blue light in different intensities, each with a possible range of 0 to 255 (00 to FF in hexadecimal). So any colour can be expressed as a six-digit hexadecimal number.

So red would be represented by FF0000 and yellow (formed by mixing red and green light) by FFFF00. You could replace 'red' with '#FF0000' and 'yellow' with '#FFFF00'—or you could mix your own colours.

Incidentally, it is possible to set these values at the time the widget is created by calling its initializer. So we could have created our label with this line, rather than using the configure method:

```
label = Label(root, bg = 'yellow', fg = 'red', text = 'Hello world')
```

The final change we made was to the line that attaches the label to the window:

```
label.pack(padx = 100, pady = 100)
```

The `padx` and `pady` parameters determine the amount of padding (in pixels) that is placed around the item—the former determines how much space there is on either side, and the latter determines the amount above and below. Here we have placed 100 pixels to the left and right, and 100 pixels above and below.

There is also another version of the `padx` and `pady` values, which could, for example, look like this:

```
padx = (10, 20)
```

This would place 10 pixels before the item and 20 after.

Similarly we could have something like:

```
pady = (30, 40)
```

This would place 30 pixels above and 40 pixels below the item.

The pack layout manager, by default, arranges the items vertically. To demonstrate this, take a look at the following program:

helloworld3.py

```
from tkinter import Tk, Label

root = Tk() # create a window
root.title('Three labels') # add a title to the window
label1 = Label(root, text = 'Hello world') # create a label
label1.configure(width = 20, height = 2, bg = 'yellow', fg = 'red') # yellow background, red foreground

label2 = Label(root, text = 'Hello world again') # create a label
label2.configure(width = 20, height = 2, bg = 'yellow', fg = 'red') # yellow background, red foreground

label3 = Label(root, text = 'Hello world again again') # create a label
label3.configure(width = 20, height = 2, bg = 'yellow', fg = 'red') # yellow background, red foreground

label1.pack(padx = 100, pady = 10) # add the label to the window with some padding
label2.pack(padx = 100, pady = 10) # add the label to the window with some padding
label3.pack(padx = 100, pady = 10) # add the label to the window with some padding

root.mainloop() # create an event loop
```

We have created three labels, `label1`, `label2` and `label3`, each showing slightly different text messages. We have then configured them as before, but with two additional arguments that set the width and height of each label. The units for width and height are text units in the case of text, and pixels in the case of images:

```
label1 = Label(root, text = 'Hello world')
label1.configure(width = 20, height = 2, bg = 'yellow', fg = 'red')

label2 = Label(root, text = 'Hello world again')
label2.configure(width = 20, height = 2, bg = 'yellow', fg = 'red')

label3 = Label(root, text = 'Hello world again again')
label3.configure(width = 20, height = 2, bg = 'yellow', fg = 'red')
```

Finally we have added each label to the widow, this time with the vertical padding set to 10.

```
label1.pack(padx = 100, pady = 10)
label2.pack(padx = 100, pady = 10)
label3.pack(padx = 100, pady = 10)
```

Fig. 11.4 By default, `pack` stacks items vertically

You can see the result of this in Fig. 11.4.

But what if we wanted our labels to line up horizontally? We need to make a change to the `pack` statements as shown in the next program, where we have also used the `minsize` method of `Tk` to ensure a width of 600 and a height of 50 so you can see more clearly how this works (changes in bold):

```
helloworld4.py

from tkinter import Tk, Label

root = Tk() # create a window

root.title(' Left alignment') # add a title to the window
root.minsize(600, 50) # set the minimum width of the window to 600 pixels and the minimum height to 50

label1 = Label(root, text = 'Hello world') # create a label
label1.configure(width = 20, height = 2, bg = 'yellow', fg = 'red') # yellow background, red foreground

label2 = Label(root, text='Hello world again ') # create a label
label2.configure(width = 20, height = 2, bg = 'yellow', fg = 'red') # yellow background, red foreground

label3 = Label(root, text='Hello world again again ') # create a label
label3.configure(width = 20, height = 2, bg = 'yellow', fg = 'red') # yellow background, red foreground

label1.pack(side = 'left', padx = 5, pady = 10) # add the label to the window with some padding
label2.pack(side = 'left', padx = 5, pady = 10) # add the label to the window with some padding
label3.pack(side = 'left', padx = 5, pady = 10) # add the label to the window with some padding

root.mainloop() # create an event loop
```

We see the result in Fig. 11.5.

The change that we made to each `pack` command was as follows:

```
label1.pack(side = 'left', padx = 5, pady = 10)
label2.pack(side = 'left', padx = 5, pady = 10)
label3.pack(side = 'left', padx = 5, pady = 10)
```

As you can see, we have added the argument `side = 'left'` to each of the instructions. This has the effect of causing the widgets to be lined up on the left, each in the next available position.

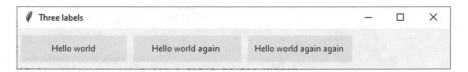

Fig. 11.5 Labels aligned to the left

Fig. 11.6 Labels aligned to the right

We could have aligned our labels to the right, as follows:

```
label1.pack(side = 'right', padx = 5, pady = 10)
label2.pack(side = 'right', padx = 5, pady = 10)
label3.pack(side = 'right', padx = 5, pady = 10)
```

The result of this is shown in Fig. 11.6.

You can try for yourself to discover the effects of lining up some labels to the left and some to the right.

Incidentally, the Tkinter module defines a number of constants, two of which are LEFT and RIGHT. We could have used these instead of the strings 'left' and 'right'. We have chosen not to do this however because, since we are importing explicitly the items that we need, we would have had to include LEFT and RIGHT in our import statement, which would add unnecessary code.

11.5 An Interactive Graphics Application

Most common applications involve controls (buttons, check boxes, entry boxes and so on) that allow the user to interact with the application by entering information. So, our next application—which is very simple—will allow the user to enter some text, and then, by clicking on a button, to see the text that was entered displayed below the button. You can see what it looks like in Fig. 11.7.

Before pushing the button

After pushing the button

Fig. 11.7 A simple interactive application

As usual, we will show you the code first and discuss it afterwards:

pushme.py

```
from tkinter import Tk, Label, Entry, Button

# method to specify the behaviour when the button is pushed
def action(event):
    label.configure(text = 'You entered: ' + entry.get()) # report what was typed
    entry.delete(0, 'end') # clear the entry field

# main body
root = Tk()
root.title('Pushme')

# create and configure the widgets
label = Label(root, fg = 'blue')
entry = Entry(root, bg = 'yellow', fg = 'red', width = 50 )
button = Button(root, bg = 'yellow', fg = 'red', text = 'Type something in the box, then push me')

# add components to window
entry.pack(padx = 100, pady = 10)
button.pack(pady = 10)
label.pack(pady = 10)

# ensure that the cursor is flashing on the entry field
entry.focus()

# specify the method that is to be called when the left-hand mouse button is clicked on the widget
button.bind('<Button-1>', action)

# start event loop
root.mainloop()
```

After the imports, you can see that we have defined a function called `action`. We will come to that in a moment, but first look at the creation of the three widgets that are going to form the basis of our application:

```
label = Label(root, fg = 'blue')
entry = Entry(root, bg = 'yellow', fg = 'red', width = 50 )
button = Button(root, bg = 'yellow', fg = 'red', text = 'Type something in the box, then push me')
```

The first one, a `Label`, is something you have already come across. This is where the text will appear after pressing the button (as in Fig. 11.7).

After that, we have an item you have not seen before—an Entry. This will be where we type our text. As well as setting its colours, we have given it a width of 50 (which is measured in characters).

Finally we create the button which will be pressed once the text has been entered.

Next we use the pack method to arrange the widgets on the window:

```
entry.pack(padx = 100, pady = 10)
button.pack(pady = 10)
label.pack(pady = 10)
```

We have chosen our padding to give the appearance that we want—but we should emphasise here once again that you should experiment with these values and see the different effects. Notice here that once we have padded the Entry widget, there is no need to pad the other items horizontally because this will determine the width of the window.

It would be nice if, when the application first starts, the cursor is flashing in the entry box—we do this by setting the focus to this item:

```
entry.focus()
```

Now we come to what could be considered the most important instruction in the whole application:

```
button.bind('<Button-1>', action)
```

What we are doing here is **binding** a component (in this case a button) to a particular event (in this case a left mouse-click). This means that we are defining the behaviour of the component that should take place when the particular event occurs.

The first argument in the brackets defines the particular event we are talking about. Here the event is <Button-1>, which is a click on the left button of the mouse. <Button-2> and <Button-3> would indicate clicks on the centre and right-hand buttons respectively. Many other events are defined, and we will come across some of these later in this chapter.

The second argument references a function—which, in this case, we have called action (we can choose any name)—that contains the instructions for what to do when the event occurs. Such a function is known as an **event-handler** or **callback**. So now let's look at this event-handler, which is defined at the beginning of the program code:

```
def action(event):
    label.configure(text = 'You entered: ' + entry.get()) # report what was typed
    entry.delete(0, 'end') # clear the entry field
```

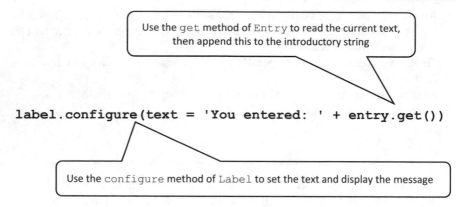

Use the `get` method of `Entry` to read the current text, then append this to the introductory string

```
label.configure(text = 'You entered: ' + entry.get())
```

Use the `configure` method of `Label` to set the text and display the message

Fig. 11.8 First line of the `action` function

The event handler will automatically be sent an object of the `Event` class, which we have named `event` in our function definition. We are not going to use this here, but the `event` object will contain information about the event, such as the coordinates of the point at which the mouse was clicked. We need to specify this parameter even if we are not going to use it.

The first line of our method transfers the text typed to the label at the bottom of the window (with a prefix). It is explained further in Fig. 11.8.

The second line of the function blanks out the entry field ready for us to enter a new value:

```
entry.delete(0, 'end')
```

We are using the `delete` method of `Entry`, which deletes the contents from a start position to an end position; here we are deleting from the first character to the end of the string (in other words the entire content).

11.6 Binding to Multiple Events

It is possible to bind a component such as a button or a window to more than one event, so that the response can be different according to the nature of the event.

In the program below we have bound a button to four different events, each with a different response. The events are a left mouse click (`'<Button-1>'`), a right mouse click (`'<Button-3>'`), a double left mouse click (`'<Double-1>'`) and a double right mouse click (`'<Double-3>'`):

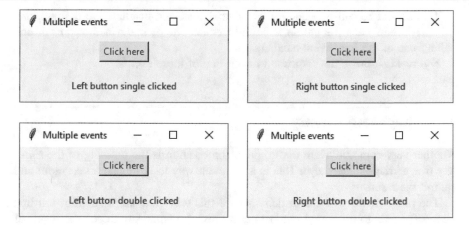

Fig. 11.9 Binding to multiple events

---

multipleevents.py

```python
from tkinter import Tk, Label, Button

# methods to specify the behaviour when different buttons are clicked
def singleLeft(event):
    label.configure(text = 'Left button single clicked')

def singleRight(event):
    label.configure(text = 'Right button single clicked')

def doubleLeft(event):
    label.configure(text = 'Left button double clicked')

def doubleRight(event):
    label.configure(text = 'Right button double clicked')


# main body
root = Tk()
root.title("Multiple events")

# create and configure the components

button = Button(root, bg = 'yellow', fg = 'red', text = 'Click here')
label = Label(root, fg = 'blue')


# add components to window

button.pack(padx = 100, pady = 10)
label.pack(pady = 10)

# specify the method that is to be called when the left-hand mouse button is single clicked
button.bind('<Button-1>', singleLeft)

# specify the method that is to be called when the right-hand mouse button is single clicked
button.bind('<Button-3>', singleRight)

# specify the method that is to be called when the left-hand mouse button is double clicked
button.bind('<Double-1>', doubleLeft)

# specify the method that is to be called when the right-hand mouse button is double clicked
button.bind('<Double-3>', doubleRight)

# start event loop
root.mainloop()
```

This should be self-explanatory. Four separate event-handlers are defined, one for each event. Then the button is bound to each one of these methods, each one calling one of the four event-handlers.

Figure 11.9 shows the response to each one of these events.

11.7   Keyboard Events

Another very common event that triggers some action is the pressing of the *Enter* key (the carriage return key). This is a common way to terminate a text input and submit the result.

The program we will use to demonstrate this will be a simple application that allows the user to enter two numbers and press the enter key to see the result of adding them together. This is shown in Fig. 11.10.

The total appears when the carriage return key is pressed on either of the two boxes. If one of the boxes is blank (or contains a string that is not a number) an error message is shown as shown in Fig. 11.11.

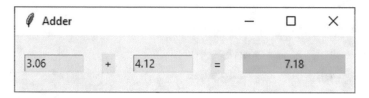

Fig. 11.10 *Adder* program

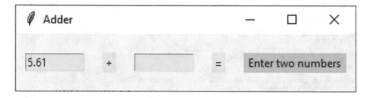

Fig. 11.11 *Adder* program showing an error

Here's the code:

adder.py

```
from tkinter import Tk, Label, Entry

def add(event):
    try:
        answer = float(first.get()) + float(second.get())
        label.configure(text = answer)
    except:
        label.configure(text = 'Enter two numbers')


# main body
root = Tk()
root.title("Adder")

# create components
plus = Label(root, bg = 'yellow', fg = 'red', text = '+')
equals = Label(root, bg = 'yellow', fg = 'red', text = '=')

first = Entry(root, bg = 'yellow', fg = 'red', width = 10 )
second = Entry(root, bg = 'yellow', fg = 'red', width = 10)

label = Label(root, bg = 'sky blue', fg = 'red',  width = 15)

# add components to window, arranged horizontally
first.pack(side = 'left', padx = 10, pady = 20)
plus.pack(side = 'left', padx = 10, pady = 20)
second.pack(side = 'left',padx = 10, pady = 20)
equals.pack(side = 'left', padx = 10, pady = 20)
label.pack(side = 'left', padx = 10, pady = 20)

first.focus()

#bind each entry widget to the carriage return (enter) key

first.bind('<Return>', add)
second.bind('<Return>', add)

root.mainloop()
```

Most of this should already be familiar to you. But let us draw your attention to the statements that bind the widgets:

```
first.bind('<Return>', add)
second.bind('<Return>', add)
```

You can see that we are binding both Entry widgets to a ' < Return > ' event—this indicates a press of the *Enter* key, so that when this key is pressed on either Entry widget the data will be submitted to the add function that we have declared at the start of the program. By the way, do not confuse ' < Return > ' with ' < Enter > '—the latter refers to a mouse entering a widget, as we shall see in a moment.

We should also take a look at the add method:

```
def add(event):
    try:
        answer = float(first.get()) + float(second.get())
        label.configure(text = answer)
    except:
        label.configure(text = 'Enter two numbers')
```

Using a **try ... except** construct here ensures that an error message is displayed if either of the Entry boxes is empty, or if the box does not contain a string in the form of a number.

The instructions in the **try** box add the two numbers (which are obtained using the get method and converted to floats) and then display the result on the label by setting its text value.

11.8   Other Common Events

Before moving on, we should draw your attention to other kinds of events that can take place. Table 11.1 shows the most common of those.

You will have an opportunity to explore these in the end of chapter exercises.

11.9   More About Labels

Before moving on to some more complex applications, it is worth taking a little more time to explore the Label widget. As you have already begun to see, this is a very useful—and as it turns out, very versatile—component for displaying information in our graphical applications. We have already seen how to set the width and height of our label and its background and foreground colours.

Another option we can use with Label is anchor. This determines how the text on the label is positioned. there are nine possibilities—eight are defined as corresponding to the cardinal and intermediate directions on a compass ('n', 'e', 'w', 's', 'nw', 'ne', 'sw', 'se'); the final one is 'center'.

So, for example, the following would position the label in the north-west corner:

```
label1.configure(anchor = 'nw')
```

The anchor could also be set when the label is created with the initialiser. As before, constants such as NW and E are provided to represent the positions, but these would need to be imported.

Figure 11.12 should make this clear.

Labels also have an attribute called relief, which can be set to different values —'sunken', 'raised', 'flat', 'groove' and 'ridge'. Figure 11.13 shows what the various options look like.

A borderwidth option is also available, and in Fig. 11.13 we have set the width of the border to 5 in each case (although it doesn't show on the flat label). So, for example, to achieve the first label in the diagram, we would have configured the label like this:

Table 11.1 Possible Tk events

Event	Description

`<Button-1>`
`<Button-2>`
`<Button-3>`
	A mouse button is pressed while the mouse pointer is on the widget. The numbers represent the left-, middle and right-hand buttons respectively

`<B1-Motion>`
`<B2-Motion>`
`<B3-Motion>`
	The mouse is moved on the widget with a mouse button being held down (dragged). As above, the numbers represent the left-, middle and right-hand buttons respectively

`<ButtonRelease-1>`
`<ButtonRelease-2>`
`<ButtonRelease-3>`
	A button is released while the pointer is on the widget. The current position of the mouse pointer is given in the x and y members of the Event object passed to the callback (so can be retrieved with event.x and event.y)

`<Double-Button-1>`
`<Double-Button-2>`
`<Double-Button-2>`
	Similar to the Button event, but the mouse is double clicked instead of single clicked

`<Enter>`	The mouse pointer entered the widget. (Don't confuse with <Return>!)
`<Leave>`	The mouse pointer left the widget
`<Return>`	The user pressed the *Enter* key
`<Key>`	The user pressed any key. The key is provided in the char member of the event object passed to the callback (this is an empty string for special keys)

Fig. 11.12 Possible
positions of text on a label

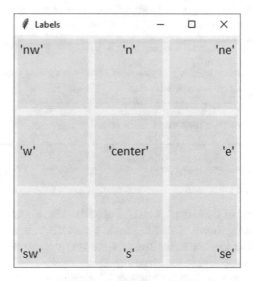

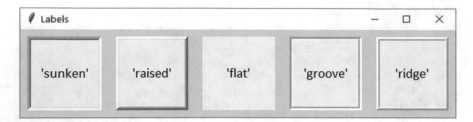

Fig. 11.13 Possible `relief` options

```
label1.configure(borderwidth = 5, relief = 'sunken')
```

Once again, constants such as SUNKEN and RAISED can also be used.

As we mentioned before, it is possible to include images on a label as well as text. An example is shown in Fig. 11.14.

This was achieved with the following code:

labelimage.py

```
from tkinter import Tk, Label, PhotoImage

root = Tk() # create a window
root.title('Label with text and image') # add a title to the window

myImage = PhotoImage(file = 'sunset.gif') # create the image file

#create the label which will include text and image
label = Label(root, image = myImage, text = 'Sunset', font = ('Calibri', 20),
                                                fg = 'red',  compound = 'bottom')

label.pack(padx = 20, pady = 20) # add the label to the window with some padding

root.mainloop() # create an event loop
```

There are two important lines here:

```
myImage = PhotoImage(file = 'sunset.gif')
label = Label(root, image = myImage, text = 'Sunset', font = ('Calibri', 20),
                                                fg = 'red',  compound = 'bottom')
```

The first of these creates an object of the PhotoImage class from the image file we are going to use. This file should be a GIF image.[1] You can also see here how we are able to choose the font for the text on the label, using one of the system fonts, and specifying the size.

Now, when we create our label (or configure it later) we can set the image option to the PhotoImage object we have created. We can also define any text that is to appear, but in order for this to be included, we must also set the compound option. The values for this are 'left', 'right', 'top', 'bottom'

---

[1] Tk also supports files in the simplistic PPM/PGM formats.

Fig. 11.14 A label
containing text and image

and 'center' (as usual, constants such as LEFT and RIGHT are also available if imported). Note that the position refers to the position of the *image* with respect to the text.

11.10 More About the *Pack* Layout Manager

We have already seen a lot of examples of the pack layout manager in operation in our previous programs. You have probably realised that this is a very powerful layout manger when used in conjunction with features such as padding.

There are in fact other features of this manager that can be used—one of which is the anchor attribute that you saw above in connection with labels. However, it is our experience that it can become quite complicated to use this feature, because the items are still stacked vertically (unless otherwise specified) and you have to work quite hard to position the components exactly where you want them.

It is our suggestion that while you are getting used to Tkinter graphics you use the pack manager in conjunction with the padding feature and place your items in this way. You can achieve an awful lot like this, particularly when you pad the widgets by different amount on each side as explained in Sect. 11.4.

A very useful widget to use with this manager (or other managers) is the Frame. A frame is an invisible window (although you could make it visible by changing its colour and so on)—you can add other items to it and arrange them how you want. It will keep them together and you can then add the frame to the main window. You will see how this works in the next section.

Once again we should emphasize that the way to get the best results is just to experiment with different settings until you get the result that looks best.

While the pack manager is very versatile, there are, as we mentioned, two other layout managers—**grid** and **place**—which we will explore later.

11.11 A Graphical User Interface (GUI) for the *Rectangle* Class

In Chap. 9, when we developed our own classes, the programs we wrote to utilize those classes were text-based programs. Now, however, we are able to create graphical user interfaces (GUIs) for our classes. Let's do this for the Rectangle class that we developed in that chapter. The sort of interface we are talking about is shown in Fig. 11.15.

Here's the code:

---
rectanglegui.py

```
from tkinter import Tk, Frame, Label, Entry, Button, Text
from rectangle import Rectangle

# function to display area and perimeter of rectangle
def calculate(event):
    try:
        display.delete(1.0, 'end')  # clear the display
        rect = Rectangle(float(lengthEntry.get()), float(heightEntry.get())) # create rectangle
        area = rect.calculateArea() # calculate area
        perimeter = rect.calculatePerimeter() # calculate perimeter
        display.insert(1.0, 'Area = %0.2f \nPerimeter = %0.2f' %(area, perimeter)) # display result
    except:
        display.delete(1.0, 'end')   # clear the display
        display.insert(1.0, 'Please enter two numbers') # show error message

# create and configure the main window
root = Tk()
root.title('Rectangle GUI')
root.geometry('300x120')
root.configure(bg = 'palegoldenrod')

# create and configure a frame
frame = Frame(root, bg = 'palegoldenrod')

# create labels and entry boxes to be added to the frame
lengthLabel = Label(frame, bg = 'palegoldenrod', fg = 'red', text = 'Length')
heightLabel = Label(frame, bg = 'palegoldenrod', fg = 'red', text = 'Height')

lengthEntry = Entry(frame, width = 10)
```

```
heightEntry = Entry(frame, width = 10)

# create the area where the results willl be displayed
display = Text(root, width = 30, height = 2)

#create a button to be added to the main window
calculateButton =  Button(root, bg = 'gold', text ='Calculate')

# add the entry items to the frame
lengthLabel.pack(side = 'left', padx = 10, pady = 5)
lengthEntry.pack(side = 'left', padx = 10, pady = 5)
heightLabel.pack(side = 'left', padx = 10, pady = 5)
heightEntry.pack(side = 'left', padx = 10, pady = 5)

# add the frame, button and display to the main window
frame.pack()
calculateButton.pack(pady = 5)
display.pack(pady = 5)

# bind the button to a left-click event
calculateButton.bind('<Button-1>', calculate)

root.mainloop()
```

The purpose of this application is that it acts as an interface to our Rectangle class and uses the methods of that class. So, we need to import that class along with the usual import statement (you will recall that this was saved in a file called rectangle.py):

```
from tkinter import Tk, Frame, Label, Entry, Button, Text
from rectangle import Rectangle
```

After the import statement we have the event-handler, which we will discuss in a moment.

Next we create and configure the main window—you can see we had some fun trying out different colours in this application. Notice we have used the geometry function here, which fixes the window to a specific width and height:

```
root = Tk()
root.title('Rectangle GUI')
root.geometry('300x120')
root.configure(bg = 'palegoldenrod')
```

Next we create a frame which is going to hold the labels and entry fields that you see in Fig. 11.15.

Fig. 11.15 *Rectangle* GUI

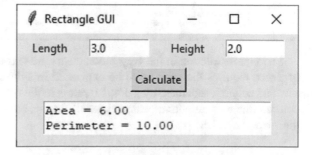

```
frame = Frame(root, bg = 'palegoldenrod')
```

Next come the labels and entry boxes—notice how they are associated with the
frame rather than the window:

```
lengthLabel = Label(frame, bg = 'palegoldenrod', fg = 'red', text = 'Length')
heightLabel = Label(frame, bg = 'palegoldenrod', fg = 'red', text = 'Height')

lengthEntry = Entry(frame, width = 10)
heightEntry = Entry(frame, width = 10)
```

The display area is going to be a Text widget. This is similar to an entry field,
but allows for many lines of text. Here we declare it so that it shows two rows, each
row containing a maximum of 30 characters:

```
display = Text(root, width = 30, height = 2)
```

Now we use the pack manager to arrange the frame, button and display area
vertically (which you will recall is the default layout for this manager).

```
frame.pack()
calculateButton.pack(pady = 5)
display.pack(pady = 5)
```

We bind the button to a left-hand click event, and to the event-handler which we
have called calculate:

```
calculateButton.bind('<Button-1>', calculate)
```

Let's take a look at the event-handler now:

```
def calculate(event):
    try:
        display.delete(1.0, 'end')  # clear the display
        rect = Rectangle(float(lengthEntry.get()), float(heightEntry.get())) # create rectangle
        area = rect.calculateArea()  # calculate area
        perimeter = rect.calculatePerimeter()  # calculate perimeter
        display.insert(1.0, 'Area = %0.2f \nPerimeter = %0.2f' %(area, perimeter))  # display result
    except:
        display.delete(1.0, 'end')  # clear the display
        display.insert(1.0, 'Please enter two numbers')  # show error message
```

The first instruction in the **try** block clears the text area—the delete method
of Text requires the position to be expressed in as two numbers representing the
row and column, separated by a dot; 1.0 refers to the cell in the first row and the first
column (the row numbering starts at zero!). In this case all the text is deleted up to
the 'end' marker.

The next three instructions exercise the methods of our Rectangle class. First the initializer, then the calculateArea and calculatePerimeter methods. The return values of the last two are assigned to the variables area and perimeter respectively. These values are used in the insert method of Text. As you can see this method expects to receive the start position followed by the string to be displayed. Notice the newline character ('\n') that we have included in the string.

```
display.insert(1.0, 'Area = %0.2f \nPerimeter = %0.2f' %(area, perimeter))
```

As usual, the **except** block displays a message if anything other than numbers has been entered, thereby avoiding a runtime error.

11.12   The *Grid* Layout Manager

The grid layout manager provides a very powerful mechanism for organizing your widgets. There is actually quite a lot to it, so once again we will not be attempting to tell you all there is to know about this geometry manger. And once again, there are many different ways of doing the same thing, so we will simply tell you what we think is the most straightforward way of doing things, and then you can go off and do some more research if you want to hone your skills.

The grid layout manager organizes the container (a window or a frame) into an invisible matrix of cells. The rows and columns start at zero. To illustrate this, we have added some different coloured labels to a grid, each named with its position, as shown in Fig. 11.16.

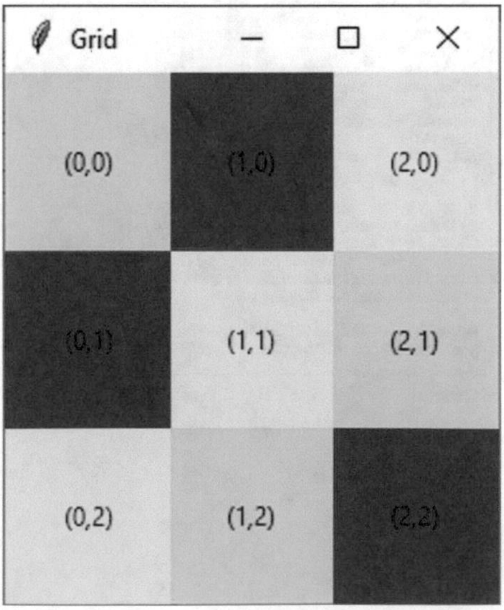

Fig. 11.16 The *grid* layout

One of the nice things about the grid manager is that the grid is built and sized as the components are added. To illustrate this we are going to create a little application that converts back and forth between metric and imperial units. This is shown in Fig. 11.17.

We created this using a grid layout. In Fig. 11.18 we have added some lines to show how the grid is laid out. There are three rows and five columns: the top left cell is at (0, 0) and the bottom right is at (2, 4).

Let's take a look at the code:

converter.py

```
from tkinter import Tk, Label, Entry, Button, Frame

# methods to specify the behaviour when the buttons are pushed
def convertCm(event):
    inchEntry.delete(0, 'end')
    inchEntry.insert(10, '%0.1f' %(float(cmEntry.get())/2.54))

def convertInches(event):
    cmEntry.delete(0, 'end')
    cmEntry.insert(10, '%0.1f' %(float(inchEntry.get()) * 2.54))

def convertKm(event):
    mileEntry.delete(0, 'end')
    mileEntry.insert(10, '%0.1f' %(float(kmEntry.get())/1.609))

def convertMiles(event):
    kmEntry.delete(0, 'end')
    kmEntry.insert(10, '%0.1f' %(float(mileEntry.get()) * 1.609))

def convertKg(event):
    poundEntry.delete(0, 'end')
    poundEntry.insert(10, '%0.1f' %(float(kgEntry.get())* 2.2))

def convertPounds(event):
    kgEntry.delete(0, 'end')
    kgEntry.insert(10, '%0.1f' %(float(poundEntry.get()) / 2.2))

# main body
root = Tk()
root.title("Converter")

# create frames to hold the buttons
frame1 = Frame(root)
frame2 = Frame(root)
frame3 = Frame(root)

# create labels and entry boxes for input
cmLabel = Label(root, text = 'cm')
cmEntry = Entry(root,  width = 10)
inchLabel = Label(root,  text = 'inches')
inchEntry = Entry(root, width = 10)
kmEntry = Entry(root,  width = 10)
kmLabel = Label(root, text = 'km')
mileLabel = Label(root,  text = 'miles')
mileEntry = Entry(root, width = 10)
kgEntry = Entry(root,  width = 10)
kgLabel = Label(root, text = 'kg')
poundLabel = Label(root, text = 'lb')
poundEntry = Entry(root, width = 10)


# create the buttons and associate them with the correct frames
cmToInch = Button(frame1, text = '--->')
inchToCm = Button(frame1, text = '<---')

kmToMile = Button(frame2, text = '--->')
mileToKm = Button(frame2, text = '<---')

kgToPound = Button(frame3, text = '--->')
poundToKg = Button(frame3, text = '<---')
```

```
# arrange the buttons on each frame
cmToInch.pack()
inchToCm.pack()

kmToMile.pack()
mileToKm.pack()

kgToPound.pack()
poundToKg.pack()

# add items to first row
cmEntry.grid( row = 0, column = 0, padx = (10, 2), pady = 10)
cmLabel.grid(sticky = 'w', row = 0, column = 1, pady = 10)
frame1.grid(row = 0, column = 2, padx = 10, pady = 10)
inchEntry.grid(row = 0, column = 3, pady = 10)
inchLabel.grid(sticky = 'w', row = 0, column = 4, padx = (2,10), pady = 10)

# add items to second row
kmEntry.grid( row = 1, column = 0, padx = (10, 2), pady = 10)
kmLabel.grid(sticky = 'w', row = 1, column = 1, pady = 10)
frame2.grid( row = 1, column = 2, padx = 10, pady = 10)
mileEntry.grid(row = 1, column = 3,  pady = 10)
mileLabel.grid(sticky = 'w', row = 1, column = 4,  padx = (2,10), pady = 10)

# add items to third row
kgEntry.grid( row = 2, column = 0, padx = (10, 2), pady = 10)
kgLabel.grid(sticky = 'w', row = 2, column = 1, pady = 10)
frame3.grid(row = 2, column = 2, padx = 10, pady = 10)
poundEntry.grid(row = 2, column = 3,  pady = 10)
poundLabel.grid(sticky = 'w', row = 2, column = 4, padx = (2,10), pady = 10)

# bind the buttons
cmToInch.bind('<Button-1>', convertCm)
inchToCm.bind('<Button-1>', convertInches)

kmToMile.bind('<Button-1>', convertKm)
mileToKm.bind('<Button-1>', convertMiles)

kgToPound.bind('<Button-1>', convertKg)
poundToKg.bind('<Button-1>', convertPounds)

# start event loop
root.mainloop()
```

Although there is quite a lot of code here, the only thing that is new is the use of the grid layout manager when adding the components. Let's look at how this is done for the first row:

```
cmEntry.grid( row = 0, column = 0, padx = (10, 2), pady = 10)
cmLabel.grid(sticky = 'w', row = 0, column = 1, pady = 10)
frame1.grid(row = 0, column = 2, padx = 10, pady = 10)
inchEntry.grid(row = 0, column = 3, pady = 10)
inchLabel.grid(sticky = 'w', row = 0, column = 4, padx = (2,10), pady = 10)
```

In each case a row and column is specified—don't forget that numbering starts at zero. We have played about with the padding to get the effect we wanted, and you can try changing some of these settings. The grid is created on the fly, so to speak, and column and row sizes are adjusted to accommodate the largest widgets.

Something you have not seen before is the `sticky` option. Possible values for this are `'n'`, `'s'`, `'e'`, `'w'`, `'ne'`, `'nw`, `'se'` and `'sw'`,[2] similar to the `anchor` values that we showed you for labels in Sect. 11.9. We have set `sticky` to `'w'` for the unit names (cm, km, etc.) so that they line up close to the entry boxes. Please do experiment with these values to see the different effects.

---

[2] Once again you can use the constants N, S, E, W, NE, NW, SE, SW, if you import them.

Fig. 11.17 *Converter*
application

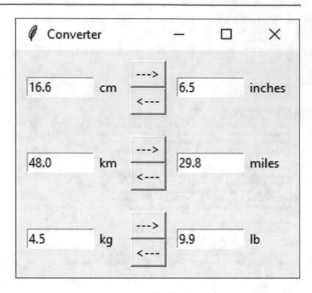

Another handy feature of the grid layout manager is the ability for a widget to span more than one column, or more than one row. To illustrate this, consider the program below:

---

spanning.py

```
from tkinter import Tk, Label

root = Tk() # create a window

root.title('Spanning example') # add a title to the window

# create five labels
label1 = Label(root, width = 20, height = 2, bg = 'pale green')
label2 = Label(root, width = 42, height = 2, bg = 'red')
label3 = Label(root, width = 20, height = 2, bg = 'pale green')
label4 = Label(root, width = 20, height = 2, bg = 'pale green')
label5 = Label(root, width = 20, height = 2, bg = 'pale green')

# add labels using a grid layout manager
label1.grid(row = 0, column = 0, padx = 4, pady = 10)
label2.grid(row = 0, column = 1, padx = 4, pady = 10, columnspan = 2) #spans two columns
label3.grid(row = 1, column = 0, padx = 4, pady = 10)
label4.grid(row = 1, column = 1, padx = 4, pady = 10)
label5.grid(row = 1, column = 2, padx = 4, pady = 10)

root.mainloop() # create an event loop
```

We have created five labels, one of which (the second one) is longer than the others and is coloured red so it stands out.

Look carefully at how the labels are added to the window:

```
label1.grid(row = 0, column = 0, padx = 4, pady = 10)
label2.grid(row = 0, column = 1, padx = 4, pady = 10, columnspan = 2) #spans two columns
label3.grid(row = 1, column = 0, padx = 4, pady = 10)
label4.grid(row = 1, column = 1, padx = 4, pady = 10)
label5.grid(row = 1, column = 2, padx = 4, pady = 10)
```

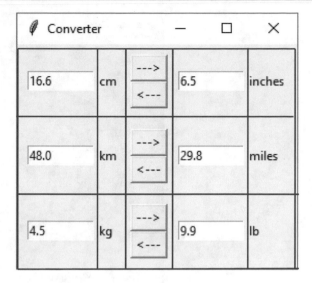

Fig. 11.18 *Converter* application uses a grid layout

Fig. 11.19 Red label spans two columns

For the second label we have an additional argument that sets the `columnspan` option to 2. The effect of this is shown in Fig. 11.19.

As you can see, the red label has been placed in the cell at row 0, cloumn 1 but spans this column and the next.

The `rowspan` option operates in a similar way—once again, you should do some experiments of your own to discover exactly how these work.

11.13 The *Canvas* Widget

The `Canvas` widget is an extremely versatile widget which enables you to draw two-dimensional shapes. Although we are going to give only a brief introduction of its capabilities here, it is actually very powerful and can be used to draw graphs, to create graphics editors or even to create custom widgets.

Fig. 11.20 Smiley face
application

In Fig. 11.20 we have created a smiley face image on a `Canvas`.

Here is the code—you can see we just need a few lines of code to produce something rather interesting and attractive:

---
smileyface.py

```
from tkinter import Tk, Canvas

root = Tk()
root.title('Smiley Face')

# create canvas
canvas = Canvas(root, width = 300, height = 350, bg = 'yellow')

# the face
canvas.create_oval(50, 75, 250, 275, outline = 'red', fill = 'yellow', width = 2)

# the right eye
canvas.create_oval(95, 135, 115, 155, outline='blue', fill = 'yellow', width = 2)

# the left eye
canvas.create_oval(180, 135, 200, 155, outline='blue', fill = 'yellow', width = 2)

# the mouth
canvas.create_arc(95, 165, 200, 250, style = 'arc', start = 0,
                                      extent = -180, outline = 'blue', fill = 'yellow', width = 2)

# the text
canvas.create_text(150, 325, font = ('Arial', 16), fill = 'blue', text = 'Smiley Face')

canvas.pack() # add canvas to window

root.mainloop()
```

So let's take a look at this. The first thing we do, once we have created our main window, is to create and configure a `Canvas` object:

```
canvas = Canvas(root, width = 300, height = 350, bg = 'yellow')
```

We then use the `create_oval` method of `Canvas` to draw the main circle for the face:

```
canvas.create_oval(50, 75, 250, 275, outline = 'red', fill = 'yellow', width = 2)
```

The first two arguments to this method represent the co-ordinates (x_1, y_1) of the top left-hand corner of an imaginary rectangle drawn around the oval. The next two represent the co-ordinates (x_2, y_2) of the bottom right corner of this rectangle. This is shown in Fig. 11.21. Remember the horizontal distance (x) is left to right starting at (0, 0), and the vertical distance (y) is measured downwards.

In our smiley face application, we have defined our co-ordinates so that the vertical and horizontal diameters are equal—in other words so that we get a circle.

The final options set the line and fill colours, and the width of the line.

The eyes are created in exactly the same way:

```
canvas.create_oval(95, 135, 115, 155, outline='blue', fill = 'yellow', width = 2) # the right eye
canvas.create_oval(180, 135, 200, 155, outline='blue', fill = 'yellow', width = 2) # the left eye
```

Incidentally, when we created this graphic, we didn't spend a long time carefully measuring each distance, but did what we suggest that you do, which is just to experiment with various values until you get what you want.

Next we draw the smiling mouth, which is a little more complicated:

```
canvas.create_arc(95, 165, 200, 250, start = 0, extent = -180,
                               style = 'arc', outline = 'blue', fill = 'yellow', width = 2)
```

The first four arguments are again the co-ordinates of the imaginary rectangle drawn around the circle of which the arc forms a part. Then come two options which set values for the attributes `start` and `extent`. The meaning of these is shown in Fig. 11.22.

The `start` angle is measured from the "quarter-past-three" position, and `extent` is the angle through which the arc is drawn. If `extent` is positive, the arc is drawn in an anti-clockwise direction, if it is negative it is drawn in a clockwise direction. In our example `extent` is set to $-180°$, to draw the smiling mouth.

Next comes the style option, which in our case is set to `'arc'`. Figure 11.23 shows all the options for this.

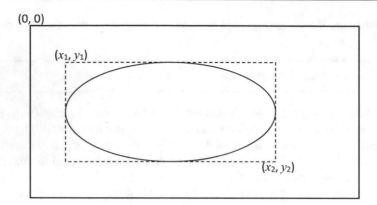

Fig. 11.21 `create_oval` method of `Canvas`

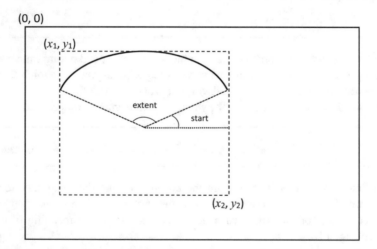

Fig. 11.22 `Arc` class

As before, the final options set the line and fill colours, and the width of the line.

The last thing we do (apart from applying the pack manager and starting the event loop) is to draw the text under the face. Here we use the `create_text` method of `Canvas`:

```
canvas.create_text(150, 325, font = ('Arial', 16), fill = 'blue', text = 'Smiley Face')
```

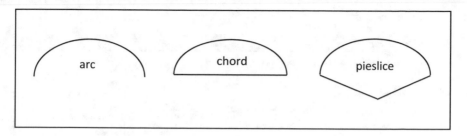

Fig. 11.23 Arc class styles

This is mostly self-explanatory—the first two arguments are the co-ordinates of the start position, and as you can see we have set the font as we did in Sect. 11.9.

Before leaving this section, we should mention two other useful Canvas methods, which do as their names suggest:

create_line(x_1, y_1, x_2, y_2):   Draws a line starting at co-ordinate (x_1, y_1) and ending at co-ordinate (x_2, y_2). The colour of the line is determined by its fill option.

create_rectangle(x_1, y_1, x_2, y_2):   Draws a rectangle whose top left vertex is co-ordinate (x_1, y_1) and whose bottom right co-ordinate is (x_2, y_2).

Arguments such as width and fill can be included as with other widgets.

11.14   The *Place* Layout Manager

The **place** layout manager does just what it says—it allows us to place an item on the screen exactly where we want it. It is less common to use this than it is to use the pack and grid managers, because it can involve a lot of work to get everything on the screen exactly where you want it. However, it can be useful and one example of when you might want to use it is when you want to place some widgets on a canvas.

We have done this here by changing our smiley face graphic from the previous section into a changing face that can smile or frown as shown in Fig. 11.24.

Here is the code:

changingface.py

```
from tkinter import Tk, Button, Canvas

root = Tk()

# action for the frown button
def frown(event):
    canvas.create_arc(95, 165, 200, 250, style = 'arc', start = 0, extent = -180,
                                         outline='yellow', fill='yellow', width=2)
    canvas.create_arc(95, 165, 200, 250, style = 'arc', start = 0, extent = 180,
                                          outline='blue', fill='yellow', width=2)

# action for the smile button
def smile(event):
    canvas.create_arc(95, 165, 200, 250, style = 'arc', start = 0, extent = 180,
                                         outline='yellow', fill='yellow', width=2)
    canvas.create_arc(95, 165, 200, 250, style = 'arc', start = 0, extent = -180,
                                          outline='blue', fill='yellow', width=2)

root.title('Changing Face')

# create canvas
canvas = Canvas(root, width = 300, height = 350, bg='yellow')

# the face
canvas.create_oval(50, 75, 250, 275, outline='red', fill='yellow', width=2)

# the right eye
canvas.create_oval(95, 135, 115, 155, outline='blue', fill='yellow', width=2)

# the left eye
canvas.create_oval(180, 135, 200, 155, outline='blue', fill='yellow', width=2)

# the mouth
canvas.create_arc(95, 165, 200, 250, start = 0, extent = -180, style = 'arc',
                                       outline = 'blue', fill = 'yellow', width = 2)
# the text
canvas.create_text(150, 325, font = ('Arial', 16), fill = 'blue', text = 'Changing Face')

# create the buttons
smileButton = Button(root, text = 'Smile', bg = 'palegreen', width = 10, height = 1)
frownButton = Button(root, text ='Frown', bg = 'palegreen', width = 10, height = 1)

# place the buttons exactly where we want them
smileButton.place(x = 65, y = 30)
frownButton.place(x = 160, y = 30)

canvas.pack() # add canvas to window

# bind the buttons
frownButton.bind('<Button-1>', frown)
smileButton.bind('<Button-1>', smile)

root.mainloop()
```

Take a look at the way we have implemented the place manager:

```
smileButton.place(x = 65, y = 30)
frownButton.place(x = 160, y = 30)
```

You can see that we have specified the absolute *x* and *y* co-ordinates of where we want each button to be placed relative to the container, root.

For those of you who wish to experiment further, there are alternative options to x and y that we can use, either on their own or in different combinations:

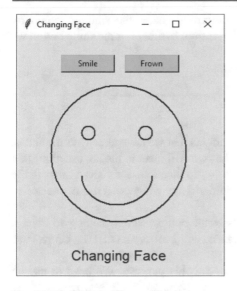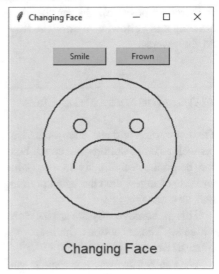

Fig. 11.24 Changing face application

height, width:	Height and width of the widget in pixels.
relheight, relwidth:	Height and width of the widget (a decimal number between 0.0 and 1.0) as a fraction of the height and width of the parent widget.
relx, rely:	Horizontal and vertical offset (a decimal number between 0.0 and 1.0) as a fraction of the height and width of the parent widget.

It is also worth taking a look at how we have implemented the event-handlers for the buttons:

```
# action for the frown button
def frown(event):
    canvas.create_arc(95, 165, 200, 250, style = 'arc', start = 0, extent = -180,
                                        outline='yellow', fill='yellow', width=2)
    canvas.create_arc(95, 165, 200, 250, style = 'arc', start = 0, extent = 180,
                                        outline='blue', fill='yellow', width=2)

# action for the smile button
def smile(event):
    canvas.create_arc(95, 165, 200, 250, style = 'arc', start = 0, extent = 180,
                                        outline='yellow', fill='yellow', width=2)
    canvas.create_arc(95, 165, 200, 250, style = 'arc', start = 0, extent = -180,
                                        outline='blue', fill='yellow', width=2)
```

The difference between the smiling mouth and the frowning mouth is that in the former case the arc is drawn clockwise (and the extent angle is therefore negative) and in the latter case the arc is drawn anti-clockwise (and the extent angle is therefore positive). So for the frown button we erase the smiling mouth by drawing it in yellow, then draw the frowning mouth in blue. For the smile button we do the reverse.

11.15   The Variable Class

There are some widgets, such as the entry widgets that we have already come across (as well as radio buttons and check boxes that we will meet in the next section) that can be connected directly to a variable in the application. This means that if the variable changes, then the corresponding option in any widget that it is connected to will also change.

This is achieved by means of some special options which belong to certain widgets. These options include: variable, textvariable, onvalue, offvalue and value.

We can't, however, use regular variables for this purpose. We have to use an object which is a subtype of a class called Variable, which is provided in the Tkinter package.

There are four possibilities:

StringVar: Holds a string. Default value is " (i.e. two single quotes, not a single double quote).

IntVar: Holds an integer. Default value is 0.

DoubleVar: Holds a decimal number. Default value 0.0.

BooleanVar: Holds a Boolean value. Default value is **False**.

To declare such a variable we would write, for example:

```
myVar = IntVar()
```

To read the current value we would call the get method:

```
x = myVar.get()
```

We could also change the value with the set method:

```
myVar.set(10)
```

This may sound a bit complicated, but the little application below should make it clear. In Fig. 11.25 we have created two entry boxes, and, as you can see, whatever we type in one box also appears in the other box.

As the code below shows, we achieved this by associating both boxes with the same Variable object:

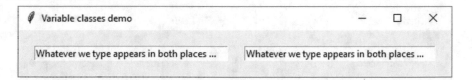

Fig. 11.25 Using the `Variable` class

```
variableclassdemo.py

from tkinter import Tk, Entry, StringVar

root = Tk()
root.title('Variable classes demo')

var = StringVar() # declare an object of StringVar

# create two Entry widget with the text option both set to the same variable
entry1 = Entry(root, textvariable = var, width = 40)
entry2 = Entry(root, textvariable = var, width = 40)

entry1.pack(side ='left', padx = (20, 10), pady = 20)
entry2.pack(side = 'left', padx = (10, 20), pady = 20)

root.mainloop
```

First we declare an object of the `StringVar` class (which we included in our `import` statement):

```
var = StringVar()
```

Now we create two `Entry` widgets:

```
entry1 = Entry(root, textvariable = var, width = 40)
entry2 = Entry(root, textvariable = var, width = 40)
```

The important thing here is that we have set *both* `textvariable` options to the same variable, `var`. Therefore, whenever this value changes, it changes in both widgets.

11.16 Check Boxes and Radio Buttons

Check boxes and radio buttons, as shown in Fig. 11.26 are very common ways of getting input from a user. Check boxes are square, whereas radio buttons are round. Usually a check box is used when more than one option can be selected, and a radio button used when only one choice is allowed. In both cases we are required to use the `Variable` class described in the previous section.

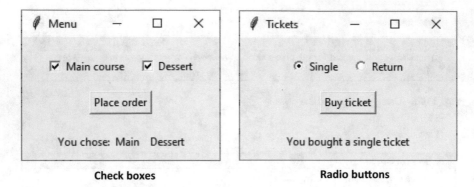

Fig. 11.26 Check boxes and radio buttons

In the check box example in Fig. 11.26 the user is asked to choose either a main course, a dessert, both or none, and submit their choice. The selection is then displayed at the bottom of the window. Here is how we achieve this:

checkbuttonexample.py

```
from tkinter import Tk, Checkbutton, IntVar, Button, Frame, Label
root = Tk()
root.title('Menu')

# event handler
def showResult():
    choice = 'You chose:   '
    if mainCourseVariable.get() == 0 and dessertVariable.get() == 0:
        choice = 'You did not order anything'
    else:
        if mainCourseVariable.get() == 1:
            choice = choice + 'Main'
        if dessertVariable.get() == 1:
            choice = choice + '    Dessert'
    displayLabel.configure(text = choice)

# declare  Variable objects
mainCourseVariable = IntVar()
dessertVariable = IntVar()

frame = Frame(root) # to hold check boxes

# create check boxes and other components
mainCourseButton = Checkbutton(frame, text = 'Main course', onvalue = 1, offvalue = 0,
                                                          variable = mainCourseVariable)
dessertButton = Checkbutton(frame, text = 'Dessert', onvalue = 1, offvalue = 0,
                                                          variable = dessertVariable)
submitButton = Button(root, text = 'Place order', command = showResult)
displayLabel = Label(root)

# arrange components
mainCourseButton.pack(side ='left', padx = 5)
dessertButton.pack(side = 'left', padx = 5)
frame.pack(padx = 20, pady = (20, 5))
submitButton.pack(pady = 10)
displayLabel.pack(pady = 10)

root.mainloop() # event loop
```

The check box widgets are called Checkbuttons in Tkinter. Because each check button is going to operate independently, we have to declare two Variable objects:

```
mainCourseVariable = IntVar()
dessertVariable = IntVar()
```

As we shall see in a moment these will hold integers, which is why we have chosen IntVar. The two check buttons are created as follows:

```
mainCourseButton = Checkbutton(frame, text = 'Main course', onvalue = 1, offvalue = 0,
                                                        variable = mainCourseVariable)
dessertButton = Checkbutton(frame, text = 'Dessert', onvalue = 1, offvalue = 0,
                                                        variable = dessertVariable)
```

Three options in the initializer are of interest here: onvalue, offvalue and variable. The variable option is the one that we associate with the variable in the main body of the program (mainCourseVariable and dessertVariable for the two buttons here). It will take the value assigned to onvalue when the check button is ticked (in this case 1), and that assigned to offvalue (in this case 0) when it is not ticked.[3]

The event handler is coded to display the correct information based on the values of mainCourseVariable and dessertVariable.

```
def showResult():
    choice = 'You chose:   '
    if mainCourseVariable.get() == 0 and dessertVariable.get() == 0:
        choice = 'You did not order anything'
    else:
        if mainCourseVariable.get() == 1:
            choice = choice + 'Main'
        if dessertVariable.get() == 1:
            choice = choice + '    Dessert'
    displayLabel.configure(text = choice)
```

Now let's look at the code for the second application shown in Fig. 11.26.

---

[3] In fact, 0 and 1 are the default values for offvalue and onvalue, so we could have got away without specifying them here.

radiobuttonexample.py

```
from tkinter import Tk, Radiobutton, IntVar, Button, Frame, Label
root = Tk()
root.title('Tickets')

# event handler
def showResult():
    choice = 'You bought '
    if var.get() == 1:
        choice = choice + 'a single ticket'
    elif var.get() == 2:
        choice = choice + 'a return ticket'
    else:
        choice = 'You did not choose a ticket'
    displayLabel.configure(text = choice)

var = IntVar() # Variable object

frame = Frame(root) # to hold radio buttons

# create radio buttons and other components
singleButton = Radiobutton(frame, value = 1, text = 'Single', variable = var)
returnButton = Radiobutton(frame, value = 2, text = 'Return',  variable = var)
submitButton = Button(root, text='Buy ticket', command = showResult)
displayLabel = Label(root)

# arrange components
singleButton.pack(side ='left', padx = 5)
returnButton.pack(side = 'left', padx = 5)
frame.pack(padx = 50, pady = (20, 5))
submitButton.pack(pady = 10)
displayLabel.pack(pady = 10)

root.mainloop() # event loop
```

In this case we have declared only one `IntVar` instead of two:

```
var = IntVar()
```

This is because the buttons are going to work in unison, so the variable should have the same value for both buttons.

Look how we have created the two buttons:

```
singleButton = Radiobutton(frame, value = 1, text = 'Single', variable = var)
returnButton = Radiobutton(frame, value = 2, text = 'Return',  variable = var)
```

Instead of there being an `offvalue` and an `onvalue` as in the check button example, there is just a single variable `value`. We have assigned this a value of 1 when the 'single' button is selected, and 2 when the 'return' button is selected (the default value is 0, so when the program starts no button will be selected). This value will be assigned to our program variable, `var`, each time this value changes.

We are therefore able to define our event handler as follows:

```
def showResult():
    choice = 'You bought '
    if var.get() == 1:
        choice = choice + 'a single ticket'
    elif var.get() == 2:
        choice = choice + 'a return ticket'
    else:
        choice = 'You did not choose a ticket'
    displayLabel.configure(text = choice)
```

11.17 Themed Widgets (and Combo Boxes)

As we explained in the introduction, Tkinter supports the newer themed (ttk) widgets which are contained in the tkinter.ttk package. Up until now we have been using only the tk widgets; now we will briefly introduce you to the ttk widgets, so that you can further research them if you would like to find out more.

To demonstrate this, we will use a combo box, which is in fact available only in the tkk package, and not in the tk package.

The application we are going to create is shown in Fig. 11.27. It might not be immediately obvious that the Label widgets are very different to the ones we have been using—but ttk widgets can be themed with user-defined styles that apply to all items of that type, or just to selected ones—this is something you can explore for yourself in the future.

Here is the code:

comboboxexample.py

```python
from tkinter import ttk, Tk
from tkinter.ttk import Combobox, Label

root = Tk()
root.title('Combo example')

# the event handler
def showChoice(event):
    if box.get() == 'Choose a day':
        display.configure(text = '')
    else:
        display.configure(text = 'You chose ' + box.get())

# create a label for displaying result
display = Label(root, width = 30, background = 'light yellow', relief = 'raised', anchor = 'center')

#define a list of days of the week
days = ['Choose a day', 'Monday', 'Tuesday', 'Wednesday', 'Thursday', 'Friday', 'Saturday', 'Sunday']

# create combo box
box = Combobox(root, values = days, width = 20)

# set current value to first item
box.current(0)

# arrange items
box.pack(padx = 100, pady = (40,10))
display.pack(pady = (0, 40))

# bind the box to an event
box.bind('<<ComboboxSelected>>', showChoice)

root.mainloop() # event loop
```

Let's start by taking a look at the import statement:

```python
from tkinter import ttk, Tk
from tkinter.ttk import Combobox, Label
```

As always, we have chosen to import only those items that we are going to use. The ttk widgets mostly have the same names as their tk counterparts, and this way of doing things shows us from the start which version we are using.

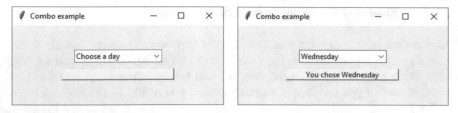

Fig. 11.27 Using a combo box

However, in many texts you will see import statements like this:

```
from tkinter import *
from tkinter import ttk
```

In this case you would need to prefix any component with `ttk` in order to specifically use the `tkk` version. For example:

```
myLabel = tkk.Label(root)
```

Another common format that you might come across is:

```
from tkinter import *
from tkinter.ttk import *
```

In this case, any `ttk` widgets such as `Button` or `Label` will automatically replace the `tk` widgets.

Take a quick look at how we created our label:

```
display = Label(root, width = 30, background = 'light yellow', relief = 'raised', anchor = 'center')
```

Most of that looks pretty familiar—except that when we chose our background colour we used the option `background`, rather than `bg`. You will sometimes find ways that `ttk` components differ from `tk` components, and this is one of them; as you might have guessed `foreground` is used instead of `fg`.

The next thing we do is to create a list, holding the various choices for the combo box:

```
days = ['Choose a day', 'Monday', 'Tuesday', 'Wednesday', 'Thursday', 'Friday', 'Saturday', 'Sunday']
```

As you can see, the first item is `'Choose a day'`—this is the text that we want to see when the application starts.

Now, when we create our combo box, we assign this list to the `values` option:

```
box = Combobox(root, values = days, width = 10)
```

The next thing we do is to set the current value to 0—the first item in the list:

```
box.current(0)
```

We want the text to appear on the display label as soon as a day of the week is selected. To do this we bind the box to a `'<<ComboBoxSelected>>'` event.

```
box.bind('<<ComboboxSelected>>', showChoice)
```

Finally, look at the way we have defined the event handler, `showChoice`:

```
def showChoice(event):
    if box.get() == 'Choose a day':
        display.configure(text = '')
    else:
        display.configure(text = 'You chose ' + box.get())
```

The current choice is retrieved by calling the `get` method of `Combo box`. We have defined the function so that if it is the first item in the list (the instruction to choose a day) that is selected, then the display label is blank. Otherwise the correct choice is displayed.

11.18   Self-test Questions

1. Briefly describe the relationship between *Tkinter* and *Tk*.
2. Describe the operation of the three layout managers (geometry managers) *pack*, *grid* and *place*.
3. Identify the widgets in the graphic below:

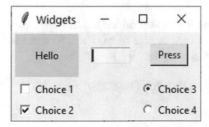

4. Consider an application that produces the following graphic:

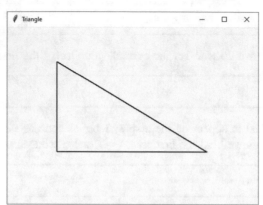

Assume that a `Canvas` object called `canvas` has been declared, and that the coordinates of the vertices are as follows:

$$(100, 70)\ (100, 250)\ (400, 250).$$

Write the line of code that will produce the hypotenuse, with a thickness of 2.

11.19 Programming Exercises

1. Implement a few of the programs that we have developed in this chapter, and experiment with different settings in order to change some the features—for example size, colour, position and so on.
2. Implement the graphic shown in self-test question 3 above.
3. Consider some changes or additions you could make to the `pushme.py` program of Sect. 11.5. For example, pushing the button could display your text in upper case—or it could say how many letters it contains. Maybe you could add some extra buttons.
4. Create an application that will produce the graphic shown in self-test question 4 above. We suggest a canvas size of 500 × 350 and the following co-ordinates for the vertices of the triangle:

$$(100, 70)\ (100, 250)\ (400, 250).$$

5. Below you see an application that produces a graphic in which two buttons can be used to change the background colour of the window:

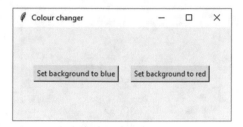

Write the code for this application.

6. Add some additional features to the `converter.py` application of Sect. 11.12. For example Celsius to Fahrenheit or litres to pints.

7. Below is a variation on the `changingface.py` application from Sect. 11.14, which has three possible moods!

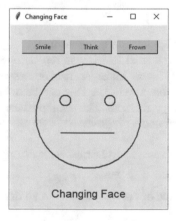

Rewrite the original code to produce this new design. You will need to use the `create_line` option described in Sect. 11.13.

8. In the application below an image is moved around the screen by means of four buttons.

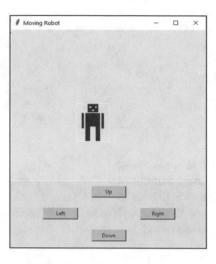

Try to create a similar application using an image of your own. In our example the image was added to a label which was repositioned each time a button was pressed, using the place layout manager. It is necessary to determine the current position of the label before moving it. This can be done by using a component's `winfo_x` and `winfo_y` methods. For example, the *x* co-ordinate of a widget called `label` can be found as follows:

$$xpos = int(label.winfo\_x())$$

Note that the return value has to be type cast to an integer, to obtain the position in pixels.

Python Case Study

12

Outcomes

By the end of this chapter you should be able to:

- *describe the activities involved the software development process;*
- ***design** an application using UML;*
- ***implement** a detailed UML design in Python;*
- *distinguish between **unit testing** and **integration testing**;*
- ***test** individual program units by creating suitable drivers;*
- *document your test results professionally using a **test log**;*
- *use pseudocode to design event-handling routines;*
- *implement a design in Tkinter using a variety of widgets;*
- *devise a testing strategy for a complete application and carry out the necessary steps to implement that strategy.*

12.1 Introduction

The process of developing software requires us to carry out several tasks. They can be summarized as follows:

- **analysis and specification**: determining what the system is required to do (analysis) and writing it down in a clear and unambiguous manner (specification);

Supplementary Information The online version contains supplementary material available at https://doi.org/10.1007/978-3-031-01326-3_12.

Q. Charatan and A. Kans, *Programming in Two Semesters*,
Texts in Computer Science, https://doi.org/10.1007/978-3-031-01326-3_12

- **design**: making decisions about how the system is to be built in order to meet the specification;
- **implementation**: turning the design into an actual program;
- **testing**: ensuring that the system has been implemented correctly to meet the original specification;
- **installation**: delivering and setting up the completed system;
- **operation and maintenance**: running the final system and reviewing it over time—in the light of changing requirements.

There was a time, some years ago, when these tasks were undertaken in order, and one task was finished before the next task was started. However, these days—helped by the advent of object-oriented development—systems tend to be developed a little bit at a time. So, for example, we can build one class and test it (maybe in the presence of the client) before moving onto the next, rather than waiting for the whole system to be developed before testing and involving the client.

In this chapter we will demonstrate this process by developing a case study that will enable you to get an idea of how a commercial system can be developed from scratch; we start with an informal description of the requirements and then specify and design the system using UML notation. From there we will go on to implement our system in Python, together with a Tkinter/tk interface. Applications such as this typically consist of many classes working together. When testing for errors, we will start with a process of **unit testing** (testing individual classes) followed by **integration testing** (testing the system as a whole, or testing two or more interdependent classes).

The system that we are going to develop will keep records of the residents of a student hostel. In order not to cloud your understanding, we have simplified things, keeping details of individuals to a minimum, and keeping the functionality fairly basic; you will have the opportunity to improve on what we have done in the practical exercises at the end of the chapter.

12.2   The Requirements Specification

The local university requires a program to manage one of its student hostels, which contains a number of rooms, each of which can be occupied by a single tenant who pays rent on a monthly basis. The program must keep a list of tenants and their monthly payments. The information held for each tenant will consist of a name, a room number and a list of all the payments a tenant has made (month and amount). The program must allow the user to add and delete tenants, to display a list of all tenants, to record a payment for a particular tenant, and to display the payment history of a tenant.

12.3 The Design

The two core classes required in this application are Tenant (to store the details of a tenant) and Payment (to store the details of a payment). We have made a number of design decisions about how the system will be implemented, and these are listed below:

- instances of the Tenant class and instances of the Payment class will each be held in separate classes, PaymentList and TenantList, respectively;
- the classes PaymentList and TenantList both store the items as lists. We could have used a dictionary in the TenantList class (as we did with our bank application in Chap. 8), and if you would like to try this alternative implementation, we have given you some hints in the end of chapter exercises.

In Chap. 11 we showed you how we could build a graphical user interface (GUI) to access and process a particular class. In that case it was the Rectangle class. We are going to do the same thing here, but on a much grander scale. The reason we have created the TenantList class above is to ensure that all the processing of the tenants can be contained within this class and kept away from the GUI, which acts purely as an interface; thus, if we wanted to change the GUI completely, it would be a simple matter to do so. Our GUI will process the TenantList class, which in turn connects to the other classes.

The class structure is shown in Fig. 12.1—it contains some new notation. There is an arrow from one class to another (Tenant to PaymentList). In UML this represents an **association**. An association is a link from objects of one class to objects of another class. For example, a *customer* might have one or more *accounts*; a *student* might have one or more *tutors*. The simplest form of association is a one-to-one relationship whereby a single instance of one class is associated with a single instance of another class—for example a *purchase transaction* and an *invoice*.

In our example, the association represented by the arrow is a one-to-one association—a Tenant requires a single instance of a PaymentList.

When one object itself consists of other objects, this relationship is called **aggregation**. This is a special type of association and is represented in UML by a diamond; it is often referred to as an *is-a-part-of* relationship. For example, the association between a car and the passengers in the car is aggregation. **Composition** (represented by a filled diamond) is a special, stronger, form of aggregation whereby the "whole" is actually dependent on the "part". For example, the association between a car and its engine is one of *composition*, as a car cannot exist without an engine. The TenantList class and the PaymentList both implement the aggregation relationship. The asterisk at the other end of the joining line indicates that the containing object contains *zero or more* of the contained objects.

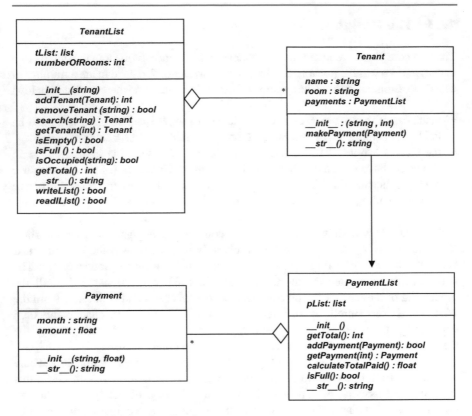

Fig. 12.1 Design of the student hostel system

The graphical interface, which will form the hostel application itself, has not yet been designed, and this will be left until later in the chapter, when we consider the overall system design and testing. However, we have given you a look ahead in Fig. 12.2, so you can see what we are aiming at:

In order to implement this application we should start with those classes that do not depend on any other, so that they can be unit tested in isolation. For example, we should not start by implementing the `Tenant` class as it requires the `Pay-mentList` class to be implemented first. You can see from the associations in Fig. 12.1 that the only class that does not require any other class for its implementation is the `Payment` class.

Fig. 12.2 *Hostel* GUI

12.4   Implementing the *Payment* Class

We are going to keep all our classes for this application in a module called
`hostelclasses.py`. The code for the `Payment` class is shown below.

Payment

```
# class to hold details of payment
class Payment:
    # the initializer
    def __init__(self, monthIn, amountIn):
        self.month = monthIn
        self.amount = amountIn

    # returns a convenient string for testing purposes
    def __str__(self):
        return('Month: %s, Amount: %0.2f' %(self.month, self.amount))
```

As you can see, this class is fairly simple and does not require much explanation. Note that we have defined a __str__ method to provide a convenient way of printing a Payment object (as discussed in Chap. 8):

```
def __str__(self):
    return('Month: %s, Amount: %0.2f' %(self.month, self.amount))
```

Before incorporating this class into a larger program you would need to test it to see if it was working reliably. Eventually, when this class is incorporated into the final program, we will have a Tkinter application to run the program, but we need to test this class before an entire suite of classes has been developed. As we indicated before, testing an individual class in this way is often referred to as *unit testing*.

In order to unit test this class we will need to implement a separate class especially for this purpose. This new class will act as a **driver** for the original class. A driver is a special program designed to do nothing except exercise a particular class. If you look back at the examples in Chaps. 8 and 9, this is exactly how we tested individual classes. Initially you should generate an object from the given class. Once an object has been generated, we can then test that object by calling its methods. In the case of the Payment class, there are no methods apart from __init__ and __str__, so we can simply use these two methods to test the class:

paymenttester.py

```
from hostelclasses import Payment

p1 = Payment('April', 550.00) # creates a new payment with __init__
print(p1) # uses the __str__ method
```

Running this program will produce the following result:

```
Month: April, Amount: 550.00
```

You can see the Payment object is displayed in the format given in our __str__ method. From this simple example, you can see just how useful this method is.

Now let's move on to the more interesting parts of this system. This system requires us to develop two kinds of list, a PaymentList and a TenantList. A TenantList requires a PaymentList class to be developed first, so let's start by looking at this PaymentList class.

12.5 Implementing the *PaymentList* Class

Figure 12.3 provides a reminder of the design of the PaymentList class.

As you can see, as well as an initializer, there are methods to add a new payment to the list and to count the total number of payments made so far. There is also a method to get a payment based on a position number. Finally, once again we have included a __str__ method for ease of testing. Take a look at the code for the PaymentList class below before we discuss it.

PaymentList

```python
#class to hold a list of payments
class PaymentList:
    # the initializer
    def __init__(self):
        self.pList = []

    # gets the total number of payments
    def getTotal(self):
        return len(self.pList)

    # adds a new payment to the end of the list
    def addPayment(self, paymentIn):
        self.pList.append(paymentIn)

    # reads the payment at the given logical (natural) position in the list
    def getPayment(self, positionIn):
        # check for valid logical position
        if positionIn < 1 or positionIn > self.getTotal():
            # no object found at given position
            return None
        else:
            # take one off logical position to get position in list
            return self.pList[positionIn - 1]

    # calculates the total payments made by the tenant
    def calculateTotalPaid(self):
        totalPaid = 0.0 # initialize totalPaid
        # loop through all payments
        for item in self.pList:
            totalPaid = totalPaid + item.amount
        return totalPaid

    # returns a convenient string for testing purposes
    def __str__(self):
        outputString = ''
        for item in self.pList:
            outputString = outputString + item.__str__() + '\n'
        return outputString
```

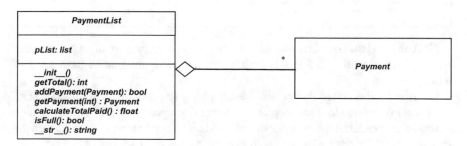

Fig. 12.3 Design of the PaymentList collection class

First of all, we should point out that we are keeping all our classes in one module, so we do not need to begin by importing `Payment`, even though the `PaymentList` class uses it.

The initializer creates an attribute `pList`, which is initialized to an empty list:

```
def __init__(self):
    self.pList = []
```

Now let's take a look at the remaining methods of this class. First the `get-Total` method:

```
def getTotal(self):
    return len(self.pList)
```

This method returns the total number of `Payments` currently in the list, by making use of the built-in `len` function.

Next, the `addPayment` method: a new payment is sent in as a parameter and is added to the list by making use of the `append` method of `list`:

```
def addPayment(self, paymentIn):
    self.pList.append(paymentIn)
```

The `getPayment` method makes use of `getTotal` to check that the validity of the parameter `positionIn`. The `positionIn` parameter is the logical position (i.e. the 'natural' position) of a payment in the list, which should be a number between 1 and the total number of items in the list. If an invalid position is sent a value of **None** is returned, otherwise the payment at the correct position is returned:

```
def getPayment(self, positionIn):
    # check for valid logical position
    if positionIn < 1 or positionIn > self.getTotal():
        # no object found at given position
        return None
    else:
        # take one off logical position to get position in list
        return self.pList[positionIn - 1]
```

Next, the `calculateTotalPaid` method computes the sum of all payments in the list. This method uses a standard algorithm for computing sums from a list of items.

In order to understand this better, we are going to introduce a common design tool called **pseudocode**. Pseudocode is a general purpose coding language which allows us to sketch out the code for our methods, without having to worry about the finer details of the particular language (e.g. using the right sort of brackets).

Pseudocode instructions are not, of course, intended to be typed in and compiled as they do not meet the syntax rules of any particular programming language. So, exactly how you write these instructions is up to you: there is no fixed syntax for them. However, each instruction conveys a well-understood programming concept and can easily be translated into a given programming language. When you read these instructions, you should be able to see how each line would be coded in Python.

```
SET totalPaid TO 0
LOOP FROM first item in list TO last item in list
    SET totalPaid TO totalPaid + amount of current payment
return totalPaid
```

It's now an easy matter to convert this to Python code:

```
def calculateTotalPaid(self):
    totalPaid = 0.0 # initialize totalPaid
    # loop through all payments
    for item in self.pList:
        totalPaid = totalPaid + item.amount
    return totalPaid
```

In this case the algorithm for calculating the total amount paid was fairly simple, and we could probably have got away fairly easily without first writing the method in pseudocode; however, in the more complex examples that follow, you will see that pseudocode is an invaluable help to us when it comes to algorithm design.

Finally, we have again written a __str__ method to allow the payment list to be displayed as a single string:

```
def __str__(self):
    outputString = ''
    for item in self.pList:
        outputString = outputString + item.__str__() + '\n'
    return outputString
```

12.6 Testing the *PaymentList* Class

As we have said before, it is always important to test classes in order to ensure that they are functioning correctly before moving on to the rest of the development. However the testing of the Payment class was an example of *unit testing*, whereas testing this PaymentList class is an example of *integration testing* as it requires the PaymentList class working in conjunction with the Payment class.

To test the `PaymentList` class, we need a driver that not only creates a `PaymentList` object, but also creates payments to add to this list.

We have quite a few methods to test in our `PaymentList` class, so we need to spend some time considering how we will go about testing these methods. Here is one possible testing strategy:

1. create a `PaymentList` object;
2. add two payments to this list, say ("Jan", 310) and ("Feb", 280) using the `addPayment` method;
3. display the list (implicitly calling the __ `str` __ method) to check the items have been added successfully;
4. add two more payments to this list, say ("March", 310) and ("April", 300) using the `addPayment` method;
5. display the list to check the items have been added successfully;
6. get details of one of the payments made (say the second payment) using the `getPayment` method.
7. attempt to retrieve a payment at an invalid position (say 5);
8. display the total number of payments made so far (using the `getTotal` method);
9. display the total of the payments made so far (using the `calculateTotalPaid` method).

Notice that the test strategy should ensure that all methods of the class are tested and all possible routes through a method are tested. So, for example, as well as ensuring that the `isFull` method is called, we provide a scenario where the method should return **True** and provide a scenario where the method should return **False**.

Once a strategy is chosen, the test results should be logged in a **test log**. A test log is a document that records the testing that took place during system development. Each row of the test log associates an *input* with an *expected output*. If the output is not as expected, reasons for this error have to be identified and recorded in the log.

Figure 12.4 illustrates a suitable test log to document the testing strategy we developed above.

Test logs such as this should be devised *before* the driver itself (and may even be developed before the class we are testing has been developed). The test log can then be used to prompt the development of the driver. As you can see by looking at the test in Fig. 12.4, we assume that the driver is a menu-driven program.

The `paymentlisttester.py` program below is one possible driver we could develop in order to process the actions given in this test log:

TEST LOG			
Purpose: To test the PaymentList class			
Run Number:	**Date:**		
Action	**Expected Output**	**Pass/ Fail**	**Reason for failure**
-	Display menu of options		
Select ADD option	Prompt for Payment details		
Enter "Jan", 310	Display menu of options		
Select ADD option	Prompt for Payment to add		
Enter "Feb", 280	Display menu of options		

Select DISPLAY option	Message:
	
	`Month: Jan, Amount: 310.00`
	`Month: Feb, Amount: 280.00`
	
	Display menu of options		

Select ADD option	Prompt for Payment to add		
Enter "March", 310	Display menu of options		
Select ADD option	Prompt for Payment to add		
Enter "April", 300	Display menu of options		

Select DISPLAY option	Message:
	
	`Month: Jan, Amount: 310.00`
	`Month: Feb, Amount: 280.00`
	`Month: Mar, Amount: 310.00`
	`Month: Apr, Amount: 300.00`
	
	Display menu of options		

Select GET PAYMENT option	Prompt for position to retrieve		
Enter 2	Message: `Month: Feb, Amount: 280.00` Display menu of options		
Select GET PAYMENT option	Prompt for position to retrieve		
Enter 5	Message: `INVALID PAYMENT NUMBER` Display menu of options		
Select GET TOTAL option	Message: `4` Display menu of options		
Select CALCULATE TOTAL PAID option	Message: `1200.0` Display menu of options		
Select EXIT option	Program terminates		

Fig. 12.4 Test log for the *PaymentList* class

paymentlisttester.py

```python
from hostelclasses import Payment, PaymentList

# ADD
def option1(listIn):
    # prompt for payment details
    month = input('Enter month: ')
    amount = float(input('Enter amount: '))
    # create new Payment object from input
    p = Payment(month, amount)
    # add payment to list
    listIn.addPayment(p) # value of false sent back if unable to add

# DISPLAY
def option2(listIn):
    print('ITEMS ENTERED')
    print(listIn) # calls __str__1 method of PaymentList


# GET PAYMENT
def option3(listIn):
    # prompt for and receive payment number
    num = int(input('Enter payment number to retrieve: '))
    # retrieve Payment object form list
    p = listIn.getPayment(num) # returns null if invalid position
    if p != None: # check if Payment retrieved
        print(p) # calls toString method of Payment
    else:
        print('INVALID PAYMENT NUMBER') # invalid position error

# GET TOTAL
def option4(listIn):
    print('TOTAL NUMBER OF PAYMENTS ENTERED: ')
    print(listIn.getTotal())


# GET TOTAL PAID
def option5(listIn):
    print('TOTAL OF PAYMENTS MADE SO FAR: ')
    print(listIn.calculateTotalPaid())


# main body

choice = ''
list = PaymentList() # create object to test
while choice != '6':      # menu
            # display options
            print()
            print('[1] ADD')
            print('[2] DISPLAY')
            print('[3] GET PAYMENT')
            print('[4] GET TOTAL')
            print('[5] CALCULATE TOTAL PAID')
            print('[6] Quit')
            print()

            # get choice
            choice = input('Enter a choice [1-6]: ')

            # process choice
            if choice == '1':
                option1(list)
            elif choice == '2':
                option2(list)
            elif choice == '3':
                option3(list)
            elif choice == '4':
                option4(list)
            elif choice == '5':
                option5(list)
            elif choice == '6':
                print('TESTING COMPLETE')
            else:
                print('1-6 only')
```

We are now in a position to run the driver and check the actions documented in the test log:

```
[1] ADD
[2] DISPLAY
[3] GET PAYMENT
[4] GET TOTAL
[5] CALCULATE TOTAL PAID
[6] Quit

Enter a choice [1-6]: 1
Enter month: Jan
Enter amount: 310

[1] ADD
[2] DISPLAY
[3] GET PAYMENT
[4] GET TOTAL
[5] CALCULATE TOTAL PAID
[6] Quit

Enter a choice [1-6]: 1
Enter month: Feb
Enter amount: 280

[1] ADD
[2] DISPLAY
[3] GET PAYMENT
[4] GET TOTAL
[5] CALCULATE TOTAL PAID
[6] Quit

Enter a choice [1-6]: 2
ITEMS ENTERED
Month: Jan, Amount: 310.00
Month: Feb, Amount: 280.00


[1] ADD
[2] DISPLAY
[3] GET PAYMENT
[4] GET TOTAL
[5] CALCULATE TOTAL PAID
[6] Quit

Enter a choice [1-6]: 1
Enter month: Mar
Enter amount: 310

[1] ADD
[2] DISPLAY
[3] GET PAYMENT
[4] GET TOTAL
[5] CALCULATE TOTAL PAID
[6] Quit
```

```
Enter a choice [1-6]: 1
Enter month: Apr
Enter amount: 300

[1] ADD
[2] DISPLAY
[3] GET PAYMENT
[4] GET TOTAL
[5] CALCULATE TOTAL PAID
[6] Quit

Enter a choice [1-6]: 2
ITEMS ENTERED
Month: Jan, Amount: 310.00
Month: Feb, Amount: 280.00
Month: Mar, Amount: 310.00
Month: Apr, Amount: 300.00


[1] ADD
[2] DISPLAY
[3] GET PAYMENT
[4] GET TOTAL
[5] CALCULATE TOTAL PAID
[6] Quit

Enter a choice [1-6]: 3
Enter payment number to retrieve: 2
Month: Feb, Amount: 280.00

[1] ADD
[2] DISPLAY
[3] GET PAYMENT
[4] GET TOTAL
[5] CALCULATE TOTAL PAID
[6] Quit

Enter a choice [1-6]: 3
Enter payment number to retrieve: 5
INVALID PAYMENT NUMBER

[1] ADD
[2] DISPLAY
[3] GET PAYMENT
[4] GET TOTAL
[5] CALCULATE TOTAL PAID
[6] Quit

Enter a choice [1-6]: 4
TOTAL NUMBER OF PAYMENTS ENTERED:
4

[1] ADD
[2] DISPLAY
[3] GET PAYMENT
[4] GET TOTAL
[5] CALCULATE TOTAL PAID
[6] Quit
```

```
Enter a choice [1-6]: 5
TOTAL OF PAYMENTS MADE SO FAR:
1200.0

[1] ADD
[2] DISPLAY
[3] GET PAYMENT
[4] GET TOTAL
[5] CALCULATE TOTAL PAID
[6] Quit

Enter a choice [1-6]: 6
TESTING COMPLETE
```

You have seen menu-driven tester programs such as this before so we will not discuss it in any detail. But do notice how the display method of our `pay-mentlisttester` (option 2 on the menu) displays the `PaymentList` object using the ___ `str` ___ method we discussed earlier:

```
def option2(listIn):
    print('ITEMS ENTERED')
    print(listIn) # calls __str__ method of PaymentList
```

If unexpected results are produced during testing, you should stop and identify the cause of the error in the class that you are testing. Both the cause of the error and how the error was fixed should be documented in the test log. The driver can then be run again with a fresh test log, and this process should continue until *all* results are delivered as predicted. In this case, however, the results were as expected, so we can now move on to developing the rest of our system. We have two more classes to look at: T enant and `TenantList`. Before we look at the `TenantList` class, we need to implement the `Tenant` class.

12.7 Implementing the *Tenant* Class

As you can see from the UML diagram of Fig. 12.1, the `Tenant` class contains three attributes:

- `name`;
- `room`;
- `payments`.

The first two of these represent the name and the room of the tenant, respectively. The third attribute, `payments`, is to be implemented as a `PaymentList` object.

Below is the code for the `Tenant` class.

Tenant

```
# class used to record the details of a tenant
class Tenant:

    # initializer
    def __init__(self, nameIn, roomIn):
        self.name = nameIn
        self.room = roomIn
        self.payments = PaymentList()

    # records a payment for the tenant
    def makePayment(self, paymentIn):
        self.payments.addPayment(paymentIn) # call method of PaymentList

    # returns a convenient string for testing purposes
    def __str__(self):
        return self.name + ', ' + str(self.room) + '\n' + self.payments.__str__()
```

The comments should be sufficient documentation for you to follow the code in this class. Also, it is worth noting that the payments attribute, being of type PaymentList, can respond to any of the PaymentList methods we discussed in Sect. 12.5. The makePayment method illustrates this by calling the addPayment method of PaymentList:

```
def makePayment(self, paymentIn):
    self.payments.addPayment(paymentIn) # call method of PaymentList
```

We will leave the testing of this class and the next TenantList class as exercises for you as end of chapter programming exercises.

12.8   Implementing the *TenantList* Class

As we explained in Sect. 12.3, the TenantList class will contain all the methods necessary for processing, such as adding and removing tenants, making payments and so on. It will also contain methods for reading and writing the records to file. The TenantList class will hold our Tenant objects in the form of a list; it will also have a numberOfRooms attribute to fix the number of tenants our hostel can accommodate. A reminder of the design of the TenantList class is shown in Fig. 12.5:

Most of the methods of the TenantList class should be familiar to you from the PaymentList collection classes that we discussed earlier. We will just take a closer look at the methods that were not mirrored in the PaymentList class. Let's start with the search method. Here is a reminder of its UML interface:

search (string): Tenant

The parameter represents the room number of the tenant that this method is searching for. We will allow string values for this, so that rooms can have names such as 1a or 2b and so on. The tenant returned is the tenant living in that particular room; if no tenant is found in that room, then **None** is returned. Here is a suitable algorithm for finding a tenant, expressed in pseudocode:

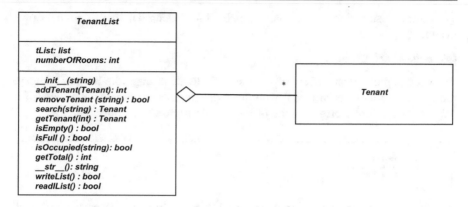

Fig. 12.5 Design of the TenantList collection class

```
LOOP FROM first tenant in list TO last tenant in list
    IF current tenant's room number = room to locate
        return current tenant
return None
```

Here is the code:

```
def search(self, roomIn):
    for item in self.tList:
        # find tenant with given room number
        if item.room == roomIn:
            return item
    return None # no tenant found with given room number
```

Now let's look at the removeTenant method. The UML interface for this method is as follows:

removeTenant(string): bool

Here the parameter represents the room number of the tenant that is to be removed from the list and the **bool** return value indicates whether or not such a tenant has been removed successfully.

The previous search method can be used here to determine if a tenant exists in that particular room (a value of **None** will be returned if no such tenant exists). If such a tenant does exist, it can be removed from the list using the remove method of list and a **bool** value of **True** can be returned, otherwise a value of **False** can be returned. Here is the code:

```
def removeTenant(self, roomIn):
    findT = self.search(roomIn) # call search method
    if (findT != None): # check tenant is found at given room
        self.tList.remove(findT) # remove given tenant
        return True
    else:
        return False # no tenant in given room
```

We have also included a convenient method for testing whether or not a room is occupied:

isOccupied(string): bool

The code is pretty straightforward—we simply iterate through the list and compare the room number of each tenant with the room number we are checking, and if it matches, we return **True**. If none of the items matches, we return **False**:

```
def isOccupied(self, roomNo):
    for item in self.tList:
        if item.room == roomNo
            return True
    return False
```

The final two methods are concerned with reading and writing the records to a file for permanent storage. Let's look first at the method for writing the file:

writeList(): bool

This is another example of when it would be very useful to design our method using pseudocode. As you read the pseudocode, bear in mind that the method will receive as an argument the current list of tenants which it will write to file.

```
OPEN file for writing
WRITE the number of rooms as first entry
LOOP FROM first tenant in list TO last tenant in list
    WRITE name
    WRITE room
    WRITE total number of payments
    LOOP FROM first payment in list TO last payment in list
        WRITE month
        WRITE amount
CLOSE file
IF operation successful
    RETURN True
ELSE
    RETURN False
```

As you can see, we start off by writing the total number of rooms in the property. After this we loop through the tenants, writing their name and room number, and then for each tenant we record the total number of payments made (which will be very useful information when it comes to reading the file), and then loop through the payments for that tenant, writing the month and the amount.

Here is the code:

```
def writeList(tenantListIn):
    try:
        f = open('tenants.txt', 'w') # open the file in write mode
        f.write(str(tenantListIn.numberOfRooms) + '\n') # write the number of rooms as the first entry
        # write the record of each tenant
        for i in range(1, tenantListIn.getTotal() + 1):
            f.write(tenantListIn.getTenant(i).name + '\n')
            f.write(tenantListIn.getTenant(i).room + '\n')
            f.write(str(tenantListIn.getTenant(i).payments.getTotal()) + '\n')
            # write the record of each payment
            for j in range(1, tenantListIn.getTenant(i).payments.getTotal() + 1):
                f.write(tenantListIn.getTenant(i).payments.getPayment(j).month + '\n')
                f.write(str(tenantListIn.getTenant(i).payments.getPayment(j).amount) + '\n')
        f.close() # close the file
        return True
    except:
        return False
```

As you saw in Chap. 10, the entire code for processing the file is placed in a **try** block—if everything is successful, the function returns **True**. If anything goes wrong with the process of writing the file, an exception occurs and a value of **False** is returned. We have already seen how the return value is used in the program.

Now for the method that reads the file:

readList(): bool

Let's begin once again with pseudocode. As you read the pseudocode, bear in mind that the method will receive as an argument a list of tenants which initially will be empty and which it will fill with the records that it reads from the file.

```
OPEN file for reading
READ the number of rooms
SET number of rooms attribute in the tenant list
READ the first name in list (read ahead)
LOOP until no more records
    READ the room number
    CREATE an empty payment list for that tenant
    READ the total number of payments
    LOOP through payments
        READ month
        READ amount
        CREATE payment
        ADD payment to payment list
    CREATE tenant using name and room number
    SET tenant's payment record to payment list
    READ next name
CLOSE file
IF operation successful
    RETURN True
ELSE
    RETURN False
```

As you will recall from the `writeList` method, the first item that was written was the number of rooms in the hostel. So this is the first item that is read and recorded in the tenant list.

After this we use the technique of reading ahead that you learnt about in Chap. 10: the name of the first tenant is read—if this is not blank, we enter a loop and continue until the name field is blank. In the loop we continue by reading the room of the tenant. We then create an empty payments list to receive the payments data that we are about to retrieve. You will remember that the total number of payments was written to the file at this point, so we now read this piece of information, which we can use to set the number of iterations of a loop that will retrieve all the payments from the file. Each time the month and amount are read, a new payment is created, and this is added to the payment list. Once this is completed, we create a new tenant and add the payment list to it. This tenant is then added to the tenant list, and the next name is read.

```python
def readList(tenantListIn):
    try:
        f = open('tenants.txt', 'r') # open the file in read mode
        maxNumberOfRooms = int(f.readline()) # read the number of rooms
        tenantListIn.numberOfRooms = maxNumberOfRooms # set number of rooms to amount read
        name = f.readline() # read ahead
        # loop though the records till an empty field is reached
        while(name != ''):
            room = f.readline() # read room number
            paymentsRead = PaymentList() # create a PaymentList object
            numberOfPayments = int(f.readline()) # read total number of payments
            # loop though the payment records
            for i in range(numberOfPayments):
                month = f.readline() # read month
                amount = f.readline() # read amount
                p = Payment(month.strip(), float(amount)) # create payment
                paymentsRead.addPayment(p) # add payment to list of payments
            t = Tenant(name.strip(), room.strip()) # create tenant
            t.payments = paymentsRead # set tenants' payments record
            tenantListIn.addTenant(t) # add tenant to list
            name = f.readline() # read name of next tenant (routine will terminate if blank)
        f.close() # close the file
        return True
    except:
        return False
```

Once again a **try ... except** construct is used to handle any exceptions that might occur—in this case the most likely cause would be that the file does not exist as the application is being run for the first time. You'll see how we handle this scenario in a moment.

The complete code for the TenantList class is now presented below. The comments provided, together with the above method descriptions, should now provide sufficient explanation of each part of this class.

TenantList

```python
# class to hold a list of tenants
class TenantList:
    # the initializer
    def __init__(self, numberOfRoomsIn):
        self.tList = []
        self.numberOfRooms = numberOfRoomsIn

    # adds a new Tenant to the list
    def addTenant(self, tIn):
        if self.isFull():
            return 1  # 1 indicates hostel is full
        elif self.isOccupied(tIn.room):
            return 2  # 2 indicates room is already occupied
        else:
            self.tList.append(tIn)
            return 0 # 0 indicates tenant successfully added

    # removes the tenant in the given room number
    def removeTenant(self, roomIn):
        findT = self.search(roomIn) # call search method
        if (findT != None): # check tenant is found at given room
            self.tList.remove(findT) # remove given tenant
            return True
        else:
            return False # no tenant in given room

    # searches for the tenant in the given room number
    def search(self, roomIn):
        for item in self.tList:
            # find tenant with given room number
            if item.room == roomIn:
                return item
        return None # no tenant found with given room number

    # reads the tenant at the given position in the list
    def getTenant(self, positionIn):
        if positionIn<1 or positionIn>self.getTotal(): # check for valid position
            return None # no object found at given position
        else:
            # remove one from logical position to get list position
            return self.tList[positionIn -1]

    # reports on whether or not the list is empty
    def isEmpty(self):
        return self.tList.size == 0

    # reports on whether or not the list is full
    def isFull(self):
        return len(self.tList) == self.numberOfRooms

    # reports on whether a particular room is occupied
    def isOccupied(self, roomNo):
        for item in self.tList:
            if item.room == roomNo:
                    return True
        return False

    # gets the total number of tenants
    def getTotal(self):
```

```
        return len(self.tList)

# returns a convenient string for testing purposes
def __str__(self):
    out = ''
    for item in self.tList:
        out = out + item.__str__() + '\n'
    return out

# writes the records to file
def writeList(self):
    try:
        f = open('tenants.txt', 'w') # open the file in write mode
        f.write(str(self.numberOfRooms) + '\n') # write the number of rooms as the first entry
        # write the record of each tenant
        for i in range(1, self.getTotal() + 1):
            f.write(self.getTenant(i).name + '\n')
            f.write(self.getTenant(i).room + '\n')
            f.write(str(self.getTenant(i).payments.getTotal()) + '\n')
            # write the record of each payment
            for j in range(1, self.getTenant(i).payments.getTotal() + 1):
                f.write(self.getTenant(i).payments.getPayment(j).month + '\n')
                f.write(str(self.getTenant(i).payments.getPayment(j).amount) + '\n')
        f.close() # close the file
        return True
    except:
        return False

# reads the records from file
def readList(self):
    try:
        f = open('tenants.txt', 'r') # open the file in read mode
        maxNumberOfRooms = int(f.readline()) # read the number of rooms
        self.numberOfRooms = maxNumberOfRooms # set number of rooms to amount read
        name = f.readline() # read ahead
        # loop though the records till an empty field is reached
        while(name != ''):
            room = f.readline() # read room number
            paymentsRead = PaymentList() # create a PaymentList object
            numberOfPayments = int(f.readline()) # read total number of payments
            # loop though the payment records
            for i in range(numberOfPayments):
                month = f.readline() # read month
                amount = f.readline() # read amount
                p = Payment(month.strip(), float(amount)) # create payment
                paymentsRead.addPayment(p) # add payment to list of payments
            t = Tenant(name.strip(), room.strip()) # create tenant
            t.payments = paymentsRead # set tenants' payments record
            self.addTenant(t) # add tenant to list
            name = f.readline() # read name of next tenant (routine will terminate if blank)
        f.close() # close the file
        return True
    except:
        return False
```

All that remains for us to do to complete our case study is to design, implement and test the GUI which will not only keep track of the tenants but will also act as the graphical user interface for the system.

The remaining code within this class will relate to the GUI for this application, so let's consider the design of the GUI now.

12.9   Design of the GUI

There will be two aspects to the design of the graphical interface. Firstly, we need to design the visual side of things; then we need to design the algorithms for our event-handling routines so that the buttons do the jobs we want them to, like adding or displaying tenants.

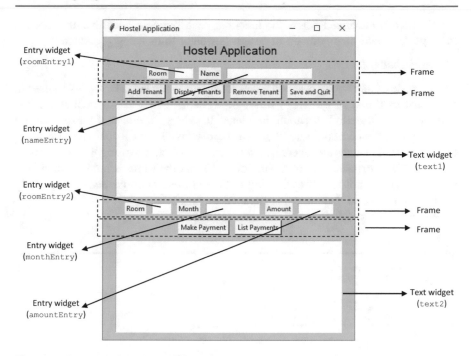

Fig. 12.6 Structure of the hostel GUI

Let's start with the visual design. We need to choose which graphics components we are going to use and how to lay them out. You have seen the overall result
in Fig. 12.2. In Fig. 12.6 we show you how we have built our graphic.

As you can see we have created four `Frames`, each of which holds a number of
components arranged side by side—we have used a simple pack manager for this.
The `Frames`, together with two `Text` widgets, are arranged vertically, again using
the pack manager.

12.10   Designing the Event-Handlers

As you saw in Fig. 12.6, there are six buttons that need to be bound to events in
order that they respond in the correct way when pressed:

- the "Add Tenant" button;
- the "Display Tenants" button;
- the "Remove Tenant" button;
- the "Save and Quit" button;
- the "Make Payment" button;
- the "List Payments" button.

We have summarized below the task that each button's event-handler method must perform and then gone on to design our algorithms using pseudocode:

The Add Tenant button

The purpose of this button is to add a new `Tenant` to the list. The values entered in `roomEntry1` and `nameEntry` must be validated; first of all neither `room-Entry1` nor `nameEntry` should be blank. If values for either of these have not been entered, then a pop-up message will be displayed (you'll see how to achieve this later). If the values are entered, however, we must check (using the return value of the `addTenant` method of `TenantList`) that the room is not occupied, and that the hostel is not full. If everything is ok and the tenant has been successfully added, a message to that effect is displayed in `text1`.

We can express this in pseudocode as follows:

```
IF roomEntry1 is blank or nameEntry is blank
    display pop-up error message
ELSE
    attempt to add tenant
    IF unsuccessful because hostel is full
        display 'Hostel is full' message in text1
    ELSE IF unsuccessful because room is already occupied
        display 'Room is already occupied' message in text1
    ELSE
        display 'Tenant added' message in text1
        blank roomEntry1 and nameEntry
```

The Display Tenants button

Pressing this button will display the full list of tenants (room number and name) in `text1`.

If all the rooms are vacant, a suitable message should be displayed; otherwise the list of tenants' rooms and names should appear under appropriate headings as can be seen in Fig. 12.2. This can be expressed in pseudocode as follows:

```
IF all rooms are unoccupied
        display 'Hostel is empty' message in text1
ELSE
    display header in text1
    LOOP FROM first item TO last item in list
        display tenant room and name in text1
```

The Remove Tenant button

Clicking on this button will remove the tenant whose room number has been entered in `roomEntry1`.

As with the *Add Tenant* button, the room number must be entered—if it is not, a pop-up message appears. Once a room number is entered, an attempt is made to remove the tenant (using the `remove` method of `TenantList`); if it fails because there is no tenant in that room, a message is displayed in `text1`. Otherwise, a confirmation message is displayed. The pseudocode for this event-handler is given as follows:

```
read roomEntry1
IF roomEntry1 is blank
   display pop-up error message
ELSE
   attempt to remove tenant from list
   IF unsuccessful
      display 'Room empty' message in text1
   ELSE
      display 'Tenant removed' message in text1
      blank roomEntry1
```

The Make Payment button

This button records payments made by an individual tenant whose room number is entered in `roomEntry2`. The values entered in `roomEntry2`, `monthEntry` and `amountEntry` must be validated as before, and if everything is okay, then a new payment record is added to that tenant's list of payments (using the `makePayment` method of `PaymentList`) and a confirmation message is displayed in `text2`. This design is expressed in pseudocode as follows:

```
read roomEntry2
IF amountEntry is not a floating point number
   display pop-up error message
ELSE
   read amountEntry
   IF roomEntry2 is blank or monthEntry is blank
      display pop-up error message
   ELSE
      search for tenant in given room
      IF no tenant is in that room
         display 'Room is empty' message in text2
      ELSE
         make payment
         display 'Payment made' message in text2
         blank roomEntry2, monthEntry and amountEntry
```

The *List Payments button*

Pressing this button causes a list of payments (month and amount) made by the tenant whose room number is entered in `roomField2` to be displayed in `displayArea2`.

After validating the values entered, each record in the tenant's payment list is displayed. Finally, the total amount paid by that tenant is displayed (we will make use of the `calculateTotalPaid` method of `PaymentList` to do this). The pseudocode is given as follows:

```
read roomEntry2
IF amountEntry is not a floating point number
    display pop-up error message
ELSE
    read amountEntry
    IF roomEntry2 is blank or monthEntry is blank
        display pop-up error message
    ELSE
        search for tenant in given room
        IF no tenant is in that room
            display 'Room is empty' message in text2
        ELSE
            make payment
            display 'Payment made' message in text2
            blank roomEntry2, monthEntry and amountEntry
```

The *Save and Quit button*

Pressing this button causes all the records to be saved to a file (it makes use of the writeFile function of TenantList). It then closes the application.

12.11   Implementing the *Hostelapplication* Program

The complete code for the hostelapplication program now appears below. Study the code and the comments carefully to make sure you understand it—in particular compare the event-handling code to the pseudocode we presented in the previous section. Notice that if any required entry field is left blank, we have made the notification appear in a pop-up dialogue (you will see how to implement this in a moment). Notice also, that if an amount of money is not entered as a floating-point number, we have used a **try . . . except** construct to flag this up as an error (again in a pop-up dialogue).

The other issue that we need to draw your attention to is our strategy for keeping permanent records of our data, for which purpose we will use the file-handling methods we developed in the TenantList class. Our strategy is that all the data will be stored to file when the program is terminated with the 'Save and quit' button —the entire contents of the file will be replaced with the current data. When the application starts, all the data will be read into memory. We are aware that this might not be the most efficient or even the most fail-safe way of storing data (e.g. what happens if the program crashes before it is closed properly?)—but it is the simplest way to do it here. You will have the opportunity to adapt this in the end of chapter exercises.

There are two issues that arise with the above strategy that we need to address. Firstly, we might want to abandon the edits we make during a particular run and not save them to file. For this purpose we have organised it so that the close button on the window (the cross-hairs in the case of Windows™, or the red button in the case of macOS™) will close the application without writing the data to file—a pop-up message will warn the user that changes will be lost.

The second issue is that the first time the program is run, there will be no file present—we don't want this to be flagged as an error, but instead we need the user to be made aware of this fact, and also to enter how many rooms there are in the hostel (this information will subsequently be recorded when the data is stored).

We will explain how we have implemented this once you have looked at the entire code below:

---

hostelapplication.py

```python
# import classes from tkinter
from tkinter import Tk, Frame, Entry, Button, Label, Text, messagebox, simpledialog, sys
# import classes from hostelclasses.py
from hostelclasses import Payment, PaymentList, Tenant,  TenantList


# EVENT HANDLERS

# adds a new tenant to the list
def addTenant(event):
    if nameEntry.get() =='' or roomEntry1.get() =='':  # name and room cannot be blank
        messagebox.showinfo(None, 'Room and name must be entered')
    else:
        tenant = Tenant(nameEntry.get(), roomEntry1.get()) # create new tenant
        result = tenantList.addTenant(tenant) # attempt to add tenant to list
        if result == 1: # addTenant method of tenantList returns 1 if hostel is full
            text1.delete(1.0, 'end') # delete existing text from text1
            text1.insert(1.0, 'Hostel is full') # display message in text1
        elif result == 2: # addTenant method of tenantList returns 2 if room is occupied
            text1.delete(1.0, 'end')  # delete existing text from text1
            text1.insert(1.0, 'Room %s is already occupied' %(roomEntry1.get()))
        else:
            text1.delete(1.0, 'end') # delete existing text from text1
            text1.insert(1.0, 'Tenant added in room %s\n' %(roomEntry1.get())) # success
            roomEntry1.delete(0, 'end') # delete text from roomEntry1
            nameEntry.delete(0, 'end') # delete text from nameEntry

# displays a list of tenants in text1
def displayTenants(event):
    if tenantList.getTotal() == 0: # if hostel is empty
        text1.delete(1.0, 'end') # delete existing text from text1
        text1.insert(1.0, 'Hostel is empty') # display message in text1
    else: # hostel is not empty
        text1.delete(1.0, 'end') # delete existing text from text1
        text1.insert(1.0, 'ROOM\tTENANT\n') # display header in text1
        # loop through tenants and display room and name in text 1
        for i in range(1, tenantList.getTotal() + 1):
            text1.insert('end', '%s\t%s\n' %(tenantList.getTenant(i).room,
                                            tenantList.getTenant(i).name ))

# removes a tenant in a particular room from the list
def removeTenant(event):
    if roomEntry1.get() == '':
        messagebox.showinfo(None, 'Room cannot be blank')
    else:
        result = tenantList.removeTenant(roomEntry1.get()) # attempt to remove tenant
        if not result: # removeTenant method of TenantList returns False if room empty
            text1.delete(1.0, 'end') # delete existing text from text1
            text1.insert(1.0, 'There is no tenant in room %s\n' %(roomEntry1.get()))
        else:
            text1.delete(1.0, 'end') # delete existing text from text1
            text1.insert(1.0, 'Tenant removed from room %s\n' %(roomEntry1.get())) # success
            roomEntry1.delete(0, 'end') # delete text from roomEntry1

# records a payment for a particular tenant
def makePayment(event):
    try:
```

```
            amount = float(amountEntry.get())
        except:
            messagebox.showinfo(None, 'Amount must be a number') # exception if value not a number
            return # end routine
        if roomEntry2.get() == '' or monthEntry.get() == '':
            messagebox.showinfo(None, 'Room and month must be entered')
        else:
            tenant = tenantList.search(roomEntry2.get()) # retrieve tenant from room
            if tenant == None: # if no tenant in room
                text2.delete(1.0, 'end') # delete existing text from text2
                text2.insert(1.0, 'There is no tenant in room %s\n' %(roomEntry2.get()))
            else:
                payment = Payment(monthEntry.get(), amount) # create new payment
                tenant.makePayment(payment) # add payment using makePayment method of Tenant class
                text2.delete(1.0, 'end') # delete existing text from text2
                # display success message in text2
                text2.insert(1.0, 'Payment of £%0.2f made for %s for room %s\n'
                                                %(amount, monthEntry.get(), roomEntry2.get()))
                roomEntry2.delete(0, 'end') # delete text from roomEntry2
                monthEntry.delete(0, 'end') # delete text from monthEntry
                amountEntry.delete(0, 'end') # delete text from amountEntry

# lists all payments made by a specified tenant
def listPayments(event):
    if roomEntry2.get() == '':
            messagebox.showinfo(None, 'Room cannot be blank')
    else:
        tenant = tenantList.search(roomEntry2.get()) # retrieve correct tenant
        if tenant == None: # if room is empty
            text2.delete(1.0, 'end') # delete existing text from text2
            text2.insert(1.0, 'There is no tenant in room %s\n' %(roomEntry2.get()))
        else:
            paymentList = tenant.payments # retrieve payments list
            text2.delete(1.0, 'end') # delete existing text from text2
            text2.insert(1.0, 'PAYMENTS FOR ROOM %s\n' %(roomEntry2.get())) # display header
            text2.insert('end', 'MONTH\t\tAMOUNT\n') # display header 2 in text2
            # loop through payments and display month and amount in text 2
            for i in range(1, paymentList.getTotal() + 1):
                text2.insert('end', '%s\t\t£%6.2f\n' %(paymentList.getPayment(i).month,
                                                        paymentList.getPayment(i).amount ))
            # display total amount paid
            text2.insert('end', '\nTotal paid so far: £%0.2f' %(paymentList.calculateTotalPaid()))
            roomEntry2.delete(0, 'end') # delete text from roomEntry2

# saves the records and terminates the application
def saveAndQuit(event):
    ok = tenantList.writeList()
    if ok:
        root.destroy()
    else:
        answer = messagebox.askquestion(None, 'There was a problem writing the file. Quit anyway?')
        if answer == 'yes':
            root.destroy()

# determines the behaviour of the system close button
def onClosing():
    answer = messagebox.askquestion(None,'Are you sure you want to quit? All changes will be lost.')
    if answer == 'yes':
        root.destroy()

# MAIN BODY

root = Tk()
tenantList = TenantList(0) # create an empty TenantList
ok = False
ok = tenantList.readList() # attempt to read file
if not ok: # no file read (first time use)
    root.withdraw() # temporarily close window
    # request number of rooms from user
    totalNumberOfRooms = simpledialog.askinteger(title = 'Initializing system',
                            prompt = '-------- How many rooms are in the hostel? --------')
    if totalNumberOfRooms != None: # user did not press cancel
        tenantList = TenantList(totalNumberOfRooms) # create new tenant list
        root.deiconify() # show window
    else:
        sys.exit() # close down system
```

```
# configure window

root.protocol('WM_DELETE_WINDOW', onClosing) # set behaviour of window close button
root.title('Hostel Application')
root.geometry('450x540')
root.configure(bg = 'sky blue')
titleLabel = Label(root, font = ('Arial', 16), bg = 'sky blue', text = 'Hostel Application')


# create frames to hold widgets
frame1 = Frame(root,bg = 'sky blue')
frame2 = Frame(root, bg = 'sky blue')
frame3 = Frame(root, bg = 'sky blue')
frame4 = Frame(root, bg = 'sky blue')

# create widgets for entering tenants and add to first frame
roomLabel1 = Label(frame1, bg = 'light yellow', text ='Room')
roomEntry1 = Entry(frame1, width = 5)
nameLabel = Label(frame1, bg = 'light yellow', text = 'Name')
nameEntry = Entry(frame1, width = 25)

# create buttons for entering and displaying tenants and add to second frame
addTenantButton = Button(frame2, bg = 'light yellow', text = 'Add Tenant')
displayTenantsButton = Button(frame2, bg = 'light yellow', text = 'Display Tenants' )
removeTenantButton = Button(frame2, bg = 'light yellow', text = 'Remove Tenant')
saveAndQuitButton = Button(frame2, bg = 'light yellow', text = 'Save and Quit')

# create text box for displaying tenant details
text1 = Text(root, width = 50, height = 10)

# create widgets for entering payments and add to third frame
roomLabel2 = Label(frame3, bg = 'light yellow', text = 'Room')
roomEntry2 = Entry(frame3, width = 5)
monthLabel = Label(frame3, bg = 'light yellow', text = 'Month')
monthEntry = Entry(frame3, width = 15)
amountLabel = Label(frame3, bg = 'light yellow', text = 'Amount')
amountEntry = Entry(frame3, width = 10)

# create buttons for entering and displaying payments and add to fourth frame
makePaymentButton = Button(frame4, bg = 'light yellow', text = 'Make Payment')
listPaymentButton = Button(frame4, bg = 'light yellow', text = 'List Payments')

# create text box for displaying payment details
text2 = Text(root, width = 50, height = 10)


# arrange items in window
titleLabel.pack(pady = 10)
roomLabel1.pack(side = 'left', padx = 5)
roomEntry1.pack(side = 'left', padx = 5)
nameLabel.pack(side = 'left', padx = 5)
nameEntry.pack(side = 'left', padx = 5)
addTenantButton.pack(side = 'left', padx = 5)
displayTenantsButton.pack(side = 'left', padx = 5)
removeTenantButton.pack(side = 'left', padx = 5)
saveAndQuitButton.pack(side = 'left', padx = 5)
roomLabel2.pack(side = 'left', padx = 5)
roomEntry2.pack(side = 'left', padx = 5)
monthLabel.pack(side = 'left', padx = 5)
monthEntry.pack(side = 'left', padx = 5)
amountLabel.pack(side = 'left', padx = 5)
amountEntry.pack(side = 'left', padx = 5)
makePaymentButton.pack(side = 'left', padx = 5)
listPaymentButton.pack(side = 'left', padx = 5)
frame1.pack(pady = 5)
frame2.pack(pady = 5)
text1.pack(pady = 5)
frame3.pack(pady = 5)
frame4.pack(pady = 5)
text2.pack(pady=5)

# bind buttons to event handlers
addTenantButton.bind('<Button-1>', addTenant)
displayTenantsButton.bind('<Button-1>', displayTenants)
removeTenantButton.bind('<Button-1>', removeTenant)
saveAndQuitButton.bind('<Button-1>', saveAndQuit)
makePaymentButton.bind('<Button-1>', makePayment)
listPaymentButton.bind('<Button-1>', listPayments)

root.mainloop() # start event loop
```

As we have said, a lot of this is familiar to you, so we will only look at the important features here. Let's start with the main body of the application. As you see, the first thing we do, once we have created the window, is to instantiate an empty tenant list:

```
tenantList = TenantList(0)
```

Having done that, we attempt to read the file containing the data and add the records to the list of tenants. We do this by calling a function called `readList` of `TenantList`. The `readList` function returns `True` if the file is read successfully and `False` otherwise:

```
ok = readList(tenantList) # attempt to read file
if not ok: # no file read (first time use)
    root.withdraw() # temporarily close window
    # request number of rooms from user
    totalNumberOfRooms = simpledialog.askinteger(title = 'Initializing system',
                        prompt = '-------- How many rooms are in the hostel? --------')
    if totalNumberOfRooms != None: # user did not press cancel
        tenantList = TenantList(totalNumberOfRooms) # create new tenant list
        root.deiconify() # show window
    else:
        sys.exit() # close down system
```

The most usual reason for the file not being read is that this is the first time that the application is being run, and no data has been created yet—in this case the user will have to let the system know how many rooms there are in the hostel. So if `readList` returns a value of `False`, the window is temporarily closed (using the `withdraw` method), and a pop-up window appears. This is achieved by calling the method `askinteger` of a class called `simpledialog`, which we imported. We chose `askinteger` because in this case the number of rooms—an integer—is required (`askfloat` and `askstring` also exist). As you can see, we have set the title and prompt by sending these values into the `askinteger` method. The result is shown in Fig. 12.7.

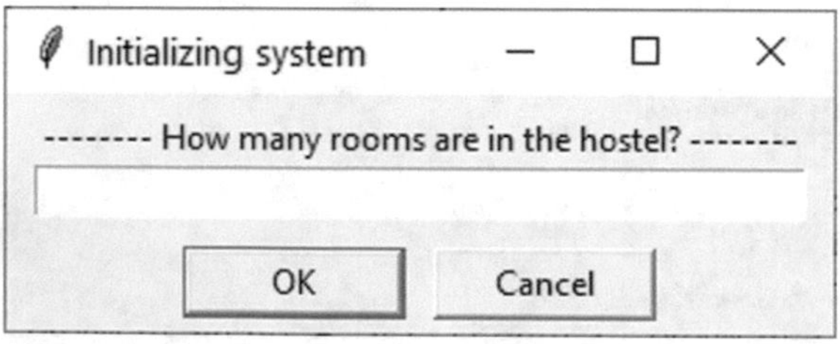

Fig. 12.7 User is asked to enter the number of rooms

If the user was expecting a file to be read, and it was not, then there is something wrong, and he or she can then press 'Cancel'. In this case a value of **None** is returned, and the system is shut down using the sys.exit () command. However, if this is indeed the first time the application is being used, the user will enter the number of rooms, a new tenant list will be created, and the window is made to appear again by calling the deiconify method.

At this point the program goes on to configure the window—most of this you are familiar with. However we should draw your attention to this instruction:

```
root.protocol('WM_DELETE_WINDOW', onClosing) # set behaviour of window close button
```

The protocol method is used to set the behaviour of the standard window icons—in this case the 'close' icon, specified by WM_DELETE_WINDOW, which we bind to a method that we have called onClosing. Let's take a look at this method now:

```
def onClosing():
    answer = messagebox.askquestion(None,'Are you sure you want to quit? All changes will be lost.')
    if answer == 'yes':
        root.destroy()
```

As we mentioned before, we want the 'close' icon to terminate the application without saving the records. But before this happens, we want the user to confirm that this is the case—we prompt the user with a pop-up message, this time using the askquestion method of messagebox. The following window that appears is shown in Fig. 12.8.

As you can see from the code, if the answer is 'yes', then the program is terminated—this time, as the window has already been created, we must use its destroy method to terminate the application.

We should now take a quick look at the event-handler for the 'Save and quit' button, which will save the data to a file before closing:

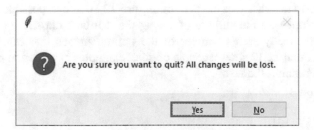

Fig. 12.8 Result of pressing the window's 'close' button

Fig. 12.9 File could not be written

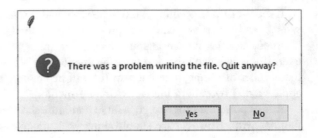

```
def saveAndQuit(event):
    ok = writeList(tenantList)
    if ok:
        root.destroy()
    else:
        answer = messagebox.askquestion(None, 'There was a problem writing the file. Quit anyway?')
        if answer == 'yes':
            root.destroy()
```

The `writeList` method of `TenantList` returns a value of **True** if the file is written successfully, or **False** otherwise; so when we call this method, we assign this return value to a variable `ok`. Then, if `ok` is `True`, the application is terminated. If it is false, a pop-up window appears as shown in Fig. 12.9.

This gives a user the opportunity to see if they can determine and fix the problem (such as creating more disk space) before trying again.

12.12   Testing the System

If you look back at the code for the hostel application, you can see that quite a bit of the event-handling code is related to the validation of data entered from the graphical interface. Much of the testing for such a system will, therefore, be geared around ensuring such validation is effective.

Among the types of validation we need to test is the display of suitable error messages when input text fields are left blank, or when inappropriate data has been entered into these text fields. Of course, as well as input validation, we also need to test the basic functionality of the system. Figure 12.10 is one possible test log that may be developed for the purpose of testing the `Hostel` class.

You have already seen examples of the pop-up menus that can be invoked. Figures 12.11 and 12.12 show a couple of other examples of what you might expect to see when running the test.

TEST LOG			
Purpose: To test the Hostel application			
Run Number:	**Date:**		
Action	**Expected Output**	**Pass/ Fail**	**Reason for failure**
Run application when file is absent	Window appears asking for number of rooms		
Press cancel	Application terminates		
Run program when file is absent	Window appears asking for number of rooms		
Enter 3	GUI appears		
Display tenants	"Empty list" message		
Add tenant: Patel, Room Number blank	"Room and name must be entered" message		
Add tenant: blank, Room Number 1	"Room and name must be entered" message		
Add tenant: Patel, Room Number 1	Confirmation message		
Add tenant: Jones, Room Number 1	Error Message: Room 1 is already occupied		
Add tenant: Jones, Room Number 2	Confirmation Message		
Add tenant: Adenike, Room Number 3	Confirmation Message		
Add tenant: Smith, Room Number 4	"Hostel is full" message		
Display tenants	ROOM TENANT 1 Patel 2 Jones 3 Adenike		
Make payment: Room blank, Month January, Amount 100	"Room and month must entered" message		
Make Payment: Room 1, Month blank, Amount 100	"Room and month must entered" message		
Make payment: Room 1, Month January, Amount £100	"Amount must be a number" message		
Make payment: Room 1, Month January, Amount 100	Confirmation message		
Make payment: Room 1, Month February, Amount 200	Confirmation message		
List payments: Room Number blank	" Room cannot be blank" message		
List payments, Room Number 1	PAYMENTS FOR ROOM 1 MONTH AMOUNT January £100.00 February £200.00 Total paid so far: £300.00		
Remove tenant: Room Number blank	"Room must be an integer" message		
Remove tenant: Room Number 1	Confirmation Message		
Display tenants	ROOM TENANT 2 Jones 3 Adenike		
List payments: Room Number 1	"Room Empty" message		
Press 'Save and quit' button	Application terminates normally		
Run application	GUI appears		
Display tenants	ROOM TENANT 2 Jones 3 Adenike		
Add tenant: Ali, Room Number 4	Confirmation message		
Display tenants	ROOM TENANT 2 Jones 3 Adenike 4 Ali		
Press window close button	Request to confirm appears		
Press 'No'	Pop-up disappears		
Press window close button	Request to confirm appears		
Press 'Yes'	Application terminates normally		
Run application	GUI appears		
Display tenants	ROOM TENANT 2 Jones 3 Adenike		

Fig. 12.10 Test log to ensure the reliability of the *Hostel* class

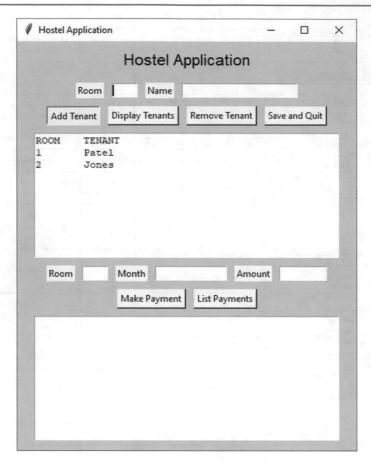

Fig. 12.11 *text1* is used to display a list of tenants entered

12.13   What Next?

Congratulations—you have now completed your first semester of programming; we hope you have enjoyed it. You may be surprised to discover just how much you have learnt—you should now be a competent Python programmer. Of course, there is even more that you can learn about Python, and for those of you who are interested—especially those of you who might eventually want to enter the world of data science, web development or artificial intelligence—you have enough background to go on to learn some more advanced aspects of Python.

But in this text, the next semester's work will be about Java, another widely used programming language, and one that in some ways is quite different to Python—although the basic programming principles you have learnt are relevant to Java, just

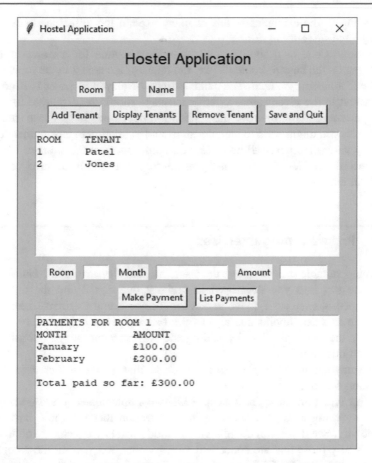

Fig. 12.12 Payments for room 1 are displayed in *text2* when the *List Payments button* is pressed

as much as they are to Python. Not only will you be developing Java programs similar to the ones we have created with Python, but you will also learn some more advanced concepts and techniques. Does that sound exciting? We think so—and we hope that you enjoy your next semester as much as we have enjoyed helping you through this one.

12.14   Self-test Questions

1 Describe the class associations given in the UML design of Fig. 12.1.
2 Develop test logs for testing the `Tenant` and `TenantList` classes.
3 Identify the benefits of adding a __ str __ method into your classes and then write a suitable __ str __ method for the `Bank` class from Chap. 8.

4   Referring to the examples in this chapter, explain the difference between *unit testing* and *integration testing*.

5   Use pseudocode to design the event-handling routine for a `search` button. Clicking on the button should display the name of the tenant in the room entered in the `roomEntry1` field. The name is to be displayed in `text1`. If no tenant is present in the given room, an error message should be displayed in `text1`.

6   How else might you improve the application developed in this case study? For example, you might want to include additional validation to ensure that negative money values are never allowed. Or you could improve the strategy for saving the records to file—for example, you could add a button to save your work without exiting.

12.15   Programming Exercises

1   Develop suitable drivers to test the `Tenant` and `TenantList` classes.

2   Use the test logs you developed in self-test question 2 and the drivers you developed in exercise 1 above to test the `Tenant` and `TenantList` classes.

3   Run the `Hostel` application against the test log given in Fig. 12.10.

4   Modify the `Hostel` class by adding the `search` button you considered in self-test question 5 above.

5   Make any additions to the `Hostel` class that you considered in self-test question 6 above.

6   As you will remember from Sect. 12.8, we implemented the `TenantList` class by using a list. We mention in that section that we could have used a dictionary. See if you can do this. The methods will have to change quite a lot— particularly those that are concerned with reading and writing the records to a file. But note that the GUI won't have to change, because all that is done in that class is to create a `TenantList` object—the internal details of which don't matter.

Java: Input, Output and Data Types

13

Outcomes

By the end of this chapter you should be able to:

- *identify some key differences between the **Java** and Python programming languages;*
- *explain how **Java** programs are compiled and run;*
- *write Java programs that display text on the screen;*
- ***declare** and **assign** values to **variables**;*
- *distinguish between the eight built-in **primitive types** of Java;*
- *create **constant** values with the keyword **final**;*
- *use the input methods of the* Scanner *class to get data from the keyboard.*

13.1 Introduction

Welcome back to the second semester of our programming course. We spent the first semester looking at how to write programs using the Python programming language and covered a number of fundamental programming concepts along the way. You learnt about variables, control structures, functions, modules and collections and then went on to look at object-oriented programming by developing your own classes and extending these classes using inheritance. You then went on to look at how to use files to save and read data, before developing applications consisting of many classes working closely together and interacting with users via attractive graphical interfaces. Along the way you also learnt about the UML notation for designing classes.

Supplementary Information The online version contains supplementary material available at https://doi.org/10.1007/978-3-031-01326-3_13.

At the beginning of that semester you probably didn't expect to come as far as you have. Well, the second semester might look equally challenging but, with some help from us along the way, you can look forward to new and more advanced challenges.

In this second semester we are going to show you how to program in another widely used and popular programming language—**Java**.

Originally named *Oak*, Java was developed in 1991 by Sun Microsystems™. The Java technology was later acquired by Oracle™ in 2010. Originally, the intention was to use Java to program consumer devices such as video recorders, mobile phones and televisions. The expectation was that these devices would soon need to communicate with each other. As it turned out, however, this concept didn't take off until later. Instead, it was the growth of the Internet through the World Wide Web that was to be the real launch pad for the language.

Java is now one of the most popular and widely used programming languages in the world. So, let's get started by looking at how writing and running a program in Java is a little bit different from writing and running a program in Python.

13.2   Programming in Java

As we discussed in Chap. 1, there are different ways in which program instructions (**source code**) can be converted into machine code, and this varies from programming language to programming language.

As we saw, in the case of Python, when a program is run, it is implicitly compiled into an intermediate low-level set of instructions (known as **byte code**) for a virtual machine, and these byte code instructions are then translated (or **interpreted**) into the relevant code for the local machine. Python allows instructions to be saved in a **.py** file or executed directly via the Python shell in **interactive mode**.

Java is implemented in a very similar way in that Java source code is first compiled to what is known as **Java byte code**—low-level instructions suitable to be run on a **Java Virtual Machine** (or **JVM** for short) as we explain below. However, unlike Python, this compilation process is explicitly required before the program can be run. The advantage of compiling instructions before they can be run is that the compiler can work hard to identify errors before the execution step. This can seem frustrating for new programmers who want to try and run their code immediately, but it does help ensure that the final code is more robust and less likely to fail. For this reason, languages such as Java are popular for applications that require high levels of reliability, such as **embedded software**.

Unlike Python instructions, which can also be executed directly in interactive mode, Java instructions must be saved in a source code file and then compiled using a Java compiler into Java byte code. Source code Java files always have a `.java` extension (e.g. `MyGame.java`), and their corresponding compiled byte code files always have a `.class` extension (e.g. `MyGame.class`). The job of the JVM (similar to the virtual machine used by Python) is to then translate and run (interpret) each Java byte code instruction for the computer it is running on. In that way, like Python programs, Java programs can be platform independent and run on any machine that has a JVM installed.

There are various ways in which a JVM can be installed on a computer. In the case of some operating systems a JVM comes packaged with the system, along with the Java **libraries**, or **packages**, (precompiled Java modules that can be integrated with the programs you create) and a compiler. Together the JVM and the libraries are known as the **Java Runtime Environment (JRE)**. If you do not have a JRE on your computer (as will be the case with any Windows™ operating system), then the entire Java Development Kit (JDK), comprising the JRE, compiler and other tools, can be downloaded from Oracle™, the owners of the Java platform.

13.3 Integrated Development Environments (IDEs)

It is very common to compile and run your Java programs by using a special program called an **Integrated Development Environment** or **IDE**. An IDE provides you with an easy-to-use window into which you can type your code; other windows will provide information about the files you are using; and a separate window will be provided to tell you of your errors.

Not only does an IDE do all these things, it also lets you run your programs as soon as you have compiled them. Depending on the IDE you are using, your screen will look something like that in Fig. 13.1.

The IDE shown in Fig. 13.1 is NetBeans™, a very commonly used compiler for Java—another widely used IDE is Eclipse™. It is also perfectly possible to compile and run Java programs without the use of an IDE—but not nearly so convenient. To start off with however, we strongly recommend that you use an IDE such as NetBeans™ or Eclipse™. For a detailed overview of these IDEs, and how to run Java programs from the command line if you choose, please refer to the Appendix.

Menu for carrying out tasks such as compiling, running and saving your programs

Code window where you type in your Java source code

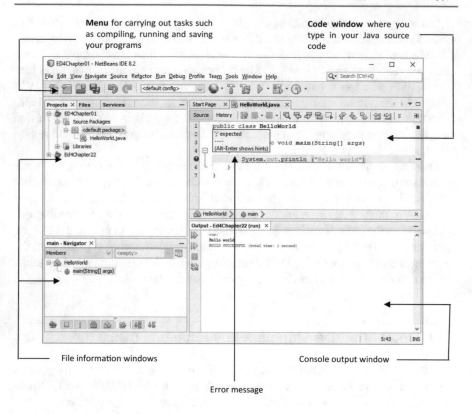

File information windows   Console output window

Error message

Fig. 13.1 Typical Java IDE screen

13.4 Your First Java Program

Now it is time to write your first Java program. The first program we showed you when you were studying Python is the first program we often write when learning a new language—a program to print "Hello world" on the screen. So, let's stick to this tradition and look at the very same program in the Java programming language. The code for the "Hello world" program is written out for you below.

HelloWorld.java

```java
public class HelloWorld
{
    public static void main(String[] args)
    {
        System.out.println ("Hello world");
    }
}
```

The first thing you will notice is that the Java program above is longer than the equivalent Python program (which contained just one instruction). Let's take a look at how this Java program is put together.

13.4.1 Analysis of the "Hello World" Program

Let's start with the really important bit—the line of code that represents the instruction *display* "*Hello world*" on the screen. The line that does this looks like this:

```
System.out.println("Hello world");
```

This is the way we are always going to get something printed on a simple text screen in Java; we use `System.out.println` and put whatever we want to be displayed in the brackets. The `println` instruction is short for "print line" and in this case we wish to print a message, which as you know is a string in programming languages. You will remember in Python we put string values in single quotes, though we could also have used double quotes. In Java, string values must *always* use double quotes (also known as speech marks) as in the case of our "`Hello world`" message.

You can see there is some additional stuff (`System.out`) to the left of the `println` instruction and you will be wondering what this is. Well, we have met the idea of classes and objects in Chaps. 8 and 9 when studying object-oriented programming in Python and we are using the dot operator again here, which is standard object-oriented notation to access something inside a class or object. In this case, `out` is an attribute in the `System` class. It refers to the standard output (the default being the screen). `System` also contains an `in` attribute which references the standard input (the default being the keyboard).

As with Python, Java is *case-sensitive*—in other words it interprets upper case and lower case characters as two completely different things. It is very important therefore to type the statements exactly as you see them here, paying attention to the case of the letters. So, for example, make sure this instruction starts with an upper case *S* at the beginning.

One important thing you should notice is the semicolon at the end of the **println** instruction. This is important; *every Java instruction has to end with a semi-colon.*

Now we can consider the meaning of the rest of the program. Unlike Python programs, Java programs *must* consist of more than just a collection of instructions. Java is a "pure" object-oriented programming language, which means *all Java code must be contained within a class.* This program introduced a class as follows:

```
public class HelloWorld
```

You can see that a class is introduced in Java simply with the keyword **class**. The simple Java programs that we will be starting off with will contain only one class (although they will interact with other classes from the "built-in" Java libraries such as System) but, as we will see in later chapters, programs often contain many classes. We always have to give a name to a class and, in this case, we have simply called our class HelloWorld. When choosing a name for a class, you can choose any name as long as:

- the name is not already a keyword in the Java language (such as **static**, **void**);
- the name has no spaces in it;
- the name does not include operators or mathematical symbols such as + and −;
- the name starts either with a letter, an underscore (_), or a dollar sign ($).

Although not a requirement, the convention is that Java class names begin with an upper case letter. So, the first line tells the Java compiler that we are writing a class with the name HelloWorld. However, you will also have noticed the word **public** in front of the word **class;** placing this word here makes our class accessible to the outside world and to other classes—so, until we learn about specific ways of restricting access, we will always include this word in the header. A **public** class should always be saved in a file with the same name as the class itself—so in this case it should be saved as a file with the name HelloWorld. java.

Notice that, unlike Python, which uses indentation to mark the beginning and end of a block of code, Java uses curly brackets (known as **braces**) that look like this { } to tell the compiler where a block of code begins and ends. In this case, we are using braces to mark the beginning and end of the class:

```
public class HelloWorld
{

}
```

The braces do not need to be aligned in the way we have presented above but doing so improves the readability of your code. Next you will see that the **println** instruction is not placed directly within this class, but instead placed inside another container piece of code called a main method:

```
public static void main(String[] args)
{
    System.out.println("Hello world");
}
```

We met the idea of a **method** when studying the Python programming language (where they are normally referred to as *functions*, unless they belong to a class). A method is just a named block of code for carrying out a particular task.

Java classes can contain many methods, and in most cases naming of these methods is left to the programmer. But the entry point of your program (i.e. the first method to be executed) must be given the name main in Java, so one class in your collection of classes must always contain this main method. As we have said, while our programs are relatively small, we will have just a single class; we will also place all our instructions in this single main method for now.

The additional syntax before the name of this method (**public static void**) and the bit in brackets after the name (**String[] args**) are necessary Java keywords that we need for the **header** (the first line) of the main method and will be explained in more detail in Chap. 15 when we return to methods in Java. This might look like quite a bit of syntax to remember, but it is worth noting that most IDEs can generate the relevant class and main method code for you when you provide a class name.

A Java program starts with the first instruction of main, then obeys each instruction in sequence (unless the instruction itself tells it to jump to some other place in the program). The program terminates when it has finished obeying the final instruction of main.[1] In this case we have only one instruction inside the curly brackets but, as you will soon see, we can have many instructions inside these braces.

By the way, you should be aware that, unlike the Python compiler, the Java compiler is not concerned about the layout of your code, just that your code meets the rules of the language. So, we could have typed the method header, the curly brackets and the println command all on one line if we wished! Obviously, this would look very messy, and it is always important to lay out your code in a way that makes it easy to read and to follow. So, throughout this book, we will lay out our code in a neat easy-to-read format, lining up opening and closing braces and indenting nested blocks in a similar way to Python's use of indentation. So, you can see that println instruction is indented inside the main method block and the main method block is indented in the **class** block (Fig. 13.2).

13.4.2 Adding Comments to a Java Program

In Chap. 1 we saw there were two ways of adding comments into Python programs: the hashtag symbol (#) for single line comments and three single quotes (''') at the beginning and the end of multiline comments. In Java, as with several other languages, we use two slashes (//) for single line comments. Multiline comments in Java are enclosed between two special symbols; the opening symbol is a slash

---

[1] In Chap. 23 you will learn to create graphics programs with a package called JavaFX, and in the case of JavaFX applications you will see that in some instances it is possible to run a JavaFX application without a main method.

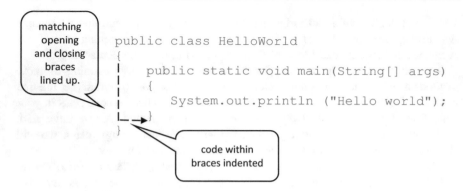

Fig. 13.2 Keeping code looking neat by aligning braces and using indentation

followed by a star (/*), and the closing symbol is a star followed by a slash (*/). The program below shows examples of both types of comment:

HelloWorld – with comments

```
// this is a short comment, so we use the first method
public class HelloWorld
{
    public static void main(String[] args)
    {
        System.out.println("Hello world");
    }

    /* this is the second method of including comments - it is more convenient to use this method here,
    because the comment is longer and goes over more than one line */

}
```

In Chap. 24 you will learn about a special tool called **Javadoc** for documenting your programs. In that chapter you will see that in order to use this tool you must comment your classes in the Javadoc style—as you will see, Javadoc comments must begin with /** and end with */.

13.5 println Versus print

As you have already seen when writing your first Java program, to output a message on to the screen in Java we use the following command:

System.out.println(*message to be printed on screen*);

There is in fact an alternative form of the System.out.println statement, which uses System.out.**print**. As we said before, println is short for *print line,* and the effect of this statement is to start a new line after displaying whatever is in the brackets (in other words it is equivalent to Python's standard print command). You can see an example of this below where we have adapted our `HelowWorld` program by adding an additional line:

HelloWorld – with an additional line

```
public class HelloWorld
{
    public static void main(String[] args)
    {
        System.out.println("Hello world"); // notice the use of println
        System.out.println("Hello world again!");
    }
}
```

When we run this program, the output looks like this:

```
Hello world
Hello world again!
```

Now let's change the first `System.out.println` to `System.out.print`:

HelloWorld – adapted to show the effect of using *print* instead of *println*

```
public class HelloWorld
{
    public static void main(String[] args)
    {
        System.out.print("Hello world"); // notice the use of 'print'
        System.out.println("Hello world again!");
    }
}
```

Now our output looks like this:

```
Hello worldHello world again!
```

You can see that the output following the `System.out.print` statement doesn't start on a new line, but follows straight on from the previous line. You will remember the equivalent was achieved in Python by using a keyworded argument as follows:

```
print('Hello world', end = '')
print('Hello world again')
```

As with Python, if you want a blank line in a Java program, then you can simply leave the brackets of the `println` command empty:

```
System.out.println(); // creates a blank line
```

We can concatenate two strings together in one `println` command using the same concatenation operator you met in Python (+). Also, as we saw with our Python programs, we are not restricted to printing out messages but can also, for example, print out the results of calculations. Unlike Python, however, we do not need to convert numeric values into strings explicitly before printing them. So, the following is possible in Java:

```
System.out.println("Result = " + 10 * 2); // result of calculation autmatically turned into a string
```

This would result in the following output:

```
Result = 20
```

In this calculation example we have used the multiplication operator (*), which is familiar to you from Python. All the Python mathematical operators from Table 2.1 in Chap. 2 are available in Java, except the exponent operator (**). Also, it is worth noting that all the formatting escape sequences that we looked at in Python (Table 2.4 in Chap. 2) are also available to you in Java.

Now let's take a look at another important difference between Java and Python, and that is how variables are created and used.

13.6   Variables in Java

One of the key differences between Python and Java is that Python is a **dynamically typed** language, whereas Java is a **statically typed** language. What do these terms mean? Put simply, Python checks the required data type of variables at run-time (and these can change during the life of the program), whereas Java checks the types of variables at compile time (and so these are fixed during the life of the program). What this means is that variables in Java need to be *declared by the programmer when writing the code* so the compiler can check that the values assigned to variables throughout the program are correct.

So, to create a variable in Java requires that we both give that variable a name *and allocate it a data type*. This process is known as **declaring** a variable. In Java there are a few simple data types that programmers can use. These simple types are often referred to as the **primitive types** of Java; they are also referred to as **scalar types**, as they relate to a single piece of information (a single real number, a single character etc.).

Table 13.1 lists the names of these types in the Java language, the kinds of value they represent and the exact range of these values.

Table 13.1 Primitive types of Java

Java type	Allows for	Range of values
`byte`	Very small integers	−128 to 127
`short`	Small integers	−32 768 to 32 767
`int`	Big integers	−2 147 483 648 to 2 147 483 647
`long`	Very big integers	−9 223 372 036 854 775 808 to 9 223 372 036 854 775 807
`float`	Real numbers	$+/-1.4 * 10^{-45}$ to $3.4 * 10^{38}$
`double`	Very big real numbers	$+/-4.9 * 10^{-324}$ to $1.8 * 10^{308}$
`char`	Characters	Unicode character set
`boolean`	True or false	Not applicable

Some of these data types will be familiar to you in Python but, as you can see, Java data types are associated with explicit ranges—so some kinds of data, namely integers and real numbers, can be kept as more than one Java type. For example, you can use the `byte` type, the `short` type or the `int` type to hold integers in Java. However, while each numeric Java type allows for both positive and negative numbers, *the maximum size of numbers that can be stored varies from type to type*. For example, the type `byte` can represent integers ranging only from −128 to 127, whereas the type `short` can represent integers ranging from −32 768 to 32 767. Unlike some programming languages, these ranges are *fixed* no matter which Java compiler or operating system you are using. Unless there is specific reason to do otherwise, however, the `int` type is normally chosen to store integer values in Java programs. Similarly, when it comes to storing real numbers, it is usual to choose the `double` type rather than the `float` type.

Notice that the `boolean` type name in Java is all lower case as are the boolean values: `true` and `false`. One type that will be unfamiliar to you is the character type, `char`. This is used to represent a single character from the **Unicode** character set that you came across in Chap. 10. This contains nearly all the characters from most known languages.

Once the name and the type of a variable have been decided upon, the variable is **declared** as follows:

```
dataType variableName;
```

where dataType is the chosen primitive type and variableName is the chosen name of the variable. The rules for naming variables are the same as those we met when discussing the rules for naming classes. However, the convention in Java programs is to begin the name of a variable with a *lower case* letter (whereas the Java convention is to start class names with an upper case letter).

Let's look at the same example we introduced in Chap. 2: a variable to store a player's score in a game. In Python we did not need to allocate this a type, it was inferred from the value we placed into it (an integer value). In Java we would need declare this variable to be in integer (an **int** data type in Java) before we could put values into it:

```
int score;
```

In this way, many variables can be declared in your programs. Let's assume that the player of a game can choose a difficulty level (A, B or C); another variable could be declared in a similar way. Now, what data type in Table 13.1 best represents the difficulty level? Since the levels are given as characters (A, B and C), the **char** type would be the obvious choice. At this point we have two variables declared: one to record the score and one to record the difficulty level.

```
int score;
char level;
```

Finally, several variables can be declared on a *single line* if they are *all of the same type*. For example, let's assume that there are penalty hits that a player can incur; the number of times a player gets hit can also be recorded. We can call this variable hits. Since the type of this variable is also an integer, it can be declared along with score in a single line as follows:

```
int score, hits; // two variables declared at once
char level ; // this has to be declared separately
```

Figure 13.3 illustrates the effect of these three declarations on the computer's memory.

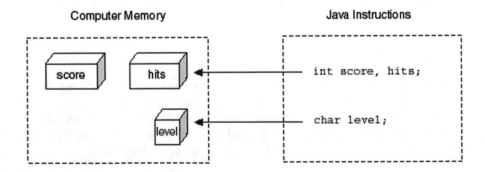

Fig. 13.3 Effect of declaring variables in Java

As you can see, variable declarations in Java set aside a small part of the computer's memory to hold that variable. You can think of these reserved spaces in memory as being small boxes, big enough to hold a value of the given data type. Figure 13.3 also illustrates that a **char** data type requires half the space in memory of an **int** type (which in turn requires half the space required by a **double** type). This is different from Python where the variable is just a **tag** that *points to* the data it is associated with. In the case of Java, the variable location also *contains* the data it is associated with. It is for this reason that Python variables can change type during a program, as this just involves pointing a tag to a new piece of data, whereas Java variable types need to remain constant throughout a program.

As with Python, the **assignment operator** (=) allows values to be put into these variables in Java. For example, to put the value zero into the variable score, the following assignment statement could be used:

```
score = 0;
```

If you wish, you can combine the assignment statement with a variable declaration to put an initial value into a variable as follows:

```
int score = 0;
```

This is equivalent to the two statements below:

```
int score;
score = 0;
```

Notice that the following declaration will not compile in Java:

```
int score = 2.5;
```

Can you think why?

The reason is that the right-hand side of the assignment (2.5) is a *real* number. This value could not be placed into a variable such as score, which is declared to hold only integers, without some information loss. In Java, such information loss is not permitted, and this statement would therefore cause a compiler error.

In Chap. 2 we introduced you to the idea of **typecasting** in Python—a technique for modifying the type of an expression at run-time. This technique can also be used in Java programs with the same syntax as in Python programs—that is putting the requested type in brackets in front of an expression. So, one way to allow the above expression to compile would be to typecast the value 2.5 into an integer as follows:

```
int score = (int)2.5; // type cast the double value to an integer
```

You may be wondering if it is possible to place a whole number into a variable declared to hold real numbers. The answer is yes. The following is perfectly legal:

```
double someNumber = 1000;
```

Although the value on the right-hand side (1000) appears to be an integer, it can be placed into a variable of type **double** because this would result in no information loss. Once this number is put into the variable of type **double**, it will be treated as the real number 1000.0.

Clearly, you need to think carefully about the best data type to choose for a particular variable. For instance, if a variable is going to be used to hold whole numbers *or* real numbers, use the **double** type as it can cope with both. If the variable is only ever going to be used to hold whole numbers, however, then although the **double** type might be adequate, use the **int** type as it is specifically designed to hold whole numbers.

When assigning a value to a character variable, you must enclose the value in single quotes. For example, to set the initial difficulty level to A, the following assignment statement could be used:

```
char level = 'A';
```

Remember: you should only declare a variable only once. You can then assign values to it as many times as you like. For example, later on in the program the difficulty level might be changed to a different value as follows:

```
char level = 'A'; // initial difficulty level
// other Java instructions
level = 'B'; // difficulty level changed
```

You may be thinking that there was no string type listed in Table 13.1. That is because Table 13.1 listed the primitive (built-in) types in Java, whereas the string type in Java (String) is a class and not a primitive type. However, Java allows us to declare and assign values to a String variable in much the same way as described above. For example, let's use the example we used when introducing strings in Python: a variable called myName to store someone's name:

```
String myName; // declare String variable
myName = "Adewale" // assign a String value
```

Notice once again that string values in Java need to be placed in double quotes. Of course, these two instructions can be combined into one single instruction:

```
String myName = "Adewale" // declare and assign a String value
```

We will explore the `String` class in more detail when we study classes and objects in Java in Chap. 17.

13.7   Creating Constants

There will be occasions where data items in a program have values *that do not change*. The following are examples of such items:

- the maximum score in an exam (100);
- the number of hours in a day (24);
- the mathematical value of π (approximately 3.1416).

In these cases the values of the items do not vary. Values that remain the same throughout a program (as opposed to variables) are referred to as **constants**. Python does not allow constants to be created, and instead the programmer is required to ensure such values do not change. In Java, however, programmers can declare and create constants by preceding a variable declaration with the keyword **final**. Once such a constant is given a value, then that value is fixed and cannot later be changed. Normally we fix a value when we initialize the constant. For example:

```
final int HOURS = 24;
```

Notice that the standard Java convention has been used here of naming constants in upper case. Any attempt to change this value later in the program will result in a compiler error. For example:

```
final int HOURS = 24; // create constant
HOURS = 12; // will not compile!
```

13.8   Expressions in Java

As with Python, the right-hand side of an assignment can use expressions involving other variables and mathematical calculations. The assignment shorthands we met in Python (+=) and (−=) are also available in Java. Java also has two assignment shorthands not available in Python: the increment (++) and decrement (– –) operators for adding 1 and subtracting 1 from a variable, respectively:

```
int x = 10; // x set to 10
x++; // x incremented to 11
x--; // x decremented back to 10
```

These shorthands are equivalent to the following:

```
int x = 10; // x set to 10
x = x + 1; // x incremented to 11
x = x - 1; // x decremented back to 10
```

13.9   The *FindCost* Program

Let's put some of what we have covered so far in this chapter together by writing a Java program similar to the findtax.py program from Chap. 2, which calculated the sales tax on a product. Here we calculate the final cost of the product after the sales tax is added.

FindCost.java

```
// a program to calculate and display the cost of a product after sales tax has been added

public class FindCost
{
    public static void main(String[] args)
    {
        System.out.println("*** Product Price Check ***");
        double price, tax;
        price = 500;
        tax = 17.5;
        price = price * (1 + tax/100);
        System.out.println("Cost after tax = " + price);
    }
}
```

Here you can see the two variables (price and tax) have been declared to be of type **double** (since they may require numbers with decimal points in them). Also, we have not had to explicitly convert the final value of price to a string before printing it (as it is implicitly converted for us in Java), and we have placed our instructions inside a main method, which is then placed within a class.

Running this program produces the following output:

```
*** Product Price Check ***
Cost after tax = 587.5
```

In Chap. 2 we went on to improve this program by incorporating user input. So, let's take a look at how to get user input into our Java programs.

13.10   Input in Java: The *Scanner* Class

Python has an `input` command for keyboard input. Java, on the other hand, provides a special class called `Scanner`, to obtain information that is typed in at the keyboard. `Scanner` is provided as part of what is known in Java as a **package**. A package is a collection of precompiled classes (a bit like a module in Python). The `Scanner` class is part of a package called `util`. In order to access a package we use a command called **import** that acts in a similar way to the **import** command in Python for accessing modules. So, to make the `Scanner` class accessible to the compiler we have to tell it to look in the `util` package, and we do this by placing the following line at the top of our program:

```
import java.util.Scanner;
```

Sometimes you might come across an **import** statement that looks like this:

```
import java.util.*;
```

This asterisk means that all the classes in the particular package are made available to the compiler. Although using the asterisk notation is perfectly acceptable, nowadays it is considered a better practice to specify only those classes that we need, as in the first statement, since this clarifies precisely which classes are being used within a program—so that is what we will do in this text.

As long as the `Scanner` class is accessible, you can use all the input methods that have been defined in this class. We are going to show you how to do this now. Some of the code might look a bit mysterious to you at the moment, but don't worry about this right now. Just follow our instructions for the time being—after a few chapters, it will become clear to you exactly why we use the particular format and syntax that we are showing you.

Having imported the `Scanner` class, you will need to write the following instruction in your program:

```
Scanner keyboard = new Scanner(System.in);
```

What we are doing here is creating an object, keyboard, of the Scanner class. You have already encountered classes and objects in Python, and we will look at Java classes and objects in more detail in Chaps. 17 and 18, but for now just note that System.in represents the keyboard, and by associating our Scanner object with System.in, we are telling it to get the input from the keyboard as opposed to a file on disk or a modem for example. Just to note that, like a variable, you can choose any name for this object, but we have chosen the obvious name here —keyboard.

The Scanner class has several input methods, each one associated with a different input type, and once we have declared a Scanner object, we can use these methods. Let's take some examples. Say we wanted a user to type in an integer at the keyboard, and we wanted this value to be assigned to an integer variable called x. We would use the Scanner method called nextInt; the instruction would look like this:

```
x = keyboard.nextInt();
```

In the case of a **double**, y, we would do this:

```
y = keyboard.nextDouble();
```

Notice that to access a method of a class you need to join the name of the method (getInt or getDouble) to the name of the object (keyboard) by using the full stop. Also, you must remember the brackets after the name of the method.

To read a string from the keyboard into a String variable called myName say, we can use the next method:

```
myName = keyboard.next();
```

However, a word of warning here—when you do this, you should *not* enter strings that include spaces, as this will give you unexpected results. We will return to this in Chap. 17 when we look at strings in more detail.

What about a character? Unfortunately, this is a little bit more complicated, as there is no nextChar method provided. Assuming c had been declared as a character, we would have to adapt the next method (which reads a whole string) and ask for the first character in that string by using a charAt method as follows:

```
c = keyboard.next().charAt(0);
```

Now let's rewrite the `FindCost` program so that it allows the user to input the values of `price` and `tax` from the keyboard. Since the type used to store the price and the tax is a **double**, the appropriate input method is `nextDouble`, as can be seen below.

FindCost2.java

```
import java.util.Scanner; // import the Scanner class from the util package

/* a program to input the initial price of a product and then calculate and display its cost after
tax has been added */

public class FindCost2
{
    public static void main(String[] args )
    {
        Scanner keyboard = new Scanner(System.in); // create Scanner object
        double price, tax;
        System.out.println("*** Product Price Check ***");
        System.out.print("Enter initial price: "); // prompt for input
        price = keyboard.nextDouble(); // input method called
        System.out.print("Enter tax rate: "); // prompt for input
        tax = keyboard.nextDouble(); // input method called
        price = price * (1 + tax/100); // perform the calculation
        System.out.println("Cost after tax = " + price);
    }
}
```

Notice that, unlike the `input` command of Python that could include a prompt message, `Scanner` methods do not allow for such a prompt to be included—so the prompts need to be included as additional output commands: for example:

```
System.out.print("Enter initial price: "); // prompt for input
price = keyboard.nextDouble(); // input method called
```

Also notice that, unlike the `input` command of Python that required us to typecast the user input from text to the required type, the individual `Scanner` methods return values of the appropriate type—so no typecasting is required:

```
price = keyboard.nextDouble(); // nextDouble returns a 'double' so no need to type-cast
```

Here is a sample run of `FindCost2`:

```
*** Product Price Check ***
Enter initial price: 120
Enter tax rate: 20
Cost after tax = 144.0
```

13.11   Self-test Questions

1. Consider a Java program called MyGame.java. How would this program be compiled and run from the command line?
2. What, precisely, would be the output of the following programs?

   (a)

```
public class Question2A
{
        public static void main(String[] args)
        {
            System.out.print("Hello, how are you? ");
            System.out.println("Fine thanks.");
        }
}
```

   (b)

```
public class Question2B
{
        public static void main(String[] args)
        {
            System.out.println("Hello, how are you? ");
            System.out.println("Fine thanks.");
        }
}
```

3. What would be the most appropriate Java data type to use for the following items of data?

   - the maximum number of people allowed on a bus;
   - the weight of a food item purchased in a supermarket;
   - the grade awarded to a student (for example 'A', 'B' or 'C').

4. Take a look at the following code fragment then answer the questions that follow:

```
int x = 75.5;
double y = 75;
```

   (a) Explain which, if any, of the lines of code above would result in a compiler error.
   (b) Use typecasting to avoid any compiler errors that you might have identified above.

5. What would be the final output from the program below if the user entered the number 10?

```
import java.util.Scanner;

public class Calculate
{
     public static void main(String[] args )
     {
          Scanner keyboard = new Scanner(System.in);
          int num1, num2;
          num2 = 6;
          System.out.print("Enter value ");
          num1 = keyboard.nextInt();
          num1 = num1 + 2;
          num2 = num1 / num2;
          System.out.println("result = " + num2);
     }
}
```

6. Identify and correct the errors in the program below, which prompts for the user's age and then attempts to work out the year in which the user was born.

```
import java.util.Scanner;

public class SomeProg
{
     public static void main (String[] args)
     {
          Scanner keyboard = new Scanner(System.in);
          final int YEAR;
          int age, bornIn;
          System.out.print(How old are you this year? );
          age = keyboard.nextDouble();
          bornIn = YEAR - age;
          System.out.println("I think you were born in " + BornIn);
     }
}
```

7. Distinguish between a **constant** and a **variable** in Java and declare a constant to hold the mathematical value of π (approximately 3.1416).

13.12 Programming Exercises

1. If you do not have access to a Java IDE go to the accompanying website (see preface) and follow the instructions for installing an IDE. You will also find instructions on the website for compiling and running programs;

2. Type and compile the *Hello World* program. If you make any syntax errors, the compiler will indicate where to find them. Correct them and recompile your program. Keep doing this until you no longer have any errors. You can then run your program;

3. Run the programs from self-test questions 2 and 5 above to check your answers to these questions;

4. Try and run the program given in self-test question 6 above. This program contained compiler errors that you should have identified in your answer to that question. Take a look at how the compiler reports on these errors then fix them so that the program can compile and run successfully;

5. In Chap. 2, you wrote three input demo programs in Python (`inputdemo1.py, inputdemo2.py, inputdemo3.py`). Rewrite these programs in Java;

6. In programming exercises 3–7 from Chap. 2, you wrote a number of Python programs. Rewrite these programs in Java.

Java Control Structures

14

Outcomes:

By the end of this chapter you should be able to:

- *use* **if** *and* **if…else** *statements to make choices in a Java program;*
- *use a* **switch** *statement to make multiple choices in a Java program;*
- *repeat a section of code with a* **for** *loop, a* **while** *loop and a* **do…while** *loop in Java;*
- *select the most appropriate loop for a particular task;*
- *develop menu-driven programs in Java;*
- *use a* **break** *statement to terminate a loop in Java;*
- *use a* **continue** *statement to skip an iteration of a loop in Java.*

14.1 Introduction

As with Python programs—and indeed all programs—Java instructions are executed in **sequence**. In Java they are executed one after the other from the beginning to the end of the `main` method, unless the programmer builds in additional forms of control. All programming languages allow programmers to control the order of execution so that they do not all necessarily need to be executed in sequence. As we saw when studying Python in Chaps. 3 and 4, the two alternative forms of control available to programmers are *selection* (making choices in programs) and *iteration* (repeating a section of code numerous times). Both of these forms of control are available in Java with very similar syntax to Python. Let's start by looking at the selection control structures of Java to allow for choices to be made in programs.

Supplementary Information The online version contains supplementary material available at https://doi.org/10.1007/978-3-031-01326-3_14.

© Springer Nature Switzerland AG 2022
Q. Charatan and A. Kans, *Programming in Two Semesters*,
Texts in Computer Science, https://doi.org/10.1007/978-3-031-01326-3_14

14.2   Making Choices in Java

In common with many programming languages, including Python, a single choice can be made with an **if** statement in Java, and a choice between two options can be implemented by using an **if...else** statement.

14.2.1   The 'if' Statement

The general form of an **if** statement in Java is given as follows:

```
if ( /* a test goes here */ )
{
       // instruction(s) inside the 'if' go here
}
```

The first thing you will notice is that the test associated with an **if** statement in Java needs to be enclosed in round brackets (and there is no colon after this test as there is in Python). Secondly, as you have seen before, indentation is not used in Java to indicate blocks of code—instead braces are used to mark the beginning and then the end of the instructions inside the **if** statement. Although, as we mentioned before, it is still a good practice to indent the code within the block to improve code readability.

As you know, when the test gives a result of **true**, the instructions inside the braces of the **if** statement are executed. The program then continues by executing the instructions after the braces of the **if** statement as normal. If, however, the **if** test gives a result of **false**, the instructions inside the **if** braces are *skipped* and not executed. Here, for example, is the rollercoaster.py program from Chap. 3, which checked the age of the customer before printing a message if the customer is a child, rewritten in Java:

RollerCoaster.java

```java
import java.util.Scanner;

// This program is an example of the use of selection in a Java program

public class RollerCoaster
{
    public static void main(String[] args)
    {
        int age;
        Scanner keyboard = new Scanner(System.in);
        System.out.print("How old are you? ");
        age = keyboard.nextInt();
        if (age < 13) // test controls if the next instruction is executed
        {
            System.out.println("Hello Junior!");
        }
        System.out.println("Enjoy your ride");// this instruction outside the if so always executed
    }
}
```

In this program there was only a *single* instruction inside the **if** statement.

```
age = keyboard.nextInt();
if (age < 13)
{
    System.out.println("Hello Junior!"); // single instruction inside 'if'
}
System.out.println("Enjoy your ride");
```

When there is only a single instruction associated with an **if** statement, the braces can be omitted around this instruction, if so desired, as follows:

```
age = keyboard.nextInt();
if (age < 13)
System.out.println("Hello Junior!"); // braces can be omitted around this line
System.out.println("Enjoy your ride");
```

The compiler will always assume that the first line following the **if** test is the instruction inside the **if**. For clarity, however, we will always use braces around instructions. In this example we have used the less than comparison operator ('<'). All the comparison operators we showed you when studying Python (in Table 3.1) are available in Java.

14.2.2 The 'if...else' Statement

As in Python, the extended form of selection in Java is the **if...else** statement that allows us to make a choice between two blocks of code:

```
if ( /* test goes here */ )
{
    // instruction(s) if test is true go here
}
else
{
    // instruction(s) if test is false go here
}
```

Here, for example, is the `displayresult.py` program (from Chap. 3) that checked whether a student has passed or failed an exam based on a mark entered, rewritten in Java:

Table 14.1 Logical operators of Java

Logical operator	Java counterpart
AND	&&
OR	||
NOT	!

DisplayResult.java

```
import java.util.Scanner;

public class DisplayResult
{
    public static void main(String[] args)
    {
        int mark;
        Scanner keyboard = new Scanner(System.in);
        System.out.print("What exam mark did you get? ");
        mark = keyboard.nextInt();
        if (mark >= 40)
        {
            // executed when test is true
            System.out.println("Congratulations, you passed");
        }
        else
        {
            // executed when test is false
            System.out.println("I am sorry, but you failed");
        }
        System.out.println("Good luck with your other exams");
    }
}
```

Again, notice that the indention of code within the **if** and **else** blocks is just to improve code readability here; it is the braces that actually mark the beginning and the end of these blocks in Java.

As discussed in Chap. 3, the tests associated with **if** statements can involve multiple conditions joined by logical operators (AND, OR and NOT). Python uses keywords for these logical operators, but Java uses operator symbols as given in Table 14.1.

Here, for example, we return to the Chap. 3 example of checking if the temperature for a given day is not hot (let's say is not greater than 18°) by using the NOT operator in Java as follows:

```
if (!(temperature > 18) ) // test to check if temperature is not hot
{
    System.out.println("Today is not a hot day!");
}
```

14.2.3   Nested 'if...else' Statements

As we have seen in Chap. 3, we can nest **if...else** statements to process multiple choices.

Here, for example, is the Java version of the timetable.py program from Chap. 3, which checked a student's group ('A', 'B', or 'C') and printed the time of that group's laboratory:

Timetable.java

```java
import java.util.Scanner;

public class Timetable
{
    public static void main(String[] args)
    {
        char group;
        Scanner keyboard = new Scanner(System.in);
        System.out.println("***Lab Times***");
        System.out.print("Enter your group (A,B,C): ");
        group = keyboard.next().charAt(0);

        // check tutorial group and display appropriate time
        if (group == 'A')
        {
            System.out.println("10.00 a.m"); // lab time for group A
        }
        else
        {
            if (group == 'B')
            {
                System.out.println("1.00 p.m"); // lab time for group B
            }
            else
            {
                if (group == 'C')
                {
                    System.out.println("11.00 a.m"); // lab time for group C
                }
                else
                {
                    System.out.println("No such group"); // invalid group
                }
            }
        }
    }
}
```

As with the Python version of this program, you can see nesting can result in code that can become difficult to read. Python allowed such code to be simplified with the use of an **elif** statement (as demonstrated in the `timetable2.py` program of Chap. 3). Java does not provide such a statement, but we can take advantage of the fact that nested **if...else** statements can be made easier to read by not including the braces associated with all the **else** branches and moving nested **if** statements onto the same line as the enclosing **else**, as in the second version of the timetable program shown below:

TimetableVersion2.java

```java
import java.util.Scanner;

public class TimetableVersion2
{
    public static void main(String[] args)
    {
        char group;
        Scanner keyboard = new Scanner(System.in);
        System.out.println("***Lab Times***");
        System.out.print("Enter your group (A,B,C): ");
        group = keyboard.next().charAt(0);

        if (group == 'A')
        {
            System.out.println("10.00 a.m");
        }
        else if (group == 'B') // nested 'if' shifted up
        {
            System.out.println("1.00 p.m");
        }
        else if(group == 'C')// nested 'if' shifted up
        {
            System.out.println("11.00 a.m");
        }
        else
        {
            System.out.println("No such group");
        }
    }
}
```

This use of nested selections is okay up to a point, but Java provides another form of control to process multiple choices that is neater and can sometimes be used in place of nested **if...else** statements: a **switch** statement.

14.2.4   The 'switch' Statement

Our next program, TimetableWithSwitch, behaves in exactly the same way as the previous program but using a **switch** instead of a series of nested **if... else** statements allows a neater implementation. Take a look at it and then we'll discuss it.

TimetableWithSwitch.java

```
import java.util.Scanner;

public class TimetableWithSwitch
{
    public static void main(String[] args)
    {
        char group;
        Scanner keyboard = new Scanner(System.in);
        System.out.println("***Lab Times***");
        System.out.print("Enter your group (A,B,C): ");
        group = keyboard.next().charAt(0);
        switch(group) // beginning of switch
        {
            case 'A': System.out.println("10.00 a.m.");
                      break;
            case 'B': System.out.println("1.00 p.m.");
                      break;
            case 'C': System.out.println("11.00 a.m.");
                      break;
            default: System.out.println("No such group");
        } // end of switch
    }
}
```

As you can see, this looks a lot neater. The **switch** statement works in exactly the same way as a set of nested **if** statements, but is more compact and readable. A **switch** statement may be used when.

- only one variable is being checked in each condition (in this case every condition involves checking the variable group);
- the check involves specific values of that variable (e.g. 'A', 'B') and not ranges (e.g. ≥ 40).

As can be seen from the example above, the keyword **case** is used to precede a possible value of the variable that is being checked. There may be many **case** statements in a single **switch** statement. The general form of a **switch** statement in Java is given as follows:

```
switch(someVariable)
{
    case value1: // instructions(s) to be executed
                 break;
    case value2: // instructions(s) to be executed
                 break;
    // more values to be tested can be added
    default: // instruction(s) for default case
}
```

where

- `someVariable` is the name of the variable being tested. This variable is most commonly of type **int** or **char**;
- `value1`, `value2`, etc., are the possible values of that variable;
- **break** is a command that forces the program to skip the rest of the **switch** statement;
- **default** is an optional (last) case that can be thought of as an "otherwise" statement. It allows you to code instructions that deal with the possibility of none of the cases above being **true**.

The **break** statement is important because it means that once a matching case is found, the program can skip the rest of the cases below. If it is not added, not only will the instructions associated with the matching case be executed, but also all the instructions associated with all the cases below it. Notice that the last set of instructions does not need a **break** statement as there are no other cases to skip.

There will be instances when a particular group of instructions is associated with more than one **case** option. As an example, consider the timetable again. Let's assume that both groups 'A' and 'C' have a laboratory at 10.00 a.m. The following **switch** statement would process this without grouping case 'A' and 'C' together:

```
// groups A and C have labs at the same time
switch(group)
{
    case 'A':   System.out.println("10.00 a.m.");
                break;
    case 'B':   System.out.println("1.00 p.m.");
                break;
    case 'C':   System.out.println("10.00 a.m.");
                break;
    default: System.out.println("No such group");
}
```

While this will work, both **case** 'A' and **case** 'C' have the same instruction associated with them:

```
System.out.println("10.00 a.m.");
```

Rather than repeating this instruction, the two **case** statements can be combined into one as follows:

```
// groups A and C have been processed together
switch(group)
{
    case 'A': case 'C':  System.out.println("10.00 a.m.");
                         break;
    case 'B':            System.out.println("1.00 p.m.");
                         break;
    default: System.out.println("No such group");
}
```

In the example above a time of 10.00 a.m. will be displayed when the group is either 'A' or 'C'. The example above combined two **case** statements, but there is no limit to how many such statements can be combined.

So far we have always used a **break** statement to avoid executing the code associated with more than one **case** statement. Since **Java 14,** an alternative version of the **switch** statement was introduced that assumes that only one option is to be executed and so does not require the **break** statement at the end of each option. The modified version of the **switch** statement also simplifies code where multiple **case**s need to be associated with a single option as in the example above. The code fragment below rewrites the example above by making use of this new version of the **switch** statement. Take a look at it, and then we will discuss it:

```
// alternative switch since Java 14
switch(group)
{
    case 'A', 'C' ->  System.out.println("10.00 a.m.");
    case 'B'      ->  System.out.println("1.00 p.m.");
    default       ->  System.out.println("No such group");
}
```

As you can see this version of the **switch** statement is considerably simplified. Grouped **case** statements are separated by commas rather than having to use the **case** keyword multiple times (in this example **case** 'A', 'C'); the colon separator is replaced by an arrow (->) and there is no need for **break** statements as each option is considered discrete (i.e. only one option will be executed). With this modified version of the **switch** statement, however, one option *must be executed;* otherwise this will result in a compiler error. Adding a **default** option will always ensure that this will be the case. Leaving out the **default** would therefore result in a compiler error in this example as the group entered may be a value other than 'A' or 'C'.

Apart from the new version of the **switch** statement only being available if you have Java 14, another reason you might want to use the standard version of the **switch** statement is that occasionally you *do* wish to execute the code associated with more than one **case** option. For example, let us assume that spies working for a secret agency are allocated different levels of security clearance, the lowest being 1 and the highest being 3. A spy with the highest clearance level of 3 can access all the secrets, whereas a spy with a clearance of level of 1 can see only secrets that have the lowest level of security. An administrator needs to be able to view the collection of secrets that a spy with a particular clearance level can see. We can implement this scenario by way of a **switch** statement in the below. Take a look at it and then we will discuss it.

```
SecretAgents.java

import java.util.Scanner;

public class SecretAgents
{
    public static void main(String[] args)
    {
        int security;
        Scanner keyboard = new Scanner(System.in);
        System.out.println("***Secret Agents***");
        System.out.print("Enter security level (1,2,3): ");
        security = keyboard.nextInt();
        switch(security) // check level of security
        {
            case 3: System.out.println("The code to access the safe is 007."); // level 3 security
            case 2: System.out.println("Jim Kitt is really a double agent."); // level 2 security
            case 1: System.out.println("Martinis in the hotel bar may be poisoned."); // level 1 security
                    break; // necessary to avoid error message below
            default: System.out.println("No such security level.");
        }
    }
}
```

You can see that there is just a single **break** statement at the end of **case** 1.

```
case 3: System.out.println("The code to access the safe is 007.");
case 2: System.out.println("Jim Kitt is really a double agent.");
case 1: System.out.println("Martinis in the hotel bar may be poisoned.");
        break; // the only break statement
```

If the user entered a security level of 3 for example, the `println` instruction associated with this case would be executed:

```
case 3: System.out.println("The code to access the safe is 007.");
```

However, as there is no **break** statement at the end of this instruction, the instruction associated with the **case** below is then also executed:

```
System.out.println("Jim Kitt is really a double agent.");
```

We have still not reached a **break** statement, so the instruction associated with the next **case** statement is then executed:

```
System.out.println("Martinis in the hotel bar may be poisoned.");
break; // the only break statement
```

Here we do reach a **break** statement. so the **switch** terminates. Here is a sample test run:

```
***Secret Agents***
Enter security level (1,2,3): 3
The code to access the safe is 007.
Jim Kitt is really a double agent.
Martinis in the hotel bar may be poisoned.
```

Because the security level entered is 3 *all* secrets can be revealed. Here is another sample test run when security level 2 is entered:

```
***Secret Agents***
Enter security level (1,2,3): 2
Jim Kitt is really a double agent.
Martinis in the hotel bar may be poisoned.
```

Because the security level is 2 the first secret is not revealed.

The last **break** statement is necessary as we wish to avoid the final error message if a valid security level (1, 2 or 3) is entered. The error message is only displayed if an invalid security level is entered:

```
***Secret Agents***
Enter security level (1,2,3): 8
No such security level.
```

14.3   Iteration in Java

As we introduced in Chap. 4, *iteration* is the form of program control that allows us to instruct the computer to carry out a task several times by repeating a section of code, and the programming structure that is used to control this repetition is often called a **loop**. There are three types of loop in Java:

- **for** loop;
- **while** loop;
- **do** … **while** loop.

We saw in Chap. 4 that Python also has a **for** loop and a **while** loop, but no **do...while** loop. We will consider each of these in turn.

14.3.1   The 'for' Loop

As with Python, we will use a **for** loop in Java if we wish to repeat a section of code a *fixed* number of times. Python uses the **range** function, in conjunction with a counter variable, to determine the number of times a **for** loop should repeat via a counter's start value, end value and step change. The Java **for** loop is controlled in a similar way—but without the convenience of a **range** function. The general form of a **for** loop in Java is given as follows:

```
for( /* start counter */ ; /* test counter */ ; /* change counter */)
{
    // instruction(s) to be repeated go here
}
```

As you can see there are three bits of information in the header of the **for** loop, each bit separated by a semicolon, which determine, respectively, the counter start value, a test to *continue the loop* and the change to the counter after each iteration.

Let's look at an example of this **for** loop in action. The program below revisits the drawpattern.py examples of Chap. 4 which displayed five rows of stars on the screen, this time using Java's **for** loop. Take a look at it and then we will discuss it:

DrawPattern.java

```
public class DrawPattern
{
    public static void main (String[] args)
    {
        for(int i = 1; i <= 5; i++) // loop to repeat 5 times
        {
            System.out.println("*****"); // instruction to display one row
        }
    }
}
```

Following the standard template for a Java **for** loop, there are three bits of information in the header of this **for** loop. All three bits of information relate to a **counter** variable (usually integer) that has to be created. In this case we have called our counter i, but of course we could give it any variable name.

First the counter is initialized to some value. Here, we have decided to initialize the counter to 1:

```
for(int i = 1; i <= 5; i++) // counter initialized to 1
{
    System.out.println("*****");
}
```

Notice that the loop counter i is *declared* as well as initialized in the header of the loop, as all variables in Java need to be declared before use. Although it is possible to declare the counter variable *prior* to the loop, declaring it within the header restricts the use of this variable to the loop itself. This is often preferable.

In the Java **for** loop the second item is a *test* that determines if the loop should *continue*. When the test returns a **boolean** value of **true,** the loop repeats; when it returns a **boolean** value of **false,** the loop ends. In this case the counter is tested to see if it is less than or equal to 5 (as we wish to repeat this loop 5 times):

```
for(int i = 1; i <= 5; i++) // counter tested
{
    System.out.println("*****");
}
```

Since the counter was initially set to 1, this test is **true** and the loop is entered. We sometimes refer to the instructions inside the loop as the **body** of the loop. As with **if** statements, the braces of the **for** loop can be omitted when only a single instruction is required in the body of the loop—but for clarity we will always use braces with our loops. When the body of the loop is entered, all the instructions within the braces of the loop are executed. In this case there is only one instruction to execute:

```
for(int i = 1; i <= 5; i++)
{
    System.out.println("*****"); // this line is executed
}
```

This line prints a row of stars on the screen. Once the instructions inside the braces are complete, the loop *returns to the beginning* where the third bit of information in the header of the **for** loop is executed. If we want the loop to repeat 5 times and we have started the counter off at 1, we should *add 1* to the counter each time we go around the loop:

```
for(int i = 1; i <= 5; i++) // counter is changed
{
    System.out.println("*****");
}
```

Notice we have used the shorthand for adding one to the counter (i++), but we could have written the full assignment here (i = i + 1). After the first increment, the counter now has the value of 2. Once the counter has been changed the test is examined again to see if the loop should repeat:

```
for(int i = 1; i <= 5; i++) // counter tested again
{
    System.out.println("*****");
}
```

This test is still **true** as the counter is still not greater than 5. Since the test is **true**, the body of the loop is entered again and another row of stars printed. This process of checking the test, entering the loop and changing the counter repeats until five rows of stars have been printed. At this point the counter is incremented as usual:

```
for(int i = 1; i <= 5; i++) // counter eventually equals 6
{
    System.out.println("*****");
}
```

Now when the test is checked, it is **false** as the counter is greater than five:

```
for(int i = 1; i <= 5; i++) // now the test is false
{
    System.out.println("*****");
}
```

When the test of the **for** loop is **false**, the loop stops. The instructions inside the loop are skipped, and the program continues with any instructions after the loop.

As with the Python **for** loop, you may start your counter at *any* value and change the counter in any way you choose when constructing your loops. For example, we could have rewritten the **for** loop of the above program so that the counter starts at 0 instead of 1. In that case, if we wish the **for** loop to still execute the instructions 5 times, the counter should reach 4 and not 5:

```
// this counter starts at 0 and goes up to 4 so the loop still executes 5 times
for(int i = 0; i <= 4; i++)
{
    System.out.println("*****");
}
```

Or we could have changed the test so that the counter should remain strictly less than 5:

```
// this counter starts at 0 and still goes up to 4, so the loop still executes 5 times
for(int i = 0; i < 5; i++)
{
    System.out.println("*****");
}
```

We can also change the way we modify the counter after each iteration. Returning to the original **for** loop, we would increment the counter by 2 each time instead of 1. If we still wish the loop to repeat 5 times, we could start at 2 and get the counter to go up to 10:

```
// this loop still executes 5 times
for(int i = 2; i <= 10; i = i+2) // the counter moves up in steps of 2
{
    System.out.println("*****");
}
```

Finally, as with Python **for** loops, Java **for** loop counters can move down as well as up. Here we rewrite the `countdown.py` program of Chap. 4, that printed out a countdown of the numbers from 10 down to 1, in Java:

Countdown.java

```
public class Countdown
{
    public static void main(String[] args)
    {
        System.out.println("*** Numbers from 10 to 1 ***");
        System.out.println();
        for (int i=10; i >= 1; i--) // counter moving down from 10 to 1
        {
            System.out.println(i);
        }
    }
}
```

Here the counter starts at 10 and is reduced by 1 each time. The loop stops when the counter falls below the value of 1.

Remember, the body of a loop can contain any number and type of instructions, including variable declarations, **if** statements, **switch** statements, or even another loop (nested loops). As an example of this consider the program DrawPattern2 below, which displays a square of stars as before, but this time uses a pair of nested loops to achieve this (compare this to its Python equivalent—`drawpattern6.py`—of Chap. 4):

DrawPattern2.java

```
public class DrawPattern2
{
  public static void main (String[] args)
  {
      for(int i = 1; i <= 5; i++) // outer loop as before
      {
          for (int j = 1; j <= 5; j++) // inner loop to display one row of stars
          {
              System.out.print("*");
          } // inner loop ends here
          System.out.println(); // necessary to start next row on a new line
      } // outer loop ends here
  }
}
```

14.3.2   The 'while' Loop

However the **for** loop is ideal for fixed repetition, the **while** loop allows for non-fixed iteration. The syntax for constructing this loop in Java is as follows:

```
while ( /* test goes here */ )
{
    // instruction(s) to be repeated go here
}
```

We have already used a **while** loop in Python. The only difference between this Java syntax and the Python syntax is the familiar differences you have now seen between these two languages: the test is in round brackets and the block of code inside the loop is marked by braces rather than indentation (although again indentation is useful to improve code readability).

We saw that a common application of the **while** loop is for *input validation*. The program below uses a Java **while** loop to ensure that an exam mark entered is within a valid range (between 0 and 100)—compare it to the Python equivalent (displayresult2.py) from Chap. 4:

```
DisplayResult2.java

import java.util.Scanner;

public class DisplayResult2
{
    public static void main(String[] args)
    {
        int mark;
        Scanner keyboard = new Scanner(System.in);
        System.out.print("What exam mark did you get? ");
        mark = keyboard.nextInt();
        // input validation
        while (mark < 0 || mark > 100) // check if mark is invalid
        {
            // display error message
            System.out.print("Invalid mark: please re-enter: ");
            // mark must be re-entered
            mark = keyboard.nextInt();
        }
        // by this point loop is finished and mark will be valid
        if (mark >= 40)
        {
            System.out.println("Congratulations, you passed");
        }
        else
        {
            System.out.println("I'm sorry, but you failed");
        }
        System.out.println("Good luck with your other exams");
    }
}
```

14.3.3 The 'do...while' Loop

There is one more loop construct in Java that we need to tell you about: the **do...while** loop. As we have already mentioned, this loop is not available in Python.

The **do...while** loop, like the **while** loop, allows for non-fixed repetitions to be implemented, but, unlike the **while** loop, the **do...while** loop has its test at the *end* of the loop rather than at the *beginning*. The syntax of a **do...while** loop is given below:

```
do
{
    // instruction(s) to be repeated go here
} while ( /* test goes here */ ); // note the semi-colon at the end
```

You are probably wondering what difference it makes if the test is at the end or the beginning of the loop. Well, there is one subtle difference. If the test is at the end of the loop, the loop will iterate *at least once*. If the test is at the beginning of the loop, however, there is a possibility that the condition will be **false** to begin with, and the loop is never executed. A **while** loop therefore executes *zero or more times,* whereas a **do...while** loop executes *one or more times.*

To make this a little clearer, look back at the **while** loop we just showed you for validating exam marks. If the user entered a valid mark initially (such as 66), the test to trap an invalid mark (mark < 0 || mark > 100) would be **false** and the loop would be skipped altogether. A **do...while** loop would not be appropriate here as the possibility of never getting into the loop should be left open.

When would a **do...while** loop be suitable? Well, any time you wish to code a non-fixed loop that must execute at least once. Usually, this would be the case when the test can take place only *after* the loop has been entered.

To illustrate this, let's look again at programs we want to keep repeating until the user chooses to quit. This would involve asking the user each time if he or she would like to continue repeating the program, or to stop.

A **for** loop would not be the best loop to choose here as this is more useful when the number of repetitions can be predicted. A **while** loop is not ideal, because the test that checks the user's response to the question would be carried out at the beginning of the loop. In Python we had no choice but to use a **while** loop, so we had to artificially initialize the user's choice before interacting with the user. Ideally, a better solution would be to move the test to the end of the loop—which is exactly what the **do...while loop** allows us to do. In outline, such a program could look something like this:

```
char response; // variable to hold user response
do // place code in loop
{
  // program instructions go here
  System.out.println("another go (y/n)?");
  response = keyboard.next().charAt(0); // get user reply
} while (response == 'y' || response == 'Y'); // test must be at the end of the loop
```

As an example of this application of the **do...while** loop, the program below revisits the findtax3.py Python program of Chap. 4, which calculated the tax on a product and allowed the user to repeat the program as often as he or she chooses. Here we have rewritten it in Java, making use of the **do...while** loop, and adapted it (as we did in the last chapter) so that this time it calculates the final cost of the product:

```
FindCost3.java

import java.util.Scanner;

public class FindCost3
{
    public static void main(String[] args)
    {
        double price, tax;
        char reply;
        Scanner keyboard = new Scanner(System.in);
        do // use 'do..while' loop to repeat program if required
        {
            // these instructions as before
            System.out.println("*** Product Price Check ***");
            System.out.print("Enter initial price: ");
            price = keyboard.nextDouble();
            System.out.print("Enter tax rate: ");
            tax = keyboard.nextDouble();
            price = price * (1 + tax/100);
            System.out.println("Cost after tax = " + price);

            // now see if user wants another go
            System.out.println();
            System.out.print("Would you like to enter another product(y/n)?: ");
            reply = keyboard.next().charAt(0);
            System.out.println();
        } while (reply == 'y' || reply == 'Y'); // test at the end of the loop
    }
}
```

In the original Python program of Chap. 4 (findtax3.py) we had to use a **while** loop with the test at the top of this block of code and artificially initialize the user reply before we got our first user response. But Java's **do..while** loop allows the test to be placed where it is really needed—at the end of the block of code.

14.3.4   Picking the Right Loop

With three types of loop to choose from in Java, it can sometimes be difficult to decide upon the best one to use in each case, especially as it is technically possible to pick *any type of loop* to implement *any type of repetition*! For example, **while** and **do...while** loops *can* be used for fixed repetitions by introducing your own counter and checking this counter in the test of the loop. However, it is always best to pick the most appropriate loop construct to use in each case, as this will simplify the logic of your code. Here are some general guidelines that should help you:

- if the number of repetitions required can be determined prior to entering the loop —use a **for** loop;
- if the number of repetitions required cannot be determined prior to entering the loop, and you wish to allow for the possibility of zero iterations—use a **while** loop;
- if the number of repetitions required cannot be determined before the loop, and you require at least one iteration of the loop—use a **do...while** loop.

14.4   Menu-Driven Programs in Java

As we saw in Chap. 4, a neat way to allow a program to be run repeatedly is to include a *menu* of options within a loop. In Python we used a **while** loop to implement such a menu-driven program and processed the menu choices using **if** and **elif** statements. In Java we can use the more appropriate **do..while** loop (as the test related to the menu choice will come at the end of this block), and we can process the menu choice itself using the neater **switch** statement.

As an example, the program below is a Java reworking of the menu-driven timetablewithloop.py Python program of Chap. 4:

TimetableWithLoop.java

```java
import java.util.Scanner;

public class TimetableWithLoop
{
    public static void main(String[] args)
    {
        char response;
        Scanner keyboard = new Scanner(System.in);
        System.out.println("***Lab Times***");
        do // put code in 'do...while' loop
        {
            // offer menu of options
            System.out.println(); // create a blank line
            System.out.println("[1] TIME FOR GROUP A");
            System.out.println("[2] TIME FOR GROUP B");
            System.out.println("[3] TIME FOR GROUP C");
            System.out.println("[4] QUIT PROGRAM");
            System.out.print("enter choice [1,2,3,4]: ");
            response = keyboard.next().charAt(0); // get response
            System.out.println(); // create a blank line
            switch(response) // process response
            {
                case '1':   System.out.println("10.00 a.m ");
                            break;
                case '2':   System.out.println("1.00 p.m ");
                            break;
                case '3':   System.out.println("11.00 a.m ");
                            break;
                case '4':   System.out.println("Goodbye ");
                            break;
                default:  System.out.println("Options 1-4 only!");
            }
        } while (response != '4'); // test for Quit option
    }
}
```

Notice that the menu option is treated as a character here, rather than an integer. So option 1 would be interpreted as the character '1' rather than the number 1, for example. The advantage of treating the menu option as a character rather than a number is that an incorrect menu entry would not result in a program crash if the value entered was non-numeric.

14.5   The 'break' and 'continue' Statements

We met the **break** statement when looking at **switch** statements in Java. The **break** statement can also be used with Java's loops to terminate a loop before it reaches its natural end, just as we also saw with loops in Python.

Here, for example, is a Java version of the `secretnumber.py` Python program of Chap. 3 that allowed the user a maximum of three attempts to guess a secret number. It makes use of a **for** loop in conjunction with the **break** statement:

SecretNumber.java

```java
import java.util.Scanner;

// This program demonstrates the use of the 'break' statement inside a 'for' loop

public class SecretNumber
{

  public static void main(String[] args)
  {
     Scanner keyboard = new Scanner (System.in);
     final int SECRET = 27; // secret number
     int num; // to hold user's guess
     boolean guessed = false; // so far number not guessed

     System.out.println("You have 3 goes to guess the secret number");
     System.out.println("HINT: It is a number less than 50!");
     System.out.println();

     // this loop contains an optionto exit early using a 'break' statement
     for (int i= 1; i <= 3; i++) // loop repeats 3 times
     {
        System.out.print("Enter guess: ");
        num = keyboard.nextInt();
        // check guess
        if (num == SECRET) // check if number guessed correctly
        {
           guessed = true; // record number has been guessed correctly
           break; // exit loop
        }
     }

     // now check to see if the number was guessed correctly or not
     if (guessed)
     {
        System.out.println("Number guessed correctly");
     }
     else
     {
        System.out.println("Number NOT guessed");
     }
  }
}
```

As with Python, the **continue** statement of Java forces a loop to skip the remaining instructions in the body of the loop and to *continue* to the next iteration. As an example, here is a Java version of the `displayeven2.py` Python program of Chap. 4 that displayed numbers from 10 down to 1, but skipped a number if it was odd. In this way, only even numbers are displayed:

DisplayEven2.java

```java
public class DisplayEven2
{
  public static void main(String[] args)
  {
     System.out.println("*** Even numbers from 10 to 1 ***");
     System.out.println();
     for(int i=10; i>=1; i--)
     {
        if (i%2 != 0) // check if number is NOT even
        {
           continue; // skips the rest of this iteration and moves to the next iteration
        }
        System.out.println(i); // even number only displayed if we have not skipped this iteration
     }
  }
}
```

14.6   Self-test Questions

1. Which selection control structure of Python is not available in Java and which Java iteration control structure is not available in Python?
2. Consider the Java program below for displaying the price of a cinema ticket:

```java
import java.util.Scanner;

public class CinemaTicket
{
    public static void main(String[] args)
    {
        double price = 10.00;
        int age;
        Scanner keyboard = new Scanner(System.in);
        System.out.print("Enter your age: ");
        age = keyboard.nextInt();
        // code to reduce ticket price for children goes here
        System.out.println("Ticket price = " + price);
    }
}
```

Replace the comment so that children under the age of 14 get half price tickets. Compare this program to the equivalent Python program in self-test question 3 of Chap. 3.

3. Consider the following program and compare it to the equivalent Python program in self-test question 4 of Chap. 3:

```java
import java.util.Scanner;

public class Colours
{
    public static void main(String[] args)
    {
        int x;
        Scanner keyboard = new Scanner(System.in);
        System.out.print("Enter a number: ");
        x = keyboard.nextInt();
        if (x > 10)
        {
            System.out.println("Green");
            System.out.println("Blue");
        }
        System.out.println("Red");
    }
}
```

What would be the output from this program if

(a) the user entered 10 when prompted?
(b) the user entered 20 when prompted?
(c) the braces used in the **if** statement are removed, and the user enters 10 when prompted?
(d) the braces used in the **if** statement are removed, and the user enters 20 when prompted?

4. Consider the following program and compare it to the equivalent Python program in self-test question 5 of Chap. 3:

```
import java.util.Scanner;

public class Colours2
{
    public static void main(String[] args)
    {
        int x;
        Scanner keyboard = new Scanner(System.in);
        System.out.print("Enter a number: ");
        x = keyboard.nextInt();
        if (x > 10)
        {
            System.out.println("Green");
        }
        else
        {
            System.out.println("Blue");
        }
        System.out.println("Red");
    }
}
```

What would be the output from this program if

(a) the user entered 10 when prompted?
(b) the user entered 20 when prompted?

5. When is it appropriate to use a **switch** statement in Java?
6. Consider the following program:

```
import java.util.Scanner;

public class Colours

{
    public static void main(String[] args)
    {
        int x;
        Scanner keyboard = new Scanner(System.in);
        System.out.print("Enter a number: ");
        x = keyboard.nextInt();
        switch (x)
        {
            case 1: case 2: System.out.println("Green"); break;
            case 3: case 4: case 5: System.out.println("Blue"); break;
            default: System.out.println("numbers 1-5 only");
        }
        System.out.println("Red");
    }
}
```

What would be the output from this program if

(a)   the user entered 1 when prompted?
(b)   the user entered 2 when prompted?
(c)   the user entered 3 when prompted?
(d)   the user entered 10 when prompted?

(e)   the **break** statements were removed from the **switch** statement and the user entered 3 when prompted?

(f)   the **default** was removed from the **switch** statement and the user entered 10 when prompted?

7. How does Python's **for** loop differ from Java's **for** loop?
8. Consider the following program:

```
public class IterationQ8
{
  public static void main(String[] args)
  {
      for(int i = 2; i <= 12;  i = i + 2)
      {
         System.out.println("YES");
      }
      System.out.println("OK");
  }
}
```

(a)   How many times does this **for** loop repeat?

(b)   What would be the output of this program?

9. Which Java loop would be appropriate to use in each of the following cases:

(a)   repeating a section of code zero or more times?

(b)   repeating a section of code a fixed number of times?

(c)   repeating a section of code one or more times?

10. Explain how **break** and **continue** statements be used in conjunction with Java's loops.

14.7   Programming Exercises

1. Implement and run the programs from self-test questions 2, 3, 4, 6 and 8 above to check your answers to these questions.
2. In programming exercises 2–8 from Chap. 3, you wrote a number of Python programs. Rewrite these programs in Java.
3. In programming exercises 9–10 from Chap. 3, you wrote two Python programs that required a multiple choice to be implemented. Rewrite these programs in Java making use of the **switch** statement in each case.
4. In programming exercises 2–7 from Chap. 4, you wrote a number of Python programs. Rewrite these programs in Java.

*Note when rewriting Chap. 4's programming exercise 6, part (d), you should use Java's **do...while** loop instead of a **while** loop.*

5. In programming exercises 8 and 9 from Chap. 4, you wrote two menu-driven Python programs. Rewrite these programs in Java making use of a **do...while** loop in conjunction with a **switch** statement in each case.

Java Methods

15

Outcomes:

By the end of this chapter you should be able to:

- **declare and define** methods in Java;
- **call** a method in Java;
- distinguish between **actual parameters** and **formal parameters**;
- define a method's **return type**;
- declare and use **overloaded** methods in Java;
- use some of the built-in methods of the Java **Math** class.

15.1 Introduction

In Chap. 5 we discussed the use of functions (a named group of instructions to carry out a particular task) in Python. Java, like many other languages, also allows us to define and use functions—but in Java we usually refer to these named group of instructions as a **method**. While methods in Java are very similar to functions in Python, there are some important differences that we shall explain to you.

Supplementary Information The online version contains supplementary material available at https://doi.org/10.1007/978-3-031-01326-3_15.

15.2   Declaring and Defining Methods

Unlike Python, all Java programs *must have* at least one method in them—that method is the `main` method. For example, in Chap. 5 we used the `dataentry.py` program in Python, which initially did not contain any of our own functions. Here is the equivalent program written in Java.

DataEntry.java

```java
import java.util.Scanner;

public class DataEntry
{
        public static void main(String[] args)// all instructions inside the main method
        {
                Scanner keyboard = new Scanner(System.in);

                int year, month, day;

                // prompt for year of birth
                System.out.println("Please enter the year of your birth");

                // display confidentiality message
                System.out.println("Please note that all information supplied is confidential");
                System.out.println("No personal details will be shared with any third party");

                // get year from user
                year = keyboard.nextInt();

                // prompt for month of birth
                System.out.println("Please enter the month of your birth as a number from 1 to 12");

                // display confidentiality message
                System.out.println("Please note that all information supplied is confidential");
                System.out.println("No personal details will be shared with any third party");

                // get month from user
                month = keyboard.nextInt();

                // prompt for day of birth
                System.out.println("Please enter the day of your birth as a number from 1 to 31");

                // display confidentiality message
                System.out.println("Please note that all information supplied is confidential");
                System.out.println("No personal details will be shared with any third party");

                // get day from user
                day = keyboard.nextInt();

                // more code here
        }
}
```

You can see that all the instructions are contained in the `main` method, whereas in the equivalent Python program you can have global program instructions not inside any function. So far, the Java programs we have shown you have just contained this `main` method. But our Java programs can be made up of a number of methods with names of your choice; however you must stick to the name of `main` for your entry method.

In Chap. 5 we rewrote the `dataentry.py` program by making use of a `displayMessage` function for displaying the confidentiality message. This is how the `displayMessage` method would be written in Java:

```
static void displayMessage()
{
    System.out.println("Please note that all information supplied is confidential");
    System.out.println("No personal details will be shared with any third party");
}
```

As usual, you can see that rather than using indentation, the body of this method in Java is contained between the two curly brackets. You will notice that there is no equivalent to Python's def keyword for introducing a method definition. Instead, the first line, which declares the method, is called the method **header** and consists of three words—let's look into each of these a bit more closely as it is a little different from the way we did things in Python:

static

You have seen this word in front of the main method many times now. However, we won't be explaining its meaning to you properly until Chap. 17. For now, all you need to know is that methods that have been declared as **static** (such as main) can only call other methods in the class if they too are **static**. So, if we did not declare displayMessage as **static** and tried to call it from the main method then our program would not compile.

void

As we saw with Python functions in Chap. 5, it is possible for a method to *send back* or *return* some information once it terminates. In Java, because it is a strongly typed language (i.e. every value we use needs to be of a specified fixed type), we need to be explicit about the type of the value returned, and this information is stated after the word **static**. This particular method simply displays a message on the screen, so we don't require it to send back any information when it terminates. The word **void** in Java indicates that the method does not return any information.

displayMessage()

This is the name that we have chosen to give our method. As with Python functions, the name of a method has to follow the same rules as naming a variable and is followed by a pair of empty brackets that can be used to send some information *into* a method. However, as the method is doing nothing more that displaying a message on the screen we do not have to send in any information and the brackets are left empty.

All the methods that we write in a Java class must reside within the curly brackets of the class. The order in which you write these methods is not important in Java, but we will always put the main method as the first method in our class and additional methods below that, as in the outline below:

```
import java.util.Scanner;

public class DataEntryWithMethods
{
        public static void main(String[] args)// main method defined first here
        {
                // code for main method here
        }

        // additional methods defined below, also within the class

        static void displayMessage()
        {
                // code for displayMessage method here
        }

}
```

15.3   Calling a Method

We call a method in Java in the same way that you would call a function in Python by simply using its name, along with the following brackets, which in this case are empty. So, in this case our method call, which will be placed at the point in the main method where we need it, looks just as it did in Python:

```
displayMessage();
```

Now we can rewrite our DataEntry program, replacing the appropriate lines of code with simple method calls. The whole program is shown below:

DataEntry2.java

```
import java.util.Scanner;

public class DataEntry2
{
        public static void main(String[] args)
        {
                Scanner keyboard = new Scanner(System.in);

                int year, month, day;

                System.out.println("Please enter the year of your birth");
                displayMessage(); // call displayMessage method
                year = keyboard.nextInt();

                System.out.println("Please enter the month of your birth as a number from 1 to 12");
                displayMessage(); // call displayMessage method
                month = keyboard.nextInt();

                System.out.println("Please enter the day of your birth as a number from 1 to 31");
                displayMessage(); // call displayMessage method
                day = keyboard.nextInt();

                // more code here
        }

        // the code for displayMessage method
        static void displayMessage()
        {
                System.out.println("Please note that all information supplied is confidential");
                System.out.println("No personal details will be shared with any third party");
        }
}
```

In most of the programs in this chapter, as in the example above, it will be the `main` method that calls other methods such as `displayMessage`. As with Python, however, it is perfectly possible for any method to call another method—and for a number of methods to be "chained", when any given method terminates, the control of the program would return to the method that called it.

15.4   Method Input and Output

As you know, it is possible to send some data into a method, and a method can send data back to the method that called it. Let's see how to do this in Java by returning to the `FindCost2` program that we showed you in Chap. 13 for adding sales tax to the price of a product:

FindCost2.java - a reminder

```
import java.util.Scanner;

/* a program to input the initial price of a product and then calculate and display its cost after
tax has been added */

public class FindCost2
{
        public static void main(String[] args)
        {
                Scanner keyboard = new Scanner(System.in);
                double price, tax;
                System.out.println("*** Product Price Check ***");
                System.out.print("Enter initial price: ");
                price = keyboard.nextDouble();
                System.out.print("Enter tax rate: ");
                tax = keyboard.nextDouble();
                price = price * (1 + tax/100);
                System.out.println("Cost after tax = " + price);
        }
}
```

In Chap. 5 we saw how to take the equivalent Python program and rewrite it to make use of a `calcTax` function to calculate the sales tax. Let's do something similar with the `FindCost2` program in Java and write an `addTax` method (as this program calculates the final price of the product). The line in the `main` method that currently calculates the new price, with the sales tax added, is this one:

```
price = price * (1 + tax/100);
```

Let's create a method that performs this calculation.

In Java we need to use parameters to send data from one method to another just as we do in Python, as variables created in one method are not visible to other methods —they only have *local* scope. So, the variables `price` and `tax` are *local* to the `main` method and are not visible to the `addTax` method; the only way to send their values to the `addTax` method is via parameters. We will also need to return the result of adding the tax to the price. Our method is going to look like this in Java:

```
static double addTax(double priceIn, double taxIn)
{
        return priceIn * (1 + taxIn/100);
}
```

You are familiar with the first word, **static**, but look at the next one; this time, where we previously saw the word **void**, we now have the word **double**. As we have said, this method must send back—or *return*—a result, the new price of the item. So, the type of data that the method is to return in this case is a **double.** In fact, what we are doing here is declaring a method of *type* **double**. Thus, in Java, the *type* of a method refers to its *return* type. It is possible to declare methods of any type—**int**, **boolean**, **char** and so on.

After the type declaration, we have the name of the method, in this case addTax —and this time the brackets aren't empty. As with Python, we send parameters to a method within these brackets. You can see that within these brackets we have two parameters, named priceIn and taxIn just as they were in our Python example in Chap. 5. But again, as Java is a strongly typed language, we must add the type information for any parameter much like declaring a variable. In this case we are declaring two variables, both of type **double**.

```
static double addTax(double priceIn, double taxIn)// parameters require types in Java
{
        // rest of method here
}
```

The variables declared in this way are known as the **formal parameters** of the method. Formal parameters are variables that are created exclusively to hold values sent in from the calling method. They are going to hold, respectively, the values of the price and the tax that are going to be sent in from the calling method (you will see how this is done in a moment). Of course, these variables could be given any name we choose, but we have called them priceIn and taxIn , respectively. We are using the convention of adding the suffix In to parameter names throughout this book.

It is worth noting that in Chap. 5 we introduced you to the idea of *global* as well as *local* variable scope in Python. Remember, global variables are variables declared *outside* of any method so are accessible throughout the program. In the examples you have seen, all our Java instructions have been within methods, so our programs *do not contain any global variables*.

Now we can turn our attention to the body of the method, which as you can see, in this case, consists of a single line:

```
return priceIn * (1 + taxIn/100);
```

As with Python, Java uses a **return** keyword to return control to the calling method and send it back a value. In this case it sends back the result of the calculation:

```
priceIn * (1 + taxIn/100)
```

You should note that if the method is of type **void**, then there is no need to include a **return** instruction—the method simply terminates once the last instruction is executed.

Now let's look at how we call this method and use its return value. The whole program appears below:

FindCost3.java

```
import java.util.Scanner;

public class FindCost3
{
    public static void main(String[] args )
    {
        Scanner keyboard = new Scanner(System.in);
        double price, tax;

        System.out.println("*** Product Price Check ***");

        System.out.print("Enter initial price: ");
        price = keyboard.nextDouble();
        System.out.print("Enter tax rate: ");
        tax = keyboard.nextDouble();

        price = addTax(price, tax); // call the addTax method
        System.out.println("Cost after tax = " + price);
    }

    static double addTax(double priceIn, double taxIn)
    {
        return priceIn * (1 + taxIn/100);
    }
}
```

The line in `main` that calls the method is this one:

```
price = addTax(price, tax);
```

You can see that this is exactly how we call a method in Python, by using its name and plugging in any data required. Since the items we need to send, `price` and `tax`, are the *actual* values that we are sending into our method, they are often referred to as the **actual parameters** of the method.

The mechanism for sending parameters from one method to another in Java varies slightly from that of Python. You know in Python the formal and actual parameters both point to the same location in memory (review Fig. 5.1 from Chap. 5 to see how this is done). In Java, however, a *copy* is made of the actual parameters and placed into the formal parameters of the called method. This process is illustrated in Fig. 15.1.

Since the formal parameters `priceIn` and `taxIn` contain copies of the actual parameters `price` and `tax` (rather than sharing the same location in memory), changing the value of formal parameters will not affect the value of the

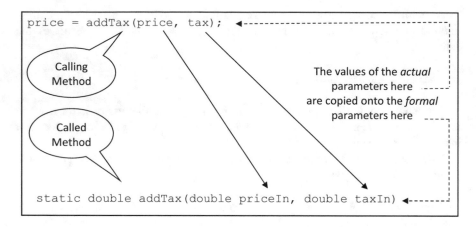

Fig. 15.1 Passing parameters from one method to another method in Java

corresponding actual parameters. So, although the underlying mechanism differs from Python to Java, the parameter passing behaviour remains the same: the ordering and numbering of parameters remain important not the names. Note however that, as Java is a strongly typed language, the *types* of corresponding actual and formal parameter must match also—otherwise this will cause a compiler error. For example, if we tried to send two **char**s to the addTax method instead of two **double**s, the compiler would flag an error:

```
price = addTax('p', 't'); // sending the wrong type of parameters will cause a compiler error!
```

Similarly, the return type of a method must be an appropriate type for the returned value. In this case we know the return type is a **double**, so if we tried to store the result in an integer variable, we could get a compiler error—for example:

```
int num = addTax(price, tax); // a double value cannot be returned and placed in an integer!
```

15.5   More Examples of Methods

To make sure you have understood how to write methods in Java and how this differs slightly from functions in Python, let us revisit a few other functions we developed in Python from Chap. 5 and rewrite them in Java, namely

- a square function;
- a max function;
- an isEven function.

The `square` function calculates the square of any number, so it should accept a single value of type **double**. Similarly, it will return a **double**. Here is our Java version of this method:

```
static double square(double numberIn)
{
        return numberIn * numberIn;
}
```

Assuming this method will be called by a `main` method, we have declared this method to be a **static** method as we will with our other examples here.

Now let's take a look at the `max` method for returning the maximum of two integers. It will receive two integers and return a single integer value.

```
static int max(int firstIn, int secondIn)
{
        if(firstIn > secondIn)
        {
                return firstIn;
        }
        else
        {
                return secondIn;
        }
}
```

As with Python, Java methods may have multiple return values.

Finally let's look at the method `isEven` that reports on whether or not a particular number is an even number. The test will be performed on integers, so we will need a single parameter of type **int**. The return value is interesting—the method will tell us whether or not a number is even, so it will need to return a value of **true** if the number is even or **false** if it is not. So, our return type is going to be **boolean**. Here is our method:

```
static boolean isEven(int numberIn)
{
        if(numberIn % 2 == 0)
        {
                return true;
        }
        else
        {
                return false;
        }
}
```

Again, as with the Python version we met in Chap. 5, there is a neater way of writing this that does not require an **if...else** statement, because the test (numberIn % 2 = = 0) is itself a boolean value:

```
static boolean isEven(int numberIn)
{
        return (numberIn % 2 == 0);
}
```

15.6   Method Overloading

In Chap. 9 we introduced you to the concept of *polymorphism*—this allows us to
have *multiple methods with the same name*, but whose *behaviour* is different. There
you met the idea of method *overriding* as one means to implement polymorphism.
Method overriding occurs when there are several methods with the same name *in
different classes*. As we will see in Chap. 18, when we look at Java applications
involving multiple classes, method overriding is also possible in Java. But also
available in Java is another form of polymorphism known as method *overloading*.

Method overloading occurs when you have two or more methods with the same
name *within the same class*. To illustrate, let's return to the `max` method of
Sect. 15.5. Here it is again:

```
static int max(int firstIn, int secondIn)
{
        if(firstIn > secondIn)
        {
                return firstIn;
        }
        else
        {
                return secondIn;
        }
}
```

As you will recall, this method accepts two integers and returns the greater of the
two. But what if we wanted to find the greatest of three integers? We would have to
write a new method, which we have shown below. We are just showing you the
header here—we will think about the actual instructions in a moment:

```
static int max(int firstIn, int secondIn, int thirdIn)
{
        // code goes here
}
```

You can see that we have given this method the same name as before—but this
time it has *three* parameters instead of two. And the really clever thing is that we
can declare and call both methods within the same class. Both methods have the
same name, but the parameter list is different—and each one will *behave* differently.
In our example, the original method compares two integers and returns the greater
of the two; the second one, once we have worked out the algorithm for doing this,
will examine three integers and return the value of the one that is the greatest of the
three. So **overloaded** methods share the same name within the same class *but are
distinguished by their parameter lists*.

The parameter list of overloaded methods can be distinguished by the number of
parameters (as in the case of the two `max` methods above) but also by the *type of*
parameters. So, for example a `max` method expecting two integer parameters can be
distinguished from a similar `max` method expecting two **double** parameters for
example. Python of course does not include type information on its parameters, and
this is why method overloading is not available in Python.

Now, you might be asking yourself how, when we call an overloaded method, the program knows which one we mean. The answer of course depends on the actual parameters that accompany the method call—they are matched with the formal parameter list, and the appropriate method will be called. So, if we made this call somewhere in a program:

```
int x = max(3, 5);
```

then the first version of max would be called—the version that returns the bigger of two integers. This, of course, is because the method is being called with two integer parameters, matching this header:

```
static int max(int firstIn, int secondIn)
```

However, if this call, with three integer parameters, was made:

```
int x = max(3, 5, 10);
```

then it would be the second version that was called:

```
static int max(int firstIn, int secondIn, int thirdIn)
```

One very important thing we have still to do is to devise the *algorithm* for this second version of our max. method above. Can you think of a way to do it? Have go at it before reading on.

One way to do it is to declare an integer variable, which we could call result, and start off by assigning to it the value of the first number. Then we can consider the next number. Is it greater than the current value of result? If it is, then we should assign this value to result instead of the original value. Now we can consider the third number—if this is larger than the current value of result, we assign its value to result. You should be able to see that result will end up having the value of the greatest of the three integers. It is helpful to express this as pseudocode:

```
SET result TO first number
IF second number > result
    SET result TO second number
IF third number > result
    SET result TO third number
RETURN result
```

Here is the code:

```
static int max(int firstIn, int secondIn, int thirdIn)
{
        int result;
        result = firstIn;
        if(secondIn > result)
        {
                result = secondIn;
        }
        if(thirdIn > result)
        {
                result = thirdIn;
        }
        return result;
}
```

Finally, here is a complete Java program that illustrates the use of our overloaded max methods:

OverloadingDemo.java

```
public class OverloadingDemo
{
        public static void main(String[] args)
        {
                int maxOfTwo, maxOfThree;
                maxOfTwo = max(2, 10);        // call the first version of max
                maxOfThree = max(-5, 5, 3); // call the second version of max
                System.out.println(maxOfTwo);
                System.out.println(maxOfThree);
        }

        // this version of max accepts two integers and returns the greater of the two
        static int max(int firstIn, int secondIn)
        {
                if(firstIn > secondIn)
                {
                        return firstIn;
                }
                else
                {
                        return secondIn;
                }
        }

        // this version of max accepts three integers and returns the greatest of the three
        static int max(int firstIn, int secondIn, int thirdIn)
        {
                int result;
                result = firstIn;
                if(secondIn > result)
                {
                        result = secondIn;
                }
                if(thirdIn > result)
                {
                        result = thirdIn;
                }
                return result;
        }
}
```

As the first call to max in the main method has two parameters, it will call the first version of max; the second call, with its three parameters, will call the second version. Not surprisingly then the output from this program looks like this:

```
10
5
```

It might have occurred to you that we could have implemented the second version of max (i.e. the one that takes three parameters) in a different way. We could have started off by finding the maximum of the first two integers (using the first version of max), and then doing the same thing again, comparing the result of this with the third number.

This version is presented below—this is an example of how we can call a method not from the main method, but from another method.

```
static int max(int firstIn, int secondIn, int thirdIn)
{
        int step1, result;
        step1 = max(firstIn, secondIn); // call the first version of max
        result = max(step1, thirdIn); // call the first version of max again
        return result;
}
```

Some of you might be thinking that if we wanted similar methods to deal with lists of four, five, six or even more numbers, it would be an awful lot of work to write a separate method for each one—and indeed it would! But don't worry—in the next chapter you will find that there is a much easier way to deal with situations like this.

15.7 Built-in Methods of the Math Class

Java comes with a large number of prewritten methods, some of which we have already used, such as println, nextInt and so on. These particular methods are, respectively, methods of the classes System and Scanner, and we access them via these classes. Methods such as println we can use at any time, since the System class is always available; others such as nextInt require us to import packages such as the util package, since the Scanner class is not always available and requires access to the util package. Actually, even classes such as System reside in a package—that package is the lang package in Java and it is always accessible without the need to explicitly import it. Within that lang package is a class called Math that contains a number of useful methods known as **static** methods which we can use at any time. We will discuss **static** methods in more detail in Chap. 17, but for now all you need to know is that **static** methods are accessed via the class name and the dot operator. Table 15.1 gives a list of some of the commonly used methods of the Math class:

You can see from Table 15.1 that the way we call a **static** method residing in another class is to append the name of the method to the class. Here for example, is how we could print out the square root of 64:

```
double answer = Math.sqrt(64); // call to sqrt method in Math class
System.out.println(answer);
```

Table 15.1 Some commonly
used methods of the Math
class

Method	Returns
Math.sqrt(x)	Square root of x
Math.pow(x,y)	x to the power of y
Math.round(x)	The closest whole number to x
Math.abs(x)	The absolute value of x
Math.max(x,y)	The maximum of two values x and y
Math.min(x,y)	The minimum of two values x and y

Notice that the square root method takes a **double** (so the 64 above is treated as 64.0), and it returns the result as a **double**. The output would be as expected:

```
8.0
```

You can also see in Table 15.1 that the Math class contains its own max method, as well as a min method. These methods are *overloaded* to take both integers and doubles (as is the abs method). The program below illustrates the use of these methods:

TestingMethodsOfMathClass.java

```
public class TestingMethodsOfMathClass
{
    public static void main(String args[])
    {
        // check square root
        System.out.println("Square root of 25 = " + Math.sqrt(25));
        // raise to the power
        System.out.println("4 to the power of 3 = " + Math.pow(4,3));
        // round to nearest whole number
        System.out.println("12.3 to nearest whole number = " + Math.round(12.3));
        // round to nearest whole number
        System.out.println("12.5 to nearest whole number = " + Math.round(12.5));
        // round to nearest whole number
        System.out.println("12.5 to nearest whole number = " + Math.round(12.7));
        // absolute value (ie positive value)
        System.out.println("Absolute value of -24.5 = " + Math.abs(-24.5));
        // maximum value
        System.out.println("Maximum value of 10 and 20 = " + Math.max(10, 20));
        // minimum value
        System.out.println("Minimum value of 10 and 20 = " + Math.min(10, 20));
    }
}
```

Below is the output that would be generated by this program:

```
Square root of 25 = 5.0
4 to the power of 3 = 64.0
12.3 to nearest whole number = 12
12.5 to nearest whole number = 13
12.7 to nearest whole number = 13
Absolute value of -24.5 = 24.5
Maximum value of 10 and 20 = 20
Minimum value of 10 and 20 = 10
```

Notice that a number which is exactly in the middle of an integer range (in the example above 12.5) is always rounded up by the round method. In Chap. 17 we will look at how you can package up your own **static** methods within a class for reuse.

15.8 Self-test Questions

1. How does the syntax of Java *methods* differ from the syntax of Python functions?
2. What would be the output of the following Java program?

```
public class MethodsQ2
{
    public static void main(String[] args)
    {
        method2();
        System.out.println("Orange");
        System.out.println("Red");
        method1();
    }

    static void method1()
    {
        System.out.println("Blue");
        method2();
    }

    static void method2()
    {
        System.out.println("Green");
    }
}
```

3. Consider the following code for a `test` method:

```
static boolean test (int numIn)
{
    return numIn > 0;
}
```

From the list of method calls that follows identify either what the output would be or, if the method call would cause a compiler error, what the error would be:

(a)

```
System.out.println( test(20) );
```

(b)

```
System.out.println( test(0) );
```

(c)

```
System.out.println( test(20.5) );
```

(d)

```
System.out.println( test() );
```

4. Consider a method, called `area`, that receives values representing the length and height of a rectangle (as **double**s), respectively, and returns the area of the given rectangle.

(a)   How many *parameters* would this method require and what *type* would they be?
(b)   What would the *return type* of this method be?
(c)   Assuming this method will be called by the `main` method of a program, write the code for this method.
(d)   Write the line of code that calls this method from the `main` method, with length and height 15.5 and 22.75, respectively, displaying the result on screen.

5. Consider the following program:

```
public class MethodsQ5
{
        public static void main(String[] args)
        {
                int x = 10;
                int y = 20;
                System.out.println( myMethod(x, y));
                System.out.println( myMethod(y));
        }

        static int myMethod(int firstIn, int secondIn)
        {
                return firstIn + secondIn;
        }

        static int myMethod(int firstIn)
        {
                return firstIn * firstIn;
        }
}
```

(a)   By referring to this program:

(i)   identify any *local* variables;
(ii)   distinguish between the terms *actual parameters* and *formal parameters*.
(iii) explain the meaning of the terms *polymorphism* and method *overloading*.

(b)   What would be displayed on the screen when this program was run?

6. What would be the output of the following program?

```
public class MethodsQ6
{
    public static void main(String args[])
    {
        System.out.println(Math.sqrt(16));
        System.out.println(Math.pow(2,4));
        System.out.println(Math.round(9.25));
        System.out.println(Math.round(10.5));
        System.out.println(Math.round(-4.7));
        System.out.println(Math.abs(-5.6));
        System.out.println(Math.max(25, 20));
        System.out.println(Math.min(25, 20));
    }
}
```

15.9 Programming Exercises

1. Implement the programs from the self-test questions 2, 5 and 6 in order to verify your answers.
2. Implement a program that includes a `main` method and the `test` method of question 3 in order to test your answers to that question.
3. Implement a program that includes a `main` method and the `area` method of question 4 in order to test your answers to that question. Add an additional method to calculate the perimeter of a rectangle and test this method by calling it from your `main` method with some test values.
4. In Sect. 5.8 of Chap. 5 we developed a circle calculation program to show you how to use functions in Python in conjunction with menu-driven programs. Rewrite this program in Java using methods.
5. In programming exercises 2, 4 and 5 from Chap. 5, we set you some programming challenges in using functions in Python. Rewrite these programs in Java making use of methods.

Java Arrays

16

Outcomes

By the end of this chapter you should be able to:

- *distinguish between an **array** in Java and a list in Python;*
- *create arrays in Java;*
- *use **for** loops to process arrays;*
- *use an enhanced **for** loop to process an array;*
- *use arrays as method parameters and return types;*
- *use arrays to send a **variable number of arguments** to a method;*
- *use methods of the **Arrays** class;*
- *distinguish between **one-dimensional** arrays and **multidimensional** arrays;*
- *create and process **two-dimensional** arrays;*
- *create **ragged arrays**.*

16.1 Introduction

In Chaps. 6 and 7 we showed you a number of Python data types such as **lists** and **dictionaries** that can be used to hold *collections* of values. Similar structures exist in Java—they are described as **collection classes** and together they form what is known as the **Java Collections Framework (JCF)**. We are going to explore these in depth in Chap. 21. However, in order to understand these, you need also to understand a number of other concepts which will be introduced to you in the coming chapters. In this chapter we are going to look at what could be described as a lower-level data type, namely the **array**. Arrays are the underlying concept on

Supplementary Information The online version contains supplementary material available at https://doi.org/10.1007/978-3-031-01326-3_16.

© Springer Nature Switzerland AG 2022
Q. Charatan and A. Kans, *Programming in Two Semesters*,
Texts in Computer Science, https://doi.org/10.1007/978-3-031-01326-3_16

which the higher-level collection classes are based, and they are a very important part of the Java language.

In Chap. 6 we showed you how to use the **list** type in Python to store and process a collection of values. Python's list type allows a collection of items to be stored, and for these items to be accessed via a common list name plus an index number. The list type in Python can store values of mixed types, is dynamic (in that it can grow/shrink as more items are added/removed) and comes packaged with a number of useful functions.

A very similar and fundamental data type in many programming languages, including Java, is an **array**. An array can also store a large collection of values that can be indexed, but the type of all elements within the array *must be the same*. Also, arrays are of a fixed size and are not dynamic. Python does not have a built-in array type (though an array type can be used in conjunction with external Python libraries such as NumPy). So, let's take a look at how to create and make use of arrays in Java to store collections of values.

One of the differences between a Java array and a Python collection that you will immediately notice is that all items in the array—unlike in a Python collection—must be of the *same type*. The other difference is that a Python collection (and indeed the Java collections that you will encounter later) can shrink and grow, whereas arrays, once they are declared, cannot change size.

16.2   Creating an Array in Java

As we have said, all the elements stored in a particular array must be of the *same type* but there is no restriction on which type this is. So, for example, an array can be used to hold a collection of **int** values or a collection of **char** values, but it cannot be used to hold a mixture of **int** and **char** values. Let's look at how to use arrays in your Java programs. First you need to know how to create an array. Array creation is a two-stage process in Java:

1. declare an array variable;
2. allocate memory to store the array elements.

An array variable is declared in much the same way as a simple variable except that a pair of square brackets is added after the type. For example, if an array were to hold a collection of integer variables, it could be declared as follows:

```
int[] someArray;
```

Here a name has been given to the array in the same way you would name any variable. The name we have chosen is someArray. If the square brackets were missing in the above declaration, this would just be a simple variable capable of holding a *single* integer value only. But the square brackets indicate this variable is an array allowing *many* integer values to be stored.

So, to declare an array temperature containing **double** values, you would write the following:

```
double[] temperature;
```

At the moment this simply declares temperature to be a variable that can be *linked* to a collection of **double** values. The temperature variable itself is said to hold a **reference** to the array elements. A reference is a variable that holds a *location* in the computer's memory (known as a memory *address*) where data is stored, rather than the data itself. This illustrated in Fig. 16.1.

At the moment the memory address stored in the temperature reference is not meaningful as the memory that will eventually hold the array elements has not been allocated yet. This is stage two.

What information do you think would be required in order to reserve enough space in the computer's memory for all the array elements?

Well, because an array is of a fixed size it would be necessary to state the size of the array, that is the *maximum* number of elements required by the array. Also, since each data type requires a different amount of memory space, it is also necessary to state the type of each individual array element (this will be the same type used in stage one of the array declaration.). The array type and size are then put together with a special **new** operator. For example, if we required an array of 10 integers, the following would be appropriate:

```
someArray = new int[10];
```

The **new** operator creates the space in memory for an array of the given size and element type.[1]

We will come back to look at this **new** operator when studying Java classes and objects in the next chapter. Once the size of the array is set it cannot be changed, so always make sure you create an array that is big enough for your purpose. Returning to the temperature example above, if you wanted the array to hold seven temperatures (one for each day of the week), you would allocate memory as follows:

```
temperature = new double[7];
```

Let's see what effect the **new** operator has on computer memory by looking at Fig. 16.2.

---

[1] Of course this size should not be a negative value. A negative value will cause an error in your program. We will discuss these kinds of errors further in Chap. 20.

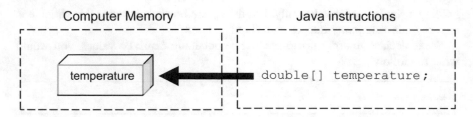

Fig. 16.1   The effect on computer memory of declaring an array reference

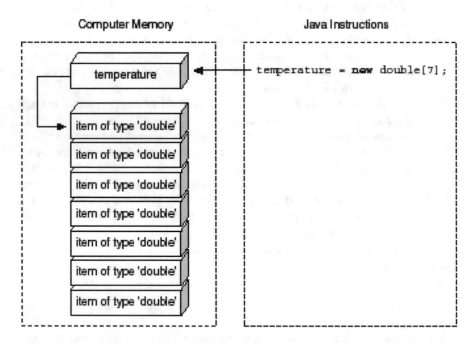

Fig. 16.2   The effect on computer memory of declaring an array of seven 'double' values

As can be seen from Fig. 16.2, the array creation has created seven continuous locations in memory. Each location is big enough to store a value of type **double**. The temperature variable is linked to these seven elements by containing the address of the very first element. In effect, the array reference, temperature, is linked to seven new variables. Each of these variables will automatically have some initial value placed in them. If the variables are of some number type (such as **int** or **double**), the value of each will be initially set to zero; if the variables are of type **char**, their values will be set initially to a special Unicode value that represents an empty character; if the variables are of **boolean** type they will each be set initially to **false**.

The two stages of array creation (declaring and allocating memory space for the elements) can also be combined into one step as follows:

```
double[] temperature = new double[7];
```

Just as with Python lists, individual elements in the array are then *uniquely identified* by an additional **index value** and again, as with Python lists, *array indices start from 0 and not from 1*. This index value is always enclosed in square brackets, so the first temperature in the list is identified as temperature[0], the second temperature by temperature[1] and so on—which is exactly how we access elements in a Python list. Similarly, if you try to access an invalid element such as temperature[7], the following program error will be generated by the system:

java.lang.ArrayIndexOutOfBoundsException

This type of error is called an *exception*. We briefly looked at Python exceptions in Chap. 4 and you will find out more about Java exceptions in Chap. 20, but you should be aware that, very often, exceptions will result in program termination.

Usually, when an array is created, values will be added into it as the program runs. If, however, all the values of the array elements are known beforehand, then an array can be created without the use of the **new** operator by initializing the array in a similar way you would initialize a Python list. For example:

```
double[] temperature = {9, 11.5, 11, 8.5, 7, 9, 8.5} ;
```

You can see that instead of enclosing these initial values in square brackets as with Python lists, initial array values are placed in braces—but they are separated by commas in Java just as list values are in Python. The compiler determines the length of the array from the number of initial values (in this case 7). Each value is placed into the array in order, so temperature[0] is set to 9, temperature[1] to 11.5 and so on. This is the only instance in which *all the elements* of an array can be assigned explicitly by listing the elements in a single assignment statement.

Once an array has been created, elements must be accessed *individually*.

16.3 Accessing Array Elements

As with Python lists, once an array has been created, its elements can be used like any other variable of the given type in Java. For example, the following command prints out the value of the *sixth* array element:

```
System.out.println(temperature[5]); // index 5 is the sixth element!
```

Now, what if you wanted to print out all the elements in the temperature array? Let's assume we have initialized the array with the seven values shown earlier—you might be tempted to do something like the following to print these values to the screen:

```
System.out.println(temperature); // trying to print the entire array?
```

We did something similar with Python lists, but unfortunately this will not produce the result expected in Java. Instead, you will see something like the following:

[D@15db9742

What is this strange looking output? Well, it is a representation of the *memory address* of the temperature array variable, not the elements of the array. Instead, if we wish to display all the elements in an array in Java, we will have to write some code to do this.

As with Python lists, very often code to process arrays involves using a **for** loop and using the *loop counter* as the *array index variable* to allow you to concisely process the entire array. For example, to print out all the items in the temperature array we could use the following **for** loop;

```
for(int i = 0; i < 7; i++) // note, loop counter runs from 0 to 6
{
        System.out.println(temperature[i]); // use loop counter as array index
}
```

Notice the loop counter follows the array indices, so starts at **0** and ends at **6** in this case; the test (i < 7) ensures the counter never reaches the invalid index of 7. Of course, if we rewrite the code to change the size of the array, we would need to change this test accordingly. To avoid having to change the tests in these **for** loops each time we resize the array, it is better to use the length attribute built into Java arrays, via the dot operator, which returns the current length of an array for us (7 in this case):

```
for(int i = 0; i < temperature.length; i++) // use the length attribute in for loops
{
        System.out.println(temperature[i]);
}
```

Given the `length` attribute makes your code more adaptable to change, we will always use it to write our **for** loops when processing arrays. Assuming the array was initialized with the seven values given earlier, this loop will produce the expected output:

```
9.0
11.5
11.0
8.5
7.0
9.0
8.5
```

16.4 The Enhanced 'for' Loop

As you can see from the examples above, when processing an entire array, a **for** loop is often required, with the loop counter used as the array index within the body of the loop. In fact, very often, when a **for** loop is required with an array, the *only* use made of the loop counter within the loop is as an array index to access all the elements of the array consecutively. Java provides an enhanced version of the **for** loop especially for the purpose of accessing the entire array, which is very similar to the iterable **for** loop provided in Python to iterate over collections such as lists.

Rather than use a counter, the enhanced **for** loop in Java consists of a variable which, upon each iteration, stores consecutive elements from the array.[2] For example, if we wished to display on the screen each value from the `temperature` array, the enhanced **for** loop could be used as follows:

```
// the enhanced for loop iterates through elements of an array without the need  for an array index
for (double item : temperature) // see discussion below
{
        System.out.println(item);
}
```

In this case we have named each successive array element as `item`. The loop header is to be read as "for each `item` in the `temperature` array". For this reason, the enhanced **for** loop is often referred to as the *for each* loop. Notice that the type of the array item also has to be specified. The type of this variable is **double** as we are processing an array of **double** values. Remember that this is the type of each *individual* element within the array.

---

[2] The enhanced **for** loop also works with other classes in Java, which act as alternatives to arrays. We will explore some of these classes in Chap. 21.

You should note that the variable item can be used only within the loop, and we cannot make reference to it outside the loop. Within the body of the loop we can now print out an array element by referring directly to the item variable rather than accessing it via an index value:

```
System.out.println(item); // 'item' is an array element
```

This is a much neater solution than using a standard **for** loop, which would require control of a loop counter in the loop header, and array look up within the body of the loop.

Be aware that the enhanced **for** loop should *not* be used if you wish to modify the array items. Modifying array items with such a loop will not cause a compiler error, but it is unsafe as it may cause your program to behave unreliably. So, you should use an enhanced **for** loop only when:

- you wish to access the *entire* array (and not just part of the array);
- you wish to *read* the elements in the array, not *modify* them;
- you do not require the array index for additional processing.

You will probably find, however, that on many occasions these three conditions do not apply—for example, you might only have a partially filled array and will therefore only need to iterate through the partially filled part of the array rather than the whole array. In those cases a standard **for** loop will be the appropriate loop to use. In the following sections we will make use of this enhanced **for** loop where appropriate.

16.5   Passing Arrays as Parameters

Just as lists in Python can be sent as parameters to functions and returned from functions, so too can arrays in Java be sent to methods and returned from methods. As an example of passing an array to a method, let's write a Temperature Readings program (similar to the temperatures.py Python program we wrote in Chap. 6) that creates a temperature array in the main method to hold seven temperature readings, then contains two methods, enterTemps and displayTemps, to enter and display temperatures, respectively. Take a look at the program and then we will discuss it:

```
TemperatureReadings.java

import java.util.Scanner;
public class TemperatureReadings
{
    public static void main(String[] args)
    {
        double[] temperature; // declare array
        temperature = new double[7]; // size array
        enterTemps(temperature); // call method to fill array
        displayTemps(temperature); // call method to display array
    }
    // method to enter temperatures
    static void enterTemps(double[] temperatureIn)
    {
        Scanner keyboard = new Scanner(System.in);
        for (int i = 0; i < temperatureIn.length; i++)
        {
            System.out.print("enter max temperature for day " + (i+1)+ ": ");
            temperatureIn[i] = keyboard.nextDouble();
        }
    }

    // method to display temperatures
    static void displayTemps(double[] temperatureIn)
    {
        System.out.println();
        System.out.println("***TEMPERATURES ENTERED***");
        System.out.println();
        for (double element : temperatureIn)
        {
            System.out.println(element);
        }
    }
}
```

Notice that when sending an array as a parameter, just as with sending lists in Python, the array name alone is required:

```
public static void main(String[] args)
{
        double[] temperature;
        temperature = new double[7];
        enterTemps(temperature); // array name used to send array
        displayTemps(temperature); // array name used to send array
}
```

To give these methods access to the array they must receive it as a parameter. Here, for example, is the header for the enterTemps method. Notice that when a parameter is declared as an array type, the size of the array is not required but the empty square brackets are:

```
static void enterTemps( double[] temperatureIn ) //method receives an array as a parameter
{
        // rest of method goes here
}
```

Now, although in the previous chapter we told you that a parameter just receives a copy of the original variable, this works a little differently with arrays. We will explain this a little later, but for now just be aware that this method will actually fill the original array. The code for the method itself is straightforward:

```
Scanner keyboard = new Scanner(System.in); // create local Scanner object
for (int i = 0; i < temperatureIn.length; i++) // loop through the array parameter
{
    System.out.print("enter max temperature for day " + (i+1) + ": ");// prompt for temperature
    temperatureIn[i] = keyboard.nextDouble(); // get value from user and place in array
}
```

Notice a standard **for** loop is being used here as the underlying array is being modified. Also, the loop counter is required to print the relevant day number (remember since the loop counter, i, starts at zero the relevant day number is i + 1). The displayTemps method will also require the array to be sent as a parameter. Here, the enhanced **for** can be used as the underlying array is not being modified. An outline of the method is given below:

```
static void displayTemps(double[] temperatureIn)
{
    for (double element : temperatureIn) // enhanced for loop to iterate over the array elements
    {
        System.out.println(element); // diplay array element
    }
}
```

Now let us return to the point we made earlier. You are aware that, in the case of a simple variable type such as an **int**, it is the *value* of the variable that is copied when it is passed as a parameter. This means that if the value of a parameter is altered within a method, the original variable is unaffected outside that method. This works differently with arrays. As we said earlier, the enterTemps method actually fills the *original* array. How can this be?

The answer is that in the case of arrays, the value sent as a parameter is not a copy of each array element but, instead, a copy of the array *reference*. In other words, the *location* of the array is sent to the receiving method not the value of the contents of the array. Now, even though the receiving parameter (temperatureIn) has a different name to the original variable in main (temperature), they are both pointing to the same place in memory so both are modifying the same array! This is illustrated in Fig. 16.3.

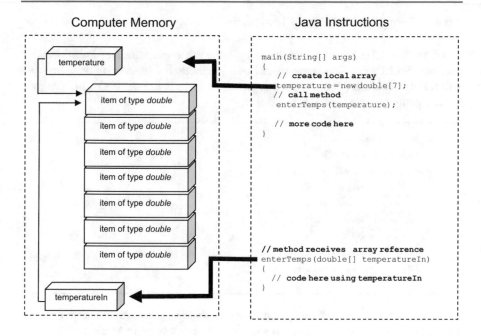

Fig. 16.3   The effect on computer memory of passing an array as a parameter

Here is a sample program run:

```
enter max temperature for day 1: 23
enter max temperature for day 2: 21.5
enter max temperature for day 3: 18.75
enter max temperature for day 4: 21
enter max temperature for day 5: 22.8
enter max temperature for day 6: 23.2
enter max temperature for day 7: 22

***TEMPERATURES ENTERED***

23.0
21.5
18.75
21.0
22.8
23.2
22.0
```

16.6   Some Useful Array Methods

Apart from the `length` feature, an array does not come with any useful built-in routines. So let's develop some of our own methods for processing an array. We will use a simple integer array for this example. Here is the outline of the program we are going to write in order to do this:

```
import java.util.Scanner;

public class SomeUsefulArrayMethods
{
    public static void main (String[] args)
    {
        Scanner keyboard = new Scanner(System.in);
        int[] someArray; // declare an integer array
        // ask user to determine size of array
        System.out.println("How many elements to store?");
        int size = keyboard.nextInt();
        // size array now
        someArray = new int[size];

        // call methods here
    }
    // methods to process an array here
}
```

As you can see, we have delayed the second stage of array creation here until the user tells us how many elements to store in the array. Now to some methods.

16.6.1   Array Maximum

The first method we will develop will allow us to find the maximum value in an array. For example, we may have a list of scores and wish to know the highest score in this list. Finding the maximum value in an array is a much better approach than the one we took in Chap. 15, where we looked at a method to find the maximum of two values and another method to find the maximum of three values. This array method can instead be used with lists of two, three, four or any other number of values. The approach we will use will be similar to the `max` method we developed in Chap. 5 for finding the maximum of three values. Here is the pseudocode again.

```
SET result TO first number
IF second number > result
  SET result TO second number
IF third number > result
  SET result TO third number
RETURN result
```

Here, the final result is initialized to the first value. All other values are then compared with this value to determine the largest value. Now that we have an array, we can use a loop to process this comparison, rather than have a series of many **if** statements. Here is a suitable algorithm:

```
SET result TO first value in array
LOOP FROM second element in array TO last element in array
        IF current element > result
                SET result TO current element
RETURN result
```

This method will need the array that it has to search to be sent in as a parameter. Also, this method will return the maximum item so it must have an integer return type.

```java
static int max (int[] arrayIn)
{
    int result = arrayIn[0]; // set result to the first value in the array

    // this loops runs from the 2nd item to the last item in the array
    for (int i = 1; i < arrayIn.length; i++)
    {
            if(arrayIn[i] > result)
            {
                result = arrayIn[i]; // reset result to new maximum
            }
    }
    return result;
}
```

Notice we did not use the enhanced **for** loop here, as we needed to iterate from the *second* item in the array rather than through *all* items, and the standard **for** loop gives us this additional control.

16.6.2 Array Summation

The next method we will develop will be a method that calculates the total of all the values in the array. Such a method might be useful, for example, if we had a list of deposits made into a bank account and wished to know the total value of these deposits. A simple way to calculate the sum is to keep a running total and add the value of each array element to that running total. Whenever you have a running total it is important to initialize this value to zero. We can express this algorithm using pseudocode as follows:

```
SET total TO zero
LOOP FROM first element in array TO last element in array
        SET total TO total + value of current element
RETURN total
```

This method will again need the array to be sent in as a parameter and will return an integer (the value of the sum), giving us the following:

```
static int sum(int[] arrayIn)
{
    int total = 0;
    for (int currentElement : arrayIn)
    {
        total = total + currentElement;
    }
    return total;
}
```

Notice the use of the enhanced **for** loop here—as we need to iterate through *all* elements within the array. We will leave the development of this complete program, along with some other useful methods, to you as end of chapter exercises.

16.7   Variable Arguments

Look back at the displayTemps method given in the TemperatureReadings program in Sect. 16.5 above. By declaring the parameter to be an array of **double** values, the displayTemps method is able to work with *any number of double values* contained in the given array parameter:

```
static void displayTemps(double[] temperatureIn) // can accept an array of any size
{
        // code to display temperatures goes here
}
```

In our TemperatureReadings program we created an array of size 7, but we could have created an array of any size—for example, an array of size 365 for each day of the year. This displayTemps method would still correctly receive this data and display all temperatures, irrespective of the size of an array.

Very closely related to the idea of sending an array to a method is a Java feature called **varargs**, which is short for **variable arguments**. Just like sending an array, the *varargs* feature allows us to send a variable number of data items to a method, as long as each item is of the same type, without having to fix the number of data items in any way. We can rewrite the displayTemps header by using the *varargs* syntax as follows:

```
static void displayTemps(double... temperatureIn) // note the varargs syntax
{
        // code to display temperatures goes here
}
```

Instead of using the array syntax of square brackets (**double**[]) we use the *varargs* syntax (**double...**). As you can see, this consists of an ellipsis (three consecutive dots). This indicates that a variable number (zero or more) of **double** values will be sent to the method. The code inside the method remains the same as the *varargs* parameter; `temperatureIn` in this case is implicitly converted into an array within the method.

```
static void displayTemps(double... temperatureIn) // temperatureIn converted to an array
{
        // code inside the method remains the same
        System.out.println();
        System.out.println("***TEMPERATURES ENTERED***");
        System.out.println();
        for (double element: temperatureIn) // enhanced for loop can still be used with varargs
        {
            System.out.println(element);
        }
}
```

You may be thinking, if *varargs* is just another notation for sending an array of values, why not just stick to array syntax? Well, while the code for the method remains the same, we are given more flexible ways of calling this method. We can send an array as before, but we can also send individual values if we wish. The `DisplayTemperaturesWithVarargs` program below illustrates this. Take a look at it and then we will discuss it.

```
DisplayTemperaturesWithVarargs.java

public class DisplayTemperaturesWithVarargs
{
    public static void main(String[] args)
    {
        double[] temperature = {7.5, 8.2, 7.7, 11.3, 10.75}; // create array with 5 readings
        System.out.println("Sending Array");
        displayTemps(temperature); // call method with a single array
        System.out.println();
        System.out.println("Sending individual items");
        displayTemps(7.5, 8.2, 7.7, 11.3, 10.75); // call method with 5 individual readings
        displayTemps(9.9); // call method with 1 value only
        displayTemps( ); // call method with no values
    }

    // method to display temperatures using varargs
    static void displayTemps(double... temperatureIn)
    {
        System.out.println();
        System.out.println("***TEMPERATURES***");
        System.out.println("Number of temperatures: "+ temperatureIn.length); // count items
        // display temperatures
        for (double element: temperatureIn)
        {
            System.out.println(element);
        }
    }
}
```

You can see that in the `main` method, and we have initialized an array with five temperature readings:

```
double[] temperature = {7.5, 8.2, 7.7, 11.3, 10.75};
```

Our `displayTemps` method has been written to accept a *varargs* collection of values:

```
// method to display temperatures using varargs
static void displayTemps(double... temperatureIn)
{
        // code to display temperatures goes here
}
```

One way to call this method is with the array of five temperatures we created:

```
displayTemps(temperature); // call method with a single array
```

However, we can also send individual values to a *varargs* parameter rather than using an array. To illustrate we have called the displayTemps method with the same values that were in our array, but sent as individual values rather than stored in an array:

```
displayTemps(7.5, 8.2, 7.7, 11.3, 10.75); // call method with 5 individual readings
```

We can send any number of values in this way, including a single value or no values at all:

```
displayTemps(9.9); // call method with 1 value only
displayTemps( ); // call method with no values
```

Here is a program run to clarify the results:

```
Sending Array

***TEMPERATURES***
Number of temperatures: 5
7.5
8.2
7.7
11.3
10.75

Sending individual items

***TEMPERATURES***
Number of temperatures: 5
7.5
8.2
7.7
11.3
10.75

***TEMPERATURES***
Number of temperatures: 1
9.9

***TEMPERATURES***
Number of temperatures: 0
```

Notice that if you wish to send additional parameters to a method as well as a *varargs* parameter, the *varargs* parameter must come last in the parameter list. So, for example, the following method header would not compile:

```
// this method header will cause a compiler error
static void someMethd(int... varargParam, int param2)
{
        // code to for method goes here
}
```

Here we have two parameters, a *vararg* collection of integers, `varagsParam`, and a single integer parameter, `param2`. This will cause a compiler error as the *varargs* parameter should be the last parameter in the list. The correct method header is given as follows:

```
// this method header will not cause a compiler error
static void someMethd(int param1, int... varargParam)
{
        // code to for method goes here
}
```

16.8 Returning an Array from a Method

A method can return an array as well as receive arrays as parameters. As an example, let us reconsider the `enterTemps` method from the `TemperatureReading` program of Sect. 16.5 again. At the moment, this method accepts an array as a parameter and fills this array with temperature values. Since this method fills the *original* array sent in as a parameter, it does not need to return a value—its return type is therefore **void**:

```
static void enterTemps(double[] temperatureIn)
{
        // code to fill the parameter, 'temperatureIn', goes here
}
```

An alternative approach would be *not* to send an array to this method but, instead, to create an array *within* this method and fill *this* array with values. This array can then be returned from the method:

```
// this method receives no parameters but returns an array of doubles

static double[] enterTemps()
{
        Scanner keyboard = new Scanner(System.in);
        // create an array within this method
        double[] temperatureOut = new double[7];
        // fill up the array created in this method
        for (int i = 0; i < temperatureOut.length; i++)
        {
           System.out.println("enter max temperature for day " + (i+1) + ": ");
           temperatureOut[i] = keyboard.nextDouble();
        }
        // send back the array created in this method
        return temperatureOut;
}
```

As you can see, we use square brackets to indicate that an array is to be returned from a method:

```
static double[] enterTemps()
```

The array itself is created within the method. We have decided to call this array temperatureOut:

```
double[] temperatureOut = new double[7];
```

After the array has been filled it is sent back with a **return** statement. Notice that, to return an array, the name alone is required:

```
return temperatureOut;
```

Now that we have changed the enterTemps method, we need to revisit the original main method also. It will no longer compile now that the enterTemps method has changed:

```
// the original 'main' method will no loger compile!
public static void main(String[] args)
{
        double[] temperature = new double[7];
        enterTemps(temperature); // this line will now cause a compiler error !!
        displayTemps(temperature);
}
```

The call to enterTemps will no longer compile as the new enterTemps does not expect to be given an array as a parameter. The correct way to call the method is as follows:

```
enterTemps(); // this method requires no parameter
```

However, this method now *returns* an array. We really should do something with the array value that is returned from this method. We should use the returned array value to set the value of the original temperature array:

```
// just declare the 'temperature' array but do not allocate it memory yet
double[] temperature;
// 'temperature' array is now set to the return value of 'enterTemps'
temperature = enterTemps();
```

As you can see, we have not sized the `temperature` array once it has been declared. Instead the `temperature` array will be set to the size of the array returned by `enterTemps`, and it will contain all the values of the array returned by `enterTemps`. The complete program, `TemperatureReadings2`, is shown below:

```
TemperatureReadings2.java

import java.util.Scanner;
public class TemperatureReadings2
{
    public static void main(String[] args)
    {
        double[] temperature ;
        temperature = enterTemps(); // call new version of this method
        displayTemps(temperature);
    }

    // method to enter temperatures returns an array
    static double[] enterTemps()
    {
        Scanner keyboard = new Scanner(System.in);
        double[] temperatureOut = new double[7];
        for (int i = 0; i < temperatureOut.length; i++)
        {
            System.out.print("enter max temperature for day " + (i+1) + ": ");
            temperatureOut[i] = keyboard.nextDouble();
        }
        return temperatureOut;
    }

    // this method is unchanged
    static void displayTemps(double[] temperatureIn)
    {
        System.out.println();
        System.out.println("***TEMPERATURES ENTERED***");
        System.out.println();
        for (double element: temperatureIn)
        {
            System.out.println(element);
        }
    }
}
```

This program behaves in exactly the same way as the previous one, so whichever way you implement `enterTemps` is really just a matter of preference.

16.9 The *Arrays* Class

Unlike lists in Python (and unlike the Java collection classes that you will encounter in Chap. 21), the built-in array type of Java does not have any predefined methods available for us to use. Instead, as we have seen, to process arrays (such as entering and printing values) we need to write code to achieve this. However, Java does provide a utility class called `Arrays` which provides a number of **static** methods that can take an array and carry out some basic processing for you. In order to use this class, we need to import it as follows:

```
import java.util.Arrays;
```

Table 16.1 lists three examples of the many **static** methods available in the `Arrays` class:

Table 16.1   Some static methods of the **Arrays** class

Method	Parameters	Return value	Description
equals	two arrays of the same type	A **boolean** value	Returns **true** if the two arrays are equal and **false** otherwise
sort	An array or primitive values	none	Sorts the given array into ascending numerical order for number arrays and alphabetical order for string arrays
toString	An array or primitive values	a String	Return a string representation of the entire array

As we saw when looking at some **static** methods in the Math class in Chap. 15, the way we access a **static** method of a class is by appending the method name onto the class name with the dot operator. The TestingArraysClass program below demonstrates these methods in action—take a look at it, and then, we will discuss it:

TestingArraysClass.java

```
import java.util.Arrays; // import Arrays class

public class TestingArraysClass
{
    public static void main(String args[])
    {
        // initialize three integer arrays
        int[] array1 = {9, 11, 5, 3, 8} ;
        int[] array2 = {11, 5, 9, 3, 8} ;
        int[] array3 = {22, -3, 27, 2, 6, 9} ;
        // use toString method to display arrays in println statements
        System.out.println("array1: " + Arrays.toString(array1));
        System.out.println("array2: " + Arrays.toString(array2));
        System.out.println("array3: " + Arrays.toString(array3));
        System.out.println();
        // check if array1 and array2 are equal
        System.out.println("array1 equals array2? "+ Arrays.equals(array1, array2));
        System.out.println();
        // sort arrays
        Arrays.sort(array1);
        Arrays.sort(array2);
        Arrays.sort(array3);
        System.out.println();
        // use toString method to display arrays again
        System.out.println("** AFTER SORTING***");
        System.out.println("array1: " + Arrays.toString(array1));
        System.out.println("array2: " + Arrays.toString(array2));
        System.out.println("array3: " + Arrays.toString(array3));
        System.out.println();
        // check if array1 and array2 are equal again
        System.out.println("array1 equals array2? "+ Arrays.equals(array1, array2));
    }
}
```

Note that, as the toString method returns a string representation of the array, this string can be printed using a println statement:

```
// string returned by toString method can be displayed on screen in a println statement
System.out.println("array1: " + Arrays.toString(array1));
```

Here is a program run to clarify how these methods work:

```
array1: [9, 11, 5, 3, 8]
array2: [11, 5, 9, 3, 8]
array3: [22, -3, 27, 2, 6, 9]

array1 equals array2? false


** AFTER SORTING***
array1: [3, 5, 8, 9, 11]
array2: [3, 5, 8, 9, 11]
array3: [-3, 2, 6, 9, 22, 27]

array1 equals array2? true
```

As you can see, the `toString` method represents the array as a collection of values, separated by commas and enclosed in square brackets (in the same way a list is presented in Python). This is a very simple way of displaying an array but of course, if you want more control of how the array looks when displayed you will have to write your own code—as we did in the `displayTemps` method earlier.

The program output above demonstrates clearly that although `array1` and `array2` contain the same values they are not initially considered equal by the `equals` method of `Arrays`, as these values are not in the same order. When the arrays are sorted (using the `sort` method of Arrays) however, `array1` and `array2` become equal as they have the same values in the same order.

16.10 Multidimensional Arrays

In the temperature reading example we used earlier in this chapter we used an array to hold seven temperature readings (one for each day of the week). Creating an array allowed us to use loops when processing these values, rather than having to repeat the same bit of code seven times—once for each different temperature variable.

Now consider the situation where temperatures were required for the four weeks of a month. We could create four arrays as follows:

```
double[] temperature1 = new double [7]; // to hold week 1 temperatures
double[] temperature2 = new double [7]; // to hold week 2 temperatures
double[] temperature3 = new double [7]; // to hold week 3 temperatures
double[] temperature4 = new double [7]; // to hold week 4 temperatures
```

How would the temperatures for these four months be entered? The obvious solution would be to write four loops, one to process each array. Luckily there is a simpler approach—create a **multidimensional** array.

A multidimensional array is an array that has *more than one* index. So far, the arrays that we have shown you have had only one index—for this reason they are very often referred to as **one-dimensional** arrays. However, an array may have as many indices as is necessary (up to the limit of the memory on your machine). In this particular example we need *two* indices to access a temperature reading (one for the week number the other for the day number). If we required temperatures for each month of the year, we may require *three* indices (one for the month number, one for the week number and one for the day number) and so on. The number of dimensions an array has corresponds to the number of indices required. Usually, no more than two indices will ever need to be used. An array with two indices is called a **two-dimensional** array.

16.10.1   Creating a Two-Dimensional Array

To create a two-dimensional (2D) array, simply provide the size of both indices. In this example we have four lots of seven temperatures:

```
double [][] temperature ; // declares a 2D array
temperature = new double [4][7]; // creates memory for a 4 by 7 array
```

As you can see, this is very similar to creating a one-dimensional array except that we have *two* pairs of brackets for a two-dimensional array. For larger dimensions we can have more pairs of brackets, 3 pairs for 3 dimensions, 4 for 4 dimensions and so on. In this example we have chosen to treat the first index as representing the number of weeks (4) and the second representing the number of days (7), but we could have chosen to treat the first index as the number of days and the second as the number of weeks.

While you would think of a one-dimensional array as a list, you would probably visualize a two-dimensional array as a table with rows and columns (although actually it is implemented in Java as an array of arrays). The name of each item in a two-dimensional array is the array name, plus the row and column index (see Fig. 16.4).

Note again that both indices begin at zero, so that the temperature for the *third* week of the month and the *sixth* day of the week is actually given as `temper-ature[2][5]`.

16.10.2   Initializing Two-Dimensional Arrays

As with one-dimensional arrays, it is possible to declare and initialize a multidimensional array with a collection of values all in one instruction. With a one-dimensional array we separated these values by commas and enclosed these values in braces. For example:

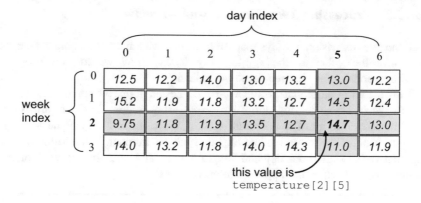

day index

Fig. 16.4 To access an element in a 2D array requires both a row and a column index

```
// this array of integers is initialized with four values
int[] a1DArray = { 11, -25, 4, 77};
```

This creates an array of size 4 with the given elements stored in the given order. A similar technique can be used for multidimensional arrays. With a two-dimensional array the sets of values in each row are surrounded with braces as above, then these row values are themselves enclosed in another pair of braces. A two-dimensional array of integers might be initialized as follows, for example:

```
// this creates a 2 dimensional array with two rows and four columns
int[][] a2DArray =   {
                        { 11, -25, 4, 77},
                        {-21, 55, 43, 11}
                     };
```

This instruction creates the same array as the following group of instructions:

```
int[][] a2DArray = new int[2][4]; // size array
// initialize first row of values
a2DArray[0][0] = 11;
a2DArray[0][1] = -25;
a2DArray[0][2] = 4;
a2DArray[0][3] = 77;
// initialize second row of values
a2DArray[1][0] = -21;
a2DArray[1][1] = 55;
a2DArray[1][2] = 43;
a2DArray[1][3] = 11;
```

As with one-dimensional arrays, however, it is not common to initialize two-dimensional arrays in this way. Instead, once an array has been created, values are added individually to the array once the program is running.

16.10.3   Processing Two-Dimensional Arrays

With the one-dimensional arrays that we have met we have used a single **for** loop to control the value of the single array index. How would you process a two-dimensional array that requires two indices?

With a two-dimensional array, a *pair* of nested loops is commonly used to process each element—one loop for each array index. Let's return to the two-dimensional array of temperature values. We can use a pair of nested loops, one to control the week number and the other the day number. In the following code fragment we've started our day and week counters at 1, and then taken 1 of these counters to get back to the appropriate array index:

```
// create Scanner object for user input
Scanner keyboard = new Scanner (System.in);

// the outer loop controls the week row
for (int week = 1; week <= temperature.length; week++)
{
    // the inner loop controls the day column
    for (int day = 1; day <= temperature[0].length; day++)
    {
        System.out.print("enter temperature for week " + week + " and day " + day + ":");

        // as array indices start at zero not 1, we must take one off the loop counters
        temperature[week-1][day-1] = keyboard.nextDouble();

    }
}
```

Notice that in a two-dimensional array, the length attribute returns the length of the *first* index (this is, what we have visualized as the number of rows):

```
// here, the length attribute returns 4 (the number of rows)
for (int week = 1; week <= temperature.length; week++)
```

The number of columns is determined by obtaining the length of a particular row. In the example below we have chosen the first row, but we could have chosen any row here:

```
// the length of a row returns the number of columns (7 in this case)
for (int day = 1; day <= temperature[0].length; day++)
```

Here we have used a pair of nested loops as we wish to process the entire two-dimensional array. If, however, you just wished to process part of the array (such as one row or one column), then a single loop may still suffice. In the next section we present a program that demonstrates this.

16.10.4   The *MonthlyTemperatures* Program

The program below provides the user with a menu of options. The first option
allows the user to enter the temperature readings for the 4 weeks of the month. The
second option allows the user to display *all* these readings. The third option allows
the user to display the reading for a particular week (e.g. all the temperatures for
week 3). The final option allows the user to display the temperatures for a particular
day of the week (e.g. all the readings for the first day of each week). Take a look at
it and then we will discuss it.

MonthlyTemperatures.java

```java
import java.util.Scanner;

public class MonthlyTemperatures
{
    public static void main(String[] args)
    {
        Scanner keyboard = new Scanner (System.in);
        char choice;

        double[][] temperature = new double[4][7]; // create 2D array
        // offer menu
        do
        {
            System.out.println();
            System.out.println("[1] Enter temperatures");
            System.out.println("[2] Display all");
            System.out.println("[3] Display one week");
            System.out.println("[4] Display day of the week");
            System.out.println("[5] Exit");
            System.out.print("Enter choice [1-5]: ");
            choice = keyboard.next().charAt(0);
            System.out.println();
            // process choice by calling additional methods
            switch (choice)
            {
                case '1':   enterTemps(temperature);
                            break;
                case '2':   displayAllTemps(temperature);
                            break;
                case '3':   displayWeek(temperature);
                            break;
                case '4':   displayDays(temperature);
                            break;
                case '5':   System.out.println ("Goodbye");
                            break;
                default: System.out.println("ERROR: options 1-5 only!");
            }
        } while (choice != '5');
    }


    // method to enter temperatures into the 2D array requires a nested loop
    static void enterTemps(double[][] temperatureIn)
    {
        Scanner keyboard = new Scanner (System.in);
        // the outer loop controls the week number
        for (int week  1; week <= temperatureIn.length; week++)
```

```java
    {
        // the inner loop controls the day number
        for (int day = 1; day <= temperatureIn[0].length; day++)
        {
            System.out.print ("enter temperature for week " + week + " and day " + day + ": ");
            temperatureIn[week-1][day-1] = keyboard.nextDouble();
        }
    }
}

// method to display all temperatures in the 2D array requires a nested loop
static void displayAllTemps (double[][] temperatureIn)
{
    System.out.println();
    System.out.println("***TEMPERATURES ENTERED***");
    // the outer loop controls the week number
    for (int week = 1; week <= temperatureIn.length; week++)
    {
        // the inner loop controls the day number
        for (int day = 1; day <= temperatureIn[0].length; day++)
        {
            System.out.println("week" +week+" day "+day+": "+ temperatureIn[week-1][day-1]);

        }
    }
}

// method to display temperatures for a single week requires a single loop
static void displayWeek (double[][] temperatureIn)
{
    Scanner keyboard = new Scanner (System.in);
    int week;
    // enter week number
    System.out.print ("Enter week number (1-4): ");
    week = keyboard.nextInt();
    // input validation: week number should be between 1 and 4
    while (week<1 || week > 4)
    {
        System.out.println("Inavlid week number!!");
        System.out.print ("Enter again (1-4 only): ");
        week = keyboard.nextInt();
    }
    // display temperatures for given week
    System.out.println();
    System.out.println("***TEMPERATURES ENTERED FOR WEEK "+week+"***");
    System.out.println();
    // week number is fixed so loop required to process day numbers only
    for (int day = 1; day <= temperatureIn[0].length; day++)
    {
        System.out.println("week "+week+" day "+day+": "+ temperatureIn[week-1][day-1]);

    }
}

// method to display temperatures for a single day of each week requires a single loop
static void displayDays (double[][] temperatureIn)
{
    Scanner keyboard  new Scanner (System.in);
    int day;
    // enter day number
    System.out.print ("Enter day number (1-7): ");
    day = keyboard.nextInt();
    // input validation: day number should be between 1 and 7
    while (day<1 || day > 7)
    {
        System.out.println("Inavlid day number!!");
        System.out.print ("Enter again (1-7 only): ");
        day = keyboard.nextInt();
    }
    // display temperatures for given day of the week
    System.out.println();
    System.out.println("***TEMPERATURES ENTERED FOR DAY "+day+"***");
    System.out.println();
    // day number is fixed so loop required to process week numbers only
    for (int week = 1; week <= temperatureIn.length; week++)
    {
        System.out.println("week "+week+" day "+day+": " + temperatureIn[week-1][day-1]);

    }
}
}
```

Here you can see that the first menu option contains the code we have just discussed for entering values into a two-dimensional array. Notice how you pass a two-dimensional array to a method. As with a one-dimensional array you do not refer to the size of the array, just its dimensions:

```
/* As with a standard 1D array, to pass a 2D array to a method the number of dimensions needs to
be indicated but not the size of these dimensions */

static void enterTemps(double[][] temperatureIn)
{
        // code for entering temperatures goes here
}
```

This method uses a pair of nested loops as we wish to process the entire two-dimensional array. Similarly, when we wish to display the entire array, we use a pair of nested loops to control the week and day number:

```
// method to display all temperatures in the 2D array requires a nested loop
static void displayAllTemps(double[][] temperatureIn)
{
    System.out.println();
    System.out.println("***TEMPERATURES ENTERED***");
    // the outer loop controls the week number
    for (int week = 1; week <= temperatureIn.length; week++)
    {
        // the inner loop controls the day number
        for (int day = 1; day <= temperatureIn[0].length; day++)
        {
            System.out.println("week " +week+" day "+day+": "+
                                            temperatureIn[week-1][day-1]);
        }
    }
}
```

However, when we need to display just one of the dimensions of an array, we do not need to use a pair of loops. For example, the displayWeek method, that allows the user to pick a particular week number so that just the temperatures for that week alone are displayed, just requires a *single* loop to move through the day numbers, as the week number is fixed by the user:

```
// method to display temperatures for a single week requires a single loop
    static void displayWeek(double[][] temperatureIn)
    {
        Scanner keyboard = new Scanner (System.in);
        int week;
        // enter week number
        System.out.print("Enter week number (1-4): ");
        week = keyboard.nextInt();
        // input validation: week number should be between 1 and 4
        while (week<1 || week > 4)
        {
            System.out.println("Inavlid week number!!");
            System.out.print("Enter again (1-4 only): ");
            week = keyboard.nextInt();
        }
        // display temperatures for given week
        System.out.println();
        System.out.println("***TEMPERATURES ENTERED FOR WEEK "+week+"***");
        System.out.println();
        // week number is fixed so loop required to process day numbers only
        for (int day = 1; day <= temperatureIn[0].length; day++)
        {
            System.out.println("week "+week+" day "+day+": "+
                                          temperatureIn[week-1][day-1]);
        }
    }
```

First the user enters the week number:

```
System.out.print("Enter week number (1-4): ");
week = keyboard.nextInt();
```

We will use this week number to determine the value of the first index when looking up temperatures in the array, so we need to be careful that the user inputs a valid week number (1 to 4) as invalid numbers would lead to an illegal array index being generated. We have used a **while** loop here to implement this input validation:

```
// input validation: week number should be between 1 and 4
while (week<1 || week > 4)
{
    System.out.println("Inavlid week number!!");
    System.out.print("Enter again (1-4 only): ");
    week = keyboard.nextInt();
}
```

Once we get past this loop, we can be sure that the user has entered a valid week number. For example, assume that we have filled the 2D array with the temperatures given in Fig. 6.4. Now assume that the user calls the option to display one week's temperature and chooses week 2. This is illustrated in Fig. 16.5.

Since array indices in Java begin at zero, the week index (1) is determined by taking one of the week number entered by the user (2). All we need to do now is to iterate through all the day numbers for that week by using a single **for** loop:

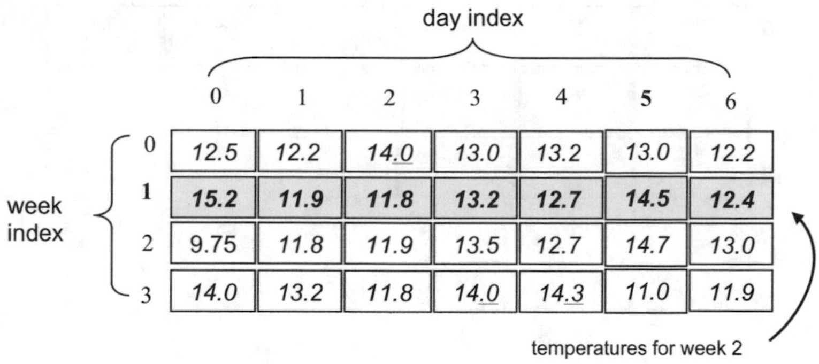

day index

Fig. 16.5 To access temperatures for a single week, the week index remains fixed and the day index changes

```
// week number is fixed by the user so a single loop is required to process day numbers only
for (int day = 1; day <= temperatureIn[0].length; day++)
{
        System.out.println("week "+ week +" day " + day + ": " +
                                temperatureIn[week-1][day-1]);

}
```

The displayDays method works in a similar way but with the day number fixed and the week number being determined by the **for** loop.

16.11 Ragged Arrays

In the examples of two-dimensional arrays discussed so far, each row of the array had the same number of columns. Each row of the two-dimensional tempera-ture array, for example, had 7 columns, and each row of a2DArray had 4 columns. Very often this will be the case. However, very occasionally, it may be necessary for rows to have a variable number of columns. A two-dimensional array with a variable number of columns is called a **ragged array**. For example, here is how we might declare and initialize a two-dimensional array of characters with a variable number of columns for each row:

```
// this creates a 2 dimensional array with a variable number of columns
char[][] animals = {
                    {'M', 'O', 'N', 'K', 'E', 'Y'}, // 6 columns
                    {'C', 'A', 'T' }, // 3 columns
                    {'B', 'I', 'R', 'D'} // 4 columns
                };
```

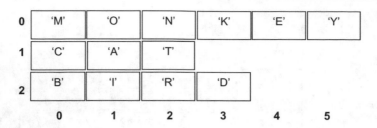

Fig. 16.6 The array 'animals' is a *ragged array*

Figure 16.6 illustrates the array created after this initialization:

To declare such an array without initialization, we need to specify the number of rows first and leave the number of columns unspecified. In the example above we have 3 rows:

```
// columns left unspecified
char[][] animals = new char[3][];
```

Now, for each row we can fix the appropriate size of the associated column. In the example above the first row has 6 columns, the second row 3 columns and the last row 4 columns:

```
animals[0] = new char[6]; // number of columns in first row
animals[1] = new char[3]; // number of columns in second row
animals[2] = new char[4]; // number of columns in third row
```

You can see clearly from these instructions that Java implements a two-dimensional array as an array of arrays. When processing ragged arrays you must be careful not to use a fixed number to control the number of columns. The actual number of columns can always be retrieved by calling the length attribute of each row. For example, the following instructions would display the number of columns for each row:

```
System.out.println(animals[0].length); // displays 6
System.out.println(animals[1].length); // displays 3
System.out.println(animals[2].length); // displays 4
```

The program below uses a pair of nested loops to display the `animals` array:

```
RaggedArray.java

public class RaggedArray
{
    public static void main(String[] args)
    {
        // initialize ragged array
        char[][] animals =
                {
                    {'M', 'O', 'N', 'K', 'E', 'Y'}, // 6 columns
                    {'C', 'A', 'T' }, // 3 columns
                    {'B', 'I', 'R', 'D'} // 4 columns
                };
        for (int row = 0; row < animals.length; row++) // row number is fixed
        {
            for (int col = 0; col < animals[row].length; col++) // column number is variable
            {
                System.out.print(animals[row][col]); // display one character
            }
            System.out.println(); // new line after one row displayed
        }
    }
}
```

Notice how the inner loop, controlling the column number, instead of being fixed to the length of one particular row, will vary each time depending upon the *current* row number:

```
for (int row = 0; row < animals.length; row++)
{
    // column number is variable and is determined by current row number
    for (int col = 0; col < animals[row].length; col++)
    {
        System.out.print(animals[row][col]);
    }
    System.out.println();
}
```

As expected this program produces the following output when run:

```
MONKEY
CAT
BIRD
```

16.12 Self-test Questions

1. Distinguish between an *array* in Java and a *list* in Python.
2. (a) When should an enhanced **for** loop *not* be used to process an array?
   (b) Describe the **varags** feature of Java.
3. Look back at the `TemperatureReadings` program from Sect. 16.5, which read in and displayed temperature readings stored in an array. Now consider an additional method, `wasHot`, which accepts two parameters, a single temperature value and the array of temperatures, and then displays all temperatures in the given array greater than the given temperature value.

(a) Write the top line of this `wasHot` method.

(b) Write the code for the `wasHot` method that makes use of a regular **for** loop

(c) Write the call to the `wasHot` method in the `main` method that sends the original temperature array and a temperature of 18°.

(d) Rewrite the code for the `wasHot` method making use of an enhanced **for** loop

(e) Rewrite the top line of the `wasHot` method making use of the *varargs* feature.

(f) Rewrite the call to the `wasHot` method by sending in values of your choice.

4. Consider the `SomeUsefulArrayMethods` program discussed in Sect. 16.6. Now:

(a) Write the code for an additional method, `contains`, that accepts the integer array and a value to search for, and returns **true** if that value is in the array and **false** otherwise.

(b) Write the code for another method, `search`, that also accepts the integer array and a value to search but returns the position of that value in the array if it is present and -999 (a "dummy" value) if it is not.

5. Assume two arrays of integers have been created, one (`lotteryNumbers`) that holds 6 winning lottery numbers, and the other (`numbersPicked`) that holds the 6 lottery numbers that a customer has picked.

(a) Use the appropriate method of the `Arrays` class to display both arrays

(b) Use the appropriate method of the `Arrays` to sort both arrays into numerical order

(c) Use the appropriate method of the `Arrays` class to check if the two arrays are equal.

6. Consider the following array declaration, to store a collection of student grades.

```
char [][] grades = new char[4][20];
```

Grades are recorded for 4 tutorial groups, and each tutorial group consists of 20 students.

(a) How many dimensions does this array have?

(b) What is the value of `grades.length`?

(c) What is the value of `grades[0].length`?

(d) Write the instruction to record the grade 'B' for the first student in the first tutorial group.

7. Consider the following scenarios and, for each, declare the appropriate array:
   - (a) `goals`: an array to hold the number of goals each team in a league scores in each game of a season. The league consist of 20 teams, and a season consists of 38 games.
   - (b) `seats`: an array to record whether or not a seat in a theatre is booked or not. There are 70 rows of seats in the theatre and each row has 20 seats.
8. Consider the `MonthlyTemperatures` program of Sect. 16.10.4. Write an additional method, `max`, that returns the maximum temperature recorded in the given two-dimensional array.
   Hint: look back at the algorithm for finding the maximum temperature in a one-dimensional array in Sect. 16.6.1.
9. Consider an application that records the punctuality of trains on a certain route.
   - (a) Declare a 2D array, `late`, to hold the number of times a train on this route was late for each day of the week, and for each week of the year.
   - (b) Write a fragment of code that adds up the total number of days in the year when a train was late more than twice in a given day.
10. A **magic word square** is a square in which a word can be formed by reading each row and each column. For example, the following is a 4 by 4 magic word square:

'P'	'R'	'E'	'Y'
'L'	'A'	'V'	'A'
'O'	'V'	'E'	'R'
'T'	'E'	'N'	'D'

   - (a) Declare and initialize a 2D array, `magicSquare`, to hold the words illustrated above.
   - (b) Write a method, `displayRow`, that accepts the `magicSquare` array and a row number and displays the word in that row.
   - (c) Write a method, `displayColumn`, that accepts the `magicSquare` array and a column number and displays the word in that column.
11. (a) Distinguish between a regular 2D array and a ragged array.
    - (b) Write instructions to create a ragged 2D array of integers, called `tri-angle`, that has the following form:

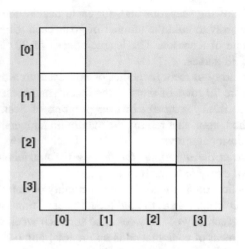

(c) Write a fragment of code to find the largest number in the triangle array.

16.13   Programming Exercises

1. Implement the TemperatureReadings program from Sect. 16.5, which read in and displayed a series of temperature readings for a given week. Now
   (a) add the wasHot method that you designed in self-test questions 3a and 3b above;
   (b) add the instruction into the main method that calls this wasHot method as discussed in self-test question 3c above;
   (c) modify the wasHot method using an enhanced **for** loop as discussed in self-test question 3d above;
   (d) modify the wasHot method again using *varargs* as discussed in self-test question 3e above;
   (e) add a call to this modified wasHot method to test your answer to self-test question 2f above;
   (f) test the *varargs* version of the wasHot method further by adding a number of calls to this method in the main method with a different number of temperature readings in each case.
2. Implement the SomeUsefulArrayMethods program discussed in Sect. 16.6 for processing an array of integers and include a menu driven interface to test the max and sum methods from that section and the contains and search methods you developed for self-test question 4 above. Include menu options and associated methods for entering values into the array and displaying the array.
3. Implement a program for storing lottery numbers and a customer's choice of numbers that tests your answers to self-test question 5 above.

4. Design and implement a magic word square program that allows you to test your answers to self-test question 10 above. The program should initialize the word square given in the question and then use the methods `displayRow` and `displayColumn` to display all the words in the magic word square.

5. Design and implement a program that allows the user to enter into an array the price of 5 products in pounds sterling. The program should then copy this array into another array but convert the price of each product from pounds sterling to US dollars. The program should allow the user to enter the exchange rate of pounds to dollars and should, when it terminates, display the contents of both arrays. Once again, make use of methods in your program to carry out these tasks.

6. Amend the program in exercise 5 above so that
   (a) the user is asked how many products they wish to purchase and the arrays are then sized accordingly;
   (b) the total cost of the order is displayed in both currencies.

7. Design and implement a program that allows you to test your answers to self-test question 11 above. The program should allow the user to enter numbers into the ragged `triangle` array and then find the largest number in the array as discussed in the question.

Object-Oriented Java: Part 1

17

Outcomes

By the end of this chapter you should be able to:

- *create and use objects in Java;*
- *use a number of methods of the String class;*
- *pass objects as parameters;*
- *create and use arrays of objects;*
- *write the Java code for a specified class;*
- *explain the difference between* **public** *and* **private** *access to attributes and methods;*
- *explain the use of the* **static** *keyword.*

17.1 Introduction

In Chap. 8 we introduced you to the **object-oriented** approach to developing programs—this is one of the most widely used paradigms among software developers today. The object-oriented approach allows us to develop programs using **classes** and **objects**, and Python and Java are two of many object-oriented programming languages in use today. In this chapter we will look at how to make use of classes and objects in Java.

Supplementary Information The online version contains supplementary material available at https://doi.org/10.1007/978-3-031-01326-3_17.

17.2   Classes and Objects in Java

So far you have been using data types such as **char**, **int** and **double** in your
Java programs. As explained in Chap. 8, in Python these types (like all types in
Python) are examples of classes, whereas in Chap. 13 we saw that in Java these
types are basic (primitive) types rather than classes. If, however, we wish to develop
new types—such as a Rectangle type or a BankAccount type—we would
need to develop these as classes in Java. Java also has a very large collection of
prewritten classes which come with the language for us to use.

In Chap. 8 we looked at how you can create and make use of Rectangle
objects from a Rectangle class that we had written for you in Python. Now let's
assume that we have written a Rectangle class for you in Java; in a moment we
will show you how to use this class to create Rectangle objects in order to carry
out some rectangle calculations. But before we do that, let's take a look at how such
a program could be written in Java *without* using an object-oriented approach:

RectangleCalculations.java

```java
import java.util.Scanner;

public class RectangleCalculations
{
        public static void main(String[] args)
        {
            double length, height, area, perimeter;
            Scanner keyboard = new Scanner(System.in);
            System.out.print("What is the length of the rectangle? "); // prompt for length
            length = keyboard.nextDouble(); // get length from user
            System.out.print("What is the height of the rectangle? "); // prompt for height
            height = keyboard.nextDouble(); // get height from user
            area = calculateArea(length, height); // call calculateArea method
            perimeter = calculatePerimeter(length, height); // call calculatePerimeter method
            System.out.println("The area of the rectangle is " + area); // display area
            System.out.println("The perimeter of the rectangle is " + perimeter); // display perimeter
        }

        // method to calculate area
        static double calculateArea(double lengthIn, double heightIn)
        {
            return lengthIn * heightIn;
        }

        // method to calculate perimeter
        static double calculatePerimeter(double lengthIn, double heightIn)
        {
            return 2 * (lengthIn + heightIn);
        }
}
```

As you can see, we have to declare several primitive variables (length and
height) and write several methods (calculateArea and calculatePerimeter) to carry out our rectangle calculations. Now let's assume we
have taken the code for creating these variables and implementing these methods
(in addition to some other useful methods) and packaged them up inside a
Rectangle **class** (just as we did in Python in Chap. 8). Remember that a class
consists of attributes (the persistent variables) and methods relevant to that particular class. As we said in Chap. 8, the advantage of packaging this code in a class
is that once it is written it acts as a blueprint to build as many objects as we like
without having to write new code for each object. Let's take a look at this
Rectangle class in Java.

17.2.1   The *Rectangle* Class

The Rectangle class we have written for you is saved in a file called Rect-angle.java, and you will need to download it from the website (see preface) in order to use it. You must make sure that it is in the right place for your compiler to find it. You will need to place it in your project folder according to the rules of the particular IDE you are using. Later in this chapter, we will look inside this class and see how it was written. For now, however, you can completely ignore the programme code, because, as you know from looking at creating objects in Python, you can use a class without knowing anything about the details.

In Chap. 8 we introduced you to the idea of **encapsulation**. Encapsulation is a feature of a class where attributes are kept hidden and secure within the class and are not directly accessible outside the class. As we have seen, encapsulation can be strongly suggested in Python classes but cannot be enforced. However, in Java classes, not only can encapsulation can be enforced, it is strongly encouraged. When we look inside our Rectangle class later, we will show you how we encapsulated its length and height attributes. For now though, you just need to know that once attributes have been encapsulated within a class the *only way* to interact with the attributes is via the methods provided in the class—we cannot access them directly. This means that in order to use a class, we do not actually need to know its attributes, all we need to know are details about its methods: their names, what the methods are expected to do, and also their **inputs** and **outputs**. Table 17.1 lists all the methods of our Rectangle class with their inputs and outputs. Take a look at and then we will discuss it.

The first method in this table is a special method known as a **constructor** in Java. Constructors in Java are very similar to **initializers** in Python, in that their job is to create (or **instantiate**) an object from the class by reserving space in memory for the object and initializing all its attributes. Constructors in Java *always take the same name as the class*, so in this case the name of the constructor is Rectangle. As you can see from Table 17.1, constructors (like initializers in Python) can take parameters. In this case, as with the equivalent initializer we showed you in our Python class, the Rectangle constructor takes two parameters allowing us to set the initial length and height of the Rectangle object. Because the Java default type for real numbers is **double**, we have referred to **double** values in Table 17.1 rather than **float**s (which is the default type for real numbers in Python).

The calculateArea and calculatePerimeter methods in Table 17.1 will be familiar to you, having seen their equivalent in the Python Rectangle class we developed in Chap. 8. But you can see we have more methods in our Java Rectangle class than we did in our equivalent Python class, as we need to provide methods to read and write to the encapsulated attributes (length and height), since we cannot access these attributes directly as we could in the equivalent Python class. We have therefore provided methods called setLength

Table 17.1 The methods of the *Rectangle* class

Method	Description	Inputs	Output
Rectangle	The constructor (see discussion below)	Two items of data, both of type **double**, representing the length and height of the rectangle, respectively	Not applicable
setLength	Updates the value of the length of the rectangle	An item of type **double**	None
setHeight	Updates the value of the height of the rectangle	An item of type **double**	None
getLength	Returns the length of the rectangle	None	An item of type **double**
getHeight	Returns the height of the rectangle	None	An item of type **double**
calculateArea	Calculates and returns the area of the rectangle	None	An item of type **double**
calculatePerimeter	Calculates and returns the perimeter of the rectangle	None	An item of type **double**

and setHeight so that we can *write* to these attributes and we have provided methods getLength and getHeight to return, or *read*, the values of the attributes. Starting the names of methods to write and read the attributes of a class with set and get is very common among Java programmers.

Now let's look at a program that makes use of this Rectangle class to create and make use of a Rectangle object for carrying out our rectangle calculations.

17.2.2   The *RectangleTester* Program

Below is a program that illustrates you how to create a Rectangle object from a Rectangle class in Java and then call some of the methods of that object. The Rectangle class will need to be available to the compiler by being placed in the same directory as this RectangleTester program. Take a look at it and then we will discuss it.

RectangleTester.java

```java
import java.util.Scanner;

public class RectangleTester
{
    public static void main(String[] args)
    {
        Scanner keyboard = new Scanner(System.in);

        // declare two variables to hold the length and height of the rectangle as input by the user
        double rectangleLength, rectangleHeight;

        // declare a reference to an Rectangle object
        Rectangle myRectangle;

        // now get the values from the user
        System.out.print("Please enter the length of your Rectangle: ");
        rectangleLength = keyboard.nextDouble();
        System.out.print("Please enter the height of your Rectangle: ");
        rectangleHeight = keyboard.nextDouble();

        // create a new Rectangle object by calling the constructor
        myRectangle = new Rectangle(rectangleLength, rectangleHeight);

        /* use the various methods of the Rectangle class to display the length, height, area, and
           perimeter of the Rectangle */
        System.out.println("Rectangle length is " + myRectangle.getLength());
        System.out.println("Rectangle height is " + myRectangle.getHeight());
        System.out.println("Rectangle area is " + myRectangle.calculateArea());
        System.out.println("Rectangle perimeter is " + myRectangle.calculatePerimeter());

        // use 'set' methods to update length and height
        myRectangle.setLength(10);
        myRectangle.setHeight(7.5);

        // display updated values and calculations
        System.out.println("UPDATED VALUES");
        System.out.println("Rectangle length is " + myRectangle.getLength());
        System.out.println("Rectangle height is " + myRectangle.getHeight());
        System.out.println("Rectangle area is " + myRectangle.calculateArea());
        System.out.println("Rectangle perimeter is " + myRectangle.calculatePerimeter());
    }
}
```

You can see that this looks very similar to the equivalent Python program we showed you in Chap. 8 (rectangletester.py). We have once again created two primitive variables to get the initial length and the height from the user (which we have declared as **double**s—the default Java type for real numbers).

```java
double rectangleLength, rectangleHeight;
```

Now to the important code that allows us to create an object from the Rectangle class.

In Java, object creation is a *two-step process*. The first step involves us *declaring the type of an object*. **The type of every object in Java is the class we will use to create the object**. For this reason, classes are often referred to as **abstract data types**. So, in this case the type of our object is Rectangle. The name you give to an object is any variable name of your choice—in this case we have chosen the name myRectangle:

```java
Rectangle myRectangle; // declaring a Rectangle object
```

Computer Memory   Java instructions

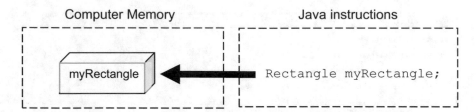

Fig. 17.1 Declaring an object reference in Java

You need to be sure that you understand what this line actually does; all it does in fact is to create a variable that holds a **reference** to an object, rather than the object itself. As explained in the previous chapter, a reference is simply a *name* for a location in memory. At this stage we have *not* reserved space for our new `Rectangle` object or initialized its data; all we have done is named a memory location `myRectangle`, as shown in Fig. 17.1.

Now of course you will be asking the question "How is memory for the `Rectangle` object going to be created, and how is it going to be linked to the reference `myRectangle`?". This is stage two of object creation in Java (sometimes called **instantiating** the object), and it is where the **constructor** method comes in. The job of the constructor method in a class is to reserve space in memory for the initial object and initialize that object's attributes in much the same way as the initializer method did in a Python class.

You can see from Table 17.1 that the constructor method (`Rectangle`) requires two parameters—representing the initial values of length and height, respectively. Rather than hard-coding these values we have got these values from the user before we call the constructor (just as we did in the equivalent Python program in Chap. 8):

```
// get the values for the rectangle length and height from the user
System.out.print("Please enter the length of your Rectangle: ");
rectangleLength = keyboard.nextDouble();
System.out.print("Please enter the height of your Rectangle: ");
rectangleHeight = keyboard.nextDouble();
```

Now that we have initial values from the user stored in variables `rectangleLength` and `rectangleHeight`, respectively, we can call the `Rectangle` constructor and link this to our object variable `myRectangle`:

```
// instantiate a new Rectangle object by calling the constructor
myRectangle = new Rectangle(rectangleLength, rectangleHeight);
```

It is worth noting that, just like arrays in Java, object variables hold a reference (that is, a memory address).

You can see that, in order to request the constructor to find space in memory to store the object in Java we have to use the **new** key word, that you met in Chap. 16

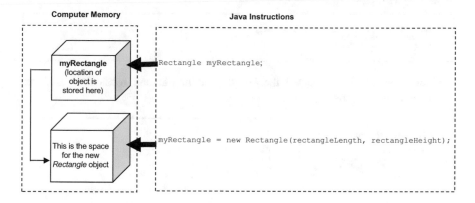

Fig. 17.2 Creating a new object in Java

for creating arrays, prior to the constructor name. The location of the new object is stored in the named location `myRectangle`. This is illustrated in Fig. 17.2.

Once an object has been instantiated by calling the constructor, we can begin to use that object's other methods using the dot operator just as we did when using objects in Python.

To retrieve the `Rectangle` object's length and height we have used the methods `getLength` and `getHeight`—remember these attributes cannot be directly accessed:

```
// use 'get' methods to retrieve the values of hidden attributes
System.out.println("Rectangle length is " + myRectangle.getLength());
System.out.println("Rectangle height is " + myRectangle.getHeight());
```

Note that you can call an object's methods (such as `getLength` and `getHeight`) only after you instantiate the object. If you tried to do so after only declaring the object, you will get a compiler error.[1]

Next, we have checked the area and perimeter of the rectangle in exactly the same way as we did in our equivalent Python program by calling the appropriate methods:

```
// check area and perimeter of rectangle using the appropriate methods
System.out.println("Rectangle area is " + myRectangle.calculateArea());
System.out.println("Rectangle Perimeter is "+ myRectangle.calculatePerimeter());
```

We have then updated the length and height of the `Rectangle` object to 10 and 7.5, respectively, by using the `setLength` and `setHeight` methods that have been provided for this purpose.

---

[1] The name of the error you will receive will be a NullPointerException. We will explore these errors in more detail in Chap. 14.

```
// use 'set' methods to update length and height
myRectangle.setLength(10);
myRectangle.setHeight(7.5);
```

Finally, we have redisplayed the length and height and recalculate area and perimeter following these changes:

```
// display updated values and calculations
System.out.println("UPDATED VALUES");
System.out.println("Rectangle length is " + myRectangle.getLength());
System.out.println("Rectangle height is " + myRectangle.getHeight());
System.out.println("Rectangle area is " + myRectangle.calculateArea());
System.out.println("Rectangle perimeter is " + myRectangle.calculatePerimeter());
```

Here is an example program run:

```
Please enter the length of your Rectangle: 4
Please enter the height of your Rectangle: 6
Rectangle length is 4.0
Rectangle height is 6.0
Rectangle area is 24.0
Rectangle perimeter is 20.0
UPDATED VALUES
Rectangle length is 10.0
Rectangle height is 7.5
Rectangle area is 75.0
Rectangle perimeter is 35.0
```

You should be aware of the fact that, just as you cannot use a variable that has not been initialized, you cannot call a method of an object if no storage has been allocated for the object via a call to the constructor; so watch out for this happening in your programs—it would cause a problem at run-time. In Java, when a reference is first created without assigning it to a new object, it is given a special value of **null**; a **null** value indicates that no storage is allocated:

```
Rectangle myRectangle; // at this point myRectangle has a null value so we cannot call any methods

myRectangle = new Rectangle (8, 12); // after allocating storage via constructor we can call methods
```

Before we go on to look at some other classes, note that the two-stage object creation process (declare object and instantiate object) can be combined into a single instruction if required. For example, if we wanted to create a Rectangle object with length 8 and height 12, we could do so as follows in one instruction:

```
// declare and instantiate object in one instruction
Rectangle myRectangle = new Rectangle (8, 12);
```

This is a very common way of creating objects in Java, and you will see this pattern often. For example, you can see that when we created Scanner objects, we followed exactly this pattern:

```
// declare and instantiate a Scanner object in one instuction
Scanner keyboard = new Scanner (System.in);
```

Now we can move on to look at using some other classes. The first is not one of our own, but the built-in `String` class provided with all versions of Java.

17.3 Strings

You know from Chap. 2 that a string is a sequence of characters—like a name, a line of an address, a car registration number, or indeed any meaningless sequence of characters such as "h83hdu2&e£8". Java provides a `String` class that allows us to use and manipulate strings. Note the name of this class (`String`) begins with a capital letter as it follows the convention that Java programmers follow of beginning the name of their classes with upper-case letters (contrast that with the `string` class of Python which begins with a lower-case letter).

As we shall see in a moment, the `String` class has a number of constructors— but in fact Java actually allows us to declare a string object in the same way as we declare variables of simple type such as **int** or **char**. For example, we could make the following declaration:

```
String name;
```

and we could then give this string a value:

```
name = "Quentin";
```

We could also do this in one line:

```
String name = "Quentin";
```

We should bear in mind, however, that this is actually just a convenient way of declaring a `String` object by calling its constructor, which we would do like this with exactly the same effect:

```
String name = new String("Quentin");
```

You should be aware that the `String` class is the only class that allows us to create new objects by using the assignment operator in this way.

In order to get a string from the keyboard, you should use the `next` method of `Scanner`. For example:

```
String name; // declaration of a String
System.out.print("What is your name? ");
name = keyboard.next(); // the 'next' method is for String input
System.out.println("Hello " + name);
```

However, a word of warning here—when you do this you should not enter strings that include spaces, as this will give you unexpected results. We will show you later in this chapter a way to get round this restriction.

17.3.1   The Methods of the *String* Class

The String class has a number of interesting and useful methods, and we have listed some of the most commonly used ones in Table 17.2.

There are many other useful methods of the String class which you can look up. The following program provides examples of how you can use some of the methods listed above; others are left for you to experiment with.

StringMethods.java

```
import java.util.Scanner;

public class StringMethods
{
    public static void main(String[] args)
    {
        Scanner keyboard = new Scanner(System.in);
        // create a new string
        String str;
        // get the user to enter a string
        System.out.print("Enter a string without spaces: ");
        str = keyboard.next();
        // display the length of the user's string
        System.out.println("The length of the string is " + str.length());
        // display the third character of the user's string
        System.out.println("The character at position 3 is " + str.charAt(2));
        // display a selected part of the user's string
        System.out.println("Characters 2 to 4 are " + str.substring(1,4));
        // display the user's string joined with another string
        System.out.println(str.concat(" was the string entered"));
        // display the user's string in upper case
        System.out.println("This is upper case: " + str.toUpperCase());
        // display the user's string in lower case
        System.out.println("This is lower case: " + str.toLowerCase());
    }
}
```

A sample run:

```
Enter a string without spaces: Europe
The length of the string is 6
The character at position 3 is r
Characters 2 to 4 are uro
Europe was the string entered
This is upper case: EUROPE
This is lower case: europe
```

Table 17.2 Some *String* methods

Method	Description	Inputs	Output
length	Returns the length of the string	None	An item of type **int**
charAt	Accepts an integer and returns the character at that position in the string. Note that indexing starts from zero, not 1! You have been using this method in conjunction with the next method of the Scanner class to obtain single characters from the keyboard	An item of type **int**	An item of type **char**
substring	Accepts two integers (e.g. m and n) and returns a copy of a chunk of the string. The chunk starts at position m and finishes at position n−1. Remember that indexing starts from zero. (Study the example below.)	Two items of type **int**	A String object
concat	Accepts a string and returns a new string which consists of the string that was sent in joined on to the end of the original string	A String object	A String object
toUpperCase	Returns a copy of the original string, all upper case	None	A String object
toLowerCase	Returns a copy of the original string, all lower case	None	A String object
equals	Accepts an object (such as a String) and compares this to another object (such as another String). It returns **true** if these are identical, otherwise returns **false**	An object of any class	A **boolean** value
equalsIgnoreCase	Accepts a string and compares this to the original string. It returns **true** if the strings are identical (ignoring case), otherwise returns **false**	A String object	A **boolean** value
startsWith	Accepts a string (say str) and returns **true** if the original string starts with str and **false** if it does not (e.g. "hello world" starts with "h" or "he" or "hel" and so on)	A String object	A **boolean** value
endsWith	Accepts a string (say str) and returns **true** if the original string ends with str and **false** if it does not (e.g. "hello world" ends with "d" or "ld" or "rld" and so on)	A String object	A **boolean** value
trim	Returns a String object, having removed any spaces at the beginning or end	None	A String object

17.3.2   Comparing Strings

When comparing two objects, such as Strings, we should do so by using a method called equals. We should *not* use the equality operator (==); this should be used for comparing primitive types only. If, for example, we had declared two strings, firstString and secondString, we would compare these in, say, an **if** statement as follows:

```
if(firstString.equals(secondString))
{
    // more code here
}
```

Using the equality operator (==) to compare strings is a very common mistake that is made by programmers. Doing this will not result in a compilation error, but it won't give you the result you expect! The reason for this is that all you are doing is finding out whether the objects occupy the same address space in memory—what you actually want to be doing is comparing the actual value of the string attributes of the objects.

Notice that an object of type String can also be used within a **switch** statement to check to see if it is equal to one of several possible String values. The simple StringCheckWithSwitch program below illustrates this by giving a meaning for three symbols on a game controller for a particular game:

StringCheckWithSwitch.java

```java
import java.util.Scanner;

public class StringCheckWithSwitch
{
    public static void main(String[] args)
    {
        Scanner keyboard = new Scanner (System.in);
        String symbol;
        // get symbol from user
        System.out.print("Enter the symbol(square/circle/triangle): ");
        symbol = keyboard.next();
        // use String object in switch
        switch(symbol)
        {
            case "square": System.out.println("ATTACK"); break;
            case "circle": System.out.println("BLOCK"); break;
            case "triangle": System.out.println("JUMP"); break;
            default: System.out.println("Invalid Choice");
        }
    }
}
```

Here is a sample run from the program:

```
Enter the symbol(square/circle/triangle): triangle
JUMP
```

Here is another sample run from the program:

```
Enter the symbol(square/circle/triangle): square
ATTACK
```

17.3.3   Entering Strings Containing Spaces

As we mentioned above there is a problem with using the `next` method of `Scanner` when we enter strings that contain spaces. If you try this, you will see that the resulting string stops at the first space, so if you enter the string "Hello world" for example, the resulting string would actually be "Hello".

To enter a string that contains spaces you need to use the method `nextLine`. Unfortunately, however, there is also an issue with this. If the `nextLine` method is used after a `nextInt` or `nextDouble` method, then it is necessary to create a separate `Scanner` object (because using the same `Scanner` object will make your program behave erratically). So, if your intention is that the user should be able to enter strings that contain spaces, the best thing to do is to declare a separate `Scanner` object for string input. This is illustrated below:

```
StringExample2.java

import java.util.Scanner;

public class StringExample2
{
    public static void main(String[] args)
    {
        double d;
        int i;
        String s;
        Scanner keyboardString = new Scanner(System.in); // Scanner object for string input
        Scanner keyboard = new Scanner(System.in); // Scanner object for all other types of input
        System.out.print("Enter a double: ");
        d = keyboard.nextDouble();
        System.out.print("Enter an integer: ");
        i = keyboard.nextInt();
        System.out.print("Enter a string: ");
        s = keyboardString.nextLine(); // use the Scanner object reserved for string input
        System.out.println();
        System.out.println("You entered: ");
        System.out.println("Double: " + d);
        System.out.println("Integer: " + i);
        System.out.println("String: " + s);
    }
}
```

Here is a sample run from this program:

```
Enter a double: 3.4
Enter an integer: 10
Enter a string: Hello world

You entered:
Double: 3.4
Integer: 10
String: Hello world
```

17.4   Our Own *Scanner* Class for Keyboard Input

It might have occurred to you that using the `Scanner` class to obtain keyboard input can be a bit of a bother:

Table 17.3 The input methods of the *EasyScanner* class

Java type	EasyScanner method
int	nextInt()
double	nextDouble()
char	nextChar()
String	nextString()

- it is necessary to create a new Scanner object in every method that uses the Scanner class;
- there is no simple method such as nextChar for getting a single character like there is for the **int** and **double** types;
- as we have just seen there is an issue when it comes to entering strings containing spaces.

To make life easier, we have created a new class which we have called EasyScanner. In Sect. 17.12 we will "look inside" it to see how it is written—for now, we will just show you how to use it. The methods of EasyScanner are described in Table 17.3.

To make life really easy we have written the class so that we don't have to create new Scanner objects in order to use it (that is taken care of in the class itself)—and we have written it so that you can simply use the name of the class itself when you call a method (you will see how to do this later in this chapter). The following program demonstrates how to use these methods. This program will need the EasyScanner class to be available to the compiler by being placed in the same directory as this EasyScannerTester program.

EasyScannerTester.java

```java
public class EasyScannerTester
{
    public static void main(String[] args)
    {
        System.out.print("Enter a double: ");
        double d = EasyScanner.nextDouble(); // to read a double
        System.out.println("You entered: " + d);
        System.out.println();

        System.out.print("Enter an integer: ");
        int i = EasyScanner.nextInt(); // to read an int
        System.out.println("You entered: " + i);
        System.out.println();

        System.out.print("Enter a string: ");
        String s = EasyScanner.nextString(); // to read a string
        System.out.println("You entered: " + s);
        System.out.println();

        System.out.print("Enter a character: ");
        char c = EasyScanner.nextChar(); // to read a character
        System.out.println("You entered: " + c);
        System.out.println();
    }
}
```

You can see from this program how easy it is to call the methods, just by using the name of the class itself—for example:

```
double d = EasyScanner.nextDouble();
```

Here is a sample run:

```
Enter a double: 23.6
You entered: 23.6

Enter an integer: 50
You entered: 50

Enter a string: Hello world
You entered: Hello world

Enter a character: B
You entered: B
```

You are now free to use the EasyScanner class if you wish. You can copy it from the website (see preface)—as usual make sure it is in the right place for your compiler to find it.

17.5 The *BankAccount* Class

In Chap. 8 we introduced you to a second class that we wrote for you in Python called BankAccount. This class allowed us to store bank account details for a customer and to deposit and withdraw money from the account. We have written an equivalent class in Java for you, which you can download. The methods of our Java BankAccount class are listed in Table 17.4.

Again, many of these methods will be familiar to you from our equivalent Python class in Chap. 8—in addition, you can see we have a BankAccount constructor and a number of get methods to access hidden attributes. We have no set methods as, once an account name and number has been created, we have not allowed these to be changed, and the deposit and withdraw methods allow us to write to the balance in a controlled way. Being able to limit the access to attributes in this way demonstrates the benefits we get with encapsulation.

The simple BankAccountTester program below, which requires the BankAccount class to be in the same directory, shows how to use some of the methods in this BankAccount class. You can explore the remaining methods in the end of chapter exercises.

Table 17.4 The methods of the *BankAccount* class

Method	Description	Inputs	Output
BankAccount	A constructor. It accepts two strings and assigns them to the account number and account name, respectively. It also sets the account balance to zero	Two String objects	Not applicable
getAccountNumber	Returns the account number	None	An item of type String
getAccountName	Returns the account name	None	An item of type String
getBalance	Returns the balance	None	An item of type double
deposit	Accepts an item of type **double** and adds it to the balance	An item of type double	None
withdraw	Accepts an item of type **double** and checks if there are sufficient funds to make a withdrawal. If there are not, then the method terminates and returns a value of **false**. If there are sufficient funds, however, the method subtracts the amount from the balance and returns a value of **true**	An item of type double	An item of type boolean

---

BankAccountTester.java

```java
import java.util.Scanner;

public class BankAccountTester
{
  public static void main(String[ ] args)
  {
      // create BankAccount object
      BankAccount account1 = new BankAccount("99786754","Crystal Ball");
      // display initial attributes
      System.out.println("INITIAL ACCOUNT ATTRIBUTES");
      System.out.println("Account number: " + account1.getAccountNumber());
      System.out.println("Account name: " +   account1.getAccountName());
      System.out.println("Starting balance: " + account1.getBalance());
      // deposit money into account
      account1.deposit(1000);
      // display new balance
      System.out.println("BALANCE AFTER DEPOSIT");
      System.out.println("New balance: " + account1.getBalance());
  }
}
```

As you can see, we have declared and instantiated a BankAccount object, account1, in a single instruction:

```java
// declare and instantiate BankAccount object with some suitable parameters
BankAccount account1 = new BankAccount("99786754","Crystal Ball");
```

The parameters to the constructor are two strings representing the account number and name, respectively. As with the equivalent Python class, our Bank-Account instructor initializes the bank balance to zero. We have checked to see that the attributes have been initialized successfully be calling the relevant get-methods to display these attributes on the screen:

```
// display initial attributes
System.out.println("INITIAL ACCOUNT ATTRIBUTES");
System.out.println("Account number: " + account1.getAccountNumber());
System.out.println("Account name: " +   account1.getAccountName());
System.out.println("Starting balance: " + account1.getBalance());
```

We then add some money into this account using the deposit method:

```
// use deposit method to deposit some money into the account
account1.deposit(1000);
```

Finally, we display the updated balance again using the getBalance method:

```
// display new balance
System.out.println("BALANCE AFTER DEPOSIT");
System.out.println("New balance: " + account1.getBalance());
```

We will leave exploring this BankAccount class further to you as an end of chapter exercise.

Here is a program run with the expected output:

```
INITIAL ACCOUNT ATTRIBUTES
Account number: 99786754
Account name: Crystal Ball
Starting balance: 0.0
BALANCE AFTER DEPOSIT
New balance: 1000.0
```

17.6   Passing Objects as Parameters

In Chap. 15 it was made clear that when a variable is passed to a method it is simply the *value* of that variable that is passed—and that therefore a method cannot change the value of the original variable. In Chap. 16 you found out that in the case of an array it is the value of the memory location (a *reference*) that is passed and consequently the value of the original array elements can be changed by the called method.

What about objects? Let's write a little program (`ParameterTest`) to test this out. Again, the `BankAccount` class will need to be in the same directory as this program.

ParameterTest.java

```
public class ParameterTest
{
    public static void main(String[] args)
    {
        // create new bank account
        BankAccount testAccount = new BankAccount("1", "Ann T Dote");
        test(testAccount); // send the account to the test method
        System.out.println("Account Number: " + testAccount.getAccountNumber());
        System.out.println("Account Name: " + testAccount.getAccountName());
        System.out.println("Balance: " + testAccount.getBalance());
    }

    // a method that makes a deposit in the bank account
    static void test(BankAccount accountIn)
    {
        accountIn.deposit(2500);
    }
}
```

The output from this program is as follows:

```
Account Number: 1
Account Name: Ann T Dote
Balance: 2500.0
```

You can see that the deposit has successfully been made—in other words the attribute of the object has actually been changed. This is because what was sent to the method was, of course, a *reference* to the original `BankAccount` object, `testAccount`. Thus `accountIn` is a *copy* of the `testAccount` reference and so points to the original object and invokes that object's methods. So, the following line of code:

```
accountIn.deposit(2500);
```

calls the `deposit` method of the original `BankAccount` object.

17.7   Arrays of Objects

In the previous chapter you learnt how to create arrays of simple types such as **int** and **char**. It is perfectly possible, and often very desirable, to create arrays of objects. To illustrate this take a look at the `ArrayOfBankAccounts` program below that instead of creating a single bank account creates several bank accounts by using an array:

ArrayOfBankAccounts.java

```
public class ArrayOfBankAccounts
{
    public static void main(String[] args)
    {
        // create an array to hold three BankAccounts
        BankAccount[] accountList = new BankAccount[3];
        // create three new accounts and place in array
        accountList[0] = new BankAccount("99786754","Susan Richards");
        accountList[1] = new BankAccount("44567109","Delroy Jacobs");
        accountList[2] = new BankAccount("46376205","Sumana Khan");

        // make various deposits and withdrawals
        accountList[0].deposit(1000);
        accountList[2].deposit(150);
        accountList[0].withdraw(500);

        // print details of all three accounts
        for(BankAccount item : accountList)
        {
            System.out.println("Account number: " + item.getAccountNumber());
            System.out.println("Account name: " + item.getAccountName());
            System.out.println("Current balance: " + item.getBalance());
            System.out.println();
        }
    }
}
```

The first line of the `main` method looks no different from the statements that you saw in the last chapter that created arrays of primitive types, except in this case we are saying that the array will hold a collection of (three) `BankAccount` objects rather than primitive types:

```
BankAccount[] accountList = new BankAccount[3];
```

We can now create new `BankAccount` objects and associate them with elements in the array as we have done with these lines:

```
accountList[0] = new BankAccount("99786754","Susan Richards");
accountList[1] = new BankAccount("44567109","Delroy Jacobs");
accountList[2] = new BankAccount("46376205","Sumana Khan");
```

Once we have created these accounts, we make some deposits and withdrawals.

```
accountList[0].deposit(1000);
accountList[2].deposit(150);
accountList[0].withdraw(500);
```

Look carefully at how we do this. To call a method of a particular array element, we place the dot operator after the final bracket of the array index. This is made clear below:

```
accountList[0].deposit(1000);
```

returns a	calls a
BankAccount	BankAccount
object	method

Notice that in this case when we call the `withdraw` method we have decided not to check the **boolean** value returned.

```
accountList[0].withdraw(500); // return value not checked
```

It is not always necessary to check the return value of a method and you may ignore it if you choose.

Having done this, we display the details of all three accounts. As we are accessing the entire array, we are able to use an enhanced **for** loop for this purpose; and since we are dealing with an array of BankAccount objects here, the type of the items is specified as BankAccount.

```
for(BankAccount item : accountList) // type of items is BankAccount
{
    System.out.println("Account number: " + item.getAccountNumber());
    System.out.println("Account name: " + item.getAccountName());
    System.out.println("Current balance: " + item.getBalance());
    System.out.println();
}
```

As you might expect, the output from this program is as follows:

```
Account number: 99786754
Account name: Susan Richards
Current balance: 500.0

Account number: 44567109
Account name: Delroy Jacobs
Current balance: 0.0

Account number: 46376205
Account name: Sumana Khan
Current balance: 150.0
```

Having looked at how to use classes to create objects, let's now take a look at how we put some of these classes together. We will start with the Rectangle class.

17.8   Implementing the *Rectangle* Class

In Chap. 8 we introduced you to the design of the Rectangle class; in this the UML class diagram reflected the fact that Python was the target language. Figure 17.3 is an updated UML class diagram for the Rectangle class, listing the

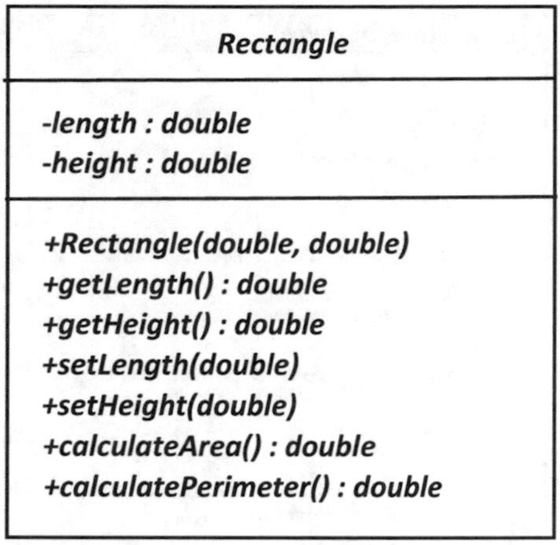

Fig. 17.3 The design of the
Rectangle class

Rectangle
-length : double -height : double
+Rectangle(double, double) +getLength() : double +getHeight() : double +setLength(double) +setHeight(double) +calculateArea() : double +calculatePerimeter() : double

attributes and methods required, targeted towards Java. As you can see, we have used the **double** type throughout here instead of **float**, as **double** is the default real number type in Java.

As we have said, when designing Java classes we often wish to build in the idea of encapsulation (keeping some parts of the class hidden within the class) and we have included this information in our UML design above. The plus and minus signs that you can see in the UML diagram in Fig. 17.3 are all to do with this idea of encapsulation; a minus sign means that the attribute (or method) is **private**—that is, it is accessible *only to methods within the same class*. A plus sign means that it is **public**—it is accessible to methods of other classes. Normally we make the attributes private and the methods public, in this way achieving encapsulation. However, methods can be declared to be private if need be (e.g. where methods are used within the class only and are not part of the external interface of the class) and attributes can be declared to be public if need be. But in most cases attributes will be private and methods public and this is what we have done with the Rectangle class. Let's now see how we implement this in Java by examining the code for our Rectangle class. Take a look at it and then we will discuss it.

The *Rectangle.java* class

```java
public class Rectangle
{
    // the attributes
    private double length;
    private double height;

    // the methods

    // the constructor
    public Rectangle(double lengthIn, double heightIn)
    {
        this.length = lengthIn;
        this.height = heightIn;
    }

    // this method allows us to read the length attribute
    public double getLength()
    {
        return this.length;
    }

    // this method allows us to read the height attribute
    public double getHeight()
    {
        return this.height;
    }

    // this method allows us to write to the length attribute
    public void setLength(double lengthIn)
    {
        this.length = lengthIn;
    }

    // this method allows us to write to the height attribute
    public void setHeight(double heightIn)
    {
        this.height = heightIn;
    }

    // this method returns the area of the Rectangle
    public double calculateArea()
    {
        return this.length * this.height;
    }

    // this method returns the perimeter of the Rectangle
    public double calculatePerimeter()
    {
        return 2 * (this.length + this.height);
    }
}
```

Let's take a closer look at this. The first line declares the `Rectangle` class:

```java
public class Rectangle
```

Next come the attributes. Unlike Python classes, attributes in Java classes need to be explicitly declared, much like variables. A `Rectangle` object will need attributes to hold values for the length and the height of the rectangle, and these will be of type **double**. The declaration of the attributes in the `Rectangle` class took the following form in our UML diagram:

-length: double

-height: double

You can see that we have indicated these attributes should be kept hidden (encapsulated) inside the class by the minus sign in front of them. In Java this is implemented as:

```
private double length;
private double height;
```

As you can see, attributes are declared like any other variables, except that they are declared *outside* of any method, and they also have an additional keyword in front of them—the word **private**, corresponding to the minus sign in the UML notation. In Java, this keyword is used to restrict the scope of the attributes to methods of this class only, as we described above.

You should note that the attributes declared outside of methods in this way (whether private or not) are always accessible to *all* the methods of the class— unlike *local* variables, which are accessible only to the methods in which they are declared. Also, while in Python variables declared outside methods become *class variables* (attributes stored once in the class and not copied into each instance of an object), in Java these attributes become *instance variables* (attributes that are stored in each instance of an object). This means that every object we create from this class will have its own length and height values stored within it. We will see later how to modify these to create class variables if we require them.

Figure 17.3 made it clear which methods we need to define within our Rectangle class. First comes the constructor. You should recall that it has the same name as the class, and note that, unlike any other method in Java, it has no return type—not even **void**! It looks like this:

```
public Rectangle(double lengthIn, double heightIn)
{
    this.length = lengthIn;
    this.height = heightIn;
}
```

The first thing to notice is that this method is declared as **public**. Unlike the attributes, we want our methods to be accessible from outside (as indicated by a plus sign in the UML design) so that they can be called by methods of other classes.

After that you can see that the code in this constructor is very similar to the equivalent initializer we showed you in the Python Rectangle class of Chap. 8, which initializes the length and height attributes based on the value of the two parameters received (lengthIn and heightIn). One thing you will notice is that we do not need to send in an additional parameter representing the name of the Rectangle object itself (a parameter we named self in Chap. 8 when looking at the equivalent Python class). Instead, Java has a standard keyword that we can use to refer to the associated Rectangle object—that keyword is **this**. The **this** keyword can be used in conjunction with the dot operator to access the attributes of the given class:

```
// the 'this' keyword referes to the object itself and can be used to refer to its attributes
this.length = lengthIn;
this.height = heightIn;
```

Attributes can also be referred to directly without using the **this** keyword, for example:

```
// accessing object attributes without the 'this' keyword
length = lengthIn;
height = heightIn;
```

However, as you can see, it is much clearer when an object attribute is being referenced by using the **this** keyword, so we will always use it when accessing object attributes in our Java classes throughout the rest of this text.

When we define a constructor like this in a class it is termed a *user-defined*[2] constructor. If we don't define our own constructor, then one is automatically and invisibly provided for us—this is referred to as the **default** constructor. The default constructor takes no parameters and when it is used to create an object—for example in a line like this:

```
Rectangle myRectangle = new Rectangle();
```

All that happens when a default constructor is called is that memory is reserved for the new object and all attributes will be given initial values according to the rules that we give you later in Sect. 17.11.

One more thing about constructors: once we have defined our own constructors, this default constructor is no longer automatically available. If we want it to be available, then we have to redefine it explicitly. In the Rectangle case we would define it as:

```
public Rectangle()
{
}
```

You can see that just like regular methods, constructers can be overloaded, and we can define several constructors in one class. When we create an object, it will be clear from the parameter list which constructor we are referring to.

Now let's take a look at the definition of the next method, getLength. The purpose of this method is simply to send back the value of the length attribute. In the UML diagram it was declared as:

+getLength(): double

In Java this becomes:

```
public double getLength()
{
    return this.length;
}
```

---

[2] Here the word *user* is referring to the person *writing* the program, not the person using it!

Once again you can see that the method has been declared as **public** (indicated by the plus sign in UML), enabling it to be accessed by methods of other classes and we use the **this** keyword to access the length attribute. A reminder that in Java we need to explicitly give a type to the return value of a method (or **void** if no value is returned), and the UML diagram makes clear the return value should be of type **double**.

The next method, getHeight, behaves in the same way in respect of the height attribute.

Next comes the setLength method:

+setLength(double)

Here you can see there is no value returned so the return type should be **void**. However, it does require a parameter of type **double** that it will assign to the length attribute. We implement this as follows:

```
public void setLength(double lengthIn)
{
    this.length = lengthIn;
}
```

The next method, setHeight, behaves in the same way in respect of height attribute.

After this comes the calculateArea method:

+calculateArea(): double

We implement this as:

```
public double calculateArea()
{
    return this.length * this.height;
}
```

Once again there are no formal parameters, as this method does not need any additional data in order to do its job; it returns a **double**. The actual code is just one line, namely the statement that returns the area of the Rectangle, calculated by multiplying the value of the length attribute by the value of the height attribute of the object.

The calculatePerimeter method is similar, and thus, the definition of the Rectangle class is now complete.

17.9   Implementing the *BankAccount* Class

The appropriate UML class diagram for the BankAccount class is shown in Fig. 17.4.

Fig. 17.4 The design of
BankAccount class

BankAccount
-accountNumber : String -accountName : String -balance : double
+BankAccount (String, String) +getAccountNumber() : String +getAccountName() : String +getBalance() : double +deposit(double) +withdraw(double) : boolean

You can see again that the attributes have been designed to be **private** and the methods **public** and we have a `BankAccount` constructor that carries out the same job as the initializer we met when looking at the equivalent Python class in Chap. 8. The code for the `BankAccount` class is now given below.

The *BankAccount.java* class

```java
public class BankAccount
{
    // the attributes
    private String accountNumber;
    private String accountName;
    private double balance;

    // the methods

    // the constructor
    public BankAccount(String numberIn, String nameIn)
    {
        this.accountNumber = numberIn;
        this.accountName = nameIn;
        this.balance = 0;
    }

    // methods to read the attributes
    public String getAccountName()
    {
        return this.accountName;
    }

    public String getAccountNumber()
    {
        return this.accountNumber;
    }

    public double getBalance()
    {
        return this.balance;
    }

    // methods to deposit and withdraw money
    public void deposit(double amountIn)
    {
        this.balance = this.balance + amountIn;
    }

    public boolean withdraw(double amountIn)
```

```
    {
        if(amountIn > this.balance)
        {
            return false; // no withdrawal was made
        }
        else
        {
            this.balance = this.balance - amountIn;
            return true; // money was withdrawn successfully
        }
    }
}
```

Having shown you how the `Rectangle` class was put together in Java from a UML design, and having described our Python `BankAccount` class in Chap. 8, the above Java `BankAccount` class should be straightforward to follow.

17.10   The *static* Keyword

You have already seen the keyword **static** in front of the names of methods in some Java classes. A word such as this (as well as the words **public** and **private**) is called a **modifier**. A modifier determines the particular way a class, attribute or method is accessed in Java.

An attribute declared as **static** in a Java class is how we create a *class variable*. We discussed class variables in Chap. 8 when looking at classes and objects in Python. You will remember from that chapter that a class variable creates only one copy of the attribute, stored in the class and makes it accessible to all objects. We can create a class variable if the value of an attribute remains the same for all objects. In Chap. 8 we described a bank account's interest rate as being a good example of a class variable, as (in this simple example) the rate of interest will be the same for all `BankAccount` objects. So, to create a class variable called `interestRate` in our `BankAccount` class we would add the **static** modifier as follows:

```
// the static modifier converts the attribute to a class variable
private static double interestRate;
```

You can see we add the **static** modifier to the left of the attribute type.

You can also see that we have kept this attribute hidden (using the **private** keyword). To allow users to access this attribute we need to provide some methods for this purpose (e.g. `getInterestRate` and `setInterestRate`). Usually, we would call methods via an object, but in the case of methods such as these which are used exclusively to read and write to the class variable, it does not make sense to have to access them via an object. For example, to set the rate of interest offered to all customers it would not make sense to have to do that via one particular customer object. Instead, it would make sense to call such methods via the class so that any changes made are made for all objects. We refer to such methods as **class methods**. To create a class method in Java we simply use the **static** modifier again, for example:

```
// the static modifier converts the method to a class method
public static double getInterestRate()
{
    return interestRate;
}
```

You can see the **static** modifier is added to the left of the method return type. As you will see in our next program, BankAccountTester2, we can call a class method by using the class name instead of the object name.

We have rewritten our BankAccount class, and called it BankAccount2. We have included three new methods as well as the new **static** attribute interestRate. The first two of these—setInterestRate and getInterestRate—are the methods that allow us to read and write to our new attribute. These have been declared as **static**. The third—addInterest—is the method that adds the interest to the customer's balance—this remains a regular method as the outcome of this is different for each customer. As can be seen in Fig. 17.5, the UML notation to underline class attributes applies to class methods too.

Here is the code for the class. The new items have been emboldened.

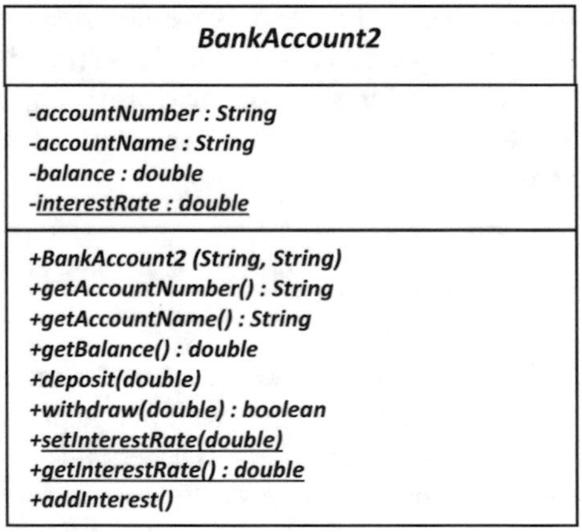

Fig. 17.5 The design of the *BankAccount2* class

BankAccount2
-accountNumber : String   -accountName : String   -balance : double   -*interestRate : double*
+BankAccount2 (String, String)   +getAccountNumber() : String   +getAccountName() : String   +getBalance() : double   +deposit(double)   +withdraw(double) : boolean   +*setInterestRate(double)*   +*getInterestRate() : double*   +addInterest()

BankAccount2.java - the modified *BankAccount* class

```java
public class BankAccount2
{
    private String accountNumber;
    private String accountName;
    private double balance;
    private static double interestRate;

    public BankAccount2(String numberIn, String nameIn)
    {
        this.accountNumber = numberIn;
        this.accountName = nameIn;
        this.balance = 0;
    }

    public String getAccountName()
    {
        return this.accountName;
    }

    public String getAccountNumber()
    {

        return this.accountNumber;
    }

    public double getBalance()
    {
        return this.balance;
    }

    public void deposit(double amountIn)
    {
        this.balance = this.balance + amountIn;
    }

            public boolean withdraw(double amountIn)
            {
                if(amountIn > this.balance)
                {
                    return false;
                }
                else
                {
                    this.balance = this.balance - amountIn;
                    return true;
                }
            }

    public static void setInterestRate(double rateIn)
    {
        interestRate = rateIn; // note that we do not use the 'this' keyword with a static variable
    }

    public static double getInterestRate()
    {
        return interestRate; // note that we do not use the 'this' keyword with a static variable
    }

    public void addInterest()
    {
        this.balance = this.balance + (this.balance * interestRate)/100;
    }
}
```

The following program, `BankAccountTester2`, uses this modified version of the `BankAccount` class.

BankAccountTester2.java

```
public class BankAccountTester2
{
    public static void main(String[] args)
    {
        // create a bank account
        BankAccount2 account1 = new BankAccount2("99786754","Gayle Forcewind");
        // create another bank account
        BankAccount2 account2 = new BankAccount2("99887776","Stan Dandy-Liver");
        // make a deposit into the first account
        account1.deposit(1000);
        // make a deposit into the second account
        account2.deposit(2000);
        // set the interest rate
        BankAccount2.setInterestRate(10);
        // add interest to accounts
        account1.addInterest();
        account2.addInterest();
        // display the account details
        System.out.println("Account number: " + account1.getAccountNumber());
        System.out.println("Account name: " + account1.getAccountName());
        System.out.println("Interest Rate " + BankAccount2.getInterestRate());
        System.out.println("Current balance: " + account1.getBalance());
        System.out.println(); // blank line
        System.out.println("Account number: " + account2.getAccountNumber());
        System.out.println("Account name: " + account2.getAccountName());
        System.out.println("Interest Rate " + BankAccount2.getInterestRate());
        System.out.println("Current balance: " + account2.getBalance());

    }
}
```

Take a closer look at the first four lines of the main method of the above program. We have created two new bank accounts which we have called account1 and account2, and have assigned account numbers and names to them at the time they were created (via the constructor). We have then deposited amounts of 1000 and 2000, respectively, into each of these accounts.

Now look at the next line:

```
BankAccount2.setInterestRate(10);
```

This line sets the interest rate to 10. Because setInterestRate has been declared as a **static** method, we have been able to call it by using the class name BankAccount2. Because interestRate has been declared as a **static** attribute this change is effective for any object of the class. Therefore, when we add interest to each account as we do with the next two lines:

```
account1.addInterest();
account2.addInterest();
```

We should expect it to be calculated with an interest rate of 10, giving us new balances of 1100 and 2200, respectively.

This is exactly what we get, as can be seen from the output below:

```
Account number: 99786754
Account name: Gayle Forcewind
Interest Rate 10.0
Current balance: 1100.0

Account number: 99887776
Account name: Stan Dandy-Liver
Interest Rate 10.0
Current balance: 2200.0
```

As you can see, class methods can be very useful indeed and we will have some more examples of them later in this chapter when we return to looking at the EasyScanner class. Of course, we have always declared our main method, and other methods within the same class as the main method, as **static**—because these methods belong to the class and not to a specific object.

17.11 Initializing Attributes

Looking back at the BankAccount2 class in the previous section, some of you might have been asking yourselves what would happen if we called the getInterestRate method before the interest rate had been set using the setInterestRate method. In fact, the answer is that a value of zero would be returned. This is because, while Java does not give an initial value to *local* variables (which is why you get a compiler error if you try to use an uninitialized variable), Java always initializes attributes. Numerical attributes such as **int** and **double** are initialized to zero; **boolean** attributes are initialized to **false** and objects are initialized to **null**. Character attributes are given an initial Unicode value of zero.

Despite the above, it is nonetheless good programming practice always to give an initial value to your attributes, rather than leave it to the compiler. One very good reason for this is that you cannot assume that every programming language initializes variables in the same way—if you were using C++, for example, the initial value of any variable is completely a matter of chance—and you won't get a compiler error to warn you! In the BankAccount2 class, it would have done no harm at all to have initialized the interestRate variable when it was declared:

```
private static double interestRate = 0;
```

Sometimes, when you initialize a class attribute you may require that value to be fixed. We would think of such an attribute as a **class constant**. You have seen in Chap. 13 that we can use the **final** keyword in Java to create a constant. For example, we considered a `CircularShape` Python class in Chap. 8 to help you carry out some circle-related calculations (such as calculating the area of a circle). Such calculations will need to use the mathematical value of pi (π)—approximately 3.1416. We could create a class constant to store this fixed value in a `CirclarShape` Java class as follows:

```
public class CircularShape
{
    // creating a class constant with the 'final' keyword
    public static final double PI = 3.1416;

    // more attrbutes and methdods here

}
```

You can see that the **final** keyword appears between the **static** keyword and the attribute's data type (**double** in this case). Notice that we have declared this class constant to be **public** rather than the usual **private** modifier for attributes. This is because it serves no purpose encapsulating a constant since there is no danger of it being modified inadvertently. For this reason, class constants are very often declared to be **public**.

Having declared a **public** class constant, we can access it in our programs using the class name and dot operator, for example:

```
// we can access public class constants in our programs via the class name
System.out.println ("value of PI = " + CircularShape.PI);
```

We will set the task of developing and testing this `CircularShape` class to you as an end of chapter exercise.

17.12 The *EasyScanner* Class

Finally, in this chapter we will return to look at the code for the `EasyScanner` class that we developed for you to make keyboard input a lot easier. We have now covered all the concepts you need in order to understand how this class works. Here it is:

The *EasyScanner.java* class

```
import   java.util.Scanner;

public class EasyScanner
{
    public static int nextInt()
    {
        Scanner keyboard = new Scanner(System.in);
        int i = keyboard.nextInt();
        return i;
    }

    public static double nextDouble()
    {
        Scanner keyboard = new Scanner(System.in);
        double d = keyboard.nextDouble();
        return d;
    }

    public static String nextString()
    {
        Scanner keyboard = new Scanner(System.in);
        String s = keyboard.nextLine();
        return s;
    }

    public static char nextChar()
    {
        Scanner keyboard = new Scanner(System.in);
        char c = keyboard.next().charAt(0);
        return c;
    }
}
```

You can see that we have made every method a **static** method, so that we can simply use the class name when we call a method. For example:

```
int number = EasyScanner.nextInt();
```

You can see that the nextString method uses the nextLine method of the Scanner class—but as a new Scanner object is created each time the method is called there is no problem about using it after a nextInt or a nextDouble method as there is with nextLine itself.

17.13   Self-test Questions

1. Consider the following line of code which makes use of the Rectangle class discussed in this chapter:

```
Rectangle rectangle1 = new Rectangle(3, 4);
```

(a) By referring to the line of code above identify the *class*, the *object* and the *constructor*.

(b) By referring to the line of code above explain the purpose of the constructor.

(c) By referring to the idea of *encapsulation*, explain why the following line of code for displaying the length of the Rectangle object created above will not compile:

```
System.out.println (rectangle1.length);
```

(d) Use the appropriate method of the `Rectangle` class to correctly display the length of the `Rectangle` object.

(e) Use the appropriate method of the `Rectangle` class to reset the length of the `Rectangle` object to 12.5.

2. (a) Write the code that will create two `BankAccount` objects, `acc1` and `acc2`. The account number and account name of each should be set at the time the object is created.

(b) Write the lines of code that will deposit an amount of 200 into `acc1` and 100 into `acc2`.

(c) Write the lines of code that attempt to withdraw an amount of 150 from `acc1` and displays the message "WITHDRAWAL SUCCESSFUL" if the amount was withdrawn successfully and "INSUFFICIENT FUNDS" if it was not.

(d) Write a line of code that will display the balance of `acc1`.

(e) Write a line of code that will display the balance of `acc2`.

3. In what way does calling methods from the `EasyScanner` class differ from calling methods from the other classes you have met (`BankAccount`, `Rectangle`, `String` and `Scanner`)?

4. Consider the following fragment of code that initializes one string constant with a password ("java") and creates a second string to hold the user's guess for the password. The user is then asked to enter their guess:

```
String final PASSWORD = "java"; // set password
String guess; // to hold user's guess
System.out.print ("Enter guess: ");
```

(a) Write a line of code that uses the `EasyScanner` class to read the guess from the keyboard.

(b) Write the code that displays the message "CORRECT PASSWORD" if the user entered the correct password and "INCORRECT PASSWORD" if not.

5. (a) Declare an array called `rooms`, to hold three `Rectangle` objects. Each `Rectangle` object will represent the dimensions of a room in an apartment.

(b) The three rooms in the apartment have the following dimensions:

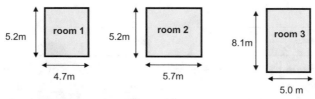

Add three appropriate `Rectangle` objects to the `rooms` array to represent these 3 rooms.

(c) Write the line of code that would make use of the `rooms` array to display the area of room 3 to the screen.

6. Consider a `Robot` class with the following UML design for its constructor and a method to move the robot right:

+Robot (int, int)
+moveRight (int)

The two integer parameters of the constructor represent the starting *x* and *y* co-ordinates of the robot on the screen, respectively, while the integer parameter of the `moveRight` method represents the number of pixels you wish to move the robot to the right.

(a) Write the method header for the `Robot` constructor.
(b) Write the method header for the `moveRight` method.
(c) Write the line of code to create a robot object, `r1`, with *x* co-ordinate 10 and *y* co-ordinate 20.
(d) Write the line of code to move the robot object you created above 25 pixels to the right.

7. Consider the `CircularShape` Python class you developed in your end of chapter exercises of Chap. 8. Below is an updated UML diagram for this class (targeted towards Java) that includes a PI class constant as discussed in Sect. 17.11.

CircularShape
– radius : double *+PI: double = 3.1416*
+CircularShape(double) *+setRadius(double)* *+getRadius( ) : double* *+calculateArea() : double* *+calculateCircumference() : double*

(a) What do the plus and minus signs in this UML class diagram indicate?
(b) Write the lines of code that declare the **radius** attribute and the PI attribute.
(c) Write the method header for each of the methods in the diagram above.

8. Consider the following class:

```
public class SomeClass
{
    private int x;

    public SomeClass( )
    {
        this.x = 10;
    }

    public SomeClass(int xIn)
    {
        this.x = xIn;
    }

    public void setX(int xIn)
    {
        this.x = xIn;
    }

    public int getX()
    {
        return this.x;
    }
}
```

(a) What would be the output from the following program?

```
public class Test1
{
    public static void main(String[] args)
    {
        SomeClass myObject = new SomeClass();
        System.out.println(myObject.getX());
    }
}
```

(b) What would be the output from the following program?

```
public class Test2
{
    public static void main(String[] args)
    {
        SomeClass myObject = new SomeClass(5);
        System.out.println(myObject.getX());
    }
}
```

(c) Explain why the following program would not compile.

```
public class Test3
{
    public static void main(String[] args)
    {
        SomeClass myObject = new SomeClass(5, 8);
        System.out.println(myObject.getX());
    }
}
```

(d) What would be the output from the following program?

```
public class Test4
{
    public static void main(String[] args)
    {
        int y = 20;
        SomeClass myObject = new SomeClass(5);
        System.out.println(myObject.getX());
        test(y, myObject);
        System.out.println(y);
        System.out.println(myObject.getX());
    }

    static void test(int z, SomeClass classIn)
    {
        z = 50;
        classIn.setX(100);
    }
}
```

17.14 Programming Exercises

In order to tackle these exercises, make sure that the classes `Rectangle`, `BankAccount` and `EasyScanner` have been copied from the website (see preface) and placed in the correct directory for your compiler to access them.

1. (a) Develop a short program to check your answer to self-test question 1(d) and 1(e) above.
   (b) Adapt the program above so that the user is able to set the length and height of the original `Rectangle` object. Make use of the `EasyScanner` class to read in the user input.
2. Develop a short program to check your answer to self-test question 2 above relating to `BankAccount` objects.
3. Consider a program to enter and confirm a suitable code name for a secret agent. Declare 2 string objects, called `codeName` and `confirm` and then
   (a) prompt the user to enter a suitable name into the `codeName` string;
   (b) use a **while** loop to ensure that the string entered is greater than 6 characters in length, if it is not print "INVALID CODENAME" and ask the user to re-enter a code name;
   (c) once a valid code name has been entered ask the user to re-enter the code name into the `confirm` string and then use an **if else** statement to ensure that the string entered matches the original code name; if it does, print a message "CODE NAME CONFIRMED" otherwise print a message saying "CODE NAME MIS-MATCH";
   (d) Use the `charAt` method to ensure that the code name ends with an 'X' character;
   (e) Finally use the `startsWith` method to ensure that, as well as being greater than 6 characters in length, the code name entered also starts with the words "Agent".

4. Write a program that creates an array of Rectangle objects to represent the dimensions of rooms in an apartment as described in self-test question 5. The program should allow the user to:

   - determine the number of rooms;
   - enter the dimensions of the rooms;
   - retrieve the area and dimensions of any of the rooms.

5. In the end of chapter exercises of Chap. 8 we asked you to develop a CircularShape class in Python. In self-test question 7 above you considered the equivalent Java class. Develop the complete CircularShape class in Java, using your answers to self-test question 7 above, then develop a tester program that creates a CircularShape object and calls various methods of this object.

6. In the end of chapter exercises of Chap. 8 you developed a Student class, a StockItem class and an IncubatorMonitor class. Update the UML diagrams produced for each of these classes so they are suitable for Java programmers then develop each of these classes in Java with suitable testers.

Object-Oriented Java: Part 2

18

Outcomes

By the end of this chapter you should be able to:

- *implement inheritance relationships in Java;*
- *distinguish between **method overriding** and **method overloading**;*
- *explain the use of the* **abstract** *modifier when applied to classes and methods;*
- *explain the use of the* **final** *modifier, when applied to classes and methods;*
- *describe the way in which all Java classes are derived from the* Object *class.*

18.1 Introduction

In Chap. 9 we introduced you to the important object-oriented concept of **inheritance**—the sharing of attributes and methods among classes. We can take a class and then define other classes based on the first one. The new classes *inherit* all the attributes and methods of the first one, but also have attributes and methods of their own. In object-oriented programming languages like Java, inheritance provides a powerful way of re-using existing classes by allowing us to extend them to meet our specific needs without our having to modify the original class. In this chapter we will look at how to utilize inheritance in Java.

Supplementary Information The online version contains supplementary material available at https://doi.org/10.1007/978-3-031-01326-3_18.

Q. Charatan and A. Kans, *Programming in Two Semesters*,
Texts in Computer Science, https://doi.org/10.1007/978-3-031-01326-3_18

18.2   The *Employee* and *PartTimeEmployee* Classes

In Chap. 9 we illustrated the use of inheritance in Python by looking at an
Employee class and showing how to extend this class to develop a Full-
TimeEmployee class and then later a PartTimeEmployee class. Here we will
look specifically at the development of a PartTimeEmployee class from an
Employee class in Java. A UML diagram, targeted at Java, illustrates the rela-
tionship between these two classes is shown in Fig. 18.1:

You can see that we have used the **double** type here throughout—as **double**
is the default real number type in Java. You can also see that both the Employee
and PartTimeEmployee classes have constructors that mirror the initializer
methods of Python given in the UML diagram we showed you in Fig. 9.2. In
addition, we have a number of get and set methods to access encapsulated
attributes.

You are familiar now with the diamond shape being used in UML to represent
an inheritance relationship with the class at the top of the hierarchy—in this case the
Employee class—referred to as the **superclass** (or **base class**) and the Part-
TimeEmployee as the **subclass** (or **derived class**). Let's now take a look at how
to implement this inheritance relationship in Java.

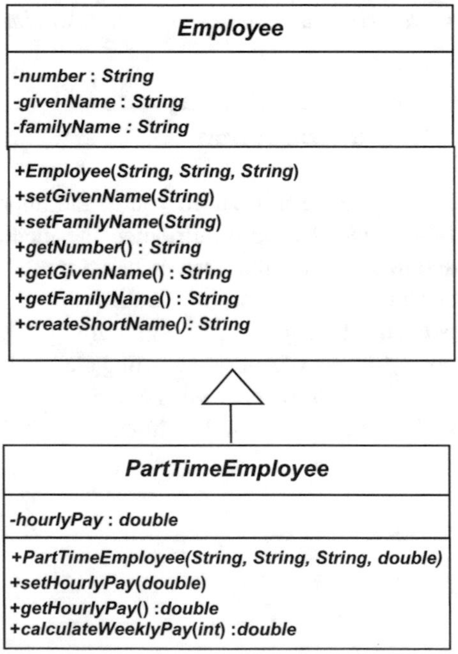

Fig. 18.1 *Employee* and
PartTimeEmployee
inheritance relationship

18.3   Implementing Inheritance in Java

The code for the Employee superclass is shown first below:

Employee.java

```java
public class Employee
{
    private String number;
    private String givenName;
    private String familyName;

    public Employee (String numberIn, String givenNameIn,  String familyNameIn)
    {
        this.number = numberIn;
        this.givenName = givenNameIn;
        this.familyName = familyNameIn;
    }

    public void setGivenName (String nameIn)
    {
        this.givenName = nameIn;
    }

    public void setFamilyName (String nameIn)
    {
        this.familyName = nameIn;
    }


    public String getNumber ()
    {
        return this.number;
    }

    public String getGivenName ()
    {
        return this.givenName;
    }

    public String getFamilyName ()
    {
        return this.familyName;
    }

    public String createShortName ()
    {
        return this.givenName.charAt(0) + "." + this.familyName;
    }

}
```

You can see that we have followed the UML design in Fig. 18.1 and encapsulated the attributes of this class (i.e. declared them as **private**). Notice how we used the charAt method of the String class to take the first character of the givenName string attribute to create a short name:

```java
public String createShortName ()
{
    return this.givenName.charAt(0) + "." + this.familyName;
}
```

There is nothing new here, so let's get on with our PartTimeEmployee subclass. We will present the code first and analyse it afterwards.

PartTimeEmployee.java

```
public class PartTimeEmployee extends Employee // this class is a subclass of Employee
{
    private double hourlyPay; // this attribute is unique to the subclass

    // the constructor
    public PartTimeEmployee(String numberIn, String givenNameIn, String familyNameIn, double hourlyPayIn)
    {
        super(numberIn, givenNameIn, familyNameIn); // call the constructor of the superclass
        this.hourlyPay = hourlyPayIn; // initialise remaining local attribute
    }

    // these methods are unique to the subclass
    public double getHourlyPay()
    {
        return this.hourlyPay;
    }

    public void setHourlyPay(double hourlyPayIn)
    {
        this.hourlyPay = hourlyPayIn;
    }

    public double calculateWeeklyPay(int noOfHoursIn)
    {
        return noOfHoursIn * this.hourlyPay;
    }
}
```

The first line of interest is the class header itself:

```
public class PartTimeEmployee extends Employee // this class is a subclass of Employee
```

Here you can see that we use of the keyword **extends** to create an inheritance relationship in Java. Using this word in this way means that the PartTimeEmployee class (the *subclass*) inherits all the attributes and methods of the Employee class (the *superclass*), that is, PartTimeEmployee *is a kind of* Employee.

One thing to bear in mind when implementing inheritance in Java is that when attributes of the superclass (Employee in this class) have been encapsulated and declared as **private** none of the PartTimeEmployee methods can directly access them directly—the subclass has only the same access rights as any other class! There are a number of possible ways around this:

1. We could declare the original attributes as **public**—but this would take away the whole point of encapsulation;
2. We could use the special keyword **protected** instead of **private**. The effect of this is that anything declared as **protected** is accessible to the methods of any subclasses. There are, however, two issues to think about here. The first is that you have to anticipate in advance when you want your class to be able to be inherited. The second problem is that it weakens your efforts to encapsulate information within the class, since, in Java, **protected** attributes are also accessible to any other class in the same *package* (you will find out much more about the meaning of the word **package** in Chap. 24);

The above remarks notwithstanding, this is a perfectly acceptable approach to use, particularly in situations where you are writing a class as part of a discrete

application, and you will be aware in advance that certain classes will need to be subclassed. You will see an example of this in Sect. 18.4;
Incidentally, in a UML diagram a **protected** attribute is indicated by a hash symbol, #'

3. The other solution, and the one we will use now, is to leave the attributes as **private**, but to plan carefully in advance which get- and set- methods we are going to provide.

After the class header we have the following declaration:

```
private double hourlyPay;
```

This declares an attribute, hourlyPay, which is unique to our subclass—but remember that the attributes of the superclass, Employee, will be inherited, so in fact any PartTimeEmployee object will have *four* attributes.

Next comes the constructor. We want to be able to assign values to the number and names at the time that the object is created, just as we do with an Employee object; so our PartTimeEmpoyee constructor will need to receive parameters that will be assigned to the number, givenName and familyName attributes of the Employee superclass.

But wait a minute! How are we going to do this? These three attributes have been declared as **private** in the superclass—so they aren't accessible to objects of the subclass. Luckily there is a way around this problem. We can call the constructor of the superclass by using the keyword **super** (in much the same way we did when looking at the equivalent Python class in Chap. 9) to initialize these superclass attributes for us. Look how this is done:

```
public PartTimeEmployee(String numberIn, String givenNameIn, String familyNameIn, double hourlyPayIn)
{
    super(numberIn, givenNameIn, familyNameIn); // call the constructor of the superclass
    this.hourlyPay = hourlyPayIn;
}
```

You can see that we send the first three parameters to the superclass constructer to initialize the superclass attributes via the call to **super**. After calling the constructor of the superclass, we need to perform one more task—namely to assign the fourth parameter, hourlyPayIn, to the hourlyPay attribute in the PartTimeEmployee class. Notice, however, that the line that calls **super** has to be the first one—if we had written our constructor like this it would not compile:

```
/* this version of the constructor would not compile - the call to super has to be the
   first instruction */
public PartTimeEmployee(String numberIn, String givenNameIn, String familyNameIn, double hourlyPayIn)
{
    this.hourlyPay = hourlyPayIn;
    super(numberIn, givenNameIn, familyNameIn);  // this call should have been the first instruction!
}
```

The remaining methods of `PartTimeEmployee` are new methods specific to the subclass:

```java
public double getHourlyPay()
{
    return this.hourlyPay;
}

public void setHourlyPay(double hourlyPayIn)
{
    this.hourlyPay = hourlyPayIn;
}

public double calculateWeeklyPay(int noOfHoursIn)
{
    return noOfHoursIn * this.hourlyPay;
}
```

The first two provide read and write access, respectively, to the `hourlyPay` attribute. The third one receives the number of hours worked and calculates the pay by multiplying this by the hourly rate attribute. The program below demonstrates the use of the `PartTimeEmployee` class—you can compare it to the equivalent `partimeemployeetester.py` Python program of Chap. 9.

PartTimeEmployeeTester.java

```java
import java.util.Scanner;
public class PartTimeEmployeeTester
{
    public static void main(String[] args)
    {
        Scanner keyboard = new Scanner(System.in);
        Scanner keyboardString = new Scanner(System.in);
        String number, givenName, familyName;
        double pay;
        int hours;
        PartTimeEmployee emp;

        // get the details from the user
        System.out.print("Employee Number? ");
        number = keyboardString.nextLine();
        System.out.print("Given name? ");
        givenName = keyboardString.nextLine();
        System.out.print("Family name? ");
        familyName = keyboardString.nextLine();
        System.out.print("Hourly Pay? ");
        pay = keyboard.nextDouble();
        System.out.print("Hours worked this week? ");
        hours = keyboard.nextInt();

        // create a new part-time employee
        emp = new PartTimeEmployee(number, givenName, familyName, pay);

        // display part-time employee's details, including the weekly pay
        System.out.println();

        // the next four methods have been inhreted from the Employee class
        System.out.println(emp.getNumber());
        System.out.println(emp.getGivenName());
        System.out.println(emp.getFamilyName());
        System.out.println(emp.createShortName());


        System.out.println(emp.calculateWeeklyPay(hours));
    }
}
```

This program will behave in exactly the same way as the `partimeemploy-eetester.py` Python program of Chap. 9.

18.4 Method Overriding

In previous chapters you were introduced to the concept of polymorphism—the idea that we can have different methods with the same name, but whose behaviour is different. You saw in Chap. 15 that one way of achieving polymorphism was by method *overloading*, which involves methods of the same class having the same name, but being distinguished by their parameter lists (e.g. two versions of the constructor in one class).

In Chap. 9 we illustrated another way of achieving polymorphism, namely by **method overriding**—two or more methods with the same name and parameter list in *different classes connected by an inheritance relationship*. We illustrated this in Python with the BankAccount superclass and GoldAccount subclass both having a withdraw method that behaved slightly differently in each class (the BankAccount method only allowed withdrawals if there was sufficient money in the account, whereas the GoldAccount customers were provided with an overdraft limit to allow for withdrawals beyond the current balance of the account). Let's take a look at this inheritance relationship in Java.

An updated UML diagram for the BankAccount and GoldAccount classes is given in Fig. 18.2.

Fig. 18.2 UML diagram for the *BankAccount* hierarchy

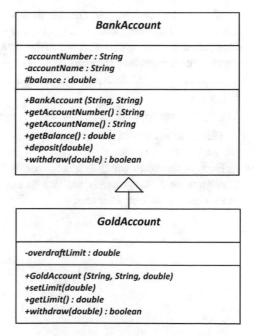

You will notice that we have made a small change to the original Bank-Account Java class design from the previous chapter. The balance attribute has a hash sign (#) in front of it instead of a minus sign. You will remember from our previous discussion that this means access to the attribute is **protected**, rather than **private**. The reason why we have decided to make this change is explained below.

You will also notice that the withdraw method appears in both classes—this, of course, is because we are going to override it in the subclass.

You might already be thinking about how to code the withdraw method in the GoldAccount class. If you are doing this, you will probably have worked out that this method is going to need access to the balance attribute, which of course was declared as **private** in the BankAccount class, and (for good reason) was not provided with a set- method.

When we developed the BankAccount class in Chap. 17, we developed it as a stand-alone class, and we didn't think about how it might be used in a larger application where it could be refined. Had we known about inheritance at that point we might have given the matter a little more thought and realized that it would be useful if any subclasses of BankAccount that were developed in future had access to the balance attribute. As we explained in Sect. 18.4, we can achieve that by declaring that attribute as **protected** instead of **private**. That is what we have done here.

The version of BankAccount that we are going to use in this chapter is, therefore, exactly the same as the previous one, with the single difference that the declaration of the balance attribute now looks like this, with the keyword **protected** replacing **private**:

```
protected double balance;
```

This new version of the BankAccount class is available on the website (see preface).

Here is the code for the GoldAccount class. You will notice that there is something new here, namely the line that reads @Override—have a look at the code, then we will explain this.

```
GoldAccount.java
```

```java
public class GoldAccount extends BankAccount
{
    private double overdraftLimit;

    public GoldAccount (String numberIn, String nameIn, double limitIn)
    {
        super (numberIn, nameIn);
        this.overdraftLimit = limitIn;
    }

    public void setLimit (double limitIn)
    {
        this.overdraftLimit = limitIn;
    }

    public double getLimit ()
    {
        return this.overdraftLimit;
    }

    @Override
    public boolean withdraw (double amountIn)
    {
        if (amountIn > this.balance + this.overdraftLimit) // customer can withdraw up to the overdraft limit
        {
            return false; // no withdrawal was made
        }
        else
        {
            this.balance = this.balance - amountIn; // balance is protected so we have direct access to it
            return true; // money was withdrawn successfully
        }
    }
}
```

The thing that we are interested in here is the `withdraw` method. As we have pointed out this is introduced with `@Override`.

```java
@Override
public boolean withdraw (double amountIn)
{
    // rest of code here
}
```

`@Override` is an example of a Java **annotation**. Annotations begin with the @ symbol and always start with an uppercase letter. Although it is not mandatory that we include this annotation, it is very good practice to do so. Its purpose is to inform the compiler that we are overriding a method from the superclass. This helps us to avoid making the common error of not giving the overridden method exactly the same name and parameter list as the method it is supposed to be overriding. Without the annotation, this would escape the notice of the compiler, and you would have simply written a new method. But with the annotation included you would get a compiler error if the method headings did not match.

As far as the method itself is concerned, the test in the **if** statement differs from the original method in the `BankAccount` class (as shown below), in order to take account of the fact that customers with a gold account are allowed an overdraft:

```
@Override
public boolean withdraw(double amountIn)
{
    if(amountIn > this.balance + this.overdraftLimit) // customer can withdraw up to the overdraft limit
    {
        return false; // no withdrawal was made
    }
    else
    {
        this.balance = this.balance - amountIn; // balance is protected so we have direct access to it
        return true; // money was withdrawn successfully
    }
}
```

Notice that, as the `balance` attribute was declared as **protected** in the `BankAccount` superclass, we can directly access it in the `withdraw` method of the `GoldAccount` subclass; we would not have been able to do so had we left that attribute as **private** in the superclass.

As we explained in Chap. 15, *overloaded* methods *within* a class share the same name and are distinguished by their parameter lists. In the case of method *overriding*, the methods have the same name *and* parameter list but belong to *different classes*—the superclass and the subclass. In this case they are distinguished by the *object with which they are associated*. Let's illustrate this in the program below, which mirrors the equivalent Python program we showed you in Sect. 9.5.

OverridingDemo.java

```
public class OverridingDemo
{
    public static void main(String[] args)
    {
        boolean ok;
        //declare a BankAccount object
        BankAccount bankAcc = new BankAccount("123", "Ordinary Account Holder");
        //declare a GoldAccount object
        GoldAccount goldAcc = new GoldAccount("124", "Gold Account Holder", 500);

        bankAcc.deposit(1000);
        goldAcc.deposit(1000);

        ok = bankAcc.withdraw(1250); // the withdraw method of BankAccount is called
        if(ok)
        {
            System.out.print("Money withdrawn. ");
        }
        else
        {
            System.out.print("Insufficient funds. ");
        }
        System.out.println("Balance of " + bankAcc.getAccountName() + " is " + bankAcc.getBalance());
        System.out.println();

        ok = goldAcc.withdraw(1250); // the withdraw method of GoldAccount is called
        if(ok)
        {
            System.out.print("Money withdrawn. ");
        }
        else
        {
            System.out.print("Insufficient funds. ");
        }
        System.out.println("Balance of " + goldAcc.getAccountName() + " is " + goldAcc.getBalance());
        System.out.println();
    }
}
```

In this program we create an object of the `BankAccount` class and an object of the `GoldAccount` class (with an overdraft limit of 500) and deposit an amount of 1000 in each:

```
BankAccount bankAcc = new BankAccount("123", "Ordinary Account Holder");
GoldAccount goldAcc = new GoldAccount("124", "Gold Account Holder", 500);
bankAcc.deposit(1000);
goldAcc.deposit(1000);
```

Next we attempt to withdraw the sum of 1250 from the `BankAccount` object and assign the return value to a **boolean** variable, `ok`:

```
ok = bankAcc.withdraw(1250);
```

The `withdraw` method that is called here will be that of `BankAccount`, because it is called via the `BankAccount` object, `bankAcc`.

Once this is done we display a message showing whether or not the withdrawal was successful, followed by the balance of that account:

```
if(ok)
{
    System.out.print("Money withdrawn. ");
}
else
{
    System.out.print("Insufficient funds. ");
}
System.out.println("Balance of " + bankAcc.getAccountName() + " is " + bankAcc.getBalance());
```

Now the `withdraw` method is called again, but in this case via the `Gold-Account` object, `goldAcc`:

```
ok = goldAcc.withdraw(1250);
```

This time it is the `withdraw` method of `GoldAccount` that will be called, because `goldAcc` is an object of this class. The appropriate message and the balance are again displayed.

The output from this program is shown below and as expected mirrors the output of the equivalent `overrdingdemo.py` Python program of Chap. 9:

```
Insufficient funds. Balance of Ordinary Account Holder is 1000.0
Money withdrawn. Balance of Gold Account Holder is -250.0
```

As expected, the withdrawal from `BankAccount` does not take place—the balance is 1000, and since there is no overdraft facility a request to withdraw 1250 is denied. In the case of the `GoldAccount`, however, a withdrawal of 1250 would result in a negative balance of 250, which is allowed, because it is within the overdraft limit of 500.

18.5   Abstract Classes

Earlier in his chapter we revisited an inheritance example from Chap. 9 of an
`Employee` superclass and its `PartTimeEmployee` subclass. In Chap. 9 the
`Employee` class was used as the superclass for two subclasses: `PartTimeEm-`
`ployee` and `FullTimeEmployee`. Figure 18.3 illustrates this inheritance
hierarchy in a UML design suitable for Java programmers:

   If you think about this inheritance relationship a bit more, it will occur to you
that *any* employee will always be either a full-time employee or a part-time
employee. There is never going to be a situation in which an individual is just a
plain old employee! So, users of a program that included all these classes would
never find themselves creating objects of the `Employee` class. In fact, it would be
a good idea to prevent people from doing this—and, as you might have guessed,
there is a way to do so, which is to declare the class as **abstract**. In order to
make our `Employee` class abstract all we have to do is to place the keyword
abstract in the header:

```
public abstract class Employee
```

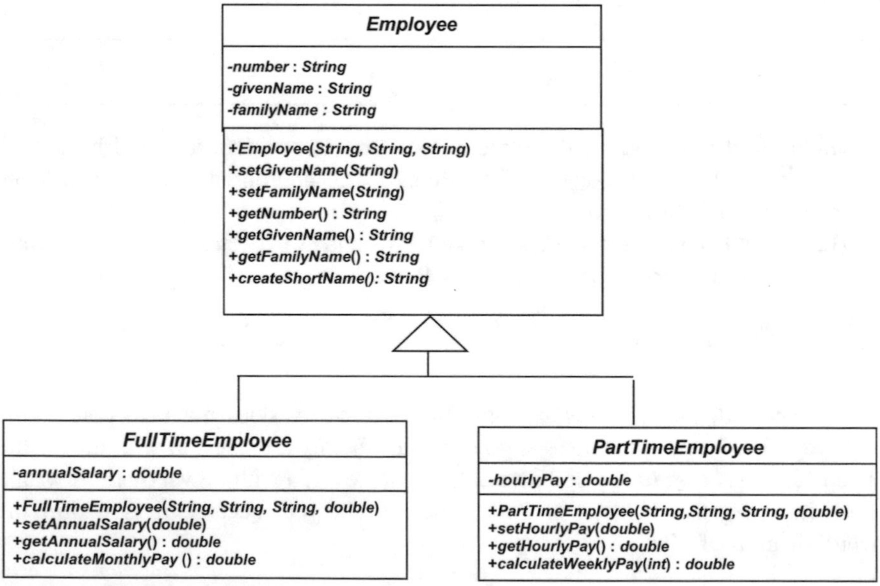

Fig. 18.3 Inheritance relationship showing the superclass *Employee* and the subclasses
FullTimeEmployee and *PartTimeEmployee*

Once a class has been declared in this way it means that you are not allowed to create objects of that class. The Employee class simply acts a basis on which to build other classes. Now, if you tried to create an object of the Employee class you would get a compiler error, for example:

```
/* this will cause a compiler error as Employee is declared to be an abstract class - its constructor
cannot be called to create Employee objects */
Employee emp = new Employee ("A123", "Sandy", "Shaw");
```

As we said before, an inheritance relationship is often referred to as an "*is-a-kind-of*" relationship. A full-time employee is a *kind of* employee, as is a part-time employee. Therefore, in Java, an object that is of type PartTimeEmployee is also considered to be of type Employee. So, an object in Java is the type of its class *and also of any of the superclasses in the hierarchy.*

Let's see how this relationship works in a Java program. Imagine a method which is set up to receive an Employee object. We know we cannot create Employee objects, as Employee has been declared to be an abstract class, but we can create PartTimeEmployee and FullTimeEmployee objects. If we call that method and send in a FullTimeEmployee object or a PartTimeEmployee object, either is absolutely fine—because both are *kinds of* Employee. We demonstrate this in the program that follows:

EmployeeTester.java

```java
public class EmployeeTester
{
    public static void main(String[] args)
    {
        FullTimeEmployee fte = new FullTimeEmployee("A123", "Aaron", "Full-Time", 25000);
        PartTimeEmployee pte = new PartTimeEmployee("B456", "Quentin", "Part-Time", 30);
        testMethod(fte); // call testMethod with a full-time employee object
        testMethod(pte); // call testMethod with a part-time employee object
    }

    static void testMethod(Employee employeeIn) // the method expects to receive an Employee object
    {
        System.out.println(employeeIn.createShortName());
    }
}
```

In this program testMethod expects to receive an Employee object. It calls the createShortName method of Employee in order to display the employee's abbreviated name.

In the main method, we create two objects, one FullTimeEmployee and one PartTimeEmployee:

```
FullTimeEmployee fte = new FullTimeEmployee("A123", "Aaron", "Full-Time", 25000);
PartTimeEmployee pte = new PartTimeEmployee("B456", "Quentin", "Part-Time", 30);
```

We then call testMethod twice—first with FullTimeEmployee object and then with the PartTimeEmployee object:

```
testMethod(fte); // call testMethod with a full-time employee object
testMethod(pte); // call testMethod with a part-time employee object
```

The method accepts either object and calls the `createShortName` method of the `Employee` class. The output is, as expected:

```
A.Full-Time
Q.Part-Time
```

Note that since we have declared the parameter to be of the type `Employee`, we are only able to call methods that belong to the `Employee` class and are unable to call methods that are specific to either `PartTimeEmployee` or `Full-TimeEmployee`. This line, for example, would cause an error:

```
System.out.println(employeeIn.getHourlyPay());
```

In this section you have already seen the code for `Employee` and `PartTimeEmployee`. We will leave developing the code for `FullTimeEmployee` to you as an end of chapter exercise.

18.6   Abstract Methods

In the last program we conveniently gave our objects the family names "Full Time" and "Part Time" so that we could easily identify them in our output. In fact, it wouldn't be a bad idea—particularly for testing purposes—if every `Employee`-type object actually had a method that returned a string telling us the kind of object we were dealing with. Adding such a method—we could call it `getStatus`—would be simple. For the `FullTimeEmployee` the method would look like this:

```
@Override
public String getStatus()
{
    return "Full-Time";
}
```

Notice that we have included the `@Override` annotation, even though it is not compulsory to do so.

For the `PartTimeEmployee`, `getStatus` would look like this:

```
@Override
public String getStatus()
{
    return "Part-Time";
}
```

It would be very useful if we could say to anyone using any of the `Employee` types that we *guarantee* that this class will have a `getStatus` method. That way, a developer could, for example, write a method that accepts an `Employee` object and call that object's `getStatus` method, even without knowing anything else about the class.

As you have probably guessed, we *can* guarantee it! What we have to do is to write an **abstract** method in the superclass—in this case `Employee`. Declaring a method as **abstract** means that any subclass is *forced* to override it—otherwise there would be a compiler error. So, in this case we just have to add the following line into the `Employee` class:

```
public abstract String getStatus();
```

You can see that to declare an **abstract** method, we use the Java keyword **abstract**, and we define the header, but no body—the actual implementation is left to the individual subclasses. Of course, **abstract** methods can only be declared in **abstract** classes—it wouldn't make much sense to try to declare an object if one or more of its methods were undefined. Now, having defined the **abstract** `getStatus` method in the `Employee` class, if we tried to compile the `FullTimeEmployee` or the `PartTimeEmployee` class (or any other class that extends `Employee`) without including a `getStatus` method we would be unsuccessful.

Once we have added the different `getStatus` methods into the `Employee` classes, we could rewrite our `EmployeeTester` program from the previous sections using the `getStatus` method in `testMethod`. We have done this with `EmployerTester2` below:

EmployeeTester2.java

```
public class EmployeeTester2
{
    public static void main(String[] args)
    {
        FullTimeEmployee fte = new FullTimeEmployee("A123", "Aaron",  "Full-Time", 25000);
        PartTimeEmployee pte = new PartTimeEmployee("B456", "Quentin", "Part-Time", 30);
        testMethod(fte); // call testMethod with a full-time employee object
        testMethod(pte); // call testMethod with a part-time employee object
    }

    static void testMethod(Employee employeeIn) // the method expects to receive an Employee object
    {
        System.out.println(employeeIn.getStatus());
    }
}
```

In the above program it was clear at the time the program was compiled which version of `getStatus` was being referred to. The first time that the `tester` method is called, a `FullTimeEmployee` object is sent in, so the `getStatus` method of `FullTimeEmployee` is called; the second time that the `tester` method is called, a `PartTimeEmployee` object is sent in, so the

getStatus method of PartTimeEmployee is called. But now have a look at
the next program (where, incidentally, we have made use of our EasyScanner
class for input).

```
EmployeeTester3.java

public class EmployeeTester3
{
    public static void main(String[] args)
    {
        Employee emp; // a reference to an Employee
        char choice;
        String numberEntered, givenNameEntered, familyNameEntered;
        double salaryEntered, payEntered;
        System.out.print("Choose (F)ull-Time or (P)art-Time Employee: ");
        choice = EasyScanner.nextChar();

        System.out.print("Enter employee number: ");
        numberEntered = EasyScanner.nextString();

        System.out.print("Enter employee given name: ");
        givenNameEntered = EasyScanner.nextString();

        System.out.print("Enter employee family name: ");
        familyNameEntered = EasyScanner.nextString();

        if(choice == 'F' || choice == 'f')
        {
            System.out.print("Enter annual salary: ");
            salaryEntered = EasyScanner.nextDouble();

            // create a FullTimeEmployee object
            emp = new FullTimeEmployee
                        (numberEntered, givenNameEntered, familyNameEntered, salaryEntered);
        }
        else
        {
            System.out.print("Enter hourly pay: ");
            payEntered = EasyScanner.nextDouble();

            // create a PartTimeEmployee object
            emp = new PartTimeEmployee
                        (numberEntered, givenNameEntered, familyNameEntered,  payEntered);
        }
        testMethod(emp); // call tester with the object created
    }

    static void testMethod(Employee employeeIn)
    {
        System.out.println(employeeIn.getStatus());
    }
}
```

In this program, we call testMethod only once and allow the user of the
program to decide whether a FullTimeEmployee object is sent in as a
parameter or a PartTimeEmployee object. You can see that at the beginning of
the program we have declared a reference to an Employee:

```
Employee emp;
```

Although Employee is an **abstract** class, it is perfectly possible to declare a
reference to this class—what we would not be allowed to do, of course, is to create
an Employee *object*. However, as you will see in a moment, we can point this
reference to an object of any subclass of Employee, since such objects, like
FullTimeEmployee and PartTimeEmployee, are kinds of Employee.

You can see that we request the employee number and names from the user and then ask if the employee is full time or part time. In the former case we get the annual salary and then create a `FullTimeEmployee` object which we assign to the `Employee` reference, `emp`.

```
if(choice == 'F' || choice == 'f')
{
        System.out.print("Enter annual salary: ");
        salaryEntered = input.nextDouble();

        // create a FullTimeEmployee object
        emp = new FullTimeEmployee
                        (numberEntered, givenNameEntered, familyNameEntered, salaryEntered);
}
```

In the latter case we request the hourly pay and then assign `emp` to a new `PartTimeEmployee` object:

```
else
{
        System.out.print("Enter hourly pay: ");
        payEntered = input.nextDouble();

        // create a PartTimeEmployee object
        emp = new PartTimeEmployee
                        (numberEntered, givenNameEntered, familyNameEntered,  payEntered);
}
```

Finally, we call the `testMethod` with `emp`:

```
testMethod(emp);
```

The `getStatus` method of the appropriate `Employee` object will then be called.

Here are two sample runs from this program:

```
Choose (F)ull-Time or (P)art-Time Employee: F
Enter employee number: 123
Enter employee given name: Sandy
Enter employee family name: Shaw
Enter annual salary: 23000
Full-Time

Choose (F)ull-Time or (P)art-Time Employee: P
Enter employee number: 876
Enter employee given name: Walter
Enter employee family name: Wall-Carpeting
Enter hourly pay: 25
Part-Time
```

As you can see, we do not know *until the program is run* whether the `getStatus` method is going to be called with a `FullTimeEmployee` object or a `PartTimeEmployee` object—and yet when the `getStatus` method is called, the correct version is executed.

The technique which makes it possible for this decision to be made at run-time is quite a complex one and differs slightly from one programming language to another.

18.7 The Final Modifier

You have already seen the use of the keyword **final** in Chap. 13, where it was used to modify a variable and turn it into a constant. It can also be used to modify a class and a method. In the case of a class it is placed before the class declaration, like this:

```
public final class SomeClass
{
    // code goes here
}
```

This means that the class cannot be subclassed. In the case of a method it is used like this:

```
public final void someMethod()
{
    // code goes here
}
```

This means that the method cannot be overridden.

18.8 The *Object* Class

One of the very useful things about inheritance is the *is-a-kind-of* relationship that we mentioned earlier. For example, when the PartTimeEmployee class extended the Employee class, it became a kind of Employee. We have seen earlier in this chapter that, in Java, if a method of some class expects to receive as a parameter an object of another class (say, for example, Vehicle), then it is quite happy to receive instead an object of a *subclass* of Vehicle—this is because that object will be *a kind of* Vehicle.

In Java, every single class that is created is in fact derived from what we might call a special "super superclass". This super superclass is called Object. So, every object in Java is in fact *a kind of* Object. Any code written to accept objects of type Object can be used with objects of any type.

The Object class has few methods that are inherited into all classes, but most of these need to be overridden to provide useful results. One example of this is the method called toString. You have seen already from Chap. 14 that the Arrays class overrides this method to allow for arrays to be converted to a String suitable for printing on the screen.

The `System.out.print` and `println` methods automatically call an object's `toString` method if they are called simply with *the name of the object itself* as an argument. If we override this method in our classes we can allow for a meaningful string representation to be printed of our entire object. For example, we could add the following `toString` method into to our `BankAccount` class:

```
@Override
public String toString()
{
    return "Name: " + this.accountName + '\n' + "Account number: " + this.accountNumber + '\n'
                                               + "Balance: " + this.balance;
}
```

Notice the use of the newline escape sequence ('\n') that is available in Java as well as Python. We can test this out with a little program—and notice how the `println` method is called simply with the name of the object:

ToStringDemo.java

```
public class ToStringDemo
{
    public static void main(String[] args)
    {
        BankAccount acc = new BankAccount("12345678", "Patel");
        System.out.println(acc);
    }
}
```

The output from this program would be:

```
Name: Patel
Account number: 12345678
Balance: 0.0
```

And if you are wondering what happens if we haven't overridden the `toString` method, the answer is that the output is simply the name of the class and its location in memory (as we saw when we tried to print an array in Chap. 14). So, the above program would have given us something like:

```
BankAccount@15db9742
```

18.9   Self-test Questions

1. In self-test question 1 of Chap. 9 we introduced a UML diagram for an inheritance relationship between two classes—`Vehicle` and `UsedVehicle`. Below is that diagram adapted so that it targets Java.

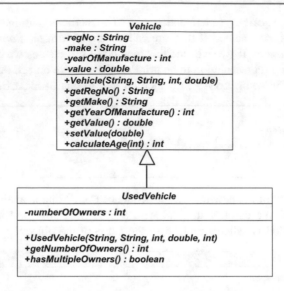

(a) Write the top line of the UsedVehicle class.

(b) Write the code for the UsedVehicle constructor.

2. (a) Consider the following classes and arrange them into an inheritance hierarchy using UML notation:

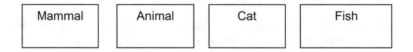

(b) Write the top line of the class declaration for each of these classes when implementing them in Java.

(c) Describe the role of the Object class in Java and add that class to the UML hierarchy you produced in part (a) of this question.

3 Consider a Sensor class developed for an application to record the reading of a pressure sensor. Now assume a SafeSensor class is developed that ensures that the pressure is never set above some maximum value. A SafeSensor *is a kind of* Sensor. The UML design is given below:

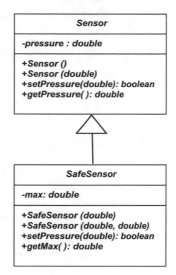

The Sensor class has two constructors. One with no parameters that sets the initial pressure to zero. Another that allows the initial pressure to be set by a parameter. The pressure should not be set to a value less than zero. Therefore, if the input parameter to the setPressure method is a negative number, the pressure should not be changed and a value of **false** should be returned. If the pressure is set successfully, a value of **true** should be returned.

The SafeSensor class also has two constructors. The first sets the maximum safe value to the given parameter and the actual value of the sensor reading to 10. The second constructor accepts two parameters, the first is used to set the maximum safe value, and the second is used to set the initial value for the reading of the sensor. The setPressure method is redefined so that only safe values (values no greater than the safe maximum value and no less than zero) are set.

(a) In the example above, distinguish between *method overriding* and *method overloading*.

(b) Below is one attempt at the Java code for the first SafeSensor constructor. Identify why it will not compile.

```
// THIS WILL NOT COMPILE!!
public SafeSensor(double maxIn)
{
        this.max = maxIn;
        this.pressure = 10;
}
```

Here is another attempt at the Java code for the first `SafeSensor` constructor. Identify why it will not compile.

```
// THIS WILL NOT COMPILE!!
public SafeSensor(double maxIn)
{
        this.max = maxIn;
        super();
}
```

Write the correct code for the first `SafeSensor` constructor.

4   By referring to the `BankAccount` class of Sect. 18.4, distinguish between **private**, **public** and **protected** access.
5   (a) Distinguish between an **abstract class** and an **abstract method**
    (b) Consider the following definition of a class called `Robot`:

```
public abstract class Robot
{
    private String id;
    private int securityLevel;

    public Robot(String IdIn, int levelIn)
    {
        this.id = IdIn;
        this.securityLevel = levelIn;
    }

    public String getId()
    {
        return this.id;
    }

    public int getSecurityLevel()
    {
        return this.securityLevel;
    }

    public abstract void calculateWarningLevel();
}
```

    (i) The following line of code is used in a program that has access to the `Robot` class:

```
Robot aRobot = new Robot("R2D2", 1000);
```

    Explain why this line of code would cause a compiler error.

(ii) Consider the following class:

```
public class CleaningRobot extends Robot
{
    public String typeOfCleaningFluid;

    public CleaningRobot(String IdIn, int levelIn, String fluidIn)
    {
        super(IdIn, levelIn);
        this.typeOfCleaningFluid = fluidIn;
    }

    public String getTypeOfCleaningFluid()
    {
        return this.typeOfCleaningFluid;
    }
}
```

Explain why any attempt to compile this class would result in a compiler error.

6   What is the effect of the **final** modifier, when applied to both classes and methods?

7   Look back at the `EmployeeTester` class from Sect. 18.5. What do you think would happen if you replaced this line of `testMethod`:

```
System.out.println(employeeIn.createShortName());
```

with the following line?

```
System.out.println(employeeIn.getAnnualSalary());
```

Give a reason for your answer.

18.10   Programming Exercises

1. (a) Implement the `Vehicle` and the `UsedVehicle` classes of self-test question 1.

You should note that:

- the `calculateAge` method of `Vehicle` accepts an integer representing the current year and returns the age of the vehicle as calculated by subtracting the year of manufacture from the current year;
- the `hasMultipleOwners` method of `UsedVehicle` should return **true** if the `numberOfOwners` attribute has a value greater than 1, or **false** otherwise.

(b) Write a tester class that tests all the methods of the `SecondHandVehicle` class.

2. (a) Implement the `Sensor` and `SafeSensor` classes of self-test question 3.

   (b) Write a tester class to test the methods of the `SafeSensor` class.

3. (a) By looking at the UML design in Fig. 18.3, implement the `FullTimeEmployee` class in Java—you will need to download the `Employee` class from the website (see preface).

   (b) Write a suitable tester program for this `FullTimeEmployee` class.

   (c) Add a suitable `toString` method to this class.

   (d) Modify the tester in part (b) of this question to test the `toString` method.

Java: Interfaces and Lambda Expressions

19

Outcomes

By the end of this chapter you should be able to:

- *explain what is meant by the term **interface** in Java*;
- *create and use your own interfaces*;
- *explain the purpose and the importance of **lambda expressions** in Java*;
- *describe the syntax of lambda expressions and utilize these expressions in a variety of contexts*;
- *create and use **generic** classes and interfaces*;
- *describe how a programming language can support **polymorphic types***;
- *summarize the ways in which polymorphism can be achieved in Java*.

19.1 Introduction

In Chaps. 9 and 10 you learnt how to create and use classes and objects in Python. In Chaps. 17 and 18 you saw how to do the same thing in Java, and you will have noticed quite a contrast in the way the two languages approach object-oriented programming, with Java being what could be described as more of a "classical" object-oriented language. As such, Java has many high-level features which we will explore some of these in this chapter.

Up until now, the Java applications we created have been fairly simple, consisting for the most part of only one or two classes. In reality, applications that are developed for commercial and industrial use comprise a large number of classes

Supplementary Information The online version contains supplementary material available at https://doi.org/10.1007/978-3-031-01326-3_19.

and are developed not by one person, but by a team. Members of the team will develop different modules which can later be integrated to form a single application. When groups of programmers work together in this way, they often have to agree upon how they will develop their own individual classes in order for them to be successfully integrated later. In this chapter we will see how these agreements can be formalized in Java programs by making use of a special kind of class called an **interface**. We will then move on to the subject of lambda expressions, which were introduced with the release of Java 8. This was a very significant addition to the language—and in this chapter you will see just how useful they can be.

19.2   An Example

It is a very common occurrence that the attributes of a class should be allowed to take only a particular set of values. Think, for example, of the BankAccount class that we developed in the last semester. It is likely that the account number should be restricted to numbers that contain, say, precisely eight digits. Similarly, a Customer class might require that the customer number comprises a letter followed by four digits. In some cases there are constraints that exist not because we choose to impose them, but because they occur "naturally"—for example, in the Rectangle class that we first introduced in Chap. 8, it would make no sense if an object of this class was to have a length or height of zero or less.

In such cases, every effort must be made when developing the class to prevent invalid values being assigned to the attributes. Constructors and other methods should be designed so that they flag up errors if such an attempt is made—and one of the advantages of object-oriented programming languages like Java is precisely that they allow us to restrict access to the attributes in this way.

The above remarks notwithstanding, it is the case that in industrial-sized projects, classes will be very complex and will contain a great many methods. It is therefore possible that a developer will overlook a constraint at some point and allow objects to be created that break the rules. It might therefore be useful if, for testing purposes, every object could contain a method, which we could call check, that could be used to check the integrity of the object.

In a particular project, people could be writing test routines independently of the people developing the modules, and these routines will be calling the check method. We need, therefore, to be able to *guarantee* that every object contains such a check method.

You learnt in Chap. 18 that the way to guarantee that a class has a particular method is for that class to inherit from a class containing an **abstract** method—when a class contains an **abstract** method, then any subclass of that class is *forced* to override that method—if it does not do so, a compiler error occurs.

Fig. 19.1 Multiple inheritance—not allowed in Java

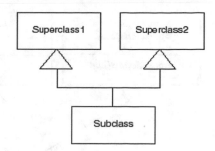

In our example, we need to ensure that our classes all have a check method which tests an object's integrity, so one way to do this would be to write a class as follows:

Checkable

```
public abstract class Checkable
{
        public abstract boolean check();
}
```

Now all our classes could extend Checkable and would compile successfully only if they each had their own check method.

While this would work, it does present us with a bit of a problem. What would happen, for example, if our Rectangle class was going to be part of a graphical application and needed to extend another class such as Application? This would be problematic, because, in Java—unlike in Python—a class is not allowed to inherit from more than one superclass. Inheriting from more than one class is known as **multiple inheritance** and is illustrated in Fig. 19.1.

One reason that multiple inheritance is disallowed in some languages (like Java) is that it can easily lead to ambiguity, and hence to programming errors. Imagine for example that the two superclasses shown in Fig. 19.1 both contained a method of the same name—which version of the method would be inherited by the subclass? Having said that, we should note that Python does, in fact, allow multiple inheritance.

Luckily, there is a way around this, because Java allows a kind of *lightweight inheritance*, made possible by a construct known as an **interface**.

19.3 Interfaces

An interface is a special class that contains **abstract** methods. When we want a class to inherit the methods of an interface, we use the word **implements**, rather than **extends**. Just as with inheritance, once a class implements an interface it has the same type as that interface, as well as being of the type of its own class. So, for example, if a class implements EventHandler, then any object of that class is a *kind of* EventHandler—in other words it is of type EventHandler, as well as being of the type of its own class.

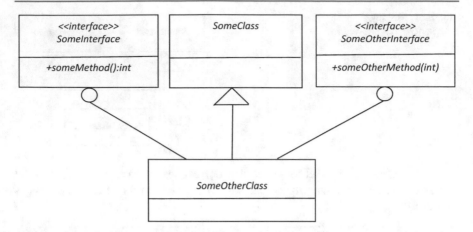

Fig. 19.2 A Class can inherit from only one superclass, but can implement many interfaces

The Java libraries, particularly those associated with graphical applications, contain a great many interfaces. And it is perfectly possible for us to write our own interfaces as we will do in a moment when we turn our Checkable class into an interface.

Figure 19.2 shows the UML notation for the implementation of interfaces—you can see that interfaces are marked with the <<interface>> tag, and that a circle is used to indicate a class implementing an interface.

As can be seen in Fig. 19.2, while it is possible to *inherit* from only one class, it is perfectly possible to implement any number of interfaces. In this case Some-OtherClass **extends** SomeClass and **implements** SomeInterface and SomeOtherInterface—because the methods are **abstract** they are not actually coded in the interface and this means that the problems with multiple inheritance that we described earlier do not arise.

Prior to the release of Java 8 an interface could contain *only* **abstract** methods—but now an interface can also contains **static** methods and **default** methods. Regular classes have always been permitted to have **static** methods (as you have seen before in Chap. 17)—now they can be included in interfaces too. A **default** method is a new concept specifically to be used in interfaces, if required. A **default** method is a regular method with a complete implementation and so is automatically inherited by all classes that implement the interface (though the implementing class may override this implementation if it chooses). Adding **default** methods into interfaces means that additions can be made to an interface without every class that implements the previous version of that interface having to change (as would be the case if we added new **abstract** methods to an inter-face[1]). We will meet interfaces with **static** and **default** methods in later

---

[1] This does give rise to issues related to multiple inheritance, but developers of the Java language thought this was a reasonable compromise for the reason given here.

chapters, but in this chapter we will focus on interfaces with **abstract** methods only.

As with inheritance, a class is *obliged* to override all the abstract methods of the interfaces that it implements. By implementing an interface we are *guaranteeing* that the subclass will have certain methods.

So, in cases where we need a class such as Checkable in which all the methods are **abstract** (apart from any **static** methods) we don't create a class—instead we create an interface.

Let's turn our Checkable class into an interface. The code looks like this:

```
Checkable.java

public interface Checkable
{
        public boolean check();
}
```

Notice the word **interface** instead of **class**—and notice also that we don't have to declare our method as **abstract**, because by definition all non-**static** and non-**default** methods of an interface are **abstract**.

Let's make the Rectangle class from Chap. 17 checkable by defining a subclass that implements the Checkable interface. We will need to override the constructor and of course to code the check method. The class will now look like this:

```
CheckableRectangle.java

public class CheckableRectangle extends Rectangle implements Checkable
{
    //override the constructor
    public CheckableRectangle(double lengthIn, double heightIn)
    {
        super(lengthIn, heightIn);
    }

    @Override
    public boolean check() // the check method of Checkable must be overridden
    {
        // the length and height must both be greater than zero
        return getLength() > 0 && getHeight() > 0;
    }
}
```

You can see that the class now implements our Checkable interface:

```
public class CheckableRectangle extends Rectangle implements Checkable
```

The check method, which the class is forced to override (note the use of the @Override annotation), returns a value of **true** if the attributes are both greater than zero and **false** otherwise:

```
@Override
public boolean check() // the check method of Checkable must be overridden
{
    // the length and height must both be greater than zero
    return getLength() > 0 && getHeight() > 0;
}
```

Other classes can implement the Checkable interface in a similar way. Do you remember the BankAccount class that we developed in Chap. 18? One of the attributes was the account number. In reality, an account number would need to obey certain rules—the most common one in the UK is that the account number should contain digits only and that it should contain exactly eight digits. Let's create a CheckableBankAccount class which checks to see if this rule is upheld.

CheckableBankAccount.java

```
public class CheckableBankAccount extends BankAccount implements Checkable
{
    // the constructor
    public CheckableBankAccount(String numberIn, String nameIn)
    {
        super(numberIn, nameIn);
    }

    @Override
    public boolean check()
    {
        // check that the account number is exactly 8 characters long
        if(getAccountNumber().length() != 8)
        {
            return false;
        }

        // check that the account number contains only digits
        for(int i=0; i <= 7; i++)
        {
            if(!Character.isDigit(getAccountNumber().charAt(i)))
            {
                return false;
            }
        }
        return true;
    }
}
```

You can see here how, in the check method, we check firstly that the string contains exactly eight characters, and then check if every character is a digit by making use of the isDigit method of the Character class (which you will hear more about in Sect. 19.5).

In the Checker class below we create five objects—two Check-ableRectangle objects and three CheckableBankAccount objects. In each case the first object is valid, but the others break the rules that we have set for these two classes.

You should notice that in each case the object—whether it is a rectangle or a bank account—is of type Checkable (as well as being a type of the particular class). This is because both CheckableRectangle and Check-ableBankAccount implement the Checkable interface.

```
Checker.java
```

```
public class Checker
{
  public static void main(String[] args)
  {
    // create two Rectangles
    CheckableRectangle Rectangle1 = new CheckableRectangle(10, 8); // valid
    CheckableRectangle Rectangle2 = new CheckableRectangle(0, 8); // invalid: first argument is zero

    // create three bank accounts

    CheckableBankAccount account1 = new CheckableBankAccount("12345678", "Smith"); // valid
    CheckableBankAccount account2 = new CheckableBankAccount("S1234567", "Patel"); // invalid: account number
                                                                                  // must contain digits only
    CheckableBankAccount account3 = new CheckableBankAccount("1234567", "Adewale"); // invalid: account number
                                                                                    // must be 8 characters long

    // send objects to the checkValidity method
    System.out.println("Rectangle1 is " + checkValidity(Rectangle1));
    System.out.println("Rectangle2 is " + checkValidity(Rectangle2));

    System.out.println("account1 is " + checkValidity(account1));
    System.out.println("account2 is " + checkValidity(account2));
    System.out.println("account3 is " + checkValidity(account3));
  }

  private static String checkValidity(Checkable objectIn) // receives any Checkable object
  {
    if(objectIn.check())  // call the check method
    {
      return "valid";
    }
    else
    {
      return "invalid";
    }
  }
}
```

As you can see, we send the five objects in turn into a method called
checkValidity which calls the object's check method and returns a String
—either "valid" or "invalid"; we append this to an initial string, and the whole
message is displayed.

The checkValidity method accepts a parameter of type Checkable—and
of course both the CheckableRectangle objects and the three CheckableBankAccount objects are of type Checkable because they both implement the Checkable interface.

As expected, the output from the program is as follows:

```
Rectangle1 is valid
Rectangle2 is invalid
account1 is valid
account2 is invalid
account3 is invalid
```

Implementing an interface is rather like making a contract with the user of a
class—it *guarantees* that the class will have a particular method or methods. In the
above case, a developer will know that any object that implements Checkable
will have a check method. This enables the developer to write methods such as
checkValidity that expect to receive an object of type Checkable, in the
certain knowledge that the object—whether it is a CheckableRectangle,
CheckableBankAccount, or any other class that implements this interface—
will have a method called check.

19.4   Lambda Expressions

Consider the rectangle example we have just talked about. The criteria for validity were that the length and height were both greater than zero. But imagine that we were writing an application in which we needed the sides of the rectangle to be no greater than 10. You might think that we would have to write a new class with a different check method. Indeed, prior to Java 8, this is what we would have had to do. We were able to make it a bit less tiresome by using mechanisms such as *inner classes* and *anonymous* classes, but nonetheless this was quite cumbersome, and not very flexible.

With Java 8 came the introduction of an important and extremely powerful innovation: **Lambda expressions**. Lambda expressions allow us to simply send in a block of code to a method as an argument, just as we would with a value of a primitive type like **int**, or an object of a class like a String or BankAccount. This means that a method like checkValidity that we saw in the last section can be called as many times as we want, each time with a new criterion to check.

In the program below, LambdaDemo, we call checkValidity twice, each time with different code for the check method of checkable. Have a quick look at this program before we take you through it. There is quite a lot here that is new—you can spot the lambda expressions by the presence of a new and unfamiliar symbol, the arrow (->). More about this when you have looked at the code.

LambdaDemo.java

```java
public class LambdaDemo
{
  public static void main(String[] args)
  {
     // create a test Rectangle
     String result;
     Rectangle testRectangle = new Rectangle (8,12);

     // this uses a lambda expression to check that the sides are greater than zero
     result = checkValidity(
                          () -> testRectangle.getLength() > 0 && testRectangle.getHeight() > 0
                          );
     System.out.println("Rectangle is " + result);

     // this uses a lambda expression to check that both sides are no greater than 10
     result = checkValidity(
                          () -> testRectangle.getLength() <= 10 && testRectangle.getHeight() <= 10
                          );
     System.out.println("Rectangle is " + result);
  }

  private static String checkValidity(Checkable objectIn)
  {
     if(objectIn.check())
     {
        return "valid";
     }
     else
     {
        return "invalid";
     }
  }
}
```

Let's begin by looking at the `checkValidity` method:

```
private static String checkValidity(Checkable objectIn)
{
    if(objectIn.check())
    {
        return "valid";
    }
    else
    {
        return "invalid";
    }
}
```

As you can see, this method returns a `String`, and, importantly, receives an object of type `Checkable`. Our `Checkable` interface is an example of a **functional interface**—that is to say, an interface that contains *only one abstract method*. Now, when a method receives an object that implements a functional interface, we are able to send it some code by means of a lambda expression—and that code is the code for the abstract method—in this case the `check` method.

As you see, the method then goes on to call the `check` method of the object that was sent in. The `check` method, as you will remember, returns a **boolean** value, and the `checkValidity` method returns "valid" if this value is **true** or "invalid" if it was **false**.

Whether the check method returns **true** or **false** will depend on the code that is sent in via the lambda expression. In the first instance we are going to get the `CheckValidity` method to determine whether or not both the length and height of the rectangle are greater than zero. So here is the first call to the `checkValidity` method, with the lambda expression highlighted:

```
result = checkValidity(
                () -> testRectangle.getLength() > 0 && testRectangle.getHeight() > 0
            );
```

As we mentioned earlier, Lambda expressions involve the use of a new symbol, the arrow symbol (`->`). There are two parts to a lambda expression, one on either side of the `->` symbol. On the left we give names to the parameters that the method expects to receive. In this case there are no parameters, so we have a pair of empty brackets. The code goes on the right of the symbol. Soon we will go into detail about the precise form in which the code is written—here, for example, there is no semicolon at the end of the statement, and the word **return** has not been included. This will be explained in the next section:

In the second call to `checkValidity`, we are going to assume that we require for some reason that the length and height of the rectangle are no greater than 10:

```
result = checkValidity(
                () -> testRectangle.getLength() <= 10 && testRectangle.getHeight() <= 10
            );
```

Since we created our rectangle with a length of 8 and a height of 12, we should expect, when we display the results, that the first call will tell us that the rectangle is valid, but that the second call will tell us it was invalid. This is exactly what we find when we run the program:

```
Rectangle is valid
Rectangle is invalid
```

To sum up: lambda expressions can be used to send a block of code to any method that expects to receive a **functional interface** as a parameter. A functional interface is an interface that contains *only one* **abstract** method. The block of code supplied in the lambda expression is the code for the **abstract** method.

Languages that are based on blocks of code being sent to methods are called *functional languages*—examples being Lisp, Clojure and Scala. And while it is true to say that the introduction of lambda expressions hasn't put Java in the same league as these, it has certainly given Java some of the same capabilities.

19.4.1   The Syntax of Lambda Expressions

You have already seen how lambda expressions are formed, with the instructions on the right side of the arrow, and the parameters on the left.

The code on the right can be a single statement (without the semicolon), or a number of statements, enclosed in braces with a semicolon at the end of each statement.

An example of the first might look like this:

```
() -> System.out.println(''Hello'')
```

However an example of the second could look like this:

```
() -> {
System.out.println(''Hello'');
System.out.println(''Goodbye'');
}
```

So, what about the left-hand side of the arrow? You have seen, as in the above two examples, that if the code for the particular method of the interface does not require parameters, then we simply place empty brackets in front of the arrow.

When a single parameter is required, we give that parameter a name and place it in front of the arrow. So, for example we might have:

```
str -> System.out.println(''Hello '' + str)
```

We don't have to specify a type for `str`, because the compiler will infer this from the header of the **abstract** method. This is an example of **type inference.**

If there is more than one parameter, then we would list them in brackets. For example:

```
(x, y) -> {
int z;
z = x + y;
System.out.println(''Sum = '' + z);
}
```

On occasion, you might find that for some reason the compiler is unable to infer the types of the variables, and you get a compiler error. To fix this you can simply place the type name in front of the variable name:

```
(int x, int y) -> {
int z;
z = x + y;
System.out.println(''Sum = '' + z);
}
```

There is one thing to watch out for when writing lambda expressions. If your code consists of a single **return** statement, you will get a compiler error if you use the single line format without the semicolon. For example, the following would give you an error:

```
x -> return 2 * x
```

There are two ways you can avoid this error. Firstly you should note that if there is a single expression on the right of the arrow, Java will evaluate this and return the value. So the above expression could be written as follows:

```
x -> 2 * x
```

We saw an example of this in the previous section.

Alternatively you could enclose the statement in braces and write:

```
x -> {
        return 2 * x;
    }
```

19.4.2 Variable Scope

Lambda expressions can access the attributes of the enclosing class. They also have access to any parameters that are passed to a method that encloses the expression and to the local variables of that method. However in the case of parameters and local variables, the lambda expression cannot change the value of these—in other words they must be **final**, or effectively **final**.[2]

19.4.3 Example Programs

In this section we will develop a few simple programs to show the various ways that lambda expressions can be written and utilized.

In each of the programs that follow we will refer to a functional interface called TestInterface that will contain one **abstract** method called test. We will redefine the header for this method in each of the programs.

For the first of our programs the test method will look like this:

```
public void test();
```

The following program uses this version:

LambdaSyntaxDemo1.java

```
public class LambdaSyntaxDemo1
{
    public static void main(String[] args)
    {
        testMethod(() -> System.out.println("Hello "));
    }

    static void testMethod(TestInterface testObjectIn)
    {
        testObjectIn.test();
    }
}
```

We call a method called testMethod, which expects to receive an object of type TestInterface. We are able simply to send the code for the test method as a lambda expression, which, since test does not require any parameters, has open brackets in front of the arrow. There is only one line of code, so we can manage without any braces.

The output from this program is simply:

```
Hello
```

The next program shows the change in syntax when more than one line of code is required.

---

[2] A variable or parameter is said to be effectively **final** if its value is not changed after its initialization.

LambdaSyntaxDemo2.java

```
public class LambdaSyntaxDemo2
{
    public static void main(String[] args)
    {
        testMethod( () -> {
                            System.out.print("Hello ");
                            System.out.println("world");
                    }
                );
    }

    static void testMethod(TestInterface testObjectIn)
    {
        testObjectIn.test();
    }
}
```

The output from this program is of course:

```
Hello world
```

For our next program we will change the test method of TestInterface to the following:

```
public String test(String stringIn);
```

The method now receives a parameter of type String. It also returns a String, and we have used this in the version of testMethod in our next program shown below.

LambdaSyntaxDemo3.java

```
public class LambdaSyntaxDemo3
{
    public static void main(String[] args)
    {
        testMethod( str -> {
                            str = "Hello " + str;
                            return str;
                    }
                );
    }

    static void testMethod(TestInterface testObjectIn)
    {
        String output = testObjectIn.test("world"); // test now requires a String argument
        System.out.println(output);
    }
}
```

As you can see, because test now requires an input, we have named the argument to this method on the left-hand side of the arrow. Our lambda expression looks like this:

```
str -> {
str = ''Hello '' + str;
return str;
}
```

testMethod now calls test with the argument "world". test obeys the instructions sent to testMethod and produces the following output:

```
Hello world
```

For our final example we will change the header for the test method to the following:

```
public void test(int firstNumber, int secondNumber);
```

Now test accepts two **int**s. We have used this version in our next version:

LambdaSyntaxDemo4.java

```
public class LambdaSyntaxDemo4
{
    public static void main(String[] args)
    {
        testMethod( (x, y) -> System.out.println("The sum is " + (x + y)) );
    }

    static void testMethod(TestInterface testObjectIn)
    {
        testObjectIn.test(10, 5);
    }
}
```

Because test now requires two arguments, we place these in brackets in front of the arrow:

```
(x, y) -> System.out.println(''The sum is '' + (x + y))
```

As we mentioned before, we don't have to specify the types for x and y, but we could do so as follows, without changing the way the program works:

```
(int x, int y) -> System.out.println(''The sum is '' + (x + y))
```

testMethod calls test with arguments of 10 and 5, so the output is:

```
The sum is 15
```

Before we leave this section, it is worth making one thing absolutely clear. While lambda expressions enable us to effectively send a block of code, what we are actually doing is sending an object which is a type of functional interface, and the code we send is the code for its **abstract** method. In LambdaSyntaxDemo4 above, for example, we could have written the instructions in the main method like this:

```
TestInterface t = (x, y) -> System.out.println("The sum is " + (x + y));
testMethod(t);
```

19.4.4 Method References—The Double Colon Operator

It is sometimes the case that a lambda expression does nothing more than reference a method of an existing class. To illustrate this, consider the following interface:

DoubleColonInterface.java

```
public interface DoubleColonInterface
{
    public void test(String s);
}
```

Now consider the following program that uses this interface:

MethodReference.java

```
public class MethodReference
{
    public static void main(String[] args)
    {
        testMethod(str -> System.out.println(str));
    }

    static void testMethod(DoubleColonInterface testObjectIn)
    {
        testObjectIn.test("Hello world");
    }
}
```

All that the lambda expression does is call the `println` method of `System.out`, with whatever parameter is specified when `test` is called. In cases such as this, a notation exists that can simplify the code. This uses a double colon to reference the method, as shown below:

DoubleColonDemo.java

```
public class DoubleColonDemo
{
    public static void main(String[] args)
    {
        testMethod(System.out::println);
    }

    static void testMethod(DoubleColonInterface testObjectIn)
    {
        testObjectIn.test("Hello world");
    }
}
```

This does exactly the same as the previous lambda expression—it calls the `println` method of `System.out` with the argument supplied to the `test` method.

Let's look at one more example. We will change the interface we are using as follows:

DoubleColonInterface.java

```
public interface DoubleColonInterface
{
    public double test(int i);
}
```

Now look at this program:

DoubleColonDemo2.java

```
public class DoubleColonDemo2
{
    public static void main(String[] args)
    {
        testMethod(Math::sqrt);
    }

    static void testMethod(DoubleColonInterface testObjectIn)
    {
        System.out.println(testObjectIn.test(25));
    }
}
```

Here we are using the `sqrt` (square root) function of Java's `Math` class. The double colon replaces the following lambda expression:

```
testMethod(i -> Math.sqrt(i));
```

In both cases, of course, the program will output `0.5`.

19.5   Wrapper Classes and Autoboxing

Before we move on to the next topic, we need to introduce you to a group of classes known as **wrapper classes**. For every primitive type, Java provides a corresponding class—the name of the class is similar to the basic type, but begins with a capital letter—for example `Integer`, `Character`, `Float`, `Double`. They are called *wrappers* because they "wrap" a *class* around the basic *type*. So an object of the `Integer` class, for example, holds an integer value. In the next section you will see why we need these classes, and in future chapters you will find that these wrapper classes also contain some other very useful methods—in fact we already used one of these in Sect. 19.3, namely the `isDigit` method of `Character`.

We can declare an object of the `Integer` class, for example, like this:

```
Integer testInt = 37;
```

Here we are using a technique known as **autoboxing**. This involves the automatic conversion of a primitive type such as an `int` to an object of the appropriate wrapper class.

Java also allows us to make use of a technique called **unboxing**, which converts from the wrapper class back to the primitive type:

```
int x = testInt;
```

Exactly the same technique would be used to store other primitive types such as `char` and `double`.

19.6 Generics

The topic of generics is a very important one. A **generic** class (or interface) has attributes and methods whose types are not defined within the class, but are left to the programmer to decide upon when an object of the class is declared. Effectively we are sending a type into a class (or interface) and for this reason we often refer to generic classes and interfaces as **parameterized types**.

This is best illustrated by way of an example. Below we have created a very simple generic class—it has only one attribute, together with a `set-` and a `get-` method.

SimpleGenericClass.java

```
public class SimpleGenericClass<T> // the angle brackets indicate that this is a generic class
{
    private T value;

    public void setValue(T valueIn)
    {
        this.value = valueIn;
    }

    public T getValue()
    {
        return this.value;
    }
}
```

The angle brackets after the class name indicate that this is a generic class. The `T` in these brackets indicates that there will be a single type chosen by the user, and we will refer to this type as `T` throughout the definition. You can think of it as a place-marker for whatever type is chosen by the user of this class. You will also see in one of the examples that follow that we can indicate more than one type in the brackets—so we could have, for example:

```
public class AnotherGenericClass<T, U, V>
```

In our `SimpleGenericClass` you can see that the single attribute, `value`, is declared as being of type `T`. Also, as we would expect, the `set-` method has a parameter of type `T` and the `get-` method returns an object of type `T`. You should note that the types have to be objects of a class—primitive types such as **int** or **double** can't be used here, so you would have to use the equivalent wrapper classes such as `Integer` and `Double` explained in the previous section.

A short program that uses this class is presented below:

```
TestGenericClass.java

public class TestGenericClass
{
    public static void main(String[] args)
    {
        SimpleGenericClass<Double> example1 = new SimpleGenericClass<>();
        SimpleGenericClass<String> example2 = new SimpleGenericClass<>();
        SimpleGenericClass<Rectangle> example3 = new SimpleGenericClass<>();

        example1.setValue(10.0);
        example2.setValue("Hello");
        example3.setValue(new Rectangle(5, 3));

        System.out.println(example1.getValue());
        System.out.println(example2.getValue());
        System.out.println(example3.getValue().calculateArea());
    }
}
```

You can see that we have declared three objects of type `Sim-pleGenericClass`, each time choosing a different type for its attribute and methods—in the third case we have used our own `Rectangle` class. Notice also that in the first case we have to use the wrapper class `Double`, rather than the primitive type.

When calling the constructor of the class, we have left the angle brackets empty:

```
SimpleGenericClass<Double> example1 = new SimpleGenericClass<>();
```

The empty brackets (sometimes referred to as the diamond) can be used in cases where it is easy for the compiler to work out what type of arguments are required; here, for example, it is apparent from the type declaration. This is another example of type inference.

We have then gone on to use the `setValue` method to give a value to the attribute for each object we created. Note that in the first case the argument of 10.0 (a **double**) is automatically typecast to `Double`.

In the last three statements we use `getValue` to return the object. In the first two examples we can display the value without having to call a method of the object (`println` is set up to automatically print the value of a `Double` or a `String`). In the final example we display the area of the `Rectangle`, using the `calculateArea` method.

The output from this program is as follows:

```
10.0
Hello
15.0
```

Collection classes and graphics classes make extensive use of generic *interfaces*, rather than classes. We could, for example, define a generic functional interface as follows:

SimpleGenericInterface.java

```
public interface SimpleGenericInterface<T, U, V>
{
    public T doSomething(U firstValue, V secondValue);
}
```

You can see that an object of type `SimpleGenericInterface` would require three types, which are referred to in the definition as T, U and V. The single **abstract** method returns an object of type T and receives objects of type U and V.

Very often, however, we don't need to define our own functional interface, because Java provides us with a number of such interfaces "out of the box". Some of these are listed in Table 19.1. Most often these reside in the `java.util.function` package. Some of these also contain **static** methods, which you can look up on the Oracle™ site.

The program that follows demonstrates how we can use one of the above interfaces—`Function`.

Table 19.1 Some common functional interfaces

Functional interface	Abstract method name	Parameter types	Return type
Supplier <T>	get	none	T
Consumer <T>	accept	T	void
BiConsumer <T, U>	accept	T, U	void
Function <T, R>	apply	T	R
BiFunction <T, U, R>	apply	T, U	R
UnaryOperator <T>	apply	T	T
BinaryOperator <T>	apply	T, T	T
Predicate <T>	test	T	boolean
BiPredicate <T, U>	test	T, U	boolean

TestGenericInterface.java

```
import java.util.function.Function;

public class TestGenericInterface
{
    public static void main(String[] args)
    {
        Function<Integer, String> str =  i -> "You entered " + i ;

        System.out.println(str.apply(10));
    }
}
```

The output from this program is:

```
You entered 10
```

Notice that in the program above we do not need to include the word **return** in the lambda expression as the code consists of a single **return** statement.

Before we move on there is one more thing to mention. If one of the types of our generic class or interface refers to the return type of a method, it is possible that we might want that method not to return any value—in other words to be of type **void**. A special class, Void, exists for this purpose. Void is simply a placeholder used to represent the keyword **void**. The method in this case would be defined so that a **null** value is returned. So a generic type such as Task<V> could be instantiated with, for example, Task<Integer >, Task<Double> or Task<Void>.

19.7   Other Interfaces Provided with the Java Libraries

Many important interfaces are provided in the Java libraries in addition to those listed in Table 19.1, and many of these are not functional interfaces, as they contain more than one **abstract** method.

In Chap. 21 you will learn much more about classes such as ArrayList, which are known as **collection classes**. As their name suggests, these are the classes designed to hold collections of objects. Collection classes implement generic interfaces such as the List interface and the Map interface, in order to provide a wealth of classes which allow us to handle different types of collections.

Also of particular interest are the interfaces provided in the JavaFX libraries which you will study in Chap. 23.

19.8 Self-test Questions

1. Consider the UML design below of a class called `MyClass`.

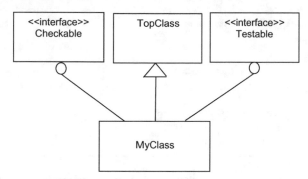

   Write the header of the `MyClass` class.

2. Consider the following interface, called `SomeInterface`:

```
public interface SomeInterface
{
    public double SomeMethod(double x);
}
```

   The following class is developed as shown below:

```
public class SomeClass implements SomeInterface
{
    private double y;

    public double SomeMethod(int x)
    {
        return 2.5 * x;
    }
}
```

   Explain why this class will not compile, and explain how it should be amended in order to rectify the problem.

3. What is meant by a *functional interface*? Explain how lambda expressions are used in conjunction with functional interfaces.

4. A lambda expression is characterized by the arrow symbol ->. What is placed to the left of this symbol, and what is placed to the right?

5. Consider the following interface:

Testable.java

```
public interface Testable
{
    public void test();
}
```

Now consider the following program:

WontCompile.java

```java
public class WontCompile
{
    public static void main(String[] args)
    {
        int x = 2;

        helper( () -> {
                          x = x * 2;
                          System.out.println(x);
                       }
              );
    }

    static void helper(Testable objectIn)
    {
        objectIn.test();
    }
}
```

As its name suggests, this program gives rise to a compiler error. Can you see why?

6. In order to tackle this exercise make sure that the classes `Rectangle` and `BankAccount` have been copied from the website (see preface) and placed in the correct directory for your compiler to access them.

Now consider the following `Resetable` interface:

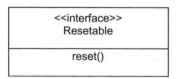

The `reset` method takes no parameters and returns no value. The intention of the `reset` method is to reset the object data to some basic initial value. For example, a rectangle object might be reset by having both sides set to 1.

(a) Write the code for the `Resetable` interface.

(b) Write a tester program to check the `Resetable` interface. An outline of the tester is given below:

Outline of a *TestResetable* program

```
public class TestResetable
{
        public static void main(String[] args)
        {
            // create a rectangle object and BankAccount Object

            // Make a deposit into the BankAccount object

            /* call the resetObject method with a lambda expression that sets
               the length and height of the Rectangle to 1 */

            /* call the resetObject method with a lambda expression that sets
               the balance of the BankAccount object to zero. You can't do this
               directly because there is no setBalance method - but you can
               withdraw the total amount that is in the account */

            /* display the length and height of the Rectangle (which should now
               be 1) and the balance of the bank account (which should now be
               zero) */
        }

    // write a resetObject method as follows:

        static void resetObject(Resetable objectIn)
        {
            objectIn.reset();
        }
}
```

7. (a) Write the code for an interface, Computable, which has a single method, compute, that accepts two **double**s and returns a **double**:

<<interface>>
Computable
+compute(double, double):double

(b) Consider the following program; a lambda expression has been replaced by a comment:

```
public class TestComputable
{
    public static void main(String[] args)
    {
        Computable comp =  /* lambda expression here */ ;
        printResult(comp);
    }

    static void printResult(Computable compIn)
    {
        System.out.println(compIn.compute(10, 5));
    }
}
```

Replace the comment with a lambda expression that causes the compute method to return the sum of the two **double**s it receives, and then test out your program with some different values in the printResult method.

(c) Change the lambda expression so that it performs other calculations such as subtraction or multiplication.

8. (a) Adapt the code for the Computable interface that you developed in
    question 7 so that it is generic interface, that is not restricted to dealing with
    doubles only.
  (b) Rewrite the TestComputable program from question 7 (b) so that it uses
    your generic interface with number types other than **double**. Don't forget
    you will have to use the wrapper classes such as Double and Integer.

19.9   Programming Exercises

1. Implement a few of the programs from this chapter in order to make sure that
   you fully understand the concepts involved.
2. A Customer class is being developed for a small business. The suggested code
   for this class is shown below:

```java
public class Customer
{
        private String customerId;
        private String name;
        private double creditLimit;

        public Customer(String IdIn, String nameIn, double limitIn)
        {
                this.customerId = IdIn;
                this.name = nameIn;
                this.creditLimit = limitIn;
        }

        public String getCustomerId()
        {
                return this.customerId;
        }

        public String getName()
        {
                return this.name;
        }

        public double getCreditLimit()
        {
                return this.creditLimit;
        }

        public void setCreditLimit(double limitIn)
        {
                this.creditLimit = limitIn;
        }
}
```

The owner of the business requires that the customer ID must comprise a single
letter followed by exactly 3 numbers.
  (a) Create a CheckableCustomer class that inherits from the Customer
    class and implements the Checkable interface that we developed in
    Sect. 19.3. The class will override the check method according to the
    above rule.
  (b) Adapt the Checker program from Sect. 19.3 so that it now checks the
    validity of a CheckableCustomer object, according to the above rule.

(c) Finally, adapt program `LambdaDemo` program from Sect. 19.4 to use a lambda expression to check the validity of a `Customer` object.

3. Implement the `Resetable` interface and the `TestResetable` class from self-test question 6.

4. Implement the `Computable` interface and the test classes you developed in self-test question 7.

5. Implement the generic version of the above classes as described in self-test question 8.

6. In Sect. 19.6 the program `TestGenericInterface` demonstrated the use one of the out of the box interfaces (`Function`) listed in Table 19.1. Design and implement some more programs to demonstrate the use of some of the other functions listed in that table.

Java: Exceptions

20

Outcomes

By the end of this chapter you should be able to:

- *explain the term* **exception**;
- *distinguish between* **checked** *and* **unchecked** *exception classes in Java*;
- *catch an exception in a* **try...catch block**;
- *use a* **try-with-resources** *construct to deal with clean-up issues*;
- *use exceptions in your own classes*;
- *utilize the* **throws Exception** *clause*;
- *throw an exception using the* **throw** *command*;
- *create and use your own exception classes*.

20.1 Introduction

As early as Chap. 4 we talked about the fact that when a program is running, there are times when something goes wrong and the program crashes, or at least doesn't behave as we would expect. In Chap. 10, when we covered file handling in Python, we saw some examples of this: when we try to open a file that doesn't exist, or to save a file when there is no space on the disk. Sometimes a printer can go wrong, or a keyboard can get stuck. Sometimes the program instructs the computer to perform an operation that causes an error—like division by zero for example. And sometimes a user can input information which causes a problem.

Supplementary Information The online version contains supplementary material available at
https://doi.org/10.1007/978-3-031-01326-3_20.

In Python we were able to use the **try ... except** construct which allows the program to anticipate these problems and organize things so that the error is dealt with smoothly and the program continues to run. Java provides a similar construct, the **try ... catch** construct. However, in Python we were not forced to use the exception handling routines that it provides (although it would be rather foolish not to do so in the case of something like file handling), whereas in Java there are times when our programs will not compile if we do not handle the exceptions that could potentially arise.

So we need to explore Java exceptions in rather more depth. Before we do so, however, we need to say a bit more about the concept so that you understand fully what exceptions are all about.

Regardless of the language that we use, unexpected situations like those that we listed above can arise and these could compromise the correct functioning of a program; programs should be written in such a way that they continue to function even if unexpected situations should arise. So far in Java we have tried to achieve this by carefully constructed **if** statements that send back error flags, in the form of **boolean** values, when appropriate. However, in some circumstances, these forms of protection against undesirable situations prove inadequate. In such cases the *exception handling* facility of Java must be used.

20.2   Predefined Exception Classes in Java

An **exception** is an event that occurs during the life of a program which could cause that program to behave unreliably. You can see that the events we described in the introduction fall into this category.

Each type of event that could lead to an exception is associated with a predefined *exception class* in Java. When a given event occurs, the Java run-time environment determines which exception has occurred and an object of the given exception class is generated. This process is known as **throwing** an exception. These exception classes have been named to reflect the nature of the exception. For example, when an array is accessed with an illegal index, an object of the ArrayIndexOutOfBoundsException class is thrown.

All exception classes inherit from the base class Throwable which is found in the java.lang package. These subclasses of Throwable are found in various packages and are then further categorized depending upon the type of exception. For example, the exception associated with a given file not being found (FileNotFoundException) and the exception associated with an end of file having been reached (EOFException) are both types of input/output exceptions (IOException), which reside in the java.io package. Figure 20.1 illustrates part of this hierarchy.

As you can see from Fig. 20.1, there are two immediate subclasses of Throwable: Exception and Error. The Error class describes internal system errors that are very unlikely ever to occur (so-called hard errors). For

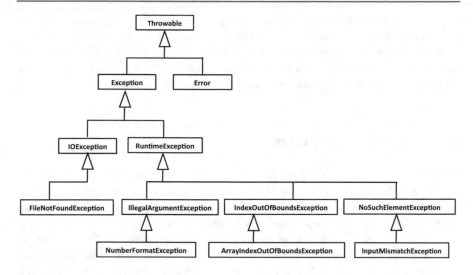

Fig. 20.1 Sample of Java's predefined exception class hierarchy

example, one subclass of `Error` is `VirtualMachineError` where some error in the JVM has been detected. There is little that can be done in the way of recovery from such errors other than to end the program as gracefully as possible. All other exceptions are subclasses of the `Exception` class, and it is these exceptions that programmers deal with in their programs. The `Exception` class is further subdivided. The two most important subdivisions are shown in Fig. 20.1: `IOException` and `RuntimeException`.

The `RuntimeException` class deals with errors that arise from the logic of a program, for example, a program that converts a string into a number, when the string contains non-numeric characters (`NumberFormatException`) or accesses an array using an illegal index (`ArrayIndexOutOfBoundsException`).

The `IOException` class deals with external errors that could affect the program during input and output. Such errors could include, for example, the keyboard locking, or an external file being corrupted.

Since nearly every Java instruction could result in a `RuntimeException` error, the Java compiler does not flag such instructions as potentially error prone. Consequently these types of errors are known as **unchecked** exceptions. It is left to the programmer to ensure that code is written in such a way as to avoid such exceptions, for example, checking an array index before looking up a value in an array with that index. Should such an exception arise, it will be due to a program error and will not become apparent until run-time.

The Java compiler *does*, however, flag up those instructions that may generate all other types of exception (such as `IOException` errors) since the programmer has no means of avoiding such errors arising. For example, an instruction to read from a file may cause an exception because the file is corrupt. No amount of program code can prevent this file from being corrupt. The compiler will not only flag such an instruction as potentially error prone, it will also specify the exact exception that could be thrown. Consequently, these kinds of errors are known as **checked** exceptions. Programmers have to include code to inform the compiler of how they will deal with checked exceptions generated by a particular instruction, before the compiler will allow the program to compile successfully.

20.3   Handling Exceptions

There are two ways an exception can be handled in a method if it occurs, either it is caught within the method (as we shall see later) or it is thrown up to the calling method to deal with. The calling method then has the same two choices. If the exception is continually thrown and never caught, it will eventually be thrown out of the main method and this will either crash the program or (in the case of graphical programs) cause it to behave erratically. If the exception is unchecked and not caught, it is automatically thrown to up to the calling method. If the exception is a checked exception and not caught, it needs to be explicitly thrown from a method by adding a **throws** clause—otherwise the method will not compile. As an example, take a look at the constructor for a class called FileWriter which we will be using in Chap. 23. As you can find out from the Java documentation, this constructor is specified with the following header:

```
public FileWriter(String fileName)throws IOException
```

The term **throws** IOException means that the method *could* cause an input/output exception in your program. The type of error that could take place while data is being written includes the loss of a network connection or insufficient space on the disk, for example.

Remember, when an exception occurs, an exception object is created. This is an unwanted object that could cause your program to fail or behave unpredictably and so should be dealt with and not ignored. Indeed, because in this case we are dealing with an IOException, we are obliged to deal with it because it is a checked exception.

The usual way to handle an exception object is to trap it in a **catch** block. In order to do this, you must surround the code that could generate the exception in a **try** block. The syntax for using a **try** and **catch** block is as follows:

```
try
{
    // code that could generate an exception
}
catch (Exception e) // type of exception must be specified as a parameter
{
    // action to be taken when an exception occurs
}
// other instructions could be placed here
```

There are a few things to note before we show you this **try** ... **catch** idea in action. First, any number of lines could be placed within the **try** block, and more than one of them could cause an exception. If none of them causes an exception, the **catch** block is missed and the lines following the **catch** block are executed. If any one of them causes an exception, the program will leave the **try** block and look for a **catch** block that deals with that exception.

Once such a **catch** clause is found, the statements within it will be executed and the program will then *continue* with any statements that follow the **catch** clause—it will *not* return to the code in the **try** clause. Look carefully at the syntax for the **catch** block:

```
catch (Exception e)
{
    // action to be taken when an exception occurs
}
```

This looks very similar to a method header. You can see that the **catch** block header has one parameter: an object, which we called e, of type Exception. Since *all* exceptions are subclasses of the Exception class, this will catch *any* exception that should arise. However, it is better to replace this exception class with the *specific* class that you are catching so that you can be certain *which* exception you have caught. As there may be more than one exception generated within a method, there may be more than one **catch** block below a **try** block—each dealing with a different exception. When an exception is thrown in a **try** block, the **catch** blocks are inspected in order—the first matching **catch** block is the one that will handle the exception.

Let's put this into practice. The program below asks the user to enter the mark that he or she gained in an aptitude test; once that is done, the user is informed about whether or not the student has been successful.

AptitudeTest.java

```java
import java.util.Scanner;

public class AptitudeTest
{
    public static void main (String[] args)
    {
        int score;
        Scanner keyboard = new Scanner(System.in);
        System.out.print("Enter aptitude test score: ");
        score = keyboard.nextInt();
        if (score >= 50)
        {
            System.out.println("You have a place on the course!");
        }
        else
        {
            System.out.println("Sorry, you failed your test");
        }
    }
}
```

Here is a sample run:

```
Enter aptitude test score: 52
You have a place on the course!
```

In this case the user entered a mark correctly and the program completed without a problem. But now look at this example:

```
Enter aptitude test score: 5w
Exception in thread "main" java.util.InputMismatchException
    at java.util.Scanner.throwFor(Scanner.java:864)
    at java.util.Scanner.next(Scanner.java:1485)
    at java.util.Scanner.nextInt(Scanner.java:2117)
    at java.util.Scanner.nextInt(Scanner.java:2076)
    at AptitudeTest.main(AptitudeTest.java:11)
```

As you can see, what has happened is that the user has entered something that isn't a number, and as a consequence an `InputMismatchException` has been thrown. As you see from Fig. 20.1, this is a derivative of `RunTimeException` so was unchecked and the compiler therefore allowed us to go ahead without catching the potential exception. But because we didn't attempt to handle the exception, the program terminated. When this happens, a **stack trace** is printed on the screen—the stack trace is a record of the various subroutines that were called and which lead to the exception being thrown. The one that is most informative is the last one that tells us the precise line in our program that caused the problem. Now while this is helpful to us, we would prefer it if the program didn't crash if the user was to inadvertently enter something that wasn't an integer. We need to catch the exception as we have done in `AptitudeTest2` below:

AptitudeTest2.java

```java
import java.util.InputMismatchException;
import java.util.Scanner;

public class AptitudeTest2
{
    public static void main (String[] args)
    {
        int score;
        Scanner keyboard = new Scanner(System.in);
        try
        {
            System.out.print("Enter aptitude test score: ");
            score = keyboard.nextInt(); // this could cause an exception to be thrown
            if(score >=50)
            {
                System.out.println("You have a place on the course!");
            }
            else
            {
                System.out.println("Sorry, you failed your test");
            }
        }
        // if the wrong type of data is entered
        catch(InputMismatchException e)
        {
            System.out.println("You entered an invalid number");
        }
    }
}
```

As you can see, the line that could cause the exception to be thrown is now placed within the **try** block. The **catch** blook looks like this:

```
catch(InputMismatchException e)
{
        System.out.println("You entered an invalid number");
}
```

Now, if the user should enter something other than integer, then the above message will be displayed. Here is a sample run:

```
Enter aptitude test score: 63tx
You entered an invalid number
```

This **catch** block is designed specifically to catch an InputMismatchException. We should note that a **catch** block will also catch any subclass of the exception specified. So we could, for example, have set it up like this:

```
catch(Exception e)
{
        // action to be taken
}
```

In this case, since Exception is at the top of the hierarchy, any exception would be caught, so if the code in the **try** block could give rise to a number of different exceptions we would have to make the message more general. Alternatively, different **catch** blocks can be provided for each possible exception.

In Chap. 4, we used Python's **try** … **except** block to validate input in conjunction with a **while** loop. AptitudeTest3 does the same thing in Java:

AptitudeTest3.java

```
import java.util.InputMismatchException;
import java.util.Scanner;

public class AptitudeTest3
{
    public static void main (String[] args)
    {
        int score;
        boolean ok = false;
        Scanner keyboard;
        while(!ok)
        {
            keyboard = new Scanner(System.in);
            try
            {
                System.out.print("Enter aptitude test score: ");
                score = keyboard.nextInt();
                if (score >= 50)
                {
                    System.out.println("You have a place on the course!");
                }
                else
                {
                    System.out.println("Sorry, you failed your test");
                }
                ok = true;
            }
            // if the wrong type of data is entered
            catch (InputMismatchException e)
            {
                System.out.println("You entered an invalid number!");
            }
        }
    }
}
```

As you can see, the whole of the **try** … **catch** block is contained within the **while** loop, which is controlled by a **boolean** variable, ok, which initially is set to **false**. If the number is entered correctly, the appropriate message is displayed and ok is set to **true**, terminating the loop. If, however, something other than a number is entered, the program will jump to the **catch** block and the message will be displayed to inform the user that data had been entered in the incorrect format. The **boolean** variable will still be **false** so the loop will continue until the data is entered successfully.

Notice that the following line is also contained within the **while** loop:

```
keyboard = new Scanner(System.in);
```

The reason for this is that if control had moved to the **catch** block, the Scanner object will still be open ready to receive input, which would simply be appended to what had previously been entered. To avoid this, we initialize a new Scanner object each time we go round the loop.

20.4   The 'try-with-resources' Construct

Very often it is necessary to close a resource before exiting a program. The best example of this is when we open a file for reading or writing as we saw when we studied file handling in Chap. 10. In Java we have a very useful construct known as **try-with-resources** which means that resources such as files are closed automatically when the program terminates without us having to worry about it. This construct was introduced in Java 8. Prior to this, it was common to add what is known as a **finally** clause after the final **catch** in which we placed such clean-up routines such as this. Try-with-resources have now largely done away with the need for such a clause.

Although we haven't yet studied file handing in Java, we can take a look ahead to a program that we will be developing in Chap. 22. Below is a method that opens a text file for writing:

```
static void writeList(List<Car> carListIn)
{
    // use try-with-resources to ensure file is closed safely
    try(
        /* create a FileWriter object, carFile, that handles the low-level details of
           writing the list to a file which we have called "Cars.txt" */
        FileWriter carFile = new FileWriter("Cars.txt");
        /* now create a PrintWriter object to wrap around carFile; this allows us to user
           high-level functions such as println */
        PrintWriter carWriter = new PrintWriter(carFile);
    )
    {
        // write each element of the list to the file
        for(Car item : carListIn)
        {
            carWriter.println(item.getRegistration());
            carWriter.println(item.getMake());
            carWriter.println(item.getPrice());
        }
    }

    // handle the exception thrown by the FileWriter methods
    catch(IOException e)
    {
        System.out.println("There was a problem writing the file");
    }
}
```

You don't need to understand the details of this method just yet—the important bit is this:

As you can see, there are two statements that are actually *contained in the brackets* of the **try** block (shown below without the comments):

```
try(
    FileWriter carFile = new FileWriter("Cars.txt");
    PrintWriter carWriter = new PrintWriter(carFile);
)
```

These two lines of code open a file and set up a stream by which to communicate with the file. It is very important to close the file and the associated stream when we are finished writing to it, or the file could be corrupted. In the past, we would have needed to ensure that we closed these resources (by specifically calling the `close` method) if, for example, an exception had occurred and the operation was not successfully completed. But enclosing them in the brackets ensures that these resources are automatically closed when the routine has finished. This is how we invoke the 'try-with-resources' mechanism—which you probably appreciate is a very useful mechanism indeed.

20.5   Exceptions in Graphical Applications

In Chap. 11, when you studied Python graphics with Tkinter, you were introduced to an `Entry` widget that enabled users of the program to input data. You will recall that when the `get` method of `Entry` was used to retrieve the data entered, this returned a string—and if the data was intended to represent a numerical value, it was necessary to typecast the string to the appropriate numerical type.

We have a similar situation with the JavaFX equivalent of Python's `Entry` widget, which—as you will discover in Chap. 23—is called a `TextField`.

In Chap. 23 you will study JavaFX to produce graphical applications. Figure 20.2 shows a JavaFX version of the hostel application that we developed in Chap. 12.

In order to convert a `String` to a **double** in Java we use a class method, `parseDouble`, of one of the wrapper classes that you learnt about in Chap. 19, namely the `Double` class; in the case of an integer we would use the `parseInt` method of the `Integer` class.

In Fig. 20.2 someone has entered '34A' in a field that expects to receive a decimal. This would result in `parseDouble` throwing a `NumberFor-matException`. As you can see in Fig. 20.1, this is a derivative of `RunTimeException` and is therefore unchecked.

Now, in a graphical application this would not cause the program to terminate. If the program was running as a stand-alone application, you would not see anything to alert you to the fact that an exception had occurred—it would be reported in a console, which is normally hidden. If you were running it in an IDE, you would see the exception being reported in the output window. Of course, although the program would not terminate, it would cause it to run incorrectly, and you would have to make sure you handled this exception properly with a **try** ... **catch** construct and a loop, so that the problem was reported somewhere within the graphic in order that the user could correct the error and move ahead.

You will see examples of this in our case study in Chap. 24.

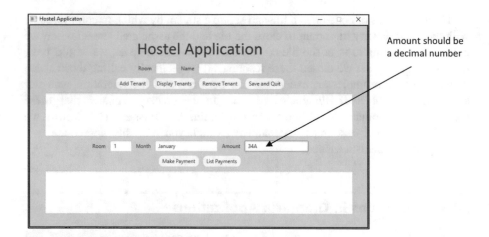

Fig. 20.2 Graphical Java application in which invalid data has been entered

20.6   Using Exceptions in Your Own Classes

So far we have been dealing with how to handle predefined exceptions that are automatically thrown by your Java programs, for example the NumberFormatException that we described above.

Sometimes, however we wish to generate an error under circumstances in which Java would not ordinarily raise an error. To illustrate this, we have devised a very simple example. We will define a class called Square, which will have one attribute (the length of the sides), a constructor that sets this attribute at the time of creation, and a method that returns the area of the square. We want to prevent anyone from setting a value of zero or less for the side, so the constructor will throw an exception if there is an attempt to do this. We will make the exception a general exception—that is, it will be of type Exception. Remember, this is a checked exception, so any program that creates a Square object will have to handle it. Had we not wanted this to be the case, we could have made our constructor throw a RunTimeException, which, as we know, is unchecked.

Here is our class, with the important parts emboldened:

Square.java

```java
public class Square
{
    private double side;

    public Square(double sideIn) throws Exception
    {
        if(sideIn <= 0)
        {
            throw new Exception();
        }
        else
        {
            this.side = sideIn;
        }
    }

    public double calculateArea()
    {
        return this.side * this.side;
    }
}
```

As you can see, in the constructor we have an **if** statement that checks whether or not the value sent in meets our criterion—if it does not, we specifically throw an exception. It is worth noting here we could not have employed the usual method of reporting an error—namely returning a **boolean** value—because a constructor does not return a value.

You will also note the words **throws** Exception in the header; this marks the fact that the method throws an exception.

Let's write a short program to test this out. Our first attempt won't compile:

TestSquare.java – won't compile

```
import java.util.Scanner;

public class TestSquare
{

    public static void main(String[] args)
    {
        Scanner keyboard = new Scanner(System.in);
        System.out.print("Enter value for the sides of the square: ");
        double side = keyboard.nextDouble();
        Square mySquare = new Square(side); // this line causes a compiler error
        System.out.println("Area of square = " + mySquare.calculateArea());
        System.out.println("End of program");
    }

}
```

The reason this won't compile is, of course, that we set up the Square class so that the constructor throws an exception—and, since we made this a checked exception, we are obliged to handle it when we create a new Square object. So let's correct this:

TestSquare2.java

```
import java.util.Scanner;

public class TestSquare2
{

    public static void main(String[] args)
    {
        Scanner keyboard = new Scanner(System.in);
        System.out.print("Enter value for the sides of the square: ");
        double side = keyboard.nextDouble();
        // handle the exception thrown by the constructor of Square
        try
        {
            Square mySquare = new Square(side);
            System.out.println("Area of square = " + mySquare.calculateArea());
        }
        catch(Exception e)
        {
            System.out.println("The side of the square must be a positive number");
        }
        System.out.println("End of program");
    }
}
```

Here is a sample run of this program when the user enters a positive number:

```
Enter value for the sides of the square: 5
Area of square = 25.0
End of program
```

But if a zero or negative number is entered, the constructor throws an exception and the **catch** block is entered.

```
Enter value for the sides of the square: 0
The side of the square must be a positive number
End of program
```

20.7   Creating Your Own Exception Classes

So far we haven't made use of the exception object received by the **catch** block. The Exception class has some useful methods which we can, if we choose, make use of in order to interrogate the object. Three of these are given in Table 20.1.

Let's see some examples. If, in TestSquare2 we wrote the **catch** block as follows:

```
catch(Exception e)
{
    e.printStackTrace();
}
```

We would get the following message instead of our own custom message when a zero or negative value was entered:

```
java.lang.Exception
    at Square.<init>(Square.java:9)
    at TestSquare2.main(TestSquare2.java:15)
```

The following version uses the toString method of Exception (remember that we just need to use the name of the object in order to invoke toString):

```
catch(Exception e)
{
    System.out.println(e);
}
```

This would result in displaying:

```
java.lang.Exception
```

This version uses getMessage:

```
catch(Exception e)
{
    System.out.println(e.getMessage());
}
```

This simply results in displaying:

```
null
```

Table 20.1 Some methods of the *Exception* class

Method	Description
printStackTrace	prints (onto the console) a stack trace of the exception
toString	returns a detailed error message
getMessage	returns a summary error message

The information provided by the `toString` and `getMessage` methods is very general and not necessarily that helpful. If you want more meaningful results from the `toString` and `getMessage` methods, then it is possible to create your own exception class.

You can create your own exception class by inheriting from any predefined exception class. Generally speaking, if you wish your exception class to be unchecked, then it should inherit from `RuntimeException` (or one of its subclasses), whereas if you wish your exception to be checked, you can inherit from the general `Exception` class or a derivative of this class such as `IOException`.

Below we have done this for our `Square` class, which extends `Exception`.:

SquareException.java

```java
public class SquareException extends Exception
{
        public SquareException() // constructor without parameter
        {
            super("zero or negative number was entered");
        }

        public SquareException (String message) // constructor with parameter
        {
            super(message);
        }

        @Override
        public String toString()
        {
            return "The sides of a square cannot be zero or negative";
        }

}
```

As you see it has two constructors, both of which call the constructor of the superclass—the first has a fixed message, and the second allows the message to be determined by the class throwing the method (as you will see in a moment). We have also overridden the `toString` method with a more detailed message.

Now for the new version of the `Square` class, which we have named `SquareVersion2`:

SquareVersion2.java

```java
public class SquareVersion2
{
    private double side;

    public SquareVersion2(double sideIn) throws SquareException
    {
        if(sideIn <= 0)
        {
            throw new SquareException();
        }
        else
        {
            this.side = sideIn;
        }
    }

    public double calculateArea()
    {
        return this.side * this.side;
    }
}
```

Now this class throws a `SquareException` instead of a general exception as before. Notice that in this case we have called the version of the constructor the does not require a parameter:

```
if(sideIn <= 0)
{
    throw new SquareException();
}
else
{
    this.side = sideIn;
}
```

We could, had we wished, have chosen our own custom message:

```
if(sideIn <= 0)
{
    throw new SquareException("Careful - sides must be positive");
}
else
{
    this.side = sideIn;
}
```

The program below tests out our new class:

TestSquare3.java
```
import java.util.Scanner;

public class TestSquare3
{
    public static void main(String[] args)
    {
        Scanner keyboard = new Scanner(System.in);
        System.out.print("Enter value for the sides of the square: ");
        double side = keyboard.nextDouble();
        // handle the exception thrown by the constructor of SquareVersion2
        try
        {
            SquareVersion2 mySquare = new SquareVersion2(side);
            System.out.println("Area of square = " + mySquare.calculateArea());
        }
        catch(SquareException e)
        {
            System.out.println(e); // calls the toString method of SquareException
        }
        System.out.println("End of program");
    }
}
```

Here is a sample run:

```
Enter value for the sides of the square: -5
The sides of a square cannot be zero or negative
End of program
```

As you would expect the message associated with the `toString` method of `SquareVersion2` has been displayed.

If we changed the `catch` block as follows:

```
catch(SquareException e)
{
    System.out.println(e.getMessage()); // calls the getMessage method of SquareException
}
```

we would get the following output instead:

```
Enter value for the sides of the square: -5
Zero or negative number was entered
End of program
```

You might be wondering, what would happen if some unexpected exception occurs during the execution of this program other than a `SquareException`? At the moment, any such exception would remain uncaught as we are only set up to catch a `SquareException`, and this would lead to a program crash. For this reason, it is always a good practice to add a final catch-all **catch** block, by catching a general `Exception`—as illustrated in `TestSquare4` below:

TestSquare4.java

```
import java.util.Scanner;

public class TestSquare4
{
    public static void main(String[] args)
    {
        Scanner keyboard = new Scanner(System.in);
        System.out.print("Enter value for the sides of the square: ");
        double side = keyboard.nextDouble();
        try
        {
            SquareVersion2 mySquare = new SquareVersion2(side);
            System.out.println("Area of square = " + mySquare.calculateArea());
        }
        catch(SquareException e) // catches SquareException only
        {
            System.out.println(e); // calls the toString method of SquareException
        }
        catch(Exception e) // catches all other exceptions
        {
            e.printStackTrace(); // prints stack trace
        }

        System.out.println("End of program");
    }
}
```

As you can see in the program above, we have printed the stack trace when catching any unexpected exception, in order to help identify the source of the error:

```
catch(Exception e)
{
     e.printStackTrace(); // prints stack trace
}
```

Note, when adding a general `Exception` **catch** block, make sure it is always last in your list of **catch** blocks, as your program will not compile if specific **catch** blocks (such as **catch** `SquareException`) are placed after a general **catch** `Exception` block, since any such specific **catch** blocks will never be reached.

Below is a test run in which the user has entered a non-numerical value for the length of the square. This error will be caught in the general `Exception` **catch** block, producing the following stack trace:

```
Enter value for the sides of the square: wewewe
Exception in thread "main" java.util.InputMismatchException
    at java.base/java.util.Scanner.throwFor(Scanner.java:939)
    at java.base/java.util.Scanner.next(Scanner.java:1594)
    at java.base/java.util.Scanner.nextDouble(Scanner.java:2564)
    at TestSquare4.main(TestSquare4.java:10)
```

20.8   Self-test Questions

1. What is an *exception*?
2. Distinguish between *checked* and *unchecked* exceptions and then identify which of the following exceptions are checked, and which are unchecked:

   - `FileNotFoundException`;
   - `NegativeArraySizeException`;
   - `NullPointerException`;
   - `NumberFormatException`;
   - `IOException`;
   - `Exception`;
   - `ArrayIndexOutOfBoundsException`;
   - `RuntimeException`.

3. Look at the program below and then answer the questions that follow:

```java
public class ExceptionsQ3
{
   public static void main(String[] args)
   {
        int[] someArray = {12,9,3,11};
        int position = getPosition();
        display (someArray, position);
        System.out.println("End of program" );
   }

   static int getPosition()
   {
       System.out.print("Enter array position to display: ");
       String positionEntered = EasyScanner.nextString(); // requires EasyScanner class
       return Integer.parseInt(positionEntered);
   }

   static void display (int[] arrayIn, int posIn)
   {
        System.out.println("Item at this position is: " + arrayIn[posIn]);
   }
}
```

   (a) Will this result in any compiler errors?
   (b) Which methods could throw exceptions?
   (c) Identify the names of the exceptions that could be thrown and the cir-
        cumstances under which they could be thrown.
4. When would you use the *try-with-resources* construct?
5. Explain why it is sometimes useful to define your own exception class?

20.9   Programming Exercises

1. Implement the program given in self-test question 3 above. Now:

   (a) Rewrite `main` so that it catches any specific exceptions it may now throw
        by displaying a message on the screen indicating the exception thrown.
   (b) Create your own exception class `InvalidPositionException` (make
        this an unchecked exception).
   (c) Rewrite   the   `display`   method   so   that   it   throws   the
        `InvalidPositionException`.
   (d) Rewrite `main` to take account of this amended display method.
   (e) Add an additional **catch** clause in `main` to catch any unaccounted for
        exceptions (within this **catch** clause print out the stack trace of the
        exception).
2. (a) Develop a new version of the `EasyScanner` class, say `EasyScan-
        nerPlus`, so that instead of throwing exceptions the methods `nextInt`
        and `nextDouble` repeatedly display an error message and allow for data
        re-entry.
   (b) Write a tester program to test out the methods of your `EasyScan-
        nerPlus` class.

3. Look back at the magic square program from self-test question 10 in Chap. 16.
   (a) Create a simple menu-driven program that asks the user for a row or column number and calls the `displayRow` method or the `displayColumn` method accordingly.
   (b) In each of the methods, add **try...catch** blocks that will respond to the possible exceptions that could be thrown by displaying a suitable message and returning the user to the menu.

The Java Collections Framework

21

Outcomes

By the end of this chapter you should be able to:

- *use the* ArrayList *class to store a **list** of objects;*
- *use the* HashMap *class to store objects in a **map**;*
- *use the* HashSet *class to store a **set** of objects;*
- *use the enhanced* **for** *loop and the* **forEach** *loop to scan through a collection;*
- *create objects of your own classes, and use them in conjunction with Java's collection classes;*
- *sort elements in a collection using existing methods.*

21.1   Introduction

In Chap. 16 you learnt about arrays as a means of holding collections of items in Java. While an array is an important data type, it does have some restrictions:

- once an array is created it must be sized, and this size is fixed;
- it contains no useful predefined methods.

When you studied Python in the first semester, you learnt about a number of mechanisms for storing collection of data, such as lists, sets and dictionaries. Similar types are available in Java, although there is one big difference: Java collections can only hold items of the same type. The classes available are generic classes, and the type has to be specified. For this reason, we needed to wait until you had studied generic classes before you learnt about Java's collection classes.

Supplementary Information The online version contains supplementary material available at https://doi.org/10.1007/978-3-031-01326-3_21.

The group of collection classes available in Java is referred to as the **Java Collections Framework (JCF)**. These collection classes are organized around several collection interfaces that define different types of collections that we might be interested in using. Three important interfaces from this group are:

- `List`;
- `Map`;
- `Set`.

The `List` and `Set` interfaces correspond to the similarly named Python types, whereas the `Map` interface corresponds to the dictionary type in Python.

As well as providing these, and other, interfaces, the Java Collections Framework also contains many classes that implement these interfaces.

21.2   The *List* Interface and the *ArrayList* Class

As with Python's **list** type, the Java `List` interface specifies the methods required to process an *ordered list* of objects. Such a list may contain duplicates. Examples of a list of objects include jobs waiting for a printer, emergency calls waiting for an ambulance and the names of players that have won the Wimbledon tennis tournament over the last 10 years. In each case ordering is important, and repetition may also be required. We often refer to such a collection as a *sequence* of objects.

There are two implementations provided for the `List` interface in the JCF. They are `ArrayList` and `LinkedList`. In this text we are only going to study the first of these, `ArrayList`.

21.2.1   Creating an *ArrayList* Collection Object

All classes in the JCF are in the `java.util` package, so to use the `ArrayList` class we require the following **import** statement:

```
import java.util.ArrayList;
```

Like all the classes in JCF, the `ArrayList` class is a generic collection class, so it can be used to store objects of any type.[1] Let's use an `ArrayList` to store a

---

[1] As we mentioned in Chap. 19, generic collections cannot store primitive types like **int** and **double**. If primitive types are required then objects of the appropriate wrapper class (`Integer`, `Double` and so on) must be used. However, as discussed in Chap. 19, *autoboxing* and *unboxing* automate the process of moving from a primitive type to its associated wrapper.

queue of jobs waiting for a printer, and let us represent these jobs by a series of Job ID `Strings`. The `ArrayList` constructor creates an empty list:

```
// creates an ArrayList object -'printQ'
ArrayList<String> printQ = new ArrayList<> ();
```

In the case of the `printQ` object, we want each element within this collection to be of type `String`. As explained in Chap. 19, type inference means that we do not need to include the `String` type in the angle brackets in the call to the constructor on the right, as the type is inferred to be `String` in this case.

Of course, the generics mechanism can be used to fix *any* object type for the elements within a collection. For example, we could use an `ArrayList` to store a collection of objects of the `BankAccount` class that we developed in Chap. 17:

```
// this will make 'bank' a list of BankAccount objects
ArrayList<BankAccount> bank = new ArrayList<>();
```

You will remember from Chap. 8, we did exactly the same thing in Python.

21.2.2 The Interface Type Versus the Implementation Type

In order to create the object `printQ` from the previous section, we used the `ArrayList` class to implement the `List` interface. What if, at some point, we decide to change to the `LinkedList` implementation? Or some other implementation that might be available in future? If we did this, then all references to the type of this object (such as in the method header of the previous section) would have to be modified to give the new class name.

There is an alternative approach. It is actually considered better programming practice to declare collection objects to be the type of the interface (`List` in this case) rather than the type of the class that implements this collection. So this would be a better way to create our `printQ` object:

```
// the type is given as 'List' not 'ArrayList'
List<String> printQ = new ArrayList<> ();
```

Notice that the interface type still needs to be marked as being a list of `String` objects using the generics mechanism. A method that receives a `printQ` object would now be declared as follows:

```
// this method receives a List<String> object
public void someMethod (List<String> printQIn)
{
    // some code here
}
```

The advantage of this approach is that we can change our choice of implementation in future (maybe by using LinkedList or some other class that might be available that implements the List interface), without having to change the type of the object (which will always remain as List). This is the approach that we will take.

Remember, all classes in the JCF reside in the util package, so to use the List interface in your code you now need to add an additional **import** statement as follows:

```
import java.util.ArrayList;
import java.util.List;
```

Now, let us look at some List methods.

21.2.3 *List* Methods

The ArrayList class provides two add methods for inserting into a list, one that inserts the item at the end of the list and one that inserts the item at a specified position in the list. Like arrays, ArrayList positions begin at zero. Below we use the former method as we are modelling a queue here. This add method requires one parameter, the object to be added onto the end of the list:

```
printQ.add("myLetter.docx");
printQ.add("myFoto.jpg");
printQ.add("results.xlsx");
printQ.add("chapter.docx");
```

Notice that, since we have marked this list as containing String objects only, an attempt to add an object of any other type will result in a compiler error:

```
// will not compile as 'printQ' can hold Strings only!
printQ.add(new Rectangle(10, 20));
```

All the Java collection types have a toString method defined, so we can display the entire list to the screen:

```
System.out.println(printQ); // implicitly calling the toString method
```

When the list is displayed, the values in the list are separated by commas and enclosed in square brackets, in a similar way to that in which Pyhton lists are displayed when we use the print command. So this println instruction would display the following list:

```
[myLetter.docx, myFoto.jpg, results.xlsx, chapter.docx]
```

As you can see, the items in the list are kept in the order in which they were inserted using the add method above.

As we said earlier, the add method is overloaded to allow an item to be inserted into the list at a particular position. When the item is inserted into that position, the item previously at that particular position and all items behind it shuffle along by one place (i.e. they have their indices incremented by one). This add method requires two parameters, the position into which the object should be inserted and the object itself. For example, let's insert a high priority job at the start of the queue:

```
printQ.add(0, "importantMemo.docx"); // inserts into the front of the queue
```

Notice that the index is provided first, then the object. The index must be a valid index within the current list, or it may be the index of the back of the queue. An invalid index throws an unchecked IndexOutOfBoundsException.

Displaying this list confirms that the given job ("ImportantMemo.docx") has been added to the front of the queue, and all other items shuffled by one place:

```
[importantMemo.docx, myLetter.docx, myFoto.jpg, results.xlsx, chapter.docx]
```

If we wish to overwrite an item in the list, rather than insert a new item into the list, we can use the set method. The set method requires two parameters, the index of the item being overwritten and the new object to be inserted at that position. Let us change the name of the last job from "chapter.docx" to "newChapter.docx". This is the fifth item in the list, so its index is 4:

```
printQ.set(4, "newChapter.docx");
```

If the index used in the set method is invalid, an IndexOutOfBoundsException is thrown once again. Displaying the new list now gives us the following:

```
[importantMemo.docx, myLetter.docx, myFoto.jpg, results.xlsx, newChapter.docx]
```

List provides a size method to return the number of items in the list, so we could have renamed the last job in the queue in the following way also:

```
printQ.set(printQ.size()-1, "newChapter.docx"); // last position is size-1
```

The indexOf method returns the index of the first occurrence of a given object within the list. It returns −1 if the object is not in the list. For example, the following checks the index position of the job "myFoto.jpg" in the list:

```
int index = printQ.indexOf("myFoto.jpg"); // check index of job
if (index != -1) // check object is in list
{
    System.out.println("myFoto.jpg is at index position: " + index);
}
else // when job is not in list
{
    System.out.println("myFoto.jpg not in list");
}
```

This would display the following from our list:

```
myFoto.jpg is at index position: 2
```

Items can be removed either by specifying an index or an object. When an item is removed, items behind this item shuffle to the left (i.e. they have their indices decremented by one). As an example, let us remove the "myFoto.jpg" job. If we used its index, the following is required:

```
printQ.remove(2);
```

Once again, an IndexOutOfBoundsException would be thrown if this was not a valid index. This method returns the object that has been removed, which could be checked if necessary. Displaying the list would confirm the item has indeed been removed:

```
[importantMemo.docx, myLetter.docx, results.xlsx, newChapter.docx]
```

Alternatively, we could have removed the item by referring to it directly rather than by its index[2]:

```
printQ.remove("myFoto.jpg");
```

This method returns a **boolean** value to confirm that the item was in the list initially, which again could be checked if necessary.

Behind the scenes you can guess how this remove method works. It looks in the list for the given String object ("myFoto.jpg"). It uses the equals method of the String class to identify a match. Once it finds such a match it shuffles items along so there are no gaps in the list.

Of course, as we have already said, these collection classes can be used to store objects of *any* type—not just Strings. For methods like remove to work properly, the contained object must have a properly defined equals method.

The get method allows a particular item to be retrieved from the list via its index position. The following displays the job at the head of the queue:

---

[2] If there were more than one occurrence of the object, the first occurrence would be deleted.

```
// the first item is at position 0
System.out.println("First job is " + printQ.get(0));
```

This would display the following:

First job is importantMemo.docx

The contains method can be used to check whether or not a particular item is present in the list:

```
if (printQ.contains("poem.docx")) // check if value is in list
{
    System.out.println("poem.docx is in the list");
}
else
{
    System.out.println("poem.docx is not in the list");
}
```

Finally, the isEmpty method reports on whether or not the list contains any items:

```
if (printQ.isEmpty()) // returns true when list is empty
{
    System.out.println("Print queue is empty");
}
else
{
    System.out.println("Print queue is not empty");
}
```

21.3 The Enhanced *for* Loop and Java Collections

In Chap. 16 we showed you how the enhanced **for** loop can be used to iterate through an entire array. The use of this loop is not restricted to arrays, and it can also be used with the List (and Set) implementations provided in the JCF. For example, here an enhanced **for** loop is used to iterate through the printQ list to find and display those jobs that end with a ".docx" extension:

```
for (String item: printQ) // iterate through all items in the 'printQ'list
{
    if(item.endsWith(".docx")) // check extension of the job ID
    {
        System.out.println(item); // display this item
    }
}
```

Notice that the type of each item in the printQ list is String. Within the loop we use the String method endsWith to check if the given job ID ends with String ".docx". Assuming we had the following printQ:

```
[importantMemo.docx, myLetter.docx, results.xlsx, newChapter.docx]
```

the enhanced **for** loop above would produce the following output:

```
importantMemo.docx
myLetter.docx
newChapter.docx
```

If we do not wish to iterate through the *entire* list, or if we wish to *modify* the items within a list as we iterate through them, then (as we have said before) the enhanced **for** loop should not be used.

For example, if we wished to display the items in the printQ that are behind the head of the queue, the enhanced **for** loop is not appropriate as we are not processing the *entire* printQ. Instead, the following standard **for** loop could be used:

```
// remember second item in list is at index 1!
for (int pos = 1; pos < printQ.size(); pos++)
{
    System.out.println(printQ.get(pos)); // retrieve item in printQ
}
```

Notice how the size method is used to determine the last index in the loop header. Within the loop, the get method is used to look up an item at the given index.

Again, if we assume we have the following printQ:

```
[importantMemo.docx, myLetter.docx, results.xlsx, newChapter.docx]
```

the for loop above would produce the following output:

```
myLetter.docx
results.xlsx
newChapter.docx
```

21.4   The *forEach* Loop

There is a very similar loop to the enhanced **for** loop known as the **forEach** loop. The **forEach** loop makes use of the forEach method, which is to be found in classes implementing the Collection interface (such as lists and sets). The forEach method requires an implementation of a Consumer interface, which can be provided via a lambda expression. Table 21.1 provides a reminder of the Consumer interface that we discussed in Chap. 19.

Table 21.1 Reminder of the Consumer interface

Functional interface	Abstract method name	Parameter types	Return type
Consumer<T>	accept	T	void

This implementation is then applied to each element in the underlying collection. For example, let's revisit the code in Sect. 21.3 for searching through our `printQ` list to display document names that end with ".docx". This time we will use a lambda expression and a **forEach** loop:

```
// using a forEach loop to iterate through a list
printQ.forEach(item ->
        {
            if(item.endsWith(".docx")) // check extension of the job ID
            {
                System.out.println(item); // display this item
            }
        });
```

As you can see, we use a **forEach** loop by calling the **forEach** method on the list object `printQ`. The parameter to the lambda expression is a name we give to one value from this collection, `item` in this case, and to the right of the lambda arrow we define how we process this value (using the same code we used in Sect. 21.3). The **forEach** loop will retrieve all the items within the collection to be processed in this way. You should note that, as with the enhanced **for** loop, the **forEach** loop should not be used to modify the underlying collection.

We will see further examples of the use of this **forEach** loop in this chapter.

21.5   The *Map* Interface and the *HashMap* Class

In Java, a map is the equivalent of a dictionary in Python. The `Map` interface, therefore, defines the methods required to process a collection consisting of *pairs* of objects. Rather than looking up an item via an index value, the first object of the pair is used. As with Python, the first object in the pair is the **key** and the second its associated **value**. Ordering is unimportant in maps, and keys are unique.

As we saw in Chap. 7, it is often useful to think of a map as a *look-up* table, with the key object the item used to look up (access) an associated value in the table. We'll use a similar example to the one we used in that chapter, namely a collection of usernames and passwords. Table 21.2 gives an example of such a look-up table.

We can look up the password of a user by looking up their username in Table 21.2. The password of *lauraHaliwell*, for example, is *unicorn*, whereas the password of *wendyHarris* is *bumble*. Notice that it is important we make usernames the key of the look-up table and *not* passwords. This is because usernames are

Table 21.2 Look-up table for users of a network

Username	Password
lauraHaliwell	unicorn
wendyHarris	bumble
bobbyMann	elephant
lucyLane	unicorn
kabirMohan	magic

unique—no two users can have the same username. However, passwords are not unique. Two or more users may have the same password. Indeed, in Table 21.2, two users (*lauraHaliwell* and *lucyLane*) do have the same password (*unicorn*).

Let's implement this kind of look-up table using a Map. There are three implementations provided for the Map interface: HashMap, TreeMap and LinkedHashMap. Here we will look at the HashMap class only.

The constructor creates the empty map:

```
Map<String, String> users = new HashMap<>();
```

As before the type of the collection is given as the interface: Map. Notice that to use the generics mechanism to fix the types used in a Map object, we must provide *two* types in the angle brackets. The first type will be the type of the key and the second the type of its associated value. In this case, *both* are String objects, but in general each may be of any object type.

21.5.1 *Map* Methods

To add a user's name and password to this map we use the put method as follows. The put method requires two parameters, the key object and the value object:

```
users.put("lauraHaliwell", "unicorn");
```

Note that the put method treats the first parameter as a key item and the second parameter as its associated value. Really, we should be a bit more careful before we add usernames and passwords into this map—only user names that are not already taken should be added. If we did not check this, we would end up overwriting a previous user's password. The containsKey method allows us to check this. This method accepts an object and returns **true** if the object is a key in the map and **false** otherwise:

```
if(users.containsKey("lauraHaliwell")) // check if username taken
{
        System.out.println("username already taken");
}
else // ok to use this username
{
        users.put("lauraHaliwell", "unicorn");
}
```

Notice we do not need to check that the password is unique as multiple users can have the same password. If we did require unique passwords the containsValue method could be used in the same way we used the containsKey method above.

Later a user might wish to change his or her password. The put method overrides the value associated with a key if that key is already present in the map. The following changes the password associated with " lauraHaliwell " to " popcorn ":

```
users.put("lauraHaliwell", "popcorn");
```

The put method returns the value that was overwritten, or **null** if there was no value before, and this can be checked if necessary.

Later, a user might be asked to enter his or her username and password before being able to access company resources. The get method can be used to check whether or not the correct password has been entered. The get method accepts an object and searches for that object among the keys of the map. If it is found, the associated value object is returned. If it is not found the **null** value is returned:

```
System.out.print("enter username ");
String nameIn = EasyScanner.nextString(); // requires EasyScanner class
System.out.print("enter password ");
String passwordIn = EasyScanner.nextString(); // requires EasyScanner class
// retrieve the actual password for this user
String password = users.get(nameIn);
// password will be 'null' if the username was invalid
if (password != null)
{
        if(passwordIn.equals(password))// check password is correct
        {
            // allow access to company resources here
        }
        else // invalid password
        {
            System.out.println ("INVALID PASSWORD!");
        }
}
else // no such user
{
        System.out.println ("INVALID USERNAME!");
}
```

As you can see, once the user has entered what they believe to be their username and password, the actual password for the given user is retrieved using the get method.

We know the password retrieved will be of type String as we created our Map by specifying that both the keys and values of the Map object would be Strings. We can then check whether this password equals the password entered by calling the equals method of the String class:

```
if(passwordIn.equals(password))
```

We have to be careful when we use the equals method to compare two objects in the way that we have done here. In this case, we are comparing the password entered by the user with the password obtained by the get method. However, the get method might have returned a **null** value instead of a password (if the key entered was invalid). The equals method of the String class does not return **false** when comparing a String with a **null** value, instead it throws a

`NullPointerException`. So, to avoid this exception, we must check the value returned by the `get` method is not **null** *before* we use the `equals` method:

```
// check password returned is not 'null' before calling 'equals' method
if (password!= null)
{
    if(passwordIn.equals(password))// now it is safe to call 'equals'
    {
        // allow access to company resources
    }
    else
    {
        System.out.println ("INVALID PASSWORD!")
    }
}
```

Note that the **null** value is always checked with primitive comparison operators (`==` for equality and `!=` for inequality).

Like all the other Java collection classes, the `HashMap` class provides a `toString` method so that the items in the map can be displayed:

```
System.out.print(users); // implicitly calls 'toString' method
```

Key and value pairs are displayed in braces. Let us assume we have added two more users: "bobbyMann" and "wendyHarris", with passwords "elephant" and "bumble", respectively. Displaying the map would produce the following output:

```
{lauraHaliwell=popcorn, wendyHarris=bumble, bobbyMann=elephant}
```

Note that the order in which the items are displayed is not determined by the order in which they were added but upon how they have been stored internally, something over which we have no control.

As with the other collections, a map provides a `remove` method. In the case of map, a key value is given to this method. If the key is present in the map both the key and value pair are removed:

```
// this removes the given key and its associated value
users.remove("lauraHaliwell");
```

Displaying the map now shows this username and associated password have been removed:

```
{wendyHarris=bumble, bobbyMann=elephant}
```

The `remove` method returns the value of the object that has been removed, or **null** if the key was not present. This value can be checked, if necessary, to confirm that the given key was in the map.

Finally, the map collection provides `size` and `isEmpty` methods that behave in exactly the same way as the `size` and `isEmpty` methods for lists.

21.5.2 Iterating Through the Elements of a Map

An enhanced **for** loop cannot directly be used with a map as it is designed for collections of single values such as arrays, lists and sets. A map, however, consists of pairs of values. To use an enhanced **for** loop with a map we can extract the *set* of keys. You are familiar with the concept of a set from Chap. 7, where we looked at Python's set collection. As you will see later in the next section, a Java Set (again a generic type) has similar properties. To extract the set of keys we use the keySet method:

```
// the keySet method returns the keys of the map as a Set object
Set<String> theKeys = users.keySet();
```

Again notice that we know this set of keys returned by the keySet method will be a set of String objects, so we mark the type of this set accordingly.

An enhanced **for** loop can now be used to iterate through the keys of the map; within the loop we can look up the associated password using the get method. For example, we might wish to display the contents of the map in our own way, rather than the format given to us by the toString method:

```
for(String username: theKeys) // iterate through the set of keys
{
    String password = users.get(item); // retrieve password value
    System.out.println(username + "\t" + password); // format output
}
```

This would display the map in the following table format:

```
lauraHaliwell          popcorn
wendyHarris            bumble
bobbyMann             elephant
```

While the enhanced **for** loop is restricted to iterating over single values, the Map class has a **forEach** method which can be used with pairs of values as well as a single value. The **forEach** method is overloaded to take a BiConsumer (see Table 21.3 for a reminder) as well as a Consumer implementation.

Here is the **forEach** implementation for displaying items in our map:

```
// the forEach loop can take two parameters, representing the key and value item of a map pair
users.forEach((username, password) -> System.out.println(username + "\t" + password));
```

Table 21.3 Reminder of the BiConsumer interface

Functional interface	Abstract method name	Parameter types	Return type
BiConsumer<T, U>	accept	T, U	void

You can see that the two parameters given to this **forEach** method represent the key and its associated value, respectively. In this case the key is the username and its associated value is a password.

21.6   The *Set* Interface and the *HashSet* Class

In most cases you will find that `ArrayList` and `HashMap` are going to be all you will need for your collections. However, we will briefly mention the `Set` interface and the corresponding `HashSet` here in case you should want to make use of a class that specifically holds unique objects. Unlike its Python equivalent, however, this class does not specifically support methods for set operations such as intersection and union.

The constructor creates an empty set. The following set, for example, could be used to store a collection of vehicle registration numbers (as `Strings`):

```
// creates an empty set of String objects
Set<String> regNums = new HashSet<>();
```

Again, notice that we have used the generics mechanism to indicate that this is a set of `String` objects, and we have given the type of this object as the interface `Set<String>`. Now we can look at some `Set` methods.

The `add` method allows us to insert objects into the set, so let us add a few registration numbers:

```
regNums.add("V53PLS");
regNums.add("X85ADZ");
regNums.add("L22SBG");
regNums.add("W79TRV");
```

We can display the entire set as follows:

```
System.out.println(regNums); // implicitly calling the toString method
```

The set is displayed in the same format as a list, in square brackets and separated by commas:

```
[W79TRV, X85ADZ, V53PLS, L22SBG]
```

Notice that, unlike lists, the order in which the items are displayed is not determined by the order in which the items were added. Instead, the set is displayed in the order in which the items are stored internally (and over which we have no control). This will not be a problem as ordering is unimportant in a set:

As with a list, the `size` method returns the number of items in the set:

```
System.out.println("Number of items in set: " + regNums.size() );
```

This would `print` the following onto the screen:

`Number of items in set: 4`

If we try to add an item that is already in the set, the set remains unchanged. Let us assume the four items above have been added into the set, and we now try and add a registration number that is already in the set:

```
regNums.add("X85ADZ"); // this number is already in the set
System.out.println(regNums);
```

When this set is displayed, `"X85ADZ"` appears only once:

`[W79TRV, X85ADZ, V53PLS, L22SBG]`

The `add` method returns a **boolean** value to indicate whether or not the given item was successfully added. This value can be checked if required.

```
boolean ok = regNums.add("X85ADZ"); // store boolean return value
if (!ok) //check if add method returned a value of false
{
        System.out.println("item already in the set!");
}
```

The `remove` method deletes an item from the set if it is present. Again, assuming that the four items given above are in the set, we can delete one item as follows:

```
regNums.remove("X85ADZ");
```

If we now display the set, the given registration will have been removed:

As with the `add` method, the `remove` method returns a **boolean** value of **false** if the given item to remove was not actually in the set. The `Set` interface also includes `contains` and `isEmpty` methods that work in exactly the same way as their `List` counterparts.

As we saw in the last section, we can iterate through a set with the enhanced **for** loop. The **forEach** method can also be used.

21.7   Using Your Own Classes with Java's Collection Classes

In the examples above, we stuck to the predefined String type for the type of objects used in the collection classes. However, objects of any class can be used inside these collections—including objects of our own classes.

21.7.1   The *Book* Class

Figure 21.1 gives the UML design for a Book class. This class consists of an ISBN number, a title and an author. An ISBN number is a unique International Standard Book Number that is allocated to each new book title. Before we deal with a *collection* of books, here is the implementation of the Book class—notice that we have included a toString method to make our testing easier.

Book.java

```java
public class Book
{
    private String isbn;
    private String title;
    private String author;

    public Book(String isbnIn, String titleIn, String authorIn)
    {
            this.isbn = isbnIn;
            this.title = titleIn;
            this.author = authorIn;
    }

    public String getISBN()
    {
            return this.isbn;
    }

    public String getTitle()
    {
            return this.title;
    }

    public String getAuthor()
    {
            return this.author;
    }

    @Override
    public String toString()
    {
        return "ISBN: " + this.isbn + "  Title: " + this.title + "  Author: " + this.author;
    }
}
```

In Chap. 8 you saw how we used a Python dictionary type to create a custom collection class to hold bank accounts. Let's do the same thing here in Java, but this time we will use our Book class and call the collection class Library:

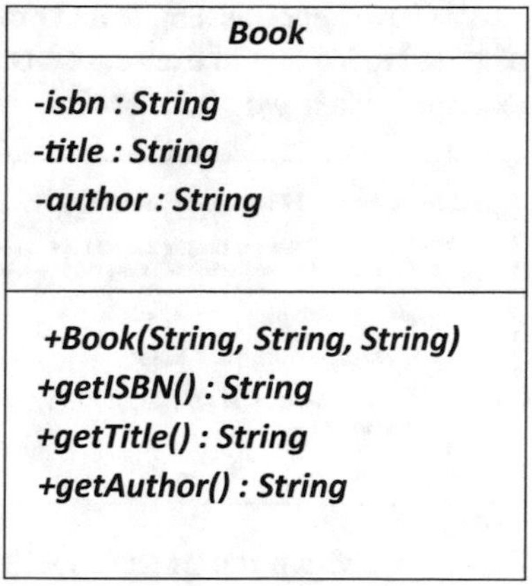

Fig. 21.1 Design of the
Book class

Book
-*isbn : String* -*title : String* -*author : String*
+*Book(String, String, String)* +*getISBN() : String* +*getTitle() : String* +*getAuthor() : String*

Library.java

```java
import java.util.Map;
import java.util.HashMap;

public class Library
{
    private Map <String, Book> books; // declare map collection

    // constructor creates empty map
    public Library()
    {
        this.books = new HashMap<> ();
    }

    // add the given book into the collection
    public boolean addBook(Book bookIn)
    {
        String keyIn = bookIn.getISBN(); // isbn will be key of map
        if (this.books.containsKey(keyIn)) // check if isbn already in use
        {
            return false; // indicate error
        }
        else // ok to add this book
        {
            this.books.put(keyIn, bookIn); // add key and book pair into map
            return true;
        }
    }

    // remove the book with the given isbn
    public boolean removeBook(String isbnIn)
    {
        Book result = this.books.remove(isbnIn);
        if (result != null) // check if item was removed
        {
            return true;
        }
        else // when item is not removed
        {
            return false;
        }
    }

    // return the book with the given isbn or null if no such book
    public Book getBook (String isbnIn)
    {
        return this.books.get(isbnIn);
    }
}
```

We have kept this simple and provided methods only to add, remove and retrieve a book. Notice that in each case a book is identified by its unique ISBN number. For example, when we add a book:

```
public boolean addBook(Book bookIn)
{
    String keyIn = bookIn.getISBN(); // isbn will be key of map
    if (this.books.containsKey(keyIn)) // check if isbn already in use
    {
        return false; // indicate error
    }
    else // ok to add this book
    {
        this.books.put(keyIn, bookIn); // add key and book pair into map
        return true;
    }
}
```

And when we retrieve a book:

```
// return the book with the given isbn or null if no such book
public Book getBook (String isbnIn)
{
    return this.books.get(isbnIn);
}
```

These methods illustrate nicely how useful a Map is in this situation—we are able to use methods such as containsKey to check if the book exists and get to retrieve the whole Book object (the value) by means of its ISBN (the key).

Here is a menu program that uses this class in a similar way to the BankApplication from Chap. 8. Note that it makes use of our EasyScanner class from Chap. 17 to obtain input:

LibraryApplication.java

```java
public class LibraryApplication
{
    public static void main(String args[])
    {
        Library library = new Library();

        char choice = '1';
        // offer menu
        while(choice != '4')
        {
            System.out.println();
            System.out.println("Library Application");
            System.out.println("1. Add new book");
            System.out.println("2. Remove a book");
            System.out.println("3. Get details of a book");
            System.out.println("4. Quit");
            System.out.println();
            System.out.print("Enter choice [1-4]: ");

            // get choice
            choice = EasyScanner.nextChar();
            System.out.println();

            // process menu options
            switch(choice)
            {
                case '1':
                    option1(library);
                    break;
                case '2':
                    option2(library);
                    break;
                case '3':
                    option3(library);
                    break;
                case '4':
                    System.out.println("Goodbye");
                    break;
                default:
                    System.out.println("Options 1-4 only");
            }
        }
    }
    // add book
    static void option1(Library libraryIn)
    {

        // get details from user
```

```
        System.out.print("Enter ISBN: ");
        String isbn = EasyScanner.nextString();
        System.out.print("Enter title: ");
        String title = EasyScanner.nextString();
        System.out.print("Enter author: ");
        String author = EasyScanner.nextString();
        // add book to list
        boolean success = libraryIn.addBook(new Book(isbn, title, author));
        if(success)
        {
            System.out.println("Book added");
        }
        else
        {
            System.out.println("Book with that ISBN already exists");
        }
    }

    // remove book
    static void option2(Library libraryIn)
    {
        // get ISBN of book to remove
        System.out.print("Enter ISBN of book to remove: ");
        String isbn = EasyScanner.nextString();
        // delete item if it exists
        boolean found = libraryIn.removeBook(isbn);
        if(found)
        {
            System.out.println("Book removed");
        }
        else
        {
            System.out.println("No such ISBN");
        }
    }

    // get book details
    static void option3(Library libraryIn)
    {
        // get ISBN of book from user
        System.out.print("Enter ISBN of book to display: ");
        String isbn = EasyScanner.nextString();
        Book book = libraryIn.getBook(isbn);
        if(book != null)
        {
            System.out.println("ISBN: " + book.getISBN());
            System.out.println("Title: " + book.getTitle());
            System.out.println("Author: " + book.getAuthor());
            System.out.println();
        }
        else
        {
            System.out.println("No such ISBN");
        }
    }
}
```

There is nothing very new here, so you should be able to understand how this works. Here is a sample run:

```
Library Application

1. Add new book
2. Remove a book
3. Get details of a book
4. Quit

Enter choice [1-4]: 1

Enter ISBN: 11111111

Enter title: Keeping Warm
Enter author: Anita Duzzit
Book added

Library Application
1. Add new book
2. Remove a book
3. Get details of a book
4. Quit

Enter choice [1-4]: 1

Enter ISBN: 22222222
Enter title: Robotics
Enter author: Ann Droid
Book added

Library Application
1. Add new book
2. Remove a book
3. Get details of a book
4. Quit

Enter choice [1-4]: 1

Enter ISBN: 33333333
Enter title: The Fall from the Cliff
Enter author: Eileen Dover
Book added
```

```
Library Application
1. Add new book
2. Remove a book
3. Get details of a book
4. Quit

Enter choice [1-4]: 3

Enter ISBN of book to remove: 22222222
ISBN: 22222222
Title: Robotics
Author: Ann Droid


Library Application
1. Add new book
2. Remove a book
3. Get details of a book
4. Quit

Enter choice [1-4]: 2

Enter ISBN of book to remove: 33333333
Book removed
 Library Application
 1. Add new book
 2. Remove a book
 3. Get details of a book
 4. Quit

Enter choice [1-4]: 3

Enter ISBN of book to remove: 33333333
No such ISBN

Library Application
1. Add new book
2. Remove a book
3. Get details of a book
4. Quit

Enter choice [1-4]: 4

Goodbye
```

21.7.2 An Alternative Implementation

Using a Map type for our Library class in the last section worked very well and is a good choice for objects that have a unique key. However, it is, of course, by no means the only way we could have implemented it. An alternative version of Library which uses an ArrayList is shown below:

AlternativeLibrary.java

```java
import java.util.ArrayList;
import java.util.List;

public class AlternativeLibrary
{
    private List <Book> books; // declare list collection

    // constructor creates empty ArrayList
    public AlternativeLibrary()
    {
        this.books = new ArrayList<> ();
    }

    // add the given book into the collection
    public boolean addBook(Book bookIn)
    {
        for(Book item : books)
        {
            if(item.getISBN().equals(bookIn.getISBN())) // book exists
            {
                return false;
            }
        }
        // ok to add this book
        this.books.add(bookIn); // add book into list
        return true;
    }

    // remove the book with the given isbn
    public boolean removeBook(String isbnIn)
    {
        for(int i = 0; i < books.size(); i++)
        {
            if(this.books.get(i).getISBN().equals(isbnIn)) // check if the item matches
            {
                books.remove(i);
                return true;
            }
        }
        return false;
    }

    // return the book with the given isbn or null if no such book
    public Book getBook (String isbnIn)
    {
        for(int i = 0; i < books.size(); i++)
        {
            if(this.books.get(i).getISBN().equals(isbnIn))
            {
                return books.get(i);
            }
        }
        return null;
    }
}
```

As you can see, we have now declared and instantiated a `List` where before we had a `Map`:

```
private List <Book> books; // declare list collection

// constructor creates empty ArrayList
public AlternativeLibrary()
{
    this.books = new ArrayList<> ();
}
```

Look through this class carefully and compare the methods with those of the previous implementation. Notice particularly how we have had to use **for** loops to iterate through the list, whereas previously we used `Map` methods. For example, when we remove a book from the list:

Original version using **Map**	New version using **List**

<pre>public boolean removeBook(String isbnIn)
{
    Book result = this.books.remove(isbnIn);
    if (result != null)
    {
        return true;
    }
    else
    {
        return false;
    }
}</pre>
	<pre>public boolean removeBook(String isbnIn)
	{
	    for(int i = 0; i < books.size(); i++)
	    {
	        if(this.books.get(i).getISBN().equals(isbnIn))
	        {
	            books.remove(i);
	            return true;
	        }
	    }
	    return false;
	}</pre>

21.8   Sorting a Collection

One of the things we often need to do with a list is to sort it. Most commonly, this involves items that have a "natural" sort order—in other words, characters, strings and numerical values.

Sorting a collection can involve complex algorithms. Luckily Java provides two classes that contain class methods to sort our ordered collections: the `Collections` class which we can use with lists and the `Arrays` class for use with arrays. Take a look at the program below:

StringSortDemo.java

```
import java.util.Collections;
import java.util.Arrays;
import java.util.List;

public class StringSortDemo
{
    public static void main(String[] args)
    {
        // create array of strings
        String[] citysArray = {"London", "Birmingham", "Manchester", "Liverpool"};
        // convert array to List using Arrays.asList
        List<String> citysList = Arrays.asList(citysArray);
        // display List
        System.out.println("Original List " + citysList);
        // sort List
        Collections.sort(citysList);
        // display List
        System.out.println("Sorted List " + citysList);
    }
}
```

The first thing we have done is to create an array of strings:

```
// create array of strings
String[] citysArray = {"London", "Birmingham", "Manchester", "Liverpool"};
```

The `Arrays` utility class has a useful class method called `asList`, which converts an array to a `List`. We have used that method here and then displayed the list:

```
// convert array to List using asList
List<String> citysList = Arrays.asList(citysArray);
// display List
System.out.println("Original List " + citysList);
```

Next we use the `sort` method to re-order our list, which we then display:

```
// sort List
Collections.sort(citysList);
// display List
System.out.println("Sorted List " + citysList);
```

As expected, the output is as follows:

```
Original List [London, Birmingham, Manchester, Liverpool]
Sorted List [Birmingham, Liverpool, London, Manchester]
```

The output from this program is shown below:

```
Original List [London, Birmingham, Manchester, Liverpool]
Sorted List [Birmingham, Liverpool, London, Manchester]
```

Note that had we wanted to sort the array, we would have used the `Arrays.sort` method.

21.8.1   Sorting Other Objects

We all know what we mean when we talk about sorting strings or numerical values. However, imagine we wanted to sort something like our Book objects. What does that mean? It could mean various things—we could sort by ISBN, by author or by title.

The List interface has a very useful method called sort, which receives an item of a functional interface called Comparator<T>. As this is a functional interface it means we can send in a lambda expression. This lambda expression would involve quite a complicated sorting algorithm, but fortunately, the whole thing has been simplified for us by the existence of a static method of Comparator called comparing, which makes it easy for us to send in the key on which we want the sort to be based.

An example will make this clear.

BookSort.java

```java
import java.util.ArrayList;
import java.util.Comparator;
import java.util.List;

public class BookSort
{
    public static void main(String[] args)
    {
        List<Book> bookList = new ArrayList<>();

        Book book1 = new Book("111111111", "Keeping Warm", "Anita Duzzit");
        Book book2 = new Book("222222222", "Falling off the cliff", "Eileen Dover");
        Book book3 = new Book("333333333", "Robotics", "Ann Droid");

        bookList.add(book1);
        bookList.add(book2);
        bookList.add(book3);

        // sort by ISBN
        bookList.sort(Comparator.comparing(Book::getISBN));
        System.out.println("Sorted by ISBN");
        for(Book item: bookList)
        {
            System.out.println(item);
        }
        System.out.println();

        // sort by title
        bookList.sort(Comparator.comparing(Book::getTitle));
        System.out.println("Sorted by Title");
        for(Book item: bookList)
        {
            System.out.println(item);
        }
        System.out.println();

        // sort by author
        bookList.sort(Comparator.comparing(Book::getAuthor));
        System.out.println("Sorted by Author");
        for(Book item: bookList)
        {
            System.out.println(item);
        }

        System.out.println();
    }
}
```

As you can see, we have created an `ArrayList` of books, to which we have added three books. We are going to sort the books by ISBN, then by title, then by author. Here is the routine that sorts according to ISBN:

```
bookList.sort(Comparator.comparing(Book::getISBN));
```

All we have had to do is to send in a lambda expression that calls the method that returns the appropriate attribute. Since all we are doing is calling a method of an existing class, we have been able to use the double colon notation that you learnt about in Chap. 19. The same format has been used in the subsequent instructions to sort on title and then on author.

The output is as expected:

```
Sorted by ISBN
ISBN: 111111111  Title: Keeping Warm  Author: Anita Duzzit
ISBN: 222222222  Title: Falling off the cliff  Author: Eileen Dover
ISBN: 333333333  Title: Robotics  Author: Ann Droid

Sorted by Title
ISBN: 222222222  Title: Falling off the cliff  Author: Eileen Dover
ISBN: 111111111  Title: Keeping Warm  Author: Anita Duzzit
ISBN: 333333333  Title: Robotics  Author: Ann Droid

Sorted by Author
ISBN: 111111111  Title: Keeping Warm  Author: Anita Duzzit
ISBN: 333333333  Title: Robotics  Author: Ann Droid
ISBN: 222222222  Title: Falling off the cliff  Author: Eileen Dover
```

The `comparing` method will work on numeric attributes too (such as **doubles**, **int**s and **long**s). In this case we should use specific `comparing` methods for these types (`comparingDouble`, `comparingInt`, `comparingLong`, etc.).

21.9   Self-test Questions

1. Distinguish between the following types of collection in the Java Collections Framework:

   - `List`;
   - `Map`;
   - `Set`.

2. Consider the following fragment of code:

```
List<Integer> someList = new ArrayList<>();

someList.add(43);
someList.add(2);
someList.add(1);
someList.add(27);
someList.add(9);
```

(a) Explain why the type of the list is Integer rather than **int**,

```
System.out.println(someList.size());
```

(b) What would be displayed as a result of executing the following line of code?

```
System.out.println(someList.get(2));
```

(c) What would happen if you tried to execute the following statement?

```
System.out.println(someList.get(6));
```

(d) Write a **for** loop that will double the value of every item in someList.
(e) Explain why, in the above example, it would not be appropriate to use an enhanced **for** loop.
(f) Use an enhanced **for** loop to display the values inside the list.
(g) Modify the enhanced **for** loop above so that only numbers greater than 2 are displayed.
(h) Write a line of code that will sort the list into numerical order.
3. Consider the following instruction:

```
Map <String, Student> javaStudents = new HashMap<>();
```

(a) Why is the type of this object given as Map and not HashMap?
(b) Assuming the object javaStudents has been created as above, why would the following line cause a compiler error?

```
javaStudents.put("u0012345", "Jeet");
```

4. In Sect. 21.6 a set called `regNums` was created to store a collection of car registration numbers.

   (a) Write a fragment of code that makes use of an enhanced **for** loop to display all registrations ending in 'S'.

   (b) Rewrite the above fragment so that it makes use of a **forEach** loop instead of a **for** loop.

5. What would be the output from the following programs? (Bear in mind that the order in which items appear is not predictable)

   (a)

Ages1.java

```java
import java.util.Map;
import java.util.Set;

public class Ages1
{
    public static void main(String[] args)
    {
        Map<String, Integer> ages = new HashMap<>();
        ages.put("Katherine", 21);
        ages.put("Abdul", 20);
        ages.put("Maria", 20);

        int sum = 0;

        Set<String> names = ages.keySet();

        for(String item: names)
        {
            sum = sum + ages.get(item);
        }
        System.out.println(sum);
    }
}
```

   (b)

Ages2.java

```java
import java.util.HashMap;
import java.util.Map;
import java.util.Set;

public class Ages2
{
    public static void main(String[] args)
    {
        Map<String, Integer> ages = new HashMap<>();
        ages.put("Katherine", 21);
        ages.put("Abdul", 20);
        ages.put("Maria", 20);

        ages.put("Abdul", 40);
        ages.put("Maria", 25);

        int sum = 0;

        Set<String> names = ages.keySet();

        for(String item: names)
        {
            sum = sum + ages.get(item);
        }
        System.out.println(sum);
    }
}
```

21.10 Programming Exercises

1. Implement the programs in this chapter in order to make sure you have understood them.
2. Implement the programs from question 5 above to check your answers.
3. In Sect. 6.4 you saw a waiting list program implemented in Python.
   (a) Rewrite this program in Java.
   (b) Design and write the code for an additional function, initialLetter, which displays all the names beginning with a particular letter (sent in as a parameter). Write a new menu option to include that will allow the user to choose the letter.
4. In Sect. 6.7 you saw the implementation of a stack in Python.
   (a) Implement the stack in Java. You will need to choose a particular data type that is held in the stack.
   (b) Convert this program to a queue.
5. Consider an application that keeps track of the registration numbers of all cars that have a permit to use a company car park. It also keeps track of the registration numbers of the cars actually in the car park at any one time. While there is no limit to the number of cars that can have permits to park in the car park, the capacity of the car park is limited. Below we give the UML design for the CarRegister class:

```
┌─────────────────────────────────────────┐
│              CarRegister                 │
├─────────────────────────────────────────┤
│ -permit : ArrayList<String>              │
│ -parked : ArrayList<String>              │
│ -capacity : int                          │
├─────────────────────────────────────────┤
│ +CarRegister(int)                        │
│ +hasPermit(String) : boolean             │
│ +isParked(String) : boolean              │
│ +isFull( ) : boolean                     │
│ +givePermit (String) : boolean           │
│ +recordParking(String) : boolean         │
│ +recordExit (String) : boolean           │
│ +numberParked() : int                    │
│ +getPermit() : List<String>              │
│ +getParked() : List<String>              │
│ +getCapacity() : int                     │
└─────────────────────────────────────────┘
```

A description of each CarRegister method is given below:

+CarRegister(int)
Initializes the permit and parked lists to be empty and sets the capacity of the car park with the given parameter.

+hasPermit(String) : boolean

Returns **true** if the car with the given registration has a permit and **false** otherwise.

+isParked(String) : boolean

Returns **true** if the car with the given registration is recorded as being parked in the car park and **false** otherwise.

+isFull() : boolean

Returns **true** if the car park is full and **false** otherwise.

+givePermit(String) : boolean

Records the registration of a car given a permit to park. Returns **false** if the car has already been given a permit and **true** otherwise.

+recordParking(String) : boolean

Records the registration of a car entering the car park. Returns **false** if the car park is full, if the car is already parked or the car has no permit to enter the car park, and **true** otherwise.

+recordExit (String) : boolean

Records the registration of a car leaving the car park. Returns **false** if the car was not initially registered as being parked and **true** otherwise.

+numberParked() : int

Returns the number of cars currently in the car park.

+getPermit() : List<String>

Returns the list of car registrations allocated permits.

getParked() : List<String>

Returns the list of registration numbers of cars in the car park.

+getCapacity() : int

Returns the maximum capacity of the car park.

(a) Implement the CarRegister class.

(b) Test the CarRegister class with a suitable tester.

Java: Working with Files

22

Outcomes

By the end of this chapter you should be able to:

- *explain the principles of **input** and **output** and identify a number of different input and output devices;*
- *explain the concept of an **I/O stream**;*
- *describe the basic file-handling techniques used in the Java language;*
- *distinguish between **text**, **binary** and **object** encoding of data;*
- *distinguish between **serial** access files and **random** access files;*
- *create and access files in Java using all the above encoding and access methods.*

22.1 Introduction

In Chap. 10 you learnt how to use Python's file-handling mechanisms—now we will learn how to do this in Java. In that chapter you were also introduced to a number of concepts and terms, and these apply generally, no matter what programming language we are using.

In this chapter we will use Java to achieve similar results to those we achieved with Python. As with Python, Java has facilities for both text and binary encoding. However, there is one additional means of encoding in Java, namely **object** encoding. This allows us to read and write whole objects—providing the files are accessed only within a Java program. In Chap. 12 you saw that the algorithms that we had to devise for reading and writing objects were quite complex, so the possibility of reading and writing whole objects really does make things a great deal easier.

Supplementary Information The online version contains supplementary material available at https://doi.org/10.1007/978-3-031-01326-3_22.

22.2   File Handling in Java

As you learnt in Chap. 10, the output process—which consists of transferring data
from memory to a file—is usually referred to as **writing**; the input process—which
consists of transferring data from a file to memory—is referred to as **reading**. We
pointed out in Chap. 10 that both of these involve some low-level detail to do with
the way in which data is stored physically on the disk, and which, as programmers,
we would prefer not to worry about any more than is necessary. As was the case
with Python, Java makes it quite easy for us to deal with these processes. As we
shall see, Java provides low-level classes which create file streams. It also provides
higher-level classes which we can "wrap around" the low-level objects, enabling us
to use methods that relate more closely to our logical way of thinking about data. In
this way we are shielded from having to know too much detail about the way our
particular system stores and retrieves data to or from a file.

22.3   Reading and Writing to Text Files

In this section we are going to use as an example a very simple class called Car; the
code for this class is given below:

Car.java

```java
public class Car
{
    private String registration;
    private String make;
    private double price;

    public Car(String registrationIn, String makeIn, double priceIn)
    {
        this.registration = registrationIn;
        this.make = makeIn;
        this.price = priceIn;
    }

    public String getRegistration()
    {
        return this.registration;
    }

    public String getMake()
    {
        return this.make;
    }

    public double getPrice()
    {
        return this.price;
    }
}
```

The program below, TextFileTester, is a simple menu-driven program that
manipulates a list of cars, held in memory as a List; it provides the facility to add new
cars to the list, to remove cars from the list and to display the details of all the cars in the
list. As it is a demonstration program only, we have not bothered with such things as
input validation, or checking if the list is empty before we try to remove an item.

The program is designed so that reading and writing to the file take place as
follows: when the quit option is selected, the list is written as a permanent text file
called Cars.txt; each time the program is run, this file is read into memory. This
is similar to the strategy that we used with our case study in Chap. 12.

The program is presented below; notice that we have provided two helper methods, `writeList` and `readList` for the purpose of accessing the file; as we shall explain, the `writeList` method also deals with creating the file for the first time. Notice also that, for convenience, we are making use of the `EasyScanner` class that we developed in Chap. 17.

TextFileTester.java

```java
// makes use of EasyScanner class

import java.io.BufferedReader;
import java.io.FileNotFoundException;
import java.io.FileReader;
import java.io.FileWriter;
import java.io.IOException;
import java.io.PrintWriter;
import java.util.ArrayList;
import java.util.List;

public class TextFileTester
{
    public static void main(String[] args)
    {
        char choice;

        // create an empty list to hold Cars
        List<Car> carList = new ArrayList<>();

        // read the list from file when the program starts
        readList(carList);

        // menu options
        do
        {
            System.out.println("\nText File Tester");
            System.out.println("1. Add a car");
            System.out.println("2. Remove a car");
            System.out.println("3. List all cars");
            System.out.println("4. Quit\n");
            choice = EasyScanner.nextChar();
            System.out.println(); switch(choice)
            {
                case '1' : addCar(carList);
                        break;
                case '2' : removeCar(carList);
                        break;
                case '3' : listAll(carList);
                        break;
                case '4' : writeList(carList); // write to the file
                        break;
                default : System.out.print("\nPlease choose a number from 1 - 4 only\n ");
            }
        }while(choice != '4');
    }

    // method for adding a new car to the list
    static void addCar(List<Car> carListIn)
    {
        String tempReg;
        String tempMake;
        double tempPrice;

        System.out.print("Please enter the registration number: ");
        tempReg = EasyScanner.nextString();
        System.out.print("Please enter the make: ");
        tempMake = EasyScanner.nextString();
        System.out.print("Please enter the price: ");
        tempPrice = EasyScanner.nextDouble();
        carListIn.add(new Car(tempReg, tempMake, tempPrice));
    }

    /* method for removing a car from the list - in a real application this would need to include
       some validation */
    static void removeCar(List<Car> carListIn)
    {
        int pos;
        System.out.print("Enter the position of the car to be removed: ");
        pos = EasyScanner.nextInt();
        carListIn.remove(pos - 1);
    }

    // method for listing details of all cars in the list
    static void listAll(List<Car> carListIn)
    {
        for(Car item : carListIn)
        {
            System.out.println(item.getRegistration()
            + " "
            + item.getMake()
```

```
                    + " "
                    + item.getPrice());
            }
        }

        // method for writing the file
        static void writeList(List<Car> carListIn)
        {
            // use try-with-resources to ensure file is closed safely
            try(
                    /* create a FileWriter object, carFile, that handles the low-level details of writing
                    the list to a file which we have called "Cars.txt" */
                    FileWriter carFile = new FileWriter("Cars.txt");
                    /* now create a PrintWriter object to wrap around carFile; this allows us to user
                    high-level functions such as println */
                    PrintWriter carWriter = new PrintWriter(carFile);
                )
            {
                // write each element of the list to the file
                for(Car item : carListIn)
                {
                    carWriter.println(item.getRegistration());
                    carWriter.println(item.getMake());
                    carWriter.println(item.getPrice()); // println can accept a double, and write it as a string
                }
            }
            // handle the exception thrown by the FileWriter methods
            catch(IOException e)
            {
                System.out.println("There was a problem writing the file");
            }
        }

        // method for reading the file
        static void readList(List<Car> carListIn)
        {
            String tempReg;
            String tempMake;
            String tempStringPrice;
            double tempDoublePrice;

            // use try-with-resources to ensure file is closed safely
            try(
                    /* create a FileReader object, carFile, that handles the lowlevel details of reading
                    the list from the "Cars.txt" file */
                    FileReader carFile = new FileReader("Cars.txt");
                    /* now create a BufferedReader object to wrap around carFile; this allows us to user
                    high-level functions such as readLine */
                    BufferedReader carStream = new BufferedReader(carFile);
                )
            {
                // read the first line of the file
                tempReg = carStream.readLine();
                /* read the rest of the first record, then all the rest of the records until the end of
                    the file is reached */
                while(tempReg != null) // a null string indicates end of file
                {
                    tempMake = carStream.readLine();
                    tempStringPrice = carStream.readLine();
                    // as this is a text file we have to convert the price to double
                    tempDoublePrice = Double.parseDouble(tempStringPrice);
                    carListIn.add(new Car(tempReg, tempMake, tempDoublePrice));
                    tempReg = carStream.readLine();
                }
            }

            // handle the exception that is thrown by the FileReader constructor if the file is not found
            catch(FileNotFoundException e)
            {
                System.out.println("\nNo file was read");
            }

            // handle the exception thrown by the FileReader methods
            catch(IOException e)
            {
                System.out.println("\nThere was a problem reading the file");
            }
        }
    }
}
```

It is only the `writeList` and `readList` methods that we need to analyse here—none of the other methods involves anything new. Let's start with `writeList`:

```
// method for writing the file
static void writeList(List<Car> carListIn)
{
    // use try-with-resources to ensure file is closed safely
    try(
            /* create a FileWriter object, carFile, that handles the low-level details of writing
               the list to a file which we have called "Cars.txt" */
            FileWriter carFile = new FileWriter("Cars.txt");
            /* now create a PrintWriter object to wrap around carFile; this allows us to user
               high-level functions such as println */
            PrintWriter carWriter = new PrintWriter(carFile);
        )
    {
        // write each element of the list to the file
        for(Car item : carListIn)
        {
            carWriter.println(item.getRegistration());
            carWriter.println(item.getMake());
            carWriter.println(item.getPrice()); // println can accept a double, and write it as a string
        }
    }
    // handle the exception thrown by the FileWriter methods
    catch(IOException e)
    {
        System.out.println("There was a problem writing the file");
    }
}
```

The first thing to notice is that we have enclosed everything in a **try** block. Here we are creating our files using the *try-with-resources* mechanism that was introduced to you in Chap. 20. We use this because the file has to be closed after we finish using it. Closing the file achieves two things. First, it ensures that a special character, the end-of-file marker,[1] is written at the end of the file. This enables us to detect when the end of the file has been reached when we are reading it—more about this when we explore the readList method. Second, closing the file means that it is no longer accessible by the program and is therefore not susceptible to being written to in error.

Using *try-with-resources* ensures that the file is always closed, no matter what other errors or exceptions may have occurred—before the advent of *try-with-resources* we would have had to specifically close the file by calling the close method of PrintWriter (this would have been done in a **finally** clause). As you can see, the instructions for opening the file have been placed in the brackets after the **try** keyword. We will use *try-with-resources* to create and open files throughout this chapter.

The file is opened by using a class called FileWriter; this is one of the classes we talked about earlier that provide the low-level communication between the program and the file. By opening a file we establish a *stream* through which we can output data to the file. We create a FileWriter object, carFile, giving it the name of the file to which we want to write the data:

```
FileWriter carFile = new FileWriter("Cars.txt");
```

---

[1] Most systems use Unicode character 26 as the end-of-file marker.

In this case we have called the file Cars.txt.[2] Creating the new File-
Writer object causes the file to be opened in output mode—meaning that it is
ready to receive data; if no file of this name exists, then one will be created.
Opening the file in this way (in output mode) means that any data that we write to
the file will wipe out what was previously there. That is what we need for this
particular application, because we are simply going to write the entire list when the
program terminates. Sometimes, however, it is necessary to open a file in **append**
mode; in this mode any data written to the file would be written after the existing
data. To do this, we would simply have used another constructor, which takes an
additional (**boolean**) parameter indicating whether or not we require append
mode:

```
FileWriter carFile = new FileWriter("Cars.txt", true);
```

The next thing we do is create an object, carWriter, of the PrintWriter
class, sending it the carFile object as a parameter.

```
PrintWriter carWriter = new PrintWriter(carFile);
```

This object can now communicate with our file via the carFile object;
PrintWriter objects have higher-level methods than FileWriter objects
(e.g. print and println) that enable us to write whole strings like we do when
we output to the screen.

Now we are ready to write each Car in the list to our file—we can use an
enhanced **for** loop for this:

```
for(Car item : carListIn)
{
    carWriter.println(item.getRegistration());
    carWriter.println(item.getMake());
    carWriter.println(item.getPrice());
}
```

On each iteration we use the println method of our PrintWriter object,
carWriter, to write the registration number, the make and the price of the car to
the file; println converts the price to a String before writing it. Notice also
that the println method inserts a newline character at the end of the string that it
prints; if we did not want the newline character to be inserted, we would use the
print method instead.

Finally we have to handle any IOExceptions that may be thrown by the
FileWriter methods:

---

[2] As we have not supplied an absolute pathname, the file will be saved in the current directory.

```
catch(IOException e)
{
    System.out.println("There was a problem writing the file");
}
```

In a moment we will explore the code for reading the file. But bear in mind that if we were to run our program and add a few records, and then quit the program we would have saved the data to a text file called Cars.txt, so we should be able to read this file with a text editor. When we did this, we created three cars and then looked inside the file using Windows™ Notepad. Figure 22.1 shows the result.

As we have written each field using the println statement, each one, as you can see, starts on a new line. If our aim was to view the file with a text editor as we have just done, then this might not be the most suitable format—we might, for example, have wanted to have one record per line; we could also have printed some headings if we had wished. However, it is actually our intention to make our program read the entire file into our list when the program starts—and as we shall now see, one field per line makes reading the text file nice and easy. So let's take a look at our readList method:

```
// method for reading the file
static void readList(List<Car> carListIn)
{
    String tempReg;
    String tempMake;
    String tempStringPrice;
    double tempDoublePrice;

    // use try-with-resources to ensure file is closed safely
    try(
            /* create a FileReader object, carFile, that handles the lowlevel details of reading
               the list from the "Cars.txt" file */
            FileReader carFile = new FileReader("Cars.txt");
            /* now create a BufferedReader object to wrap around carFile; this allows us to user
               high-level functions such as readLine */
            BufferedReader carStream = new BufferedReader(carFile);
        )
    {
        // read the first line of the file
        tempReg = carStream.readLine();
        /* read the rest of the first record, then all the rest of the records until the end of
           the file is reached */
        while(tempReg != null) // a null string indicates end of file
        {
            tempMake = carStream.readLine();
            tempStringPrice = carStream.readLine();
            // as this is a text file we have to convert the price to double
            tempDoublePrice = Double.parseDouble(tempStringPrice);
            carListIn.add(new Car(tempReg, tempMake, tempDoublePrice));
            tempReg = carStream.readLine();
        }
    }

    // handle the exception that is thrown by the FileReader constructor if the file is not found
    catch(FileNotFoundException e)
    {
        System.out.println("\nNo file was read");
    }

    // handle the exception thrown by the FileReader methods
    catch(IOException e)
    {
        System.out.println("\nThere was a problem reading the file");
    }
}
```

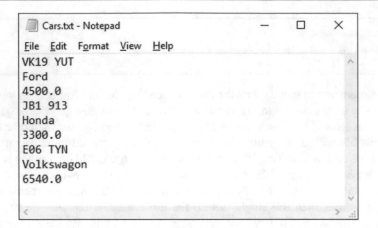

Fig. 22.1 Viewing a text file with Windows Notepad

First, we have declared some variables to hold the value of each field as we progressively read through the file. Remembering that this is a text file we have declared three `Strings`:

```
String tempReg;
String tempMake;
String tempStringPrice;
```

The last of these will have to be converted to a **double** before we store it in the list, so we also need a variable to hold this value once it is converted:

```
double tempDoublePrice;
```

Now, as before, we put everything into a **try** block, as we are going to have to deal with the exceptions that may be thrown by the various methods we will be using. Again we are using *try-with-resources*, so the process of opening the file is place in the brackets after the **try**. As you can see from the code, we start by creating an object—carFile—of the class `FileReader` which deals with the low-level details involved in the process of reading a file. The name of the file, `Cars.txt`, that we wish to read is sent in as a parameter to the constructor; this file is then opened in read mode.

```
FileReader carFile = new FileReader("Cars.txt");
```

Now, in order that we can use some higher-level read methods, we wrap up our carFile object in an object of a class called `BufferedReader`. We have called this new object carStream.

```
BufferedReader carStream = new BufferedReader(carFile);
```

Now we are going to read each field of each record in turn, so we will need some sort of loop. The only problem is to know when to stop—this is because the number of records in the file can be different each time we run the program. There are different ways in which to approach this problem. One very good way (although not the one we have used here), if the same program is responsible for both reading and writing the file, is simply to write the total number of records as the first item when the file is written. Then, when reading the file, this item is the first thing to be read —and once this number is known, a **for** loop can be used to read the records.

However, it may well be the case that the file was written by another program (such as a text editor). In this case it is necessary to check for the end-of-file marker that we spoke about earlier. In order to help you understand this process we are using this method here, even though we could have used the first (and perhaps simpler) method.

This is what we have to do: we have to read the first field of each record, then check whether that field began with the end-of-file marker. If it did, we must stop reading the file, but if it didn't we have to carry on and read the remaining fields of that record. Then we start the process again for the next record.

Some pseudocode should make the process clear; we have made this pseudocode specific to our particular example:

```
READ the registration number field of the first record
LOOP while the field just read does not contain the end-of-file marker
    READ the make field of the next record
    READ the price field of the next record
    CONVERT the price to a double
    CREATE a new car with details just read and add it to the list
    READ the registration number field of the next record
```

The code for this is shown below:

```
tempReg = carStream.readLine();
while(tempReg != null) // a null string indicates end of file
{
    tempMake = carStream.readLine();
    tempStringPrice = carStream.readLine();
    tempDoublePrice = Double.parseDouble(tempStringPrice);
    carListIn.add (new Car(tempReg, tempMake, tempDoublePrice));
    tempReg = carStream.readLine();
}
```

Notice that we are using the readLine method of BufferedReader to read each record. This method reads a line of text from the file; a line is considered anything that is terminated by the newline character. The method returns that line as a String (which does not include the newline character). However, if the line read consists of the end-of-file marker, then readLine returns a **null**, making it very easy for us to check if the end of the file has been reached. In Sect. 22.5 you will be able to contrast this method of BufferedReader with the read method, which reads a single character only.

Finally, we must handle any exceptions that may be thrown by the methods of `FileReader`; first, the constructor throws a `FileNotFoundException` if the file is not found:

```
catch(FileNotFoundException e)
{
    System.out.println("\nNo file was read");
}
```

All the other methods may throw `IOExceptions`:

```
catch(IOException e)
{
    System.out.println("\nThere was a problem reading the file");
}
```

22.4   Reading and Writing to Binary Files

As we know from Chap. 10, when we refer to binary files, we are usually referring to non-text files such audio, video or image files—although of course, as we mentioned in Chap. 10, all files, including text files, are stored in binary format, so the process below can be used for any file. The following program makes a copy of an image file, `sunset.jpg`, to a new file `sunsetCopy.jpg`.

CopyBinaryFile.java

```java
import java.io.FileInputStream;
import java.io.FileNotFoundException;
import java.io.FileOutputStream;
import java.io.IOException;

public class CopyBinaryFile
{
    public static void main(String[] args)
    {
        // use try-with-resources
        try(FileInputStream  picFileIn = new FileInputStream("sunset.jpg"); // open for reading
            FileOutputStream picFileOut = new FileOutputStream("sunsetCopy.jpg");) //open for writing
        {
            byte[] buffer = new byte[10]; // create a 10 byte buffer
            int bytesRead = picFileIn.read(buffer); // read ahead
            while(bytesRead > 0) // stop when no more data available
            {
                picFileOut.write(buffer, 0, bytesRead); // write bytesRead number of bytes
                bytesRead = picFileIn.read(buffer);
            }
        }

        // handle exceptions
        catch(FileNotFoundException e)
        {
            System.out.println("\nFile not found");
        }

        catch(IOException e)
        {
            System.out.println("There was a problem writing the file");
        }

    }
}
```

Our strategy is to read and write the files in 10 byte chunks.

The low-level classes that allow us to read and write binary files are `FileInputStream` and `FileOutputStream`, respectively. The `read` method of `FileInputStream` receives an array of bytes and reads the number of bytes indicated by the length of that array and places them into the array. If the number of bytes remaining is less than the array length, the array will be partially filled; the method returns the number of bytes read.

So let's take a look at the **try** block:

```
// use try-with-resources
try(FileInputStream  picFileIn = new FileInputStream("sunset.jpg"); // open for reading
    FileOutputStream picFileOut = new FileOutputStream("sunsetCopy.jpg");)  //open for writing
{
    byte[] buffer = new byte[10]; // create a 10 byte buffer
    int bytesRead = picFileIn.read(buffer); // read ahead
    while(bytesRead > 0) // stop when no more data available
    {
        picFileOut.write(buffer, 0, bytesRead); // write bytesRead number of bytes
        bytesRead = picFileIn.read(buffer);
    }
}
```

As you can see, we have opened the files within a try-with-resources construct and associated them with the image files that we want to read and write.

We have declared an array of 10 bytes, called `buffer`, to hold the bytes read.

We read ahead and place the number of bytes read into a variable called `bytesRead`. We then begin a **while** loop that ends when the number of bytes last read is zero. Within the **while** loop we call the `write` method of `FileOutputStream`. The version we have used takes three parameters. The first is the byte array that is to be written. The second is the start position (index zero), and the final one is the position before which we stop. For example if the buffer contained seven bytes (index 0 to index 6), our start position would be 0, and our end position would be 7, since the end position is not included. The reason we have used this version, rather than writing the whole buffer every time, is that on the final iteration the buffer might contain fewer than ten bytes, because the total number of bytes is unlikely to be a multiple of 10.

Once we have written to our buffer, we read the next 10 bytes. This continues until there is no more data to read.

So in our case we continuously read 10 bytes from `sunset.jpg` and write them to `sunsetCopy.jpg` until the end of the file is reached.

Two **catch** blocks are defined to handle read and write exceptions, respectively.

If you run this program, you will see that a copy of your original file will appear.

22.5   Reading a Text File Character by Character

As you will have realized by now, there are many ways in which we can deal with handling files, and the methods we choose will depend largely on what it is we want to achieve.

In the last section we showed you how to read a specific number of bytes from a binary file. In this section we will show you how to read a text file character by character—this is a useful technique if we do not know anything about the structure of the file.

We have written an application which reads a text file, Poem.txt, character by character—each time the character is read it is displayed on the screen. The process continues until the end of the file is reached.

The output from our program using the particular file in question is shown below:

```
The moving finger writes and having writ
Moves on; nor all thy piety nor wit
Shall lure it back to cancel half a line,
Nor all thy tears wash out a word of it.
```

Here is the code for the application:

CharacterByCharacter.java

```java
import java.io.FileReader;
import java.io.BufferedReader;
import java.io.IOException;

public class CharacterByCharacter
{
  public static void main(String[] args)
  {
    try( // use try-with-resources to ensure file is closed safely
         FileReader testFile = new FileReader("Poem.txt");
         BufferedReader textStream = new BufferedReader(testFile);
       )
    {
       int ch; // to hold the integer (Unicode) value of the character
       char c; // to hold the character when type cast from integer
       ch = textStream.read(); // read the first character from the file
       c = (char) ch; // type cast from integer to character
       // continue until the end of the file is reached (-1 is returned)
       while( ch != -1)
       {
           System.out.print(c);
           ch = textStream.read(); // read the next character
           c = (char) ch; // type cast from integer to character
       }
       System.out.println();
    }

    catch(IOException ioe)
    {
       System.out.println("There was a problem reading the file\n");
    }
  }
}
```

The main thing to notice here is that we are using the read method of BufferedReader; this method reads a single character from the file and returns an integer, the Unicode value of the character read. If the character read was the end-of-file marker then it returns −1, making it an easy matter for us to check whether the end of the file has been reached. We are once again using the technique of reading ahead before entering the **while** loop. As you can see, after each read operation, we typecast the integer to a character, which we then display on the screen.

22.6 Object Serialization

If you are going to be dealing with files that will be accessed only within a Java program, then one of the easiest ways to do this is to make use of two classes called ObjectInputStream and ObjectOutputStream. These classes have methods called, respectively, readObject and writeObject that enable us to read and write whole objects from and to files. The process of converting an object into a stream of data suitable for storage on a disk is called **serialization**.

Any class whose objects are to be read and written using the above methods must implement the interface Serializable. This is a type of interface that we have not actually come across before—it is known as a **marker** and in fact contains no methods. Its purpose is simply to make an "announcement" to anyone using the class, namely that objects of this class can be read and written as whole objects. In designing a class we can, then, choose not to make our class Serializable—we might want to do this for security reasons (e.g. to stop whole objects being transportable over the Internet) or to avoid errors in a distributed environment where the code for the class was not present on every machine.

In the case of our Car class, we therefore need to declare it in the following way before we could use it in a program that handles whole objects:

```
public class Car implements Serializable
```

The Serializable interface resides within the java.io package.

Now we can rewrite the writeList and readList methods of TextFileTester so that we manipulate whole objects. First the writeList method:

```
static void writeList(List<Car> carListIn)
{
    // use try-with-resources to ensure file is closed safely
    try(
            FileOutputStream carFile = new FileOutputStream("Cars.dat");
            ObjectOutputStream carStream = new ObjectOutputStream(carFile);
    )
    {

        for(Car item : carListIn)
        {
            carStream.writeObject(item);
        }

    }
    catch(IOException e)
    {
        System.out.println("There was a problem writing the file");
    }
}
```

You can see how easy this is—you just need one line to save a whole object to a
file by using the `writeObject` method of `ObjectOutputStream`.

Now the `readList` method:

```
static void readList(List<Car> carListIn)
{
    boolean endOfFile = false;
    Car tempCar;

    // use try-with-resources to ensure file is closed safely
    try(
        // create a FileInputStream object, carFile
        FileInputStream carFile = new FileInputStream("Cars.dat");
        // create an ObjectInputStream object to wrap around carFile
        ObjectInputStream carStream = new ObjectInputStream(carFile);
    )
    {

        // read the first (whole) object with the readObject method
        tempCar =  (Car) carStream.readObject();
        while(endOfFile != true)
        {
            try
            {
                carListIn.add(tempCar);
                // read the next (whole) object
                tempCar = (Car) carStream.readObject();
            }

            /* use the fact that readObject throws an EOFException to
               check whether the end of the file has been reached */
            catch(EOFException  e)
            {
                endOfFile = true;
            }
        }

    }

    catch(FileNotFoundException e)
    {
        System.out.println("\nNo file was read");
    }

    catch(ClassNotFoundException e) // thrown by readObject
    {
        System.out.println("\nTrying to read an object of an unknown class");
    }

    catch(StreamCorruptedException e) // thrown by the constructor
    {
        System.out.println("\nUnreadable file format");
    }

    catch(IOException e)
    {
        System.out.println("There was a problem reading the file");
    }

}
```

Again you can see how easy this is—a whole object is read with the read-
`Object` method.

We should draw your attention to a few of the exception handling routines we
have used here—first notice that we have made use of the fact that `readObject`
throws an `EOFException` to check for the end of the file. Second, notice that
`readObject` also throws a `ClassNotFoundException`, which indicates that
the object just read does not correspond to any class known to the program. Finally,
the constructor throws a `StreamCorruptedException`, which indicates that
the input stream given to it was not produced by an `ObjectOutputStream`
object—underlining the fact that reading and writing whole objects are comple-
mentary techniques that are specific to Java programs.

One final thing to note—if an attribute of a `Serializable` class is itself an object of another class, then that class too must be `Serializable` in order for us to be able to read and write whole objects as we have just done. You will probably have noticed that in the case of the `Car` class, one of its attributes is a `String`— fortunately the `String` class does indeed implement the `Serializable` interface, which is why we had no problem using it in this way in our example.

Before moving on, it is worth noting that all the Java collection classes such as `HashMap` and `ArrayList` are themselves `Serializable`.

22.7   Random Access Files

All the programs that we have looked at so far in this chapter have made use of serial access. For small applications this will probably be all you need—however, if you were writing applications that handled very large data files it would be desirable to use random access methods. Fortunately Java provides us with this facility.

The class that we need is called `RandomAccessFile`. This enables us to open a file for random access. Random access files can be opened in either read–write mode or in read-only mode; the constructor therefore takes, in addition to the name of the file, an additional `String` parameter which can be either "rw" or "r", indicating the mode in which the file is to be opened.

`RandomAccessFile` has methods such as `readChar` and `writeChar`, `readInt` and `writeInt`, `readDouble` and `writeDouble`. It also has methods called `readUTF` and `readUTF` for writing strings. UTF stands for *Unicode Transformation Format*, and the methods are so-called because, when they write and read strings string to or from a file, the Unicode characters (which are used in Java) are converted to the machine-specific format and vice versa.

In addition, `RandomAccessFile` has a method called `seek`. This takes one attribute, of type `long`, which indicates how many bytes to move the file pointer before starting a read or write operation.

So now we have the question of how far to move the pointer—we need to be able to calculate the size of each record. Table 22.1 shows the amount of storage space taken up on disk when the different types are written with a particular method.

As you can see from the table a `String` object will occupy one byte of space per character, plus two extra bytes (at the beginning) which an integer representing the length of the string.

There is a slight problem here, because the size of a `String` object varies according to how many characters it contains. So we have to restrict the length of each string to a given amount.

To demonstrate this, we are going to define a class called `Building`, which might be used by an estate agent for example.

Table 22.1 Size of the Java types on disk

Java type	Method used for writing	Storage on disk
byte	writeByte	1 byte
short	writeShort	2 bytes
char	writeChar	2 bytes
int	writeInt	4 bytes
long	writeLong	8 bytes
float	writeFloat	4 bytes
double	writeDouble	8 bytes
boolean	writeBoolean	1 byte
String	writeUTF	1 byte per character plus 2

Building.java

```java
public class Building
{
    private String id;
    private char typeOfProperty;
    private int squareMeterage;
    private double price;

    public Building(String idIn, char typeOfPropertyIn, int squareMeterageIn, double priceIn)
    {
        this.id = idIn;
        this.typeOfProperty = typeOfPropertyIn;
        this.squareMeterage = squareMeterageIn;
        this.price = priceIn;
    }

    public String getId()
    {
        return this.id;
    }

    public char getTypeOfProperty()
    {
        return this.typeOfProperty;
    }

    public int getSquareMeterage()
    {
        return this.squareMeterage;
    }

    public double getPrice()
    {
        return this.price;
    }
}
```

In the program that follows are going to restrict the length of the ID to exactly four characters (giving as string length of 6). This will enable us to calculate the size of each record as follows:

id (4-character `String`)	6 bytes
typeOfProperty (`char`)	2 bytes
squareMeterage (`int`)	4 bytes
price (`double`)	8 bytes
Total	20 bytes

The program below takes a rather different approach to the one we have used so far in this chapter. Two options (as well as a *Quit* option) are provided. The first, the option to add a building, simply adds the building to the end of the file. The second, to display the details of a building, asks the user for the position of the building in the file then reads this record directly from the file. You can see that there is now no need for a `List` in which to store the items.

Study the program carefully—then we will discuss it. Note that we have once again made use of our `EasyScanner` class here.

RandomFileTester.java

```
import java.io.FileNotFoundException;
import java.io.IOException;
import java.io.RandomAccessFile;

public class RandomFileTester
{
    static final int SIZE = 20; // each record will be 20 bytes

    public static void main(String[] args)
    {
        char choice;
        do
        {
            System.out.println("\nRandom File Tester");
            System.out.println("1. Add a building");
            System.out.println("2. Display a building");
            System.out.println("3. Quit\n");
            choice = EasyScanner.nextChar();
            System.out.println();
            switch(choice)
            {
                case '1' : addBuilding();
                        break;
                case '2' : displayBuilding();
                        break;
                case '3' : break;
                default : System.out.print("\nChoose 1 - 3 only please\n ");
            }
        }while(choice != '3');
    }

    static void addBuilding()
    {
        String tempId;
```

```java
        char tempType;
        int tempMeterage;
        double tempPrice;
        System.out.print("Please enter the ID: ");
        tempId= EasyScanner.nextString();

        while(tempId.length() != 4) // make sure that the ID is exactly 4 characters
        {
            System.out.print("Four characters only - please re-enter: ");
            tempId = EasyScanner.nextString();
        }

        // get the price of the building from the user
        System.out.print("Enter single character indicating (F)lat or a (H)ouse: ");
        tempType = EasyScanner.nextChar();

        // get the square meterage of the building from the user
        System.out.print("Please enter the square meterage: ");
        tempMeterage = EasyScanner.nextInt();

        // get the price of the building from the user
        System.out.print("Please enter the price: ");
        tempPrice = EasyScanner.nextDouble();

        // write the record to the file
        writeRecord(new Building(tempId, tempType, tempMeterage, tempPrice));
    }

    static void displayBuilding()
    {
        int pos;
        // get the position of the item to be read from the user
        System.out.print("Enter the building's position in the list: ");
        pos = EasyScanner.nextInt(); // read the record requested from file
        Building tempBuilding = readRecord(pos);
        if(tempBuilding != null)
        {
            System.out.println(tempBuilding.getId()
            + " "
            + tempBuilding.getTypeOfProperty()
            + " "
            + tempBuilding.getSquareMeterage()
            + " "
            + tempBuilding.getPrice());
        }
        else
        {
            System.out.println("Invalid postion") ;
        }
    }

    static void writeRecord(Building tempBuilding)
    {
        // use try-with-resources to ensure file is closed safely
        try(
                // open a RandomAccessFile in read-write mode
                RandomAccessFile buildingFile = new RandomAccessFile("Buildings.rand", "rw");
            )
            {

            // move the pointer to the end of the file
            buildingFile.seek(buildingFile.length());

            // write the four three fields of the record to the file
            buildingFile.writeUTF(tempBuilding.getId());
            buildingFile.writeChar(tempBuilding.getTypeOfProperty());
            buildingFile.writeInt(tempBuilding.getSquareMeterage());
            buildingFile.writeDouble(tempBuilding.getPrice());
        }
        catch(IOException e)
        {
            System.out.println("There was a problem writing the file");
        }
    }

    static Building readRecord(int pos)
    {
        String tempId;
        char tempType;
```

```
        int tempMeterage;
        double tempPrice;
        Building tempBuilding = null; // a null value indicates there was a problem reading the record

        // use try-with-resources to ensure file is closed safely
        try(
                // open a RandomAccessFile in read-only mode
                RandomAccessFile buildingFile = new RandomAccessFile("Buildings.rand","r");
        )
        {
            // move the pointer to the start of the required record
            buildingFile.seek((pos-1) * SIZE);
            // read the three fields of the record from the file
            tempId = buildingFile.readUTF();
            tempType = buildingFile.readChar();
            tempMeterage = buildingFile.readInt();
            tempPrice = buildingFile.readDouble();
            // use the data just read to create a new Building object
            tempBuilding = new Building(tempId, tempType, tempMeterage, tempPrice);
        }
        catch(FileNotFoundException e)
        {
            System.out.println("\nNo file was read");
        }

        catch(IOException e)
        {
            System.out.println("There was a problem reading the file");
        }
        // return the record that was read
        return tempBuilding;
    }
}
```

You can see that in the addBuilding method we have called writeRecord with a Building object as a parameter.

```
writeRecord(new Building(tempId, tempType, tempMeterage, tempPrice));
```

Let's take a closer look at the writeRecord method. First the line to open the file in read–write mode:

```
RandomAccessFile buildingFile = new RandomAccessFile("Buildings.rand", "rw");
```

Now the instruction to move the file pointer:

```
buildingFile.seek(buildingFile.length());
```

You can see how we use the `seek` method to move the pointer a specific number of bytes; here the correct number of bytes is the size of the file (as we want to write the new record at the end of the file), so we use the `length` method of `RandomAccessFile` to determine this number.

Now we can move on to look at the `readRecord` method. You can see that this is called from within the `displayBuilding` method, with an integer parameter, representing the position of the required record in the file:

```
Building tempBuilding = readRecord(pos);
```

The file is opened in read-only mode:

```
RandomAccessFile buildingFile = new RandomAccessFile("Buildings.rand","r");
```

Then the `seek` method of `RandomAccessFile` is invoked as follows:

```
buildingFile.seek((pos-1) * SIZE);
```

You can see that the number of bytes through which to move the pointer has been calculated by multiplying the size of the record by one less than the position. This is because in order to read the first record we don't move the pointer at all; in order to read the second record we must move it 1×20 bytes; for the third record 2×20 bytes; and so on.

Here is a test run from the program (starting off with an empty file):

```
Random File Tester
1. Add a building
2. Display a building
3. Quit

1

Please enter the ID: A123
Enter single character indicating (F)lat or a (H)ouse: F
Please enter the square meterage: 80
Please enter the price: 250000

Random File Tester
1. Add a building
2. Display a building
3. Quit

1

Please enter the ID: B345
Enter single character indicating (F)lat or a (H)ouse: H
Please enter the square meterage: 75
Please enter the price: 299000

Random File Tester
1. Add a building
2. Display a building
3. Quit

2

Enter the building's position in the list: 2

B345 H 75 299000.0

Random File Tester
1. Add a building
2. Display a building
3. Quit

3
```

Unlike our examples with sequential files, we are accessing the file directly each time we read or write a record. So, how would we delete a record? One strategy that is used in large databases is to mark a record as deleted and to purge deleted records at a later date, essentially by making a copy of the file without the deleted records. In this case we could, for example, change the ID of the building to "0000". This is left as an end of chapter exercise.

22.8   Self-test Questions

1. Identify and explain the types of encoding provided by Java classes for reading and writing files.
2. Explain why we have used the *try-with-resources* construct throughout this chapter to create and open files.
3. The `TextFileTester` of Sect. 22.3 is to be adapted so that the user is simply asked to enter a number of cars, which, when that process is finished, saves those cars to a text file. The program then terminates. The file does not have to be read from within the program, but should be able to be read by a text editor such as Windows™ Notepad. The format should be as follows:

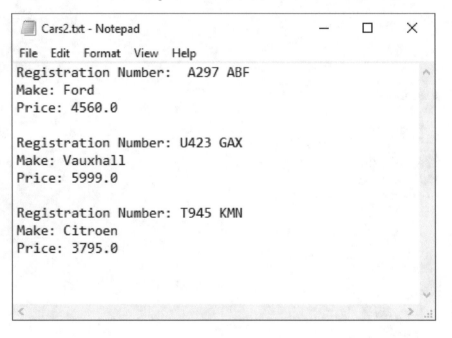

Adapt the `writeList` method accordingly.
Hint: remember that a blank line is obtained by calling `println` *with no parameters.*
4. What is the difference between *serial access* files and *random access* files?
5. Explain the purpose of the `Serializable` interface.
6. Calculate the number of bytes required to store an object of a class, the attributes of which are declared as follows:

```
private int x;
private char c;
private String s;
```

You can assume that the String attribute will always consist of exactly 20 characters.

22.9 Programming Exercises

1. Adapt the TextFileTester so that it behaves in the way described in question 3 of the self-test questions.
2. Implement the CopyBinaryFile program from Sect. 22.4 using a binary file such as an image or sound file. Then try the same thing with a text file.
3. Implement the CharacterByCharacter program from Sect. 22.5, using a text file that you have created.
4. Adapt the TextFileTester so that it uses object encoding, as explained in Sect. 22.6 (don't forget that the Car class must implement the Serializable interface).
5. Adapt the Library application of Chap. 21 so that it keeps permanent records
   (a) using text encoding;
   (b) using object encoding (remember that the Book class must be serializable).
6. (a)At the end of Sect. 22.7, we discussed how records could effectively be removed from a random access file by marking them as deleted (e.g. by changing their ID to something like "0000"). Add an option to the menu of RandomFileTester to implement this.
   (b) (This is more difficult.) See if you can add an option to purge the deleted records from the file. You will need to copy the records from the old file to a new file, omitting those that are marked for deletion. The new file would then have to be renamed outside the program and the old file deleted.

Hint: You can calculate the number of records by dividing the file length by the length of each record; you could then use a **for** loop,

Introducing JavaFX

23

Outcomes

By the end of this chapter you should be able to:

- *briefly describe the history of graphics programming in Java;*
- *explain the structure and life cycle of a **JavaFX** application;*
- *produce 2D graphical shapes in **JavaFX**;*
- *build an interactive graphics application in **JavaFX** using common components such as buttons, text fields and labels;*
- *program a **JavaFX** control to listen for events using a **lambda expression**;*
- *make use of a variety of different **JavaFX** containers;*
- *create borders, fonts and colours;*
- *format decimal numbers so that they appear in an appropriate form in a graphics application;*
- *write applications that offer choices via **combo boxes**, **check boxes** and **radio buttons**.*

23.1 Introduction

In Chap. 11 you learned how to create graphical applications using Python and Tkinter. Now we are going to learn how to create similar programs using the latest of Java's graphics libraries, **JavaFX**. We should mention here that since the release of Java 11, JavaFX is not packaged with Java and has to be downloaded and used as a separate module. This makes the process of creating JavaFX programs a little more complicated, but the various ways of doing this are clearly explained in the Appendix.

Supplementary Information The online version contains supplementary material available at https://doi.org/10.1007/978-3-031-01326-3_23.

© Springer Nature Switzerland AG 2022
Q. Charatan and A. Kans, *Programming in Two Semesters*,
Texts in Computer Science, https://doi.org/10.1007/978-3-031-01326-3_23

We will use some of the same applications that you produced in Chap. 11, so that you can compare and contrast JavaFX with Tkinter. But we will also produce some new applications.

23.2 JavaFX: An Overview

In this chapter we will be using JavaFX exclusively for our graphics applications, rather than using the earlier packages (which were **AWT** and **Swing**). So first, some terminology. Firstly, you need to know that a JavaFX program is referred to as an **application**. Your JavaFX class will extend the `Application` class, for which you need the following **import** statement:

```
import javafx· application ·Application
```

The top-level window in which the application runs is called a **stage**—but if, as you can do with many JavaFX applications, you run the program in full-screen mode, then the screen becomes the stage. Some applications can be made to run in a browser, in which case the browser is the stage. The contents of the stage—the graphic itself—are called a **scene** and are often referred to as a **scene graphic**. The items that make up the scene are referred to as **nodes**. They are very commonly the kind of components that allow interaction with the user, such as buttons, text fields, labels and check boxes, which are often referred to collectively as **controls**. They can also be 2D or 3D graphics shapes. But nodes can also be **containers**. Containers are components that hold other nodes, and each container arranges the nodes in a particular way—for example, vertically, horizontally, in a grid, or stacked one on top of the other. Normally, we would not see the container, but it is perfectly possible to put a border around it if we want to. Importantly, containers can contain other containers, so we can develop a hierarchy in our scene. We normally place a single top-level node in our scene, and this is referred to as the **root** node. We use the terms **parent** and **children** for the containing and contained nodes, respectively. You will notice here the similarities between JavaFX and Tkinter.

Figure 23.1 should make this clear. Here we have a sample scene in which the root node is a `VBox`—this is a container that arranges its child nodes vertically. We have given it a black border so that you can see it. The `VBox` has three children—a `TextField`, a `Label` and an `HBox`, around which we have again put a border. As you can probably guess, an `HBox` is similar to a `VBox`, but arranges its child nodes horizontally. In this case it has three child nodes which are `Button`s. All of these components will become familiar to you as you proceed through this chapter —in particular you will see how we have made extensive use of the `VBox` and `HBox` to construct our scene graphics.

To help you understand the way that a scene is constructed in a hierarchal way, we have shown you in Fig. 23.2 the hierarchy that makes up the scene graphic in the above example.

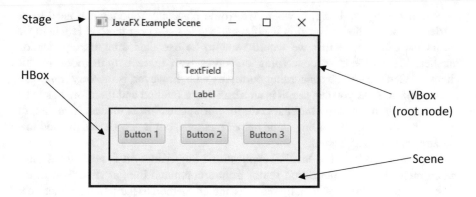

Fig. 23.1 A hierarchical scene

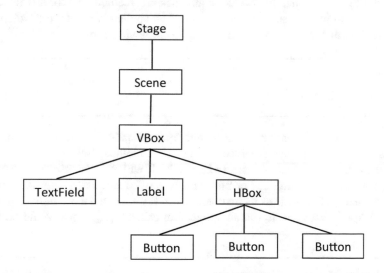

Fig. 23.2 The hierarchical structure of the scene in Fig. 23.1

When a JavaFX application begins, there are three methods that are called in order. These are as follows:

```
void init()
abstract void start(Stage stage)
void stop()
```

The first of these, init, is where we would place any routines that need to be carried out before the application itself starts, while the stop method is where we would place any code that we would want to be executed after the application finishes. We will not be concerning ourselves with these two methods in this chapter. What we will be concerning ourselves with, however, is the very important start method. As you can see, it is an **abstract** method and therefore has to be coded. It is in this method that the code for our application is placed. You can, of course, break this up by adding some helper methods, but it is with this method that the application itself begins.

So how do we launch a JavaFX application? Surprisingly it is not always via a main method. If the application is run from a command line, as described in the appendix, then it does not actually require a main method to launch it. Neither does it need a main method if it is deployed as a .jar file, which is something we describe in the next chapter. But if you run your program within an IDE, as most of you will be doing at first, then we do require a main method, and for that reason we have chosen to include such a method with each application that we develop here. You will see that the main method takes the following form:

```
public static void main(String[] args)
{
    launch(args);
}
```

As you can see the main method calls the application's launch method and passes to it any arguments received by the main method itself.

The launch method is a **static** method, and we can use it to launch a JavaFX application from another program. It is overloaded to accept the name of the compiled .class file as its first parameter. If we wanted a program called, say, LaunchApplication to run an application called MyApp, we would do it like this:

```
import javafx.application.Application;

class LaunchApplication
{
    public static void main(String[] args)
    {
        Application.launch(MyApp.class, args);
    }
}
```

So now that you know how a JavaFX application is structured, and you are aware of the sequence in which its methods are called; we can go on to develop our first graphics application.

23.3   2D Graphics: The *SmileyFace* Class

Our first graphics application is going to use 2D graphics and is going to create a smiley face, as shown in Fig. 23.3. You will remember a similar application from Chap. 11.

Although it is a rather simple application, in that there is no user interaction, it nonetheless introduces many new concepts. In particular it shows you how to create a scene, to add items to the scene and to add the scene to a stage. It also introduces you to 2D graphics, which enables you to draw two-dimensional shapes such as circles, lines, ellipses, rectangles and arcs. Here we draw circles for the face and eyes and an arc for the mouth. You will also see how to create text which you can configure using different colours and fonts.

As explained in the previous section, we have included a `main` method which launches the application. The complete code is shown below. Take a look at it, and then we will discuss it with you:

Fig. 23.3 The Smiley Face application

SmileyFace.java

```java
import javafx.application.Application;
import javafx.scene.Group;
import javafx.scene.Scene;
import javafx.scene.paint.Color;
import javafx.scene.shape.Arc;
import javafx.scene.shape.ArcType;
import javafx.scene.shape.Circle;
import javafx.scene.text.Font;
import javafx.scene.text.Text;
import javafx.stage.Stage;

public class SmileyFace extends Application
{
    @Override
    public void start(Stage stage)
    {
        // create and configure the main circle for the face
        Circle face = new Circle(125, 125, 80);
        face.setFill(Color.YELLOW);
        face.setStroke(Color.RED);

        // create and configure the circle for the right eye
        Circle rightEye = new Circle(86, 100, 10);
        rightEye.setFill(Color.YELLOW);
        rightEye.setStroke(Color.BLUE);

        // create and configure the circle for the left eye
        Circle leftEye = new Circle(162, 100, 10);
        leftEye.setFill(Color.YELLOW);
        leftEye.setStroke(Color.BLUE);

        // create and configure a smiling mouth
        Arc mouth = new Arc(125, 150, 45, 35, 0, -180);
        mouth.setFill(Color.YELLOW);
        mouth.setStroke(Color.BLUE);
        mouth.setType(ArcType.OPEN);

        // create and configure the text
        Text caption = new Text(80, 240, "Smiley Face");
        caption.setFill(Color.BLUE);
        caption.setFont(Font.font("Verdana", 15));

        // create a group that holds all the features
        Group root = new Group(face, rightEye, leftEye, mouth, caption);

        // create and configure a new scene
        Scene scene = new Scene(root, 250, 275, Color.YELLOW);

        // add the scene to the stage, then set the title
        stage.setScene(scene);
        stage.setTitle("Smiley Face");

        // show the stage
        stage.show();
    }

    public static void main(String[] args)
    {
        launch(args);
    }
}
```

There are a number of new concepts here. First, let us take a look at the **import** clauses, which show you that all of our classes come from a package called javafx, which as you can see has many subpackages including scene and stage.

```java
import javafx.application.Application;
import javafx.scene.Group;
import javafx.scene.Scene;
import javafx.scene.paint.Color;
import javafx.scene.shape.Arc;
import javafx.scene.shape.ArcType;
import javafx.scene.shape.Circle;
import javafx.scene.text.Font;
import javafx.scene.text.Text;
import javafx.stage.Stage;
```

Now look at the class header:

```
public class SmileyFace extends Application
```

As we explained, all JavaFX programs run as an application, and we therefore have to extend the `Application` class. `Application` requires you to code the `start` method, which we talked about in the previous section. Let us take a look at this now, starting with the header:

```
public void start(Stage stage)
```

When `start` is called, it is automatically sent an object of the `Stage` class, which will be the main container for our graphic.

The first thing we do within the `start` method is to create and configure the main circle for the face:

```
Circle face = new Circle(125, 125, 80);
face.setFill(Color.YELLOW);
face.setStroke(Color.RED);
```

The `Circle` class, which resides in a the `javafx.scene.shape` library, has a number of constructors (which you can look up on the OracleÔ site). The constructor we are using here takes three parameters of type **double**.

The first two of these parameters represent, respectively, the *x* and *y* positions of the centre of the circle (with respect to the top left-hand corner of the parent node), measured in pixels. The third parameter represents the radius of the circle, also in pixels. You will see later that we have chosen our initial scene to be 250×275 pixels, so that our circle with its centre at (125, 125) will be horizontally centred, but will leave enough vertical room for a caption.

We have used two other methods of `Circle`, namely `setFill` and `setStroke`, to set the fill colour and line colour of the circle. To each of these we have passed a predefined attribute of the `Color` class (note the American spelling), which resides in `javafx.scene.paint`. The `paint` library provides a great many colours that you can use, and which you can look up—or which you can choose from the list of suggestions that your IDE will make after pressing the full stop.

In a similar manner we draw the right eye and the left eye:

```
Circle rightEye = new Circle(86, 100, 10);
rightEye.setFill(Color.YELLOW);
rightEye.setStroke(Color.BLUE);

Circle leftEye = new Circle(162, 100, 10);
leftEye.setFill(Color.YELLOW);
leftEye.setStroke(Color.BLUE);
```

You might be wondering how we decided upon the exact position in which to draw these circles. In theory it is possible to calculate exactly where you want everything to be on a graphic—but often it is easier (and actually quite good fun) simply to make an estimate and see how it looks, then change the values until you are happy. That is what we did here. We strongly recommend that once you have got the application up and running, you experiment with the different values to explore what they do. This is the best way to become familiar with all of the graphics objects.

Now we come to the smiling mouth, which is a little more complicated.

```
Arc mouth = new Arc(125, 150, 45, 35, 0, -180);
mouth.setFill(Color.YELLOW);
mouth.setStroke(Color.BLUE);
mouth.setType(ArcType.OPEN);
```

Creating an object of the Arc class draws part (or all) of an ellipse. The constructor we have used is specified on the Oracle™ website like this:

```
Arc(double centreX, double centreY, double radiusX, double radiusY, double
startAngle, double length)
```

The names of the parameters mostly speak for themselves. The first two represent the position of the centre of the ellipse. The next two are the horizontal and vertical radii, respectively. startAngle represents the angle at which we start drawing the arc. The only confusing name is the last one, length, which represents the size of the angle through which the arc is drawn. Figure 23.4 should make it clear.

In our case we have chosen the radii to give us an arc of an ellipse which is somewhat wider than it is high. We have chosen a start angle of 0°, and you will notice that the value of the final angle (the length parameter) is set to −180. The negative sign indicates that this angle is formed by moving from the start angle in a clockwise direction (so that the mouth is smiling). A positive sign indicates an anticlockwise direction (as, e.g. in Fig. 23.4).

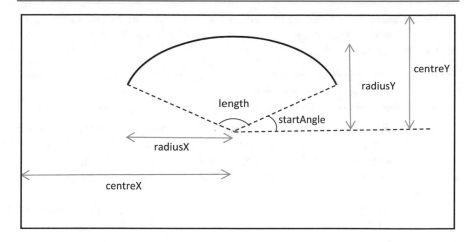

Fig. 23.4 The Arc class

The next lines of code set the fill colour and line colour (referred to as the stroke colour) of the mouth. The final line of code selects the type of arc we want, which in this case is ArcType.OPEN. Two other types exist (ArcType.CHORD and ArcType.ROUND), and these are demonstrated in Sect. 23.5.

The next thing we do is to add a caption:

```
Text caption = new Text(80, 240, "Smiley Face");
caption.setFill(Color.BLUE);
caption.setFont(Font.font("Verdana", 15));
```

For this purpose we are creating an instance of the Text class, which resides in javafx.scene.text. The constructor takes three parameters—two **double**s and a String. The first two are used to position the text (they are the co-ordinates of the beginning of the String), and the final one holds the value of the text itself.

We have gone on to set the colour, using the setFill method, and then we have set the font, with the setFont method. You can look at the syntax to see how we select the name and size of the font—in this case "Verdana", 15 points.

Now that we have defined all of our features, we want them to stay together as a group. We can do this with the Group class from the javafx.scene package. This class acts like an invisible container—it is very useful when we have already defined the position of our shapes (as we have done here), so we do not have to worry any further about how they will be laid out within the container:

```
Group root = new Group(face, rightEye, leftEye, mouth, caption);
```

We are using the convention of naming the first node that we add to our scene root, as it is the root node. In this case it is the only node. We have created our new scene like this:

```
Scene scene = new Scene(root, 250, 275, Color.YELLOW);
```

Here we have chosen to use the constructor that allows us to set the size (width and height) of the initial scene, together with the background colour. If you do not set these values initially, the Scene class (and other graphics components) has many set-methods such as setMinWidth and setMaxHeight that you can code later.

Now all that remains to complete the start method is to add the scene to the stage, set the title and finally make the stage visible, which we do by calling its show method:

```
stage.setScene(scene);
stage.setTitle("Smiley Face");
stage.show();
```

As we mentioned before, we have included a main method (and will continue to do so) in order that you can run the application in any environment.

```
public static void main(String[] args)
{
     launch(args);
}
```

23.4   Event-Handling in JavaFX: The *ChangingFace* Class

The SmileyFace class that we developed in the last section was "passive" and did not involve any interaction with the user. In practice of course, graphics applications will normally require input from the user in the form of clicking a button, entering text and so on.

Just as you saw in Chap. 11 when you studied Tkinter, in response to the user performing an action (such as clicking a mouse button) an Event object is generated. This object is sent to an EventHandler which we attach to a particular control and supply it with the instructions for what to do when the action occurs. There are many actions that the user could perform, such as pressing a key, dragging a mouse and so on, but for the moment we will concern ourselves only with a simple mouse click on a button.

Our first application will modify our `SmileyFace` class and turn it into a `ChangingFace` class that can change its mood so it can be sad as well as happy —just as we did in Chap. 11. We are going to add a couple of buttons, as shown in Figs. 23.5 and 23.6.

Fig. 23.5 The *ChangingFace* class (still smiling)

Fig. 23.6 The *ChangingFace* class (frowning)

You can see that we have now changed our title and caption from "Smiley Face" to "Changing Face"—because, when we have finished, we will be able to click on the *Frown* button and get the face to look like the one you see in Fig. 23.6. Clicking the *Smile* button will get the face to smile again.

The code for our class is shown below. There are quite a lot of new concepts and techniques here, so we will discuss it in detail once you have had a look at it.

```
ChangingFace.java
import javafx.application.Application;
import javafx.scene.Group;
import javafx.scene.Scene;
import javafx.scene.control.Button;
import javafx.scene.layout.Background;
import javafx.scene.layout.HBox;
import javafx.scene.layout.VBox;
import javafx.scene.paint.Color;
import javafx.scene.shape.Arc;
import javafx.scene.shape.ArcType;
import javafx.scene.shape.Circle;
import javafx.scene.text.Font;
import javafx.scene.text.Text;
import javafx.stage.Stage;
import javafx.geometry.Pos;

public class ChangingFace extends Application
{
    @Override
    public void start(Stage stage)
    {
        // create and configure the main circle for the face
        Circle face = new Circle(125, 125, 80);
        face.setFill(Color.YELLOW);
        face.setStroke(Color.RED);

        // create and configure the circle for the right eye
        Circle rightEye = new Circle(86, 100, 10);
        rightEye.setFill(Color.YELLOW);
        rightEye.setStroke(Color.BLUE);

        // create and configure the circle for the left eye
        Circle leftEye = new Circle(162, 100, 10);
        leftEye.setFill(Color.YELLOW);
        leftEye.setStroke(Color.BLUE);

        // create and configure a smiling mouth (this is how it will start)
        Arc mouth = new Arc(125, 150, 45, 35, 0, -180);
        mouth.setFill(Color.YELLOW);
        mouth.setStroke(Color.BLUE);
        mouth.setType(ArcType.OPEN);

        // create and configure the text
        Text caption = new Text(68, 240, "Changing Face");
        caption.setFill(Color.BLUE);
        caption.setFont(Font.font ("Verdana", 15));

        // create a group that holds all the features
        Group group = new Group(face, rightEye, leftEye, mouth,  caption);

        // create a button that will make the face smile
        Button smileButton = new Button("Smile");

        // create a button that will make the face frown
        Button frownButton = new Button("Frown");
```

```
        // create and configure a horizontal container to hold the buttons
        HBox buttonBox = new HBox(10);
        buttonBox.setAlignment(Pos.CENTER);

        //add the buttons to the horizontal container
        buttonBox.getChildren().addAll(smileButton, frownButton);

        // create and configure a vertical container to hold the button box and the face group
        VBox root = new VBox(10);
        root.setBackground(Background.EMPTY);
        root.setAlignment(Pos.CENTER);

        //add the button box and the face group to the vertical container
        root.getChildren().addAll(buttonBox, group);

        // create and configure a new scene
        Scene scene = new Scene(root, 250, 275, Color.YELLOW);

        // supply the code that is executed when the smile button is pressed
        smileButton.setOnAction(e -> mouth.setLength(-180));

        // supply the code that is executed when the frown button is pressed
        frownButton.setOnAction(e -> mouth.setLength(180));

        // add the scene to the stage, then set the title
        stage.setScene(scene);
        stage.setTitle("Changing Face");

        // show the stage
        stage.show();
    }

    public static void main(String[] args)
    {
        launch(args);
    }
}
```

We have proceeded as before when it comes to creating the face. Once we have done this, we have created two instances of the `Button` class. A button is an extremely common feature of graphics programming, and the `Button` class, along with many other similar components, is to be found in `javafx.scene.control`. Here is the code for the buttons:

```
Button smileButton = new Button("Smile");
Button frownButton = new Button("Frown");
```

You can see that we have used a version of the constructor that allows us to set the text that appears on the button. You can also use the `setText` method of `Button` for this purpose.

Having created our two buttons, we now go on to create a container to hold them:

```
HBox buttonBox = new HBox(10);
buttonBox.setAlignment(Pos.CENTER);
```

We have created an instance of an HBox. As we mentioned earlier, this is a container that arranges the contained nodes horizontally. The constructor we have used takes a parameter that sets the distance between the items, in this case 10 pixels. We have then gone on to use its setAlignment method, into which we send a predefined constant, an attribute of the Pos class which is found in the package javafx.geometry. The constant we have chosen is Pos.CENTER in order to centre the components that the HBox contains. There are a number of other options, and these are demonstrated in Sect. 23.9.1.

Having created our HBox, we need to add our buttons to it. We do this by calling a method of HBox, called getChildren, which returns a list of all the child nodes. This list has two methods for adding the nodes: the add method will add a single item, and addAll a list of items. As we need to add two buttons, we have used the latter:

```
buttonBox.getChildren().addAll(smileButton, frownButton);
```

So now we have an HBox containing our buttons and a Group containing the shapes that make up our face. We need to organize these so that the face is placed vertically below the buttons, so we use a VBox which lines the items up vertically, just as the HBox does horizontally. We have given the name root to this instance of VBox, because this will be the root node that we add to our scene.

```
VBox root = new VBox(10);
root.setBackground(Background.EMPTY);
root.setAlignment(Pos.CENTER);
root.getChildren().addAll(buttonBox, group);
```

You will notice that we have done something else here, which is to add an empty background to the VBox—this is so that the yellow colour of the scene is not hidden.

Now we can add the HBox containing the buttons, and the group containing the face, to the VBox. We then add this VBox to the scene graphic:

```
root.getChildren().addAll(buttonBox, group);
Scene scene = new Scene(root, 250, 275, Color.YELLOW);
```

We are almost ready to take the final step of adding the scene to the stage.

Almost but not quite! There is one really vital thing we have to do, which is to enable the buttons to respond when they are pressed and to provide the code that tells the buttons what to do when this happens. At the beginning of this section, we explained that a control can be programmed to generate an `Event` object in response to some action taken by the user. The type of `Event` that we are interested in here is called an `ActionEvent`, which is the one that handles a simple mouse click. We need to add an `EventHandler` to each button, which means it will generate the `ActionEvent` as soon as the mouse is clicked. Effectively we are programming our button to "listen out" for a mouse click.

`EventHandler` has a method called `handle`, and it is the code for this method that we need to supply in order that the button knows what to do when the mouse is clicked.

Now, you might think that all this sounds rather complicated—but lambda expressions make this very simple. The code for doing this for each button is shown below. Have a look at it, then we will explain it to you:

```
smileButton.setOnAction(e -> mouth.setLength(-180));
frownButton.setOnAction(e -> mouth.setLength(180));
```

You can see that a `Button` has a method called `setOnAction`. This is an example of what is known as a **convenience method**, a feature of JavaFX. It certainly is convenient, because it means that all we have to do in order to add an `EventHandler` is to supply the code it needs for its `handle` method. Most controls have these convenience methods, all starting with `setOn-`. Other examples are described in Sect. 23.10.

You can see that the code is sent directly into the method by means of a lambda expression. In each case we are using the `setLength` method of `Arc` to redraw the mouth. As we have seen, giving this a negative value draws it clockwise, so that the mouth smiles, and giving it a positive value makes the mouth frown. So the instructions for the `smileButton` and `frownButton`, respectively, are `mouth.setLength(-180)` and `mouth.setLength(180)`. Our lambda expressions therefore look like this:

```
e -> mouth.setLength(-180)  //smile
```

```
e -> mouth.setLength(180)   //frown
```

Fig. 23.7 Some more 2D
shapes

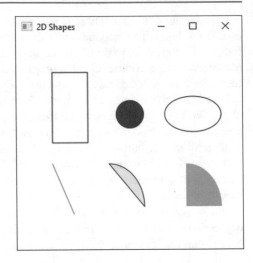

23.5   Some More 2D Shapes

Before we move away from 2D graphics, we will draw your attention to a some
more shapes that will increase your repertoire.

We have shown a few examples in Fig. 23.7.

You can see that we have experimented with different colours and with using the
`setFill` and `setStroke` methods.

The rectangle that you see in the top left-hand corner was created with the
following code:

```
Rectangle = new Rectangle(50, 50, 50, 100);
```

In this constructor, the first two parameters (all of which are of type **double**)
represent the x and y co-ordinates of the top left-hand corner, and the next two
represent the width and height of the rectangle, respectively.

The line underneath was created using the following constructor:

```
Line = new Line(50, 180, 80, 250);
```

The first two parameters are the x and y co-ordinates of the start position, and the
last two are the co-ordinates of the end position.

The ellipse that you see in the top right hand corner was drawn simply by creating an `Arc` and drawing the line through an angle of 360°. In our previous examples you saw the effect of choosing `ArcType.OPEN` for our arc type. The two arcs you see on the bottom row show the effect of choosing `ArcType.CHORD` and `ArcType.ROUND`, respectively.

All of the above shapes reside in `javafx.scene.shape`. You can check out the many other constructors and methods of these and other shapes on the Oracle™ website.

23.6 An Interactive Graphics Class

Most common applications involve controls (buttons, check boxes, text fields and so on) rather than graphical shapes. In Chap. 11 we created an application called PushMe using Python and Tkinter, so now let us do the same thing in JavaFX.

As with the Python version, it will allow the user to enter some text and then, by clicking on a button, to see the text that was entered displayed below the button. You can see what it looks like in Fig. 23.8.

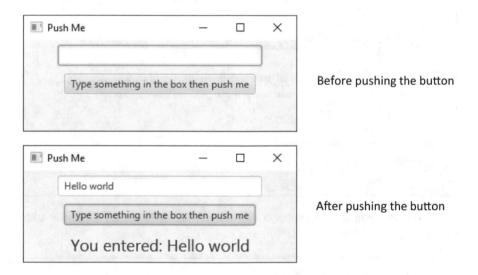

Fig. 23.8 The *PushMe* class

As usual we will show you the code first and discuss it afterwards:

PushMe.java

```java
import javafx.application.Application;
import javafx.geometry.Pos;
import javafx.scene.Scene;
import javafx.scene.control.Button;
import javafx.scene.control.Label;
import javafx.scene.control.TextField;
import javafx.scene.layout.VBox;
import javafx.scene.paint.Color;
import javafx.scene.text.Font;
import javafx.stage.Stage;

public class PushMe extends Application
{
    @Override
    public void start(Stage stage)
    {
        // create and configure a text field for user entry
        TextField pushMeTextField = new TextField();

        pushMeTextField.setMaxWidth(250);

        // create and configure a label to display the output
        Label pushMeLabel= new Label();
        pushMeLabel.setTextFill(Color.RED);
        pushMeLabel.setFont(Font.font("Arial", 20));

        // create and configure a label which will cause the text to be displayed
        Button pushMeButton = new Button();
        pushMeButton.setText("Type something in the box then push me");
        pushMeButton.setOnAction(e -> pushMeLabel.setText("You entered: "
                                             + pushMeTextField.getText()));

        // create and configure a VBox to hold our components
        VBox root = new VBox();
        root.setSpacing(10);
        root.setAlignment(Pos.CENTER);

        //add the components to the VBox
        root.getChildren().addAll(pushMeTextField, pushMeButton, pushMeLabel);

        // create a new scene
        Scene scene = new Scene(root, 350, 150);

        //add the scene to the stage, then configure the stage and make it visible
        stage.setScene(scene);
        stage.setTitle("Push Me");
        stage.show();
    }

    public static void main(String[] args)
    {
        launch(args);
    }
}
```

The box into which we type our text is called a `TextField`. This allows us to type in one line of text:

```java
TextField pushMeTextField = new TextField();
pushMeTextField.setMaxWidth(250);
```

You can see that we have set the maximum width of our `TextField` to 250—if we had not done this, it would simply have filled the width of its parent container. You might want to explore a similar class, `TextArea`, that allows you to add several rows of text—you will see an example of this in the Sect. 23.8.

When the button is pressed, the text entered will be displayed underneath the button on a `Label`. As its name suggests, its purpose is simply to display some chosen text. We have created and configured it with the following lines of code (notice how we set the font):

```
Label pushMeLabel= new Label();
pushMeLabel.setTextFill(Color.RED);
pushMeLabel.setFont(Font.font("Arial", 20));
```

Next we have the code for the `Button`:

```
Button pushMeButton = new Button();
pushMeButton.setText("Type something in the box then push me");
pushMeButton.setOnAction(e -> pushMeLabel.setText("You entered: " + pushMeTextField.getText()));
```

We have already seen how to create and code a button, so this should be familiar to you. Look carefully at the lambda expression, which is explained in Fig. 23.9.

Having done all this, we create and configure a `VBox`, add the three components and then add the `VBox` to the scene.

```
VBox root = new VBox();
root.setSpacing(10);
root.setAlignment(Pos.CENTER);

root.getChildren().addAll(pushMeTextField, pushMeButton, pushMeLabel);

Scene scene = new Scene(root, 350, 150);
```

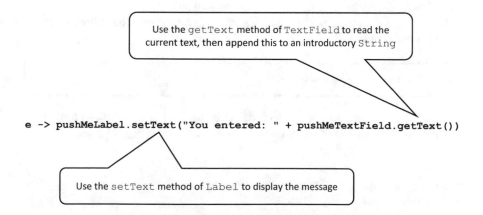

Fig. 23.9 The lambda expression explained

Finally we add the scene to the stage, then add a title and make it visible.

```
stage.setScene(scene);
stage.setTitle("Push Me");
stage.show();
```

23.7   Number Formatting

We are now going to take a quick diversion and tell you about a technique that is not specifically related to JavaFX, but is something you will often want to use in your graphics applications, or even in text-based applications. We frequently need our numerical output to appear in a suitable format—for example with no more than two numbers after the decimal point—or perhaps with *exactly* two numbers after the decimal point. In order to do this, we make use of the `DecimalFormat` class that resides in the `java.text` package. We would need the following import statement:

```
import java.text.DecimalFormat;
```

Once you have access to this class you can create `DecimalFormat` objects in your program. These objects can then be used to format decimal numbers for you. The `DecimalFormat` constructor has one parameter, the format string. This string instructs the object on how to format a given decimal number. Some of the important elements of such a string are given in Table 23.1.

In the example in the next section we are going to create the following `DecimalFormat` object:

```
DecimalFormat df = new DecimalFormat("0.0#");
```

Here the `DecimalFormat` object, `df`, is being informed on how to format any decimal numbers that may be given to it, as shown in see Fig. 23.10.

Table 23.1 Special DecimalFormat characters

Character	Meaning
.	Insert a decimal point
,	Insert a comma
0	Display a single digit
#	Display a single digit or empty if no digit present

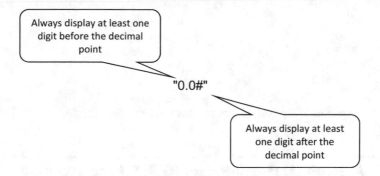

"0.0#"

Fig. 23.10 A format `String` used with the *DecimalFormat* class

Having created a `DecimalFormat` object, we could then create a `String`, s, from a **double**, d, as follows:

```
String s = df.format(d);
```

The program below shows some examples:

NumberFormatExample.Java

```
import java.text.DecimalFormat;

public class NumberFormatExample
{
    public static void main(String[] args)
    {
        double number = 4376.7863;

        DecimalFormat df1 = new DecimalFormat("###,##0.0#");
        DecimalFormat df2 = new DecimalFormat("###000.00");
        DecimalFormat df3 = new DecimalFormat("00.0");
        DecimalFormat df4 = new DecimalFormat("000000.00000");
        DecimalFormat df5 = new DecimalFormat("000,000.00####");

        System.out.println(df1.format(number));
        System.out.println(df2.format(number));
        System.out.println(df3.format(number));
        System.out.println(df4.format(number));
        System.out.println(df5.format(number));
    }
}
```

The output from the above program is as follows:

```
4,376.79
4376.79
4376.8
004376.78630
004,376.7863
```

We will use the `DecimalFormat` class in the next section.

23.8 A Graphical User Interface (GUI) for the *Rectangle* Class

Up till now, when we wanted to write programs that utilize our classes, we have written text-based programs. In many cases, however, you will be wanting to create graphical user interface (GUI) for your classes. Let us do this for the `Rectangle` class that we developed in Chap. 17, just as we did with Tkinter in Chap. 11. The sort of interface we are talking about is shown in Fig. 23.11.

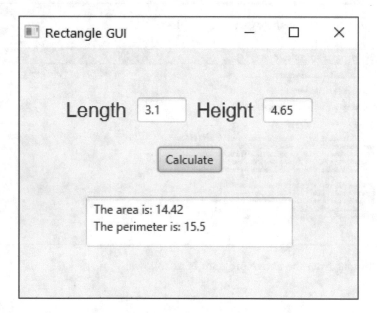

Fig. 23.11 A GUI for the *Rectangle* class

Here is the code for the GUI:

RectangleGUI.java

```java
import java.text.DecimalFormat;
import javafx.application.Application;
import javafx.geometry.Pos;
import javafx.scene.Scene;
import javafx.scene.control.Button;
import javafx.scene.control.Label;
import javafx.scene.control.TextArea;
import javafx.scene.control.TextField;
import javafx.scene.layout.HBox;
import javafx.scene.layout.VBox;
import javafx.scene.paint.Color;
import javafx.scene.text.Font;
import javafx.stage.Stage;


public class RectangleGUI extends Application
{
    // create an object of the Rectangle class as an attribute
    private Rectangle testRectangle = new Rectangle(0, 0);

    @Override
    public void start(Stage stage)
    {
        DecimalFormat df = new DecimalFormat("0.0#");
        // create and configure text fields for input
        TextField lengthField = new TextField();
        lengthField.setMaxWidth(50);

        TextField heightField = new TextField();
        heightField.setMaxWidth(50);


        // create and configure a non-editable text area to display the results
        TextArea display = new TextArea();
        display.setEditable(false);
        display.setMinSize(210,50);
        display.setMaxSize(210,50);


        // create and configure Labels for the text fields
        Label lengthLabel = new Label("Length");
        lengthLabel.setTextFill(Color.RED);
        lengthLabel.setFont(Font.font("Arial", 20));

        Label heightLabel= new Label("Height");
        heightLabel.setTextFill(Color.RED);
        heightLabel.setFont(Font.font("Arial", 20));


        // create and configure a button to perform the calculations
        Button calculateButton = new Button();
        calculateButton.setText("Calculate");
        calculateButton.setOnAction( e ->
            {
                // check that fields are not empty
                if(lengthField.getText().isEmpty() || heightField.getText().isEmpty())
                {
                    display.setText("Length and height must be entered");
                }
                else
                {
                    // convert text input to doubles and set the length and height of the Rectangle
                    this.testRectangle.setLength(Double.parseDouble(lengthField.getText()));
                    this.testRectangle.setHeight(Double.parseDouble(heightField.getText()));

                    // use the methods of Rectangle to calculate the area and perimeter
                    display.setText("The area is: " + df.format(this.testRectangle.calculateArea())
                                    + "\n" + "The perimeter is: "
                                    + df.format(this.testRectangle.calculatePerimeter()));

                }
            }
                                );

        // create and configure an HBox for the labels and text inputs
        HBox inputComponents = new HBox(10);
        inputComponents.setAlignment(Pos.CENTER);
        inputComponents.getChildren().addAll(lengthLabel, lengthField, heightLabel, heightField);
```

```
    // create and configure a vertical container to hold all the components
    VBox root = new VBox(25);
    root.setAlignment(Pos.CENTER);
    root.getChildren().addAll(inputComponents, calculateButton, display);

    // create a new scene and add it to the stage
    Scene scene = new Scene(root, 350, 250);
    stage.setScene(scene);
    stage.setTitle("Rectangle GUI");
    stage.show();
}

public static void main(String[] args)
{
    launch(args);
}

}
```

In order to connect a GUI to a class, we create an object of that class within the GUI class—and as you can see that is what we have done here. We have declared an attribute, testRectangle, which we have initialized as a new Rectangle with a length and height of zero (since the user has not entered anything yet):

```
private Rectangle testRectangle = new Rectangle(0,0);
```

After this we declare the graphics components; the only one of these that you have not yet come across is the TextArea, which is the large text area that you see in Fig. 23.11, where the area and perimeter of the rectangle will be displayed. As you can see, it is a useful component for entering and displaying text, although this time we are using it only to display text, not to enter it. We have declared and configured it as follows:

```
TextArea display = new TextArea();
display.setEditable(false);
display.setMinSize(210,50);
display.setMaxSize(210,50);
```

We have prevented the possibility of entering text by the use of the setEditable method, and we have given it a fixed size by calling both the setMinSize and setMaxsize methods.

Something we need to draw your attention to is the lambda expression that we have sent into the setOnAction method of the calculate button.

```
calculateButton.setOnAction( e ->
          {
                  // check that fields are not empty
                  if(lengthField.getText().isEmpty() || heightField.getText().isEmpty())
                  {
                          display.setText("Length and height must be entered");
                  }
                  else
                  {
                          // convert text input to doubles and set the length and height of the Rectangle
                          this.testRectangle.setLength(Double.parseDouble(lengthField.getText()));
                          this.testRectangle.setHeight(Double.parseDouble(heightField.getText()));

                          // use the methods of Rectangle to calculate the area and perimeter
                          display.setText("The area is: " + df.format(this.testRectangle.calculateArea())
                                            + "\n" + "The perimeter is: "
                                                  + df.format(this.testRectangle.calculatePerimeter()));
                  }
          }
                          );
```

The first thing that we do here is to check that something has actually been entered. We do this by reading the `String` that is currently in the `TextField` by calling its `getText` method and then calling the `isEmpty` method of `String`.

If either one of the fields is empty then an error message is displayed; otherwise we continue with the task. We could have, if we had wanted to, done some more input validation—for example we could have checked that zeros or negative numbers had not been entered.

If there is no error, we use the `setLength` and `setHeight` methods of `Rectangle` to set the length and the height of `testRectangle` to the values entered. However, these methods expect to receive **double**s—but the `getText` method of `TextField`, which we use to see what has been entered, returns a `String`. We must therefore perform a conversion, which we do with the `parseDouble` method of the `Double` class.

```
this.testRectangle.setLength(Double.parseDouble(lengthField.getText()));
this.testRectangle.setHeight(Double.parseDouble(heightField.getText()));
```

It might have occurred to you that if the `String` did not contain a number, then this would cause an exception to be thrown, as we explained in Chap. 20. In the end of chapter exercises we have given you an opportunity to improve on this by handling the exception smoothly.

You should note that had we wanted to convert the `String`s to **int**s, we would have used the `parseInt` method of the `Integer` class.

Incidentally, if you want to do this the other way round and convert a **double** or an **int** to a `String`, you can do so simply by concatenating it onto an empty `String`, as shown in the examples below:

```
String s = "" + 3;
```

or:

```
String s = "" + 3.12;
```

You will probably have noticed that at the beginning of the start method we have created a DecimalFormat object as follows:

```
DecimalFormat df = new DecimalFormat("0.0#");
```

The code that displays the result in the setOnAction method uses this to ensure that the output is formatted in the way that we want (at least one digit is always displayed after the decimal point with a second displayed if it is non-zero—see the example in Fig. 23.11):

```
display.setText("The area is: " + df.format(this.testRectangle.calculateArea())
                         + "\n" + "The perimeter is: "
                              + df.format(this.testRectangle.calculatePerimeter())));
```

If you take a look at the rest of the code you will see that we have arranged our items by using an HBox to hold the labels and fields for input, so they are lined up horizontally, and then used a VBox to line this up vertically with the button and the display area. This is something you should be getting used to by now, so we can move on to the next section where we explain more about how to use these boxes, as well as other containers, each of which lays out the components in a different way.

23.9   Containers and Layouts

You have already seen how much we can achieve just with an HBox and a VBox—we have found these containers to be very versatile, and for simple applications you can do an enormous amount just with these two containers. So we start this section telling you a bit more about what we can do with these, and then we go on to show you some other containers with different layout policies.

23.9.1   More About *HBox* and *VBox*

In Fig. 23.12 you can see twelve VBoxes (although they could have been HBoxes because each one contains only one component), organized in four groups of three. We have drawn a border around each one and coloured the background (we will show you how to do this in a moment). Each box contains a Button—the presence of the border shows the effect of setting the alignment to different values.

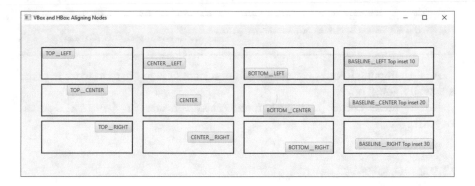

Fig. 23.12 Aligning nodes

You will recall that the only alignment we have seen so far is Pos.CENTER, but there are 11 others that we can choose from. Most are self-explanatory—but the three on the right need a little explanation. Pos.BASELINE_LEFT, Pos.BASE-LINE_CENTER and Pos.BASELINE_RIGHT place the component in the lowest position available and are most relevant to text fields where we want the text to appear at the bottom of a window—as in a chat application, for example. In our diagram we have set our boxes to have a top inset, and the buttons are then positioned accordingly.

To set some insets on a component we use the setPadding method, with a statement such as this:

```
box.setPadding(new Insets(10, 20, 10, 20));
```

The parameters to the Insets constructor are all **double**s and define the insets for the top, right, bottom and left insets, respectively. A single parameter would set all four insets to the same value.

Here box could be any component such as a VBox or HBox, or a Button, Label or TextField for example, as all these inherit the setPadding method from a higher level class.

We also promised to show you how to create a border and background colour. To get the black borders that you see in the diagram we did the following:

```
box.setBorder(new Border(new BorderStroke(Color.BLACK, BorderStrokeStyle.SOLID,
                          new CornerRadii(0),new BorderWidths(2)))));
```

This does seem to be a rather complicated process, but if you study it, you can easily see what is going on. The setBorder method requires an object of the class Border. To create this we have to send the constructor an object of Bor-derStroke, which requires four arguments. The argument names should speak for themselves, except perhaps for ConerRadii, which determines the roundness of the corners; in this example a value of zero produces square corners. To achieve the background colour we did this:

```
box.setBackground(new Background(new BackgroundFill(Color.LIGHTYELLOW,
                                        new CornerRadii(0), new Insets(0))));
```

Again, although it looks complicated at first sight, it is not hard to work out what is actually going on.

All of these border and background classes reside in `javafx.scene.layout`.

23.9.2   GridPane

A `GridPane` is a very useful container. As its name suggests, it lays out the components in a matrix of rows and columns, as shown in Fig. 23.13.

The following lines of code would create a `GridPane` object, and configure it to position the components in the centre of each cell, and to leave a 10 pixel vertical gap (the gap between rows) and a 5 pixel horizontal gap (the gap between columns).

```
GridPane pane = new GridPane();
pane.setAlignment(Pos.CENTER);
pane.setVgap(10);
pane.setHgap(5);
```

The really good thing about a `GridPane` is its flexibility—it is sized dynamically as you insert the components, as are the individual cells. For example we could insert a `Button`, `myButton`, to the above `GridPane` object as follows:

`pane.add(myButton, columnIndex, rowIndex);`

`columnIndex` and `rowIndex` are **int**s—we start counting from zero, so the following line of code would add the button in column 4, row 6:

`pane.add(myButton, 3, 5);`

Fig. 23.13 Using a *GridPane*

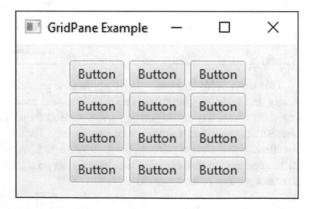

Because of its flexibility, GridPane can be very versatile and will allow you to create quite complex presentations—the best thing you can do, as usual, is to try some experiments of your own.

23.9.3   StackPane

A StackPane, as its name suggests, stacks components on top of each other. In Fig. 23.14 we have created three different coloured rectangles, each one smaller than the previous one, and added them to the StackPane from largest to smallest.

The components are added as before by calling the getChildren method inherited by StackPane. Here we have chosen to align them in the centre of the pane. You can see that there is a lot of potential here for drawing interesting shapes, and as before you should conduct your own experiments.

23.10   Key Events

The other common input event is a key event. A key event occurs whenever a key is pressed or released. One of the common applications of this event is to check if the key pressed was the <Enter> key, which indicates that the entry is completed.

There are three common types of key event which are summarised in Table 23.2.

Fig. 23.14 Using a
StackPane

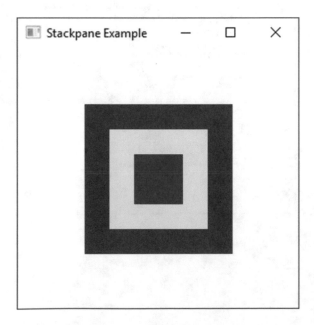

We have developed a little application to demonstrate this. The application, which we have called `TextConverter`, allows the user to type something into a text field, and when <Enter> is pressed the content of the text field is displayed below in upper case. This is shown in Fig. 23.15—you can see we have used a similar interface to the `PushMe` class, but this time there is no button, as the application responds to a key press rather than a mouse click.

Here is the code for the class:

TextConverter.java

```java
import javafx.application.Application;
import javafx.geometry.Pos;
import javafx.scene.Scene;
import javafx.scene.control.Label;
import javafx.scene.control.TextField;
import javafx.scene.layout.VBox;
import javafx.scene.paint.Color;
import javafx.scene.text.Font;
import javafx.stage.Stage;

public class TextConverter extends Application
{
    @Override
    public void start(Stage stage)
    {
        // create and configure a text field for user entry
        TextField textField = new TextField();
        textField.setMaxWidth(250);

        // create and configure a label to display the output
        Label label= new Label();
        label.setTextFill(Color.RED);
        label.setFont(Font.font("Ariel", 20));

        // display the contents of textField in upper case when <Enter> is pressed
        textField.setOnKeyTyped(e ->
                            {
                                if(e.getCharacter().equals("\r"))
                                {
                                    label.setText(textField.getText().toUpperCase());
                                }
                            }
                        );
        // create and configure a VBox to hold the components
        VBox root = new VBox();
        root.setSpacing(10);
        root.setAlignment(Pos.CENTER);

        //add the components to the VBox
        root.getChildren().addAll(textField, label);

        // create a new scene
        Scene scene = new Scene(root);

        //add the scene to the stage, then configure the stage and make it visible
        stage.setScene(scene);
        stage.setTitle("Text Converter");
        stage.setHeight(150);
        stage.setWidth(350);
        stage.show();
    }

    public static void main(String[] args)
    {
        launch(args);
    }
}
```

The only thing we need to draw your attention to is this:

```
textField.setOnKeyTyped(e ->
                        {
                            if(e.getCharacter().equals("\r"))
                            {
                                label.setText(textField.getText().toUpperCase());
                            }
                        }
                        );
```

We are using the convenience method setOnKeyTyped to program the response to a key stroke. The event is triggered when the key is pressed and released. You can see that the lambda expression deals with the possibility that the <Enter> key has been pressed. In order to do this, we have made use of the getCharacter method of e, the KeyEvent parameter that is sent into the handle method of EventHandler when the event concerned is a key event.

After a KEY_TYPED event, the getCharacter method returns a string which holds the value of the character returned. We have checked to see if this is the special character (\r) which represents the <Enter> key (Unicode 13). If it was the <Enter> key, the entire string is converted to upper case and copied from the text field to the label.

23.11   More Input Options

In all the examples we have seen so far the user has entered information via a TextField. In this section we are going to show you three additional input methods, with which you are already familiar—combo boxes, check boxes and radio buttons.

Table 23.2 Types of key event

KEY_TYPED	This event occurs when a key has been typed (pressed and released)
KEY_PRESSED	This event occurs when a key has been pressed
KEY_RELEASED	This event occurs when a key has been released

Fig. 23.15 The *TextConverter* application

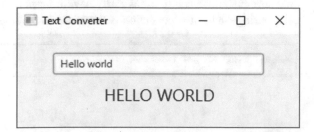

23.11.1   Combo Boxes

A combo box is a very common way of offering choices. Our example is shown in
Fig. 23.16.

Here is the code:

ComboBoxExample.java

```java
import javafx.application.Application;
import javafx.geometry.Insets;
import javafx.geometry.Pos;
import javafx.scene.Scene;
import javafx.scene.control.ComboBox;
import javafx.scene.control.Label;
import javafx.scene.layout.VBox;
import javafx.stage.Stage;

public class ComboBoxExample extends Application
{
    @Override
    public void start(Stage stage)
    {
        final double WIDTH = 400;
        final double HEIGHT = 150;

        // declare a String type combo box
        ComboBox<String> box = new ComboBox<>();

        // add the choices
        box.getItems().addAll("Small", "Medium", "Large", "Extra large");

        // set the intitial text
        box.setValue("Chooose your size");

        Label message = new Label();

        // display the user's choice

        box.setOnAction(e -> message.setText("You have chosen: " + box.getValue()));

        VBox root = new VBox(10);


        root.setPadding(new Insets(20, 20, 20, 20));
        root.setAlignment(Pos.TOP_CENTER);

        root.getChildren().addAll(box, message);

        Scene scene = new Scene(root, WIDTH, HEIGHT);
        stage.setScene(scene);
        stage.setTitle("Combo Box Example");
        stage.show();
    }

    public static void main(String[] args)
    {
        launch(args);
    }
}
```

The only new thing here is the combo box itself. The `ComboBox` class is a
generic class, so that the type of items held can vary—most commonly the box will
hold strings, but we could just as easily have images for example. In our case we are
using strings, and the declaration is therefore as follows:

```java
ComboBox<String> box = new ComboBox<>();
```

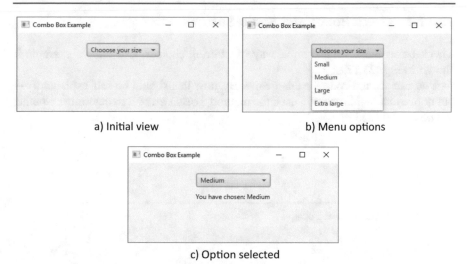

a) Initial view   b) Menu options

c) Option selected

Fig. 23.16 Combo box example

The menu items are added by using the `getItems` method:

```
box.getItems().addAll("Small", "Medium", "Large", "Extra large");
```

We want the box to start off displaying the instruction, so we use the `setValue` method for this purpose:

```
box.setValue("Chooose your size");
```

The other point to note is the use of the `getValue` method to retrieve the current item displayed—we use this to display the choice made by the user:

```
box.setOnAction(e -> message.setText("You have chosen: " + box.getValue()));
```

23.11.2   Check Boxes and Radio Buttons

Check boxes are a very familiar way of offering choices. Our simple example is shown in Fig. 23.17.

You can see the code for this below. By now this should be self-explanatory— but notice that in this case we used the method isSelected to determine whether the box is selected or not.

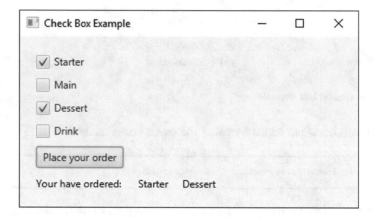

Fig. 23.17 Check box example

CheckBoxExample.java

```java
import javafx.scene.control.Button;
import javafx.application.Application;
import javafx.geometry.Insets;
import javafx.geometry.Pos;
import javafx.scene.Scene;
import javafx.scene.control.CheckBox;
import javafx.scene.control.Label;
import javafx.scene.layout.VBox;
import javafx.stage.Stage;

public class CheckBoxExample extends Application
{
    @Override
    public void start(Stage stage)
    {
        final double WIDTH = 400;
        final double HEIGHT = 200;

        // create four check boxes
        CheckBox starter = new CheckBox("Starter");
        CheckBox mainCourse = new CheckBox("Main");
        CheckBox dessert = new CheckBox("Dessert");
        CheckBox drink = new CheckBox("Drink");

        Button submitButton = new Button("Place your order");
        Label message = new Label();

        // clicking the button
        submitButton.setOnAction(e -> {
                            String yourOrder = "Your have ordered: ";

                            if(!starter.isSelected()&& !mainCourse.isSelected()
                                    && !dessert.isSelected() && !drink.isSelected())
                            {
                                    yourOrder = "You did not select anything";
                            }
                            else
                            {
                                    if(starter.isSelected())
                                    {
                                        yourOrder = yourOrder + "      Starter";
                                    }

                                    if(mainCourse.isSelected())
                                    {
                                        yourOrder = yourOrder + "      Main";
                                    }
                                    if(dessert.isSelected())
                                    {
                                        yourOrder = yourOrder + "      Dessert";
                                    }
                                    if(drink.isSelected())
                                    {
                                        yourOrder = yourOrder + "      Drink";
                                    }
                            }
                                message.setText(yourOrder);
                        }
                    );

        VBox root = new VBox(10);
        root.setPadding(new Insets(20, 20, 20, 20));
        root.setAlignment(Pos.CENTER_LEFT);

        root.getChildren().addAll(starter, mainCourse, dessert, drink, submitButton, message);

        Scene scene = new Scene(root, WIDTH, HEIGHT);

        stage.setScene(scene);
        stage.setTitle("Check Box Example");
        stage.show();
    }

    public static void main(String[] args)
    {
        launch(args);
    }
}
```

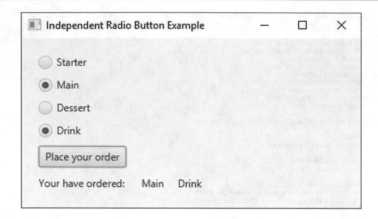

Fig. 23.18 Independent radio buttons

Radio buttons are very similar to check boxes, although they are round instead of square. They can operate in exactly the same way as check boxes, but can also be made to operate as a group, so that only one item can be selected at a time; if a box is selected and then the user chooses another box, the first one is cleared.

Figure 23.18 shows an example of radio buttons working independently. You can see that it is the same as our check box example, with the check boxes replaced by radio buttons.

All we needed to do was to replace the declarations of the four check boxes with the following code:

```
RadioButton starter = new RadioButton("Starter");
RadioButton mainCourse = new RadioButton("Main");
RadioButton dessert = new RadioButton("Dessert");
RadioButton drink = new RadioButton("Drink");
```

Figure 23.19 shows an example of radio buttons acting together in a group—only one item can be selected.

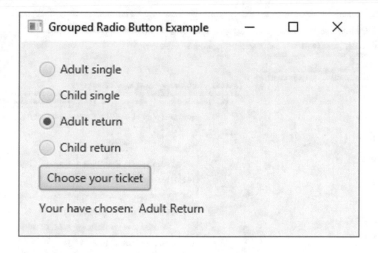

Fig. 23.19 Grouped radio buttons

Here is the code:

```
GroupedRadioButtonExample.java

import javafx.application.Application;
import javafx.geometry.Insets;
import javafx.scene.Scene;
import javafx.scene.control.Button;
import javafx.scene.control.Label;
import javafx.scene.control.RadioButton;
import javafx.scene.layout.VBox;
import javafx.stage.Stage;
import javafx.geometry.Pos;
import javafx.scene.control.ToggleGroup;

public class GroupedRadioButtonExample extends Application
{
    @Override
    public void start(Stage stage)
    {
        final double WIDTH = 350;
        final double HEIGHT = 200;

        // declare the radio buttons
        RadioButton adultSingle = new RadioButton("Adult single");
        RadioButton childSingle = new RadioButton("Child single");
        RadioButton adultReturn = new RadioButton("Adult return");
        RadioButton childReturn = new RadioButton("Child return");

        // add the radio buttons to a toggle group
        ToggleGroup group = new ToggleGroup();
```

```
    group.getToggles().addAll(adultSingle, childSingle, adultReturn, childReturn);

    Button submitButton = new Button("Choose your ticket");
    Label message = new Label();

    // clicking the button
    submitButton.setOnAction(e-> {
                                String yourOrder = "Your have chosen: ";
                                if(!adultSingle.isSelected()&& !childSingle.isSelected()
                                    && !adultReturn.isSelected() && !childReturn.isSelected())
                                {
                                        yourOrder = "You did not chose a ticket";
                                }
                                else
                                {
                                        if(adultSingle.isSelected())
                                        {
                                                yourOrder = yourOrder + " Adult Single";
                                        }
                                        else if(childSingle.isSelected())
                                        {
                                                yourOrder = yourOrder + " Child Single";
                                        }
                                        else if(adultReturn.isSelected())
                                        {
                                                yourOrder = yourOrder + " Adult Return";
                                        }
                                        else if(childReturn.isSelected())
                                        {
                                                yourOrder = yourOrder + " Child Return";
                                        }
                                }
                                message.setText(yourOrder);
                            }
                    );

    VBox root = new VBox(10);
    root.setPadding(new Insets(20, 20, 20, 20));
    root.setAlignment(Pos.CENTER_LEFT);
    root.getChildren().addAll(adultSingle, childSingle, adultReturn, childReturn,
                                                submitButton, message);

    Scene scene = new Scene(root, WIDTH, HEIGHT);
    stage.setScene(scene);
    stage.setTitle("Grouped Radio Button Example");
    stage.show();
    }

    public static void main(String[] args)
    {
        launch(args);
    }
}
```

As you can see we have declared a `ToggleGroup` and added our radio buttons to it:

```
ToggleGroup group = new ToggleGroup();
group.getToggles().addAll(adultSingle, childSingle, adultReturn, childReturn);
```

The buttons now act as one unit—if a button is already selected when another button is chosen, then the first button is cleared.

23.11.3 Drop-Down Menus

A drop-down menu, or pull-down menu, is a very common way to offer choices to the user of a program. In Fig. 23.20 we see a very simple example indeed.

Fig. 23.20 Drop-down menu example

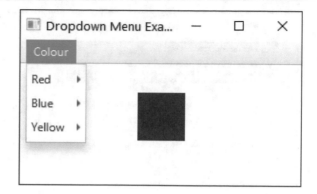

The program allows the user to choose the colour of a square shape by means of a pull-down menu on the top bar.

The code for this class is presented below:

MenuExample.java

```java
import javafx.application.Application;
import javafx.geometry.Insets;
import javafx.scene.Scene;
import javafx.scene.control.Menu;
import javafx.scene.control.MenuBar;
import javafx.scene.layout.Background;
import javafx.scene.layout.VBox;
import javafx.scene.paint.Color;
import javafx.scene.shape.Rectangle;
import javafx.stage.Stage;
import javafx.geometry.Pos;
import javafx.scene.layout.HBox;

public class MenuExample extends Application
{
    @Override
    public void start(Stage stage)
    {
        final double WIDTH = 300;
        final double HEIGHT = 150;

        // create and configure a menu bar
        MenuBar bar = new MenuBar();

        // create drop-down menu
        Menu rectMenu = new Menu("Colour");

        // add the drop-down menu to the menu bar
        bar.getMenus().add(rectMenu);

        // create menu items
        Menu red = new Menu("Red");
        Menu blue = new Menu("Blue");
        Menu yellow = new Menu("Yellow");

        // add menu items to drop-down menu
        rectMenu.getItems().addAll(red, blue, yellow);

        // create the rectangle
```

```
        Rectangle rect = new Rectangle(WIDTH/6, HEIGHT/3);

        // set initial colour
        rect.setFill(Color.RED);

        // define the behaviour for each menu item
        red.setOnAction(e ->  rect.setFill(Color.RED));
        blue.setOnAction(e -> rect.setFill(Color.BLUE));
        yellow.setOnAction(e -> rect.setFill(Color.YELLOW));

        // create and configure an HBox to hold the rectangle
        HBox box = new HBox();
        box.setPadding(new Insets(30));
        box.setAlignment(Pos.CENTER);

        // create VBox to hold the menu bar and the HBox
        VBox root = new VBox();
        root.setAlignment(Pos.TOP_LEFT);
        root.setBackground(Background.EMPTY);
        box.getChildren().add(rect);
        root.getChildren().addAll(bar, box);

        // create the scene and add the VBox
        Scene scene = new Scene(root, WIDTH, HEIGHT);

        // configure the stage
        stage.setScene(scene);
        stage.setTitle("Dropdown Menu Example");
        stage.show();
    }

    public static void main(String[] args)
    {
        launch(args);
    }
}
```

You can see that the menu is constructed by creating a menu bar, creating a menu to add to that bar and then creating the menu items and adding them to the menu (with getItems as opposed to getChildren):

```
// create and configure a menu bar
MenuBar bar = new MenuBar();

// create drop-down menu
Menu rectMenu = new Menu("Colour");

// add the drop-down menu to the menu bar
bar.getMenus().add(rectMenu);

// create menu items
Menu red = new Menu("Red");
Menu blue = new Menu("Blue");
Menu yellow = new Menu("Yellow");

// add menu items to drop-down menu
rectMenu.getItems().addAll(red, blue, yellow);
```

We are now able to add the event handlers to the menus, using the convenience method setOnAction that we have seen before:

```
red.setOnAction(e ->  rect.setFill(Color.RED));
blue.setOnAction(e -> rect.setFill(Color.BLUE));
yellow.setOnAction(e -> rect.setFill(Color.YELLOW));
```

Here we have only one menu in our menu bar. It is, however, perfectly possible to have more than one menu as we see in Fig. 23.21.

Fig. 23.21 Drop-down menu
example with two menus

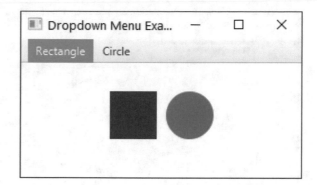

We have left the implementation of this for you to complete as an end of chapter exercise.

23.11.4 Pop-Up Dialogues

JavaFX provides a very useful control class called `Dialog`, which has subclasses called `Alert`, `ChoiceDialog` and `TextInputDialog`. These provide pop-up windows which allow the user to view or enter information. One of the very useful aspects of this is that we can begin an application by showing a pop-up window that gets some information from the user before showing the main scene graphic.

The program below demonstrates how a couple of these classes work.

```java
DialogDemo.java
import java.util.Optional;
import javafx.application.Application;
import static javafx.application.Application.launch;
import javafx.geometry.Pos;
import javafx.scene.Scene;
import javafx.scene.control.Alert;
import javafx.scene.control.Alert.AlertType;
import javafx.scene.control.TextField;
import javafx.scene.control.Button;
import javafx.scene.control.Label;
import javafx.scene.control.TextInputDialog;
import javafx.scene.layout.VBox;
import javafx.stage.Stage;

public class DialogDemo extends Application
{
    private String name;
    @Override
    public void start(Stage stage)
    {
        this.name = getUserName(); // get the user name by calling a text input dialog

        Label label = new Label("Enter your name");
        TextField entry = new TextField();
        entry.setMaxWidth(100);
```

```
            Button button = new Button ("Check name");

            // call a choice dialog
            button.setOnAction(e ->
                                {
                                    if(this.name.equals(entry.getText()))
                                    {
                                        showCorrect();
                                    }
                                    else
                                    {
                                        showIncorrect();
                                    }
                                }
                            );

        VBox root = new VBox(10);
        root.setAlignment(Pos.CENTER);
        root.getChildren().addAll(label, entry, button);

        Scene scene = new Scene(root);
        stage.setScene(scene);
        stage.setTitle("Demo");
        stage.setWidth(250);
        stage.setHeight(250);
        stage.show();
    }

    private String getUserName()
    {
        TextInputDialog dialog = new TextInputDialog();
        dialog.setHeaderText("Enter your name");
        dialog.setTitle("Text Input Dialog");
        Optional<String> response = dialog.showAndWait();
        return response.get(); // extract the string from the Optional object
    }

    private void showCorrect() // show information alert
    {
        Alert alert = new Alert(AlertType.INFORMATION);
        alert.setHeaderText("Information");
        alert.setContentText("That is correct");
        alert.showAndWait();
    }

    private void showIncorrect() // show warning alert
    {
        Alert alert = new Alert(AlertType.WARNING);
        alert.setHeaderText("Warning");
        alert.setContentText("That is not your name");
        alert.showAndWait();
    }

    public static void main(String[] args)
    {
        launch(args);
    }
}
```

As you can see, the first thing that happens, even before the scene is configured and shown, is that a helper method getUserName is called. This causes the following popup to appear as shown in Fig. 23.22.

The code for getUserName is as follows:

```
private String getUserName()
{
    TextInputDialog dialog = new TextInputDialog();
    dialog.setHeaderText("Enter your name");
    dialog.setTitle("Text Input Dialog");

    Optional<String> response = dialog.showAndWait();
    return response.get();
}
```

Fig. 23.22 A text input
dialogue

As you can see from the code, we create and configure a `TextInputDialog` and then call its `showAndWait` method, which does exactly what it says—it shows the dialogue and waits for a value to be entered. The value entered is returned as an object of a special class called `Optional`. This is a generic wrapper class, and it is designed to allow whatever value it holds to be **null**, thus avoiding many instances where a `NullPointerException` is thrown. In this case our return item will be of type `Optional<String>`. The `String` value is retrieved with the `get` method of `Optional`.

Once the dialogue is closed, the main graphic appears (Fig. 23.23).

The code for the button causes one of two helper methods to be called—either `showCorrect` or `showIncorrect`:

```
private void showCorrect() // show information alert
{
    Alert alert = new Alert(AlertType.INFORMATION);
    alert.setHeaderText("Information");
    alert.setContentText("That is correct");
    alert.showAndWait();
}

private void showIncorrect() // show warning alert
{
    Alert alert = new Alert(AlertType.WARNING);
    alert.setHeaderText("Warning");
    alert.setContentText("That is not your name");
    alert.showAndWait();
}
```

There are a number of different types of `Alert`, and the particular type is provided as a parameter to the constructor. Here we are using `AlertType.INFORMATION` and `AlertType.WARNING`. The results are shown in Fig. 23.24.

Fig. 23.23 Dialogue demo application

Fig. 23.24 An information alert and a warning alert

There are other types of dialogue, and it is possible to vary the icons and messages. There is too much to cover in this chapter, but there is a lot that more to explore for those who are keen to do so. You can also see these in action in the next chapter.

23.12 Self-test Questions

1. Briefly describe the history of graphics programming in Java.
2. What are the names of the three methods that are called when a JavaFX application is launched? What is the purpose of each?
3. Which containers have been used in the following two scene graphics?

(a) 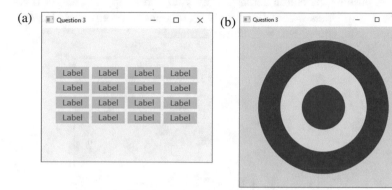 (b)

4. Describe how the following containers lay out the nodes that they contain:
   (a) a VBox   (b) an HBox   (c) a GridPane   (d) a StackPane
5. Explain how a number of *radio buttons* can be made to work together.
6. The diagram below shows the choices available under the "Select a country" option in a particular application.

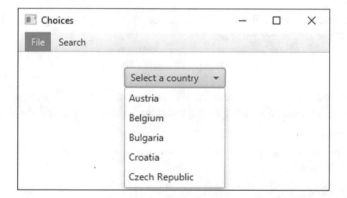

Referring to the above diagram, explain how you would begin a conditional statement that would execute some code if Bulgaria had been chosen.

23.13   Programming Exercises

1. Implement a few of the programs that we have developed in this chapter and experiment with different settings in order to change some the features—for example size, colour, position and so on.

2. Consider some changes or additions you could make to the PushMe class. For example, pushing the button could display your text in upper case—or it could say how many letters it contains. Maybe you could add some extra buttons.

3. The application shown below produces a triangle:

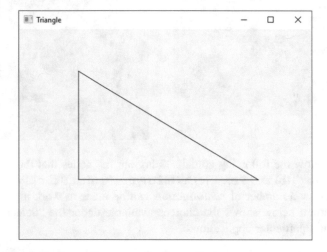

See if you can write the code to produce this triangle using three lines. We suggest the following vertices:

$$(100, 70) \quad (100, 250) \; (400, 250)$$

4. Below you see an application called ColourChanger which produces the following graphic in which two buttons can be used to change the background colour:

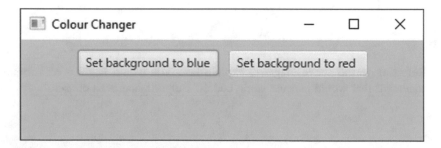

Write the code for this application.

5. Below is a variation on the ChangingFace class, which has three possible moods!

Rewrite the original code to produce this new design.

Hint: *The easiest way to achieve the "thinking" mouth is to set the* radius *attribute of* Arc *to zero.*

A more difficult approach would be to draw a line, but then you would have to create three different mouths, and each time check which was the current mouth, remove that and add the mouth you require. It is perfectly possible to do this because the list of nodes returned by the getChildren *method has methods named* contains *and* remove *as well as the* add *and* addAll *methods that you are used to.*

6. (a) Look back at the RectangleGUI that we developed in Sect. 23.8. Modify the code so that as well as checking that the values have been entered, and it also checks that the values entered are positive numbers.
   (b) Further modify the code so that the application handles exceptions thrown as a result of the user entering something other than a number for the length and height of the rectangle.
7. Create a graphical user interface for the Library class that we developed in Chap. 21. Make use of the many JavaFX features discussed in this chapter.
8. Implement the drop-down menu example with two menus as shown in Fig. 23.21.

Java Case Study

24

Outcomes

By the end of this chapter you should be able to:

- *identify the role of **packages** in organizing classes;*
- *specify system requirements by developing a **use case model**;*
- *annotate a **composition** association on a UML diagram;*
- *specify **enumerated types** in UML and implement them in Java;*
- *develop test cases from **behaviour specifications** found in the use case model;*
- *use the* `TabPane` *class to create an attractive user interface;*
- *add **tool tips** to JavaFX components.*

24.1 Introduction

You have now covered many aspects of the Java language. In this chapter we are going to take stock of what you have learnt by developing a Java application that draws upon all these topics. We will implement interfaces; we will catch and throw exceptions; we will make use of the collection classes in the `java.util` package; and we will store objects to file. We will also make use of many JavaFX components to develop an attractive graphical interface.

As with the Python case study we presented to you in the first semester, we will discuss the development of this application from the initial stage of requirements analysis, through to final implementation and testing stages. Along the way we will look at a few new concepts.

Supplementary Information The online version contains supplementary material available at https://doi.org/10.1007/978-3-031-01326-3_24.

Before we begin, however, we are going to make two quick diversions. First we will take a look at Java's **package** facility, which allows us to bundle together related classes, because we are going to make use of this in our case study. Second, we will describe Javadoc, which—as we briefly mentioned in Chap. 13—is a tool for professionally documenting Java classes.

24.2   Packages

A **package**, in Java, is not dissimilar to a module in Python; it is a *named collection* of *related classes*. In fact, you have already been using packages to access prewritten classes. For example, to store objects in an ordered collection you made use of the ArrayList class, which resides in the util package. To read and write to files you used classes in the io package. To organize the layout of your JavaFX applications you used classes such as Scene and Group from the scene package. Giving meaningful names to a set of related classes in this way makes it easy for programmers to locate these classes when required. Packages can themselves contain other packages. For example, as well as containing classes for organizing the layout of your JavaFX applications, the scene package also contains the control package, which contains JavaFX control classes such as Button and Label, since this group of classes is still logically related to JavaFX's collection of scene-related files.

The package name actually corresponds to the *name of the directory* (or folder as some operating systems call it) in which all the given classes reside. All the core Java packages themselves reside in a global Java directory, named simply java. This directory is not itself a package but a store for other packages. Since Java was launched a few additional global directories have been developed. In particular, the javafx directory contains all the packages and classes required for JavaFX development. Figure 24.1 illustrates part of this hierarchy of packages.

As you can see from Fig. 24.1, packages contain class files (that is the compiled Java byte code), not source files (the original Java instructions). This means the location of the original Java source files is unimportant here. They may be in the same directory as the class files, in another directory or, as in the case of the predefined Java packages, they may even no longer be available. It is worth reminding you that since the release of Java 11 the JavaFX package is not packaged with the core Java packages.

The most common way to access a class in a package is to add an **import** statement above the class. For example:

```
import java.io.FileReader; // allows compiler to find the FileReader.class file
```

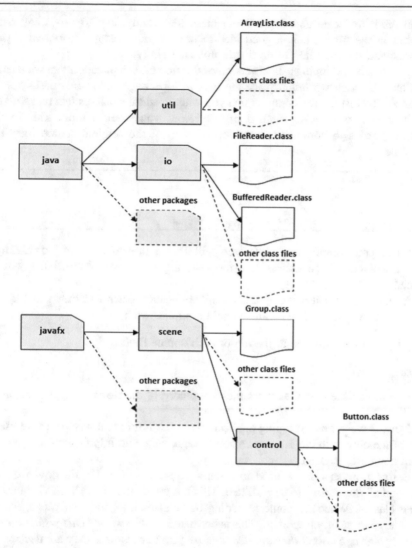

Fig. 24.1 A sample of the Java package hierarchy

You can see how the **import** statement matches the directory structure we illustrated in Fig. 24.1. Effectively the compiler is being told to look for the FileReader class in the io directory (package), which in turn is in the java directory (whose location is already known to the Java run-time system).

All the classes that you have developed so far actually already reside in a *single* package. This may seem strange as you did not instruct the compiler to add your classes to any package. In fact, what actually happens is that if you do not specifically ask your classes to be put in a package, then they all get added to some large unnamed package.

In order to locate and deploy your class files easily, and to avoid any name clashes in the future, it is a good idea to use named packages to organize your classes, and we are going to do that in this case study.

If we were developing a Java version of the `Hostel` application that we created in Chap. 12, then we might place the files in a package called `hostelApp`, for example. To instruct the compiler that you wish to add the classes that make up the application into a package called `hostelApp`, you would simply add the following **package** command at the top of each of the original source files. For example:

```
package hostelApp; // add this line to the top of the source file

public class Payment
{
    // more code here
}
```

When you compile this class, you will find a directory called `hostelApp` which will have been created and the resulting `Payment.class` file will be placed into this directory.[1]

All the classes that make up this *Hostel* application (such as `Tenant`, `Hostel` and so on) would need to be amended in a similar way:

1. add the following line to the top of each source file

```
package hostelApp;
```

2. ensure that the compiled class files are placed in the `hostelApp` directory.

Now, if we were developing applications in the future that wish to make use of any of the classes in our `hostelApp` package, we could import them like classes from any other package.

Before moving on, we need to discuss *package scope*. Up till now we have declared all our classes to be **public**. This has meant they have been visible to all other classes. When we come to adding our classes into our own packages, this becomes particularly important. This is because *classes can be made visible outside of their package only if they are declared as* **public**. Unless they are declared as **public**, classes by default have what is known as **package** scope. This means that they are visible *only to other classes within the same package*.

---

[1] If you are developing a class from scratch that you wish to add into a package, your Java IDE can be used so that the package line is inserted into your code for you and the required directory structure is created. If you are using your Java IDE to *revisit* classes previously written outside of a package (as in this example), you may need to ensure that the resulting directory structure is reflected in the project you are working in. Refer to your IDE's documentation for details about how to do this.

Not all classes in the package need be declared as **public**. Some classes may be part of the implementation only and the developer may not wish them to be made available to the client. These classes can have **package** scope instead of **public** scope. To give a class package scope, simply remove the **public** modifier from in front of the class declaration.

Packages provide a very good way of making your applications available to clients—this is done by converting them to JAR files. A JAR file (short for Java Archive) has the extension .jar and is simply a compressed file.

If you are working in a graphics environment, and there is a Java Runtime Environment installed on your computer, then it is also possible to create a JAR file that will run the program by double-clicking on its icon. We call such a JAR file an *executable* JAR file. All common IDEs provide very simple tools to both create a JAR file and to make this JAR file executable if you choose. We provide instructions on the accompanying website on how to do this for a popular Java IDE.

24.3   Javadoc

The Java Development Kit contains a tool, Javadoc, which allows you to generate documentation for classes in the form of HTML files. In order to use this tool you must comment your classes in the Javadoc style. As we mentioned in Chap. 1, Javadoc comments must begin with /** and end with */. Javadoc comments can also contain 'tags'. Tags are special formatting markers that allow you to record information such as the author of a piece of code. Table 24.1 gives some commonly used tags in Javadoc comments.

The @author and @version tags are used in the Javadoc comments for the class as a whole. For example, in the Runway class that you will see later:

```
package airportSys; // add class to package
import java.io.Serializable;

/**
 * This class is used to store details of a single runway.
 *
 * @author Charatan and Kans
 * @version 1st August 2021
 */

public class Runway implements Serializable
{
    // attributes and methods go here
}
```

Table 24.1 Some Javadoc tags

Tag	Information
@author	The name(s) of the code author(s)
@version	A version number for the code (often a date is used here)
@param	The name of a parameter and its description
@return	A description of the return value of a method
@throws	Any exceptions that may be thrown

The @param, @return and @throws tags can be used in the Javadoc comments preceding each method. The @param tag is used to name and describe the purpose of a given parameter. The @return tag is used to describe the value returned by a method. Here for example are the Javadoc comments for the leave method of the Airport class that you will encounter later:

```java
/**
 * Records a plane taking off from the airport
 *
 * @param   flightIn The plane's flight number
 * @throws  AirportException if plane not plane not not previously registered
 *                 or if plane not yet recorded as landed
 *                 or if the plane has not previously been recorded as ready for take off
 */

private void leave (String flightIn)
{
    // get plane associated with given flight number
    Plane plane = this.getPlane(flightIn); //  if not registered
    // throw exceptions if plane is not ready to leave airport
    if (plane.getStatus().compareTo(PlaneStatus.LANDED)<0)
    {
        throw new AirportException ("flight "+flightIn+" not yet landed");
    }
    if (plane.getStatus()==PlaneStatus.LANDED)
    {
        throw new AirportException ("flight "+flightIn+" must register to board");
    }
    // process plane leaving airport
    plane.vacateRunway(); // runway now free
    this.planes.remove(flightIn); // remove plane from list
}
```

Note that when Javadoc comments run over several lines it is common (though not necessary) to begin each line with a leading asterisk.

We will use Javadoc to document our classes throughout the remainder of this chapter.

The Javadoc HTML documentation is easily invoked directly by using the tools provided by any common IDE. Figure 24.2 gives part of the documentation generated as a result of the Javadoc comments within one of the classes that you will meet soon, Plane class.

24.4 System Overview

Now we can start to think about our case study. The application that we will develop will keep track of planes using a particular airport. So as not to over-complicate things, we will make a few assumptions:

- there will be no concept of *gates* for arrival and departure—passengers will be met at a runway on arrival and be sent to a runway on departure;
- planes entering airport airspace and requesting to land are either called in to land on a free runway or are told to join a queue of circling planes until a runway becomes available;
- once a plane departs from the airport it is removed from the system.

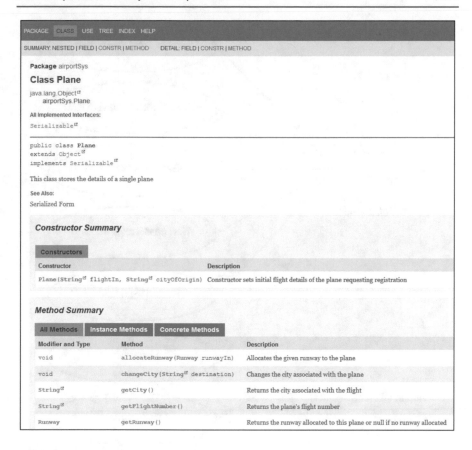

Fig. 24.2 Javadoc documentation generated for the *Plane* class

24.5 Requirements Analysis and Specification

Many techniques are used to determine system requirements. Among others, these include interviewing the client, sending out questionnaires to the client, reviewing any documentation if a current system already exists and observing people carrying out their work. A common way to document these requirements in UML is to develop a **use case model**. A use case model consists of **use case diagrams** and **behaviour specifications**.

A *use case diagram* is a simple way of recording the *roles* of different users within a system and the services that they require the system to deliver. The users (people or other systems) of a system are referred to as **actors** in use case diagrams and are drawn as simple stick characters. The roles these actors play in the system are used to annotate the stick character. The services they require are the so-called *use cases*. For example, in an ATM application an actor may be a customer and one

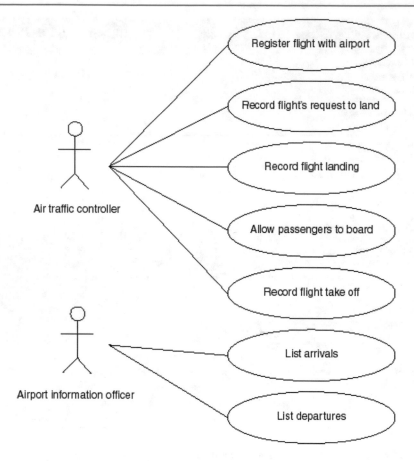

Fig. 24.3 A use case diagram for the airport application

of the use cases (services) required would be to withdraw cash. A very simple use case diagram for our application is given in Fig. 24.3.

Figure 24.3 depicts the actors in this application (air traffic controllers and information officers) and the services these actors require (registering a flight, listing arrivals and so on). Once a list of use cases has been identified, *behaviour specifications* are used to record their required functionality. A simple way of recording behaviour specifications is to give a simple textual description for each use case. Table 24.2 contains behaviour specifications for each use case given in Fig. 24.3. Note that the descriptions are always given from the user's point of view.

As the system develops, the use case descriptions may be modified as detailed requirements become uncovered. These descriptions will also be useful when testing the final application, as we will see later.

Table 24.2 Behaviour specifications for the airport application

Register flight with airport	An air traffic controller registers an incoming flight with the airport by submitting its unique flight number and its city of origin. If the flight number is already registered by the airport, the software will signal an error to the air traffic controller
Record flight's request to land	An air traffic controller records an incoming flight entering airport airspace, and requesting to land, by submitting its flight number. As long as the plane has previously registered with the airport, the air traffic controller is given an unoccupied runway number on which the plane will have permission to land. If all runways are occupied however, this permission is denied and the air traffic controller is informed to instruct the plane to circle the airport. If the plane has not previously registered with the airport, the software will signal an error to the air traffic controller
Record flight landing	An air traffic controller records a flight landing on a runway at the airport by submitting its flight number and the runway number. If the plane was not given permission to land on that runway, the software will signal an error to the air traffic controller
Allow passengers to board	An air traffic controller allows passengers to board a plane currently occupying a runway by submitting its flight number and its destination city. If the given plane has not yet recorded landing at the airport, the software will signal an error to the air traffic controller
Record flight take off	An air traffic controller records a flight taking off from the airport by submitting its flight number. If there are planes circling the airport, the first plane to have joined the circling queue is then given permission to land on that runway. If the given plane was not at the airport, the software will signal an error to the air traffic controller
List arrivals	The airport information officer is given a list of planes whose status is either due-to-land, waiting-to-land or landed
List departures	The airport information officer is given a list of planes whose status is currently waiting-to-depart (taking on passengers)

24.6   Design

The detailed design for this application is now presented in Fig. 24.4. It introduces some new UML notation, which was briefly referred to in Chap. 12. Have a look at it and then we will discuss it.

As you can see from Fig. 24.4, an Airport class has been introduced to represent the functionality of the system as a whole. The **public** methods of the Airport class correspond closely to the use cases identified during requirements analysis and specification. Notice we have provided two constructors: one that will allow us to create an empty Airport object and another that allows us to provide a filename (as a String) and load data stored in the given file. The **private** methods of the Airport class are there simply to help implement the functionality of the class.

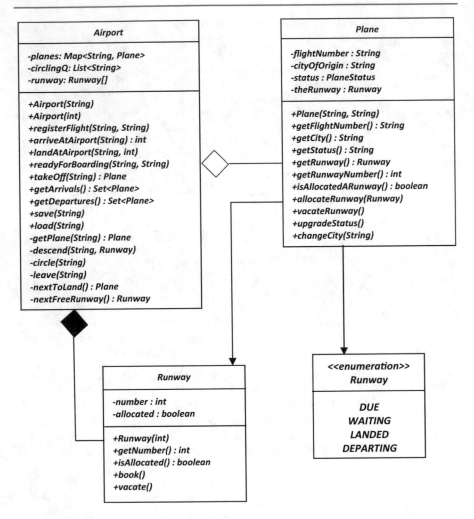

Fig. 24.4 Detailed design for the airport application

The requirements made clear that there would be *many* planes to process in this system. Since the airport exists regardless of the number of planes at the airport, the relationship between the `Airport` and `Plane` class is one of containment, as indicated with a hollow diamond. It makes sense to consider the collection classes in the `java.util` package at this point. As we record planes in the system, and process these planes, we will always be using a plane's flight number as a way of identifying an individual plane. A Map is the obvious collection to choose here, with flight numbers the *keys* of the Map and the planes associated with these flight numbers as *values* of the Map.

The one drawback with a Map, however, is that it is not ordered on input. When considering which plane in a circling queue of planes to land, ordering is important, as the first to join the queue should be the first to land. So we have also introduced a List to hold the flight numbers of circling planes.

The new notation that we referred to above is the filled diamond. The airport will also consist of a number of runways. In fact the airport cannot exist without this collection of runways. The airport is said to be *composed of* a number of runways as opposed to *containing* a number of planes. Notice that the UML notation for **composition** is the same as that for containment, except that the diamond is filled rather than hollow. We use an array to hold this collection of Runway objects.

Turning to the contained classes, the Runway class provides methods to allow for the runway number to be retrieved and for a runway to be booked and vacated. The Plane class also has access to a Runway object, to allow a plane to be able to book and vacate runways. You can see that as well as each plane being associated with a runway, the plane also has a flight number, a city and a status associated with it. The arrows from the Plane class to the PlaneStatus and Runway classes indicate the direction of the association. In this case a Plane object can send messages to a Runway and PlaneStatus object, but not vice versa.

The status of a plane is described in the PlaneStatus diagram. This diagram is the UML notation for an *enumerated type*, which is a type we have not met before.

24.7   Enumerated Types in UML

A type that consists of a few possible values, each with a meaningful name, is referred to as an **enumerated type**. The status of a plane is one example of an enumerated type. This status changes depending upon the plane's progress to and from the airport:

- when a plane registers with the airport, it is *due* to land;
- when a plane arrives in the airport's airspace, it is *waiting* to land (this plane may be told to come in and land, or it may have to circle the airport until a runway becomes available);
- when a plane touches down at the airport, it has *landed*;
- when a plane starts boarding new passengers, it is *departing* the airport.

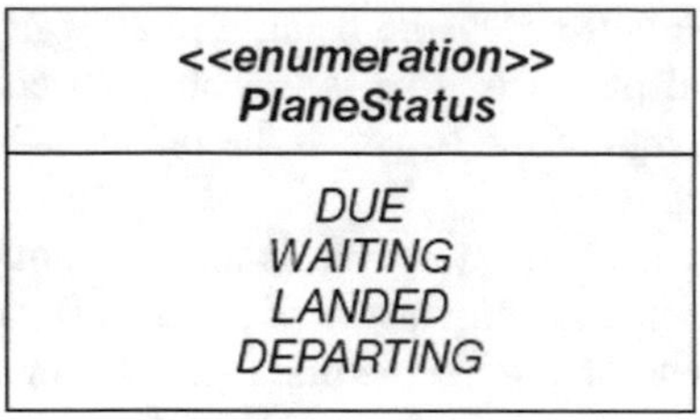

```
          <<enumeration>>
           PlaneStatus

              DUE
            WAITING
            LANDED
           DEPARTING
```

Fig. 24.5 The UML design of the enumerated *PlaneStatus* type

You can see from the design of the system that such a type is captured in UML by marking this type with <<enumeration>> as shown in Fig. 24.5.

We need to mark this UML diagram with <<enumeration>> so that it is not confused with a normal UML class diagram. With a normal UML class diagram, attributes and methods are listed in the lower portion. With an enumerated type diagram, the possible values of this type are given in the lower portion of the diagram, with each value being given a meaningful name. An attribute that is allocated a PlaneStatus type, such as status in the Plane class, can have any one of these values.

This completes our design analysis, so now let us turn our attention to the Java implementation.

24.8   Implementation

Since we are developing an application involving several classes, it makes sense to bundle these classes together into a single package. We will call this package airportSys. This means that all our classes will begin with the following **package** statement:

```
package airportSys;
```

It is a good idea to create a custom exception class to allow for application-specific errors to be flagged, so we have defined our own AirportException class.

```
AirportException.java

package airportSys; // add to package

/**
 * Application Specific Exception
 *
 * @author Charatan and Kans
 * @version 1st August 2021
 */

public class AirportException extends RuntimeException
{
    /**
     * Default Constructor
     */
    public AirportException ()
    {
        super("Error: Airport System Violation");
    }

    /**
     * Constructor that accepts an error message
     * @param msg
     */

    public AirportException (String msg)
    {
        super(msg);
    }
}
```

Now let us consider the remaining classes. First of all, we will look at the implementation of the enumerated PlaneStatus type.

24.8.1 Implementing Enumerated Types in Java

In order to define an enumerated type such as PlaneStatus, the **enum** keyword is used. The PlaneStatus type can now be implemented simply as follows:

```
// this is how to definine an enumerated type in Java
public enum PlaneStatus
{
    DUE, WAITING, LANDED, DEPARTING
}
```

You can see how easy it is to define an enumerated type. When defining such a type, do not use the **class** keyword, use the **enum** keyword instead. The different values for this type are then given within the braces, separated by commas.

These values create class constants, with the given names, as before. The type of each class constant is PlaneStatus and variables can now be declared of this type. For example, here we declare a variable of the PlaneStatus type and assign it to one of these class constant values:

```
PlaneStatus status; // declare PlaneStatus variable
status = PlaneStatus.DEPARTING; // assign variable a class constant
```

The variable `status` can take no other values, apart from those defined in the enumerated `PlaneStatus` type. Each enumerated type you define will also have an appropriate `toString` method generated for it, so values can be displayed on the screen:

```
System.out.println("Value = " + status);
```

Assuming we created this variable as above, this would display the following:

```
Value = DEPARTING
```

As well as a `toString` method, a few other methods are generated for you as well, and the **switch** statement can be used in conjunction with enumerated type variables. We will see examples of these features when we look at the code for the other classes in this application.

Of course, we must remember to add this `PlaneStatus` type into our `airportSys` package and to add the `Javadoc` comments:

PlaneStatus.java

```java
package airportSys; // add to package

/**
* Enumerated plane status type.
*
* @author Charatan and Kans
* @version 1st August 2021
*/

public enum PlaneStatus
{

    /**
     * Plane is due
     */
    DUE,

    /**
     * Plane is waiting
     */
    WAITING,

    /**
     * Plane has landed
     */
    LANDED,

    /**
     * Plane is departing
     */
    DEPARTING
}
```

24.8.2 The *Runway* Class

Here is the code for the `Runway` class, take a look at it and then we will discuss it.

Runway.java

```java
package airportSys; // add class to package
import java.io.Serializable;

/**
* This class is used to store details of a single runway.
*
* @author Charatan and Kans
* @version 1st August 2021
*/

public class Runway implements Serializable
{
    // attributes
    private int number;
    private boolean allocated;

    /**
     * Constructor sets the runway number
     *
     * @param numberIn
     */

    public Runway (int numberIn)
    {
        if (numberIn <1)
        {
            throw new AirportException ("invalid runway number "+numberIn);
        }
        this.number = numberIn;
        this.allocated = false;
    }

    /**
     *  Returns the runway number
     *  @return Returns the runway number
     */
    public int getNumber()
    {
        return this.number;
    }

    /**
     *  Checks if the runway has been allocated
     *  @return  Returns true if the runway has been allocated and false otherwise
     */
    public boolean isAllocated()
    {
        return this.allocated;
    }

    /**
     *  Records the runway as being booked
     */
    public void book()
    {
        this.allocated = true;
    }

    /**
     *  Records the runway as being vacant
     */
    public void vacate()
    {
        this.allocated = false;
    }
}
```

There is not much that needs to be said about this class. As we may wish to save and load objects from our system, we have to remember to indicate that this class is `Serializable`.

```
public class Runway implements Serializable
```

Notice that we have defined this as a **public** class so that it is accessible outside of the package. We did this as a runway is a generally useful concept in many applications; declaring this class **public** allows it to be reused outside of the `airportSys` package. In fact, we have declared most of our classes **public** for this reason.

24.8.3   The *Plane* Class

Here is the code for the `Plane` class. Have a close look at it and then we will discuss it.

```
Plane.java
package airportSys;

import java.io.Serializable;

/**
 * This class stores the details of a single plane
 *
 * @author Charatan and Kans
 * @version 2nd August 2021
 */
public class Plane implements Serializable
{

   // attributes
   private String flightNumber;
   private String city;
   private PlaneStatus status;
   private Runway theRunway; // to implement Runway association

   // methods

   /**
    * Constructor sets initial flight details of the plane requesting registration
    *
    * @param   flightIn      The flight number of the plane to register
    * @param   cityOfOrigin  The city of origin of the plane to register
    */
   public Plane(String flightIn, String cityOfOrigin)
   {
```

```
      this.flightNumber = flightIn;
      this.city = cityOfOrigin;
      this.status = PlaneStatus.DUE; // initial plane status set to DUE
      this.theRunway = null; // indicates no runway allocated
  }

  /**
   * Returns the plane's flight number
   * @return Returns the flight number
   */
  public String getFlightNumber()
  {
    return this.flightNumber;
  }

  /**
   * Returns the city associated with the flight
   * @return Returns the city
   */
  public String getCity()
  {
    return this.city;
  }

  /**
   * Returns the current status of the plane
   * @return Retuns the status
   */
  public PlaneStatus getStatus()
  {
    return  this.status;
  }

  /**
   * Returns the runway allocated to this plane or null if no runway allocated
   * @return Returns the runway
   */
  public Runway getRunway()
  {
    return  this.theRunway;
  }

  /**
   * Returns the runway number allocated to this plane
   * @return Returns the allocated runway number
   * @throws    AirportException if no runway allocated
   */
  public int getRunwayNumber()
  {
    if (this.theRunway == null)
    {
      throw new AirportException ("flight "+flightNumber+" has not been allocated a runway");
    }
    return this.theRunway.getNumber();
  }

  /**
   * Checks if the plane is allocated a runway
   * @return     Returns true if the plane has been allocated a runway
   *             and false otherwise
   */
  public boolean isAllocatedARunway()
  {
    return this.theRunway!=null;
  }

  /**
   * Allocates the given runway to the plane
   *
   * @param runwayIn The number of the runway to allocate
   * @throws     AirportException if runway parameter is null or runway already allocated
   */
  public void allocateRunway(Runway runwayIn)throws AirportException
  {
    if (runwayIn == null) // check runway has been sent
    {
      throw new AirportException ("no runway to allocate");
```

```
        }
        if (runwayIn.isAllocated())
        {
            throw new AirportException ("runway already allocate");
        }
        this.theRunway = runwayIn;
        this.theRunway.book();
    }

    /**
     * De-allocates the current runway
     *
     * @throws    AirportException if no runway allocated
     */
    public void vacateRunway()
    {
        if (this.theRunway==null)
        {
            throw new AirportException ("no runway allocated");
        }
        this.theRunway.vacate();
    }

    /**
     * Returns the String representation of the plane's status
     * @return Returns String representatnion of the plane's status
     */
    public String getStatusName()
    {
        return this.status.toString();
    }


    /**
     * Upgrades the status of the plane.
     */
    public void upgradeStatus()
    {
        switch(this.status)
        {
            case DUE: this.status =PlaneStatus.WAITING; break;
            case WAITING: this.status =PlaneStatus.LANDED; break;
            case LANDED: this.status =PlaneStatus.DEPARTING; break;
            case DEPARTING: throw new AirportException("Cannot upgrade DEPARTING status");
        }
    }

    /**
     * Changes the city associated with the plane
     * @param destinationIn The destination of the plane
     */
    public void changeCity (String destinationIn)
    {
        this.city = destinationIn;
    }

    /**
     * Returns a string representation of a plane
     * @return Returns String representation of plane
     */
    @Override
    public String toString()
    {
        String out =    "number: "+ this.flightNumber+  "\tcity: "+ this.city+  "\tstatus:
                                                        "+this.status;
        if (this.theRunway!=null)
        {
            out = out +"\trunway: "+ this.theRunway;
        }
        return out;
    }
}
```

Again, most of the points we raised with the `Runway` class are relevant to this `Plane` class. It needs to be `Serializable`, and it is declared **public**.

In addition you should look at the way in which we dealt with the `status` attribute. During class design we declared this attribute to be of the enumerated `PlaneStatus` type, so it has been implemented as follows:

```
private PlaneStatus status;
```

We can then assign this attribute values from the enumerated `PlaneStatus` type. For example, in the constructor, we initialize the status of a plane to DUE:

```
public Plane(String flightNumberIn, String cityOfOrigin)
{
    this.flightNumber = flightNumberIn;
    this.city = cityOfOrigin;
    this.status = PlaneStatus.DUE;
    this.theRunway = null;
}
```

The `getStatus` method returns the value of the `status` attribute, so the appropriate return type is `PlaneStatus`:

```
public PlaneStatus getStatus()
{
    return this.status;
}
```

The `upgradeStatus` method is interesting as it demonstrates how the **switch** statement can be used with enumerated type variables such as `status`:

```
public void upgradeStatus()
{
    switch(status) // this is an enumerated type variable
    {
        // 'case' statements can check the different enumerated values
        case DUE: this.status = PlaneStatus.WAITING; break;
        case WAITING: this.status = PlaneStatus.LANDED; break;
        case LANDED: this.status = PlaneStatus.DEPARTING; break;
        case DEPARTING: throw new AirportException("Cannot upgrade DEPARTING status");
    }
}
```

Here we are upgrading the status of a plane as it makes its way to, and eventually from, the airport. Notice that the value of the `status` attribute is checked in the **case** statements, but this value is *not* appended onto the `PlaneStatus` class name. For example:

```
// just use a status name in 'case' test
case DUE: this.status = PlaneStatus.WAITING; break;
```

However, in all other circumstances, such as assigning to the `status` attribute, the enumerated value *does* have to be appended onto the `PlaneStatus` class name:

```
// use class + status name in all other circumstances
case DUE: this.status = PlaneStatus.WAITING; break;
```

You can see that we should not be upgrading the status of a plane if its current status is DEPARTING, so an exception is thrown in this case:

```
case DEPARTING: throw new AirportException ("Cannot upgrade DEPARTING status");
```

Before we leave this class, also notice that by adding a runway attribute, theRunway, into the `Plane` class we can send messages to (access methods of) a `Runway` object, for example:

```
public void allocateRunway(Runway runwayIn)
{
    // some code here
    this.theRunway.book(); // 'book' is a 'Runway' method
}
```

24.8.4 The *Airport* Class

The `Airport` class encapsulates the functionality of the system. It does not include the interface to the application. As we have done throughout this book, we have kept the interface of an application separate from its functionality. That way, we can modify the way we choose to implement the functionality without needing to modify the interface, and vice versa. Examine it closely, being sure to read the comments, and then we will discuss it.

Airport.java

```
package airportSys;

import java.util.Map;
import java.util.HashMap;
import java.util.List;
import java.util.ArrayList;
import java.util.Set;
import java.util.HashSet;
import java.io.IOException;
import java.io.FileOutputStream;
import java.io.ObjectOutputStream;
import java.io.FileInputStream;
import java.io.ObjectInputStream;

/**
 * Class to provide the functionality of the airport system
 *
 * @author Charatan and Kans
 * @version 4th August 2021
 */
public class Airport
{

    // attributes
    private Map<String, Plane> planes;  // registered planes
    private List<String> circlingQ; //flight numbers of circling planes
    private Runway []runway; // runways allocated to the airport

    // methods

    /**
     * This Constructor allows airport data to be loaded from a file
     *
     * @param    filenameIn The name of the file
     * @throws   IOException if problems with opening and loading given file
```

```
 * @throws  ClassNotFoundException if objects in file not of the right type
 */
public Airport(String filenameIn)throws IOException, ClassNotFoundException
{
    load(filenameIn);
}


/**
 * This Constructor creates an empty collection of planes,
 * and allocates runways to the airport
 *
 * @param   numIn The number of runways
 * @throws  AirportException if negative runway number used
 */
public Airport (int numIn)
{
  try
  {
      // intialise runways
      this.runway = new Runway [numIn];
      for (int i = 0; i<numIn; i++)
      {
        this.runway[i] = new Runway (i+1);
      }
      // initially no planes allocated to airport
      this.planes = new HashMap<>();
      this.circlingQ = new ArrayList<>();
  }
  catch (Exception e)
  {
      // notice throwing an excpetion from a catch clause
      throw new AirportException("Invalid Runway Number set, application closing");
  }
}

/**
 * Registers a plane with the airport
 *
 * @param   flightIn The plane's flight number
 * @param   cityOfOrigin The plane's city of origin
 * @throws  AirportException if flight number already registered.
 */
public void registerFlight (String flightIn, String cityOfOrigin)
{
    if (this.planes.containsKey(flightIn))
    {
      throw new AirportException ("flight "+flightIn+" already registered");
    }
    Plane newPlane = new Plane (flightIn, cityOfOrigin);
    this.planes.put(flightIn, newPlane);
}

 /**
 * Records a plane arriving at the airport
 *
 * @param   flightIn The plane's flight number
 * @throws  AirportException if plane not previously registered
 *              or if plane already arrived at airport
 * @return Returns booked runway number or 0 if no runway available
 */
public int arriveAtAirport (String flightIn)
{
    Runway vacantRunway = nextFreeRunway(); // get next free runway
    if (vacantRunway != null) // check if runway available
    {
      descend(flightIn, vacantRunway); // allow plane to descend on this runway
      return vacantRunway.getNumber(); // return booked runway number
    }
    else // no runway available
    {
      circle(flightIn); // plane must join circling queue
      return 0; // indicates no runway available to land
    }
}

/**
```

```
 * Records a plane landing on a runway
 *
 * @param   flightIn The plane's flight number
 * @throws  AirportException if plane not previously registered
 *                           or if the runway is not allocated to this plane
 *                           or if plane has not yet signalled its arrival at the aiport
 *                           or if plane is already recorded as having landed.
 */
public void landAtAirport (String flightIn)
{
  Plane plane = getPlane(flightIn);
  if (plane.getStatus()== PlaneStatus.DUE)
  {
    throw new AirportException ("flight "+flightIn+" not signalled its arrival");
  }
  if (plane.getStatus().compareTo(PlaneStatus.WAITING)>0)
  {
    throw new AirportException ("flight "+flightIn+" already landed");
  }
  plane.upgradeStatus(); // upgrade status from WAITING to LANDED
}


/**
 * Records a plane boarding for take off
 *
 * @param   flightIn The plane's flight number
 * @param   destination The city of destination
 * @throws  AirportException  if plane not previously registered
 *                            or if plane not yet recorded as landed
 *                            or if plane already recorded as ready for take off
 */
public void readyForBoarding(String flightIn, String destination)
{
  Plane plane = getPlane(flightIn); // if not registered
  if (plane.getStatus().compareTo(PlaneStatus.LANDED)<0)
  {
    throw new AirportException ("flight "+flightIn+" not landed");
  }
  if (plane.getStatus()== PlaneStatus.DEPARTING)
  {
    throw new AirportException ("flight "+flightIn+" already registered to depart");
  }
  plane.upgradeStatus(); // upgrade status from LANDED to DEPARTING
  plane.changeCity(destination); // change city of origin to city of destination
}

/**
 * Records a plane taking off from the aiprort
 *
 * @param   flightIn The plane's flight number
 * @return  Returns next plane to take off or null if no plane is circling
 * @throws  AirportException    if plane not previously registered
 *                              or if plane not yet recorded as landed
 *                              or if the plane not previously recorded as taken off
 */
public Plane takeOff (String flightIn)
{
  leave(flightIn); // remove from plane register
  Plane nextFlight = nextToLand(); // return next circling plane to land
  if (nextFlight != null) // check circling flight exists
  {
    Runway vacantRunway = nextFreeRunway();
    descend(nextFlight.getFlightNumber(), vacantRunway); // allocate runway to circling plane
    return nextFlight; // send back details of next plane to land
  }
  else // no circling planes
  {
    return null;
  }
}


/**
 * Returns the set of planes due for arrival
 * @return Returns the set of planes due to arrive
 */
public Set<Plane> getArrivals()
```

```
    {
        Set<Plane> planesOut = new HashSet<>();
        Set<String> items = this.planes.keySet();
        for(String thisFlight: items)
        {
            Plane plane = this.planes.get(thisFlight);
            if (plane.getStatus() != PlaneStatus.DEPARTING)
            {
                planesOut.add(plane); // add to set
            }
        }
        return planesOut;
    }

    /**
     * Returns the set of planes due for departure
     * @return Returns the set of planes due to depart
     */
    public Set<Plane> getDepartures()
    {
        Set<Plane> planesOut = new HashSet<>();
        Set<String> items = this.planes.keySet();
        for(String thisFlight: items)
        {
            Plane plane = this.planes.get(thisFlight);
            if (plane.getStatus()==PlaneStatus.DEPARTING)
            {
                planesOut.add(plane); // add to set
            }
        }
        return planesOut;
    }

    /**
     * Returns the number of runways
     * @return Returns the number of runways
     */
    public int getNumberOfRunways()
    {
        return this.runway.length;
    }

    /**
     * Saves airport object to file
     *
     * @param    fileIn The name of the file
     * @throws   IOException if problems with opening and saving to given file
     */
    public void save(String fileIn)throws IOException
    {
        // notice try-with-resources to ensure file closes safely
        try ( FileOutputStream fileOut = new FileOutputStream(fileIn);
              ObjectOutputStream objOut = new ObjectOutputStream (fileOut))
        {
            objOut.writeObject(this.planes);
            objOut.writeObject(this.circlingQ);
            objOut.writeObject(this.runway);
        }
    }

    /**
     * Loads airport object from file
     *
     * @param    fileName The name of the file
     * @throws   IOException if problems with opening and loading given file
     * @throws   ClassNotFoundException if objects in file not of the right type
     */
    public void load (String fileName) throws IOException, ClassNotFoundException
    {
        // notice try-with-resources to ensure file closes safely
        try ( FileInputStream fileInput = new FileInputStream(fileName);
              ObjectInputStream objInput = new ObjectInputStream (fileInput))
        {
            this.planes = (Map<String, Plane>) objInput.readObject();
            this.circlingQ = (List<String>) objInput.readObject();
            this.runway = (Runway[])objInput.readObject();
        }
```

```
}


/**
 * Helper method to find next free runway
 *
 * @Returns the next free runway or null if there is none
 */

private Runway nextFreeRunway()
{
    for (Runway nextRunway : runway)
    {
        if (!nextRunway.isAllocated())
        {
            return nextRunway;
        }
    }
    return null;
}

/**
 * Returns the registered plane with the given flight number
 * @param flightIn The flight number of the plane
 * @throws AirportException if flight number not yet registered
 */
private Plane getPlane(String flightIn)
{
    if (!this.planes.containsKey(flightIn))
    {
        throw new AirportException ("flight "+flightIn+" has not yet registered");
    }
    return this.planes.get(flightIn);
}


/**
 * Records a plane descending on a runway
 *
 * @param    flightIn The plane's flight number
 * @param    runwayIn The runway the plane will be landing on
 * @throws AirportException      if plane not previously registered
 *                               or if plane already arrived at airport
 *                               or if plane already allocated a runway
 */
private void descend (String flightIn, Runway runwayIn)
{
  Plane plane = getPlane(flightIn); // if not registered
  if (plane.getStatus().compareTo(PlaneStatus.WAITING)>0)
  {
      throw new AirportException
         ("flight "+flightIn+" already at airport has status of " + plane.getStatusName());
  }
  if (plane.isAllocatedARunway())
  {
     throw new AirportException
        ("flight "+flightIn+" has already been allocated runway "+ plane.getRunwayNumber());
  }
  plane.allocateRunway(runwayIn);
  if (plane.getStatus()==PlaneStatus.DUE) // updraged status from DUE to WAITING
  {
      plane.upgradeStatus();
  }
}

/**
 * Records a plane joining the planes circling the airport
 *
 * @param    flightIn The plane's flight number
 * @throws AirportException if plane not previously registered
 *                          or if plane already arrived
 */
private void circle (String flightIn)
{
  Plane plane = getPlane(flightIn); // if not registered
  if (plane.getStatus()!= PlaneStatus.DUE)
  {
```

```
        throw new AirportException ("flight "+flightIn+" already at airport");
    }
    plane.upgradeStatus(); // updraged status from DUE to WAITING
    this.circlingQ.add(flightIn);
}


/**
 * Records a plane taking off from the airport
 *
 * @param    flightIn The plane's flight number
 * @throws   AirportException if plane not plane not not previously registered
 *                    or if plane not yet recorded as landed
 *                    or if the plane has not previously been recorded as ready for take off
 */

private void leave (String flightIn)
{
    // get plane associated with given flight number
    Plane plane = this.getPlane(flightIn); //  if not registered
    // throw exceptions if plane is not ready to leave airport
    if (plane.getStatus().compareTo(PlaneStatus.LANDED)<0)
    {
        throw new AirportException ("flight "+flightIn+" not yet landed");
    }
    if (plane.getStatus()==PlaneStatus.LANDED)
    {
        throw new AirportException ("flight "+flightIn+" must register to board");
    }
    // process plane leaving airport
    plane.vacateRunway(); // runway now free
    this.planes.remove(flightIn); // remove plane from list
}

/**
 * Locates next circling plane to land
 *
 * @return     Returns the next circling plane to land
 *                    or null if no planes
 */
private Plane nextToLand()
{
    if (!this.circlingQ.isEmpty()) // check circling plane exists
    {
        String flight =  this.circlingQ.get(0);
        this.circlingQ.remove(flight);
        return getPlane(flight); // could throw exception of not in list
    }
    else // no circling plane
    {
        return null;
    }
}

}
```

There is not a lot that is new here, but we draw your attention to a few implementation issues.

First, notice we have provided two constructors, as specified in Fig. 24.4. The first receives the name of a file and loads data from this given file (using the **private** load method to be found later in this `Airport` class); the associated exceptions are passed on if an error occurs during this process:

```
public Airport(String filenameIn)throws IOException, ClassNotFoundException
{
   this.load(filenameIn); // call private method to load airport data

}
public Airport (int numIn)
{
   try
   {
      // intialise runways
      this.runway = new Runway [numIn];
      for (int i = 0; i<numIn; i++)
      {
         this.runway[i] = new Runway (i+1);
      }
      // initially no planes allocated to airport
      this.planes = new HashMap<>();
      this.circlingQ = new ArrayList<>();
   }
   catch (Exception e)
   {
      // notice throwing an exception from a catch clause
      throw new AirportException("Invalid Runway Number set, application closing");
   }
}
```

The second constructor receives the number of runways associated with this airport and initializes all data to be empty.

Within this constructor you can see that we catch a general exception, in case something goes wrong when allocating the array, and throw our application-specific exception when this occurs. This can be useful if we wish to suppress the name of Java specific expectations and stick to the names of our own user-defined exceptions.

Most of the other **public** methods simply check for a list of exceptions and then upgrade the plane's status as it makes its way to and eventually from the airport.

Here, for example, is the method that records a plane that has previously landed at the airport, being ready to board new passengers for a new destination:

```
/**
 * Records a plane boarding for take off
 *
 * @param   flightIn The plane's flight number
 * @param   destination The city of destination
 * @throws  AirportException  if plane not previously registered
 *                            or if plane not yet recorded as landed
 *                            or if plane already recorded as ready for take off
 */
public void readyForBoarding(String flightIn, String destination)
{
   Plane plane = getPlane(flightIn); // if not registered
   if (plane.getStatus().compareTo(PlaneStatus.LANDED)<0)
   {
      throw new AirportException ("flight "+flightIn+" not landed");
   }
   if (plane.getStatus()== PlaneStatus.DEPARTING)
   {
      throw new AirportException ("flight "+flightIn+" already registered to depart");
   }
   plane.upgradeStatus(); // upgrade status from LANDED to DEPARTING
   plane.changeCity(destination); // change city of origin to city of destination
}
```

The first thing we need to do in this method is to check whether or not an AirportException needs to be thrown. The Javadoc comments make clear that there are three situations in which we need to throw such an exception.

First, an exception needs to be thrown if the given flight number has not been registered with the airport. At some point we also need to retrieve the `Plane` object from this flight number. Calling the helper method `getPlane` will do both of these things for us, as it throws an `AirportException` if the flight is not registered.

```
// retrieves plane or throws AirportException if flight is not registered
Plane thisPlane = getPlane(flightIn);
```

To check for the remaining exceptions, we need to check that the plane currently has the appropriate status to start taking on passengers. The `getStatus` method of a plane returns the status of a plane for us. We know from the previous section that this method returns a value of the enumerated type `PlaneStatus`.

An enumerated type will automatically have a number of methods generated. As we said earlier, it has a `toString` method—it also has a `compareTo` method. This latter works in exactly the same way as it does for `Strings`—it returns 0 when the two values are equal, a negative number when the first value is less than the second value and a positive number when the first value is greater than the second value. But what does it mean for a particular value of an enumerated type to be less than or greater than another value? The answer is that each value represents an integer, starting from zero for the first value to be declared and increasing by 1 for each value. So in the case of `PlaneStatus`, `DUE` represents 0, `WAITING` represents 1, `LANDED` represents 3, and `DEPARTING` represents 4. If a plane has a status that is less than `LANDED` it has not yet landed, so cannot be ready to board passengers—an `AirportException` is thrown:

```
// use 'compareTo' method to compare two status values
if (thisPlane.getStatus().compareTo(PlaneStatus.LANDED)<0)
{
    throw new AirportException ("flight "+flightIn+" not yet landed");
}
```

We also need to throw an `AirportException` if the plane already has a status of `BOARDING`. Although the `compareTo` method can be used to check for equality as well, with most classes it is common to use an `equals` method to do this. An `equals` method is generated for any enumerated type, such as `PlaneStatus`, that you define. However, because of the way enumerated types are implemented in Java, the simple equality operator (`==`) can also be used to check for equality:

```
// equality operator can be used to check if 2 enumerated values are equal
if (thisPlane.getStatus()== PlaneStatus.DEPARTING)
{
    throw new AirportException ("flight "+flightIn+" already registered to depart");
}
```

Having checked for exceptions, we can now indicate that this plane is ready for boarding by upgrading its status (from LANDED to DEPARTING) and by recording the flight's new destination city:

```
// we have cleared all the exceptions so we can update flight details now
thisPlane.upgradeStatus(); // upgrades status from LANDED to DEPARTING
thisPlane.changeCity(destination); // changes city to destination city
```

The inequality operator (! =) can also be used with enumerated types, to check for inequality of two enumerated type values. An example of this can be seen in the implementation of the arrivals method:

```
/**
 * Returns the set of planes due for arrival
 * @return Returns the set of planes due to arrive
 */
public Set<Plane> getArrivals()
{
    Set<Plane> planesOut = new HashSet<>();
    Set<String> items = this.planes.keySet();
    for(String thisFlight: items)
    {
      Plane plane = this.planes.get(thisFlight);
      if (plane.getStatus() != PlaneStatus.DEPARTING)
      {
            planesOut.add(plane); // add to set
      }
    }
    return planesOut;
}
```

Here we create an empty set of planes. We then add planes into this set if they do not have a status of DEPARTING:

```
// use inequality operator to check if status does not equal some value
if (thisPlane.getStatus() != PlaneStatus.DEPARTING)
{
    planesOut.add(thisPlane);
}
```

We have used an enhanced **for** loop in this method, but you might consider using a **forEach** loop. We leave this as end of chapter exercises for you.

Before we leave this section, let us take a look at the save and load methods that allow us to save and load the attributes in our application. We have three attributes here, planes (the Map of registered planes), circlingQ (the List of flight numbers of the planes circling the airport) and runway (the array of runways).

Since we have declared our Plane and Runway classes to be Serializable, and because enumerated types such as PlaneStatus and collection classes such as Map and List are already Serializable, it is a simple matter to write these objects to a file and read them from a file. Here is the save method:

```
/**
 * Saves airport object to file
 *
 * @param     fileIn The name of the file
 * @throws    IOException if problems with opening and saving to given file
 */
 public void save(String fileIn) throws IOException
 {
     // notice try-with-resources to ensure file closes safely
     try ( FileOutputStream fileOut = new FileOutputStream(fileIn);
         ObjectOutputStream objOut = new ObjectOutputStream (fileOut))
     {
         objOut.writeObject(planes);
         objOut.writeObject(circlingQ);
         objOut.writeObject(runway);
     }
 }
```

You can see we have used a *try-with-resources* construct here to ensure the file is closed once the method terminates.

Here is the `load` method:

```
/**
 * Loads airport object from file
 *
 * @param     fileName The name of the file
 * @throws    IOException if problems with opening and loading given file
 * @throws    ClassNotFoundException if objects in file not of the right type
 */
public void load (String fileName) throws IOException, ClassNotFoundException
{
    // notice try-with-resources to ensure file closes safely
    try ( FileInputStream fileInput = new FileInputStream(fileName);
        ObjectInputStream objInput = new ObjectInputStream (fileInput))
    {
        planes = (Map<String, Plane>) objInput.readObject();
        circlingQ = (List<String>) objInput.readObject();
        runway = (Runway[])objInput.readObject();
    }
}
```

Again, we have used a *try-with-resources* construct to ensure our file is closed upon termination. Notice that when we load the attributes from file, we must indicate their type. The collection class types need to be marked using the generics mechanism:

```
// indicate the type of each collection using generics mechanism
planes = (Map<String, Plane>) objInput.readObject();
circlingQ = (List<String>) objInput.readObject();
runway = (Runway[])objInput.readObject();
```

There is nothing particularly new in the remaining methods. Take a look at the comments provided to follow their implementation.

24.9 Testing

In Chap. 12 we looked at the concepts of unit testing and integration testing. We have left unit testing to you as a practical task, but we will spend a little time here considering integration testing. A useful technique to devise test cases during integration testing is to review the behaviour specifications of use cases, derived during requirements analysis.

Remember, a use case describes some useful service that the system performs. The behaviour specifications capture this service from the point of view of the user. When testing the system you take the place of the user, and you should ensure that the behaviour specification is observed.

Often, there are several routes through a single use case. For example, when registering a plane, either the plane could be successfully registered, or an error is indicated. Different routes through a single use case are known as different **scenarios**. During integration you should take the place of the user and make sure that you test *each* scenario for *each* use case. Not surprisingly, this is often known as **scenario testing**. As an example, reconsider the "*Record flight's request to land*" use case:

An air traffic controller records an incoming flight entering airport airspace, and requesting to land at the airport, by submitting its flight number. As long as the plane has previously registered with the airport, the air traffic controller is given an unoccupied runway number on which the plane will have permission to land. If all runways are occupied however, this permission is denied and the air traffic controller is informed to instruct the plane to circle the airport. If the plane has not previously registered with the airport, an error is signalled.

From this description three scenarios can be identified:

Scenario 1

An air traffic controller records an incoming plane entering airport airspace and requesting to land at the airport, by submitting its flight number, and is given an unoccupied runway number on which the plane will have permission to land.

Scenario 2

An air traffic controller records an incoming plane entering airport airspace and requesting to land at the airport, by submitting its flight number. The air traffic controller is informed to instruct the plane to circle the airport as all runways are occupied.

Scenario 3

An air traffic controller records an incoming plane entering airport airspace and requesting to land at the airport, by submitting its flight number. An error is signalled as the plane has not previously registered with the airport.

Similar scenarios can be extracted for each use case. During testing we should walk through each scenario, checking whether the outcomes are as expected.

24.10   Design of the JavaFX Interface

Figure 24.6 illustrates the interface design we have chosen for the *Airport* application. A few new JavaFX features have been highlighted.

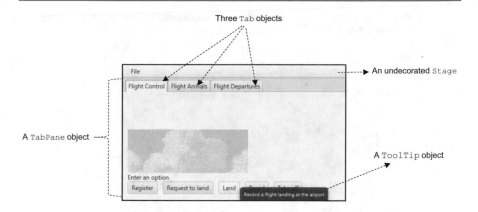

Fig. 24.6 Some new JavaFX features in the *Airport* JavaFX interface

Apart from the features highlighted in Fig. 24.6, the remaining JavaFX components will be familiar to you. The three new JavaFX features are a layout component known as a **tab pane**; some text that appears when you keep your cursor over a component—known as that component's **tool tip;** and a Stage with no icons for minimizing/maximizing/closing—known as an **undecorated** stage. We will return to look at tool tips and undecorated stages later in the chapter but we will look at a tabbed pane now—it is implemented in JavaFX using a TabPane class.

24.11 The *TabPane* Class

The TabPane class provides a very useful JavaFX component for organizing the user interface. You can think of a TabPane component as a collection of overlapping tabbed "cards", on which you place other user interface components. A particular card is revealed by clicking on its **tab**. This allows certain parts of the interface to be kept hidden until required, thus reducing screen clutter.

A TabPane component can consist of any number of tabbed cards. Each card is actually a *single* component of your choice. If you use a container component such as a VBox, you can effectively associate many components with a single tab (see Fig. 24.7).

We can construct a TabPane component by calling the empty constructor as follows:

```
TabPane tabbedPane = new TabPane();
```

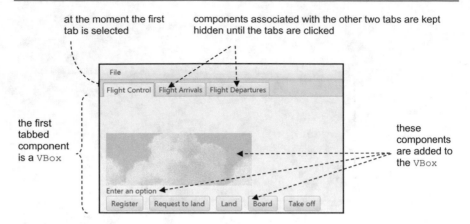

at the moment the first
tab is selected

components associated with the other two tabs are kept
hidden until the tabs are clicked

the first
tabbed
component
is a VBox

these
components
are added to
the VBox

Fig. 24.7 A `TabPane` allows parts of the interface to be revealed selectively

A `TabPane` can be associated with any number of individual tabbed cards. To do this we use the `Tab` class for each individual tabbed card. We need three tabbed cards, one for the main screen shown in Fig. 24.7, one for the arrival information and one for the departure information:

```
Tab tab1 = new Tab("Flight Control"); // main flight control tab
Tab tab2 = new Tab("Flight Arrivals"); // arrivals tab
Tab tab3 = new Tab("Flight Departures"); // departures tab
```

The strings provided to the constructors are the titles displayed on each tab.

We can now add tabbed components to the `TabPane`. When adding a tabbed component to a `TabPane`, you call the `getTabs` method to access the link to the collection of tabbed cards and then the tabs themselves can be set using the `addAll` method:

```
tabbedPane.getTabs().addAll(tab1, tab2, tab3);
```

The order in which the tabs are given to the `addAll` method is the order in which they will appear on the screen.[2] As we mentioned, each tabbed card is associated with a single component. So to add multiple components to a tab we can use a container such as a `VBox` or a `HBox`. For example, to create the main tab

---

[2] By default, the tabs you add will appear at the top left of the TabPane (as in Fig. 24.8). A `setSide` method can be used to choose an alternative side (the top right, the bottom, the left or the right).

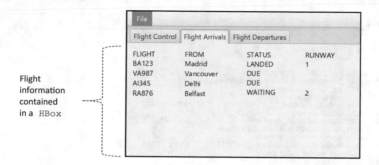

Fig. 24.8 Both "Flight Arrivals" and "Flight Departures" tabs consist of flight information in a HBox

shown in Fig. 24.5, we have 3 components highlighted—a cloud image (named `imageView` in the code), a label (named `label` in the code) and a collection of buttons (stored in a HBox named `controls` in the code). We add all three of these to a VBox (named `box` in the code):

```
// add cloud image, label and button collection to VBox
box.getChildren().addAll(imageView,label, controls);
```

We then use the `setContent` method of a tabbed card to add this VBox component to a given tab:

```
// add VBox to tab1
tab1.setContent(box);
```

The "Flight Arrivals" and "Flight Departures" each contain a HBoxes (each of which contains a series of VBox columns) to display arrival and departure information, respectively. Figure 24.8 shows the airport GUI after selecting the "Flight Arrivals" tab.

24.12 The *AirportFrame* Class

We now present the complete code for the JavaFX class. Take a look at it and then we will point out a few features:

AirportFrame.java

```java
package airportSys; // add class to package

import java.util.Optional;
import java.util.Set;

import javafx.application.Application;
import static javafx.application.Application.launch;
import javafx.application.Platform;
import javafx.geometry.Insets;
import javafx.geometry.Pos;
import javafx.scene.Scene;
import javafx.scene.control.Alert;
import javafx.scene.control.Alert.AlertType;
import javafx.scene.control.Button;
import javafx.scene.control.ButtonType;
import javafx.scene.control.Label;
import javafx.scene.control.Menu;
import javafx.scene.control.MenuBar;
import javafx.scene.control.Tab;
import javafx.scene.control.TabPane;
import javafx.scene.control.TextInputDialog;
import javafx.scene.image.Image;
import javafx.scene.image.ImageView;
import javafx.scene.layout.HBox;
import javafx.stage.Stage;
import javafx.scene.layout.VBox;
import javafx.scene.text.Text;
import javafx.scene.control.Tooltip;
import javafx.scene.layout.Border;
import javafx.scene.layout.BorderStroke;
import javafx.scene.layout.BorderStrokeStyle;
import javafx.scene.layout.BorderWidths;
import javafx.scene.layout.CornerRadii;
import javafx.scene.paint.Color;
import javafx.stage.StageStyle;

/**
 * Class to provide the JavaFX interface of the airport system
 *
 * @author Charatan and Kans
 * @version 6th August 2021
 */

public class AirportFrame extends Application
{
    // declare Airport object
    private Airport myAirport;
    // additional data required for the airport system
    private int numberOfRunways ;
    private final String FILENAME = "airport.dat";

    // create arrival and departure visual components that need global access

    // arrivals information displayed in a HBox
    private HBox arrivals = new HBox(50);
    // include columns for arrivals information
    private    VBox arrivalsColumn1 = new VBox();
    private    VBox arrivalsColumn2 = new VBox();
    private    VBox arrivalsColumn3 = new VBox();
    private    VBox arrivalsColumn4 = new VBox();
    // departures information displayed in a HBox
    private    HBox departures = new HBox(60);
    // include columns for departures information
```

```
private    VBox departuresColumn1 = new VBox();
private    VBox departuresColumn2 = new VBox();
private    VBox departuresColumn3 = new VBox();

// methods

/**
 * The start method to initialise the screen and the airport data
 *
 * @param stage The Stage object
 */
@Override
public void start(Stage stage)
{
    // check if data is to be loaded from file
    Alert alert = new Alert(  AlertType.INFORMATION, "Do you want to restore your data?",
                              ButtonType.YES, ButtonType.NO);
    String response = alert.showAndWait().get().getText();
    if (response.equals("Yes")) // load data from file
    {
        try
        {
            this.myAirport = new Airport(FILENAME); // call file loading constructor
            listArrivals(); // update arrivals tab
            listDepartures(); // update departures tab
            showInfo("Planes loaded");
        }
        catch (Exception e) // file loading errors
        {
            showError("File Opening error");
            System.exit(1); // indicates exit with error
        }
    }
    else // initialise an empty airport
    {
        this.numberOfRunways = getNumberOfRunways(); // request number of runways
        try
        {
            this.myAirport = new Airport (numberOfRunways); // create an empty Airport object
        }
        catch (AirportException ae) // error initialising Airport object
        {
            showError(ae.getMessage());
            System.exit(1); // indicates exit with error
        }
        catch (Exception e) // in case of any unforseen error
        {
            showError(e.getMessage());
            System.exit(1); // indicates exit with error
        }
    }
    // set up three Tab objects in a TabPane
    TabPane tabbedPane = new TabPane();
    Tab tab1 = new Tab("Flight Control"); // main flight control tabs
    Tab tab2 = new Tab("Flight Arrivals"); // arrivals tab
    Tab tab3 = new Tab("Flight Departures"); // departures tab
    tabbedPane.getTabs().addAll(tab1, tab2, tab3);
    // ensure tabs remain open
    tab1.setClosable(false);
    tab2.setClosable(false);
    tab2.setClosable(false);

    // creat a VBox to hold all scene components
    VBox root = new VBox();

    // set up menu bar and items
    MenuBar bar = new MenuBar();
    bar.setMinHeight(25);
    Menu item = new Menu("File");
    Menu saveAndContinueOption = new Menu("Back-up and continue");
    Menu saveAndExitOption = new Menu("Back-up and exit");
    Menu exitWithoutSavingOption = new Menu("Exit without backing-up");
    item.getItems().addAll(saveAndContinueOption, saveAndExitOption, exitWithoutSavingOption);
    bar.getMenus().add(item);

    // create and customise a VBox to organise flight control screen
    VBox box = new VBox();
```

```
        box.setPadding(new Insets(10));
        box.setMinHeight(215);
        // add Vbox to tab1
        tab1.setContent(box);
        box.setAlignment(Pos.BOTTOM_LEFT);
        // create a cloud image
        Image image = new Image("clouds.png");
        ImageView imageView = new ImageView(image);
        // create an instructional label
        Label label = new Label("Enter an option");
        // create a HBox to hold main flight control buttons
        HBox controls = new HBox(10);
        // create flight control buttons and add tooltips
        Button button1 = new Button("Register");
        button1.setTooltip(new Tooltip("Register a flight with the airport"));
        Button button2 = new Button("Request to land");
        button2.setTooltip(new Tooltip("Record a flight requesting to land at the airport"));
        Button button3 = new Button("Land");
        button3.setTooltip(new Tooltip("Record a flight landing at the airport"));
        Button button4 = new Button("Board");
        button4.setTooltip(new Tooltip("Record a landed flight ready for boarding new passengers"));
        Button button5 = new Button("Take off");
        button5.setTooltip(new Tooltip("Record a flight leaving the airport"));
        // add buttons to HBox
        controls.getChildren().addAll(button1, button2, button3, button4, button5);
        // add cloud image, label and button collection to VBox
        box.getChildren().addAll(imageView,label, controls);
        try
        {
            // code button responses by calling private methods
            button1.setOnAction(e -> register());
            button2.setOnAction(e -> requestToLand());
            button3.setOnAction(e -> land());
            button4.setOnAction(e -> board());
            button5.setOnAction(e -> takeOff());
            // code menu responses
            saveAndContinueOption.setOnAction(e -> save(FILENAME));
            saveAndExitOption.setOnAction(e ->{
                                            save(FILENAME);
                                            Platform.exit();
                                        });
            exitWithoutSavingOption.setOnAction(e -> exitWithoutSaving());
        }
        catch(Exception e) // for any unforseen errors
        {
            showError("Invalid Operation");
        }

        // customise look of arrivals tab
        this.arrivals.setPadding(new Insets(10));
        this.arrivals.getChildren().addAll( arrivalsColumn1, arrivalsColumn2, arrivalsColumn3,
                                    arrivalsColumn4);
        tab2.setContent(this.arrivals);
        // customise look of departures tab
        this.departures.setPadding(new Insets(10));
        this.departures.getChildren().addAll(departuresColumn1,
                                                departuresColumn2, departuresColumn3);
        tab3.setContent(this.departures);
        // customise root object and add menu and tabbed pane
        root.setBorder( new Border(new BorderStroke(Color.BLACK, BorderStrokeStyle.SOLID,
                        new CornerRadii(0), new BorderWidths(2))));
        root.getChildren().addAll(bar, tabbedPane);
        // customise frame
        Scene scene = new Scene(root,450, 275);
        stage.setScene(scene);
        stage.setTitle("Airport System");
        stage.initStyle(StageStyle.UNDECORATED); // for undecorated frame

        stage.show();
    }

    /**
    *  private method to request and return the number of runways
    *  @return Returns number of runways selected or -1 if none available
    */
    private int getNumberOfRunways()
    {
```

```
        Optional<String> response;
        boolean ok = false;
        int choice = -1;
        try
        {
            TextInputDialog dialog = new TextInputDialog();
            dialog.setHeaderText("Enter number of runways");
            dialog.setTitle("Runway Information Request");
            response = dialog.showAndWait();
            if(!response.isPresent()) // user pressed cancel
            {
                return -1;
            }
            choice= Integer.parseInt(response.get());
            ok = true;
        }

        catch(NumberFormatException e)
        {
            showError("Invalid runway number");
        }
    return choice;
}


/**
 *  private method to register new flight with the airport
 */
private void register()
{
    String flightNo, city;
    boolean cancelled = false;
    Optional<String> result;
    try
    {
            TextInputDialog dialog = new TextInputDialog();
            dialog.setHeaderText("Enter flight number");
            dialog.setTitle("Registration form");
            result = dialog.showAndWait();

            if(!result.isPresent()) // user pressed cancel
            {
                return;
            }
            flightNo = result.get();
            //  if no flight entered
            checkIfEmpty(flightNo, "No flight number entered");

            dialog = new TextInputDialog();
            dialog.setHeaderText("Enter city of origin");
            dialog.setTitle("Registration form");
            result = dialog.showAndWait();
            if(!result.isPresent()) // user pressed cancel
            {
                return;
            }
            city = result.get();
            //  if no city entered
            checkIfEmpty(city, "No city entered");

            // register flight
            this.myAirport.registerFlight(flightNo, city);
            showInfo("confirmed:\nflight "+flightNo +" registered from "+city);

    }
    catch(AirportException ae) // catch airport exceptions
    {
            showError(ae.getMessage());
    }

    listArrivals();  // update arrivals tab

}

/**
```

```
 *  private method to record a flight's request to land
 */
private void requestToLand()
{
    String flightNo, message;
    Optional<String> result;
    try
    {
        TextInputDialog dialog = new TextInputDialog();
        dialog.setHeaderText("Enter flight number");
        dialog.setTitle("Request to land form");

        result = dialog.showAndWait();
            if(!result.isPresent()) // user pressed cancel
            {
                return;
            }
        flightNo = result.get();
        //  if no flight entered
        checkIfEmpty(flightNo, "No flight number entered");

        // record flight's request to land and get runway number
        int runway = this.myAirport.arriveAtAirport(flightNo);
        // check runway number
        if (runway == 0)
        {
            message = " no runway available, circle the airport";
        }
        else
        {
            message = " has permission to land on runway "+runway;
        }
        showInfo("confirmed:\nflight "+flightNo + message);
    }
    catch(AirportException ae) // catch airport exceptions
    {
        showError(ae.getMessage());
    }
    listArrivals(); // update arrivals tab
}

/**
 *  private method to record a flight landing at the airport
 */
private void land()
{
    String flightNo, runwayIn;
    int runway;
    Optional<String> result;
    try
    {
        TextInputDialog dialog = new TextInputDialog();
        dialog.setHeaderText("Enter flight number");
        dialog.setTitle("Landing form");
        result = dialog.showAndWait();
        if(!result.isPresent()) // user pressed cancel
        {
            return;
        }
        flightNo = result.get();
        //  if no flight entered
        checkIfEmpty(flightNo, "No flight number entered");

        myAirport.landAtAirport(flightNo);
        showInfo("confirmed:\nflight " + flightNo + " has landed");
        listArrivals();
    }

    catch (AirportException ae) // catch airport exceptions
    {
        showError(ae.getMessage());
    }

}
```

```java
/**
 * private method to register a flight boarding passengers at the airport
 */
private void board ()
{
    String flightNo, city;
    Optional<String> result;

    try
    {
        TextInputDialog dialog = new TextInputDialog();
        dialog.setHeaderText("Flight number");
        dialog.setTitle("Boarding form");
        result = dialog.showAndWait();
        if(!result.isPresent()) // user pressed cancel
        {
            return;
        }
        flightNo = result.get();
        // if no flight entered
        checkIfEmpty(flightNo, "No flight number entered");

        dialog = new TextInputDialog();
        dialog.setHeaderText("Enter destination city");
        dialog.setTitle("Boarding form");
        result = dialog.showAndWait();
        if(!result.isPresent()) // user pressed cancel
        {
            return;
        }
        city = result.get();
        // if no city entered
        checkIfEmpty(city, "No city entered");

        // record flight boarding
        this.myAirport.readyForBoarding(flightNo, city);
        showInfo("confirmation:\nflight "+flightNo+" boarding to "+city);
    }
    catch (AirportException ae) // catch airport exceptions
    {
        showError(ae.getMessage());
    }
    listArrivals(); // update arrivals tab
    listDepartures(); // update departures tab
}

/**
 * private method to register a flight leaving the airport
 */
private void takeOff ()
{
    String flightNo;
    Optional<String> result;

    try
    {
        TextInputDialog dialog = new TextInputDialog();
        dialog.setHeaderText("Flight number");
        dialog.setTitle("Take off form");
        result = dialog.showAndWait();
        if(!result.isPresent()) // user pressed cancel
        {
            return;
        }
        flightNo = result.get();
        // if no flight entered
        checkIfEmpty(flightNo, "No flight number entered");

        // record flight taking off
        this.myAirport.takeOff(flightNo);
        showInfo("confirmation:\nflight "+flightNo+" Removed from system");
    }
    catch (AirportException ae) // catch airport exceptions
    {
        showError(ae.getMessage());
    }
```

```java
      listDepartures(); // update departures tab
      listArrivals();  // update arrivals tab
   }

   /**
    *  private method to update arrivals tab information
    */
   private void listArrivals()
   {
      // get arrivals information
      Set<Plane> arrivalsList = this.myAirport.getArrivals();
      // clear current arrivals information
      this.arrivalsColumn1.getChildren().clear();
      this.arrivalsColumn2.getChildren().clear();
      this.arrivalsColumn3.getChildren().clear();
      this.arrivalsColumn4.getChildren().clear();
      this.arrivalsColumn1.getChildren().add(new Text("FLIGHT"));
      this.arrivalsColumn2.getChildren().add(new Text("FROM"));
      this.arrivalsColumn3.getChildren().add(new Text("STATUS"));
      this.arrivalsColumn4.getChildren().add(new Text("RUNWAY"));
      // re-populate arrivals information
      for (Plane thisPlane: arrivalsList)
      {
         this.arrivalsColumn1.getChildren().add(new Text(thisPlane.getFlightNumber()));
         this.arrivalsColumn2.getChildren().add(new Text(thisPlane.getCity()));

         this.arrivalsColumn3.getChildren().add(new Text(thisPlane.getStatusName()));
         try
         {
            // throws exception if no runway set
            this.arrivalsColumn4.getChildren().add(
                                    new Text(Integer.toString(thisPlane.getRunwayNumber())));
         }
         catch(Exception e) // catch exception and leave runway column blank
         {
             this.arrivalsColumn4.getChildren().add(new Text(""));
         }
      }
   }

   /**
    *  private method to update departures tab information
    */
   private void listDepartures()
   {
      // get departures information
      Set<Plane> departuresList = myAirport.getDepartures();
      // clear current departures information
      this.departuresColumn1.getChildren().clear();
      this.departuresColumn2.getChildren().clear();
      this.departuresColumn3.getChildren().clear();
      this.departuresColumn1.getChildren().add(new Text("FLIGHT"));
      this.departuresColumn2.getChildren().add(new Text("TO"));
      this.departuresColumn3.getChildren().add(new Text("RUNWAY"));
      // re-populate departures information
      for (Plane thisPlane: departuresList)
      {
         this.departuresColumn1.getChildren().add(new Text(thisPlane.getFlightNumber()));
         this.departuresColumn2.getChildren().add(new Text(thisPlane.getCity()));

         try
         {
            // throws exception if no runway set
            this.departuresColumn3.getChildren().add(
                                    new Text(Integer.toString(thisPlane.getRunwayNumber())));
         }
         catch(Exception e) // catch exception and leave runway column blank
         {
             this.departuresColumn3.getChildren().add(new Text(""));
         }
      }
   }

   /**
    *  private method to exit application without saving data
    */
   private void exitWithoutSaving()
```

```
          Alert alert = new Alert(  AlertType.WARNING, "Are you sure? Your work could be lost.",
                                    ButtonType.YES, ButtonType.CANCEL);
          alert.setTitle("Confirmation reqired");
          String response = alert.showAndWait().get().getText();

          if(response.equals("Yes"))
          {
              Platform.exit();
          }
      }

      /**
       * private method to load airport data from a file
       * @param   fileName The name of the file to open
       */
      private void open(String fileName)
      {
          try
          {
              this.myAirport.load(fileName); // may throw an exception
              listArrivals(); // update arrivals tab
              listDepartures(); // update departures tab
              showInfo("Planes Loaded");
          }
          catch (Exception e) // catch file related exceptions
          {
              showError("File Opening error");
              System.exit(1); // indicates exit with error
          }
      }

      /**
       * private method to save airport data to a file
       * @param   fileName The name of the file to save
       */
      private void save(String fileName)
      {
          try
          {
              this.myAirport.save(fileName); // may throw exception
              showInfo("Planes saved");
          }
          catch (Exception e) // catch file related exceptions
          {
              showError("Error saving data");
          }
      }

      /**
       * private method to show an error message
       * @param   msg The error message
       */
      private void showError(String msg)
      {
          Alert alert = new Alert(AlertType.ERROR);
          alert.setHeaderText("Airport Error Alert");
          alert.setContentText(msg);
          alert.showAndWait();
      }

      /**
       * private method to show an information message
       * @param   msg The information message
       */
      private void showInfo(String msg)
      {
          Alert alert = new Alert(AlertType.INFORMATION);
          alert.setHeaderText("Airport Information Alert");
          alert.setContentText(msg);
          alert.showAndWait();
      }

      /**
       * Private method to check if a string is empty
       * @param   s The string to check
       * @param   errorMessage The error message to include in an exception
```

```
 *   @ if string is empty
 */
private void checkIfEmpty(String s, String errorMsg)
{
    if (s.equals(""))
    {
        throw new AirportException (errorMsg);
    }
}

/**
 * @param args
 */

public static void main(String[] args)
{
    launch(args);
}
}
```

As you can see, although this class has more code than those we have met before, it follows a familiar pattern. Most of the code will therefore be familiar to you, and the `Javadoc` comments and additional supplementary comments should be sufficient to follow what we have done here. We will just draw your attention to one or two JavaFX features that we have decided to incorporate into our implementation that will be new to you and that we mentioned in the introduction.

First, we have added **tool tips** to our buttons. A tool tip is an informative description of the purpose of a GUI component. This informative description is revealed when the user places the cursor over the component. Figure 24.9 shows the tool tip that is revealed when the cursor is placed over the "Land" button.

Adding a tool tip to a JavaFX component is easy; just use the `setTool-TipText` method and provide a tool tip message as a parameter to the `ToolTip` class:

```
// create a Land button
Button button3 = new Button("Land");
// add a tool tip to the Land button using the setToolTip method
button3.setTooltip(new Tooltip("Record a flight landing at the airport"));
```

We also mentioned that we have made our frame an undecorated frame. An undecorated frame has no icons to minimize or maximize (or close) the frame. This ensures the frame remains the same size and cannot be altered. To do this we use the `initStyle` method of our `stage` object and pass an enumerated type constant `StageStyle.UNDECORATED` as a parameter:

Fig. 24.9 A tool tip is revealed when the mouse is placed over the "Land" button

Fig. 24.10   An `Alert` dialogue to allow users to load data from a file

```
stage.initStyle(StageStyle.UNDECORATED);
```

Finally we draw your attention to a few things related to the functionality of this class.

When the application opens the user is given the option to load data from a file via an `Alert` dialogue (see Fig. 24.10).

If the user chooses to load data from a file, the airport interface (as given in Fig. 24.10) is activated once the data is loaded. If the user chooses not to load data from a file, the system needs to be initialized by asking the user for the number of runways associated with this airport. A `TextInputDialog` is used for this purpose (see Fig. 24.11).

Again, the airport interface (as given in Fig. 24.5) is activated once the user has entered the number of runways. The user can then use the buttons on the flight control tab to register, request to land, land, board and take off flights at the airport —with arrival and departure information being always available in the arrivals and departures tabs.

We have created two **private** methods, `listArrivals` and `listDepartures`. These methods update the information in the arrivals and departures tabs, respectively. Whenever the airport data is modified (i.e. when a

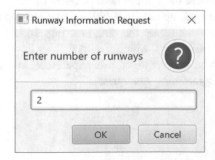

Fig. 24.11   A `TextInputDialog` to allow users to specify the number of runways

button is pressed in the main control tab) these methods need to be called to update the arrivals and departures tabs so when these tabs are revealed they always show the current state of flights in the system.

For example, when a flight registers at the airport the arrivals tab only needs to be updated before we exit the method. Here is the outline of the code for processing the register button response:

```
/**
 *  private method to register new flight with the airport
 */
private void register()
{
        // code to register flight at airport here

        this.listArrivals();  // update arrivals tab
}
```

However, when a flight is ready for boarding, it needs to be removed from the arrivals tab and added to the departures tab, so both listArrivals and listDepartures need to be called.

```
/**
 *  private method to register a flight boarding passengers at the airport
 */
private void board()
{
        // code to record flight as ready for boarding

        this.listArrivals();     // update arrivals tab
        this.listDepartures();   // update departures tab
}
```

When a flight takes off from the aiport, it only needs to be removed from the departures tab:

```
/**
 *  private method to record a flight leaving the airport
 */
private void takeOff()
{
        // code to record flight leaving the airport

        this.listDepartures();  // update departures tab only
}
```

Finally, the user can use the file menu to back-up the data to a file and continue with the application, to back-up data to a file and exit the application or simply exit the application without backing up the data (see Fig. 24.12).

That concludes our case study, which means that we have come to the end of the course. We hope that you have enjoyed this experience, and we wish you the very best in your future programming enterprises.

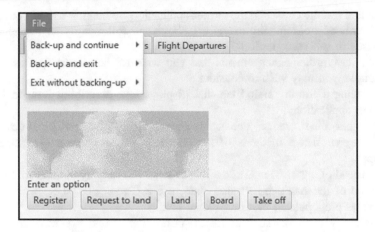

Fig. 24.12 Menu options to allow users to back-up data and exit the application as required

24.13 Self-test Questions

1. What is the difference between *containment* and *composition* in UML?
2. Consider an enumerated type, `Light`. This type can have one of three values: RED, AMBER and GREEN. It will be used to display a message to students, indicating whether or not a lecturer is available to be seen.
   (a) Specify this type in UML.
   (b) Implement this type in Java.
   (c) Declare a `Light` variable, `doorLight`;
   (d) Write a **switch** statement that checks `doorLight` and displays "I am away" when `doorLight` is RED, "I am busy" when `doorLight` is AMBER and "I am free" when `doorLight` is GREEN.
3. Identify the benefits offered by the `TabPane` component.
4. How can the tool tip *"This button stops the game"* be added to a `Button` called `stop`?
5. Develop test plans for the `Runway`, `Plane`, `Airport` and `AirportFrame` classes.

24.14 Programming Exercises

Copy, from the accompanying website, the classes that make up the airport application and then tackle the following exercises:

1. Develop `toString` methods for the `Runway`, `Plane` and `Airport` classes and then develop testers for these classes.

2. Run and test the classes in the airport application by making use of your testing programs of programming exercise 1 above and following your test plans you devised in self-test question 5.

3. Make any further enhancements that you wish to the airport application. For example, you may wish to consider

(a) adding a fourth "Help" tab that displays text describing how to use the airport application;

(b) rather than use an enhanced **for** loop in the getArrivals and getDepartures methods of the Airport class make use of **forEach** loops;

(c) instead of a TextInputDialog to enter the runway number in the land method of the AirportFrame class, use a ChoiceDialog with a list of runways prepopulated in a drop-down box;

(d) identify methods, such as nextFreeRunway and nextToLand in the Airport class, that could return **null** values and then modify the code in the airport application to make use of the Optional type to avoid returning these **null** values;

(e) design your own skin for the AirportFrame by creating a cascading style sheet.

4. Create an executable JAR file to run the airport application.

5. Look back at the hostel application that we developed in Chap. 12 using Python and Tkinter. Now see if you can implement the same system with Java and JavaFX.

Appendix
Compiling and Running Java Programs

Introduction

In this appendix we are going to take you through the various ways in which you can compile and run your Java programs.

In order to compile and run a Java application you will need a **Java Standard Edition Development Kit**, usually referred to simply as a **Java SE Development Kit** or **JDK**. This comes as a downloadable executable file which contains a great many programs and tools that enable you to compile and run Java programs. Among the most important of these are a program called **javac.exe** which compiles your java source code, and a program called **java.exe** which runs the programs. Also included is a **Java Runtime Environment (JRE)**, which is the virtual machine that runs your Java programs as we explained in Chap. 13. However, in most cases you will not be using these programs directly because you will be using an **Integrated Development Environment (IDE)** as explained below; instructions for downloading and installing the JDK and an IDE are provided on our website (see preface).

Before moving on we should mention that new versions of Java are being released (and then updated) quite rapidly. At the time of writing, the latest release is Java 17, but this is likely to change quite quickly. For each release there is a corresponding release of the JDK, which is named accordingly (including the number of the latest update). So, for example, at the time of writing, the latest JDK is *Java SE 17.0.1* and the corresponding executable installation file for Windows, for example, is *jdk-17.0.1_windows-x64_bin.exe*.

We should also mention here that the latest graphics package, **JavaFX**, that we use in Chaps. 23 and 24 is not packaged with any releases of Java higher than Java 8. So, if you are using later versions of the JDK then you also have to download the

© Springer Nature Switzerland AG 2022
Q. Charatan and A. Kans, *Programming in Two Semesters*,
Texts in Computer Science, https://doi.org/10.1007/978-3-031-01326-3

JavaFX software development kit (JavaFX SDK 17 is the latest at the time of writing). Although this can make life a bit more difficult when it comes to using an IDE to create graphical applications, we offer some simple advice below about how to simplify this process.

Integrated Development Environments (IDEs)

Using an IDE is the most common way to compile and run Java programs—you saw what this looks like for NetBeans in Chap. 13 (Fig. 13.1), and other IDEs have a similar look. In this section we are going to take a look at some of the IDEs commonly in use. For a couple of these we also provide instructions on the website (see preface) for downloading, installing and using the product.

Apache NetBeans

In 2016, Oracle, the owners of NetBeans™, handed the product over to the Apache Software Foundation, making it an open-source product. At the time of writing the latest release of Apache NetBeans™ is 12.6.

Although Apache NetBeans™ now has a lot more features than before, the basic operations for setting up a simple Java application are not very different from those of its predecessor. You will need to download and install the JDK before installing Apache NetBeans™.

As we have said, instructions for downloading and installing the JDK and Apache NetBeans™ are provided on the website (see preface).

You should be aware that if you use NetBeans™ with any version of Java later than Java 8, then creating JavaFX applications requires that you download the JavaFX SDK separately and go through a number of steps to configure the IDE to run JavaFX applications; instructions for doing this are included with the instructions on our website (see preface).

However, with NetBeans it is still possible to use Java 8. Although this is an older version of Java it has the advantage that JavaFX is packaged with it. In fact, almost everything in this book[1] can be implemented in Java 8—and because it is so useful for students and personal users, Oracle have committed to supporting Java 8 until at least 2030. As a new user, you might well choose to work with Java 8 rather than a later version.

---

[1]The only feature that is not available in Java 8 is the enhanced **switch** statement described in Chap. 14—and, as explained in that chapter, this simply provides a more convenient way of using an existing feature, rather than introducing a new feature.

Other Popular IDEs

Along with NetBeans™ there are some other very popular IDEs that we should mention here—Eclipse™, Visual Studio Code™ and IntelliJ™; you might easily find that your particular college or university uses one of these, in which case you will be given instructions on how to use them. These also require you to download the JDK. In the case of IntelliJ, a JavaFX plugin has recently been developed so that you no longer have to configure it for this purpose (see instructions on our website). Instructions for configuring Eclipse and Visual Studio Code for JavaFX can be found on the JavaFX website: https://openjfx.io/openjfx-docs/.

Web-Based Compilers

A recent innovation which is particularly useful for new Java students has been the emergence of online compilers. These are easy to use and have the advantage of not requiring the user to download a JDK or IDE. Examples of popular web-based compilers are JDoodle™, Codiva™ and Repl™.

One of the limitations of online compilers is that it is not possible to use them for creating graphical applications (Chaps. 23 and 24 of this book). They are also somewhat limited when it comes to creating and reading files (Chap. 22) because the files have to be stored online as part of your project, rather than in a location of your choice.

Compiling and Running Programs from the Command Line

It is perfectly possible to compile and run Java programs without the use of an IDE by using a command line in a console window; using a command line interface is something that is more commonly done by those who work with operating systems such as Unix™ or Linux™, and it is not something we would recommend for beginners.

As mentioned above, the compiler that comes as part of the JDK is called *javac. exe*, and to compile a file called, for example, *MyProgram.java*, you would write at the command prompt.

javac MyProgram.java

This would create a file called *MyProgram.class*, which is the compiled file in Java byte code. The name of the JVM is *java.exe,* and to run the program you would type:

java MyProgram.

Project Management Tools

Large-scale commercial and industrial projects are seldom produced by a single developer, but rather by several people working together and collaborating on different parts of the application; in many cases they will not all be using the same platform to develop their classes, and management of the project as a whole can easily become unwieldy. To assist in this process there are a number of project management tools which help an individual or team in organizing and managing their projects and tasks. Project management software enables the developer (or developers) to both build and manage applications, by organizing and documenting all the resources needed for a particular project. Two of the most common Java management tools are Maven™ and Gradle™, both of which are supported by the IDEs that we spoke about here, so that a Maven™ or Gradle™ project can be developed via IDEs such as NetBeans™, as well as independently via the project management tool itself. This won't be something that you will need for this text, but it is important to be aware of project management tools as you move further in your careers.

Index

© Springer Nature Switzerland AG 2022
Q. Charatan and A. Kans, *Programming in Two Semesters*,
Texts in Computer Science, https://doi.org/10.1007/978-3-031-01326-3

Printed in the United States
by Baker & Taylor Publisher Services